THE IRISH PENITENTIALS

SCRIPTORES LATINI HIBERNIAE

VOLUME V

THE IRISH PENITENTIALS

EDITED BY

LUDWIG BIELER

WITH AN APPENDIX BY

D. A. BINCHY

DUBLIN

THE DUBLIN INSTITUTE FOR ADVANCED STUDIES

1975

First Published 1963
Reprinted 1975

Printed in Great Britain
at the University Press, Oxford
by Vivian Ridler
Printer to the University

PREFACE

THE present edition of the Irish Penitentials has a limited aim: to put before the reader the basic documents relating to the administration of penance in Ireland during the early Middle Ages, and to bring together some material for their literal and historical interpretation. To do this is the first step towards that great desideratum—a fully documented history of penance in early Christian Ireland. The scholar best qualified to write on this subject, the Right Rev. Mgr. Gerard Mitchell, President of St. Patrick's College, Maynooth, has unfortunately, under pressure of other work, been obliged to abandon the project of contributing to this volume an exposé of Irish penitential history which he had kindly promised. I myself have not been able to do more than give a brief analysis of each text, sketch the manuscript tradition of the Penitentials, and make some general comments on their Latinity.

I have refrained also from commenting on the legal matter of such texts as *Canones Wallici* or *Canones Hibernenses* in relation to Welsh and Irish secular law; my notes on these compilations are concerned merely with the Latin texts here edited and with the linguistic background of their wording.

All the texts of the present edition have been transcribed or collated from photos or microfilms of the original manuscripts; these reproductions have been consulted for the checking of details at every stage of my work. The correction of transcripts and proofs has been shared bravely and patiently by my wife, who has detected numerous errors that might otherwise have gone unnoticed.

In plan and layout this volume follows its predecessors, except that, in view of the uncertainty of some texts with regard to details, manuscript variants have been quoted in the indexes more frequently.

Some readers might feel that the *Index rerum uerborum locutionum* has grown out of proportion. Its fullness can, I think, be justified on several grounds. This index is meant to serve a double purpose: to be a subject index to the Latin texts, and to present in detail the vocabulary and phraseology of their authors. The need for a subject index is obvious; to fuse this *Index rerum* with the *Index uerborum* has seemed convenient as well as economical. In my support I quote McNeill–Gamer, *Medieval Handbooks of Penance*, p. 70: 'It would be a great help to have indexes or glossaries for the penitentials. A comparison of parallel passages has illumined many a hidden meaning and cleared away many a doubt.' The demands of Ludwig Traube, *Einleitung in die lateinische Philologie des Mittelalters*, Munich, 1911, p. 80, go even farther: editions of medieval Latin texts should be accompanied by '*indices*, womöglich *pleni, plenissimi*, nicht *glossaria*'.

In a review of *Scriptores Latini Hiberniae*, vol. ii, *S. Columbani Opera*, ed. G. S. M. Walker, which appeared in *Classica et Mediaevalia*, vol. xxi, Signor Mario Esposito asks the question (pp. 196 f.) what precisely I mean by 'Hibernian Latin'; chapter iii of the introduction here following contains as full an answer as can at present be given.

It is a pleasant duty to acknowledge the generous assistance of scholars and librarians in many lands. I owe a special debt of gratitude to the Lord Abbot of San Girolamo, Dom Pierre Salmon, and to the Prior of the same monastery, Dom Jean Gribomont; to the Rev. Professor Dr. A. Kalsbach, lately Librarian of the Dombibliothek at Cologne; to the Rev. Librarian of the Stiftsbibliothek of Saint Gall, Dr. Johannes Duft; to Dr. François Masai, Keeper of Manuscripts at the Bibliothèque Royale, Brussels; to the authorities of the British Museum and, personally, to Mr. R. A. Wilson, Keeper of Printed Books, and Mr. D. H. Turner, Assistant Keeper of Manuscripts; to Dr. R. W. Hunt, Keeper of Manuscripts in the Bodleian Library, Oxford; to the library staff of the Institute for Advanced Study, Princeton, and of the Firestone Library, Princeton, where some part of my work was done. Here in Dublin Dr. R. J. Hayes, Director of the National Library of Ireland, and his staff have been most helpful in every possible way; especially, the collection of manuscripts on microfilm which Dr. Hayes is building up has been of inestimable value. Dr. William O'Sullivan, Keeper of Manuscripts in the Library of Trinity College, Dublin, and the library staffs of University College, Dublin, of the Royal Irish Academy, and of Marsh's Library have been untiring in their efforts to meet my often heavy demands.

For information or expert opinion on particular problems I am greatly obliged to Professor Bernhard Bischoff of Munich; to Dr. Bonifaz Fischer, Director of the Vetus Latina Institute, Beuron; to my colleague, the Rev. Professor Dermot Ryan of University College, Dublin; to Dom E. Dekkers of Sint Pietersabdij, Steenbrugge; and to Dr. Cyril Vogel, Strasbourg. Above all, I am most grateful to Dr. D. A. Binchy of the Institute for Advanced Studies, Dublin, for the active interest he has taken in this publication from the very beginning. Not only has he contributed annotated translations of two important penitential texts in Old Irish; he has also given most generously of his unique knowledge in fields of learning which lie outside my province.

Several publishers have put me under a great obligation by permitting me to reproduce here, verbatim or nearly so, English translations of penitential texts the copyright of which is theirs. I wish to thank the Columbia University Press, New York, for their permission to use the translations of McNeill–Gamer (*Medieval Handbooks of Penance*, 1938, pp. 75–134, 169–78, 369–82, 425 f.) as basis of my own translations; the editors of *Ancient Christian Writers* as well as the Newman Press, Westminster,

Md., and Messrs. Longmans, Green & Co., London, for permission to reprint, with small changes, my translation of the 'First Synod of St. Patrick', published in vol. xvii of their series, pp. 50–54; I am most grateful also to Dr. G. S. M. Walker, of the University of Leeds, for allowing me to use in a similar manner his translation of the Penitential of St. Columbanus (*S.L.H.*, vol. ii, pp. 169–81).

To conclude this Preface, let me thank most sincerely the authorities of all those libraries not yet mentioned whose manuscripts I have been allowed to use for the establishment of the texts here edited. These manuscripts are scattered over a wide area: Austria, England, France, Germany, Italy, Switzerland—the area once visited by the *Scotti peregrini*; the present custodians of the surviving documents of their zeal and learning, whose co-operation has made it possible to reunite these *membra disiecta*, may rest assured of our deep gratitude.

LUDWIG BIELER

University College, Dublin

CONTENTS

INTRODUCTION

I. THE LATIN TEXTS

1

THE present edition includes all known Irish penitentials and penitential canons (those in Latin both in the original and in an English translation, those in Old Irish in translation only); some Welsh canons that have a bearing on the history of Penance in Ireland; and the so-called *Paenitentiale Bigotianum*. Included also are certain texts which, for the greater part, are not penitential but legal in character, viz. the so-called *Canones Wallici* and *Canones Hibernenses*.

One text that might be expected to be found here has not been included—Pseudo-Cummean (Kenney, no. 77). This work would seem to have no better claim to a place in the present edition than have some other Irish-influenced penitentials of the eighth and ninth centuries which are mentioned by Kenney, p. 243. However, Ps.-Cummean has been used extensively for the restoration of the badly transmitted texts of the genuine *Penitential of Cummean* and of the *Bigotianum*.

To introduce these texts is no easy task. 'La date, l'origine, la forme primitive de ces pénitentiels restent, malgré de nombreuses recherches, pleines d'incertitude.'[1] In the following, I shall merely put together what little can be asserted with some confidence, and point out difficulties which remain to be solved. My discussion will be restricted to penitentials in Latin: the Old-Irish penitential texts will be discussed at the end of this introduction by Professor D. A. Binchy.

General literature on the subject has been listed by J. T. McNeill–H. M. Gamer, *Medieval Handbooks of Penance* (Records of Civilization xxix, Columbia Univ. Press, 1938), pp. 453 ff.; see also below, p. 52. Literature on individual texts is found in McNeill–Gamer and Kenney *suis locis*. My own references are mainly to these two books; there have been few occasions for going beyond them.[2]

2

The document generally known as the *First Synod of St. Patrick* (Kenney, no. 30) is a circular letter to the clergy of Ireland by the

---

[1] P. Fournier–G. Le Bras, *Histoire des collections canoniques en occident*, i (1931), p. 52.

[2] Fournier–Le Bras, i. 50–56, 84 ff.; G Le Bras, *Pénitentiels*, in *Dictionnaire de théologie catholique*, xii/1 (1933), cols. 1162–72, and *Les Pénitentiels irlandais*, in Daniel–Rops, *Le Miracle irlandais* (1956), pp. 172–90; L. Gougaud, *Christianity in Celtic Lands* (1932), pp. 276–87; R. Buchner, *Die Rechtsquellen* (Wattenbach–Levison, *Deutschlands Geschichtsquellen im Mittelalter. Vorzeit und Karolinger: Beiheft*, Weimar, 1953), pp. 67 f., do not go into details.

bishops Patricius, Auxilius, and Iserninus. Technically speaking, it is
not a penitential. Its inclusion in this volume seems justified on the
grounds that it is, to our knowledge, the earliest surviving document
concerning ecclesiastical discipline in Ireland, and that it contains, *inter
alia*, penitential matter in the narrower meaning of the term.

According to the Irish Annals, the bishops Secundinus, Auxilius, and
Iserninus[1] came to Ireland in 439; their obits are given as 447, 459, and
468 respectively. If these canons were decreed at a synod, its date would
fall after the death of Secundinus, who is not included in the formula
of greeting, and before the death of Auxilius in 459. Assuming that
a reference to a *senodus Patricii* underlies the annalistic obit of *senex
Patricius*,[2] I have suggested that this synod was held in 457. This date
would fall within the Irish mission of St. Patrick according to Carney's
chronology as well as to Bury's.

Fourteen of these canons are quoted under the name of Patricius in
the *Collectio Hibernensis*. An early date of the document is borne out
also by the unsettled state of ecclesiastical affairs in Ireland to which
many of its decrees refer. Since Bury it has been generally believed
that these canons are in their majority authentic; only canons 25, 30,
33, 34, and a clause in canon 6 might be interpolated. This is not to say
that Patrick was necessarily responsible for the actual wording but
merely that the document, or whatever portion of it is authentic, was
issued with his express approval.[3]

The order of the decrees as they stand is not strictly logical; it need
not in every detail represent the order of the original. There are three
major groups: decrees concerning clerics and monks (cc. 5–11); decrees
concerning Christians at large (cc. 12–22); and decrees dealing with
ecclesiastical jurisdiction (cc. 23–30, 33). Canons 4 and 5 should probably be read together with canon 1;[4] canons 2 and 3 are then intruders
in their present place. Out of place are also canons 31 and 32, which
concern the civil conduct of clerics. Other canons seem to have been
grouped together by mere association, e.g. 11–13, 27–28, 33–34. In the
circumstances it seems impossible to reconstruct the original order.

Literature: J. B. Bury, *The Life of St. Patrick* (1905), pp. 233–45; Kenney,
pp. 169 f.; McNeill–Gamer, pp. 75 f.; L. Bieler, *The Life and Legend of St.
Patrick* (1949), pp. 34–36.

---

[1] Muirchú, *Vita s. Patricii*, i. 9, relates that Auxilius and Iserninus received minor
orders when Patrick was ordained bishop. Some traditions concerning Iserninus have
been recorded in the Book of Armagh, fol. 18[r].

[2] *Ir. Eccl. Record*, 5th ser., lxxxv. 188.

[3] The same is possibly the case with the Penitential of St. Columbanus and the
Canons of Adamnan, see below, pp. 5 and 9.

[4] Certainly so if, as I assume, *praetium* in c. 4 means 'ransom' as it does in c. 32;
cf. also Patricius, *Conf.* 53. For a different interpretation see H. Leclercq, *Histoire des
Conciles*, ii. 2, 889 f.

3

The four short texts known as the *Preface of Gildas on Penance*, the Decrees of the *Synods of North Britain* (Brevi) and of the *Grove of Victory*, and the *Excerpts from a Book of David* (Dewi) are preserved, in this order, in the twin MSS. Cambrai 625 and Paris, Bibl. Nat. Lat. 3182 (*Codex Bigotianus*). They purport to be of Welsh origin and to date from the early sixth century. The ascriptions and historical associations of these canons depend entirely on the evidence of the two manuscripts in which they are found. The part which St. David is supposed to have played in the synods of Brevi and *Lucus Victoriae* has no other authority than the late and untrustworthy Life of that saint by Rhigyfarch (eleventh century), whose account of these synods is intrinsically improbable.[1] There is, on the other hand, no inherent reason why the four texts should not have originated in the early Welsh Church;[2] a positive argument for their early Welsh origin is perhaps the laying down of penances for acting as guide to the 'barbarian invaders', obviously the Angles and Saxons, in Luc. Vict. c. 4.[3] Supporting evidence may be found in the references to Roman liquid measures in Gildas, cc. 1 and 2, and in David, c. 11.[4]

These four texts are thus the earliest penitential documents of the Celtic Church that have survived. It would appear that this particular penitential system originated in Wales, and that it was adopted and further developed in Ireland.[5]

The *Preface of Gildas on Penance* and the *Synod of North Britain* concern penances of monks and clerics only; the other two documents apply to both clergy and laity. Common to all four texts is the grading of the penances according to ecclesiastical status. The penances are mild in comparison with the rigorous practice of the later Irish Church.

4

The earliest Irish penitential now in existence is the *Penitential of Vinnian*[6] (Kenney, no. 72). It cannot be dated with any degree of accuracy except that it must be prior to the *Penitential of St. Columbanus*,

[1] See McNeill–Gamer, p. 169; Nora K. Chadwick in *Studies in the Early British Church* (1958), p. 134.

[2] As Prof. Binchy points out, *ferculo* Gi 1, Da 7, is a continental scribe's misreading of *serculo* (Ir. *sercol*). These two texts might, then, be Irish; they would, to say the least, owe their present form to an Irish redactor.

[3] The recurrence of this decree in Cumm. (IX) 13 is most naturally understood as a borrowing from the Welsh document.

[4] Characteristically, these measures are equated, after the Irish manner, with the capacity of so many egg-shells, in the parallel passage Cumm. II. 2 (R).

[5] See Kenney, pp. 239 f.

[6] The author's name is given as *Vinniaus* in the postscript to the Penitential in MS. V; as *Vinnianus* in the title of the work in MS. S, and in the *Catalogus Sanctorum Hiberniae* (ed. P. Grosjean, *Anal. Boll.* lxxiii. 197–213), c. 2 ex. (A); as *Vennianus* in Columbanus, Epist. i. 7.

who, though without acknowledging his source,[1] draws largely on Vinnian's work. Columbanus in all probability wrote his Penitential on the Continent; it would then fall after 575, or even, according to the more probable chronology of Columbanus' life, after 591.[2] The latter date may be taken as a reasonably safe *terminus ad quem* for the *Penitential of Vinnian*.

Vinnian, so he tells us in a postscript to his work, was abbot of some monastery, and compiled his Penitential in the first place for the benefit of his own monks. As his sources he names the Scriptures and *opiniones quorundam doctorum*. These 'learned men' remain largely unknown except for some echoes of Cassian and for St. Columbanus's testimony to the effect that *Vennianus auctor* consulted Gildas on a point of discipline and that the latter replied. Most scholars regard this Penitential as the work of either St. Finnian of Clonard (d. 549) or St. Finnian of Mag-Bile (Moville), d. 579. A decision between the two alleged authors seems impossible.[3]

The composition of the Penitential is clear in outline but not very careful in detail. Canons 1–4 establish the distinction between sins by thought and sins by deed. There follows (5–9) a section on strife, wounding, and homicide; penances are fixed differently for clerics and lay people. Canons 10–29 concern penances of clerics; here the author deals with fornication, the killing of the offspring of a sinful union, magic practised in connexion with these two crimes, perjury, homicide, theft, marital relations of clerics with their former wives, greed, and anger. At the end of c. 29 he states the principle *contraria contrariis curare* in terms reminiscent of Cassian. Canon 30 refers to the diversion of ecclesiastical property; in codex S this is contemplated expressly as a sin committed by a cleric. Canons 31–48 are concerned with sinners among the laity: 31–35 give general directions (c. 34, in particular, on deathbed repentance); 36–38 deal with fornication; 39–48 treat at some length of the duties of the married state and of sins against it. Canons 49–53 are miscellaneous; they are followed by the epilogue already mentioned.[4]

Literature: Kenney, pp. 240 f.; M. Esposito, *Hermathena*, xx. 236–40; McNeill–Gamer, pp. 86 f.

---

[1] There is, however, a reference to *Vennianus auctor* in the saint's letter to Pope Gregory, Epist. i. 7.

[2] On the chronology of St. Columbanus cf. Dr. Walker's edition (SLH, vol. ii), pp. x–xii.

[3] The argument of Seebass (endorsed by Esposito) in favour of Finnian of Moville (cf. *Hermathena*, xx. 238 f.) is not convincing. Even if a visit to Ireland by Gildas in or about 565 may be considered historical, it does not follow that *Vennianus auctor* could not have consulted Gildas at some earlier date; the fact that Gildas replied in writing (*rescripsit*) would rather suggest that he answered a letter. The Irish teachers of Columbanus, SS. Sinell and Comgall, were pupils of St. Finnian of Clonard; in the same direction points a reminiscence of a Bangor hymn in Vinnian's postscript, see p. 245.

[4] Canons 46–53 and the epilogue are missing in codex S; see below, pp. 17 and 92.

5

The *Penitential of St. Columbanus* (Kenney, no. 46, pp. 199 f.) has been discussed very fully by Dr. Walker[1] and especially by Dom Jean Laporte.[2] Contrary to the accepted opinion, which has some foundation in the manuscript tradition (see below), viz. that the Penitential is extant in two recensions (Seebass's A and B), Dom Laporte has proved that it is all of a piece. It falls into three parts: a penitential for monks (A 2–8), one for the secular clergy (B 1–12), and one for the laity (B 13–23); these are preceded by a short prologue (A 1). To this nucleus, which in my opinion dates from the saint's early days at Annegray and Luxeuil, additions were made at various times; they have resulted in a slight overlapping of the disposition. The two paragraphs concerning participation in pagan or heretical rites, especially in those of the followers of Bonosus (B 24 and 25), were probably added in Burgundy early in the seventh century, when the heresy of Bonosus was in its zenith; two sections on minor trespasses of monks (A 9–12, B 26–30) are dated by Laporte to *c.* 608; four rubrics (hardly by Columbanus himself) were inserted at a time when the Penitential contained already the other accretions. There is reason for believing that at an early date the non-monastic section (B), which was of wider pastoral application, had become separated from the monastic section (A); the former was given a new prologue (*Diuersitas culparum* . . .).

Dependence on Vinnian is evident throughout, not only in numerous provisions concerning particular sins but also in the general concept of penance, which may be described as a transition from the idea of vindictive penance to that of remedial penance. Both authors know and endorse Cassian's principle *contraria contrariis curare*, but they do not (as does Cummean) make Cassian's ogdoad of capital sins the basis of their classification. Authorship of St. Columbanus in a strictly literary sense need not be assumed for every detail of the text; there is little doubt, however, that—except for the rubrics, and possibly for the 'B-prologue'—it is substantially his.

6

The penitential ascribed to *Cummean*[3] (Kenney, no. 73) is, with the exception of the Old Irish *Penitential of Tallaght*,[4] the most comprehensive of the Irish penitentials. In its main body, penances are grouped according to the eight capital sins as formulated by Cassian. These

[1] *Sancti Columbani Opera* (SLH, vol. ii), pp. lii–lv.
[2] *Le Pénitentiel de Saint Colomban. Introduction et édition critique.* Tournai, 1958. See also my review, *J.T.S.*, N.S. xii (1961), pp. 106–12.
[3] The name is spelt variously *Com(m)ianus*, *Cum(m)ianus*, *Com(m)eanus*, *Cum(m)eanus*, and even *Commenianus* or *Comminianus*; cf. the titles and colophons in the manuscripts mentioned below, pp. 18 f., and *Cat. Sanctorum Hiberniae*, c. 3 ex. (US).
[4] See Dr. Binchy's account, below, pp. 47–49.

eight chapters are followed by three others: on minute offences, on misdemeanours of boys, on questions concerning the Host. The two groups are separated by a short list of 'commutations', (VIII) 25–28; only the first of these is known also from Can. Hib. II. 6 and the *Old-Irish Table of Commutations*, § 16. The two groups differ also in details of syntactical usage;[1] they were probably combined in this work for the first time. The compilation draws substantially on the early Welsh texts discussed in section 3 of this chapter; to a lesser degree it depends on Vinnian, and for the remainder on sources that can no longer be determined.[2] The whole is prefaced by a homily on the 'twelve remissions of sins'—an extract from earlier patristic sources (Origen, Cassian); in two manuscripts (LF) this preface is ascribed to St. Caesarius.[3] In the epilogue, confessors are urged to enjoin penances with due regard to the state and particular condition of each individual sinner. Both prologue and epilogue may once have been independent pieces, as were the several introductory sections of the *Paenitentiale Bigotianum*.

The titles in MSS. E and N respectively, *Incipit sancti Basilii Penitentiale ad Cumiani Longii* and *Expositio sancti Basilii inquisitio acumiani Longii*, both obviously incorrect in wording, could be derived from such an original title as *Sancti Basilii expositio ad inquisitionem Cumiani Longii*, which might have referred to the prologue only. The name of St. Basil here is hard to account for, but it is not more surprising than is the name of St. Gregory of Nazianzus in the title of Can. Hib. I.

The name-form in MSS. EN, viz. Cumianus Longius, helps to identify the author as the Cummaine Fota who is quoted as an authority in the *Old-Irish Table of Commutations*, § 31, and in the *Old-Irish Penitential*;[4] according to the Annals of Ulster, he died in his seventy-second year in 662. This Cummaine Fota may be further identified with the Cumineus Longus, bishop of Clonfert, who is named as author of the hymn *Celebra Iuda* in the *Liber Hymnorum*.[5] There is no evidence to show that our Cummean is identical with the author of the Letter on the Easter date (Kenney, no. 57). Even less evidence is there for identifying him with either Cumine Ailbe of Iona or the eighth-century bishop Cummean of Bobbio.

---

[1] See Chapter III below, pp. 33 f.

[2] These sources are partly the same as those of the so-called Penitential of Theodore; besides, Cummean seems to make use of monastic rules: Fournier–Le Bras, i. 54, n. 3.

[3] It has been printed among the works of St. Caesarius in Migne, *PL* lxvii. 1075; see, however, Dom G. Morin, *S. Caesarii Arelatensis Opera*, i. 2 (1937), p. 930; 2nd ed., by Dom C. Lambot (*Corpus Christianorum*, vol. civ, 1953), pp. 980 f.

[4] Cf. E. J. Gwynn, *Ériu*, vii. 128 f. Cumoine (*sic*) Fota is quoted in the following canons: OI II. 21 (cf. Cumm. II. 7—but the Latin text says 'three years' where the Irish has 'four'); OI III. 2 (= Cumm. III. 1. 2). 12 (cf. Cumm. III. 8). 15 (no parallel in the Latin text). Further, OI II. 31. 33. 34 and IV. 7, which are not attributed to Cumoine, have parallels in Cumm. (X) 5. 8. 9 and (VIII) 6.

[5] Bernard–Atkinson, i. 18–21; cf. ii. 108–12.

The *Penitential of Cummean* was much circulated on the Continent during the eighth and ninth centuries. Substantial extracts, enlarged with matter from 'Theodore'[1] and from other sources, were combined in the *Excarpsus Cummeani* ('Pseudo-Cummean'), which is preserved in manuscripts from the late eighth century onwards.[2] Much of Cummean's Penitential has found its way also into the early-ninth-century *Capitula Iudiciorum*.[3]

Literature: J. Zettinger, *Archiv für katholisches Kirchenrecht*, lxxxii (1902), pp. 501–40; M. Esposito, *Hermathena*, xx. 245–50 (most of the manuscripts listed by Esposito are copies of the *Excarpsus* or Ps.-Cummean); McNeill–Gamer, pp. 98 f.

7

The so-called *Canones Wallici* are preserved in two slightly different recensions, which I label A-text and P-text. They are not a penitential but a collection of laws of some rural community (*Gemeinderecht*). Only the three canons A 59–61, which are a later addition, have a penitential character. However, not only have *Canones Wallici* been transmitted together with a body of penitential literature, but they also provide interesting parallels to the elements of traditional secular law in the Irish penitentials and related texts and thus help to recreate their social background.

That this legal text is essentially Welsh can be inferred from the inclusion of some of its provisions in the Latin version of the Laws of Hywel Dda, and from frequent references to Welsh institutions, in particular to compurgation. At the same time the title of the A-text (four out of five manuscripts), *Incipiunt excerpta de libris Romanorum et Francorum*, and a number of parallels and verbal resemblances between *Canones Wallici* and *Lex Salica*, would seem to indicate some connexion with the Continent. From the fact that the manuscript tradition of *Canones Wallici* is mainly Breton one might conclude that an early Welsh text (which Haddan and Stubbs date to 550–650) was brought to Brittany by Welsh refugees and that it took its present shape in their new surroundings. The 'Romans' of the title would then be the Roman Britons who had settled in Brittany, as distinct from their Frankish overlords.[4]

Literature: Haddan–Stubbs, *Councils and ecclesiastical documents relating to Great Britain and Ireland*, i. 127 ff.; McNeill–Gamer, pp. 372 f.

---

[1] On Finsterwalder's tentative equation of the *Penitential of Cummean* with the *libellus Scottorum* referred to by 'Theodore' (Discipulus Humbrensium, Preface and I. 7, 5) see Fournier–Le Bras, i. 55 f.

[2] See the list of MSS., McNeill–Gamer, pp. 437 f.   [3] See Kenney, p. 243.

[4] See my article 'Towards an interpretation of the so-called "Canones Wallici"', in *Medieval Studies presented to A. Gwynn, S.J.* (Dublin, 1961), pp. 387–92.

8

The six texts printed by Wasserschleben under the collective title of *Canones Hibernenses* (Kenney, no. 78) are not transmitted as a unit. Texts I and II have a different manuscript tradition from the remainder.[1] All of them, except Text II, are introduced as decrees of some Irish synod.[2] There is, however, no evidence to show (as is the opinion of McNeill and Gamer) that the six texts are the outcome of a teamwork of ecclesiastical and lay persons that was finally sanctioned by one particular synod. It is even questionable whether they ever formed a whole.

Text I has three main sections: penances for various forms of homicide, fornication, and the destruction of the embryo; penances for the eating or drinking of forbidden food; penances for illicit companionship of religious with lay people, and for keening, which is obviously considered a pagan custom.

Text II is entitled *De arreis*. It is a list of commutations of long penances into shorter and harder ones (on this principle cf. '*Synodus II S. Patricii*', c. 3). This piece is related to the *Old-Irish Table of Commutations*; some canons are common to both. Similar commutations are found in Cumm. (VIII) 25–28 and in the *Bigotian Penitential*, pr. 5. The word *arra, arreum*, occurs only here and in the Old-Irish texts from Tallaght.[3]

Text III (Wasserschleben VI)[4] enforces the offering of certain ecclesiastical tithes, on the authority of Exodus and Leviticus. The last paragraph, a piece of biblical exegesis, would seem to be derived from a different source.

Text IV (Wasserschleben III) fixes punishments of a secular nature for offences or attacks on ecclesiastical personages. Only the last paragraph, which is introduced by the words *Patricius dixit*, provides for penance as an alternative to the established fine for various crimes against a king or a bishop or a *scriba*.

Secular also are the sanctions for the refusal of hospitality,[5] especially to the clergy, as laid down in Text V (Wasserschleben IV). This list of sanctions is preceded by a number of *exempla*; one of these is not known to me from any other source.

A piece of purely secular legislation is the law of dogs (Text VI, Wasserschleben V). One of the original tracts of the *Senchas Már* was called *Conslechta* 'Dog-classes' (cf. *ZCP* xviii. 361). Only some

---

[1] See below, p. 26.

[2] The reference to St. Gregory of Nazianzus in the title of Text I is still an unsolved problem.

[3] See Dr. Binchy, below, pp. 49 f.

[4] I follow the order of the texts in the manuscripts, which differs from that in Wasserschleben.   [5] See below, n. 1 on Can. Hib. V.

fragments of the text survive in later commentaries. One is tempted to regard the present section as derived from a latinized version of the lost tract, but there seems to be no correspondence between it and the surviving Irish fragments. One thing at least is certain: this set of 'canons' is in no sense a piece of 'ecclesiastical' legislation. All the same, these provisions, like those concerning tithes, are said to have been issued on the authority of a *sinodus sapientium*.

The date, or dates, of these canons cannot be accurately determined. II. 6, which is identical with Cumm. (VIII) 25, is quoted in the *Penitential of 'Theodore'*, I. 7, 5. IV. 8 and VI. 1–2 are quoted in the *Collectio Hibernensis* (c. 725). If Monochoma, named as an authority in I. 3, is correctly interpreted as Manchán, and if this is the Manchán of Liath-Mancháin who died in 665 (AU), we should have an approximate date at least for Text I; but all this remains quite uncertain. None of the six texts, however, with the possible exception of *De arreis* (Text II),[1] would seem to be later than the middle of the seventh century.

Literature: Kenney, p. 244; McNeill–Gamer, pp. 117 f.

9

The collection of twenty canons that have been transmitted in a number of manuscripts under the name of *Adamnan* (Kenney, no. 80) are regulations concerning clean and unclean food. They are based in part on similar regulations embedded in the Mosaic Law. Their attribution to Adamnan of Iona (d. 704) has no other authority than that of the manuscripts, none of which is earlier than the ninth century. The style, pedestrian and at the same time involved, bears little resemblance to the style of *De locis sanctis* or of the *Life of St. Columba*. It is just possible that these canons were enacted on the authority of Adamnan although their wording is not his. On this assumption, such phrases as c. 16 *sic idem interpraetatus est* (cf. also canons 17, 19, 20) might be understood as invoking the (real or alleged) authority of the great Irish churchman.

Literature: Kenney, p. 245; McNeill–Gamer, pp. 130 f.

10

The so-called *Second Synod of St. Patrick* (Kenney, no. 79)[2] does not seem to have anything to do with the Apostle of Ireland. I am not certain that c. xxvii must be so interpreted as to contradict St. Patrick's Confession, c. 42, as is the opinion of Haddan–Stubbs, Bury, Kenney, Dom Gougaud, and McNeill–Gamer. The canon in question requires

---

[1] II. 7 could be a misunderstanding of the eighth-century *Table of Commutations*, § 16A.

[2] The attribution to St. Patrick rests mainly on the colophon (in all manuscripts of the complete text): *Finit Patricii sinodus*.

the father's consent to his daughter's marriage; it states nothing
expressly about her entering the religious life, with which alone the
passage in the *Confessio* is concerned. A much stronger argument
against a fifth-century date of our document is the fact that, while twelve
of the thirty-one canons are quoted in the *Collectio Hibernensis*, only
one of them is attributed to Patrick; all the others are introduced as
decrees of a *sinodus Romana*, or *Romanorum*, or of the *Romani*, that is,
of the Roman party in seventh-century Ireland. On these grounds Bury
concluded that these canons were formulated at some Irish synod of the
seventh century.

Literature: Bury, *Life of St. Patrick*, pp. 237–9; Kenney, p. 245; McNeill–
Gamer, pp. 75 f.

11

The Penitential listed in Kenney as no. 74 has been labelled *Bigotianum*
because until now it has been known only from a *Codex Bigotianus* (Paris,
Bibl. Nat. Lat. 3182).[1] It is closely related to the *Old-Irish Penitential*
and to the *Penitential of Cummean*. However, it is not purely Irish. Its
main body is based on Cummean I–VIII (or on some unknown text
that was closely parallel), with which it agrees as regards composition
and chapter headings; but it also contains material that derives from
Canones Hibernenses I, the *Vitae Patrum* Book V (*Verba Seniorum*),
and 'Theodore'. Among the prefatory matter we find, side by side with
two pseudo-patristica of unmistakable Irish character and extracts from
Cassian and Isidore—authors well known in Ireland—an entire chapter
(c. 4) of the Rule of St. Benedict, of which, as far as I can see, there is
no trace in the early Irish Church. Moreover, the two manuscripts in
which this text is preserved place the *Bigotian Penitential*, together with
miscellaneous Welsh and Irish matter, between the *Collectio Dionysio-
Hadriana* and a copy of *Lex Salica*. Apparently this Penitential had
come to the Continent before it took the form in which we now read it.[2]
At the same time the *Bigotianum* is far less contaminated with English
or continental matter than are the 'mixed' penitentials of eighth- and
ninth-century France.

Literature: Kenney, p. 241; McNeill–Gamer, p. 148.

12

This brief survey of the Irish penitentials in Latin may be concluded
by some remarks on the text of their biblical quotations.

The number of quotations which are sufficiently explicit for textual

[1] I have since identified this text in another manuscript: Cambrai 625, of the late
ninth century; see above, p. 3; below, pp. 13, 21 ff.

[2] See below, p. 22.

comparison is 105. Their distribution over the several parts of the Bible and over its principal Latin versions is shown in the table here following:

	Vulgate or near-Vulgate	*Non-Vulgate*	*Inaccurate or conflate*
O.T.	17 (4 = or ∼ A)	17 (includ. 5 Psalt. Vet.)	3
Gosp.	15 (1 = A)+6 'Irish' (all Mt)	3	2
St. Paul	15[1] +4 'Irish' (D)	10 (6 distinctly Vet. Lat.)	2[2]
Cath. Ep.	7 +1 = AD	3 (1 distinctly Vet. Lat.)	0
	54 +11 = 65	33	7 (Total: 105)

The general picture shows a strong leaning towards the Vulgate. If the 'Irish' text of the New Testament is included,[3] the Vulgate or near-Vulgate quotations make up almost two-thirds of the total. The Vulgate text is most prominent in the Gospels, less so in the remainder of the New Testament, and least of all in the Old Testament, where the ratio of Vulgate and non-Vulgate is 1:1. However, distinct *Vetus Latina* readings are rare. This is due largely to our imperfect knowledge of the *Vetus Latina* for the greater part of the Old Testament; it is significant that the five distinct *Vetus Latina* quotations are all from the Psalms. Of the remaining twelve non-Vulgate quotations one-half are traceable to patristic or liturgical sources; others, especially 3 Reg. 21, 29; Ier. 3, 1; Ezech. 18, 20, have no close parallels. *Vetus Latina* readings are comparatively frequent in quotations from the Epistles, in particular from those of St. Paul.

It seems worth mentioning that nine passages (four from the Old Testament, two from the Gospels, and three from the Epistles) are quoted with a text either identical with, or very similar to, the text of Caesarius of Arles; four of these quotations occur in Vinnian, four in the prologue of Cummean, and one in the prologue of the *Bigotianum*. I would also call attention to the fact that Vinnian quotes three times 2 Petr. 1, 13 with a variant known to me only from St. Patrick (*Confessio*, 20 and 44), and that both Adamnan, c. 15, and '*Synodus II S. Patricii*', c. ii, quote Eccli. 34, 23 with the characteristically 'Hibernian' variant *reprobat* for *non probat* (see my apparatus to Patricius, *Epist.* 8). Finally, I observe that the more unusual or untraceable variants are, with one exception, found in two texts only—the prologues of Cummean and of the *Bigotianum*, which seem to have been prefixed *tels quels* to the respective penitentials.

[1] Including 4+1 quotations in a section derived from Gregory's *Moralia*.

[2] Including Gal. 5, 22–24, a passage with a very confused text tradition. The text as quoted in the prologue of the *Bigotianum* is clearly different from the Vulgate but has no particular affinity with any set of variants in the apparatus of Wordsworth–White.

[3] '*Synodus II S. Patricii*' has more 'Irish' quotations than have all the other texts with biblical quotations together (6:5).

II. THE MANUSCRIPT TRADITION

1

The Latin texts among the Irish penitentials are presented here in critical editions based on the complete evidence of all available manuscripts. Some of these have been collated here for the first time: Cambrai 625 for Gildas and the other early Welsh pieces, for Adamnan, *Canones Hibernenses*, and the *Bigotianum*; Oxford, Bodl. 311, for Cummean, whose Penitential was known so far from Vat. Pal. 485 only (for the prologue of Cummean six more manuscripts have been collated); the '*Second Synod of St. Patrick*', all previous editions of which derive ultimately from Sirmond's apographum of a *Codex Andegavensis*, is here edited from six manuscripts, three of which date from the eighth century; *Canones Wallici*, of which only the P-text has been printed, are here presented also in the parallel version (A-text), edited from all the five manuscripts in which it is known to be contained.

I have disregarded only a manuscript of the fifteenth and sixteenth centuries, Cambridge, CCC 298, which on foll. 57ᵛ–60ʳ contains a transcript of '*Synodus I S. Patricii*' made for Archbishop Parker (16th c.) from MS. Cambridge, CCC 279.

2

I first give a handlist of the manuscripts that have been consulted.[1]

A   Orléans 221 (193), saec. VIII–IX, from Fleury. Insular (Breton) minuscule. Scribe: Iunobrus (see colophon on p. 212). Cf. *Catalogue Général des Manuscrits des Départements*, 8°, vol. 12 (1889), pp. 114 f. (Ch. Cuissard). Contains:

> *Canones Wallici*: pp. 206–12.
> *Canones Adamnani*: p. 212 (beginning only, same text as *Codex Bigotianus*, p. 164).

B   Paris, Bibl. Nat. Lat. 3182 (*Codex Bigotianus*), saec. xᴵ.[2] Written by a Breton scribe named Maeloc; has Breton glosses. Was later at Fécamp (Normandy). Analysed by F. Maassen, *Geschichte der Quellen und Literatur des kanonischen Rechtes*, i (1870), pp. 784–6. A detailed analysis of contents will be given below. Contains:

> *Canones Wallici*: pp. 160–4.
> *Canones Adamnani*: p. 164 (beginning only, same text as Orléans 221); pp. 173–5 (complete text); p. 283 (end only, same text as Cambrai 625).
> *Vinnian* (extracts): pp. 176–7.
> *Canones Hibernenses* (II–VI Wasserschleben): pp. 177 f., 279–80, 302, 305–7, 312.

---

[1] See also H. Gamer in McNeill–Gamer, pp. 55–68, 432–50.

[2] The date commonly given ('saec. XI') seems too late (Bischoff: 's. x²').

Praefatio Gildae, Synodus Aquilonalis Brittanniae, Synodus Luci Victoriae, Excerpta de Libro Dauidis: pp. 280–3.
Paenitentiale Bigotianum: pp. 286–99.

C   Cambrai 625 (576), saec. IX ex. Provenance: Cambrai Cathedral. Cf. *Catalogue Général des Manuscrits des Départements*, 8°, vol. 17 (1891), pp. 242–4 (A. Molinier). Contains:

      Canones Hibernenses (III, IV, VI Wasserschleben): foll. 51^v–52; 68^{r-v}; 70^v–71^v.
      Praefatio Gildae, &c., as in *Codex Bigotianus*: foll. 52^r–54^v.
      Canones Adamnani (end only, as in *Cod. Bigot.*, p. 283): fol. 54^v.
      Paenitentiale Bigotianum: foll. 56^v–66^r.

D   Brussels, Bibliothèque Royale 10127–44, saec. VIII ex., from Saint-Pierre, Ghent. A collection of liturgical and canonistic texts, including the *Collectio Andegavensis*. For a detailed analysis see J. van den Gheyn, *Bibliothèque Royale de Belgique, Catalogue des Manuscrits*, i (1901), pp. 191–4. Contains: '*Synodus II S. Patricii*': foll. 45^v–48^r.

E   Oxford, Bodleian Library, Bodl. 311, in a continental minuscule saec. X. (Colophon, fol. 85^r: *Iohannes me scripsit.*) A collection of penitential texts. Was in England as early as saec. XI, as is proved by an Old English entry, now half erased, on fol. 1. Was presented to the Bodleian Library by the Dean and Chapter of Exeter in 1602. Cf. Madan–Craster, *Summary Catalogue*, ii. 1 (1922), p. 220; N. R. Ker, *Catalogue of MSS. containing Anglo-Saxon* (1957), no. 307; M. Esposito, *Hermathena*, xx (1930), pp. 246 f. Contains:

      Paenitentiale Cummeani: foll. 37^v–50^v.

F   Dijon, Bibliothèque Municipale, Anc. Fonds 42 (24), saec. XII ex., from Cîteaux. A theological miscellany. Cf. *Catalogue Général des Manuscrits des Départements*, 8°, vol. 5 (1889), pp. 11 f. Contains:

      Praefatio Cummeani: foll. 171^{r-v}.

G   Milan, Biblioteca Ambrosiana, C. 79 sup., saec. XII. A miscellaneous manuscript. Contains:

      Praefatio Cummeani: foll. 110^v–111^r.

H   Oxford, Bodleian Library, Hatton 42 (section A), saec. IX². Has Breton glosses. Cf. Madan–Craster, *Summary Catalogue*, ii. 2 (1937), pp. 848 f. Contains:

      Canones Wallici: foll. 130^r–132^v.
      Canones Adamnani: foll. 132^v–133^v.

I   Stuttgart, Württembergische Landesbibliothek HB VI. 112, saec. X, from Weingarten. Cf. J. F. von Schulte, *Sitzungsberichte Wien, phil.-hist. Kl.* 117 (1889), xi, pp. 15–22. *Collectio Andegavensis, Excarpsus Cummeani*, then, separately:

      '*Synodus II S. Patricii*': foll. 68^v–70^v.

J   Stuttgart, Württembergische Landesbibliothek HB VI. 109,first third of saec. IX, from Weingarten. Cf. J. F. von Schulte, op. cit., pp. 22–23. A collection of canons, including the *Collectio Andegavensis*. Contains:
   '*Synodus II S. Patricii*': foll. 94^v–100^r.

K   Cologne 91, saec. VIII–IX. 'Origin probably Burgundy': E. A. Lowe, *CLA* viii. 1155. Cf. Ph. Jaffé and G. Wattenbach, *Ecclesiae Metropolitanae Coloniensis Codices Manuscripti* (1874), p. 34; New Palaeographical Society, Ser. I, plate 57 with text. *Collectio Andegavensis*, Ps.-Cummean, *alia*. Contains:
   '*Synodus II S. Patricii*': foll. 54^r–57^v.

L   Milan, Ambrosianus L. 28 sup., saec. X.
   Contains on fol. 48 the Praefatio Cummeani (*De remediis uulnerum Cesarii episcopi*): cf. G. Morin, *Caesarii Opera*, i. 2 (1937), p. 930.

M   Montecassino 372, in Beneventan script, saec. XI in., from S. Nicola della Cicogna, see E. A. Lowe (Loew), *The Beneventan Script* (1914), p. 75.
   Contains on foll. 28^v–29^v the Praefatio Cummeani, lines 5–37 (*Ex coñ abbati iscotti. Medicina anime*). Collated from a microfilm obtained through the great kindness of his Lordship, Dom Pierre Salmon, San Girolamo, Rome.

N   Vatican Library, Vat. Lat. 1349. Collection of canons. Beneventan script, saec. XI. Cf. E. A. Lowe, *The Beneventan Script*, p. 362. Contains:
   Praefatio Cummeani: foll. 193^{r-v}.

O   London, British Museum, Cotton Otho E. XIII, saec. X in. Has Breton glosses. Cf. Th. Smith, *Catalogus codicum Bibliothecae Cottonianae* (1696), p. 79. A more detailed description will be given below. Contains:
   Canones Wallici: foll. 139^r–141^v.
   Canones Adamnani: foll. 141^v–143^v.

P   Paris, Bibl. Nat. Lat. 12021 (Sangermanensis 121), saec. X in., from Corbie.[1] Written in Brittany, by the scribe Arbedoc for abbot Haeb-Hucar (see colophon on fol. 139^r). Has also Breton glosses. Analysed by F. Massen, op. cit., pp. 786 f. A more detailed analysis will be found below. Contains:
   Canones Adamnani: foll. 132^v–133^v.
   Vinnian (extracts): foll. 134^v–135^r.
   Canones Wallici: foll. 135^r–138^r.
   Canones Hibernenses (I, II Wasserschleben): foll. 138^r–139^r.

Q   Paris, Bibliothèque Nationale, Lat. 1603, saec. VIII ex. *Collectio Andegavensis, Penitential of 'Theodore', Excarpsus Cummeani, alia*. Cf. *Catalogue Général des Manuscrits Latins* 2 (1940), pp. 85–86; Lowe, *CLA* v. 531. Contains:
   '*Synodus II S. Patricii*': foll. 74^r–78^v.

---

[1] This manuscript is often dated as of either saec. IX or X. I am convinced that it is earlier (but not much earlier) than Paris 3182.

R Vatican Library, Palat. Lat. 485, saec. IX, from Lorsch. Cf. H. Stevenson, *Codices Palatini Latini Vaticani*, i (1886), pp. 155–8; H. Ehrensberger, *Libri Liturgici Bibliothecae Apostolicae Vaticanae* (1897), pp. 396 ff. Contains:
   Paenitentiale Cummeani: foll. 101^r–107^v.

S St. Gall, Stiftsbibliothek 150, saec. IX. Cf. G. Scherrer, *Verzeichnis der Handschriften der Stifsbibliothek von Sankt Gallen* (1875), pp. 55–57. Contains:
   Praefatio Cummeani: pp. 285–7.
   Penitentiale Vinniani (incomplete at the end): pp. 365–77.

Ti Turin, Biblioteca Nazionale, G. VII. 16, saec. IX^2 (Bischoff: 'last quarter'), from Bobbio. Contains:
   Paenitentiale Columbani: foll. 62^v–70^v.

Tii Turin, Biblioteca Nazionale, G. V. 38, saec. IX–X or X in., from Bobbio. Contains:
   Paenitentiale Columbani: foll. 125^r–130^v.
   Cf. C. Cipolla, *Codici Bobbiesi* (1907), pp. 127–8, 140–1. Cipolla's dating of these two manuscripts seems more probable than the later dates that are usually given. See also my remarks *SLH*, vol. ii, pp. lxxiii f., and, against Dom Laporte's return to the late dating, *JTS*, N.S. xii (1961), p. 111.

V Vienna, National Library, Lat. 2233 (Theol. Lat. 725), *c*. 800, from Salzburg (?).[1] Cf. *Tabulae codicum in Bibliotheca Palatina Vindobonensi asservatorum*, ii (1868), p. 40; a more detailed analysis has been given by F. W. H. Wasserschleben, *Die Bussordnungen der abendländischen Kirche* (1851), pp. 494–7. Contains:
   Penitentiale Vinniani: foll. 25^v–58^v.

W Cambridge, CCC 279 (O. 20), saec. IX^2. Written on the Continent ('near Tours or under Turonian influence': Bischoff); was later at Worcester Cathedral. Cf. M. R. James, *Catalogue of Manuscripts of Corpus Christi College, Cambridge*, ii (1912), pp. 42–44. Contains:
   '*Synodus I S. Patricii*': pp. 1–10.
   Canones Hibernenses (III and an extract from IV Wasserschleben): pp. 156–7.

X Cambridge, CCC 265 (K. 2), saec. X–XI, from Worcester. Cf. M. R. James, op. cit., pp. 14–21; M. Bateson, *EHR* x (1895), pp. 712–31. Contains:
   Three Irish Canons: pp. 96–97.
   Canones Wallici (with many omissions): pp. 100–4.
   '*Synodus I S. Patricii*', can. 6: p. 104.

---

[1] On the early date of this manuscript (against the accepted later dating) Prof. Bischoff and I agree. As regards my guess concerning its Salzburg origin, Prof. Bischoff writes to me: 'Bei Wien 2233 . . . halte ich es für höchst wahrscheinlich, dass er und das aufs engste verwandte Sermones-Fragment in Donaueschingen B. III. 15 in Salzburg geschrieben sind; zu gänzlicher Sicherheit konnte ich noch nicht gelangen, und leider fehlt ja das erwünschte Argument zweiter Ordnung, die Salzburger Provenienz.' As an alternative possibility, Prof. Bischoff would think of Rheims.

Y   Paris, Bibliothèque Nationale, Lat. 3859, saec. ix middle to third quarter.[1] Given to Bonneval Abbey by an abbot named Godo (foll. 55ᵛ–56ʳ). '*Collectio Bonnaevallensis*'.[2] Contains:
'*Synodus II S. Patricii*': foll. 51ᵛ–52ᵛ.

Most of the manuscripts here listed are referred to in Wasserschleben, Kenney, and McNeill–Gamer.

A manuscript often mentioned in this connexion, but erroneously so, is Lyons 203. It has been said to contain the *Canones Wallici* and the *Canones Adamnani*. In actual fact it is a late medieval collection of privileges of the Dominican order, and has nothing to do with the present subject. The references to this manuscript in Wasserschleben, Kenney, and McNeill–Gamer are all derived from a note by Dr. J. L. Klee in *Serapaeum*, iii. 120, which in turn is a misinterpretation of G. Libri, *Journal des Savants*, 1842, p. 43, n. 2. Libri speaks of MS. Orléans 221 (193). The error was detected by H. Bradshaw (Wasserschleben, *Die irische Kanonensammlung*, 2nd ed., 1885, p. lxvii), but his words have passed unnoticed.

Many of these manuscripts show insular symptoms of one sort or another, especially in the matter of abbreviation.

3

From the point of text tradition, the Irish penitentials fall into two large groups: works which in their transmission are linked up with the *Collectio Hibernensis*, and works which have a text tradition of their own.

The second group can be dealt with rather briefly.

(1) The *Penitential of Columbanus* in found in two Bobbio MSS. (Ti and Tii), of ninth–tenth-century date, together with some other of the saint's works. The two copies differ but little; they are probably derived from the same exemplar. G. V. 38 (Tii), the later of the two, which is incomplete at the end, would appear to be the more faithful copy; the scribe of G. VII. 16 (Ti) has, I think, made some feeble attempts at 'editing' his *Vorlage*. From the same exemplar as these two codices obviously derives the lost manuscript used by P. Fleming, *Collectanea Sacra* (Louvain, 1667), pp. 94–97. Which of Fleming's individual readings come from his manuscript, and which are his own, it is impossible to say. Fleming's edition was reproduced by Wasserschleben. An independent edition is that of Seebass, *Zeitschrift für Kirchengeschichte*, xiv (1894), pp. 441–8. More recently new editions of the Penitential of Columbanus were published by G. S. M. Walker, in *Sancti Columbani Opera* (vol. ii of this series), pp. 168 ff., and by Dom Laporte (see

---

[1] So Prof. Bischoff (private communication).
[2] Prof. Bischoff writes (cf. note 1); 'Wenn ich auch mit der Datierung der Capitalis der Godo-Verse ins IX. Jh. recht haben sollte, könnte Godo sogar als Urheber in Betracht kommen.'

above, p. 5, n. 2). Both editors use the same manuscript sources as I do (my Ti = Ti Walker = T² Laporte; my Tii = T Walker = T¹ Laporte); our editions differ only in minutiae. However, for the sake of completeness it has seemed advisable to include that text also in this collection.

The other texts of this group—Vinnian, Cummean, and the so-called *Synodus II S. Patricii*—are transmitted in collections of canons. All these manuscripts except EY contain also either the *Penitential of 'Theodore'*, or the *Excarpsus Cummeani*, or both.[1]

(2) The *Penitential of Vinnian* (except for the extracts in P and B) is preserved in MSS. V and S. V is not only the sole manuscript of Vinnian that is complete; it has also the older, and more authentic, text. A considerable portion of the text is, however, taken out of its context and scattered over a larger compilation—mainly a combination of Vinnian and Ps.-Cummean—according to subject-matter. The original order is preserved in S, but Vinnian's diction has often been 'polished' and the spelling has been more or less normalized. S breaks off shortly before the end. P and B derive their extracts from a common source, which reproduces, with some variants, the S-text; both manuscripts have also readings of their own. Our edition will follow the order of S and the wording of V except where the latter is demonstrably wrong.

(3) The *Penitential of Cummean* (as distinct from the *Excarpsus Cummeani* or Ps.-Cummean) is commonly believed to have survived in a single ninth-century manuscript from Lorsch, R. The scribe of R worked rather carelessly, and his text teems with blunders. Many of these are obvious enough to be easily corrected. Of the remainder, much can be emended from later texts in which Cummean has been used: *Bigotianum*, Ps.-Cummean, the *Iudicia Cummeani* in the St. Gall Tripartitum, &c. In doing so one might even go beyond the first editor, J. Zettinger (*Zeitschrift für katholisches Kirchenrecht*, lxxxii (1902), pp. 501–40).

However, the genuine text of Cummean is preserved also in the tenth-century continental MS. Bodl. 311, for which I use the symbol E.[2] The text of Cummean (INCIP SCI BASILII PENITENTIALE AD CUMIANI LONGII) extends from fol. 37ᵛ to fol. 50ᵛ. It is followed by a number of extracts from various penitential sources, the first of which, with the title *Item de modis penitentie*, is a parallel to Cumm. (VIII) 25–28 and to the corresponding section in the prologue of Ps.-Cummean. The whole compilation, which ends on fol. 62ʳ, is divided into 223 short paragraphs the titles of which are united in a *capitulatio* prefixed to the *Penitential of Cummean* (fol. 33ʳ–37ᵛ); this *capitulatio*, too, is headed by the lemma

---

[1] The *Praefatio Cummeani* as a separate piece has been transmitted also in some miscellaneous MSS, see below, pp. 18 f.

[2] This manuscript is listed among the texts of Ps.-Cummean by McNeill–Gamer, p. 438. The particulars given by Esposito (*Hermathena*, xx. 246 f.) and by Madan–Craster, ii. 1, p. 220, however, make it abundantly clear that it contains the genuine text of Cummean.

INCIP̄ SC̄I BASILII PENITENTIALE AD COMIANI LONGII DE REMEDIIS. The chapter division of Cummean is abandoned, but the titles of the several chapters (though in ordinary minuscule, and not standing out from the text) have been retained. Textually, E is in some respects a rather free rendering of the original: there are many omissions of words and short phrases, changes of word order, filling up or abridgement of formulas, mutual substitution of such alternatives as *qui, si quis, qui si; in* or *cum pane et aqua; autem, uero,* &c. There is much hesitation between accusative and ablative forms, especially in indications of time. In many instances a vulgar Latin spelling of R has been normalized; in others, E has vulgar Latin spellings of its own. However, in spite of all this and of a number of scribal blunders pure and simple, E is of some help for the restoration of Cummean's text. It is certainly independent of R. In the prologue, where alone comparison with other manuscripts is possible, E stands half-way between R and SLMNFG (see below); a number of peculiar readings are common to E and LF. In the body of the work, E often sides with the text underlying Ps.-Cummean. In my apparatus I give a complete collation of E for the prologue and epilogue, and throughout the text all those variants which are in any way relevant either textually or linguistically. To give a complete collation of E would have encumbered the apparatus beyond all reasonable limits. In the circumstances, no E-reading must be inferred *ex silentio*, except that wherever an R-variant is found in the apparatus the text represents the reading of E. I have abandoned R only where this seemed absolutely necessary. This is not to say that E might not (or in actual fact does not) more often represent the true reading of Cummean than where I have followed it in my text; at the present stage, however, that is, in the absence of critical editions of 'Theodore', Ps.-Cummean, the *Capitula Iudiciorum,* and other related works, I have thought it safer to edit as far as possible the text of R.

The prologue, which is an extract from earlier patristic sources (Origen, Cassian), is preserved also separately in the ninth-century manuscript St. Gall 150 (S), in a tenth-century manuscript (L), in two eleventh-century manuscripts, M and N, and in two twelfth-century manuscripts, F and G. In L and F it is ascribed to St. Caesarius;[1] in S and N, to Cummean, and the same ascription is suggested by the heading in M: *Ex coñ abbati iscotti,* i.e. *Ex Commeano abbate in Scottia.* The heading of N agrees substantially with that of E; it reads: *Expositio sancti basilii Inquisitio acumiani longii.*[2] The prologue has also been incorporated in the preface of Ps.-Cummean, where it follows, without a break, on the prologue of Columbanus 'B' (*Diuersitas culparum* . . .); both are anonymous there, except that in MS. St. Gall 550, p. 163, after the initial words of the Cummean prologue (*et de*

---

[1] See above, p. 6. [2] Cf. Zettinger, p. 524; McNeill–Gamer, p. 98.

remediis uulnerum . . . conpendii racione intimemus) the text is interrupted
by a new lemma: PREFACIO CV̄MEANI ABBATIS IN SCOTHIA ORTVS, after
which the prologue starts again from the beginning: *De remedis*, &c.[1]
The prologue as contained in Ps.-Cummean has some characteristic
textual variants, especially *latroni crucifixo* for *latroni cruento* in the
'twelfth remission'. With regard to other variant readings, SLMNFG
in the prologue, and E throughout the work, in varying degrees desert R
in the direction of Ps.-Cummean.

(4) The so-called *Synodus II S. Patricii* has come down to us as an
addition to the *Collectio Andegavensis*,[2] but not in all its manuscripts.
This collection is named after an Angers codex, known to J. Sirmond,
but now untraceable; Sirmond's apographum has been the basis, either
directly or indirectly, of all previous editions of the '*Synodus II*'. The
present edition is based on five manuscripts of the *Collectio Andegavensis*
(KQDJI) and on the incomplete text (see note 2) in the *Collectio
Bonnaevallensis* (Y), which derives from the former. With the exception
of *I*, all these manuscripts date from the late eighth and ninth centuries.
The text is in a bad state; a number of corruptions in all six manuscripts
must go back to the exemplar which came to be incorporated in the
original collection. The *Textgeschichte* of the *Collectio Andegavensis* has
not, to my knowledge, been written yet;[3] my tentative classification of
manuscripts KQDJIY is based exclusively on the short text with which
we are concerned.

K, and to a slightly lesser degree Q, seems to keep very close to the
archetype; they are independent of one another but derive from an inter-
mediate copy (cf. p. 184, 13, *apciorē* K, *abciorem* Q, for *aptior est*; p. 192,
11 *ad altaris* KQ, *ad alteris* DJI, deest Y: the correct reading *ad alterius* had become *ad alteris* already in the archetype, *ad altaris* is a
secondary variant based on *ad alteris*). DJ and IY respectively are also
twin manuscripts. For DJ compare the apparatus at pp. 190, 18 sq. 21;
192, 8. 12 sq.; 194, 4. 13. 15 (deest Y, except for the last two references);
for IY, p. 186, 21 is characteristic: instead of *ad reorum defensionem*,
Y reads *hereorum defensione*, I reads *hebreorum difinitione*! IY have also

---

[1] The lemma is identical with that in MS. St. Gall 150, p. 285, but the text exhibits
a number of variant readings; it is substantially the text of Ps.-Cummean. Wasserschleben, pp. 461 f., erroneously quotes the Incipit and Explicit of the prologue in
St. Gall 150 as from St. Gall 675 (this has been kindly pointed out to me by the Rev.
Librarian of St. Gall, Dr. J. Duft).

[2] In MSS. Paris Lat. 1603 (Q) and Stuttgart HB VI. 112 (I) it is title LXUI, in MS.
Stuttgart HB VI. 109 (J) it is title LXIII (scribal blunder for LXUI?); in two other
manuscripts it is unnumbered. A shortened version (17 of the 31 canons) is included, as
title XXX, in the first collection of a Bonneval codex saec. IX[2] (see above, p. 16), now
Paris Lat. 3859 (Y).

[3] Valuable preliminary work has been done by F. Maassen, *Geschichte der Quellen
und Literatur des kanonishen Rechts*, 1 (1870), pp. 821 ff., J. F. von Schulte (see above,
in the description of MSS. I and J, pp. 13 f.), and G. Le Bras, in *Revue historique du
droit*, 4 sér., 8 (1929), pp. 767 ff.

a number of normalizations in common (the tenth-century manuscript I alone has many more). On the other hand, Y (or rather the parent of IY) derives directly from the archetype; this is proved by the occasional agreement of QI (p.194, 7 *superstis*: *super histis* Q. *super istis* I.deest Y), QY (p. 186, 2: omission of *et mensa*), and KY (p. 188, 5 *mysterium* for *ministerium*); most revealing is p. 188, 2; *confugerunt* KQ. *confugiunt* DJ. *confugerint* I. *confugierunt* Y: *confugierunt*, a typical 'Hibernicism', was normalized in KQ and 'corrected' in different ways by the parent of DJ and by I.

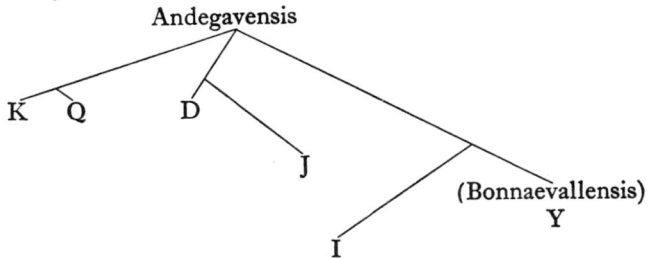

In my edition I reproduce the text of K, except for its evident *errores proprii*, with all its peculiarities of spelling and grammar;[1] the *errores communes* of the text tradition have, as far as possible, been emended, partly from the *Collectio Hibernensis*, in which twelve of our canons are quoted, partly by adopting corrections suggested by previous editors or translators (Spelman, Ware, Wilkins, Haddan–Stubbs, McNeill–Gamer).[2]

4

The manuscripts of the first group are more closely connected, and form, as it were, a unit. Whereas in the group that has been discussed above manuscripts of known origin come from a number of central European scriptoria with Irish, or at least insular, connexions (Bobbio, St. Gall, Salzburg (?), Weingarten, and Lorsch), most manuscripts to be considered here point to one district as centre of dissemination— Brittany. Three of these manuscripts (ABP) were written by Breton

[1] Occasionally other manuscripts, in particular Q, have 'irregular' forms where K is 'normal'; none of these forms, however, with the possible exception of p. 188, 2 *confugierunt* Y, may be claimed confidently for the archetype, let alone the original. In the circumstances, I prefer to follow K throughout.

[2] A copy of *Codex Andegavensis* was sent by Sirmond to David Rothe, bishop of Ossory, and was forwarded by the latter to Primate Ussher. This transcript was the basis of the *editio princeps* by Spelman, and, independently, of the edition by James Ware. J. Hardouin (*Conciliorum Collectio Regia* I, 1715, cols. 1793–6; reprinted, with few changes, by Mansi vi. 522–8) gives his text 'ex bibliotheca Andegavensi et apographo P. Jacobi Sirmondi', but quotes also *codex Bonnaevallensis*. Wilkins based his text on Spelman and Ware, Haddan–Stubbs on all three. McNeill–Gamer avowedly (see p. 76) translate, with some emendations of their own, the text of Haddan–Stubbs. (Editions, except Hardouin's and Mansi's, are listed by Kenney, p. 245). In my *apparatus* 'Spelman' inevitably covers three different things: readings of the Angers MS., the corrections (or otherwise) of Sirmond's amanuensis, and the emendations of Spelman.

scribes; for two others (HO) a Breton origin, or in any event, a Breton exemplar, is evidenced by the presence of Breton glosses.[1]

Another, and even more important, link between these manuscripts is their similarity as regards contents. They all contain the *Collectio Hibernensis* with certain accretions of a similar nature. The core of this group is the five manuscripts already mentioned, ABPHO. To these must be added Cambrai 625 (C), which runs parallel to the last section of B, and MS. Cambridge CCC 279 (W), which contains partly the same texts as ABO. Besides, W is our sole witness for the '*Synodus I S. Patricii*'. Less closely connected with this group is MS. Cambridge CCC 265 (X), which, for its greater part, is an entirely different collection (Egbert, Halitgar, Ps.-Theodore, Ps.-Romanum).

A key to the relationship of manuscripts ABCHOP is provided by the fact that they all contain, either wholly or in part, the *Canons of Adamnan*. The text is complete in HOP and once in B (pp. 173–5). B, however, has parts of this text also in two other places. On p. 164 we read the beginning (can. 1–7), followed by a paragraph of apparently different origin, similar to the last paragraph of *Canones Wallici*. The same seven canons together with this addition are found in A, p. 212. Further, on p. 283, B has can. 19–20 (ITEM ADOMPNANUS. Medullas . . .); the same extract, with the same heading, in the same context, is found in C, fol. 54ᵛ. Labelling the three texts of Adamnan in B as B¹ (the complete text), B² (1–7), and B³ (19–20), we state a close textual relation (with only minor individual variants) of AB² and CB³ respectively; of the four complete texts, HO often stand against PB¹, but H and O differ more widely in their readings than do B¹ and P.

A comparative study of the contents of ABCP, which was suggested by these findings, has yielded the following result:

A (Orléans 221)		B (Paris 3182)
pp. 1–16	*Liber ex lege Moysi*	pp. 1–12
pp. 16–20	*Computus* (Adam–Stilicho, interrupted by a paragraph on Narcissus of Jerusalem, and a chapter headed *Incipiunt remissiones peccatorum*). The same computus, with the Narcissus paragraph but without the *Remissiones*, is found in P, fol. 139ᵛ.	pp. 13–16
pp. 21–23	*Incipiunt uirtutes* . . . . ²; 2 canons concerning bishops	pp. 17–19
pp. 23–206	*Collectio Hibernensis* (A-text), without Preface	pp. 20–160
pp. 206–12	*Canones Wallici* (last paragraph omitted in A)	pp. 160–4
p. 212	*Canones Adamnani*, 1–7, followed by a short paragraph: *Equus aut pecus si percuserit hominem*	p. 164

[1] See H. Bradshaw, in Wasserschleben, *Kanonensammlung*, 2nd ed., p. lxxii.
[2] Edited by Rev. R. E. McNally in *Mediaeval Studies*, xxii (1960), 355–61.

P (Paris 12021)		(B)
foll. 127^v–132^v	*Iudicia Theodori* (different *explicit* and no colophon in B)	pp. 164–73
foll. 132^v–133^v	*Canones Adamnani* (no title in B)	pp. 173–5
foll. 133^v–135^v	*Canons of Ancyra and Neocaesarea*, followed by extracts from Vinnian (B has one paragraph less than P)	pp. 175–7
foll. 135^r–138^r *Canones Wallici* (P-text)		
foll. 138^r–139^r	*Canones Hibernenses* I, II (B has only title of I and text of II)	pp. 177–8
fol. 139^v *Computus* (cf. AB above)		pp. 178–83 Miscellaneous additions
C (Cambrai 625)		
foll. 1–51^v	*Collectio Dionysio-Hadriana*, with additions, the last of which is:	pp. 184–279
foll. 51^v–52^r	*Canones Hibernenses* VI Wass. (*De decimis*)	pp. 279–80
foll. 52^r–54^v	*Praefatio Gildae*, &c.	pp. 280–3
fol. 54^v	*Canones Adamnani*, 19–20	pp. 283
foll. 54^v–71^v (foll. 56^v–66^r)	A miscellaneous collection of canons, with *Paenitentiale Bigotianum* as its major item: contains also:	pp. 283–312 (pp. 286–99)
(fol. 68^{r-v})	*Canones Hibernenses* III Wass.	(p. 302)
(fol. 70^v–71^v)	*Canones Hibernenses* III (abridged). IV Wass.	(p. 305–7) p. 312 *Canones Hibernenses* V Wass.
foll. 71^v–80^v (incomplete)	*Lex Salica* (followed by the *Penitential of Egbert* in B)	p. 312–56

B is a compilation of three different collections of texts. Its first section (pp. 1–164) is, for all practical purposes, identical with A; section II (pp. 164–83) is closely parallel to the last part of P (foll. 127^v–139^r); section III (pp. 184–356) is almost identical with C (which has some minor omissions).

Textually, B is not a copy of either A or P or C; in all its three sections, B and its companion derive from a common exemplar. ABi and CBiii are almost identical in respect of contents. The relationship of P and Bii is not quite so close. Two texts of P are missing in B: the *Canones Wallici* (copied, in a different recension, at the end of Bi), and the first section of *Canones Hibernenses*, perhaps because of their resemblance to *Canones Adamnani*, by which they are preceded. Of *Canones Hibernenses* II (*De arreis*), which PBii have in common, either manuscript represents a different redaction. CBiii is substantially a Frankish compilation, as is proved by the inclusion of the *Lex Salica*; Frankish, I think, is also the *Bigotianum* in its present form (including as it does an extract from the *Regula Benedicti*, which seems to have been unknown in ancient Ireland).

H and O, as regards both contents and variants, are less closely related with ABCP as well as with each other. O contains much the same texts as ABi: *Liber ex lege Moysi, Collectio Hibernensis* (A-text), *Canons Wallici,*[1] *Canones Adamnani* (complete!); the computus and the *uirtutes* are missing, except for some of the 'inserts'. There follows a supplement from the B-text of the *Hibernensis*. This supplement forms a link with H, which contains the *Collectio Hibernensis* (B-text), *Canones Wallici, Canones Adamnani,* and several other texts with which we are not concerned.

A step farther removed is W. This manuscript starts with '*Synodus I S. Patricii*'. Next comes a collection of canons that is similar to, but not identical with, the *Hibernensis*; it gives an idea of the material out of which the standard collection was made.[2] After this follows the *Liber ex lege Moysi*, and extracts from the *Collectio Hibernensis* and from *Canones Hibernenses* III and IV. About the Worcester MS., X, enough has been said above.

All these manuscripts, it would appear, derive ultimately from a common repository (though not necessarily from one identifiable collection). The main text is the *Collectio Hibernensis* in either of its two recensions; around this have clustered some minor texts of a similar nature, partly Irish, partly Welsh. In point of time, this combination of texts would fall between the date of the latest item, the *Collectio Hibernensis* (*c.* 725), and that of the earliest manuscript, A (*c.* 800).

The common stock has branched out into several fairly distinct collections. One collection consists of *Liber ex lege Moysi*, the *Computus*[3] (with Narcissus and *Remissiones*), *Virtutes* etc., *Collectio Hibernensis* (either A or B), *Canones Wallici, Canones Adamnani*; its main area of circulation was Brittany.

In Brittany we can locate also a second collection, represented for us by P, and partly by Bii: *Collectio Hibernensis* (A-text), the *Penitential of 'Theodore'* ('Capitula Dacheriana'), *Canones Adamnani*, excerpts from Vinnian, a second recension of *Canones Wallici* (P-text),[4] and *Canones Hibernenses* I and II. Its original relation with the first collection is proved by the presence in P of the ABi computus.

Quite different is the collection of CBiii, which contains a number of texts not known from other sources: *Canones Hibernenses* III–VI (except

[1] *Canones Wallici* are incomplete. This is partly the result of damage which the manuscript suffered by fire in 1731. There are also omissions where the manuscript is not damaged; they are not identical with those in X, but overlap.

[2] P. Fournier, *Nouvelle Revue historique du droit français et étranger*, xxiii (1899), pp. 4 f., is inclined to regard this section as an abridgement of the *Collectio Hibernensis*, but leaves the question open.

[3] The fact that the computus comes to an end with Stilicho is possibly indicative of its ultimate Welsh origin.

[4] This recension is different in arrangement, wording, and occasionally in subject-matter from that of the other manuscripts.

for III and a short extract from IV in W), the group of early Welsh canons headed by the *Praefatio Gildae*, and the *Bigotianum* (to retain this traditional name, which now proves a misnomer). This collection can be located only tentatively. The earlier of the two manuscripts, C, comes from the Cathedral of Cambrai. The manuscript has no recognizable links with either Wales or Brittany. The presence in this distinctly Frankish collection (Dionysio-Hadriana, *Lex Salica*) of the Welsh and Irish items would seem to be the result of direct contacts with the Irish mission, for which there was ample opportunity in northern France. There is no reason why this collection should not have been made at Cambrai. The same source has left a trace in W—*Canones Hibernenses* III and a short extract from IV. Another Irish item in the same manuscript is the '*Synodus I S. Patricii*'.

At this point it might be useful to present the contents of ABCHOPWX in tabular form. The texts here edited are printed in italics.

X Cambridge, CCC 265	W Cambridge, CCC 279	H Hatton 42	O Otho E. XIII	A Orléans 221
Collect. canonum				
	'*Synod. I S. Patr.*'			
	Coll. Proto-Hibern.			
	Liber Moysi		Liber Moysi	Liber Moysi
			(See p. 23, top)	Computus, &c.
	Coll. Hib. A (extr.)	Coll. Hib. B	Coll. Hib. A	Coll. Hib. A
3 Irish canons				
Canones Wallici		*Can. Wall.*	*Can. Wall.*	*Can. Wall.*
'*Synod. I S. Patr.*'				
(can. 6)		*Adamnan*	*Adamnan*	*Adamnan* (1–7);
		Gaius		*Equus . . .*
			Coll. Hib. B	
			(supplement)	
	Can. Hib. IV. V (ex- tract)[1]			

B i Bi (Par. 3182)	P Par. 12021	B ii Bii (Par. 3182)	B iii Biii (Par. 3182)	C Cambrai 625
	Comm. in Matth.		Coll. Dionysio-Hadriana	
			Can. Hib. III	*Can. Hib. III*
Liber Moysi				
Computus, &c.				
Coll. Hib. A	Coll. Hib. A			
	Theodore (Dach.)	Theodore (Dach.)		
	Adamnan	*Adamnan* (no title)		
	Can. Ancyr.	Can. Ancyr.		
	Vinnian (extr.)	*Vinnian* (extr.)		
Can. Wall.	*Can. Wall.* (P-text)			
			Gildas, &c.	Gildas, &c.
Adamnan (1–7);			*Adamnan* (19 f.)	*Adamnan* (19 f.)
Equus . . .			Bigotianum	Bigotianum
	Can. Hib. I, II	*Can. Hib. I* (title), *II*	*Can. Hib. IV* (*bis*), *V*	
		Additions	*Can. Hib. VI*	
	Computus, &c.		Lex Salica	
			(lacuna)	
			Egbert	

[1] The numbering of *Canones Hibernenses* here is that of the present edition, not Wasserschleben's. Our Can III is Wass. VI; our IV = Wass. III; V = Wass. IV; VI = Wass. V.

5

Little need be said about individual items.

(1) '*Synodus I S. Patricii*' has been edited by a number of scholars from Spelman to Haddan–Stubbs. They all, and also McNeill–Gamer, have helped to make the text intelligible. Quotations in the *Collectio Hibernensis* are frequent, but of less value for emendation than are those from '*Synodus II*'. All editions are based, either directly or indirectly, on W.

None of the other texts in this group has ever been edited critically. Of previous editors only Wasserschleben deserves to be mentioned. We are indebted also to McNeill–Gamer. For the present edition, two important manuscripts, A and C, have been used for the first time.

(2) *Canones Wallici* have come down to us in two recensions, which will be printed one after the other. The one is preserved in ABHOX (A-text), the other in P only (P-text). Some paragraphs of the A-text have been incorporated in *Leges Walliae* (II. 49, 2–17). The manuscripts of the A-text fall clearly into two groups: AB and HO. Among particular agreements of HO I mention an omission by *homoiotes* in 60, and the transposition of canons 54 and 55; besides, there are many characteristic group-readings of AB and HO respectively. X sides partly with AB, partly with HO, and partly with only one manuscript or the other of either group. The text of these canons must have had many variants, not only of formulation, but also alternative provisions. The arrangement is not entirely satisfactory in either recension, but the A-text seems slightly more orderly.

(3) The text tradition of *Canones Adamnani* has already been discussed. It may be added here that PB^1 and HO have many significant group-readings, HO also a strange common omission, which, I think, represents one line of the archetype left out by the scribe of their exemplar. Of the remaining groups, which contain only sections of the text, AB^2 are nearer to HO than to PB^1; CB^3 render the text rather freely.

The complete *Canones Adamnani* were first printed by Luc d'Achéry (*Spicilegium*, i (Paris 1723), pp. 490 f.) from P; Martène and Durand (*Thesaurus novus anecdotorum*, iv (Paris, 1717), col. 11, 18, 19), who used B, gave only canons 1–7, 19, 20 (that is, B^2+B^3); Wasserschleben's text (pp. 120–3) is based on B^1 ('a') and P ('b'). Haddan–Stubbs (ii. 1, pp. 111–14), who on the whole reproduce the text and apparatus of Wasserschleben, allegedly add variants from O ('c'). These 'c'-references, however, are restricted to the paragraphs which are also in Martène, and agree more often with B^2+B^3 than with O. In actual fact the 'c'-readings of Haddan–Stubbs are derived almost entirely from the edition in J. Robertson's *Concilia Scotiae* (Bannatyne Club, Edinburgh,

1863), ii. 229 f.;[1] this, however, is the incomplete text of Martène imperfectly collated with O. The present edition is based on a collation of all the manuscripts mentioned above, p. 21.

(4) *Canones Hibernenses* I is extant in P only. The text is in a very bad condition, my emendations are merely tentative. Canons II is found in P and B—two different recensions, which will be printed in parallel columns. Canons VI (Wasserschleben V) is known only from B; its first two paragraphs are quoted in the *Collectio Hibernensis*.

(5) The remaining texts (*Canones Hibernenses* III, IV, V = Wasserschleben VI, III, IV; *Gildas*, &c.; *Bigotianum*) are found only in CB (the greater part of IV and an extract from V also in W). C and B derive from a common exemplar with a badly corrupt text. A limited number of corrections are offered by parallel texts, especially Cummean and Ps.-Cummean.

6

In the circumstances, I have thought it best to follow in every instance the earliest complete manuscript of the respective text, and to abandon it, even in matters of spelling, only for very definite reasons, in particular where other manuscripts have distinct 'Hibernicisms'. All variants are listed except, as a rule, the substitution of *æ ę e œ*. I have always expanded *e caudata* as *æ*, and *p̄* as *prae*—including such words as *praelium praetium*, which are normally so spelled in our sources when written in full.

Fontes and *Similia* are given under the text where this has seemed helpful for the study of either the text tradition or the Hibernian Bible text.

The biblical references do not claim to constitute an *apparatus biblicus* deserving this name; they are merely indications of textual affinity. In my presentation of the material I follow the method adopted in my *Libri Epistolarum S. Patricii*.

Some of the penitentials here described have a certain amount of material in common. The *Penitential of Vinnian*, which, as far as we

---

[1] At the beginning of their apparatus, Haddan–Stubbs declare: 'the same part as Martène's [was edited] by Robertson (*Stat. of Ch. of Scotl.*, pp. 229, 230) from a Cotton MS., Otho E. XIII, fol. 155*b*, 157*b*, of which a transcript is also in Bishop Marsh's Library in Dublin (*Reeves ad Adamn.*, p. 179 note), and which is almost the same in text with Martène's MS.' This statement is partly erroneous and partly misleading. To begin with, the reference to Robertson's publication is cryptic; it is an English translation of the Latin subtitle of *Concilia Scotiae*, viz. *Ecclesiae Scoticanae Statuta* (it was resolved by Kenney, p. 245, as 'State of the Church of Scotland'!). Secondly, Robertson's procedure is described very inaccurately. Robertson says in the preface to his work that the *Canones Adamnani* were reprinted by him from Martène and Durand, but that their text had been collated for him by Mr. James Gairdner with MS. Cotton Otho E. XIII, foll. 155*b*, 137*b* (not 157*b*, as in Haddan–Stubbs; the two folios are now 141ᵛ and 142ᵛ). The manuscript in Marsh's Library referred to by Reeves is Z. 3. 1. 14—an inaccurate transcript of Cotton Otho E. XIII, foll. 141ᵛ–143ᵛ (present foliation). In the clarification of this matter I have been greatly assisted by Mr. R. A. Wilson, Keeper of Printed Books, and Mr. D. H. Turner, Assistant Keeper of Manuscripts, in the British Museum.

can see, is an original composition, i.e. not dependent on known sources, has been largely drawn upon, though not *verbatim*, by St. Columbanus. Cummean includes in his Penitential a number of Welsh canons in their original wording. The *Paenitentiale Bigotianum* is in its main section parallel to Cummean and to the *Old-Irish Penitential* but borrows also from Columbanus and *Canones Hibernenses* I (and from other sources with which we are not concerned here). These borrowings are often so literal that the several texts, all more or less corrupt, can in some measure be mutually corrected by comparison. A concordance of these parallel passages will be found at the end of the volume.

III. REMARKS ON THE LATINITY

It is not my intention to discuss here the Latinity of the penitentials exhaustively and systematically. A study of this kind would have to place its subject against the background of Hibernian Latin in all its aspects. For such an endeavour the time has not yet come. I shall do no more than briefly survey the material presented in the linguistic indexes, and point out some problems to which it gives rise.

I

Spelling is very irregular; it often violates the classical rules. Some of our texts survive in manuscripts that were written before the Carolingian revival. Even the later penitential manuscripts show as a rule little or no trace of linguistic normalization. Penitentials served a strictly practical purpose, and nobody would bother to touch them up; an important group of such texts was brought together and copied in Brittany, where the influence of the Frankish schools made itself felt but slowly and where it was never particularly strong.

To classify these spellings is no easy task. Too many of the relevant phenomena defy linguistic analysis because they are functionally ambiguous. Are such forms as *absteneant, contenentes, redemi* (infinitive) instances of Vulgar Latin vocalism or of recomposition? Is the confusion of the case-endings *-e* and *-em*, so frequent in Cu(E)[1] and in Pa II, phonetic or syntactic? Is *effunderit* (Wa A 50, Bi II. 1, 2) an analogical formation after the present stem, or is the insertion of the nasal merely a 'hyper-correct' spelling? Sometimes one can decide at least on grounds of probability: the plural accusatives (all in Pa II) *absoluendus lapsus, monachus, subditus* are hardly heteroclitic; the infinitives *furare moechare* are in all probability active counterparts of the deponents *furari moechari*. Many cases, however, remain doubtful; sometimes one cannot even be sure what exactly the text is meant to say.

[1] I use in this chapter the same abbreviations for texts as in the Indexes, see list of abbreviations, p. 284.

Thus Wa A 58 *intercidendo* (*intercedendo* HO, cf. P 67) *litem* might be taken at its face value and be translated 'by trying to break up a brawl'; the variant reading, however, which has the support of the P-version suggests that we ought to understand *intercedendo liti* 'by interfering with a brawl'. More problematical is Pa II. 12 *qui . . . in uita sua sacrificium non meretur accipere, quomodo post mortem illi poterit adiuuare?* We may either take the words as they stand and acknowledge the impersonal use of *potest* (cf. *si può, il se peut*) and a dative construction with *adiuuare* after the analogy of *subuenire succurrere*, or else we may read *illi* as *ille* and *adiuuare* as *adiuuari*. At Pa II. 17, *superhabundantia . . . diuiditur* is the reading of KQI—possibly a reminiscence of Acts 2, 45; 4, 35; but DJ read *diuitetur* (that is, *deuitetur*), and the same interpretation is possible for the reading of KQI. Is *scupa* Cu (XI) 24 (E) a Latin phonetic variant, or does it reflect Irish *scúap?*[1]

Analogical spellings are frequent here as they are elsewhere. In some cases the analogy is, I think, lexicographical. This need not amount to more than a subconscious verbal echo: *capud* follows *apud* (and inversely, *aput* follows *caput*), *obduratur* echoes *durus*, *relinquid* is possibly prompted by *quid*, *scriptulum* is modelled on *scriptum*, *summere* on *summa*, and, perhaps, even *sodomitta* on *mittere*. One cannot help feeling, however, that the *concupina* of Wa A 59 (B) got her *p* from *concupiscere*.[2]

The picture is complicated by the fact that the manuscript tradition of our texts is not uniform, and especially that groups of texts by different authors and of different date have been transmitted in the same manuscripts. Many spellings are characteristic of certain manuscripts rather than of particular texts. Most interesting from the point of spelling are MSS. K and Q of the *Collectio Andegavensis* and *Codex Bigotianus* (B), with ACDEHJOPRTiiVW as close runners-up.

This raises the problem of the relation between Vulgar Latin, Hibernian Latin, and Merovingian Latin. Not one of the manuscripts used for the present edition was written in Ireland. Most of the earlier copies were made either in France or in western Germany; an important group, containing, *inter alia*, texts which were originally composed in Wales, can be located in Brittany. The scribes of these manuscripts, unbridled by Alcuinian discipline, indulge, some more and some less so, in vagaries of spelling that are characteristic of the Merovingian period; but they copy texts that were originally written in a different

[1] Cf. also Welsh *ysgub*. Ir. *úa* from *ō* could not be earlier than *c.* 650; it is thus barely possible that *scupa* was the original spelling of Cummean, but it is more probable that this spelling, found only in the tenth-century manuscript E, is peculiar to this manuscript or to its immediate exemplar.

[2] Generally speaking, *tt* and *p* could, in accordance with OI orthography, represent unlenited *t* and *b* respectively. But (see below, pp. 29 f.) these and other 'Hibernian' spellings of Latin are far from regular, and are found most commonly in a limited number of individual words; one is therefore inclined to look for a special cause at least as a contributing factor.

environment with spelling traditions of its own. Can we separate these layers? Can we 'strain off' the Merovingian element?

Both Hibernian Latin and Merovingian Latin stem from Late Latin. They have thus many non-classical features in common, not excepting details of spelling. There is, however, this important difference: the Latin of late antiquity persists in Merovingian France without a break; to the Irish schools Latin was introduced from abroad as a learned and sacred language. During the first 150 years of growth in its new habitat it was nourished from at least two sources: the Latin of Gaul and the Latin of Wales.[1] To these must be added the powerful impact, even in such minor things as spelling, of the biblical and liturgical manuscripts which had reached Ireland with the first missionaries. It stands to reason that the native language would also exercise a certain influence. All this might be expected to show in details of spelling as much as in other grammatical features. Unfortunately the Welsh and Gaelic elements are largely unknown factors, and the Merovingian element, which is more tangible, remains, to say the least, an unknown quantity. It would thus be hazardous to declare as Hibernian this or that general type of spelling. There are, however, certain spellings of which Irish writers of Latin and Irish copyists of Latin texts seem to have been particularly fond. Below, I give a selected list of such spellings in the Irish penitentials:

accussantis cassu Casianus centissimi, &c. (cf. Matth. 13, 23 LQR), effussio effussus heressis ingresor inlessi inlissi Isserninus Issiodorus (com-, de-, di-, per-, pro-)misserit remissisti misa miso (omisa permisione remisio) occassum occissio occissus paradisso parruchia percusio percusor percuserit possitus, &c., pussilanimitas subdiuissionibus ussus[2] Solamone—iecite iectus iectio—ce(cę-)nubium aec(c)lesia aelimosina aequus (= equus) caeterum praetium—adherit—Grecos Gregis letus merens sepe—ancella demedium senum (= sinum)—acciperit susciperit—Grigori— dispectione dispicere disperare dispoliat disponsata distituta distruatur Contracted genitives in *-i* of the type *bardigi eloqui fili,* &c. fruntibus prumptum renuetur—habundat heremi hostiarium hostium (= ostium)[3] caticumini—quoaequalia quohabitatione.

Characteristically Hibernian are also such spellings as *cremina commonis*

---

[1] There is little, if any, difference between the Latinity of Welsh and Irish writers. See also below, section 7.

[2] In OI an original simple *-s-* between vowels was lenited and disappeared completely. Hence, where intervocalic *-s-* appears, it invariably represents older *-ss-*; this is written *-s-* or *-ss-* indifferently. Against this background must be seen the tendency to write *-ss-* for intervocalic *-s-* (and vice versa) in Hibernian Latin. This tendency is very strong indeed, but again certain words are more commonly so spelt than others.

[3] This phenomenon also is common to Latin (especially late Latin) and OI, where (cf. Thurneysen, *Grammar,* § 25) *h* had no phonetic value and is often arbitrarily prefixed to a word beginning with a vowel; in Latin loanwords it is sometimes inserted sometimes omitted (*óre* and *hóre,* gen. of *úar* from Lat. *hora*).

excommonis commotauerit. These are neither phonetic spellings on the grounds of Vulgar Latin pronunciation nor inverse spellings of the ordinary type. They might be 'inverse spellings of the second degree', that is to say, they might be due to a desire of avoiding such spellings as *uirum* for *uerum* or *putu* for *potu*; on the other hand, they might reflect an open pronunciation in early Ireland of Latin *i* and *u*, in the same way as the frequent substitution of *ae* for *e* (*aepiscopus, aecclesia, caena, aequus,* &c.) seems to indicate an open pronunciation of Latin *e*.[1]

Studying Latin texts and manuscripts of Irish origin one gets the impression of a distinct partiality for certain Late Latin spellings of particular words: *acciperit caena cremen demedium missit hostium parruchia,* &c. These spellings are as such not peculiar to Ireland; it is their frequency, if not regularity, that makes them Hibernicisms. Why just these words and a limited number of others? In the present state of our knowledge I can only raise the question.

2

The vocabulary of the penitentials is primarily technical. In this category fall, *inter alia*, the numerous abstract feminine nouns in *-io* (see Index grammaticus). Apart from technical terms, its most striking feature is a number of rare words, some of doubtful meaning, with a sprinkling of corrupt Greek; they will be discussed below under 'Hibernicisms'. The vocabulary of *Canones Wallici* stands a little apart. This results largely from the different subject-matter: *Canones Wallici* are a *legal* text. In some respects their vocabulary seems slightly more classical than the rest; there certainly is a basis of Roman legal tradition.

An interesting detail are the synonyms for 'all' and 'each'. The classical *cunctus* is found only twice, in Columbanus: B. pr. *cuncta cognoscere, curare* (a highly stylized phrase—was this prologue really composed by Columbanus?), and B. 20 *uti . . . cibis . . . cunctis*. The normal word for 'all' is, of course, *omnis*; the Romance *totus* = *omnis* is rare.[2] A borderline case is Lu 9: *totum hoc quod diximus* (the penances for three types of *scelus uirile* as stated in the preceding paragraph), *si post uotum perfectionis fuerit homo; si ante uotum, annus diminuitur de omnibus his tribus.* The two phrases *totum remanet aurum* Bi pr. 15 and *totus*

---

[1] Cf. St. Patrick's *exagaellias* (*Confessio* 14) and the remarks of K. Mras, *Anzeiger der Österr. Akademie der Wiss.*, phil.-hist. Kl., 1953, p. 108, n. 38. In OI the ligature *æ* is sometimes written for *ĕ*, thus *æclis* = *ecclesia*, but *ae* for *ĕ* is very rare (even for *ē* it is unusual). On the other hand, the continental copyists may have written *ae* for *æ* of their insular exemplar; see Thurneysen, § 24, 1.

[2] One must, of course, exclude passages where the whole is contrasted with a part: *annum totum abstineat se* Vi 3. 6 (as contrasted with the six months of stricter penance); similarly Cu II. 22 *tribus annis peniteat; in primo . . . et in totis . . .*; slightly different is Bi I. 9, 1 (he who fasts on a Sunday) *ebdomadam totam debet ieiunare*. Even this use of *totus* is not frequent; both Vi and Co prefer *annum(-o) integrum(-o)*.

plumbeus ibid. 16 are half-way in the direction of the Romance pole; the only indisputable instances occur in Columbanus B (20 *totas res suas uendat*; 29 *toti . . . sint conglobati*)—a text that was probably penned on the Continent, in a 'Romance' environment. *Omnis* 'each' has a rival in the more individualizing *unus quisque*, but both expressions are used without distinction of meaning, cf. Gi 1 = Cu II. 2 *ueniam omni hora roget . . . in una quaque hebdomada*; we find *in omni hora* Hi II. 2 (B) twice, *in una quaque hora* Hi II. 2 (P), 9 (B), cf. 4 (B) twice; *omni anno* Hi III. 1 twice, *in uno quoque anno* Hi III. 2 twice. Occasionally *singulus, -i* is preferred to either *omnis* or *unus quisque*: *per singula cremina* Pa I. 14; *in anno singulo* Vi 46; *in singulis hebdomadibus* Hi II. 8 (P), where B has *uni cuique ebdomadae*.

Facere is the basic verb *par excellence*. We read, *inter alia*, the expressions *cenam faciat* (= *paret*) *seruis Dei* Vi 35; *cremen* (Pa I. 16), *homicidium* (6 times), *parricidium* (twice), *scelus uirile* (Lu 8) *facere* for *cremen*, &c., *committere*, *perpetrare*. Other phrases of this type are circumlocutions or equivalents for more specific verbs, for example *peccatum facere* Gi 4 = *peccare*, *dolum facere* Da 7 = *fallere*, *fornicationem facere* (four times) = *fornicari*, *furtum facere* (eight times) = *furari*, *iudicium facere* Pa II. 5 = *iudicare*, *osculum facere* Cu (X) 2 = *osculari*, *rixam facere* Vi 5 = *rixari*, *uomitum facere* Bi I. 2, 1. 4 = *uomere*;[1] also, *in bonam partem*, Pa I. 28 *orationem facere*, Gi 1. 20 = Cu II. 2; (IX) 9, and Vi 4 *superpos(s)itionem, -es facere* beside the more frequent *orare, superponere*; Gi 20 *triduanum* (i.e. *ieiunium?*) *facere* apparently for *triduum ieiunare*. This might be in the nature of artless diction (a sort of 'basic Latin'), which does not bother about the *mot juste* but is content with a few clichés; more probably, however, it is an element of legal style, which tends to emphasize the act by the use of a noun.[2]

3

The gender of *dies* is but rarely determinable. We find *in illo die* Da 8; Vi 9 ex. (PB); *in quo die* Bi pr. 21; *uno (.i. R) die uel duos (.ii. R)* Cu (VIII) 14 (E); *uno (.i. R) die* Cu (VIII) 17 (E); *octauo (-a I) die* Pa II. 19; *intra dies paucos* Wa A 15; and, if my supplementation is accepted, *in duobus <diebus> legitimis* Cu II. 30. *Dies* is feminine only in the phrases *septima, octaua die(s)*, twice each, in Bi pr. 19–21. More interesting is perhaps the distribution of *(dies) dominicus* and *dominica*: on the one hand, *die dominico* Gi 1 (= *dominico die* Cu II. 2); *in dominico* Cu II. 30; *de, in die dominico* Bi I. 9 tit.; 9, 1; *in dominico* Bi II. 10 tit. and text; on the other hand, *die dominica* Pa I. 30; *in die dominica* Da 7; *ad . . . diem*

---

[1] Is it mere chance that so many of the verbs thus avoided are deponents?

[2] Examples are found as early as the *Twelve Tables*, e.g. XII. 2 *si seruus furtum faxsit*. On elements of legal style in the Penitential of St. Columbanus, see *SLH*, vol. ii, p. lxxxi.

dominicam, die dominica Co B 28, 29. The texts written in Ireland and Wales reflect the uncertainty regarding the gender of *dies* in late Latin. The consistent treatment of *dies* as a masculine noun in the *Bigotianum* (the archetype of which is Frankish) and as a feminine in the *Penitential of St. Columbanus* (which survives only in Bobbio MSS.) might be related to the regional differentiation of the 'Romania' (cf. French *dimanche* and Italian *domenica*); but the basis for arguing this point is rather narrow.[1]

Extension in time (in particular of the duration of penances) is expressed as often by the accusative as by the ablative (the latter occasionally with *in*).[2] Both constructions are used indiscriminately, even side by side in one sentence, e.g. Pa I. 15 *demedium peniteat, .xx. diebus cum pane*; Vi 20 *dimedium annum . . . peniteat et duobus annis* (PB: *.ii. añ* VS) *abstineat*; Vi 26 *annis tribus peniteat, primo anno . . ., et duos alios abstineat se*; Cu (VIII) 14 (E) *uno die uel duos*. In other places our manuscripts read variously: Vi 24 *tres annos* V, *tribus annis* SP (similarly Vi 23); Vi 25 *anno integro* V, *annum integrum* S. Frequently some or all manuscripts of a text express the numeral by a figure that is followed by the suspension *añ*; this would seem to have been a common practice, and the compilers of penitential canons as well as their copyists would regard the two constructions as interchangeable. They may not even have felt accusative and ablative as two different cases; the spoken language knew only one *obliquus*. Indifferent use of the two cases is most common after prepositions. Some scribes have their idiosyncrasies: in Vinnian, for example, MS. V writes consistently *per mensura* where the other manuscripts have the more classical *per mensuram*.

The ablative absolute is still employed in the classical manner in such passages as Gi 1 = Cu II. 2 *praelato ante monachi uoto*; Co B 14 *toro proximi uiolato*; ibid. 16 *reddito . . . humiliationis eius praetio parentibus*; 19 *data . . . ante pauperibus de suo labore helemosina*; 28 *altero pedes suos lauante*; Cu (XI) 27 *linteamina . . . abluat . . . calice subter posito*; Wa P 13 *si quis ad alterum lanceam misserit inlesso homine*; Wa A 37 (P 46) *commisso delicto*; Wa P 57 *flumine transmisso*; cf. also the elliptical phrase, Wa A 30 *si (tributo) mense ante praedicto (tributum reddere) neglexerit*. It should be noted, however, that all these examples are taken from the earlier texts, and four out of ten from St. Columbanus. On the whole there is a tendency to restrict this construction to a small number of set types which often function as formulae: *inconsultu (suo) abbate* Pa I. 34 twice; *nullo audiente* Gi 16; *praesente Petro*, &c., Bi IV. 7; — *uiris nominatis* Wa P 3. 32; *inuocatis ex omnibus .iiii.* Wa P 34; *indictis iuratoribus* Wa A 43 (P 45); — *iudice sacerdote* ten times, cf. also *sacerdote*

---

[1] See also my remarks in *SLH*, vol. ii, pp. lxxviii f.

[2] In OI duration of time can be expressed either by the accusative or by the dative, which in Irish has taken over most of the functions of the ablative; see Thurneysen, §§ 249, 3; 251, 3.

iudicante Bi V. 3, 1;[1] — *exundante uentre* Gi 7; *concepto semine* Cu II. 30; *omni dimisso saeculo* Co B 20; *relictis (reiectis* E) *armis* Cu (IV) 5, (IX) 13; *reiectis armis* Lu 4; — *impleto anno* Pa I. 14; *impletis .x. annis* Vi 23; *anno emenso* Aq 6 = Cu (VIII) 12; *una interueniente nocte* Cu (VIII) 27; — phrases with *excepto (-a, -is)*: Gi 1 = Cu II. 2, Gi 16, Co B 20. 29 (twice).

An ablative absolute is often used in introducing biblical quotations: *Solamone dicente* Pa I pr.; *Domino dicente* Cu pr. 5; *psalmista testante* Cu pr. 6; similarly Cu pr. 7. 8. 11. 12. 13. Pa II. 22. 25; in this category also falls *Deo auctore*, Vi 46.

I find only two instances of *post* with the accusative as a substitute for the ablative absolute: *post paenitentiam transactam* Co B 18, and *post abscisam . . . aurem* Ad 20.

4

The so-called analytical conjugation figures in our texts so largely[2] as to deserve a brief discussion. All examples are of the type *mortuus fuit = mortuus est*.[3] The text-to-text ratio of regular passive or deponent perfects and those formed with the help of *fui* may be seen from the conspectus here following:

	Type: *mortuus fuit*	Type: *mortuus est*
Pa I	7+2 (?)	3
Gi	2	0
Aq	1	0
Lu	0	1
Da	0	3
Vi	16	12
Co	6 (3 in MS. Ti only)	4
Cu	I–(VIII): 1 (+4 in quotations) (IX)–(XI): 10 (+1 in a quotation) Postscript: 0	I–(VIII): 5 (+2 in quotations) (IX)–(XI): 2 (+1 in a quotation) Postscript: 1
Wa A	18 (none in 59–63)	2 (copula omitted) +1 in 63
P	19	0
Hi IV	1	0
V	2	0
Ad	1	6+1 (copula omitted)
Pa II	1	3+1 (copula omitted)
Bi pr.	2	5 (+1 in a quotation)
(text)	2 (+1 in a quotation)	6 (+5 in quotations) +2 (copula omitted)

[1] A rival formula is *iudicio* (or *ad iudicium*) *sacerdotis*; see the references in the Index uerborum.

[2] In the entire works of St. Columbanus there are *c.* 40 examples of analytical conjugation, in Adamnan's *De locis sanctis* there are 13; in our texts I count about 100.

[3] The only instance of a perfect with the function of a present (other than the

It is perhaps worth noting that in the latest of our texts the ratio is strongly in favour of the normal type; that the ratio in Vi and Co is very nearly the same (4:3–3:2);[1] that, quotations apart, there is a great difference between the ratio in the first eight chapters of Cummean and the ratio in the last three;[2] and that, while the number of 'analytical' perfects in Wa is very great (Wa has the highest ratio of all the texts here edited), there is not a single instance in the alien matter appended to Wa A (59–63). Even such compilations as these, which were made without literary ambition, have their linguistic individuality.

5

Conditional clauses,[3] inevitably, are very numerous; they reproduce, as might be expected, a limited number of set types. However, they are not without their own problems. I shall analyse in some detail those in the *Penitential of Vinnian*, which is fairly representative of its *genre*. The commonest type is *si* (less often a relative pronoun) with the future perfect (rarely another tense) in the protasis, and the subjunctive of the present (alternatively, the future,[4] the indicative of the present, *debere* or *oportere* with the infinitive, or a gerundive construction) in the apodosis: Vi 1 *Si quis in corde suo per cogitationem peccauerit . . ., percutiat pectus suum . . . et sanus sit*. The place of the protasis might be taken by a present participle or the perfect participle of a deponent, as in Vi (2)–(4). Since the decrees are all in the third person, it is often impossible to decide whether a form should be interpreted as future perfect or subjunctive of the perfect; the latter can be understood as an 'aorist' *pendant* of the subjunctive of the present, which, in a number of instances, is used with little difference in meaning from the indicative. Thus, in 41 *si . . . manseremus* (i.e. *manserimus*, cf. in the same paragraph

common type of *scriptum est* 'it is written', &c.) is Bi IV. 2, 1 (a quotation from 'Theodore') *Deo relinquendum est hoc iudicium et non ausi sumus orare pro eo*, where I am strongly inclined to write *non ausi simus*. 'In Irish, as in the other Celtic languages, the normal—one might almost say, the only—way of saying "he died" is Ir. *ba marb*, Welsh *bu farw*, lit. "he was (preterite) dead". On the other hand, Ir. *is* (present = Lat. *est*) *marb* means "he *is* dead". Perhaps the old scribes came to regard *mortuus est* as an equivalent to *is marb*, and hence substituted *fuit* (= Ir. *ba*, Welsh *bu*) when they meant "he died".' (Prof. Binchy.)

[1] Vinnian and Columbanus are also the only authors of penitentials who frequently use *si quis* with a noun: see below, p. 36.

[2] See the analysis of Cummean's Penitential, above, p. 6.

[3] See also my remarks on this subject in Dr. Walker's *Sancti Columbani Opera* (SLH, vol. ii), pp. lxxix–lxxxi, and P. B. Corbett, *The Latin of the Regula Magistri* (Louvain 1958), pp. 260 ff.

[4] For the parallel use of the future (future perfect) and the subjunctive cf. Vi 6 *peniteat . . . et sic . . . reconciliabitur* (*-atur* S); 44–45 (S) *decet suscipi eam . . . sed dotem ei non dabit et seruiet . . . uicem . . . ancille expleat . . . expectabit*; 46 *abstineant se . . . non intrabit*; (V) *regnabunt . . . accipiant*. The two forms are variants at 23 *recipiatur* (*-etur* P) and 41 ex. *suscipiemus* (*-amus* S); they correspond in the protasis and apodosis of a conditional period in 50 (V) *si . . . accipiant . . . cur non babtizabunt?* Cf. also, in Vinnian's postscript, *si . . . inueniat aut si proferet . . . uel scripseret*.

beati sunt si permanserint) fideles in his quecumque dederit Deus siue pro-sperum siue contrarium . . . *suscipiemus gloriam Dei*, I am inclined to term *manseremus = manserimus* a future perfect, but I would term *dederit*, in accordance with the common late Latin construction of generalizing relative clauses, a subjunctive. Other instances are even more doubtful, e.g. 34 *si conuersus fuerit* . . . *impleat quod uouerit Deo*. In general, scribes would feel at liberty to substitute alternative forms for one another, and they may be excused on the grounds that there seems to be rarely a difference in meaning or even in nuances of expression. In the final clause of 23, for example, VS read *si* . . . *non satis egerit, non recipiatur,* but P has *si* . . . *non satis faciat, non recipietur.* Occasionally the indicative of the perfect seems to be used for distinguishing between the hypothetical and the factual elements of a case. For example, in 4 *si quis uerbo peccauerit* . . . *et statim penituerit et non per difinitionem tale aliquid locutus est, submittere se debet ad penitentiam,* the cola *uerbo peccauerit* and *statim penituerit* are mere assumptions but, on these assumptions, *non per difinitionem* . . . *locutus est* is an inference of fact. Again, in 6–7 *si quis surrexerit ad scandalum et disposuit in corde suo proximum percutere* . . . *si clericus fuerit dimedium annum peniteat* . . .; *si quis autem laicus fuerit* . . ., we have to do with a double assumption, a general one (*si quis surrexerit ad scandalum*) and a particular one (*si clericus fuerit* . . ., *si laicus fuerit* . . .), which are both given in the future (subjunctive) perfect; only the phrase *et disposuit in corde suo*, &c., has the verb in the 'historical' perfect: the decision of the will has actually taken place in the (presumed) case of a man *qui surgit ad scandalum.* Similar instances are 10 *si semel contigerit et celatum est hominibus;* 11 *si* . . . *in consuetudine* . . . *fuerunt (fuerat S) et* . . . *non uenerit;* 24 *si* . . . *subito occiderit et amici fuerunt ante;* 25 *si* . . . *furtum fecerit* . . ., *id est si furatus est ouem,* &c. (the act of stealing is merely assumed but not so the specification of the theft); 47 *si quis fuerit cuius paruulus absque babtismum abscesserit et per neglegentiam perierat* (but only V is available here); 51 *si quis fuerit cuius uxor fornicata est.* On the strength of these observations I have ventured to write in 30 (S) *quecumque inuenta fuerint (fuer̃ S) apud eum ex his que congregauit* (V reads: *quae traxit*); also, I write in 3 *si* . . . *cogitauerit (cogitaū V) et uoluerit (uoluit S) facere et non potuit* (last three words omitted in S); in 15, *si* . . . *multarum feminarum habuerit familiaritatem* . . . *et oscolis inlecebrosis seipsum dederat (dederit S), sed* . . . *se seruauit a ruina (dederat* is relative to the 'factual' *seruauit,* and the reading of S can be understood as analogical levelling).[1] The perfect throughout is used only in 16–17. Manuscript variants add to the

---

[1] An 'absolute' pluperfect is found in 23 *si* . . . *comprobatus fuerit testimonium* (sic) *abbatis* . . . *cui commissus fuerat* (so S: *fuerit* V), and *satis faciat amicis eius quem occiderat;* 47 *cuius paruulus absque babtismum abscesserit et* . . . *perierat.* More difficult to explain are the pluperfects in 18–19 *si* . . . *deciperat (deceperint B), si* . . . *non deciperat (-it S)* and in 11 *si* . . . *fuerat (fuerunt V).*

confusion; a suspension mark, in the shape of a simple dash, would often be the only difference between such forms as *dixit* and *dixerit* in a scribe's exemplar. The result can be seen in such passages as these: 20 *si* . . . *partum* . . . *perdiderit* (*perdidit* P, but cf. *deciperit* S); 21 *si* . . . *genuerit* . . . *filium et manifestum peccatum eius fuerit* (*fuit* S)—to decide between *fuit* and *fuerit* is difficult, cf. above, 11 and 24, but I prefer to give V the benefit of the doubt;[1] 21 *clericus qui cecidit* (*ceciderit* S)—a clear case of an attributive relative clause, cf. *qui cecidit*, without variant, a little later in the same paragraph; 23 *si* . . . *homicidium fecerit* (*fecit* V) *et occiderit proximum suum et mortuus fuerit* (*et occ.—fuerit* om. V)— I follow S here because of the overwhelming number of parallels where there is no variant; 26 *si* . . . *in consuetudine longa fecit* (*fecerit* S), where V is confirmed by the parallel in 11 *si in consuetudine fuerunt*; in 38 I write *si autem non genuerit* (*geñ* V, *genuerunt* S) because of the parallel *si* . . . *genuerit* in 37 and 40.

At this point some remarks must be made concerning the use of *si quis* and *si qui*. This type of protasis is not found in Aq Lu Da Ad Pa II; it is rare in Gi Cu Hi and Bi; it is comparatively frequent in Pa I and Ca, and is the normal protasis in Vi, Co, and Wa. All the texts in which this type is represented, with the sole exception of Vi, use only *si quis*, which may or may not be followed by a noun or substantival adjective. In the majority of texts the former is rather the exception; *quis* has then, as a rule, its individualizing force[2] (cf. Pa I. 24 *si quis aduena*; 26 *si quis clericus*;[3] Gi 2 = Cu II. 3 *si quis* . . . *monachus*; Wa A 5 *si quis seruus*; Wa A 6 (O) = P 5 *si quis dominus*; sim. A 7 = P 6; A 27 = P 21. 22; A 33 = P 38; A 56 = P 66; A 61; P 18;[4] Ca 3 *si quis tirannus*; Bi I. 1 ('Theodore') *si quis episcopus*). The picture changes when we turn to Vinnian. Here we find both *si quis* and *si qui* either alone or with a noun. The latter, however, is found only in MS. V. MS. S has *q̄* throughout, only in Vi 1 *quis* is written in full letters. I have always resolved *q̄* as *quis*; Columbanus, who makes ample use of Vinnian, always writes *si quis*, whether or not this is followed by a noun. MS. V has *quis* by the first hand at Vi 5 (?), 10, 27, 47, 51, 52; *q̄* (= *quis?*) at 16, 29; *qui*, with an *s* either inserted, or added above the line, at 1, 5 (?), 6, 7 (*om.* SPB), 18; *autem* in the place of *q̄* (S) at 3; in all other places it has *qui*. This results in the following distribution:[5]

[1] In this as in other matters the editor has no choice but to select one manuscript and follow it unless there is a special reason for the contrary.

[2] See my remark on 'inverse' *quis* and *qui* in *Lingua* vi. 111.

[3] Compare the partitive phrases *si quis presbiterorum*, sim., Pa I. 23. 28. 29. 32; *si quis* . . . *e duobus clericis*, 31. *Quislibet* with a similar function as *si quis* is used Pa I. 27; cf. 30.

[4] As against these fourteen instances (7 in A and 7 in P) of *si quis*+noun there are in Wa 84 instances of *si quis* without a noun (A: 44; P: 40).

[5] Doubtful are Vi 7 *si quis* (*qui* V*: om.* SPB) *laicus fuerit*, and 27 *si quis fuerit clericus* (*de clericis* S).

Si qui alone: 1 (V*). 4 (V). 5 (V*?). 6 (V*). 12 (V). 14 (V). 22 (V). 28 (V). 34 (V). 39 (V). 41 (V).
Si qui clericus: 18 (V*). 23 (V: *om.* P). 25 (V). *laicus* 35 (V). 36 (V). 37 (V).
Si quis alone: 1 (VᶜS). 3 (S). 4 (S). 5 (VSPB). 6 (VᶜSPB). 10 (VS). 12 (S). 14 (S). 22 (S). 27 (VS). 28 (S). 30 (S). 34 (S). 35 (S). 37 (S). 41 (S). 47 (V: *deest* S). 51 (V: *deest* S). 52 (V: *deest* S).
Si quis clericus: 16 (VS). 18 (VᶜSPB). 23 (S: *om.* P). 25 (S). 29 (VS). *laicus* 36 (S). 39 (S).

It should be noted that the only nouns used with *qui(s)* in Vi are *clericus* and *laicus*. To go by the evidence of MS. V, Vinnian seems to use *si qui* and *si quis* without distinction, and to specify them, where necessary, by the addition of either *clericus* or *laicus*: 'if anyone, being a cleric (layman) . . .'.

6

Distinct Hibernicisms other than 'Hibernian' spellings are fewer than one might expect. The vocabulary includes *arreum* Hi II passim, *bardicatio* Bi IV. 6, 2, *bardigium* (?) Hi I. 26, †*capalbia* (meaning unknown, possibly corrupt) Hi I. 26, *clentella* (*glantella*, sim.)—see note 12 on Vinnian, *singa* 'tent' (?) Hi I. 24. *Caballus, capallus* (fourteen times in Wa) and *ceruis(s)a* (Gi 22, Da 11, Cu I. 1, Hi II. 12 P) are common Celtic words that were known also to the ancients. The few Irish words in Hi are probably glosses that have crept into the text. The forms of certain Greek words (*caraxare* Bi pr. 6, *ebibatus* Da 10, *eglotas* Bi pr. 6, *aetia*—if related to ἔτειος 'yearling'—Wa P 17, *pilax* Bi I. 5, 8) might be either 'Hibernian' or 'Hisperic'. A more specific Hibernicism than the 'Hibernian' spellings considered in paragraph 1 is possibly the spelling *scupa* Cu (XI) 24 (E), cf. OI *scúap*.

There are some instances of *alius* = *aliquis* (Ir. *alaile*): Wa P 32 *si quis . . . alium suspectum habuerit*; Bi IV. 3, 2. 4 *si quis . . . alium occiderit*; probably also Pa I. 11 *quicumque clericus . . . excommonicatus fuerit et alius eum susciperit*.[1] There is a tendency to substitute *alter* for *alius* not only in the genitive and dative, where the substitution is classical, but also in other cases, cf. Pa I. 30 *aepiscopus . . . qui de sua in alteram progreditur parruchiam*; Cu (VIII) 10 *si te non audierit, uoca alterum*; Ad 16 (*meretricis*) *maritus illa uiuente alteram non suscipiet*; Pa II. 16 *qui non . . . electus est ab altero episcopo est damnandus*; Pa II. 26 *se* (= *si*) *ducat alteram* (*uxorem*); uncertain is the interpretation of *altera sinodus* in the title of Lu. Inversely, we read in Co B3 (*Sodomita*) *non maneat cum alio in aeternum*, where *alius* can mean only his partner in sin. In Wa (and there only) *alter* = *alius* stands several times for *aliquis*: A 50 *si*

---

[1] In Pa I. 5 *si quid supra manserit . . . detur ali indigenti* the pronoun might have its normal meaning; Bi VII. 2 *qui aliam doctrinam extra scripturas . . . praesummit* is ambiguous: either *aliam* = *aliquam*, or a pleonasm (*aliam . . . extra*).

D

quis alterum fuste ferierit; P 35 *si quis percusserit alterum*; P 36 *si alterum in faciem alapa ferierit*; P 53 *si quis alterum flagillo percusserit.*[1]

Irish and Welsh idiom almost certainly accounts for the choice of prepositions in the following passages: *ad* (Ir. *do*) *aruspicem iurare* Pa I. 14; *si quis caballum ante* (Welsh *rhag*) *latronem excusserit* Wa P 57; *omnia quaecumque inuenta fuerint apud* (Ir. *la*) *eum* Vi 30 (S); *cum uestimento circa* (Ir. *imm*) *se* Hi II. 3 (P). 4 (B), cf. Muirchú, i. 20 (*erga*); *anathema sit cum* (Ir. *la*) *omnibus Christianis* Vi 31 (S); *sacerdotis cum quo paenituit* Co B 1.

7

Another Hibernicism is, possibly, the present indicative of *a*-verbs used apparently with the force of a subjunctive. It was d'Arbois de Jubainville who, in his study of the verse prayer to Aed mac Bricc,[2] explained the frequent occurrence in that poem of such forms as a trace of the Old Irish *a*-subjunctive.[3] Isolated instances elsewhere need not, of course, be so interpreted.[4] In the texts here edited, however, the number of instances, real or apparent, of this '*a*-subjunctive' is large enough to call for a discussion of the phenomenon under the aspect of a possible influence of Irish on Latin.

I shall proceed by a process of elimination. We may dismiss at the outset those cases where an indicative was probably intended. Cu ps. 1 reads: *intuendum est quanto quis tempore in delictis remaneat, qua inpugnatur passione, qualis existat fortitudine, qua uidetur adfligi lacrimabilitate, quali compulsus est grauatione peccare.* Here we have a sequence of indirect questions, some in the subjunctive, some in the indicative (there can be no doubt as regards *uidetur* and *compulsus est*); it would, then, seem most natural to take *inpugnatur* as an indicative pure and simple. The indicative in indirect questions is well known from both early and late Latin, including 'Hibernian' Latin.[5] The rendering of our Cummean passage in Bi pr. 2, though different in minor details, e.g. *exstat* for *existat*, *remansit* for *remaneat*, *affligitur* for *uidetur adfligi*, shows the same mixture of indicatives and subjunctives used indiscriminately. We might see an indicative also in Pa II. 1 *si bos es* (K: *sis* cett.) *et trituras . . ., non obduratur tibi os et dignus es mercedem tuam,*

---

[1] The same substitution is found in *Lex Salica*, xvii. 1. 2. 3. *al*. In the language of Roman Law *alter* is used for *alius* and sometimes approaches the meaning of *aliquis*.

[2] *Revue celtique*, xxi (1900), p. 268.

[3] On the Irish subjunctive see Strachan–Bergin, *Old Irish Paradigms*, 3rd ed., Dublin, 1929, pp. 38 ff.; Thurneysen, *Grammar of Old Irish*, Dublin 1946, pp. 380 ff.

[4] For example, Patricius, *Conf.* 23 *ut uenias et adhuc ambulas inter nos*; see my comments, *Classica et Mediaevalia*, xii. 151.

[5] The indicative is common in the Latin writings of St. Columbanus, see *SLH* ii. 239; cf. also iii. 146 (Adamnan).

where the mood of *obduratur* (= *obturatur*) is confirmed by *es*.[1] Pa II. 15 *licet periclitatur* (*-etur* Y) would also seem to be a real indicative; *licet* has become a concessive particle and might take the indicative as well as the subjunctive.[2] Finally, Cu (XI) 17 *ter quinis diebus concauum cruciat in ieiunio stomachum*—a passage with a certain 'Hisperic' flavour—might have been taken over from a context where *cruciat* was an ordinary indicative.

Some other instances are better left out of the discussion because manuscript evidence is either divided or uncertain. Cu I. 2 *qui cogit aliquem . . . ut inebriatur* rests on the authority of two faulty manuscripts (R and E); Ps.-Cummean I. 8 has *inebrietur*, and Cummean's source, Da 3, has *ebrietur*. Vi 20 *sex quadragissimas ieiunat* is found only in the inferior MSS. PB; S has the normal subjunctive *ieiunet*, and in V the verb is omitted. Vi 27 *non peniteant simul sed separantur* is the reading of V; but S has *separatim*. Cu (IV) 12 *placat* and (XI) 20 *saluat* are in all probability scribal blunders of R; codex E and the parallel texts read *placeat* and *soluat*.[3] Pa II. 29 *ut quattuor genera diuidantur* is a case in point only on the assumption (though a probable one) that we are to understand *deuitantur* (cf. the variants at Pa II. 17). Also doubtful is Bi II. 5, 1 *ab uxore propria ieiunat* (so C: *ieiunet* B; immediately following, *ieiunet* CB).—Similar cases arise in the non-Irish *Canones Wallici*. A 15 *restaurantur* is the variant of a single manuscript (H) for *restituantur*; besides, the form might be explained in more than one way. Slightly better attested is the *a*-form in A 53 *nullus alterius siluam . . . deuorat* (*deuoret* XHO; *deteneat* P 61). The text of P 24 *si quis . . . uenire noluerit hoc testibus adprobatur* is uncertain; the parallel provision, A 29, reads *ut in testibus probetur*.

In a considerable number of instances an '*a*-subjunctive' could be the result of *Fernassimilation* or *Reimzwang*.[4] Progressive assimilation is at work in such passages as Cu I. 5 = Bi I. 4, 3 *qui anticipat . . . uel . . . sum(m)at*; Cu (V) 2 = Bi V. 3, 1 *si . . . non . . . deponat, . . . emendat*; Cu (XI) 22 *sumatque sacrificium et . . . emendat* (*-et* E) *culpam*; Cu (XI) 26 *tabula radatur, igni sumatur, ut supra diximus celatur* (after the analogy of *abscondatur?*); Bi II. 1, 7 *surgat cantatque* (but *cantat* alone Bi II. 1, 8); Bi VIII. 1 *primo satis faciat eis, deinde ieiunat* (Cu (VIII) 3 has *ieiunet*); Bi VIII. 4 *inobediens maneat extra concilium . . . et pulsat* (*pulset* Cu). Regressive assimilation is found in Pa I. 16 *quam ut . . .*

---

[1] A real indicative might be recognized also in Wa P 62 *si quis fecerit aliud reprobatur*, where the action of *reprobare* could be referred to the legislator; a list of *uerba dispositiua* in Wa will be found under 'Formulae' in the Index grammaticus.

[2] Cf. *SLH* ii. 238.

[3] Cf. also Cu I. 10 *cantat* R, *cantet* E (*canet* Bi I. 3, 3); (X) 9 *ieiunat* E, *ieiunet* R; (XI) 24 *mundatur* E, *mundetur* R (supported by the following *comburetur*).

[4] See my article 'Fernassimilation und Reimzwang' in *Classica et Mediaevalia*, xv. 120–3.

reuocat[1] *et . . . agat*; Pa I. 24 *non ante baptizat neque offerat*; Cu (VIII) 12 (= Aq 6) *sociantur . . . relinquantur.*[2]

The same phenomenon occurs in passages where there can be no question of an 'Irish' *a*-subjunctive, e.g. Pa I. 9 *non commaneant nec . . . discurreant nec . . . exerceant*: Vi 34 *adfectandum et nitandum* (so S: *nitendum* V); Cu (XI) 24 *locus . . . mundetur et stramen . . . comburetur*; Bi V. 1, 2 *cum . . . contristant et . . . inducant*; (regressive) Pa II. 15 *mittetur* (so DJY: *mittitur* K) *. . . iubetur*.

There remain the following instances: Cu (VII) 2 *iactans in suis benefactis humiliat se* (cf. Bi VII. 3); Cu (VIII) 28 (R) *paenitentiam aegris statuunt ut elemosinam dant* (but *ut* with the indicative instead of the subjunctive is found occasionally); Cu (X) 1 *.iii. superpositionibus emendantur*; Cu (X) 7 (R) *separantur et peniteant* (similarly E); Cu (XI) 16 (R) *emendatur ieiunio* (*idomata ieiuno* E); Cu (XI) 29 (R) *.l. plagis emundatur*; Pa II. 26 *adultera lapidatur* (so DJY: *lapidetur* K);[3] Bi I. 9, 2 *qui . . . non communicauerint excommunicantur*; Bi VI. 1, 1 *otiosus. . . laborat* (in the biblical model, Eph. 4, 28, only a single manuscript of Wordsworth–White's apparatus, V, reads *laborat*); Bi VII. 2 *qui . . . heressim praesummit alienatur ab ecclesia* (after the analogy of *abscidatur*? Cf. Cu. III. 13; (IV) 16; (V) 3; Bi III. 6, 1; V. 3, 1). I append a list of similar passages from texts whose background is Welsh: Gi 10 *caena priuatur*; Wa A 21 *quicquid dampni pertullerit sine dubio restauratur* (*-abitur* O); A 23 *in .iii. prouinciis iurat* (*iuret* P 16); A 37 *aepiscopi iudicant inter illos* (*ueniant arbitrio* P 40); A 61 *donec delictum emendat*; P 23 *res ipsius . . . signatur* (*consignetur* A 28).

In a number of these instances the *-a*-form might have come to the writer's (or scribe's) mind after the analogy of a synonym: *emendatur emundatur* after *puniatur*, *separantur* after *seiungantur*, *cantat* after *canat*, &c.; forms that can be so explained make up more than one third of the total. Most examples could even be understood as real indicatives: instead of issuing a command, the law is laid down in the form of a simple statement; this, in any event, seems the only possible interpretation of Pa I. 28 *Si quis clericorum excommonis fuerit, solus non in eadem domo cum fratribus orationem facit nec offerre nec consecrare ei licet.* It should also be remembered that the material of our last group is drawn almost entirely from Cu, Bi (and Wa), the text tradition of which is extremely bad.[4]

In the circumstances I hesitate to be dogmatic. This is not as clear

---

[1] Codex W corrects *reuocet* to *reuocat*!

[2] From *Canones Wallici* I add: A 26 *quicquid delinquat aut furatur* (but in late Latin both indicative and subjunctive are used in generalizing relative clauses); P 29 *adequant . . . diuidant* (but the meaning of this clause is not quite certain).

[3] Cf. also Pa II. 24 *ut . . . testetur* KQ (*testatur* DJI).

[4] I have not found a single instance in either Co or Hi; this may or may not be accidental.

a case as is the prayer to Aed mac Bricc.[1] However, even for the penitentials some influence, at least as a contributing factor, of the Old Irish *a*-subjunctive on these Latin forms cannot be excluded.

8

Among the stylistic peculiarities of our texts the most striking one is ellipsis. The commonest form in which it appears has its root in the technical nature and practical purpose of these compilations.[2] As often as not the verb *paenitea(n)t* or a synonym is left unexpressed, e.g. Vi (2) *in terga uero fornicantes, si pueri sint, annos ii, si uiri, iii* (taking up the *peniteat* of Vi (1)); Vi 17 *penitentia eius haec est: xl dies cum pane et aqua* (*peniteat* is inserted in S); Vi 20 *duobus annis abstineat a uino et a carnibus et sex quadragissimas cum pane et aqua* (one has to supply either *uiuat* or, with S, *ieiunet*); Cu (IX) 2–3 *Qui communicauerit . . . excommunicato, xl peniteat. Sic qui manducauerit morticinam inscius.* Bolder is the ellipsis in Gi 15: *Si cui inponitur opus aliquod et contemptus gratia illud non fecerit, cena careat. Si uero obliuione* (viz. *illud non fecerit*), *demedium cotidiani uictus* (*habeat? careat?*), or Lu 9 *Totum hoc quod diximus* (viz. *ualet*), *si post uotum perfectionis fuerit homo,* or Cu (XI) 21 *Si cum consummatione saporis decoloratur sacrificium, .xx. diebus expleatur ieiunium; conglutinatum uero* (= *si uero sacrificium conglutinatum est*), *.vii. diebus.* Not infrequently one has to supply an element of the title immediately preceding, e.g. Wa A 32 *si capallum* stands for *si quis capallum perdiderit et suspicionem habuerit,* cf. 31 *si quis ancellam aut seruum perdiderit,* &c.; Wa P 6 *Si quis ingenuus seruum alterius sine culpa occiderit, seruos duos domino* (supply: *se nouerit rediturum* as in 5). More capricious still is Vi 24 *Si autem subito occiderit et non ex odio, et amici fuerunt ante, sed instincto diabuli per obreptione, tres annos peniteat,* &c. We have to understand (from 23) *si clericus occiderit proximum suum subito,* &c., and have again to supply *occidit eum* after *obreptione.* Loosely constructed rather than elliptic is Pa II. 1 *Cum huiusmodi* (public sinners) *nec cybum quidem sumere. Non eius esca, sed cum eo simul ad mensam.* The second sentence is an interpretation of the apostolic command (1 Cor. 5, 11): it is not forbidden to accept food from a sinner but to sit down with him at his table. The meaning of the comment is clear, but it is formulated without even the slightest regard for grammatical construction; it reads like a gloss, which originally it might have been. Harsh rather than syntactically peculiar is the omission of the verb of saying at the end of Hi III (supplied above the line by a gloss in both manuscripts, C and B): *Ubi sunt in lege praecepta quae Deus non praecipit? Iethro socer Moysi elegere .lxx. principes,* &c. Evidently, we have to understand *praecepit* (cf. the gloss *s. dixit* in CB) as the verb on which *elegere* depends; it would be

---

[1] Best edition: *Acta Sanctorum*, Nov. IV. 503 (by P. Grosjean).
[2] Cf. McNeill–Gamer, pp. 70 f.

easy to insert it in the text before *Iethro*, but such an emendation is hardly called for in a set of jottings at the end of a text.

Peculiar to Wa, as far as I can see, is the ellipsis of the pronominal object, e.g. A 17 *Si quis fornicatus fuerit cum alterius uxore . . . morte moriatur; qui autem occiderit* (sc. *eum*), *nullam causam timeat habere*; cf. A 27; A 37 *si quis commisso delicto . . . ad confessionem uenerit sacerdoti, a nullo condempnari praecipimus*; similarly 40. 41. 45. P 50. 54. 67. The word omitted is in all instances the accusative of the demonstrative, which, as a rule, takes up a preceding *si quis*; this form of ellipsis is thus related to the suppression of the antecedent to a relative clause.

The type of ellipsis that occurs in these texts most frequently is ellipsis of the subject. There are about twenty-five instances in Wa alone. Most of them are of the type (A 6 = P 5) *Si autem dominus seruo arma portare commisserit et* (the slave) *ingenuum hominem occiderit, ipsum et alium seruum se nouerit* (the master) *rediturum.* Other instances are A 21 = P 14, A 22 = P 15, A 25 = P 19, A 35, A 47 (last sentence), A 49 = P 56, A 51, A 53, A 58 = P 67 (beginning), A 59, A 63, P 13 (?), P 30, P 63. One is reminded of the language of the Twelve Tables: *Si in ius uocat, ni it, antestamino* (I. 1) 'If (plaintiff) summons (defendant), if (defendant) does not go, (plaintiff) shall call witnesses.'[1] We are not concerned here with the linguistic explanation of the phenomenon[2] but merely with the fact that it is met unexpectedly in a Welsh (or Breton?) law text of the sixth century. It is found also in the slightly earlier *Lex Salica*, cf. I. 2 *ille uero qui alium mannit* (summons) *et ipse* (defendant) *non uenerit, si eum sunnis non tricauerit* (if he is not prevented by some valid impediment), *ei qui manebit* (= *manniuit*) *XV solidos culpabilis iudicetur.* 3 *Et ille qui alium mannit cum testibus ad domum illius ambulare debet; et si praesens non fuerit* (the defendant), *sic aut uxorem aut quaecumque* (= *quemcumque*) *de familia illius apellit, ut illi faciat notum quod ab eum mannitus est.* II. 12 *Si quis maiale uotiuo furauerit et*[3] (the owner) *hoc testibus quod uotiuus fuit potuerit adprobare,* &c. It seems out of the question that the linguistic basis of the construction in the Twelve Tables (the indefinite use of the third person singular) should have either persisted or reasserted itself in the sixth century A.D.; this stylistic peculiarity was felt strange by the Romans as early as the second century B.C. Clumsiness or carelessness in formulation would hardly have resulted in the revival of a set type of a thousand years ago. There must be some historical connexion.[4] Did the young scholars of the

---

[1] On the text, see D. Daube, *Forms of Roman Legislation*, Oxford, 1956, pp. 28 f. Similar formulations are found in Tables I. 2. 3. 6. 7–8; III. 1–6; VII. 7; VIII. 12; X. 9.   [2] See the lucid comment of Daube, loc. cit., pp. 57–61.

[3] Some manuscripts insert here: *ille qui illum perdidit.*

[4] Even the double condition of *Twelve Tables*, I. 1 and elsewhere, is found in *Canones Wallici*. A 25 *si porci in glande ingressi, quotiens capti, porcastrum reddat*; cf. Can. Hib. V. 7 *si quis occiderit episcopum . . ., si accipiatur ab eo praetium sanguinis eius, .l. ancellas reddat.*

Romania memorize the Twelve Tables as did the schoolboys of the Roman Republic? Did the codifiers of *Salic Law* and those 'Romans' who formulated the so-called *Canones Wallici* deliberately imitate this apparent, and to them inexplicable, oddity of an archaic legal style?

Traces of this sort of ellipsis are found even in the penitentials proper. Pa I. 22 *Si quis tradiderit filiam suam uiro honestis nuptis et* (the daughter) *amauerit alium et* (the father) *consentit filiae suae* . . . . Vi 23 *Si quis clericus* . . . *occiderit proximum suum et* (his fellow) *mortuus fuerit* . . . . Vi 37 *Si* . . . *laicus puellam Dei maculauerit et* (the virgin) *coronam suam perdiderit et* (the layman) *genuerit filium ex ea* . . . . Cu (XI) 26 *si* . . . *de calice aliquid* . . . *stillauerit in terra* . . ., *tabula radatur,* (what is scraped off) *igni sumatur,* (the ashes) *ut supra diximus celatur,* (the priest who spilled the wine) *.l. diebus peniteat.* Hi IV. 1 *Sanguis episcopi* . . . *qui ad terram effunditur, si* (the wound, or the bishop) *colirio indiguerit* . . .; cf. 4. Hi V. 7 *Si quis occiderit episcopum et* (the bishop) *mortuus fuerit, si accipiatur ab eo* (the murderer) *praetium sanguinis eius* (the bishop's) . . .; possibly also Pa II. 15 *Docenda patria prius per exemplum Domini et derelinquenda postea, si non proficiat, iuxta exemplum apostuli* (the subject of *proficiat* might be *patria,* or the verb might be impersonal, but in view of the clause immediately following, *sed qui potest proficere* . . . *doceat,* it seems more probable that the subject of *proficiat* is the teacher: 'if he has no success').

Identical in form only is another type: Gi 26 *Qui sarculum perfrangit et ante fracturam non habuit, illud extraordinario opere restituat*; Wa P 19 *si quis seruum* . . . *uel rem quamlibet conparauerit et cum ipso fuerit consignatum*; A 52 *Si quis ancellam alterius adpraehenderit fugientem et a domino suo potuerit euadere.* Here the *et*-clause is equivalent to a relative clause, and the construction is loose rather than elliptic.

A form of ellipsis for which Hiberno-Latin writers have a foible is the suppression of the copula *est.*[1] Examples might be quoted from most of the texts here published; their total number is 46. On examination it is found that, allowance being made for a reasonable amount of analogical extension, most instances fall in one or another category of Latin 'verbless' clauses that were either inherited from Indo-European or had for a long time been sanctioned by Latin usage. Most frequent of all is the case of the simple gerund(ive) for the gerund(ive) with *est,* e.g. *egenis et pauperibus fenerandum* Vi 32 (S); similarly, Vi 34. 53; Cu (VIII) 25; Hi III. 1; Ad 2. 6. 8 (u. app.) 10. 18; Bi pr. 3 (three times). 26. IV. 3, 2; add Wa A 24. P 17. 58. Cf. also Pa I. 10 *ab ecclesia excludendus*; 16 *in ecclesiam recipiendus*; Pa II. 31 *ut fidelis peccator iudicandus*; Bi II. 2, 5 *iuniores leuius uindicandi*; IV. 6, 1 *clamor dolore excitatus non praetermittendus.* True to type are also such formulations as Co B 30 *tribunal Christi altare*; Bi VI. 2, 1 *somnus assiduus emitatio mortis*;

---

[1] See, *inter alia,* P. Grosjean, *Anal. Boll.* lxx (1952), p. 321, n. 1.

Bi pr. 5 *praetium anni .vii. diebus ieiunare*; Pa II. 7 *baptizati, qui symbuli traditione acciperunt*; analogously, we find Vi 7 *quia homo seculi huius est, culpa leuior in hoc mundo et premium minus in futuro*; Vi 47 (V) *nullum crimen quod non potest ridimi*; Vi 11 (S) *non minus peccare coram Deo quam coram hominibus*, cf. 27 (S). Vi 23 *Ecce ego uobis pro filio uestro* is modelled on biblical phrases, see my *Libri Epistolarum S. Patricii*, ii. 142. The ellipsis of the copula in conditional clauses (e.g. Gi 2 *si quis inferiore gradu possitus monachus*; similarly Vi 29; Cu (X) 21; (XI) 20; Wa A 25. 41; cf. *si filius . . ., si filia . . .* Cu II. 31) and in equivalent relative clauses (Cu II. 30 *qui in matrimonio*; (XI) 18 *quod intinctum a familiari bestia*; Bi II. 3, 1 *qui cum matre uel sorore fornicatus*) is in line with the technical character of our texts. The only instances that are more or less unusual are the following: Lu 4 *si . . . uoluerit et non ad uota sibi*; Ad 6 *cum . . . decreuerit et ad pristinam maciem reuersa* (u. app.); Cu ps. 1 = Bi pr. 2 *qua eruditione inbutus*; and Pa I. 25 *sicut mos antiquis ordinare*, where we must supply a past tense. It is the frequency of the phenomenon rather than the peculiar character of individual instances that gives the ellipsis of *esse* a place among Hibernicisms.

9

Brachylogy can take other forms than ellipsis. In Cu (VII) 1 = Bi VII. 1 *Contentiosus etiam alterius sententiae subdat se* the particle *etiam* implies an idea that remains unexpressed: it is not enough for the self-assertive monk to restrain himself; he shall, in addition, accept the authority of another. Similar is the function of *tamen* in the following example, Cu (IV) 12–14: *Fratrem cum furore maledicens . . . .* (13) *Qui uerba aceruiora protulerit in furore . . . .* (14) *Si autem cum pallore uel rubore uel tremore tacuit tamen . . . .* The angry monk may use bad language, or just harsh language, or may betray his emotion merely by bodily reactions and, in spite of these signs of anger, keep silent. Of a different kind is the following brachylogy, Bi IV. 6, 7: *Iacob . . . in Egypto luctatus est et . . . in terra Canaan; et Christus in Nouo, plorauerunt eum feminae*. The term 'in the Old Testament', to which *in Nouo* forms a contrast, is not expressed at all; it must be inferred from the Old Testament parallel.

The non-literary character of the penitentials appears also in a number of loose constructions; in a leaning towards variation, which is not an element of style but rather a symptom of stylistic indifference— of the absence of any striving for balance or symmetry; lastly in the frequent use of 'formulae', of repeated phrases, of clichés of all sorts. Details are given in the Index grammaticus under these headings. Here I shall comment only on some peculiarities that cannot be easily classified.

Vinnian is particularly rich in formulae and repetitive phraseology, much of which has passed into the *Penitential of St. Columbanus*.[1] One of Vinnian's clichés is interesting because of its structure: Vi 3 *si uoluerit facere et non potuit, sed facultas prohibuit eum*; cf. 17 *si . . . concupiuit et non potuit, sed non suscipit eum mulier.* The contrasting *non potuit* is both times specified by a *sed*-clause of identical pattern. A similar pattern is found in Columbanus B 23 *si . . . adulterare uoluerit . . . et non fecerit . . ., tamen paratus fuit ad fornicandum.* Here, however, the *tamen*-clause is in contrast only to *non fecerit*, and takes up the *si adulterare uoluerit* of the beginning; the result is a pattern *a–b–a.* A variation of this pattern is Hi III ps.: *populus Israel debuerat constringui .x. mandatis legis dum causa ipsorum percusit Deus Egyptum .x. plagis; ideo decim mandata sunt.* Such cyclic structure is an age-old form of set speech.

10

By way of conclusion I should like to call attention to two characteristic phenomena which are on the borderline of language and subject-matter, and which might be of some interest to the historian of ideas.

Whereas the majority of penances are enjoined for a definite period (so many days, or weeks, or months, or years), there are a number of canons which provide for an indefinite penance according to the duration of the sin. The principle is formulated in general terms by Gildas, c. 14: *quanto quis tempore moratur in peccatis tanto ei augenda* (i.e. *agenda?*) *penitentia est.* It is applied to certain particular sins in the *Penitential of Cummean.* This is a penance appropriate to attitudes rather than to acts, e.g. to the sins of disobedience, anger, despondency. In substance it is a form of the *principium talionis.* Vi 29 gives it a slightly different turn: a cleric who is either angry or envious or an informer or greedy or despondent should do penance as long as these sins are rooted in his heart. From this there is but one step to the maxim *contraria contrariis sanari*, which, in the footsteps of Cassian, was adopted by Vinnian and in the prologue of Cummean.[2]

Other passages advocate a real *talio* in the sense of a retaliation. Aq 7 provides that if a monk has accused another wrongly but afterwards confesses the truth, then *quantum laboris alteri intulit tantum sibi multiplicetur.* Outside the monastery, a person confessing perjury is to do penance by undergoing what the victim of his sin has suffered (Cu III. 12 *quale fratri inposuit tali iudicio damnetur iudice sacerdote*). To the same effect is Co B 21: if a layman has shed another person's blood and has either wounded or maimed him, he shall pay compensation according

---

[1] Among the remaining texts Pa II and Bi are more stereotyped than are the others; both have formulae of their own. *Canones Wallici* stand apart with their wealth of *formulae iudiciales.*

[2] See n. 14 on Vinnian.

to the harm done; if he is unable to pay, he shall do his neighbour's job until the latter is fit again to work.[1] In the case of homicide, the murderer, beside his performance of an appropriate penance, is bound to fulfil the obligations of a son to his victim's parents (Vi 23; Co B 1). The idea of *talio* is expressed in the stereotype forms *tantum—quantum, quanto (tempore)—tanto (tempore)*; once only (Vi 29) we read *tamdiu—quam*, and once (Cu III. 12) *quale—tali*.[2]

The second phenomenon is the frequent occurrence of metaphors taken from medicine. The idea that ignorance or vice is an illness of mind or soul which can be cured by instruction and correction is, of course, widespread. In Greek and Roman antiquity medical metaphors are anything but rare. As early as the fifth century B.C. Nicias in the *Histories* of Thucydides (vi. 14), demanding of the Assembly that a previous decree in favour of the Sicilian campaign should be rescinded, addresses the presiding magistrate as follows: 'If you put my motion to the vote you will, I think, become a physician of our city.' Such metaphors belong in particular to philosophical and theological literature. Protagoras in Plato's dialogue (357 e) is termed a physician of ignorance. Philo of Alexandria speaks of God as a physician of sins, and St. Ignatius (ad Ephes. 7, 2) applies this title to Christ. In the Gospel Jesus compares himself to a physician (Matth. 9, 12; Luc. 5, 31). Christ the Physician is a favourite theme of early Christianity.[3] Patristic writers of a later time are fond of medical metaphors when referring to the correction and the correctors of moral faults.[4] In the penitentials, the 'cure' for sin is, of course, penance; the physician, ultimately Christ Himself, is, *hic et nunc*, the priest who enjoins the penance, the confessor (Ir. *anmchara*). The most elaborate comparison of penance to a medical cure is found in the prologue to the 'B-text' of the *Penitential of Columbanus;* it was later incorporated in other penitentials, including Ps.-Cummean. Isolated medical metaphors occur in almost all the texts of the present collection. The list here following, though not complete, will give some idea of the range of variation of which this theme is capable:

> Debet hoc indicare abati, non tamen accussantis sed medentis afectu Gi 18; cf. medendi animas Bi pr. 28.
>
> Medicina penitentiae Vi 22. medicina salutaris animarum Cu pr. tit. sancti eloqui medicamina Cu pr. 1.[5]

---

[1] Cf. the *Old-Irish Penitential*, V. 8. This provision is merely 'lifted' from the native customary law of 'sick-maintenance', see D. A. Binchy, *Ériu*, xii. 115 f.

[2] See Index grammaticus sub 'Formulae'.

[3] Literature on the subject is given by Walter Bauer, *Griechisch-deutsches Handwörterbuch zu den Schriften des Neuen Testaments*, 4th ed., 1952, s.u. ἰατρός; Grosjean–Deanesly, *JEH* x (1959), p. 17.

[4] For Latin, see the articles *medela, mederi, medicamen(tum), medicina*, and *medicus* in the *Thesaurus Linguae Latinae*.

[5] In a different context (Gi 1 = Cu II. 2; cf. Pa II. 22) the 'medicine' is the Eucharist: *caelestis medicina*.

Penitentiae remedia Vi ps. remedia uulnerum Cu pr. 1; Bi pr. 6. de remediis uitiorum Bi tit.

Spiritales medici Co B pr. mala non recipientium sanitatem retractans . . . medicus aestimandus est Cu (VIII) 16. tanto maior potentia medici quanto magis creuit morbus egroti Bi pr. 1. animarum uulnera morbos dolores aegritudines infirmitates sanare Co B pr. morbi languentis[1] animae Co B 30. superbiae morbus Co A 11. inuidia lepra esse in lege iudicatur Vi 29. E contrariis contraria curet Vi 28. Cf. 29. uitia contrariis remediis sanantur Cu pr. 15. uarietas curandorum Vi ps. diuersa curationum genera Co B pr. uitium curatur Bi VII. 4. Sanus sit Vi 1. 2. cor sanum Co B 30. elemosyna et ieiunio sanetur Cu III. 3. Cf. (V) 1; (VI) 2; (VIII) 5; Bi V. 3, 1. VI. 2, 2; 3, 1. VIII. 4. 5.

IV. PENITENTIAL TEXTS IN OLD IRISH

Like all other Irish ecclesiastical works of the period, the early penitentials, even those which clearly reflect the influence of native customary law, were composed in Latin. The two OI tracts printed in translation as an appendix to the present volume are not merely later in date but are also based exclusively on earlier Latin texts. Though the vernacular was doubtless used in religious verse, as well as in explanatory glosses on Latin, from the seventh century on, complete prose treatises on religious or ecclesiastical subjects do not seem to have been composed before the second half of the eighth. Robin Flower has already suggested that the earliest religious works written in Irish, including the *Old-Irish Penitential* (P), were a product of the reform movement associated with the rise of the *Céli Dé* or 'Culdees'.[2] I am inclined to accept his view, and would add to the corpus of vernacular literature which he ascribes to this movement the second tract appended here, that on the *arrai* or Commutations (A).

The most important centre of the 'Culdee' movement was the monastery of Tallaght, south-west of Dublin. Its first abbot Mael Ruain, who died in 792, is honoured as the founder and patron saint of the 'Culdees'. Around his name and that of his monastery there grew up a considerable quantity of Irish religious literature: this includes, apart from our two tracts, a Mass-book (the Stowe Missal), two Martyrologies (that of Tallaght, where only the names of Irish saints are in the vernacular, and that of Oengus Céle Dé, a calendar in OI verse, composed about 800), a monastic rule ('The Rule of the Céli Dé'), and the remarkable account of the teaching and practice of Mael Ruain and his associates

---

[1] Cf. Aug. Sermo 299, 6 (*PL* xxxviii. 1372) *medicus magnus, hoc est Iesus, medicus magnus ad regionem ueniens languidorum,* quoted by W. Schmid, 'Boethius and the Claims of Philosophy', in *Studia Patristica,* ii (1957), p. 375, n. 1. See also the same author's paper 'Philosophisches und Medizinisches in der Consolatio des Boethius', in *Festschrift Bruno Snell* (Munich, 1956), pp. 113–44; R. Arbesmann in *Traditio,* x (1954), pp. 1–28.

[2] 'The Two Eyes of Ireland', in *The Church of Ireland, 432–1932,* pp. 71 f.; cf. also *The Irish Tradition* (1947), pp. 29 f.

edited by Edward Gwynn under the title of 'The Monastery of Tallaght'
(*PRIA* xxix. 115–80).[1] It is difficult to study P and A in isolation from
the other works produced by the reform movement: linguistically as
well as psychologically they all belong together, and each of them is
complementary to the others. Thus much additional information about
penances is found in the Rule of the Céli Dé (§§ 7, 17, 26, 32, &c.) and
in the 'Monastery of Tallaght' (§§ 9, 11, 36, &c.).

A study of the literature associated with Tallaght makes it abundantly
clear that the 'Culdee' reform represented a sharp reaction against the
laxity and corruption of the ancient monastic communities, 'the people
of the old churches' (*lucht na sencheld*, Mon. Tall., § 26) or 'the lax folk'
(*lax-aes*, § 57, *sic leg.*), who are always mentioned with obvious dis-
approval. Hence its insistence on the renewal of ascetic practice and
strict monastic discipline. In this exalted spiritual climate it was natural
that interest in the ancient records of penitential discipline should be
revived. The tradition which assigns the authorship of P to Mael Ruain
himself cannot be traced back farther than the seventeenth century (see
Gwynn, *Rule of Tallaght*, pp. xviii f.); linguistically at least there is no
reason why it should not be correct.

On the other hand, I find it impossible to accept a theory concerning
the precise date of P and the circumstances of its composition which was
first tentatively advanced by Gwynn (op. cit., p. xx) and later endorsed
much more emphatically by Flower (op. cit., pp. 67 f.). Under the year
779 (*recte* 780) the Annals of Ulster have the following entry:

Congressio senodorum nepotum Neill Laginentiumque in opido Temro
ubi fuerunt ancorite 7 scribe multi quibus dux erat Dublitter.

Since the last-named is undoubtedly the celebrated abbot of Finglas
(†796), who figures prominently in some of the Tallaght documents
(e.g. Mon. Tall., §§ 5–7, &c.), it has been inferred that P was drawn up
at a 'joint synod' of the (Southern) Uí Néill and the Leinstermen held
in Tara under his presidency. In support of this Gwynn and Flower
quote the opening words of P: 'The elders of Ireland have ordained
(*concemdetar*) . . . a Penitential.' But the whole context of the annal is
heavily against their theory. The background to the 'congressio' is the
invasion of Leinster by Donnchad King of Tara in this very year,
followed by a savage war during which *uastauit 7 combussit fines eorum et
aeclesias.* Hence the Tara meeting was clearly an attempt by the clerical
leaders of both states (not all of them necessarily adherents of the
'Culdee' reform) to secure an end, or at least a truce, to hostilities; they

---

[1] A seventeenth-century redaction by John Colgan of this and some further material
which has since disappeared has been published by Gwynn in 'The Rule of Tallaght'
(*Hermathena*, xliv, 2nd supplemental volume, Dublin, 1927), pp. 2–63; this volume
also contains (pp. 64–87) a revised edition and translation of the Rule of the Céli Dé.

thus had more urgent matters to deal with than the drafting of a Penitential in the vernacular. Again, it would be rash to attach any special significance to the opening words of P: they are common form in a number of legal tracts which were certainly never adopted by any 'assembly', lay or clerical. On the contrary, it is more than probable that 'the elders (*sruithi*) of Ireland' are those spiritual leaders of the past—Colum Cille, Finian, Cummaine Fota, and the rest—upon whose Latin words P is based. Like all other OI 'laws', both ecclesiastical and secular, this is a private compilation, and it was almost certainly made in Tallaght or one of the houses associated with it in the 'Culdee' reform movement.

We have already seen that this movement produced the earliest corpus of ecclesiastical literature in Irish prose. What lay behind the departure from Latin? Here we can only speculate. The provision in A (§§ 12, 21, 27) of certain 'commutations' of traditional penances 'for one who cannot read' shows that some members of the community were ignorant of Latin; accordingly the preparation of an Irish version of some earlier work or works on penitential discipline may well have been undertaken to cater for their needs. At all events it is certain that P is in no sense an 'original' work. Nearly all its rules are substantially, and often verbally, identical with one or other of the Latin penitentials printed in this volume, though occasionally (as in II. 14) we find a formulation of practices which may have been peculiar to Tallaght. The question whether P is an eclectic arrangement of material drawn from a number of these works or whether the compiler's exemplar was a later composite penitential now lost is difficult to decide. So far as I am competent to judge, I regard the former as slightly more probable.

Was it the only penitential written in Irish? A glossary in the well-known legal codex TCD, H 3. 18 (now no. 1337), pp. 623 f. cites several lemmata purporting to come from a penitential (*pennadóir*), but, as Gwynn has pointed out (*Ériu*, xii. 248), such of them as can be identified are quotations from the Rule of Mo-Chuta (edited by Meyer in *Archiv f. celt. Lexicographie*, iii. 312–20). On the other hand, in the sole reference to P contained in O'Davoren's Glossary (ibid. ii. 443, no. 1389) it is called '*the* Penitential'. The balance of evidence seems to be against the existence of any other document of this kind.

The *Table of Commutations* (A) has not hitherto been reckoned among the products of the 'Culdee' reform. Nevertheless, I think there are weighty reasons for affiliating it to the Tallaght school. The longer and better recension of the text is contained in the same manuscript (RIA, 3 B 23, now 1227) that provides our only copy of both P and the 'Monastery of Tallaght'. Further, the only OI sources besides A which use the word *arre* in the specialized sense of 'commutation' (of a penance or other religious duty) are all associated with Tallaght; thus we find it not merely in P (II. 27 (*bis*), III. 15 (*bis*), IV. 3), but also in the 'Monastery of Tallaght' (§ 80), the Rule of the Céli Dé (§ 23), and the Martyrology of Oengus (epilogue 177. 179. 181. 186). Finally, both in content and in style A bears a close resemblance to the first three of these works, and its linguistic forms are contemporary with theirs. An upper limit for the date of its composition is furnished by the reference to Mo-Cholmóc mac Commain (§ 31), who died in 751; on the other hand, the linguistic evidence will hardly allow us to date the text any later than 800.

Since the term *arreum* is found only in section II of the *Canones Hibernenses* (pp. 162–6 *infra*), Du Cange rightly took it to be the latinized form of an Irish word, though his suggestion that this word was in turn borrowed from Anglo-Saxon *arian* is altogether wide of the mark. OI *arr(a)e*, in later orthography *arra*, is the verbal noun of *ar-ren* 'pays for, pays instead of', and the various senses in which later glossators interpret it—'equivalent, substitute, price, salary', &c.—are all derived from this primary meaning.[1] In the OI law of sale (or rather barter) the *a.* of an object 'sold' means the specifically stipulated object (or class of object) for which it is 'purchased'. Somewhat closer to the meaning in our text is the institution known as *arra cuir* 'substitute for an oath' (transl. 'Eidesgutmachung' by Thurneysen, *Cóic Conara Fugill*, Abh. d. preuss. Ak., 1925, phil.-hist. Kl., Nr. 7, p. 67), by which a person who is disqualified from making proof by oath in person provides a number of compurgators to take his place. (Note, however, that here the *a.* is much more complicated and cumbersome than what it replaces.) The use of *a.* for the commutation of a penance is confined, as already stated, to the Tallaght documents; in them it figures as a substitute not merely for penance but for any religious duty—thus in the epilogue to the Martyrology of Oengus (l. 177) we are told that the reading aloud of the whole poem 'is an *arrae* of seven Masses'. Are we then to regard this system of commutation as a product of the 'Culdee' reform? If so, we should be compelled to fix the end of the eighth century as an upper limit for dating the section *De Arreis*, which would thus be considerably later than the remainder of these Canons (p. 9 *supra*). Since neither manuscript of *De Arreis* (P and B, cf. pp. 12, 14) is earlier than the tenth century, this is not impossible. Yet I think it is extremely unlikely for several reasons. The references in A itself (§§ 31–33) to some well-known saints of the sixth century as the 'authors' of certain commutations suggests that the institution was considerably older. Further, the shortening (and in some cases, as we shall see, the alleviation) of a traditional penance are unlikely to have commended themselves to a reform movement which aimed at the restoration of the strictest asceticism.

[1] Meyer, in his *Contributions to Irish Lexicography* (p. 127) distinguishes two words: (1) *arra* = Lat. *arreum*, (2) *arra* = Lat. *arrha*, but there is no foundation whatever for this distinction.

Previous writers on the penitentials (e.g. McNeill, *Rev. Celt.* xl. 329) have seen in this system of 'commutation' the influence of native Irish custom with its fixed tariff of compensations for various breaches of law. I must confess I can see no analogy whatever. If one could find in Irish law any rule under which, instead of the traditional compensatory penalty, a smaller amount payable within a shorter period of time may be substituted, this would correspond roughly to the ecclesiastical *arre*. But I do not know of a single example of this kind. For the same reason I fail to see how the 'estimations' in Lev. xxvii, which Fournier (*Rev. Celt.* xxx. 233) regards as 'legitimizing' the Irish *a.*, have any relevance here: in no case does the *a.* consist of a payment, but rather of a shorter (and sometimes more intensive) form of penance. In the present state of our knowledge we can say no more than that the system of *a.* originated in Ireland, as its name clearly shows, but would seem to have been evolved independently of native and biblical precedents alike. Even the name itself has been invested with a specialized meaning which occurs nowhere else among our extant Irish sources.

An examination of 'the four reasons why the commutations are practised' (§ 6) shows that these apply only to commutations of a protracted period of penance. On the other hand, the numerous commutations of a one-day or three-day fast (§§ 9–13. 21–25) or of a week's strict penance (§§ 26. 27) can hardly have been dictated by any of the considerations set forth in § 6, nor can any of them have been intended for the sick or infirm. In *De arreis*, however, all the commutable penances except the first two are of a year's duration. One is tempted to infer that the earliest type of *a.* was designed to replace a protracted period of penance by a shorter and more intensive discipline,[1] and that the other commutations which tend to mitigate the rigours of a comparatively brief penance, as well as the *arrai* 'which rescue a soul out of hell' (§§ 1–4), are later accretions. But all such questions are better left to specialists in the history of theology and ecclesiastical institutions.[2]

[1] Bieler refers me to '*Synodus II S. Patricii*', c. 3: *apcior est . . . siuera* (= *seuera*) *paenitentia breuis quam longa et remissa.*

[2] Since the above was written, I have published a more detailed account of the *arra* in *Ériu* XIX (1962), pp. 47–72.

EXPLANATIO SIGNORUM

⟨ ⟩   uoces et litterae ab editore suppletae (in apparatu: a scriba additae)

[ ]   uoces et litterae ab editore deletae

†   locus corruptus

A*   A ante correcturam (similiter B* et rell.)

A^c A correctus (similiter B^c et rell.)

EDITIONES

Haddan–Stubbs	A. W. Haddan and W. Stubbs, *Councils and Ecclesiastical Documents relating to Great Britain and Ireland*, ii. 2 (1878).
Schmitz	H. J. Schmitz, *Die Bussbücher und die Bussdisziplin der Kirche* (1883).
Spelman	H. Spelman, *Concilia . . . Orbis Britannici*, i (1639).
Ware	J. Ware, *S. Patricio . . . adscripta opuscula* (1656).
Wasserschleben	F. W. H. Wasserschleben, *Die Bussordnungen der abendländischen Kirche* (1851).
Wilkins	D. Wilkins, *Concilia Magnae Britanniae et Hiberniae*, i (1737).
McNeill–Gamer	John T. McNeill and Helena M. Gamer, *Medieval Handbooks of Penance*. (Records of Civilization, XXIX, 1938).
Capitula Iudiciorum	H. J. Schmitz, *Die Bussbücher und das kanonische Bussverfahren* (1898), pp. 204–51.
Coll. Hib.	F. W. H. Wasserschleben, *Die irische Kanonensammlung*. 2nd ed. (1885).
Ps.-Cummean.	F. W. H. Wasserschleben, *Die Bussordnungen* (u. supra), pp. 460–93. (Textum hic illic correxi ex codicibus antiquis, imprimis ex codice Coloniensi 91.)

TEXT AND TRANSLATION

'SYNODUS I S. PATRICII'

INCIPIT SINODUS EPISCOPORUM ID EST PATRICI AUXILII
ISSERNINI

Gratias agimus Deo Patri et Filio et Spiritui Sancto.
Presbiteris et diaconibus et omni clero Patricius Auxilius Isserninus
episcopi salutem.   5
  Satius nobis neglegentes praemonere ⟨quam⟩ culpare que facta sunt
Solamone dicente: *Melius est arguere quam irasci.*
  Exempla difinitionis nostrae inferius conscripta sunt et sic inchoant:
  1. Si quis in questionem captiuis quesierit in plebe suo iure sine
permisi⟨one⟩ meruit excommonicari.   10
  2. Lectores denique cognoscant unus quisque aecclesiam in qua psallat.
  3. Clericus uagus non sit in plebe.
  4. Si quis permissionem acciperit et collectum sit praetium non plus
exigat quam quod necessitas poscit.
  5. Si quid supra manserit ponat super altare pontificis ut detur ali 15
indigenti.
  6. Quicumque clericus ab hostiario usque ad sacerdotem sine tunica
uisus fuerit atque turpitudinem uentris et nuditatem non tegat, et si
non more Romano capilli eius tonsi sint, et uxor eius si non uelato capite
ambulauerit, pariter a laicis contempnentur et ab ecclesia separentur.   20
  7. Quicumque clericus ussus neglegentiae causa ad collectas mane
uel uespere non occurrerit alienus habeatur nisi forte iugo seruitutis sit
detentus.
  8. Clericus si pro gentili homine fideiusor fuerit in quacumque
quantitate et si contigerit, quod mirum non †potest, per astutiam aliquam 25
gentilis ille clerico fallat, rebus suis clericus ille soluat debitum. Nam si
armis conpugnauerit cum illo, merito extra ecclesiam conputetur.
  9. Monachus et uirgo unus abhinc et alia ab aliunde in uno hospitio
non conmaneant nec in uno curru a uilla in uillam discurrant nec
adsidue inuicem confabulationem exerceant.   30

6–7 Satius–irasci: cf. Coll. Hib. LXVI. 18 (Patricius)   7 cf. Eccli. 20, 1 quam
bonum est (melius est Coll. Hib.) arguere quam irasci   9–10 can. 1: cf. Coll. Hib.
XLII. 25c (Patricius)   13–16 can. 4. 5: Coll. Hib. XLII. 26a (Patricius)
17–20 can. 6: cf. Coll. Hib. LII. 7 (Patricius) *Hic canon in cod. Cantabr.* 265 Coll.
Corp. Christi, p. 104 sic legitur: CAN(ON) ROMAN(U)S. Quicumque clericus ab hostiario
usque ad sacerdotem sine tonica uisus fuerit quę turpitudinem corporis et nuditatem
tegat. et si non more romano capillos et barbam tonderit. excommunicetur   24–27
can. 8: Coll. Hib. XXXIV. 2b (Patricius)

Codex: W

6 quam *suppl. Spelman; cf. Coll. Hib.*   9 in–quesierit: redemptionem captiui
inquisierit *Coll. Hib.*   10 permisi W: *suppl. Ware; cf. can. 4. 24; Coll. Hib. XLII.*

'FIRST SYNOD OF ST. PATRICK'[1]

HERE BEGINS THE SYNOD OF THE BISHOPS, NAMELY, PATRICK,
AUXILIUS, ISERNINUS

We give thanks to God the Father, and the Son, and the Holy Ghost.

To the priests, deacons, and all the clergy—Patrick, Auxilius, Iserninus, the bishops, greetings.

We deem it better to forewarn the negligent rather than to condemn accomplished deeds, as Solomon says: *It is better to reason than to be wroth.*

Copies of our decisions are given below, and begin thus:

1. If anyone has collected money for captives in his community on his own, and without permission, he has deserved to be excommunicated.

2. Lectors[2] should acquaint themselves with the church in which each is to sing.

3. There should be no vagrant cleric in the community.

4. If anyone has obtained permission, and money has been collected, he should not ask for more than is needed.

5. If anything is left over, he should lay it on the bishop's altar, to be given to some (other) needy person.

6. Any cleric, from ostiary to priest, that is seen without a tunic and does not cover the shame and nakedness of his body, and whose hair is not shorn after the Roman custom, and whose wife goes about with her head unveiled, shall both likewise be held in contempt by the laity and be removed from the Church.

7. Any cleric who, when summoned, in neglect of the custom fails to appear at the meetings for matins and vespers shall, except he be held under the yoke of servitude, be considered a stranger.

8. If a cleric has given surety[3] for a pagan in whatsoever amount, and it so happens—as well it might—that the pagan by some ruse defaults upon the cleric, the cleric must pay the debt from his own means; should he contend with him in arms, let him be reckoned to be outside the Church, as he deserves.

9. A monk and a virgin, the one from one place, the other from another, shall not take lodging in the same inn, nor travel in the same carriage from village to village, nor carry on prolonged conversations together.

[1] For Notes on Translation, see pp. 240 ff.

25c   21 ussus neglegentiae causa, *i.e.* usum deuotionis neglegens   25 potest: est *Ware* (quod mirum non est, ut . . . *Coll. Hib.*)   29 discurreant *perperam per analogiam, cf. can. 16. 24*

10. Si ⟨quis⟩ incoeptum boni operis ostenderit in psallendo et nunc intermisit et comam habeat, ab ecclesia excludendus nisi statui priori se restituerit.

11. Quicumque clericus ab aliquo excommonicatus fuerit et alius eum susciperit, ambo coaequali penitentia utantur.   5

12. Quicumque Christianus excominicatus (*sic*) fuerit, nec eius elimosina recipiatur.

13. Elimosinam a gentibus offerendam in ecclesiam recipi non licet.

14. Christianus qui occiderit aut fornicationem fecerit aut more gentilium ad aruspicem iurauerit, per singula cremina annum peni- 10 tentiae agat; impleto cum testibus ueniat anno penitentiae et postea resoluetur a sacerdote.

15. Et qui furtum fecerit demedium peniteat, .xx. diebus cum pane, et si fieri potest rapta repraesentet; sic in ecclesiam renuetur.

16. Christianus qui crediderit esse lamiam in saeculo, quae inter- 15 praetatur striga, anathemazandus quicumque super animam famam istam inposuerit, nec ante in ecclesiam recipiendus quam ut idem creminis quod fecit sua iterum uoce reuocat et sic poenitentiam cum omni diligentia agat.

17. Uirgo quae uouerit Deo permanere kasta et postea nubserit 20 carnalem sponsum excommonis sit donec conuertatur; si conuersa fuerit et dimiserit adulter[i]um penitentiam agat et postea non in una domo nec in una uilla habitent.

18. Si quis excommonis fuerit nec nocte pascharum in ecclesiam non introeat donec penitentiam recipiet.   25

19. Mulier Christiana quae acciperit uirum honestis nuptis et postmodum discesserit a primo et iunxerit se adulter[i]o, quae haec fecit excommonis sit.

20. Christianus qui fraudat debitum cuiuslibet ritu gentilium excom- monis sit donec soluat debitum.   30

21. Christianus cui dereliquerit aliquis et prouocat eum in iudicium et non in ecclesiam ut ibi examinetur causa, qui sic fecerit alienus sit.

22. Si quis tradiderit filiam suam uiro honestis nuptis et amauerit alium et consentit filiae suae et acceperit dotem, ambo ab aecclesia excludantur.

23. Si quis presbiterorum aecclesiam aedificauerit, non offerat ante- 35 quam adducat suum pontificem ut eam consecret, quia sic decet.

4–5 can. 11: Coll. Hib. XXXIX. 10b (Patricius)   6–7 can. 12: *cf.* Coll. Hib. XL. 8 (Patricius); Patricius, Epist. c. 7.   9–12 can. 14: Coll. Hib. XXVIII. 10c (Patricius)   13–14 can. 15: Coll. Hib. XXIX. 8a (Patricius) 29–30 can. 20: Coll. Hib. XXXIII. 1e (Sinodus Romana)

1 quis *suppl. Haddan–Stubbs*   4 ab aliquo: *lege* ob aliquod? *cf. Can. Hib. IV. 9* 13 demedium ⟨annum⟩ *Coll. Hib.*   14 renuetur, *i.e.* renouetur, ecclesiae restituatur 15 saeculo: speculo *Spelman*   16 anathemazandus *conflatum uidetur esse ex* ana- thematizandus (*sic editores*) *et* anathemandus   18 reuocat (cat *super* cet) W; *cf.* *can. 24*   20 permanere *Wilkins*: permanet W   22 adulterium W: *corr. Wilkins*

10. If anyone has made a good beginning as a psalmist, and then quits and lets his hair grow, he is to be excluded from the Church, unless he returns to his former status.

11. If any cleric has been excommunicated by someone (?) and some other person receives him, both are to perform the same penance.

12. If a Christian has been excommunicated, not even his alms are to be accepted.[4]

13. Alms offered by pagans are not to be accepted for the Church.

14. A Christian who has committed murder, or committed adultery, or sworn before a druid as pagans do, shall do a year's penance for each of these crimes; the year of penance completed, he shall present himself, accompanied by witnesses, and then be freed of his obligation by a priest.

15. And he that commits theft shall do penance for half a year; twenty days on bread only; and, if possible, he shall restore the stolen goods; thus shall he be restored to the Church.

16. A Christian who believes that there is such a thing in the world as a vampire,[5] that is to say, a witch, is to be anathematized—anyone who puts a living soul under such a reputation; and he must not be received again into the Church before he has undone by his own word the crime that he has committed, and so does penance with all diligence.

17. A virgin who has made a vow to God to remain chaste and afterwards has taken a spouse in the flesh, shall be excommunicated until she changes her ways; if she converts and dismisses the adulterer, she shall do penance; and afterwards they shall not live in the same house or in the same village.

18. If a person is excommunicated he shall not enter the church even on Easter night, until he pledges himself to a penance.

19. A Christian woman who has taken a man in honourable marriage and afterwards deserts the same and gives herself to an adulterer, she who does this shall be excommunicated.

20. A Christian who, acting like a pagan, fails to pay a debt shall be excommunicated until he pays the debt.

21. A Christian whom someone has wronged and who calls that person to court, and not to the Church, for the case to be tried, he who does this shall be a stranger.

22. If anyone has given his daughter to a man in honourable marriage and she loves another, and he connives with her and receives a bride-price,[6] both shall be excluded from the Church.

23. If a priest has built a church, he shall not offer the holy sacrifice in it before he has his bishop come to consecrate it; for so it is proper.

---

23 domo *ex* -u W; *cf. p.* 58, 13   27 adulterio W: *corr. Spelman*   31 dereliquerit: *cf.* Ezech. 3, 21 (Lucifer); '*probably error for* delinquo': *A. Souter, Glossary of Later Latin* (*1949*) *s.u.*   28 *lege* fecerit? *cf.* 32   31 in iudicium *Spelman*: imductum W   34 *scribere malim* acciperit, *cf. can. 4. 19. 30;* (susciperit) *can. 11*

24. Si quis aduena ingressus fuerit plebem non ante baptizat neque offerat nec consecret nec aecclesiam aedificet †nec permissionem accipiat ab episcopo, nam qui a gentibus sperat permissionem alienus sit.

25. Si que a religiosis hominibus donata fuerint diebus illis quibus pontifex in si⟨n⟩gulis habitauerit aecclesis pontificalia dona, sicut mos 5 antiquis ordinare, ad episcopum pertinebunt siue ad ussum necessarium siue aegentibus distribuendum, prout ipse episcopus moderabit.

26. Si quis uero clericus contrauenerit et dona inuadere fuerit depraehensus, ut turpis lucri cupidus ab ecclesia sequestretur.

27. Clericus aepiscopi in plebe quislibet nouus ingresor, baptizare et 10 offerre illum non licet nec aliquid agere; qui si sic non faciat excommonis sit.

28. Si quis clericorum excommonis ⟨fuerit⟩, solus non in eadem domo cum fratribus orationem facit nec offere nec consecrare ⟨ei⟩ licet donec se faciat emendatum; qui si sic non fecerit, dupliciter uindicetur.   15

29. Si quis fratrum accipere gratiam Dei uoluerit non ante baptizetur quam ut .xl. mum agat.

30. Aepiscopus quislibet qui de sua in alteram progreditur parruchiam nec ordinare praesumat nisi permissionem acciperit ab eo qui in suo principatu est. Die dominica offerat tantum susceptione et obsequi 20 hic contentus sit.

31. Si quis conduxerit e duobus clericis quos discordare conuenit per discordiam aliquam prolatum uni e duobus hostem ad interficiendum, homicida congruum est nominari; qui clericus ab omnibus rectis habetur alienus.   25

32. Si quis clericorum uoluerit iuuare captiuo, cum suo praetio illi subueniat. Nam si per furtum illum inu[i]olauerit, blasfemantur multi clerici per unum latronem. Qui sic fecerit excommonis sit.

33. Clericus qui de Britanis ad nos uenit sine epistola, etsi habitet in plebe, non licitum ministrare.   30

34. Diaconus nobiscum similiter qui inconsulto suo abbate sine litteris in aliam parruchiam †adsentiat, nec cibum ministrare decet et a suo presbitero quem contempsit per penitentiam uindicetur.

Et monachus inconsultu abbate uagulus decet uindicari.

FINIUNT SINODI STATUTA   35

1–3 can. 24: Coll. Hib. XLIII. 4 (Sinodus Patrici)   13–15 can. 28: *cf*. Coll. Hib. XL. 9 (Patricius)   22–25 can. 31: *cf*. Coll. Hib. X. x   34 *cf*. Coll. Hib. XXXIX. 11 (Patricius)

1 baptizat: *cf. can. 16*   2 nec (3) : quam *Spelman*; ⟨do⟩nec, *collata Coll. Hib. XLIII. 4* (donec . . . acceperit), *Ware; fort*. quam ut, *cf. can. 16. 29*   13 fuerit *suppl. Spelman; cf. Coll. Hib.* domo *ex* -u W   14 facit: faciat *Coll. Hib.* ei *suppleui ex Coll. Hib.* (liceat ei), *sed cf.* 30   17 *lege* .xl. mam?   19 acciperit: i (1) *ex* e W   20 principatum (m *del*.) W   23 prolatum: *lege* probatum? (*Coll. Hib.*: uel adprobatum fuerit uni uel duobus prouocasse hostem)   32 adsentiat: absentat *Ware* 35 STATUTA *ego*: DISTITUTA W

24. If a new-comer joins a community, he shall not baptize, or offer the holy sacrifice, or consecrate, or build a church, until he receives permission from the bishop. One who looks to laymen for permission shall be a stranger.

25. If gifts are made by pious people on days when the bishop stays in the several churches, they shall, as the ancients used to decree, be the bishop's to dispose of as pontifical gifts, either for his own needs or for distribution among the poor, as the bishop himself will decide.

26. But if a cleric contravenes and is caught encroaching on the gifts, he shall be cut off from the Church as one greedy for sordid gain.

27. Any cleric who is a new-comer in a bishop's community is not allowed to baptize, or to offer the holy sacrifice, or to perform any functions; if he does not abide by this, he shall be excommunicated.

28. If a cleric has been excommunicated, he shall say prayer alone, and not in the same house with his brethren; nor is he allowed to offer the holy sacrifice or to consecrate until he has corrected himself; if he does otherwise he shall be doubly punished.

29. If one of the brethren wishes to receive the grace of God, he shall not be baptized before he has kept the forty days' fast.

30. Any bishop who goes from his own parish[7] to another must not presume to ordain unless he has received permission from him who holds jurisdiction in the place; on the Lord's Day he shall offer the holy sacrifice only if he is invited to do so,[8] and he shall be content to comply in this matter.

31. If one of two clerics who happen to be at odds over some matter of dispute hires an enemy of the other who has offered to kill him, he is rightly called a murderer; such a cleric is regarded as excommunicated by all righteous people.

32. If a cleric wishes to come to the aid of a captive, he should assist him with his own money; for if he kidnaps him, many clerics will be blamed because of one thief. He who does this shall be excommunicated.

33. A cleric who comes from the Britons without a letter, even though he lives in a community, is not allowed to minister.[9]

34. Similarly, if one of our deacons goes away to another parish without consulting his abbot,[10] and without a letter, he should not even be given food; and he shall be punished with penance by the priest whom he has disobeyed.

Also a monk who goes wandering without consulting his abbot is to be punished.

HERE END THE STATUTES OF THE SYNOD

INCIPIT PRAEFATIO GILDAE DE POENITENTIA

1. Praesbiter aut diaconus faciens fornicationem naturalem siue sodomitam praelato ante monachi uoto .iii. annis peniteat. Ueniam omni hora roget, superpos⟨s⟩itionem faciet in una quaque hebdomada exceptis .l. diebus post passionem; pane sine mensura et ferculo 5 aliquatenus butero inpinguato die dominico, caeteris uero diebus paxmati panis mensura et misso parum inpinguato, horti holeribus, ouis paucis, Britannico formello utatur, himina Romana lactis pro fragilitate corporis istius eui, tenuclae uero uel battuti lactis sextario Romano sitis gratia et aquae talimpulo, si operarius est; lectum non multo feno 10 instructum habeat; per .iii. xlmas superaddat aliquid prout uirtus eius admiserit. Semper ex intimo corde defleat culpam suam; obedientiam prae omnibus libentissime excipiat. Post annum et dimedium euchari- stiam summat, ad pacem ueniat, psalmos cum fratribus canat, ne penitus anima tanto tempore caelestis medicinae ⟨ieiuna⟩ intereat. 15

2. Si quis inferiore gradu possitus monachus, .iii. annis poeniteat, sed mensura grauetur panis. Si operarius, sextarium de lacte Romanum et alium de tenucla et aquam quantum sufficiat pro sitis ardore summat.

3. Si uero sine monachi uotu presbiter aut diaconus peccauerit, sicut monachus sine gradu sic peniteat. 4. Si autem peccatum uoluerit 20 monachus facere, anno et dimedio. Habet tamen abas huius rei mode- randae facultatem, si oboedientia eius placita fuerit Deo et abati suo.

5. Antiqui patres .xii. presbitero et .vii. diacono poenitentiae statuere.

6. Monachus furatus uestem uel aliquam rem .ii. annis ut supra poeniteat, si iunior est; si senior, anno integro. Si uero monachus non 25 fuerit eque anno et maxime in .iii. xlsimis.

7. Si monachus exundante uentre euomerit sacrificium in die, cenam suam non praesummat; et si non infirmitatis causa, vii. superpossitioni- bus, si infirmitatis et non uoracitatis, .iiii. superpossitionibus deleat culpam. 8. Si autem non sacrificium, diei superpossitione et multa 30 increpatione plectatur.

Codices: C B

2 presbyter C   3 sodomittam C: *lege* sodomiticam? monachii C   4 super- positionem B. superpossessionem C   5 ferculo: serculo (*i.e. Hib.* sercol) *in exemplari fuisse euidenter coniecit Binchy; cf. Lib. Dauid. c. 7*   6 butiro B   cęteris C. ceteris B 7 miso B. misoclo (*i.e. tenui ferculo) Martène; malim intelligere* missu '*dish*' '*course*', *cf. Souter, Glossary, s.u.* parum: paruum B. *s.l.* aďo C. a ďo B; *cf.* C, fol. 57ᵛ, b: perpetuo,*s.l.* AD (*i.e. aduerbium*); aequale .i. aďu B, *Can. Wall. A 20*   8 himana C 9 battuti *scripsi, cf. Cumm. II. 2*: balthutae B. -e C   10 et–talimpulo: etque talimpulo C   lecturum C   14 sumat B   ⟨et⟩ ad B   15 ieiuna *suppleui; cf. Cumm. II. 2*   16 inferiore C   positus C   manachus B*   18 sumat B 20–21 si autem post peccatum uoluerit monachus fieri *Cumm. II. 5*   21 dimedium C   anno et dimedio: *ellipsim statuunt McNeill–Gamer p. 71, collato Cumm. II. 5*

HERE BEGINS THE PREFACE OF GILDAS ON PENANCE

1. A presbyter or a deacon committing natural fornication or sodomy who has previously taken the monastic vow shall do penance for three years. He shall seek pardon every hour and keep a special fast[1] once every week except during the fifty days following the Passion.[2] He shall have bread without limitation and a titbit[3] fattened slightly with butter on Sunday; on the other days a ration of dry bread and a dish enriched with a little fat, garden vegetables, a few eggs, British cheese, a Roman half-pint of milk in consideration of the weakness of the body in this age, also a Roman pint of whey or buttermilk for his thirst, and some water if he is a worker.[4] He shall have his bed meagrely supplied with hay. For the three forty-day periods[5] he shall add something as far as his strength permits. He shall at all times deplore his guilt from his inmost heart. Above all things let him show the readiest obedience. After a year and a half he may receive the eucharist and come for the kiss of peace and sing the psalms with his brethren, lest his soul perish utterly from lacking so long a time[6] the celestial medicine.

2. If any monk of lower rank (does this), he shall do penance for three years, but his allowance of bread shall be increased. If he is a worker, he shall take a Roman pint of milk and another of whey and as much water as the intensity of his thirst requires.

3. If, however, it is a presbyter or a deacon without monastic vow who has sinned, he shall do the same penance as a monk not in holy orders.

4. But if a monk (merely) intends to commit (such) a sin,[7] (he shall do penance) for a year and a half. The abbot has authority, however, to modify this if his obedience is pleasing to God and the abbot.

5. The ancient fathers commanded twelve (years) of penance for a presbyter and seven for a deacon.

6. A monk who has stolen a garment or any (other) thing shall do penance for two years as stated above, if he is a junior; if a senior, one entire year. If, however, he is not a monk, likewise a year, and especially the three periods of forty days.

7. If a monk after loading his stomach vomits the host during the day, he shall not venture to take his supper; and if it is not on account of infirmity he shall wipe out his offence with seven special fasts; if it is from infirmity, not from gluttony, with four special fasts. 8. But if it is not the host, he is to be punished with a special fast of one day and with much reproach.

---

22 facundatem B   28 superpositionibus B. -posit- C   29 uoracitatis: *s.l.* i. causa
CB   superpositionibus C   deleat: *cf. p.* 62, 5   30 die superpositionem C

9. Si casu neglegens quis sacrificium aliquod perdat, per .iii. xlmas, relinquens illud feris et alitibus deuorandum.

10. Si quis autem ebrietatis causa psallere non potest, stupens elinguis, caena priuatur.

11. Peccans cum pecode anno; si ipse solus, .iii. xlmas deluat 5 culpam.

12. Qui communicauerit a suo abate excommunicato, xl.

13. Manducans morticinam inscius, xl.

14. Sciendum est tamen quod quanto quis tempore moratur in peccatis tanto ei augenda penitentia est. 10

15. Si cui inponitur opus aliquod et contemptus gratia illud non fecerit, cena careat. Si uero obliuione, demedium cotidiani uictus.
16. Si autem summat alterius opus, illud notum faciat abati cum reuerentia, excepto eo nullo audiente, et sic peragat, si iubetur.

18. Offensus quis ab aliquo debet hoc indicare abati, non tamen 15 accussantis sed medentis afectu, et abas decernat. 17. Nam qui iram corde multo tempore retinet, in morte est.

Si autem confitetur peccatum, xl ieiunet, et si ultra in peccato persistat, .ii. xl, et si idem fecerit, abscidatur a corpore sicut membrum putredum, quia furor homicidium nutrit. 20

19. Qui non occurrit ad ⟨secundi psalmi⟩ consummationem, canat .viii. in ordine psalmos. Si excitatus ueniat post misam, quicquid cantauerunt replicet ex ordine fratres. Si uero ad secundam uenerit, caena careat.

20. Si quis errans commotauerit aliquid de u⟨e⟩rbis ubi periculum 25 adnotatur, triduanum aut .iii. superpositiones faciat.

21. Si sacrum terra tenus neglegendo ceciderit, caena careat.

22. Qui uoluntate obsceno liquore maculatus fuerit dormiendo, si ceruisa et carne habundat cenubium, .iii. noctis horis stando uigilet, si sane uirtutis est. Si uero pauperem uictum habet, .xxviii. aut .xxx. 30 psalmos canet stando suplex aut opere extraordinario pendat.

23. Pro bonis regibus sacra debemus offerre, pro malis nequaquam.

24. Presbiteri uero pro suis episcopis non prohibentur offerre.

25. Qui arguitur pro aliquo delicto et quasi inconsultans refrenatur, cena careat. 35

1 casu aliquo . . . sacrificium perdat *Cumm. (IX) 1*   xlmas: *s.l.* i. peniteat CB   4 elinguis: et linguis C   cẹna B. cena C   5 pectans C   diluat B; *cf. p.* 60, 29   7 cummunicauerit B   excommunicato: dā (*i.e.* datiuus) *s* com C 9 quanto: quando CB; *corr. Wasserschleben*   10 augenda, *i.e.* agenda; *cf. Cumm. (IX) 4*   13 illiud C   14 iubentur C   *can. 17 et 18 mutato ordine tradita esse suspicor* 16 accuˢsantis B. accusantis C   sed: sunt C   affectu B   21 secundi psalmi *cum Haddan–Stubbs addidi, cf. Cumm. (IX) 6; Poenit. XXXV Capit., can. 31 (p. 524 Wasserschleben)*   22 missam C   24, 27 cẹna B. cena C   28 qui: quid B 29 *post* cenubium (cẹ- B) *add.* .ē. CB   34 *exspectes* et quasi insultans refragatur

9. If someone by a mishap through carelessness loses a host, leaving it for beasts and birds to devour, he shall do penance for three forty-day periods.

10. But if on account of drunkenness someone is unable to sing the psalms, being benumbed and speechless, he shall be deprived of his supper.

11. One who sins with a beast shall expiate his guilt for a year; if by himself alone, for three forty-day periods.

12. One who holds communion with one who has been excommunicated by his abbot, forty days.

13. One who unwittingly eats carrion, forty days.

14. It is to be understood, however, that as long a time as a person remains in sin so long is he to do penance.

15. If a certain task has been enjoined on one and through contempt he leaves it undone, he shall go without supper; but if through an oversight, he shall go without half his daily portion. 16. But if he undertakes another's task, he shall modestly make this known to the abbot, none else hearing it, and he shall perform it if he is commanded to do so.

18. One who has been offended by anyone ought to make this known to the abbot, not indeed in the spirit of an accuser, but of a physician; and the abbot shall decide. 17. For he that for a long time holds anger in his heart is in (a state of) death.

But if he confesses his sin, he shall fast for forty days; and if he still persists in his sin, two forty-day periods. And if he does the same thing again, he shall be cut off from the body as a rotten member, since wrath breeds murder.

19. One who has not arrived by the end of the second psalm shall sing eight psalms in order. If when he has been aroused he comes after the reading,[8] he shall repeat in order whatever the brethren have sung. But if he comes at the second reading,[9] he shall go without supper.

20. If in error anyone has changed any of the words where 'danger'[10] is noted (he shall do penance) for three days or perform three special fasts.

21. If by neglect the host has fallen to the ground (the offender) shall go without supper.

22. He who willingly has been defiled in sleep, if the monastic house is abundantly supplied with beer and flesh, shall make a standing vigil for three hours of the night if his health is strong. But if it has poor fare, standing as a suppliant he shall sing twenty-eight or thirty psalms or make satisfaction with extra work.

23. For good rulers we ought to offer the sacrifice, for bad ones on no account.

24. Presbyters are indeed not forbidden to offer for their bishops.

25. One who is accused of any fault and is checked as an inconsiderate person[11] shall go without supper.

26. Qui sarculum perfrangit et ante fracturam non habuit, aut illud extraordinario opere restituat aut superponat.

27. Qui uiderit aliquem ex fratribus abatis transgredi praecepta, debet abatem non caelare; sed ante admoneat peccantem ut solus quod male agit confiteatur abati. Non tam dilator quam ueritatis regulae exsecutor 5 inueniatur.

HUCUSQUE GILDAS

4 celare B   quod: pro (*per compendium*) C

26. One who has broken a hoe which was not broken before, shall either make amends by an extraordinary work or perform a special fast.

27. One who sees any of his brethren violate the commands of the abbot ought not to conceal the fact from the abbot, but he ought first to admonish the offender to confess alone to the abbot the wrong he is doing. Let him be found not so much an informer as one who truly practises the rule.

THUS FAR GILDAS

INCIPIT NUNC SINODUS AQUILONALIS BRITANIAE

1. Cum muliere uel cum uiro peccans quis expellatur ut alterius patriae cenubio uiuat, et peniteat confessus .iii. annis clausus, et postea frater illius altari subiectus anno uno diaconus, .iii. presbiter, .vii. episcopus et abbas suo quisque ordine priuatus doctoris iudicio peniteat.

2. Qui se ipsum quoinquinauerit, annum clausus poeniteat, puer .xii. annorum xl, .xx. annorum .iii. xlmis; diaconus anno clausus et cum fratribus poeniteat demedio; sacerdos uno anno clausus et cum fratribus altero.

3. Monachus consecrata furatus anno, et altero cum fratribus peniteat; si autem iterauerit, exilium patietur.

4. Furatus cybum xl; si iterato, .iii. xlmas; si tertio, anno; si quarto, iugi exilio sub alio abate peniteat.

5. Dilatus et dilator consimili persona iudicentur. Si dilatus negauerit, anno simul uno paenitea⟨n⟩t, in septimana .ii. diebus pane aquaque et biduano in fine cuiusque mensis omnibus fratribus subponentibus et Deum eis iudicem contestantibus. 6. Permanentes autem in obstinatione anno emenso altaris communioni sub iudice flamma sociantur et Dei iudicio relinquantur. 7. Si quando alter fuerit confesus, quantum laboris alteri intulit tantum sibi multiplicetur.

---

2 BRITANNIAE B   4 causus C   5 .vii.: .iiii. B   8 .xx. *om.* B   11 *lege* anno ⟨clausus⟩? *cf.* 8 *et* 9; *s.l. add* .i. exilio CB. anno in exilio *Wasserschleben*   12 intrauerit B   patiętur C   16 anno simili paeniteat CB: *correxi ex Cumm.* (*VIII*) 11   17 aquaque: et aquae C (et aqua *Cumm.*)   sobponentibus C   19 abstinatione CB: *cf. Cumm.* (*VIII*) 12   19 altaris *Cumm. l.c.*: alterius CB   20 quando: q̄m C confessus C

HERE BEGINS THE SYNOD OF NORTH BRITAIN[1]

1. Anyone who sins with a woman or with a man shall be sent away to live in a monastery of another country and shall do penance, after he has confessed, for three years in confinement; and afterwards, as a brother subject to the altar of that monastery he shall do penance at the discretion of his teacher; if he is a deacon, for one year; if a presbyter, for three years; if a bishop or abbot, for seven[2] years; each being deprived of his order.

2. Whoever has defiled himself shall do penance in confinement for a year; a boy of twelve years, for forty (days); one of twenty years, three forty-day periods. A deacon shall do penance for a year in confinement, and for half a year with his brethren; a priest, for one year in confinement and for another year with his brethren.

3. A monk who has stolen consecrated things shall do penance for a year ⟨in confinement⟩ and another year with his brethren; but if he repeats the offence he shall suffer exile.

4. He who steals food shall do penance for forty days; if a second time, for three forty-day periods; if a third time, for a year; if a fourth time, he shall do penance in permanent exile under another abbot.[3]

5. He who is informed on and he who lays the information shall be adjudged as persons of the same status. If he who is informed on denies (his guilt) they shall do penance together for a year, two days a week on bread and water, and two days at the end of each month, all the brethren pledging them and calling upon God as their judge. 6. But if they persist in their obstinacy, after the lapse of a year they shall be joined to the communion of the altar, under the risk of (eternal) fire, and left to the judgement of God.[4] 7. If at any time one of them confesses, to the extent to which he has inflicted hardship on the other his own (hardship) shall be increased.

INCIPIT ALTERA SINODUS LUCI UICTORIE

1. Faciens furtum semel, anno uno; si plura, duobus annis.

2. Qui occidit fratrem suum non ex odii meditatione, si iracondia subita, triannio peniteat.

3. Adulter quoque et ipse triannio.

4. Qui praebent ducatum barbaris, .xiii. annis, tamen si non acciderit stragis Christianorum et sanguinis effussio et dira captiuitas. Si autem euenerit, agant residuo uitae penitentiam reiectis armis. Si autem uoluerit et non ad uota sibi barbaros ad Christianos educere, residuo uite suae peniteat.

5. Qui periurium iurat, .iiii. annis. Qui deducit alium in periurium ignorantem, .vii. annis. Qui autem deductus est ignorans et postea scit, anno uno. Qui uero suspicatur quod in periurium deducitur, tamen iurat pro consensu, .ii. annis.

6. Qui mechator matris est, .iii. annis cum peregrinatione perenni.

7. Qui cum cane uel cum quocumque peccauerit animali, .ii. annis et dimedio.

8. Qui facit scelus uirile ut Sodomite, .iiii. annis. Qui uero in femoribus, .iii. annis; manu autem siue alterius siue sua, .ii. annis.

9. Totum hoc quod diximus, si post uotum perfectionis fuerit homo. Si autem ante uotum, annus diminuitur de omnibus his tribus; de reliquis uero ut debet minuitur dum non uouit.

---

2 furtum: fructum C   3 si: *lege* sed?   6 .xiiii. B   8 reiectis C. *Ps.-Cumm. VI 28*: relictis B. *Cumm.* (*IX*) *13*   9 non: *lege* hoc?   11 educit C   12 autem *om.* B   15 mechatur B. medichatur C   19 siue (2): si C   20 fuerit: fecerit B

HERE BEGINS ANOTHER SYNOD, (THAT) OF THE GROVE OF VICTORY

1. He who commits theft once shall do penance for one year; more than once, for two years.

2. He who slays his brother not with malice aforethought, if[1] from sudden anger, shall do penance for three years.

3. Likewise shall an adulterer do penance for three years.

4. They who afford guidance to the barbarians,[2] thirteen[3] years, provided there be no slaughter of Christians or effusion of blood or dire captivity. If, however, such things do take place the offenders shall perform penance, laying down their arms for the rest of life. But if one planned to conduct the barbarians to the Christians, and did so according to his will, he shall do penance for the remainder of his life.[4]

5. He who swears a false oath, four years. He who leads another into perjury unknowingly, seven years. He who is led into (perjury) unknowingly and later knows of it, one year. He who suspects that he is being led into perjury and yet swears, on account of his agreement to do so, two years.

6. He who defiles his mother, three years with perpetual pilgrimage.

7. He who sins with a dog or with any animal, two years and a half.

8. [In substance:] He who is guilty of sodomy in its various forms shall do penance for four, three, or two years according to the nature of the offence.

9. All that we have just said applies if a man has made the vow of perfection. But if he sins before the vow, a year is deducted from each of the three above; as to the rest, a reduction is made as it ought to be so long as he has not taken the vow.

INCIPIUNT EXCERPTA QUEDAM DE LIBRO DAUIDIS

1. Sacerdotes in templo Dei ministraturi gule gratia uinum aut siceram per neglegentiam et non per ignorantiam bibentes .iiii. diebus peniteant. Si autem per contemptum arguentium, xl.

2. Inebriati autem per ignorantiam .xv. diebus; si per neglegentiam, xl; si per contemptum, .iii. x⟨l⟩mis.

3. Qui cogit aliquem humanitatis gratia ut ebrietur, similiter ut ebrius peniteat. 4. Qui uero effectu hodii seu luxuriae ut turpiter confundat uel irrideat ad ebrietatem alios cogit, si non satis penituerit, sic peniteat ut homicida animarum.

5. Cum muliere disponsata Christo maritoue siue cum iumento uel cum masculo fornicantes de reliquo mortui mundo Deo uiuant. 6. Qui autem cum uirgine uel uidua necdum disponsata peccauerit, dotem det parentibus eius et anno uno peniteat. Si non habuerit dotem, .iii. annis peniteat.

7. Episcopus homicidium uoluntate faciens uel quamlibet fornicationem dolumue .xiii. annis peniteat; presbiter autem .vii. cum pane et aqua et ferculo in die dominica uel sabati; diaconus autem .vi., sine gradu monachus .iiii., nisi infirmitas inpediat illos.

8. Qui in sompnis cum uoluntate pollutus est surgat canatque .vii. psalmos et in die illo in pane et aqua uiuat; sin autem, .xxx. psalmos canat. 9. Uolens in sompnis peccare sed non potuit, .xv. psalmos. Si autem peccauit sed non pollutus est, .xxiiii. Si sine uoluntate pollutus est, .xvi.

10. Antiqui decreuere sancti ut episcopus pro capitalibus peccatis .xxiiii. annis peniteat, presbiter .xii., diaconus .vii., sic uirgo lectorque et relegiosus, ebibatus autem .iiii.

11. Nunc autem presbiteri ruentis poenitentia est diaconique et subdiaconi uirginisque et cuiuslibet hominis hominem ad mortem tradentis et cum pecodibus uel cum sua sorore uel cum mariti uxore fornicantis et uenenis hominem occidere uolentis triennium: primo anno super terra, secundo lapidi capud inponendum, tertio super axem iaceat; solo pane et aqua et sale et leguminis talimpulo uescatur. Ceterique malint .xxx. triduanos †uel cum superpositionibus cum cybo lectoque supra dicto. annona ad nonam usque alteram.† Alia est paenitentia

25 ebibati (epibati, epiuati, *recte* epibatae) laici *Corp. Gloss. Lat.* iv. 512, 28; v. 290, 15; 358, 20; 548, 2; 597, 57

3 ciceram B   per ignorantiam: pignorantiam B   4 arguentium *om.* C 8 hodii: ho C   9 ebrię̨tatem C   satis penituerit: *locus uix sanus; lege* satis fecerit?   11 cum in iumento C   17 ferculo *pro* serculo: *u. Gildas c.* 1   sabbati B   autem *om.* B   18 impediat C   illis C*   19 somnis C   20 in ⟨aqua⟩ die C sin: si C   21 uolens ⟨autem⟩ B   .xu. salpmos C   22 est (1) *om.* C .xv. B 25 religiosus C   26 et–27 uirginisque *om.* C   28 pę̨codibus B   30 terram C 31 talimpolo B*   33 usque ⟨ad⟩ B   32–33 *fort. lege* triduanos cum cybo lectoque supra dicto uel cum superpositionibus a nona ad nonam usque alteram

HERE BEGIN CERTAIN EXCERPTS FROM A BOOK OF DAVID

1. Priests who are about to minister in the temple of God, who through greediness drink wine or strong drink negligently, not ignorantly, shall do penance for four days; but if they do so out of contempt of those who censure them, forty days.

2. Those who become drunk through ignorance, fifteen days; through negligence, forty days; through contempt, three forty-day periods.

3. One who constrains another to get drunk for the sake of good fellowship shall do the same penance as the drunken man. 4. But one who under the influence of hatred or of wantonness constrains others to drunkenness that he may basely put them to confusion or ridicule, if he has not done adequate penance,[1] shall do penance as a slayer of souls.

5. Those who commit fornication with a woman who has become vowed to Christ or to a husband, or with a beast, or with a male, for the remainder (of their lives) dead to the world shall live unto God. 6. But one who sins with a virgin or a widow not yet betrothed, shall pay the bride-price[2] to her parents and do penance for a year. If he has not the bride-price, he shall do penance for three years.

7. A bishop who wilfully commits murder or any kind of fornication or fraud shall do penance for thirteen years; but a presbyter seven years on bread and water, and a titbit on Sunday or Saturday; a deacon, six years; a monk not in holy orders, four years—unless they are hindered by infirmity.

8. He who intentionally has become polluted in sleep shall get up and sing seven psalms and live on bread and water for that day; but if he does not do this he shall sing thirty psalms. 9. If he desired to sin in sleep but could not, fifteen psalms; if, however, he sinned but was not polluted, twenty-four. If he was unintentionally polluted, sixteen.[3]

10. The saints of old decreed that for capital sins a bishop should do penance for twenty-four years; a presbyter, twelve; a deacon, seven; a virgin, a reader, and a monk, the same; but a layman, four years.

11. Now, however, the penance of a presbyter, a deacon, a sub-deacon or a virgin who falls, as well as of anyone who puts a man to death, who commits fornication with beasts or with his sister or with another's wife, or who plans to kill a man with poisons, is three years. During the first year he shall lie upon the ground; during the second his head is to be laid upon a stone; during the third, upon a board; and he shall eat only bread and water and salt and some pease porridge. Others might prefer thirty periods of three days, with food and bed as aforesaid, or with special fasts from nones to the next nones.[4] Another

.iii. annis, sed himina de ceruissa uel lacte cum pane saleque altera e
duabus noctibus cum prandii ratione, et ordine .xii. horis noctium
dierumque Deum suplicare debent.

12. Hinc autem presbitero offerre sacrificium uel diacono tenere
calicem non licet aut in sublimiorem gradum ascendere.   5

13. Usuram accipiens perdat ea quae accipit.

14. Praeda uel fraude uescit, semiannus.

15. Uirgini osculum in secreto praebens triduanum peniteat.

16. In aecclesia mendacium iurans quadruplum pro quo iurauerat
reddat.   10

2 cum prandinatione C. cum prandii natione B: *corr. Wasserschleben*   noxium
(*s.l.* l– c) B   3 suplicare C   7 semiannus: i. peniteat *s.l.* CB   9 eclesia B
mendatium C*

penance is for three years, but with a half-pint of beer or milk with bread and salt every second night with a ration of dinner; and they ought to supplicate God regularly in the twelve hours of the nights and of the days.

12. But thenceforth it is not permitted to a priest to offer the sacrifice or for a deacon to hold the chalice or to rise to higher rank.

13. He who receives interest shall give up what he has received.

14. He who enjoys the fruits of robbery or fraud, half a year.

15. He who kisses a virgin in secret shall do penance for three days.

16. He who takes a false oath in the church shall restore four times that for which he made the oath.

PENITENTIALIS VINNIANI

(1) Puer qui sacrificium communicat peccans cum pecode .c. dies peniteat cum pane et aqua.

(2) In terga uero fornicantes, si pueri sint, annos ii, si uiri, iii; si autem in consuetudine uertunt, ⟨.vii.⟩ et modus paenitentia⟨e⟩ addatur iudicio sacerdotis. 5*

(3) Desideria suis labiis conplentes iii annos. Si in consuetudine fuerint adsueti, vii annos.

(4) Puer de seculo ueniens cum aliqua puella fornicari nitens nec coinquinatus est, xx dies; si autem coinquinatus est, .c. dies; si uero, ut moris est, compleat suam uoluntatem, annum peniteat. 10*

In nomine Dei Patris et Filii et Spiritus Sancti.

1. Si quis in corde suo per cogitationem peccauerit et confestim penituerit, percutiat pectus suum et petat a Deo ueniam et satis faciat et sanus sit.

2. Si autem frequenter cogitat et dubitat facere, aut uictor aut uictus 5 fuerit, petat a Deo adiutorium per orationem et ieiunium diebus ac noctibus donec euanescat maligna cogitatio et sanus sit.

3. Si autem cogitauerit et uoluerit facere et non potuit sed facultas prohibuit eum, unum est peccatum sed non eadem penitentia; uerbi gratia, si fornicationem uoluit aut homicidium, quia effectus non 10 expleuit, uoluntate iam peccauit in corde suo sed celeritate penitentiae potest adiuuari. Penitentia eius ipsa est: dimedium annum peniteat cum pane et aqua per mensura et annum totum abstineat se a uino et a carnibus.

4. Si qui⟨s⟩ uerbo peccauerit per inreptionem et statim penituerit 15 et ⟨non⟩ per difinitionem tale aliquid locutus est, submittere se debet ad penitentiam, sed superpositionem unam faciat; sed post haec caueat se de reliquo ne amplius peccet.

5. Si quis rixam facit de clericis aut de ministris Dei, ebdomadam peniteat dierum cum pane et aqua et sale et petat ueniam a Deo suo et 20

Codices: VSPB

Titulus in S solo
1*–10* V 25ᵛ–26ʳ, *sub titulo*: XII NUNC DE PRIORUM STATUTA NOSTRORUM PATRUM PROPON⟨AMUS⟩. *Desunt ceteri codices. Leguntur isdem fere uerbis apud Cummeanum, Penit.* (X) 5. *15–17. De Vinniano auctore dubitat Wasserschleben, Bussordnungen, p. 108, adn. 1; p. 119, adn. 2. Quae si ad Vinnianum pertinent fortasse post can. 13 inserenda sunt, cf. Cummeani Paenit. II. 6 sqq.* 5* .vii. *suppleui ex Cumm.* (X) *15* paenitentia V

VS (V *29ʳ–31ʳ*)   1 DE COGITATIONIBUS *titulus in* V   In–Sancti *om.* S
2 quis: s *s.l.* V   3 percutiet S   4 et: ut S   5 cogitauerit S   dubitet S
6 adiutorium: ueniam S   8 autem: quis S   cogitaū V   uoluit S   et non
potuit *om.* S   ⟨sa (*i.e.* sua)⟩ facultas S   9 est *om.* S   eandem V. eodem
S   10 uoluerit S   q² V. quia S; *lege* quod?   11 uoluntatem S   celeritate

PENITENTIAL OF FINNIAN

(1)[1] A boy who communicates in the sacrament although he has sinned with a beast, shall do penance for a hundred days on bread and water.

(2) Those practising homosexuality, if they are boys, two years, if men, three; if, however, it has become a habit, seven, and in addition, the manner of penance shall be decided according to the judgement of a priest.

(3) Those who satisfy their desires with their lips, three years. If it has become a habit, seven years.

(4) A boy coming from the world who intends to commit fornication with a girl, and has not been polluted, 20 days; if he has been polluted, 100 days; if, however, as it commonly happens, he fulfils his intention, he shall do penance for a year.

In the name of the Father and of the Son and of the Holy Ghost.

1. If anyone has sinned by thought in his heart and immediately repents, he shall beat his breast and seek pardon from God and make satisfaction, and (so) be whole.

2. But if he frequently entertains (evil) thoughts and hesitates to act on them, whether he has mastered them or been mastered by them, he shall seek help[2] from God by prayer and fasting day and night until the evil thought departs and he is whole.

3. If, however, he has thought evil and intended to do it and has not been able to do it, since opportunity has failed him, it is the same sin but not the same penance; for example, if he intended fornication or murder, he has, by his intention, already committed the sin in his heart which he did not complete by a deed; but if he quickly does penance, he can be helped. His penance is this: half a year he shall do penance on an allowance of bread and water, and he shall abstain from wine and meat for a whole year.

4. If anyone has sinned in word by inadvertence and immediately repented, and has not said any such thing of set purpose, he ought to submit to penance, but he shall keep (only) one special fast; but thereafter let him be on his guard throughout his life, lest he commit further sin.

5. If one of the clerics or ministers of God makes strife, he shall do penance for a period of seven days with bread and water and salt, and

---

penitentiae: celeriter S   12 potest: post V   est: sē S   dimidium S   peniteat
–13 aqua *om.* S   13 per mensura V *semper ubi plenis litteris scribitur*; per mensuram
semper SPB   15 qui V   inredemptionem S   16 non *om.* V.   difficionem
S   17 unam *om.* S   se *om.* S   18 peccat S
'SPB   19–*p. 76, 17 extant in* PB   19 faciat SPB   de (2) *om.* SPB   ebd- V. ebdomades P   20 dierum peniteat SPB   et sale *om.* SPB   per mensuram *add.* PB
a deo suo (*om.* PB) ueniam SPB

proximo plena confessione et humilitate et sic potest Deo reconciliari et proximo.

6. Si quis surrexerit ad scandalum et disposuit in corde suo proximum percutere aut occidere, si clericus fuerit dimedium annum peniteat cum pane et aqua per mensura et annum totum abstineat se a uino et a 5 carnibus et sic altario reconciliabitur; 7. si quis autem laicus fuerit ebdomadam dierum peniteat; quia homo seculi huius est, culpa leuior in hoc mundo et premium minus in futuro.

8. Si autem clericus fuerit et percusserit fratrem suum aut proximum et sanguinem effuderit, unum est ut occiderit eum, sed non eadem 10 penitentia: annum integrum peniteat cum pane et aqua et sale et sine ministerio clericatus; et orare [se] debet cum fletu et lacrimis ut misericordiam consequatur a Deo, quia dicit scriptura: _Qui odit fratrem suum homicida est_; quanto magis qui percutit. 9. Si autem laicus fuerit, xl dies peniteat et det aliquam pecuniam quem percutit, quantum arbitratus 15 fuerit sacerdos aut iustus quisque. Clericus autem pecuniam dare non debet aut illi aut illę.

10. Si quis autem ruina fornicationis ceciderit et clericus fuerit ⟨et⟩ coronam suam perdiderit, si semel contigerit et celatum est hominibus sed notuit coram Deo, annum i. peniteat cum pane et aqua per mensura 20 et duobus annis abstineat se a uino et a carnibus, sed officium clericatus sui non amittat. Dicimus enim in absconso absolui esse peccata per penitentiam et per studium diligentius cordis et corporis. 11. Si autem in consuetudine peccati multo tempore fuerunt et in notitiam homonum non uenerit, tribus annis peniteat cum pane et aqua et officium clericatus 25 amittat et aliis tribus abstineat se a uino et a carnibus, quia non minus est peccare coram Deo quam coram hominibus.

12. Si qui⟨s⟩ autem clericorum ruina maxima ceciderit et genuerit filium et ipsum occiderit, magnum est crimen fornicatio et homicidium, sed redimi potest per penitentiam et misericordiam Dei. Tribus annis 30 peniteat cum pane et aqua per mensura in fletu et ⟨lacrimis atque⟩

13 sq 1 Ioh. 3, 15

---

1 proximo ⟨suo⟩ SPB   et ⟨1⟩ _om._ PB   potest: petaens P. petḗns B   a deo B   reconciliare S. reconsiliari B   2 proximo ⟨suo⟩ SB   3 quis: s _ins._ V   ad scandalum surrexerit SPB   deposuit B   proximum ⟨suum⟩ SPB   4 aut: auet V   dimidium SP   annum SP*. añ V. anni PᶜB   4 peniteat–5 mensura: cum pane . . . secundum mensuram peniteat PB   6 alt̄o P. altio B   reconciliatur S. reconsiliabitur B   quis (s _ins._) V: _om._ SPB, _nescio an recte_   7 huius saeculi P   est et culpa eius P   10 et: aut S   sanguinem ⟨eius⟩ P   effunderit S   _post_ est _add._ illi peccatum P, peccatum B   eum _om._ PB   11 intigrum P*   et sale _om._ SPB   et sine: Ce sene in S   12 se debet: se _deleui._ ⟨pro⟩ se debere S   ut: et B   13 a deo consequatur S   14 homicidia P   quando P*B   percuserit B   autem _om._ PB   dierum S   15 de (_sic_) pecuniam aliquam S. aliquam _om._ PB. pecŏniam P   quem: qui S. cui PB   percuˢsit P. percuserit B   quantum: quando B   16 quisq; S. quisquem V. quisquam PB   pecŏniam P   16–17 non debet dare P   17 ille SPB. _hic addunt_ PB: igitur peniteñ (penī B; _lege_ peniteat?) suplicatione (suppl- B) necessaria. Qui conuersus

seek pardon from God and his neighbour, with full confession and humility; and thus can he be reconciled to God and his neighbour.

6. If anyone has decided on a scandalous deed and plotted in his heart to strike or kill his neighbour, if (the offender) is a cleric, he shall do penance for half a year with an allowance of bread and water and for a whole year abstain from wine and meat, and thus he will be reconciled to the altar; 7. but if he is a layman, he shall do penance for a period of seven days; since he is a man of this world, his guilt is lighter in this world and his reward less in the world to come.

8. But if he is a cleric and strikes his brother or his neighbour and sheds blood, it is the same as if he had killed him, but the penance is not the same: he shall do penance with bread and water and salt and be deprived of his clerical office for an entire year, and he must pray with weeping and tears, that he may obtain mercy of God, since Scripture says: *Whosoever hateth his brother is a murderer*; how much more he who strikes him. 9. But if he is a layman, he shall do penance forty days and give some money to him whom he has struck, according as some priest or arbiter determines. A cleric, however, ought not to give money to either man or woman.[3]

10. But if one who is a cleric falls miserably through fornication and loses his crown,[4] if it happens once (only) and it is concealed from men but known before God, he shall do penance for an entire year with an allowance of bread and water and for two years abstain from wine and meat, but he shall not lose his clerical office. For, we say, sins can be absolved in secret by penance and by very diligent devotion of heart and body. 11. If, however, they have long been in the habit of sin and it has not come to the notice of men,[5] he shall do penance for three years with bread and water and lose his clerical office, and for three years more he shall abstain from wine and meat, since it is not a smaller thing to sin before God than before men.

12. But if one of the clerical order falls to the depths of ruin and begets a son and kills him, great is the crime of fornication with homicide, but it can be expiated through penance and God's mercy. He shall do penance three years with an allowance of bread and water, in weeping and tears, and prayers by day and night, and shall implore the mercy

ingemuit et cum deo aeterno pactum iniuit in (init l- P) illo igitur (*om.* B) die non commemorabuntur (-bitur P) ⟨eius B⟩ dilecta (delicta B) quae gessit in saeculo. *Fortasse
legend.*: Clericus autem pecuniam dare non debet. Illi igitur penitentia (*aut* ille igitur
peniteat) supplicatione necessaria. Qui ⟨si⟩ conuersus, *etc.*

⟨VS⟩ (V *49ᵛ–50ᵛ*: 18 Item alio loco. Si quis–*p.* 78, 7 penitentia)   18 ⟨et⟩ *suppleui,*
cf. p. 88, 4   19 si semel: et si seni hec S   contingeret S (contingerit *in exemplari?*)
20 i. V: integrum S   aque V   mensuras S   21 a (2) *om.* S.   21–22 clericatus
sui non: clericatis nono S   24 multo tempore peccati fuerat S   in notitiam: in
nocentiam S   hominum S   25 clericatum V   26 ammittat S   alius V   27 est
om. S   quam: quia V   coram (2) *om.* S   28 qui V   ruinam S   30 remedi
S. (redemi *in exemplari? cf. pp.* 78, 27; 80, 15)   Dei *om.* S   31 lacrimis atque *om.* V

orationibus die ac nocte et postulet de Domini misericordia si forte habeat remissionem peccatorum et tribus aliis abstineat se a uino et a carnibus sine officio clericatus et quadragisimas in tribus annis nouissimis ieiunet cum pane et aqua ⟨et⟩ extorris existat de patria sua donec impleatur numerus .vii. annorum et ita iudicio episcopi uel sacerdotis 5 suo officio restituatur. 13. Si autem non occiderit filium, minus peccatum sed eadem penitentia.

14. Si qui⟨s⟩ autem ex clericis habuerit familiaritatem alicuius femine et ipse nihil mali fecerit cum ea nec commanendo nec oscolando illecebroso, penitentia haec est: quamdiu habeat abstineat se a communione 10 altaris et peniteat xl diebus et noctibus cum pane et aqua et consortium femine de corde suo absciderit et ita restituatur altario.

15. Si autem multarum feminarum habuerit familiaritatem et earum commansionibus et oscolis inlecebrosis seipsum dederat, sed ipse, ut dicat, se seruauit a ruina, dimedium annum peniteat cum pane et aqua 15 per mensura et dimedium aliud abstineat se a uino et a carnibus, sed non amittat officium clericatus, et post annum integrum penitentiae ita iungat se altario.

16. Si quis clericus concupiuit uirginem aut aliquam feminam in anima sua sed non dixit per labia, ⟨si⟩ semel tantum concupiuit debet 20 penitere .vii. dies cum pane et ⟨aqua per mensura⟩. 17. Si autem perseueranter concupiuit et non potuit, sed non suscipit eum mulier, siue erupuit dicere, iam mechatus est eam in corde suo, sed in corde non in corpore; unum est peccatum per corpus et animam sed non eadem penitentia. Penitentia eius haec est: xl dies ⟨peniteat⟩ cum pane et aqua. 25

18. Si quis clericus uel si qua mulier malifica uel malificus si aliquem maleficio suo deciperat, inmane peccatum est sed per penitentiam redimi potest; sex annis peniteat, tribus cum pane et aqua per mensura et in residuis .iii. annis abstineat a uino et a carnibus. 19. Si autem non deciperat aliquem sed pro inlecebroso amore dederat alicui, annum 30 integrum peniteat cum pane et aqua per mensura.

20. Si mulier maleficio suo partum alicuius perdiderit, dimedium

---

1 de *om.* S   3 quadragisimas: xl V   4 et *suppl. Wasserschleben*   ectoris S de: in S   5 impleauit S
(V 31ᵛ–32ᵛ)   8 qui V   ⟨qui⟩ habuerit S   9 manendo S   inosculando S 10 habet S   12 abscideret S   13 eorum V   14 commansionibus: cum mansionibus V. cūmansionibus S   osculis S   dederit seipsum S   sed: se S   15 dimidium S   16 dimidium S   aliūd S   sed: Et S   17 dimittat S   ita *om.* S 18 iungat se: iungantur S   19 concupiscit S   feminam aliquam S   20 animo suo S   si *suppleui*   21 aqua per mensura *om.* V   perseuerant S   22 sed: quia S   suscepit S   23 erubuit S   ⟨et⟩ non S   24 per–animam *om.* S 25 penitentia ⟨est⟩ pen. S   peniteat *om.* V
VSPB   26–*p.* 80, 4 annis *extant in* PB   26 quis (s *ins.*) V   clericus uel si qua mulier malificacus (l- *in marg.*) V; *cf. p.* 86, 10: clericus maleficus (*om.* B) uel si qua mulier malefica SPB   27 deceperint B   27 inmane–28 potest *om.* PB 27 redemi S   28 sex: vii B   peniteat *om.* B. penitentiam agat S   *post* tribus *add.* annis S, de his PB   per mensura *om.* PB   29 residuis .iii. annis: caeteris P.

of the Lord, if he may perchance have remission of sins; and he shall abstain for three more years from wine and meat, deprived of his clerical office, and for the forty-day periods[6] in the last three years he shall fast with bread and water; and (he shall) be an exile from his own country, until a period of seven years is completed, and so by the judgement of a bishop or a priest he shall be restored to his office. 13. If, however, he has not killed the child, the sin is less, but the penance is the same.

14. But if one of the clerical order is on familiar terms with any woman and he has himself done no evil with her, neither by cohabiting nor by lascivious embraces, this is his penance: For such time as he has her he shall withdraw from the communion of the altar and do penance for forty days and nights with bread and water and tear out of his heart his fellowship with the woman, and so be restored to the altar.

15. If, however, he is on familiar terms with many women and has given himself to association with them and to their lascivious embraces, but has, as he says, preserved himself from ruin, he shall do penance for half a year with an allowance of bread and water, and for another half year he shall abstain from wine and meat, but he shall not lose his clerical office; and after an entire year of penance, he shall join himself to the altar.[6a]

16. If any cleric lusts after a virgin or any woman in his heart but does not speak with his lips, if he sins thus but once he ought to do penance for seven days with an allowance of bread and water. 17. But if he continually lusts and is unable to indulge his desire, since the woman does not admit him or since he is ashamed to speak, still he has committed adultery with her in his heart—yet it is in his heart, and not in his body; it is the same sin whether in the heart or in the body, yet the penance is not the same. This is his penance: let him do penance for forty days with bread and water.

18. If any cleric or woman who practises magic have led astray anyone by their magic, it is a monstrous sin, but it can be expiated by penance. (Such an offender) shall do penance for six years, three years on an allowance of bread and water, and during the remaining three years he shall abstain from wine and meat. 19. If, however, such a person has not led astray anyone but has given (a potion) for the sake of wanton love to someone, he shall do penance for an entire year on an allowance of bread and water.

20. If a woman by her magic destroys the child she has conceived of

ceteris B. .iii. *om.* S   abstinea⟨n B⟩t ⟨se⟩ SPB   a *ante* carnibus *om.* P   30 deciperit
S   illecebro P   alicui: aliqui S   31 intigrum P   cum . . . aqua peniteat B
per mensura *om.* PB
(V *26ʳ–27ʳ* 32 Si mulier–*p.* 80, 13 suum)   32 Si ⟨aliqua⟩ SPB   mulier
om. P   alicuius ⟨femine (-ę B)⟩ SPB   perdidit P. deciperit S   demedium S.
dimidium P

annum cum pane et aqua peniteat per mensura et duobus annis abstineat
a uino et a carnibus et sex quadragissimas ⟨ieiunet⟩ cum pane et aqua.

21. Si autem genuerit, ut diximus, filium et manifestum peccatum
eius fuerit, ui. annis, sicut iudicatum est de clerico, et in septimo
iungatur altario, et tunc dicimus posse renouare coronam et induere 5
uestimentum album debere et uirginem nuncupare. Ita clericus qui
cecidit eodem modo in septimo anno post laborem penitentie debet
accipere clericatus officium sicut ait scriptura: *Septies cadit iustus et
resurgit*, id est post ⟨septem⟩ annos penitentie potest iustus uocari qui
cecidit et in octauo non obtinebit eum malum, sed de cetero seruet se 10
fortiter ne cadat, quia, sicut Solamon dicit, *sicut canes reuertens ad
uomitum suum hodibilis fit ita qui* per neglegentiam suam *reuertitur ad
peccatum suum.*

22. Si qui⟨s⟩ iurauerit iuramentum falsum, magnum est crimen; aut
uix aut non potest redimi, sed tamen melius est penitere et non dispe- 15
rare. Magna est enim misericordia Domini. Penitentia eius haec est:
in primo numquam in uita sua iurare debet, quoniam *uir multum iurans*
non iustificabitur *et plaga de domo eius non discedet*, id est quecumque
boni fecerit peribit et poena in futuro de tabernaculo eius non discedet;
sed in presenti tempore caeleri medicina penitentiae preuenire oportet 20
[de] perpetuas poenas in futuro et agere penitentiam .uii. annorum et de
reliquo uite suae bene facere et ancillam siue seruum liberare siue
pretium eius pauperibus et egenis dare.

23. Si qui⟨s⟩ clericus homicidium fec⟨er⟩it ⟨et occiderit proximum
suum et mortuus fuerit,⟩ .x. annis exterrem fieri de patria sua oportet et 25
agat penitentiam vii annorum in alia urbe, tres ex his cum pane et aqua
et sale per mensura et .iiii. abstineat se a uino et a carnibus et ieiunet

8 Prou. 24, 16 (*sic* A. Fulg. Cassian *bis.* Caes.Arel. *ter, mutato uerborum ordine*: cadet
et resurget VULG *cum* LXX: cadit et resurget Lucif.)   11–13 Prou. 26, 11 sicut
canis qui reuertitur ad uomitum suum sic imprudens qui iterat stultitiam suam VULG:
sed Lucif. pro s. Athanas. i. 29 sicut canis qui conuertitur ad uomitum suum et odibilis
efficitur ita stultus sua malitia conuersus ad suum peccatum (= LXX, *excepto* qui *pro*
ὅταν); Caes.Arel. hom. 12, 6; 32, 2 sicut canis odibilis est quando reuertitur (redit
12, 6) ad uomitum suum ita et (sic 32, 2) peccator quando reuertitur ad peccatum
suum; *cf.* hom. 30, 4 (sicut odibilis fit canis), 237, 3; ne reuertamur quasi *canes* ad
uomitum 97, 5. *Cf.* 2 Petr. 2, 22 ⟨sicut *m*⟩ canis reuersus (reuertens *m*) ad uomitum
suum   17–18 Eccli. 23, 12 uir multum iurans im(re-)plebitur iniquitate et non
discedet a (de Caes.Arel. *ter*) domo illius plaga

    1 añ VSP: anni B; *cf.* p. 76, 4   peniteat cum pane et aqua SPB   per mensura
om. PB   et (2) *om.* P   ii añ VS   abstineat ⟨se⟩ SPB   2 a (2) *om.* P   sex: iii B
quadragissimas: xlmas VPB   ieiunet *om.* V: ieiunat PB   3 si ⟨mulier⟩ B   ut
diximus *om.* B   filium ut diximus P   3 et–4 fuerit *om.* PB   3–4 fuit
peccatum eius S   4 ui. annis ⟨peñ cum pañ et aq̄⟩ S. iii. ⟨ut diximus de clerico⟩ añ ⟨peñi⟩
PB. *Desinunt* PB

VS   5 iungantur S   renouari S   6 noncupari S   7 ceciderit S   penitentiae S   8 scriptura ait S   cadet S   9 resurget S   septem *om.* V
penitentię S   potest ⟨esse⟩ uocari iustus S   10 octauo ⟨anno⟩ S   11 ne:

somebody,[7] she shall do penance for half a year with an allowance of bread and water, and abstain for two years from wine and meat and fast for the six forty-day periods with bread and water.

21. But if, as we have said, she bears a child and her sin is manifest, ⟨she shall do penance⟩[8] for six years ⟨with bread and water⟩,[8] as is the judgement in the case of a cleric, and in the seventh year she shall be joined to the altar, and then we say her crown can be restored and she may don a white robe and be pronounced a virgin. So a cleric who has fallen ought likewise to receive the clerical office in the seventh year after the labour of penance, as saith Scripture: *Seven times a just man falleth and ariseth*, that is, after seven years of penance he who fell can be called 'just' and in the eighth year evil shall not lay hold on him, but for the remainder (of his life) let him preserve himself carefully lest he fall, since, as Solomon saith, *as a dog returning to his vomit becomes odious, so is he who* through his own negligence *reverts to his sin.*

22. If one has sworn a false oath, great is the crime; it can hardly, if at all, be expiated, but none the less it is better to do penance and not to despair: for great is the mercy of God. This is his penance: first, he must never in his life take an oath, since *a man who swears much* will not be justified and *the scourge shall not depart from his house*, that is, whatever good he has done will perish, and in future punishment will never leave his tent; but in the present time one must, by the medicine of immediate penance, prevent perpetual pains in the future, and do penance for seven years and for the rest of one's life do right, ⟨not take oaths,⟩[8] and set free a maidservant or manservant or give the value of one to the poor and needy.

23. If any cleric commits murder and strikes down his neighbour and he is dead, he must become an exile from his country for ten years and do penance seven years in another city,[9] three years of this time on an allowance of bread and water and salt, and for four years he shall abstain from wine and meat, and fast during the forty-day periods on ⟨an

nec S   salamon S   canis S   12 odilibilis S   fit: sit V; *cf. Caes. hom. 30, 4* (γένηται *LXX*)

(V 55ʳ–56ʳ ITEM ALIO LOCO. Si–23 dare)   14 qui V. quis ⟨autem⟩ S
15 redemi S   *post* penitere *uersus et dimidius erasi sunt in* V   16 enim *om.* S
17 debere S   18 discendat S; *cf.* V *ad l. 19.* (*In codice* V *sequitur rasura trium fere uersuum*)   18 id–19 discedet *om.* S   19 discendet V*   20 tempore *om.* S   celeri S   21 de *om.* S   penas perpetuas S   22 uitę suę S   facere ⟨et non iurare⟩ S   23 et: aut S

(V 58ʳ⁻ᵛ Item si quis–*p. 82, 9* patria)   24–*p. 82, 9 extant in* P   24 qui V. *om.* P   fecit V   et–25 fuerit *om.* V   25 extorem S; *de forma* exterris, *cf. Isid. Etym. x. 85 sq.; Schol. Stat. Theb. ix. 578*   exterrem–de: excidat (i *corr. in* e) a P   de patria sua *om.* S   oportet *om.* P   26 alio orbe S   ui V: ⟨et S⟩ tribus SP   ex ipsis SP   27 et sale *om.* SP   per mensura *om.* P. per mensuram ⟨peniteat⟩ S   et .iiii.–*p. 82, 1* sal: et tribus (tres aᵃlis P) xlmas ieiunet (-at P) cum pane et aqua ⟨per mensuram S⟩ et ⟨in aliˢ P⟩ quatuor abstineat se a uino et a (*om.* P) carnibus SP xlmas cum pane et aqua et sal, et sic impletis .x̃. annis, si bene egerit et comprobatus fuerit testimonium abbatis siue sacerdotis cui commissus fuerit, recipiatur in patria sua et satis faciat amicis eius quem occiderat et uicem pietatis et oboedientie reddat patri et matri eius si adhuc in corpore sunt et dicat: 'Ecce ego uobis pro filio uestro; quecumque dixeritis mihi 5 faciam.' Si autem non satis egerit, non recipiatur in aeternum.

24. Si autem subito occiderit et non ex odio, et amici fuerunt ante, sed instincto diabuli per obreptione, tres annos peniteat cum pane et aqua per mensura et .iii. alios abstineat se a uino et a carnibus, et non in sua patria.

25. Si qui⟨s⟩ autem clericus furtum fecerit semel aut bis, id est si 10 furatus est ouem proximi sui aut suem aut aliquod animal, anno integro peniteat cum pane et aqua per mensura et reddat quadruplum proximo suo. 26. Si autem non semel uel bis sed in consuetudine longa fecit, annis tribus peniteat, primo anno cum pane et aqua et sale per mensura et duos alios abstineat se a uino et a carnibus. 15

27. Si quis fuerit clericus diaconis uel alicui⟨us⟩ gradus et laicus ante fuerit ⟨et⟩ cum filiis et filiabus suis et cum clentella habitet et redeat ad carnis desiderium et genuerit filium ex clentella propria sua, ut dicat, sciat se ruina maxima cecidisse et exsurgere debere; non minus peccatum eius est ut esset clericus ex iuuentute sua et ita est ut cum puella aliena 20 peccasset, quia post uotum suum peccauerunt et postquam consecrati sunt a Deo et tunc uotum suum inritum fecerunt. III. annos peniteant cum pane et aqua per mensura et alios .iii. abstineant se a uino et a carne et non peniteant simul sed separantur, et tunc in uii anno iungantur altario et accipiant gradum suum. 25

28. Si qui⟨s⟩ autem auarus clericus fuerit, crimen hoc magnum est *auaritia*, quia *idolatria* nuncupatur, sed largitate et elymosinis et humilitate emendatur. Haec est penitentia huius criminis ut e contrariis contraria curet et emendet.

---

10 *can. 25 breuiter laudatur, sub Vinniani nomine, in* Coll. Hib. XXIX. 8b   27 Col. 3, 5 auaritia quae est simulacrorum (idolorum *d e g* Cypr. Ambrst. Hier. Aug. Sed. Caes.Arel. H) seruitus (quae est idolatria D. Iren. Tert. Ambr.; *cf.* Orig.)

---

1 impletis–2 fuerit *om.* P   2 cum probatus VS; *cf. adn. ad p.* 78, 14   testimonio S; *lege* per testimonium? seu S   cui: qui S   cummissus V. cūmissus S; *cf. adn. ad l.* 2 *in.* 3 fuerat S   faciat satis P   eius: huius uiri P   3–4 et uicem–eius *om.* P 4 obedientiae S   et (2): aut S   5 sint P   filio: amico P   6 faciat V* autem *om.* P   egerit: faciat P   recipietur P   7 ex *om.* S   sed ⟨occiderint⟩ P   8 instinctu SP   diaboli S   inreptionem SP   iii. añ V. tribus annis S. vi. annos (*ex* -um) P   8–9 per mensura *om.* P   9 .iii. alios: tribus aliis (alias P) SP a (2) *om.* P   et (3): sed SP   patria sua SP. *Hic in* P *additur*: Quod si per inuidiam aut empti causa muneris hominem interfecerit ancellas (e *corr. in* i) vii. et seruos .iiii. (*suppl.* liberet). *Desinit* P
VS   (V 27ʳ⁻ᵛ Si–15 carnibus)   10 qui V   autem *om.* S   fecerit *om.* S   si *om.* S   11 aut (2) *om.* S   annum integrum S   13 uel: aut S   fecerit S 14 primo–15 carnibus *om.* S
(V 44ʳ⁻ᵛ Si–25 suum)   16 clericus: de clericis S   diaᶜ S   uel: aut S   alicui V   17 fuerit *om.* S   et *suppleui*   et cum *post* suis *om.* S

allowance of⟩⁸ bread and water and salt; and having thus completed the ten years, if he has done well and is approved by testimonial of the abbot or priest to whom he was committed, he shall be received into his own country and make satisfaction to the friends of him whom he slew, and compensate his father and mother, if they are still in the flesh, by filial piety and obedience and say: 'Lo, I am in the place of your son; I will do for you whatever you tell me.'¹⁰ But if he does not fulfil his obligation he shall not be received back for ever.

24. But if he kills him suddenly and not from hatred—the two having formerly been friends—but by the prompting of the devil ensnaring him, he shall do penance for three years on an allowance of bread and water, and for three more years he shall abstain from wine and meat, and not (stay) in his own country.¹¹

25. If a cleric commits theft once or twice, that is, steals his neighbour's sheep or hog or any animal, he shall do penance an entire year on an allowance of bread and water and shall restore fourfold to his neighbour. 26. If, however, he does it, not once or twice, but of long habit, he shall do penance for three years, the first year on an allowance of bread and water and salt, and for the other two he shall abstain from wine and meat.

27. If anyone is a cleric of the rank of a deacon or of any rank, and if he formerly was a layman, and if he lives with his sons and daughters and with his mate¹² and if he returns to carnal desire and begets a son with his own mate, as he might say, let him know that he has fallen to the depths of ruin and ought to rise; his sin is not less than it would be if he had been a cleric from his youth and sinned with a strange girl, since they have sinned after their vow¹³ and after they were consecrated to God, and then they have made their vow void. They shall do penance for three years on an allowance of bread and water and shall abstain for three years more from wine and meat, and they shall not do penance together, but separately, and then in the seventh year they shall be joined to the altar and shall receive their rank.

28. But if a cleric is covetous, this is a great offence, for covetousness is declared idolatry, but it is corrected by liberality and alms and humility. This is the penance for his offence, that he cure and correct contraries by contraries.¹⁴

---

17 cleuentella ⟨sua propria⟩ S   reddat S   18 carnale S   cleuentella S   propria *om.* S   19 ruinā S   et–debere *om.* S   20 est (1) *om.* S   ita est ut *om.* S 21 postquam: post S   22 a Deo VS: *lege* Deo? *cf. Columbanus B. 8*   tribus annis S 23 alios .iii.: tribus aliis S   abstineat S   carnibus S   24 peniteant simul: ambo S   separantur: separatim S, *fortasse recte, cf. p.* 90, 30; *sed cf. p.* 88, 23 uii–25 suum: anno uii iunguntur et suum gradum recipiant S

(V 27ᵛ–29ʳ DE AVARITIA. Si–*p.* 86, 3 fenerandum est)   26 qui V   clericus auarus S crimen: clem S (*lege* cremen?)   27 quia *om.* S   idolatrie S   nuncupantur (no- S) V*S   helymosinis S (h. *s.l.*)   et humilitate *om.* S   28 huius: eius S

29. Si quis clericus iracundus aut inuidus aut detractor aut tristis aut cupidus, magna sunt peccata haec et capitalia et occidunt animam et demergunt eam in profundum inferni. Sed haec est penitentia eorum donec euellantur et eradicentur de cordibus nostris per auxilium Dei et per studium nostrum [diuinum]: petamus ueniam de Dei misericordia 5 et de his uictoriam, [et] tamdiu in penitentia constituti in fletu et lacrimis die ac nocte quam diuuersantur haec in cordibus nostris. Sed e contrariis, ut diximus, festinemus curare contraria et mundemus ea de cordibus nostris et insinuamus uirtutes caelestes pro illis: patientia pro ira, mansuetudo et dilectio Dei et proximorum pro inuidia, pro de- 10 tractione continentia cordis et lingue, pro tristitia gaudium spiritale, pro cupiditate largitas nasci debet. Dicit enim scriptura: *Iracundia uiri iustitiam Dei non operatur*, et inuidia lepra esse in lege iudicatur, detractio anathema, si⟨cu⟩t in scripturis dicitur: Qui detrahit proximo suo eradicabitur de terra uiuentium; scilicet tristitia occidit uel con- 15 sumit animam; *cupiditas radix omnium malorum* est, sicut apostolus dicit.

V 26ʳ:

30. Qui monasteria dispoliat se falso dicens captiuos redimere .i. annum cum pane et aqua peniteat et omnia quae traxit pauperibus det et iibus annis sine uino et carnibus peniteat.

S:

30. Si quis clericorum sub falso nomine redemptionis captiuorum inuentus fuerit et dispoliare eccle- 20 sias et monasteriis (*sic*), arguatur usque dum confundatur. Si con- uersus fuerit, annum integrum peniteat cum pane et aqua per mensuram et omnia quecumque 25 inuenta fuer*int* apud eum ex his quę congregauit pauperibus erogentur et fenerentur, et duobus annis abs- tineat se a uino et a carnibus.

31. Si autem non conuersus fuerit, excommunicetur et anathema sit 30 cum omnibus Christianis; exterminabitur de patria sua et uirgis uir- geatur usquequo conuertatur si conpunctus fuerit.

12–13 Iac. 1, 20 ira (iracundia *ff s*) uiri iustitiam Dei non operatur. 13 (inuidia) *cf*. Prou. 14, 30; Sap. 6, 25 14–15 *cf*. Iac. 4, 11 qui detrahit fratri; Ps. 100, 5 (R) detrahentem proximo suo; Eccli. 21, 5 substantia superbi eradicabitur; Is. 53, 8 abscissus est de terra uiuentium 15–16 *Cf*. Eccli. 30, 25; 2 Cor. 7, 10 16 1 Tim. 6, 10 radix enim omnium malorum est cupiditas (cupiditatem . . . quae omnium malorum radix est Caes.Arel. hom. 189, 4) 18–23 V = Cumm. (IX) 14; *cf*. Pen. Rom. IX. 7 (*p. 371 Wasserschl*.) qui monasteria expoliant falso se dicentes captiuos redimere iii annos poeniteant et omnia quae abstraxerunt pauperibus donent; Pen. Merseb. a. 88 (*p. 400 Wasserschl*.) si qui monasteria spoliant iii annos peniteant, i ex his in pane et aqua, ii sine carne et uino, et omnia quae subtraxit det pauperibus

1 ⟨DE IRACONDIA ET DIUERSIS UITIIS⟩ Si . . . V detractatur S 2 peccata·hęc est capitalia S 3 eam *om*. S in: ad S haec–eorum: penitentia eorum hęc sunt S 4 Dei: dñi S 5 studium ⟨et exercicium⟩ S diuinum

29. If a cleric is wrathful or envious or backbiting or gloomy or greedy, great and capital sins are these, and they slay the soul and cast it down to the depth of hell. But there is this penance for them, until they are plucked forth and eradicated from our hearts through the help of God and through our own zeal: let us seek pardon from the mercy of God and victory over these things, continuing in a state of penance, in weeping and tears day and night, so long as these things dwell in our hearts. But by contraries, as we said, let us make haste to cure contraries and to cleanse away these faults from our hearts and introduce heavenly virtues in their places: patience must arise for wrathfulness; kindliness, or the love of God and of one's neighbour, for envy; for detraction, restraint of heart and tongue; for dejection, spiritual joy; for greed, liberality. For Scripture saith: *The anger of man worketh not the justice of God*, and envy is judged as leprosy by the law, detraction as anathema, as is said in the Scriptures: *He that detracteth his neighbour shall be cast out of the land of the living*; gloom certainly devours or consumes the soul; *covetousness is the root of all evil*, as saith the Apostle.

30 (V): He who despoils monasteries, falsely saying that he is collecting money for the redemption of captives, shall do penance for one year with bread and water, and all that he has gathered he shall give to the poor, and for two years he shall do penance without wine and meat.

30 (S). If any cleric under the false pretence of the redemption of captives is found to be despoiling churches and monasteries, he shall be reprimanded until he is confounded. If he repents[15] he shall do penance for an entire year on an allowance of bread and water and all the goods that were found with him of those things which he has gathered shall be given to the poor and (so) be made fruitful;[16] and for two years he shall abstain from wine and meat.

31. But if he does not repent he is to be excommunicated and be anathema to all Christians; he shall be driven from the bounds of his country and beaten with rods until he is converted,—if he has compunction.[17]

om. S ; (*fortasse lege*: per auxilium diuinum et per studium nostrum)   petimus dñi misericordiam S   6 et *deleui*   7 diuuersantur (u *prima expuncta*) V. diuuersatur S   corde nostro S   8 mundemus ea: uitia mundemus S 9 corde nostro S   uirtutes insinuamus (*om.* caelestes) S   illis ⟨et⟩ S   10 ira: iracundia S   et (1): l- S   proximi S   11 linguę S   12 iracundia: ira S 13 esse: ē S   ⟨dicitur l-⟩ iudicatur S   14 *sicut scripsi*: sit V. *om.* S   15 de— scilicet: scilicet de terra uiuentium S   15 occidit: comedit S   16 apostolus dicit: ait apostolus S   28 et (2) *ego*: in S   30–32 *in* S *solo extant*   30–*p.* 86, 3: 31 Capitiuis–fenerandum est. 32 Si autem–fuerit, *contra testimonium codicis* S, *Was-serschleben, quem Schmitz et McNeill–Gamer secuti sunt*   30 c̄uersus S, *cf. p.* 78, 14; 82, 2.

G

32. Captiuis redimendis communicandum esse precipimus et exortamur. Ecclesiastico dogmate egen[en]is et pauperibus fenerandum est.

33. Et basilicis sanctorum ministrandum est et ex facultatibus nostris omnibus qui sunt in necessitatibus constituti conpatiendum est nobis et 5 in domibus nostris suscipiendi sunt nobis peregrini, sicut preceptum est a Domino; infirmi s⟨unt⟩ uisitandi et in uinculis constitutis ministrandum est et omnia Christi mandata *a minoribus usque ad maiora* implenda sunt.

34. Si qui⟨s⟩ in ultimo spiritu constitutus fuerit uel si qua constituta sit licet peccatrix uel peccator fuerit et exposcerit communionem 10 Christi, non negandum ei dicimus si promiserit uotum suum Deo et bene agat et accipiatur ab eo. Si conuersus fuerit in hunc mundum, impleat quod uouerit Deo; sin autem non impleat uotum quod uouerit Deo, in caput suum erit et nos quod debemus non negabimus ei. Non cessandum est eripere predam ex ore leonis uel draconis, id est de ore 15 diabuli, qui predam nostre anime deripere non desinit, licet in extremo line uite hominis adfectandum ⟨et⟩ nitendum sit.

35. Si qui⟨s⟩ autem laicus ex malis actibus suis conuersus fuerit ad Dominum et omne[m] malum egerit, id est fornicando et sanguinem effundendo, tribus annis peniteat et inermis existat nisi uirga tantum in 20 manu eius et non maneat cum uxore sua, sed in primo anno cum pane et aqua et sale ieiunet per mensura et non maneat cum uxorem; post penitentiam trium annorum det pecunia⟨m⟩ pro redemptionem anime sue et fructum penitentie in manu[s] sacerdotis et cenam faciat seruis Dei et in cena consummabitur et recipietur ad communionem; intret ad 25 uxorem suam post integram et perfectam penitentiam suam et si ita libuerit iungatur altario.

36. Si qui⟨s⟩ laicus maculauerit uxorem proximi sui aut uirginem, annum integrum peniteat cum pane et aqua et non intret ad uxorem suam propriam et post annum penitentiae tunc recipiatur ad com- 30 munionem et det elymosinam pro anima sua et non intret amplius fornicari cum extranea femina *quamdiu fuerit in hoc corpore*; uel si

---

6 cf. Matth. 25, 35–36. 42–43   8 cf. Heb. 8, 11   32 2 Petr. 1, 13 quamdiu sum (fuero: Patricius *bis*) in hoc corpore

---

(1–3: V 29ʳ)   1 captiuos redimendi s̄ S   2 docmate S   3 est *om.* S
(V 32ᵛ–35ʳ)   4 Et *om.* S   est ministrandum S   et ex *om.* S   5 ⟨et⟩
omnibus S   est nobis *om.* S   6 peregrini in domibus . . . sunt (*om.* nobis)
S   preceptum: scriptum S   7 infirmis uisitandi V. infirmos uisitandi sunt
S (*cf.* 1)   8 a min.–sunt: a maioribus usque ad minora x̄p̄i mandata
inplenda sunt S   9 qui V   fuerit *om.* S   constituta *om.* S   10 peccatrix
uel peccator: peccatrix (1- *in marg.*) V   11 ⟨nom̄⟩ non S   dicimus ⟨esse⟩ S
Deo *om.* S   12 recipiatur S   13 deo uouerit S   sin: si S   impleat
uotum quod *om.* S   14 capud Sᶜ   negamus S   15 est cessandum S
16 diabulum V. diaboli S   16–17 fine extremo S   17 adfectandam S   et *om.*
V   nitandum S   sit: de laicis S. (*in exemplari titulus canonis 35?*)   18 qui
V   autem laicus *om.* S   19 omne S   ⟨antea⟩ egerit S   20 inhermis S

32. We prescribe and urge contributing for the redemption of captives. By the teaching of the Church, money is to be spent fruitfully on the poor and needy.

33. We are also obliged to serve the churches of the saints and, within our means, have pity on all who are in need; pilgrims are to be received into our houses, as the Lord has commanded; the infirm are to be visited; those who are in chains are to be ministered to; and all commandments of Christ are to be performed, *from the least unto the greatest.*

34. If any man or woman is nigh unto death, although he (or she) has been a sinner, and asks for the communion of Christ, we say that it is not to be denied to such a person if that person promise God to take the vow, and do well and be received by Him. If he is restored to this world, let him fulfil that which he has vowed to God; but if he does not fulfil the vow which he has vowed to God, (the consequences) will be on his own head, and we will not refuse what we owe to him: we are not to cease to snatch prey from the mouth of the lion or the dragon, that is of the devil, who ceases not to snatch at the prey of our souls, even though we may have to follow up and strive (for his soul) at the very end of a man's life.

35. If one of the laity is converted from his evil-doing unto the Lord, and if he has wrought every evil deed, by committing fornication, that is, and shedding blood, he shall do penance for three years and go unarmed except for a staff in his hand, and shall not live with his wife, but in the first year he shall fast on an allowance of bread and water and salt and not live with his wife; after a penance of three years he shall give money for the redemption of his soul and the fruit of his penance[18] into the hand of the priest and make a feast for the servants of God, and in the feast (his penance) shall be ended and he shall be received to communion; he may then resume relations with his wife after his entire and complete penance, and if it is so decided he shall be joined to the altar.

36. If any layman defiles his neighbour's wife or virgin daughter, he shall do penance for an entire year on ⟨an allowance of⟩[19] bread and water, and he shall not have intercourse with his own wife, and after a year of penance he shall be received to communion, and shall give alms for his soul; and *so long as he is in this body*, he shall not go in to commit fornication again with a strange woman; or if (he defiles) a virgin, two years

---

uirgā S   21 anno ⟨peniteat⟩ S   22 et sale ieiunet *om.* S   uxore ⟨sua⟩ S
p̄ V. post S   23 det pecunia: p̈ecuniam d̈abit S   redemptione S   suę S
24 manu S, *cf.* 19   cęnam S   25 recipiatur S*   intret: et intrabit S; *lege* et
intret? *cf.* 29. 31; *p.* 88, 6. 8. 11. 25–26   26 integram penitentiam et perfectam S
28 XX. Si qui V   29 aqua ⟨per mensuram⟩ S   intrabit S   31 hely-
mosinam S   32 quandodiu S   hoc *om.* S   uel–*p.* 88, 3 sacerdotis *om.* S

uirginem, duorum penitentia est annorum, primo cum pane et aqua, in alio xlmas ieiunet et abstineat se a uino et a carnibus et det elimosinas pauperibus et fructum penitentie in manu[s] sacerdotis.

37. Si qui⟨s⟩ laicus puellam Dei maculauerit et coronam suam perdiderit et genuerit filium ex ea, tribus annis peniteat ille laicus, i. 5 annum cum pane et aqua per mensura et inermis existat et non intret ad uxorem suam propriam, et in duobus annis abstineat se a uino et a carnibus et non intret ad uxorem suam. 38. Si autem non genuerit ex ea filium, sed tamen maculauit, annum integrum et dimedium peniteat, sed annum integrum cum pane et aqua et dimedium abstineat se a uino et a 10 carnibus et non intret ad uxorem suam donec impleatur penitentia eius.

V 51^r: S:

39. Si qui⟨s⟩ intrat ad ancellam suam, uenundet eam et annum peniteat.

39. Si quis laicus cum uxore propria intrauerit ad ancillam suam et †ita debet fieri, ancillam 15 uenundari, et ipse per annum integrum non intrabit ad uxorem suam propriam. 40. Si autem

40. Si genuerit filium ex ea, liberet eam.

genuerit ex illa ancilla filium unum aut duos uel tres, oportet †eum 20 libera fieri ancilla, et si uoluerit uenundari eam, non permittatur ei, sed separentur ab inuicem et peniteat annum integrum cum pane et aqua per mensuram; et 25 non intret amplius ad concubinam suam, sed iungatur propriae uxori.

41. Si qui⟨s⟩ habuerit uxorem sterilem non debet demittere uxorem suam propter sterilitatem suam, sed ita debet fieri, ambo manere in continentiam suam, et beati sunt si permanserint casti corpore usquequo 30 iudicauerit Deus illis iudicium uerum et iustum. Credo enim si tales fuerint quales fuerunt Abraham et Sarra siue Isaac et Rebecca et Anna mater Samuhel uel Elis[h]abet mater Iohannis, bene illis in nouissimo †diregetur; dicit enim apostolus: *Et qui habent uxores sic sint quasi non habentes. Preteriit enim figura mundi huius.* Si autem manseremus fideles 35

34–35 1 Cor. 7, 29 ut ⟨et *c d e f g m* TEST HKLMNᶜOPVZ⟩ qui habent (et qui habent, *om.* ut, Caes.Arel. hom. 51, 3) tamquam non habentes sint (sint quasi (tamquam: Caes.Arel.) non habentes Tert. Zeno Hier. Caes.Arel.)   35 praeterit (-iit *d e* N¹O*Z*) enim figura huius mundi (mundi huius *g* Tert.)

3 manu *scripsi, cf. p.* 86, 24   4 qui V   laicus *om.* S   5–6 i. annum: sed in primo anno S   6 intrabit S   7 propriam–8 suam *in marg.* V 7 annis ⟨aliis⟩ S   8 intrabit S   geñ V. genuerunt S   9 tañ VS; tantum *Wasserschleben*   annum–dimedium *om.* S   sed *om.* S   10 dimidium ⟨annum⟩ S   11 intrabit S   suam *om.* S   13–19 V = *Cumm.* II 26. 27; *Ps.-Cumm.* III 32   15 *lacunam in* S *indicaui, quam sic suppleas:* et ⟨non genuerit ex ea filium,⟩   20 *lege* ⟨per⟩ eum?

shall be his penance: the first with bread and water, in the other (year) he shall fast during the forty-day periods and abstain from wine and meat; and he shall give alms to the poor and the fruit of his penitence into the hands of his priest.

37. If any layman has defiled a vowed virgin and she has lost her crown and he has begotten a child by her, let such a layman do penance for three years; in the first year he shall go on an allowance of bread and water and unarmed and shall not have intercourse with his own wife, and for two years he shall abstain from wine and meat and shall not have intercourse with his wife. 38. If, however, he does not beget a child of her, but nevertheless has defiled the virgin, he shall do penance for an entire year and a half, an entire year on an allowance of bread and water, and for half a year he shall abstain from wine and meat, and he shall not have intercourse with his wife until his penance is completed.

39 (V). If anyone has intercourse with his female slave, he shall sell her and do penance for a year.

39 (S). If any layman with a wife of his own has intercourse with his female slave,[20] the procedure is this: the female slave is to be sold, and he himself shall not have intercourse with his own wife for an entire year. 40. But if

40 (V). If he begets a child of her he shall set her free.

he begets by this female slave one, two, or three children, he is to set her free, and if he wishes to sell her it shall not be permitted to him, but they shall be separated from each other, and he shall do penance an entire year on an allowance of bread and water; and he shall have no further intercourse with his concubine but be joined to his own wife.

41. If anyone has a barren wife, he shall not turn away his wife because of her barrenness, but this is what shall be done: they shall both dwell in continence, and blessed they are if they persevere in chastity of body until God pronounces a true and just judgement upon them. For I believe that if they be as Abraham and Sarah were, or Isaac and Rebecca, or Anna the mother of Samuel, or Elizabeth the mother of John, it will come out well for them at the last.[21] For the Apostle saith: *And let those that have wives be as if they had none. For the fashion of this world passeth*

(V 35^{r-v}) 28 XXI. Si qui V   sterelem S   debet demittere: dimittat S
29 sterelitatem S   fieri *om*. S   manere ambo S   30 continentia S   suam
om. S   permanserint: perseuerauerint S   31 Deus illis: illi deus S   32 siue:
seu S   33 elis habet V. elysabet S   34 dirigetur S; *lege* di⟨e⟩ geretur ?
35 huius mundi S   manserimus S

in his quecumque dederit Deus si⟨ue⟩ prosperum siue contrarium, semper suscipiemus gloriam Dei in gaudio.

V 51ʳ:

42–45. Si ab aliquo discesserit sua uxor et iterum reuersa fuerit, suscipiat eam, et ipsa annum .i. cum pane et aqua peniteat uel ipse si aliam duxerit.

S:

42. *Uxorem a uiro non discedere* dicimus, sed *si discesserit manere* 5 *innuptam aut uiro reconciliari* secundum apostolum. 43. Si alicuius uxor fornicata fuerit et habitet cum alio uiro, non oportet adducere uxorem aliam quandiu 10 fuerit uxor eius uiua (44) prima, si forte conuersa fuerit ad penitentiam, et decet suscipi eam, si satis ac libenter expeterit; sed dotem ei non dabit et seruiet uiro 15 suo priori *quandiu fuerit in corpore:* uicem serui uel ancille expleat in omni pietate atque subiectione. 45. Sic et mulier, si dimissa fuerit ex uiro suo, non oportet alio uiro 20 copolari *quandiu fuerit* uir eius *in corpore* prior, sed expectabit eum innupta in omni patientia et cas⟨ti⟩tate, si forte det Deus penitentiam in corde uiri eius; sed 25 penitentia eorum hęc est, id est uiri fornicarii siue mulieris fornicarię: annum integrum peniteant cum pane et aqua per mensuram separatim nec in uno lecto 30 maneant.

46. Continentiam esse in matrimonio precipimus et exortamur, quia matrimonium sine continentia non ligitimum sed peccatum est et non

---

4–8 V: *cf. Cumm. II 29 (Ps.-Cumm. III 31; Merseb. a. 104)* Si ab aliquo sua discesserit uxor et iterum reuersa fuerit, suscipiat (-et *Ps.-Cumm.*) eam ⟨sine dote *Cumm.*⟩ et ipsa .i. annum cum pane et aqua peniteat, uel ipse si (si ipse *Ps.-Cumm.* similiter et ille si *Merseb.*) aliam duxerit   4–6 S 1 Cor. 7, 10–11 (a uiro suo VULG: suo *om., cum* GR, *d e f g m* Tert. Cypr. Sed.)   7–31 S: *cf. Coll. Hib. XLVI. 32b* Patricius: Si alicuius uxor fornicata fuerit cum alio uiro, non ducat aliam uxorem quamdiu uiua fuerit uxor prima; si forte conuersa fuerit et agat penitentiam, suscipiet eam et seruiet ei quamdiu uiua fuerit in uicem ancillae, et annum integrum in pane et aqua per mensuram peniteat nec in uno lecto permaneant   16. 21–22 2 Petr. 1, 13; *cf. p.* 86, 32   17–18 *Cf.* 1 Tim. 2, 2. 11   23–24 *Cf.* 2 Tim. 4, 2; 1 Tim. 2, 2; 5, 2

---

1 in his *om.* S   quęcumque S   si V. siue in S   2 suscipiemus–gaudio: in gaudia suscipiamus S   11 fuerat S*   uiua; Prima S   (44. Prima

away. But if we remain faithful in that which God hath given, whether it be prosperity or adversity, we shall always receive with joy the glory of God.

42–45 (V). If someone's wife goes away from her husband and comes back again, he shall take her back, and she shall do penance for one year with bread and water, or he shall do so if he takes another wife.

42 (S). We declare that *a wife must not leave her husband*; but *if she has left him, that she remain unmarried or be reconciled to her husband* according to the Apostle. 43. If a man's wife commits fornication and cohabits with another man, he ought not to take another wife while his first wife is alive, (44) in the hope that, perchance, she be converted to penance, and it is becoming to take her back, if she fully and freely seeks this; but he shall not make any payment to her,[22] and she shall go into service to her former husband *as long as he is in the body*: she shall make amends in the place of a male (?) or a female slave, in all loyalty and subjection. 45. So also a woman, if she has been sent away by her husband, must not mate with another man *so long as* her former husband *is in the body*, but should wait for him, unmarried, in all patience and chastity, in the hope that God may perchance put penance in the heart of her husband. But the penance of these persons is this—that is, of a man or woman who has committed fornication: they shall do penance for an entire year on an allowance of bread and water separately and shall not sleep in the same bed.

46. We prescribe and exhort that there be continence in marriage, since marriage without continence is not lawful, but sin, and (marriage),

si forte ... *editores priores*)   17 *lege* serue?   22 expectabatS*   26 penitentia: patientia S
(V 35ᵛ–38ᵛ)   32 in–quia *bis in* S   33 matrimonium: in matrimonio S
non (1): **nec** S   legitimam S   sed–est: est sed peccatum S

ad libidinem sed causa filiorum Deo auctore concessum est, sicut
scriptum est: *Et erunt duo in carne una*, id est in unitate carnis per
generationem filiorum et non libidine concupiscentie carnalis. Oportet
enim tres quadragisimas in anno singulo abstinere se inuicem ex consensu ad tempus ut possint orationi uacare pro salute animarum suarum, 5
et in nocte dominica uel sabbati abstineant se ab inuicem, et postquam
conceperit uxor non intrabit ad eam usquequo genuerit filium et iterum
ad hoc ipsum conueni[r]ent sicut apostolus dicit. Si autem perficerent
secundum istam sententiam, tunc digni sunt Domini corpore, si cum
bonis operibus expleant matrimonium, id est cum elimosinis et mandatis 10
Dei implendis et uitiiis expellendis, et in futuro cum Christo regnabunt
cum sanctum Abraham et Isaac et Iacob Iob Noe omnibus sanctis, et
tunc accipiant xxx^m fructum quem Saluator in euangelio enumerans et
coniugiis deputauit.

47. Si quis fuerit cuius paruulus absque babtismum abscesserit et per 15
neglegentiam perierat, magnum est crimen animam perdere, sed per
penitentiam redimi potest, quia nullum crimen quod non potest ridimi
per penitentiam *quamdiu sumus in hoc corpore*; annum integrum peniteant
parentes cum pane et aqua et non maneant in unum lectum.

48. Si autem clericus non susciperit paruulum, si ex una plebe fuerit, 20
annum integrum peniteat cum pane et aqua.

49. Non debet uocari clericus aut diaconus qui non potest babtizare
neque accipere dignitatem clerici aut diaconi in ecclesia.

50. Monachi autem non debent babtizare neque accipere elimosinam.
Si autem accipiant elimosinam, cur non babtizabunt?   25

51. Si quis fuerit cuius uxor fo⟨r⟩nicata est cum alio, non debet intrare
ad eam donec peniteat secundum illam penitentiam quam supra
posuimus, id est post annum integrum penitentiae. Sic et mulier non
debet intrare ad uirum suum si fornicatus est cum alia muliere donec
peniteat equali penitentia.   30

52. Si quis creaturam uel benedictionem Dei perdiderit, vii dies peniteat.

53. Non intrandum ad altare donec penitentia impleatur. FINIT.

DEO GRATIAS

Haec, amantissimi fratres, secundum sententiam scripturarum uel
opinionem quorundam doctissimorum pauca de penitentiae remediis 35

---

2 Gen. 2, 24; Matth. 19, 5; Marc. 10, 8; Eph. 5, 31   3–8 *cf.* 1 Cor. 7, 5
13 Matth. 13, 8   13 sq. *cf.* 'Syn. II S. Patr.', c. 18.   18 2 Petr. 1, 13; *cf.*
p. 86, 32   27–28 *cf. p.* 90, 28

V   3 libidini concupiscentiae carnis S   4 xlmas V   ex consensu: et consensu S. consensum V   6 inuicem *desinit* S   8 perficerent: *i.e.* perfecerint   11
regnabis V: *cf.* *McNeill–Gamer*   21 aque V   24 XXXIII. Monachi V
26 XXIIII. Si V

by the authority of God, is permitted not for lust but for the sake of children, as it is written, *And they shall be two in one flesh*, that is, in unity of the flesh for the generation of children, not for the lustful concupiscence of the flesh. Married people, then, should mutually abstain during the three forty-day periods in each single year, by consent for the time being, that they may be able to have time for prayer for the salvation of their souls; and on Sunday night or Saturday night they shall mutually abstain; and after the wife has conceived he shall not have intercourse with her until she has borne her child, and they shall come together again for this purpose, as saith the Apostle. But if they shall fulfil this instruction, then they are worthy of the Lord's body, if by good works they fulfil matrimony, that is, with alms and by fulfilling the commands of God and expelling their faults, and in the life to come they shall reign with Christ, with holy Abraham, Isaac, Jacob, Job, Noah, all the saints; and there they shall receive the thirtyfold fruit which the Saviour in the Gospel, in his account (of rewards), has set aside for married people.

47. If the child of anyone departs without baptism and was lost through negligence, great is the crime of occasioning the loss of a soul, but its expiation through penance is possible, since there is no crime which cannot be expiated through penance *so long as we are in this body*; the parents shall do penance for an entire year with bread and water and not sleep in the same bed.

48. But if a cleric does not receive a child (to baptism), if it is a child of the same parish, he shall do penance for an entire year on bread and water.

49. He is not to be called a cleric or a deacon who is not able to baptize, nor is he to receive the dignity of a cleric or a deacon in the Church.

50. Monks, however, are not to baptize, nor to receive alms. Else, if they do receive alms, why shall they not baptize?

51. If there is anyone whose wife has committed fornication with another man, he ought not to hold intercourse with her until she does penance according to the penalty which we laid down above, that is, after an entire year of penance. So also a woman is not to hold intercourse with her husband, if he has committed fornication with another woman, until he performs a corresponding penance.

52. If anyone loses a consecrated object[23] or a blessing of God, he shall do penance for seven days.

53. One must not go to the altar until one's penance has been completed. HERE IS THE END.

THANKS BE TO GOD

These few things concerning the remedies of penance, my dearly beloved brethren, according to the pronouncement of Scripture and to

uestro amore conpulsus supra possibilitatem meam potestatemque temptaui scribere. Sunt preterea aliaque uel de remediis aut de uarietate curandorum testimonia, quae nunc breuitatis causa uel situs loci aut penuria ingenii non sinit nos ponere. Sed si qui diuine lectionis scrutator ipse magis inueniat aut si proferet meliora uel scripseret, et nos con- 5 sentimus et sequeremur.

Finit istud opusculum quod coaptauit Uinniaus suis uisceralibus filiis dilectionis gratia uel religionis obtentu de scripturarum uenis redundans, ut ab omnibus omnia deleantur hominibus facinora.

7 uisceralibus filiis: *cf.* 1 Tim. 1, 2 (*g*)

4 scrutat' V   6 sequeremur: *lege* sequemur ?

the opinion of some very learned men, I have tried to write down, compelled by love of you, beyond my ability and authority. There are still other authoritative decisions concerning either the remedies or the several kinds of those (things?) who (*or:* that?) are to be cured, which now a concern for brevity, or the situation of the place, or the poverty of my talent does not permit me to set down. But if any diligent searcher of divine reading should for himself find out more, or bring forth and write down better things, we, too, shall agree and follow him.

Here ends the little work which Finnian adapted for the sons of his bowels, out of affection and in the interest of religion, overflowing with the waters of the Scriptures, in order that by all men all evil deeds might be destroyed.[24]

PAENITENTIALE S. COLUMBANI

[A:]

INCIPIT DE PENITENTIA

1. Paenitentia uera est paenitenda non admittere sed admissa deflere. Sed quia hanc multorum fragilitas, ut non dicam omnium, rumpit, mensurae noscendae sunt paenitentiae, quarum sic ordo a sanctis traditur 5 patribus ut iuxta magnitudinem culparum etiam longitudo statuatur paenitentiarum.

2. Si quis igitur per cogitationem peccauerit, id est concupierit hominem occidere aut fornicari aut furari aut clam commedere et inebriari uel certe aliquem percutere siue discedere uel alia his facere 10 similia, et paratus ad haec corde conplenda fuerit, maiora demedio anno, minora quadraginta diebus in pane et aqua paeniteat.

3. Si quis autem peccatis praeualentibus facto peccauerit, si homicidium aut sodomiticum fecerit peccatum, .x. annis paeniteat; si fornicauerit semel tantum, tribus annis †monachus † paeniteat; si saepius, 15 septem annis. Si discesserit et uota fregerit, si cito paenitens redierit, tribus quadragesimis, si autem post annos, tribus annis paeniteat.

4. Si quis furauerit anno paeniteat.

4a. Si quis periurauerit, vii annis paeniteat.

5. Si quis percusserit per rixam fratrem suum et sanguinem fuderit, 20 .iii. annis paeniteat.

6. Si quis autem inebriauerit se et uomuerit aut saturatus nimis sacrificium per hoc euomuerit, xl diebus paeniteat. Si uero per infirmitatem sacrificium uomere cogatur, vii diebus paeniteat. Si ipsum sacrificium quis perdiderit, anno paeniteat. 25

7. Si quis se ipsum quoinquinauerit, anno paeniteat si iunior sit.

8. Si quis falsum testimonium testificatus fuerit sciens, duobus annis paeniteat cum illius rei perditione uel redintegratione. Haec de causis casualibus. Caeterum de minutis morum inconditorum.

9. Qui facit per se aliquid sine interrogatione uel qui contradicit et 30 dicit 'non facio' uel qui murmorat, si grande sit, tribus superpositionibus,

---

c. 1 Paenitentia–deflere: *cf.* Ambr. De Quadrag. sermo 9; Greg. Magn. Homil. in Euang. ii. 34, 15; Gennad. De eccl. dogm. 54, *PL* xlii. 1218 (et admissa)   c. 2 *cf.* Vinnianus c. 1–3   c. 3 *cf.* Vinnianus c. 12. 23   c. 4 *cf.* Columbanus B. 7. 19; Vinnianus c. 25   c. 4a *cf.* Columbanus B. 5. 20; Vinnianus c. 22   c. 5 *cf.* Columbanus B. 9 c. 6 *cf.* Columbanus B. 12 ; Regula coen. c. 15; Gildas c. 7   c. 7 *cf.* Columbanus B. 10; Syn. Aquil. Brit. c. 2   c. 9 *cf.* Columbanus, Regula coenob. c. 8. 10. 15

Codices: Ti Tii

11 demidio Tii[c]. dimidio Ti   15 *uocem q.e.* monachus *loco errasse suspicor; lege* si fornicauerit semel tantum, tribus annis paeniteat, si saepius, septem annis. Monachus si discesserit, *etc.*   18 furauerit: furatus fuerit Ti, *cf. Columbanus B. 7. 19*   19 c. 4a *om.*

PENITENTIAL OF ST. COLUMBANUS*

[A:]

ON PENANCE HERE BEGINS

1. True penance is not to commit things deserving penance but to lament such things as have been committed. But since this is broken by the weakness of many, not to say of all, the measures of penance must be known.[1] A scheme of these has been handed down by the holy fathers, so that in accordance with the greatness of the offences the length also of the penances should be ordained.

2. Therefore, if anyone has sinned in thought, that is, has desired to kill a man, or to commit fornication, or to steal, or to feast in secret and be drunken, or indeed to strike someone, or to desert, or to do anything else like this, and has been ready in his heart to carry out these sins: let him do penance for the greater ones half a year, for the lesser ones forty days on bread and water.

3. But if anyone has sinned in act with the common sins, if he has committed the sin of murder or sodomy, let him do penance for ten years; if he has committed fornication once only, let him do penance three years, if oftener, seven years. If a monk[2] has deserted and broken his vows, if he repents and returns at once, let him do penance three forty-day periods, but if after a period of years, three years.

4. If anyone has stolen, let him do penance for a year.

4a. If anyone has perjured himself, let him do penance for seven years.

5. If anyone has struck his brother in a quarrel and spilt blood, let him do penance for three years.

6. But if anyone has got drunk and has vomited, or, being overfed, for this reason has vomited the sacrifice, let him do penance forty days. However, if he is forced by ill health to vomit the sacrifice, let him do penance seven days. If anyone has lost the sacrifice itself, let him do penance for a year.

7. If anyone has defiled himself, let him do penance for a year, if he is a junior.

8. If anyone has borne false witness knowingly, let him do penance for two years, together with the loss or restitution of the object in dispute.

So much about matters of importance; now about small matters of disorderly behaviour.[3]

9. He who does something by himself without asking, or who contradicts and says: 'I am not doing it', or who murmurs, if the matter is

---

Fleming, McNeill–Gamer   22 uomerit Tii* (*cf.* euomerit *Gildas c. 7*): evomuerit
Fleming   26 coinquinauerit Ti   27 testificauerit, *ut uid.,* Tii*   31 murmurat Ti

si paruum, una paeniteat. Uerbum uero contra uerbum simpliciter
prumptum .l. plagis uindicandum est, uel si ex contentione, silentii
superpositione. Nam si rixa, septimana paeniteatur.

10. Qui autem detrahit aut libenter audit detrahentem, tribus superpositionibus paeniteat; si de eo qui praeest, septimana paeniteat.   5

11. Qui autem per superbiam suum praepositum dispexerit aut
regulam blasphemauerit, foras repellendus est nisi confestim dixerit
'penitet me quod dixi'. Si autem se non bene humiliauerit, xl diebus
paeniteat, quia superbiae morbo detenetur.

12. Uerbosus uero taciturnitate damnandus est, inquietus mansue-   10
tudine, gulosus ieiunio, somnolentus uigilia, superbus carcere, destitutor repulsione; unusquisque iuxta quod meretur quoaequalia sentiat,
ut iustus iuste uiuat. AMEN.

[B:]

Diuersitas culparum diuersitatem facit paenitentiarum. Nam et · corporum medici diuersis medicamenta generibus conponunt. Aliter enim 15
uulnera, aliter morbos, aliter tumores, aliter liuores, aliter putredines,
aliter caligines, aliter confractiones, aliter conbustiones curant. Ita igitur
etiam spiritales medici diuersis curationum generibus animarum uulnera
morbos [culpas] dolores aegritudines infirmitates sanare debent. Sed
quia haec paucorum sunt, ad purum scilicet cuncta cognoscere, curare, 20
ad integrum salutis statum debilia reuocare, uel pauca iuxta seniorum
traditiones et iuxta nostram ex parte intellegentiam (ex parte namque
prophetamus et ex parte cognoscimus) aliqua proponamus.

De capitalibus primum criminibus, quae etiam legis animaduersione
plectantur, sanciendum est.   25

1. Si quis clericus homicidium fecerit et proximum suum occiderit, x
annis exul paeniteat; post hos recipiatur in patriam, si bene egerit paenitentiam in pane et aqua testimonio conprobatus episcopi uel sacerdotis
cum quo paenituit et cui conmissus fuit, ut satis faciat parentibus eius
quem occidit uicem filii reddens et dicens 'quaecunque uultis faciam 30
uobis'. Si autem non satis fecerit parentibus illius nunquam recipiatur
in patriam, sed more Cain uagus et profugus sit super terram.

2. Si quis ruina maxima ceciderit et filium genuerit, septem annis
peregrinus in pane et aqua paeniteat; tunc primum sacerdotis iudicio
iungatur altario.   35

---

c. 10 *cf.* Columbanus, Regula coen. c. 7. 10   cc. 11–12 *cf.* Columbanus, Regula
coen. c. 15 (textus auctus), pp. 166, 31–168, 3 Walker   B: 14–23 *cf.* Ps.-Cumm.,
Praefatio; Gregor. Magn., Reg. past. iii. 36   22 *cf.* 1 Cor. 13, 9   c. 1 *cf.* Vinnianus c. 23; *cf. etiam* infra, c. 13   32 *cf.* Gen. 4, 12   c. 2 *cf.* Vinnianus c. 12; infra, c. 14

---

1 una *Rossetti*: uno TiTii (anno *s.l. add* Ti^c)   2 promptum TiTii^c   ex
contentione: extentione TiTii (in *super* -xt- Ti^c), *cf.* Columbanus, *Regula coen. c. 15*
3 nam *uix sanum*   paenitea*tur Tii. poeniteat *Fleming, nescio an recte, cf.* 5   6 propositum Ti   9 detinetur TiTii^c   11 distitutor Tii*?   12 quo aequalia TiTii:
corr. Seebass, cf. p. 96, 26   13 AMEN *om.* Ti   19 culpas *ut glossema deleui*

serious, let him do penance with three special fasts, if slight, with one. Simple contradiction of another's word is to be punished with fifty strokes; if out of contention, with an imposition of silence. If it is made in a quarrel, the penance should be for a week.

10. He who slanders or willingly hears a slanderer, let him do penance with three special fasts; if it concerns the superior, let him do penance for a week.

11. He who has despised his superior in pride, or has spoken evil of the rule, is to be cast out, unless he has said immediately: 'I am sorry for what I said'; but if he has not truly humbled himself, let him do penance for forty days, because he is infected with the disease of pride.

12. The talkative is to be punished with silence, the restless with the practice of gentleness, the gluttonous with fasting, the sleepy with watching, the proud with imprisonment, the deserter with expulsion; let each suffer exactly in accordance with his deserts, that the just may live justly.[4] AMEN.

[B:]

Diversity of offences causes diversity of penances. For doctors of the body also compound their medicines in diverse kinds; thus they heal wounds in one manner, sicknesses in another, boils in another, bruises in another, festering sores in another, eye diseases in another, fractures in another, burns in another. So also should spiritual doctors treat with diverse kinds of cures the wounds of souls, their sicknesses, [offences], pains, ailments, and infirmities. But since this gift belongs to few, namely to know to a nicety all these things, to treat them, to restore what is weak to a complete state of health, let us set out even a few prescriptions according to the traditions of our elders, and according to our own partial understanding, for we prophesy in part and we know in part.

First we must enact concerning capital sins, which are punished even by the sanction of the law.

1. If any cleric has committed murder and killed his neighbour, let him do penance for ten years in exile; after these, let him be restored to his native land, if he has performed his penance well on bread and water, being approved by the testimonial of the bishop or priest with whom he did penance and to whose care he was entrusted, on condition that he make satisfaction to the relatives of the slain, taking the place of a son, and saying: 'Whatever you wish I will do for you.' But if he does not make satisfaction to his relatives, let him never be restored to his native land, but like Cain let him be a wanderer and fugitive upon the earth.

2. If anyone has fallen to the depth of ruin and begotten a child, let him do penance as an exile for seven years on bread and water; then only, at the discretion of the priest, let him be restored to the altar.

---

20 cognoscere, curare: *cf. Ps.-Cumm.* cognoscere et curare   24 animuaduersione, *ut uid.*, Tii*   25 plectuntur *Fleming*   santiendum (sa *in ras.?*) Tii   28 sacerdotes Tii   29 ut: et *Vinnianus*   34 paeniteiat Tii

3. Si quis autem fornicauerit sicut sodomitae fecerunt, .x. annis paeniteat, iii primis cum pane et aqua, vii uero aliis abstineat se a uino et carnibus et non maneat cum alio in aeternum.

4. Si quis uero fornicauerit quidem cum mulieribus sed non filium generauerit et in notitiam hominum non uenerit, si clericus, iii annis, si 5 monachus uel diaconus, .v. annis, si sacerdos, vii, si episcopus, xii annis.

5. Si quis periurauerit, vii annis paeniteat et numquam iuret postea.

6. Si quis maleficio suo aliquem perdiderit, iii annis paeniteat cum pane et aqua per mensuram et iii aliis annis abstineat se a uino et 10 carnibus et tunc demum in septimo anno recipiatur in communionem. Si autem pro amore quis maleficus sit et neminem perdiderit, annum integrum cum pane et aqua clericus ille paeniteat, laicus dimidium, diaconus duos, sacerdos tres; maxime, si per hoc mulieris partum quis[que] deceperit, ideo vi quadragesimas unus quisque insuper augeat, 15 ne homicidii reus sit.

7. Si quis clericus furtum fecerit, id est bouem aut aequum aut ouem aut aliquod animal proximi sui furauerit, si semel aut bis fecit, reddat proximo suo primum et anno integro in pane et aqua paeniteat; si hoc consueuit et reddere non potuerit, iii annis paeniteat cum pane et aqua. 20

8. Si quis autem clericus aut diaconus uel alicuius gradus, qui laicus fuit in saeculo cum filiis et filiabus, post conuersionem suam iterum suam cognouerit clientelam et filium iterum de ea genuerit, sciat se adulterium perpetrasse et non minus peccasse quam si ab iuuentute sua clericus fuisset et cum puella aliena peccasset, quia post uotum suum peccauit 25 postquam se domino consecrauit et uotum suum irritum fecit; idcirco similiter vii annis in pane et aqua paeniteat.

9. Si quis clericus per rixam proximum suum percusserit et sanguinem fuderit, annum integrum paeniteat; si laicus, xl diebus.

10. Si quis per se ipsum fornicauerit aut cum iumento, ii. annis 30 paeniteat, si gradum non habet; si autem gradum aut uotum, iii annis paeniteat, si aetas non defendit.

11. Si quis concupiscit mulierem et non potest facere, id est, non suscipit eum mulier, dimidium annum in pane et aqua peniteat et toto se abstineat anno a uino et carnibus et communione altaris. 35

12. Si quis sacrificium perdiderit, anno paeniteat. Si per aebrietatem aut uoracitatem illud euomuerit et neglegenter illud dimiserit, iii

c. 3 *cf.* infra, c. 15   c. 4 *cf.* Vinnianus c. 11; David c. 7   c. 5 *cf.* Columbanus A. 4a   c. 6 *cf.* Vinnianus c. 18–20   c. 7 *cf.* Vinnianus c. 25. 26; infra, c. 19 c. 8 *cf.* Vinnianus c. 27   c. 9 *cf.* Columbanus A. 5; Vinnianus c. 8. 9   c. 10 *cf.* A. 7 et infra, c. 17   c. 11 *cf.* Vinnianus c. 17; infra, c. 23   c. 12 *cf.* A. 6; Regula coen. c. 15, p. 162, 15 Walker

3 carne Ti   14 diacon^vos Ti   15 quisq; TiTii. quisquam *Fleming* augeat: *i.e.* agat? *cf. p.* 106, 5   17 aut (2) *om.* Tii, *ins.* Ti; *cf. infra, c. 19* 18 furauerit: furatus fuerit Ti; *cf. p.* 96, 18   20 pot^uerit Tii   23 clientellam, *ut uid.*, Tii*   34 anni *Fleming*   36 ebrietatem Ti   37 ^euomuerit Ti *cf. p.* 96, 22

3. But if anyone has committed fornication as the Sodomites did, let him do penance for ten years, for the three first on bread and water, but for the seven others let him refrain from wine and meat, and let him never again live with the other man.

4. However, if anyone has committed fornication with women, but has not begotten a child, and it has not become known among people: if he is a cleric, three years, if a monk or deacon, five years, if a priest, seven, if a bishop, twelve years.

5. If anyone has perjured himself, let him do penance seven years, and never take an oath again.

6. If anyone has destroyed someone by his magic art, let him do penance three years on an allowance of bread and water, and for three other years let him refrain from wine and meat, and then finally in the seventh year let him be restored to communion. But if anyone has used magic to excite love, and has destroyed no one, let him do penance on bread and water for a whole year, if a cleric, for half a year, if a layman, if a deacon for two, if a priest for three; especially if anyone has thus produced abortion, on that account let each add on six extra forty-day periods, lest he be guilty of murder.

7. If any cleric has committed theft, that is, has stolen an ox or a horse, a sheep or any beast of his neighbour's, if he has done it once or twice, let him first make restitution to his neighbour, and do penance for a whole year on bread and water; if he has made a practice of this, and cannot make restitution, let him do penance three years on bread and water.

8. But if any cleric or deacon, or a man in any orders, who in the world was a layman with sons and daughters, after his profession has again known his mate, and again begotten a child of her, let him know that he has committed adultery, and has sinned no less than if he had been a cleric from his youth, and had sinned with a strange girl, since he sinned after his vow, after he consecrated himself to the Lord, and made his vow void; therefore let him likewise do penance seven years on bread and water.

9. If any cleric has struck his neighbour in a quarrel and spilt blood, let him do penance for a whole year; if a layman, for forty days.

10. If anyone has defiled himself or sinned with a beast, let him do penance two years, if he is not in orders; but if he is in orders or under a vow, let him do penance three years, if his age does not forbid.

11. If anyone desires a woman and cannot commit the act, that is, if the woman does not admit him, let him do penance half a year on bread and water, and for a whole year let him refrain from wine and meat and the communion of the altar.

12. If anyone has lost the sacrifice, let him do penance for a year. If through drunkenness or greed he has vomited it up and cast it carelessly

H

quadragisimas in pane et aqua paeniteat; si uero per infirmitatem, vii diebus paeniteat. Sed haec de clericis et monachis mixtim dicta sunt. Caeterum de laicis.

13. Quicunque fecerit homicidium, id est, proximum suum occiderit, iii annis inermis exsul in pane et* aqua paeniteat, et post iii annos 5 reuertatur in sua reddens uicem parentibus occisi pietatis et officii et sic post satisfactionem iudicio sacerdotis iungatur altario.

14. Si quis laicus de alterius uxore filium genuerit, id est adulterium commiserit toro proximi sui uiolato, iii annis paeniteat abstinens se a cybis suculentioribus et a propria uxore, dans insuper praetium puditi- 10 tiae marito uxoris uiolatae, et sic culpa illius per sacerdotem abstergatur.

15. Si quis uero laicus fornicauerit sodomitico ritu, id est cum masculo coitu faemineo peccauerit, vii. annis paeniteat, iii primis cum pane et aqua et sale et fructibus horti siccis, quattuor reliquis abstineat se a uino et carnibus et ita dimittatur illi sua culpa et sacerdos oret pro 15 illo et sic iungatur altario.

16. Si quis autem fornicauerit de laicis cum mulieribus a coniungio liberis, id est uiduis uel puellis, si cum uidua, uno anno, si cum puella, duobus annis, reddito tamen humiliationis eius praetio parentibus eius, paeniteat; si autem uxorem non habuit, sed uirgo uirgini coniunctus est, 20 si uolunt parentes eius, ipsa sit uxor eius, ita tamen ut anno ante paeniteant ambo et ita sint coniugales.

17. Si quis autem laicus cum iumento fornicauerit, anno paeniteat, si uxorem habuit; si autem non habuit, dimidio anno, sic et qui uxorem habens propriis menbris se ipsum uiolauerit paeniteat.   25

18. Si quis laicus infantem suum oppraesserit uel mulier, anno integro in pane et aqua paeniteant et duobus aliis abstineant se a uino et carnibus et ita primum altario sacerdotis iudicio iungantur et suum torum tunc licito maritus ille cognoscat. Sciendum est enim laicis quod tempore paenitentiae illis traditae a sacerdotibus non illis liceat suas cognoscere 30 uxores nisi post paenitentiam transactam; demedia namque paenitentia non debet esse.

19. Si quis laicus furtum fecerit, id est bouem aut aequum aut ouem aut aliquod animal proximi sui furauerit, si semel aut bis fecit, reddat primum proximo suo dampnum quod fecit et tribus xlmis in pane et 35 aqua peniteat; si autem saepe furtum facere consueuit et reddere non

c. 13 *cf.* Vinnianus c. 35; Ps.-Cumm. VI 17   cc. 14–15 *cf.* supra, cc. 2–3 12 sq. *cf.* Leu. 20, 13   c. 16 *cf.* Dauid c. 6   c. 17 *cf.* supra, c. 10   c. 18 *cf.* Ps.-Cumm. VI 20   c. 19 *cf.* supra, c. 7; Vinnianus c. 25

p. 100, 37–102, 1 trib; quadragisimas (i *corr. in* e) Tii. iii quadragisimis Ti. tribus quadragisimis *Fleming*   2 sunt: sint Ti   4 Quicumque Ti   5 ex/sul Tii. exul Ti   10 cibis Ti   11 uxorisui uiolatae Tii   13 fęmineo Tii. fe- Ti 14 aquae. sale Tii   15 dimitatur Tii*   17 coniugio Ti   25 membris Ti 31 trasactam Tii   de media Ti. dimidia Tii[c]   32 non debet esse *om. Fleming* 34 furauerit: furatus fuerit Ti; *cf. p.* 96, 18; 100, 18   35 damnum Ti   *post* tribus *des.* Tii

aside, let him do penance three forty-day periods on bread and water; but if through ill health, let him do penance seven days. But these provisions are made for clerics and monks collectively; now for laymen.

13. Whoever has committed murder, that is, has killed his neighbour, let him do penance three years on bread and water as an unarmed exile, and after three years let him return to his own, rendering the compensation of filial piety and duty to the relatives of the slain, and thus after making satisfaction let him be restored to the altar at the discretion of the priest.

14. If any layman has begotten a child by another's wife, that is, has committed adultery in violating his neighbour's bed, let him do penance for three years, refraining from the more appetizing foods and from his own wife, giving in addition the price of chastity to the husband of the violated wife, and thus let his guilt be wiped off by the priest.

15. But if any layman has committed fornication in sodomite fashion, that is, has sinned by effeminate intercourse with a male, let him do penance for seven years, for the three first on bread and water and salt and dry produce of the garden, for the remaining four let him refrain from wine and meat, and thus let his guilt be remitted to him, and let the priest pray for him, and so let him be restored to the altar.

16. But if any of the laity has committed fornication with women who are free from wedlock, that is, with widows or virgins, if with a widow, let him do penance for one year, if with a virgin, for two years, provided that he pays her relatives the price[5] of her disgrace; yet if he has no wife, but has lain as a virgin with the virgin, if her relatives agree, let her be his wife, but on condition that both first do penance for a year, and so let them be wedded.

17. But if any layman has committed fornication with a beast, let him do penance for a year, if he has a wife; yet if he has not, for half a year; likewise also let him do penance who, having a wife, has defiled himself with his own hands.

18. If any layman or lay woman has misused their[6] child, let them do penance for a whole year on bread and water, and for two others let them refrain from wine and meats, and so first let them be restored to the altar at the discretion of the priest, and then let such a husband use his bed lawfully. For the laity must know, that in the period of penance assigned to them by the priests it is not lawful for them to know their wives, except after the conclusion of the penance; for penance ought not to be halved.

19. If any layman has committed theft, that is, has stolen an ox or a horse or a sheep or any beast of his neighbour's, if he has done it once or twice, let him first restore to his neighbour the loss which he has caused, and let him do penance for three forty-day periods on bread and water; but if he has made a practice of stealing often, and cannot

potuerit, anno et .iii. xlmis peniteat et deinceps nequaquam facere promittat et sic in Pascha alterius anni communicet, id est post duos annos, data tamen ante pauperibus de suo labore helemosina et sacerdoti paenitentiam iudicanti epula et ita abremitatur illi malae consuetudinis culpa.   5

20. Si quis laicus periurauerit, si per cupiditatem hoc fecerit, totas res suas uendat et donet pauperibus et conuertatur ex integro ad Dominum et tundatur omni dimisso saeculo et usque ad mortem seruiat Deo in monasterio; si autem non per cupiditatem, sed mortis timore hoc fecit, iii annis inermis exul peniteat in pane et aqua et duobus adhuc 10 abstineat se a uino et carnibus et ita animam pro se reddens, id est, seruum aut ancillam de seruitutis iugo absoluens, et helemosinas multas faciens per duos annos, in quibus illi licito uti facile cibis est cunctis excepta carne, post vii^{mum} communicet annum.

21. Si quis laicorum per scandalum sanguinem fuderit aut proximum 15 suum uulnerauerit aut debilitauerit, quantum nocuit tantum reddere cogatur; si autem non habet unde soluat, opera proximi sui primum agat quamdiu ille infirmus est medicumque quaerat et post sanitatem eius xl dies in pane et aqua peniteat.

22. Si quis laicus inebriauerit se aut usque ad uomitum manducauerit 20 aut biberit, septimana in pane et aqua peniteat.

23. Si quis laicus adulterare uoluerit aut fornicare cum sponsa et concupierit mulierem proximi sui et non fecerit, id est, non potuerit quia mulier eum non suscepit, tamen ille paratus fuit ad fornicandum, confiteatur culpam suam sacerdoti et ita xl diebus in pane et aqua peniteat. 25

24. Si quis autem laicus manducauerit aut biberit iuxta fana, si per ignorantiam fecerit, promittat deinceps quod numquam reiteret et xl diebus in pane et aqua peniteat; si uero per contemptum hoc fecerit, id est, postquam sacerdos illi praedicauit quod sacrilegium hoc erat, et postea mensae daemoniorum communicauerit, si gulae tantum uitio hoc 30 fecerit aut repetierit, iii quadragesimis in pane et aqua peniteat; si uero pro cultu daemonum aut honore simulacrorum hoc fecerit, iii annis peniteat.

25. Si quis laicus per ignorantiam cum Bonosiacis aut ceteris haereticis communicauerit, stet inter catecuminos, id est, ab aliis separatus 35 Christianis, xl diebus et duabus aliis quadragesimis in extremo Christianorum ordine, id est, inter paenitentes, insanae communionis culpam diluat; si uero per contemptum hoc fecerit, id est, postquam denuntiatum

---

c. 20 *cf.* Vinnianus c. 22; Ps.-Cumm. V 4 c. 21 *cf.* supra, c. 9; Vinnianus cc. 8–9 c. 23 *cf.* supra, c. 11; Vinnianus c. 17 c. 25 *cf.* Ps.-Cumm. XI 18

(Ti) 8 .tundatur *Fleming*; tondatur (o *ex* u *aut uice uersa*) Ti   30 singulę (n *eras.*)

Ti: si gulae *Fleming* 35 catecuminis Ti 37 insanae–38 diluat: et sic culpam suam diluat *Ps.-Cumm.*

make restitution, let him do penance for a year and three forty-day periods, and further undertake not to repeat it, and thus let him communicate at Easter of the second year, that is, after two years, on condition that, out of his own labour, he first gives alms to the poor and a meal to the priest who adjudged his penance, and so let the guilt of his evil habit be forgiven.

20. If any layman has perjured himself, if he did it out of greed, let him sell all his property and give it to the poor, and devote himself wholly to the Lord, and receive the tonsure, bidding farewell to the entire world, and until death let him serve God in a monastery; yet if he did it, not out of greed, but in fear of death, let him do penance for three years on bread and water as an unarmed exile, and for two more let him refrain from wine and meat, and thus by offering a life for himself, that is, by freeing a slave or maidservant from the yoke of bondage, and by doing many alms throughout two years, in which he may quite lawfully use all foods except meat, let him communicate after the seventh year.

21. If any of the laity has shed blood in a brawl, or wounded or maimed his neighbour, let him be compelled to restore all the damage he has done; but if he has nothing to pay with, let him first attend to his neighbour's work, while he is sick, and call in a doctor, and after his recovery, let him do penance for forty days on bread and water.

22. If any layman has become intoxicated, or eaten or drunk to the extent of vomiting, let him do penance for a week on bread and water.

23. If any layman has desired to commit adultery or fornication with a married woman, and has lusted after his neighbour's wife, and not committed the act, that is, has not been able to, because the woman did not admit him, yet he was ready to fornicate, let him confess his guilt to the priest, and so let him do penance for forty days on bread and water.

24. But if any layman has eaten or drunk beside temples, if he did it through ignorance, let him undertake forthwith never to do it again, and let him do penance forty days on bread and water; but if he did it in derision, that is, after the priest has declared to him that this was sacrilege, and if then he communicated at the table of demons, if it was only through the vice of greed that he did or repeated it, let him do penance for three forty-day periods on bread and water; but if he did it in worship of the demons or in honour of idols, let him do penance for three years.

25. If any layman in ignorance has communicated with the followers of Bonosus[7] or other heretics, let him rank among the catechumens, that is, separated from other Christians, for forty days, and for two other forty-day periods in the lowest rank of Christians, that is, among the penitents, let him wash away the guilt of his unsound communion; but if he did this in derision, that is, after he was warned and forbidden by

illi fuerat a sacerdote ac prohibitum, ne se communione sinistrae partis macularet, anno integro peniteat et iii xlmis, et duobus aliis annis abstineat se a uino et carnibus et ita post manus inpositionem catholici episcopi altario iungatur.

Postremo de minutis monachorum augendum est sanctionibus.   5

26. Si quis uallum apertum in nocte dimiserit, superpositione peniteat; si uero in die, xxiiii percussionibus, si non aliis superuenientibus apertum dimiserit. Si quis hunc ipsum [absolute] praecesserit, superpositione peniteat.

27. Si quis lumentum petens solus absolute lauauerit, superpositione 10 paeniteat. Si quis uero lauans licito coram fratribus stando hoc fecerit, si non necessitate luti largius abstergendi xxiiii plagis emendetur.

28. Si quis uero etiam sedendo in lumento genua aut brachia discooperuerit absque necessitate luti lauandi, vi diebus non lauet, id est, usque ad alteram diem dominicam inhonestus ille lauator pedes non 15 lauet. Soli autem monacho secrete stando pedes lauare licet; seniori uero etiam publice, sed altero pedes suos lauante, licet stando lauari.

29. Ante praedicationem uero die dominica toti exceptis certis necessitatibus simul sint conglobati, ut nullus desit numero praeceptum audientium excepto coco ac portario; qui et ipsi si possint satis agant, ut 20 adsint quando tonitruum euangelii auditur.

30. Confessiones autem dari diligentius praecipitur maxime de commotionibus animi antequam ad missam eatur, ne forte quis accedat indignus ad altare, id est, si cor mundum non habuerit; melius est enim expectare donec cor sanum fuerit et alienum a scandalo ac inuidia fuerit 25 quam accedere audacter ad iudicium tribunalis. Tribunal enim Christi altare, et corpus suum inibi cum sanguine iudicat indignos accedentes. Sicut ergo a peccatis capitalibus et carnalibus cauendum est antequam communicandum sit, ita etiam ab interioribus uitiis et morbis languentis animae abstinendum est ac abstergendum ante uerae pacis coniunctionem 30 et aeternae salutis conpaginem. FINIT.

5 augendum *i.e.* agendum (*sic Fleming*)   8 absolute *del. McNeill–Gamer,* *cf.* 10   praecesserit *Fleming*: processerit Ti, *cf. p.* 98, 6.

the priest not to pollute himself with the communion of an evil faction, let him do penance for a whole year and three forty-day periods, and for two other years let him refrain from wine and meat, and thus after imposition of hands by a Catholic bishop let him be restored to the altar.

Finally we must deal with the minor sanctions for monks.

26. If anyone has left the enclosure open during the night, let him do penance with a special fast; but if during the day, with twenty-four blows, if others were not following behind when he left it open. If someone has gone immediately in front of himself, let him do penance with a special fast.

27. If anyone, desiring a bath, has washed alone naked,[8] let him do penance with a special fast. But if anyone, while washing lawfully in presence of his brethren, has done this standing, unless through the need for cleansing dirt more fully, let him be corrected with twenty-four strokes.

28. But if anyone, even while sitting in the bath, has uncovered his knees or arms, without the need for washing dirt, let him not wash for six days, that is, let that immodest bather not wash his feet until the following Lord's Day. Yet a monk, when standing privately alone, is permitted to wash his feet; while a senior even publicly, but with another washing his feet, is permitted to be washed standing.

29. But before sermon on the Lord's Day let all, except for fixed requirements, be gathered together, so that none is lacking to the number of those who hear the exhortation, except for the cook and porter, who themselves also, if they can, are to try hard to be present, when the gospel bell[9] is heard.

30. It is ordained that confessions be made carefully, especially of mental disturbances, before going to Mass, lest perhaps any should approach the altar unworthily, that is, if he does not have a clean heart. For it is better to wait until the heart is healed, and becomes a stranger to offence and envy, than rashly to approach the judgement of the throne. For Christ's throne is the altar, and His Body there with His Blood judges those who approach unworthily. Therefore, just as we must beware of mortal and fleshly sins before we may communicate so we must refrain and cleanse ourselves from interior vices and the sicknesses of the ailing soul before the covenant of true peace and the bond of eternal salvation. THE END.

PAENITENTIALE CUMMEANI

INCIPIT PROLOGUS DE MEDICINAE SALUTARIS ANIMARUM

1. De remediis uulnerum secundum priorum patrum diffinitiones
dicturi sacri tibi eloqui, mi fidelissime frater, antea medicamina conpendi ratione intimemus.
2. Prima itaque est remisio qua baptizamur in aqua secundum illud: 5
*Nisi quis renatus fuerit ex aqua et Spiritu Sancto, non potest uidere regnum
Dei.* 3. Secunda caritatis affectus, ut est illud: *Remittuntur ei peccata
multa, quia dilexit multum.* 4. Tertia elymosinarum fructus secundum
hoc: *Sicut ignem extinguit aqua ita elymosina extinguit peccatum.* 5. Quarta
profusio lacrimarum Domino dicente: *Quia Achab fleuit in conspectu meo* 10
et ambulauit tristis coram me, non inducam mala in diebus eius. 6. Quinta
criminum confessio psalmista testante: *Dixi 'confitebor aduersum me
iniustitiam meam Domino' et tu remisisti impietatem peccati mei.* 7. Sexta
adflictio cordis et corporis apostolo consolante: *Dedi huiusmodi hominem
satanae in interitum carnis, ut spiritus saluus fiat in die Domini nostri Iesu* 15
Christi. 8. Septima emendatio morum, hoc est abrenuntiatio uitiorum,
euangelio contestante: *Iam sanus factus es, noli ultra peccare, ne quid tibi*

Ad Prologum cf. Origenem, Homil. in Leuiticum ii. 4; Cassian. Coll. xx. 8.

6–7 Ioh. 3, 5 (Spiritu ⟨Sancto⟩ a ff₂ m r aur CDERTW vg.; uidere *pro* intrare in: aur
cum GRℵ*M) 7–8 Luc. 7, 47 (remittuntur a r δ aur Ƒ DEJKMTOVWZ vg.;
quia b f Y) 9 Eccli. 3, 33: sicut aqua extinguit ignem ita elimosina extinguit
peccatum Cass. Coll. XX. 8, 2; Caes.Arel. *ter* (*a* VULG *prorsus differt*)
Reg. 21, 29 *a* VULG *prorsus differt* (quia . . . fleuit in conspectu meo: *cf.* ὅτι ἔκλαυσεν ἀπὸ
προσώπου μου g y Chrysostomus; *uerba* et ambulauit tristis coram me *alibi non inueni*)
12–13 Ps. 31, 5 (*sic* GALL, *cf.* H: iniustitias meas ΨB*, Rom. cordis mei, *cum* GRBSA,
PsVetᵖˡ, Rom. GALLᴸ) 14–16 1 Cor. 5, 5 *a* VULG *satis differt* (dedi:
cf. dedendum Tert. *bis*; huiusmodi ⟨hominem⟩ TESTᵖˡ; fiat *pro* sit: R Orig. Hil.
Cass.; Iesu ⟨Christi⟩ c f g VULGᵖˡ vg. TESTᵃˡᑫ *cum* GR (AFGP *al.*)) 17–*p.* 110, 1
Ioh. 5, 14 iam sanus factus es, noli peccare ne quid tibi deterius contingat Caes.Arel.
ter; ⟨ultra⟩ peccare: *cf.* ne iam ultra pecca δ

Codices: R E; (*Praefatio:*) SLN (1–*p.* 110, 21), MFG (1–*p.* 110, 14). *Codex G textum exhibet breuiatum, qui ad Ps.-Cumm. proxime accedit; lectiones selectas tantum
inter uncinos adnotaui.*

1–4 Ex coñ abbati iscotti. Medicina anime. per quas peccata delebuntur duodecim
sunt M Sententia scĩ cęsarii epĩ de duodecim remissionibus peccatorum F. De .XII.
remissionibus. Duodecim sunt remissiones peccatorum G 1 INCIP. SCĨ BASILII
PENITENTIALE AD CUMIANI (COMIANI *fol. 33ʳ*) LONGII E. PREFATIO CŪMEANI ABBATIS in
Scothia ortus S. Incip(it) de remediis penitentię exposit(io) sancti basilii Inquisitio
acumiani longii. Inprimis de remediis uulnerum N. I *in marg. adscribit* R 1–2 DE
REMEDIIS VULNERUM CESARII EPISCOPI. Secundum priorum, *etc.*, L 2 diffiniᵉonis E.
-es Eᶜ. diffinitionem S. definitiones N. definitionibus L 3 eloquii L sacris . . .
eloquis S mi *om.* LN, *Ps.-Cumm.* mini (*i.e.* eloquimini) E* *ante* ELN medicaminᵉ S
conpendii SL. cōpetendi N 4 rationem L. -is E 5 *remissiones numeris distinguuntur in S, ubi haec in margine adscribuntur:* I Ad nicodemum. II Simoni de maria. III in
solomone. VIIII in epistole iacobi. VIIII in euangelio. X in epistola iacobi. XI in epistola
ad corintheos. XII secundum iohannem secundum lucam ïtaque *om.* F *remissio*
ESLF. remissi M. *om.* N peccatorum *add.* F illut S. illud ⟨quod scriptum est⟩
ELF 6 sancto *om.* F(G) 7 Secunda remissio SLF *In* LF *uox* remissio *additur*

PENITENTIAL OF CUMMEAN

HERE BEGINS THE PROLOGUE ON THE MEDICINE FOR THE
SALVATION OF SOULS[1]

1. As we are about to tell of the remedies of wounds according to the ruling of the fathers before us, let us first, my most faithful brother, indicate in a concise manner the medicines of Holy Scripture.

2. The first remission then is that by which we are baptized in water, according to this (passage): *Unless a man be born again of water and of the Holy Spirit, he cannot see the Kingdom of God.* 3. The second is the emotion of charity, as this (text) has it: *Many sins are remitted unto her for she hath loved much.* 4. The third is the fruit of alms, according to this: *As water quencheth fire so doth alms extinguish sin.* 5 The fourth is the shedding of tears, as saith the Lord: *Since Ahab wept in my sight and walked sad in my presence I will not bring evil things in his days.* 6. The fifth is the confession of crimes, as the Psalmist testifies: *I said, I will confess against myself my injustice to the Lord, and thou hast forgiven the iniquity of my sin.* 7. The sixth is affliction of heart and body, as the Apostle comforts us: *I have given such a man to Satan unto the destruction of the flesh, that his spirit may be saved in the day of our Lord Jesus Christ.* 8. The seventh is the amendment of one's ways, that is, the renunciation of vices, as the Gospel testifies: *Now thou art whole, sin no more, lest some worse thing happen to thee.* 9. The eighth is the intercession of the saints, as this (text) states: *If any be sick, let him bring the priests of the church and let them pray for him and lay their hands upon him, and anoint him with oil in the name of the Lord, and the prayer of faith shall save the sick man and the Lord shall raise him up, and if he be in sins they shall be forgiven him,* and so forth, and: *the continual prayer of a just man availeth much before the*

post numerale l. 8. 9. 11. 13. 16. p. 110, 1. 5. 7. 13; in F solo p. 110, 11   affectum N illut S   remittentur, cum VULG, e corr. E   8 ęlemosynarum S. elemosinarum ELF(G). helemosinarum M. elemosynarum N   9 hoc: illud F   aqua exting(u)it ignem ESLMNF(G), Ps.-Cumm.; cf. app. bibl. ita ⟨et⟩ E   elęmosyna S. elemosina ELF. helemosina M. elemosyna N   extinguet L   peccata L cum GR   extinguit peccatum: resistit peccatis (= VULG) M   10 perfusio RSLNF(G), Ps.-Cumm. fusio M (effusio Sang. 550)   Quia: qua L   Achab om. ESLMNF(G), Ps.-Cumm.; cf. GR uar. lect.   11 ambulabuit (b eras.) S   coram me tristis EL, (tristris) F. coram me om. N (tristis om. G)   malum LF   diebus: conspectu M   12 criminum om. E   psalmi (s.s. te) stante N   adtestante L. att- MF   Dixi et aduersum me om. MN   13 ⟨in⟩ iniustitiam E   iniustitias meas MN, Ps.-Cumm.   Domino om. E   remissisti NF   impietatem om. R. impietate MN (deest G)   peccati: cordis SMN; cf. app. bibl.   14 afflictio ENF(G)   et corporis om. N   consolante: consonante M. dicente S. consolante et dicente N   dedi–15 satanae: uidebit (lege uidelicet?) h. h. satane tradentem M (tradere VULG)   15 satane ELM. -em S. sathane F   in om. L   spiritu N   saluos E   fiet E. sit S (G). om. N   diem L, Ps.-Cumm.; cf. d e Pacian. F*N(VULG)   16 Septima remissio est L   hoc– uitiorum om. M. uitiorum om. R   17 euangelio: euangelista LF, Ps.-Cumm. contestante: testante F, Ps-Cumm.   euang.–iam: dicente dño ecce N   Iam–ultra: Ecce factus es sanus (= VULGR), iam noli M cum VULG *deterius accedat.* 9. Octaba intercessio sanctorum, ut est illud: *Si quis infirmatur, inducat presbiteros ecclesiae et orent pro eo ⟨et⟩ inponent ei manus et unguentes eum oleo in nomine Domini, et oratio fidei saluauit infirmum et alleuauit eum Dominus et si in peccatis sit dimittuntur ei,* et reliqua, et *multum ualet apud Deum depraecatio iusti assidua.* 10. Nona ⁵ misericordiae et fidei meritum, ut est hoc: *Beati misericordes, quoniam ipsi misericordiam consequentur.* 11. Decima conuersio et salus aliorum Iacobo confirmante: *Quoniam qui conuerti fecerit peccatorem de errore uitae suae, saluauit animam suam a morte et cooperit multitudinem peccatorum suorum*; sed melius est tibi si infirmus fueris uitam solitariam ₁₀ ducere quam perire cum plurimis. 12. Undecima indulgentia et remissio nostra, ueritate promittente et dicente: *Dimittite et dimittetur uobis.* 13. Duodecima passio martyrii spe unica salutis indulgente et latroni cruento Deo respondente: *Amen dico tibi, hodie mecum eris in paradiso.*

14. His ergo de canonis auctoritate prolatis patrum etiam statuta ₁₅ Domini ore subrogatorum inuestigare te conuenit secundum illud: *Interroga patrem tuum et adnuntiauit tibi, seniores tuos et dicent tibi*; item: *causa deferatur ad eos.* 15. Statuunt itaque ut octo principalia uitia humanae saluti contraria his octo contrariis remediis sanantur. Uetus namque prouerbium est: Contraria contrariis sanantur. Qui enim inlicita ₂₀ licenter commisit, a licitis licet cohercere se debuit.

I. INCIPIT DE GULA

1. Inebriati igitur uino siue ceruisa contra interdictum Saluatoris, ut dicitur, *Adtendite ut non grauentur corda uestra in crapula et ebrietate aut in curis huius uitae, ne forte superueniat in uos repentina dies illa; tamquam* ₂₅ *laqueus enim ueniet super omnes qui habitant super faciem omnis terrae,* apostolique: *Nolite inebriari uino, in quo est luxoria,* si uotum sanctitatis

1–5 Iac. 5, 14–16 a VULG *satis differt* (si quis infirmatur inducat: Orig. in Leu. ii. 4; Caes.Arel. Serm. 19. 184, pp. 87, 7; 710, 20 sq. Morin; et inponent ei manus et Orig. *l.c., alibi omittuntur*; dimittuntur VULGᵃˡ𐞥 Cass. Caes.Arel. *bis*); enim *post* multum [5] *om.* ff, Pelag.)   6–7 Matth. 5, 7   8–10 Iac. 5, 20 quoniam qui conuerti fecerit peccatorem ab errore uitae (AD: uiae, *cum* GR, VL.VULGᶜᵉᵗᵗ·; *sic et Bigotianum cum* Caes.Arel. *et* Cass.) suae, saluabit animam eius a morte et cooperit (AC: operit VULGᵖˡ) multitudinem peccatorum ⟨suorum D⟩   12 Luc. 6, 37 (dimittetur *uel* dimittitur uobis: c e r aur JKOVX*Z. Caes. Arel. *bis*)   14 Luc. 23, 43   17 Deut. 32, 7 (adnuntiauit AO; seniores *pro* maiores: ΛᴴB. Hier. ep. 53, 3; Cass. Coll. ii. 15; *alii*) 18 *cf.* Exod. 22, 9   24–26 Luc. 21, 34. 35 (*textus non ad uerbum expressus*)   27 Eph. 5, 18

1 accidat SMF. fiat N. (contingat G.) *utraque uox u. l. in Ps.-Cumm.* (accedat *Sang. 550*)   octaua ESLNF(G) intercessio: intertio L   2 infirmauerit L   ecclē S. ęcclę F. *om.* MN   et (1): ut N   inponent–5 reliqua *om.* ES*LMNF(G), *Ps.-Cumm.* (& rel- *s.s.* S. et reliqua et multum, *etc.*, *Sang. 550*)   5 reliqua: rel- q· R. et: et alibi M. quia F. (*om.* G)   multum ⟨enim⟩ S(G)(= VULG)   apud Deum *om.* MN   depraecatio: oratio LF   asidua S*. adsidua E. assiduę M   6 misericordia (G), *Ps.-Cumm.* et fidei *om.* N   ut est: secundum ESLF   hoc: illud N   7 ipse S*. *om.* RN   consecuntur N   ali***orum S. (alienorum *Ps.-Cumm.*) iustorum M   8 Iacobo ⟨apostolo⟩ LF   affirmante F. (attestante G.)   Quoniam *om.* ESLMN(G), *Ps.-Cumm.* quia F   conuerti fec.: conuertitur S*   peccatores N   de: ab ESLMNF(G), *Ps.-Cumm.* errorę S   9 uitae: ui(a)e SLMNF, *Ps.-Cumm.* suę suę N   saluabit ESF (= VULG)

Lord. 10. The ninth is the merit of mercy and faith, as this says: *Blessed are the merciful for they shall obtain mercy.* 11. The tenth is the conversion and salvation of others, as James assures us: *He who causeth a sinner to be converted from the error of his life² shall save his soul from death and cover a multitude of sins;* but it is better for thee, if thou art weak, to lead a solitary life than to perish with many. 12. The eleventh is our pardon and remission, as He that is the Truth has promised, saying: *Forgive and ye shall be forgiven.* 13. The twelfth is the passion of martyrdom, as the one hope of our salvation (then) grants pardon; and God replies to the cruel robber: *Amen I say to thee this day thou shalt be with me in paradise.*

14. Therefore, since these things are cited on the authority of the Canon,³ it is fit that thou shouldst search out, also, the decrees of the fathers who were chosen by the mouth of the Lord, according to this passage: *Ask thy father and he will declare unto thee, thy elders and they will tell thee,* moreover: *Let the matter be referred to them.* 15. And so they determine that the eight principal vices contrary to human salvation shall be healed by the eight remedies that are their contraries. For it is an old proverb: Contraries are cured by contraries. For he who without restraint commits what is forbidden ought to restrain himself even from what is permissible.

I. HERE BEGINS OF GLUTTONY⁴

1. Those who are drunk with wine or beer, contrary to the Saviour's prohibition—as it is said: *Take heed that your hearts be not overcharged with surfeiting and drunkenness or with the cares of this life lest perchance that day come upon you suddenly; for as a snare shall it come upon all that dwell upon the face of the whole earth,* and (that) of the Apostle: *Be not drunk with wine wherein is luxury*—if they have taken the vow of sanctity,

suam: eius SLMNF(G), *Ps.-Cumm.*   operit MNF, *Sang. 550, Ps.-Cumm.* (*uar. lect.*); *cf. app. bibl.*   10 suorum *om.* LNF   set N   est tibi: tibi est L   fueris: fuerit S* (sis *Ps.-Cumm.*)   si–fueris: infirmus esse N   ⟨et⟩ uitam N, *Ps.-Cumm.* 11 indulgentia et *om.* MN   11–12 rem. nostra: nostra rem. F. remissio**E   12 nostra: peccatorum S*. *om.* E   nostra, ueritate: diuersitatis culparum uoce dominica M. ueritate–dicente: dicente dño N   promittente: pollicente S, *Sang. 550* et dicente *om.* ESLMF   13 martiri L. -ii EM(G)   spes ScMF(G), *Sang. 550.* spem N indulgentiae (-ę) SLM. ⟨et⟩ indulgentię (-e) F(G). indulgentes N (et *om.* G)   14 cruento: crucifixo (G), *Ps.-Cumm.*   Deo *om.* ESLMNF(G)   respondenti M. resp. ⟨domino⟩ ELF. ⟨dno⟩ dicente (G); *sed* dō respondente *Ps.-Cumm.*   ⟨quia⟩ hodie L, *Ps.-Cumm.*   paradyso SNF. *hic desinunt* MFG   15 canonum SN. canonicis auctoritatibus L, (-te) E   16 ora E   prorogatorum EL   uestigare L te *om.* ESN, *Sang. 550*   illut N   17 adnuntiabit S. annuntiabit N   seniores–tibi *om.* L   seniores: presbiteros ES (*s.s.* maiores E), *Ps.-Cumm.*   item: iste N   18 causas deferantur L, cause deferatur N   ad deos S, *Sang. 550*   Statuunt–19 sanantur: hunc ergo salutis contraria uitia contrariis remediis sanentur N   18 itaque S   printipalia S   19 humane EL   salutis S, *Sang. 550* (N, *u. supra*)   contrariis: concurris R. contrariis sanentur (-untur E) remediis ESL, *Sang. 550* (sanentur *etiam* N, *u. supra*)   20 est *s.s.* S   contrarii sanantur N   sanentur SL, *Sang. 550.* sanuntur E   21 licentur L   ommisit L   iicet: licete (*corr. in* licite) S. *om.* N, *Sang. 550*   coherceri Sc   se *om.* S   debuit: debet SLN, *Ps.-Cumm.* (debent *Sang. 550*)   EXP(LICIT) P(RAE)FATIO CU(*ex* O?)MEANI abbatis S   23 siue: sine R 23–27 saluatoris apostolique si uomitum (*sic*) sanctitatis, &c. E; *cf. Pen. Hib.* I. 7

habuerint, .xl. diebus cum pane et aqua culpam deluant, laici uero .vii. diebus.

2. Qui cogit aliquem humanitatis gratia ut inebriatur, similiter ut ebrius peniteat. 3. Si odii causa, ut homicida iudicetur.

4. Qui psallere non potest stupens elinguis, superponat. 5

5. Qui anticipat horam canonicam uel suauiora ceteris sumat gulae tantum obtentu, cena careat uel duobus diebus in pane et aqua uiuat.

6. Qui autem superfluam uentris distentionem doloremque saturitatis sentit, .i. diem. 7. Si autem ad uomitum infirmitate sine, .vii. diebus.

8. Si uero sacrificium euomerit, .xl. diebus. 9. Si autem infirmitatis 10 causa, .vii. diebus. 10. Si in ignem proiecerit, .c. psalmos cantat. 11. Si uero canes lambuerint talem uomitum, .c. diebus qui euomit peniteat.

12. Furat cibum, .xl. diebus; si iterum, .iii. xlmas; si tertio, annum; si uero quarto, iugi exilio sub alio abbate paeniteat.

13. Paruulus decem annorum aliquid furti faciens .vii. diebus peniteat. 15

14. Si uero postea .xx. annorum aliquid modici furti huic accederit, .xx. uel .xl. diebus.

II. DE FORNICATIONE

1. Episcopus faciens fornicationem degradatus .xii. annos paeniteat.

2. Presbiter aut diaconus faciens fornicationem naturalem praelato 20 ante monachi uotu .vii. ann(os) peniteat. Ueniam omni hora roget, superpositionem faciet in una quaque ebdomada exceptis lme diebus; post superpositionem pane sine mensura utatur et ferculo aliquatenus butero inpinguato [hoc est quadrante], et dominico die sic uiuat, ceteris uero diebus paxmatiui [.i. xii pol(entarum) plenum uas de farina] panis 25 mensura et miso parumper inpinguato, horti oleribus, ouis paucis, Brittanico formello, c⟨h⟩immina [plenitudo .vi. ouorum gall(inaceorum)] Romana lactis pro fragilitate corporum istius eui, tenucle uero uel batuti lactis [.xii. plenitudo ouorum gall(inaceorum)] sextario Romano sitis gratia et aquae talimpulo, si operarius est, et lectum non multo foeno 30 instructum habeat; per .iii. quadragesimas anni superaddat aliquid prout

---

1 culpam suam diluant E 3 aliquem: aliquam R 4 Si–causa: si per odium hoc fecerit E 5 stupense (e *eras.*) linguis E. stupens se linguis R: *correxi ex Praefatione Gildae, can. 10* 7 ⟨et⟩ uel E 8 satiuitatis RE: *corr. Zettinger* 9 sine infirmitate ⟨hoc fecerit⟩ E 11 cantet ⟨et si psalmus non habet peniteat iuxta qualitatem suam⟩ E 12 canis E lambuerint: *s.s.* l- lamberint E euomerit E peniteatur R dimidium in pane et aqua ipsos denumeras (*lege* -ans?) dies peniteat *add.* E 13 *lege* furatus *cum Big.?* (qui furatur *Ps.-Cumm.*) 14 quarto ⟨perpetratus fuerit furare⟩ E 16 post E 17 uel .xl. *om.* E 19 degradatur (*s.s.* aut) E annos: añs E. annum R 21 .vii.: .iii. E ⟨in terra⟩ omni ⟨iam⟩ hora E 22 faciat E 23 postea R ferculo: *i.e.* serculo, *u. adn. ad Gildam c. 1* 24 *hic et infra* (25. 27. 29.) *quae uncinis includuntur, glossae uidentur esse; desunt in Praefatione Gildae, quam Cummeanus exscribit, desunt etiam, exceptis uerbis* 24 hoc est quadrante, *in* E *et in Ps.-Cumm.* 25 paximatiui E 26 misso E parumper: paruum E 27 himina E 28 baptuti E 29 ouorum *scripsi*: vi R 30 et (2)–multo: lectuq non multum E 31 instructo R tria xlma E annis R

they shall expiate the fault for forty days with bread and water; laymen, however, for seven days.

2. He who compels anyone, for the sake of good fellowship, to become drunk shall do penance in the same manner as one who is drunk. 3. If he does this on account of hatred, he shall be judged as a homicide.

4. He who is not able to sing psalms, being benumbed and speechless, shall perform a special fast.

5. He who anticipates the canonical hour,[5] or only on account of appetite takes something more delicate than the others have, shall go without supper or live for two days on bread and water.

6. He, however, who suffers excessive distention of the stomach and the pain of satiety (shall do penance) for one day. 7. If he suffers to the point of vomiting, though he is not in a state of infirmity, for seven days.

8. If, however, he vomits the host, for forty days. 9. But if (he does this) by reason of infirmity, for seven days. 10. If he ejects it into the fire, he shall sing one hundred psalms. 11. If dogs lap up this vomit, he who has vomited shall do penance for one hundred days.

12. (One who) steals food (shall do penance) for forty days; if (he does it) again, for three forty-day periods; if a third time, for a year; but if a fourth time, he shall do penance in permanent exile under another abbot.

13. A boy of ten years who steals anything shall do penance for seven days, (14) but if afterward (at the age) of twenty years he happens to commit a small theft, for twenty or forty days.

II. OF FORNICATION

1. A bishop who commits fornication shall be degraded and shall do penance for twelve years.

2. A presbyter or a deacon who commits natural fornication, having previously taken the vow of a monk, shall do penance for seven years. He shall ask pardon every hour; he shall perform a special fast during every week except in the fifty days (between Easter and Pentecost). After the special fast he shall use bread without limitation and a titbit spread with some butter [that is to say, a quarter-measure][6] and he shall live in this way on Sunday; on other days on a ration of dry bread [made from a twelve-*polentae*[7] vessel full of flour] and a dish enriched with a little fat, garden vegetables, a few eggs, British cheese, a Roman half-pint [the capacity of six hen's eggs] of milk on account of the weakness of bodies in this age; a Roman pint of whey or buttermilk [the capacity of twelve hen's eggs] for his thirst, and some water, if he is a worker; and he shall have his bed provided with a small amount of hay. Through the three forty-day periods of the year he shall add something, as far as

uirtus eius a⟨m⟩miserit; semper ex intimo corde defleat culpam suam
oboedientiamque prae omnibus libentissimę excipiat. Post annum autem
et dimidium eucharistiam sumat et ad pacem ueniat et psalmos cum
fratribus canat, ne penitus anima tanto tempore caelestis medicinae
ieiuna interiat.   5

3. Si inferiori gradu quis positus sit monachus, .iii. quidem annos
peniteat, sed iam mensura non grauetur panis; si operarius est, sextarium
de lacte Romanum et alium de tenucla et aqua quantum sufficiat pro
sitis ardore sumat.

4. Si uero sine monachi uoto presbiter aut diaconus sic peccauerint, 10
sicut monachus sine gradu peniteant. 5. Si autem post peccatum uoluerit
monachus fieri, in districto proposito exalii anno et dimedio peniteat sic;
habet tamen abbas huius rei moderande facultatem, si oboedientia eius
placita fuerit Deo et abbati suo.

6. Peccans cum pecode ann⟨um⟩ peniteat; si ipse solus, .iii. xlmas; 15
si cum gradu, ann⟨o⟩; puer .xv. annorum xl.

7. Moechator matris suae ann⟨is⟩ .iii. cum peregrinatione perenni
peniteat.

8. Moechantes in labiis, .iiii. ann⟨is⟩ peniteant; si in consuetudine
fuerint adsueti, .vii. ann⟨is⟩ peniteant.   20

9. Sic qui faciunt scelus uirile ut Sodomite, .vii. ann⟨is⟩ peniteant.
10. Si uero in femoribus, .ii. ann⟨is⟩.

11. Qui concupiscit mente tantum fornicari sed non potuit, .i. ann⟨o⟩
peniteat, maxime in tribus xlmis. 12. Qui per turpiloquium uel aspectu
coinquinatus est, non tamen uoluit fornicari corporaliter, .xx. uel .xl. 25
diebus iuxta qualitatem peccantis peniteat. 13. Si autem inpugnatione
cogitationis uiolenter coinquinatus est, .vii. diebus peniteat. 14. Qui diu
inluditur fornicari a cogitatione tepidius ei repugnans, .i. uel .ii. uel
pluribus diebus, quantum exierit diuturnitas cogitationis, peniteat.

15. Qui in somnis uoluntate pullutus est, surgat canatque genua 30
flectendo .viiii. in ordine psalmos, in crastino cum pane et aqua uiuat;
uel .xxx. psalmos flectendo genua unius cuiusque in fine canat. 16.
Uolens in somno peccare siue pullutus sine uoluntate, [xii] .xv. psalmos;
peccans ⟨sed⟩ non pullutus, .xxiiii.

17. Clericus semel fornicans anno .i. cum pane et aqua; si genuit 35
filium, .vii. ann⟨os⟩ peniteat exul; sic et uirgo.

1 amiserit, *i.e.* ammiserit, R. adm- E   2 oboediens iamque R. obsedientiam q̃ E
4 cantet E   penitus: petitus R   5 ieiunia R; *cf.* '*Synodus II S. Patricii*', *can.*
xxii; Ps.-Cumm. II 23   6 annos E (-is *Gildas c. 2*): annum R   7 iam *om.*
E   non *om. Gildas, Pen. Hib. II. 6*   9 situs R   10 sic] si E   11
penitet E   12 p̄posito R   ex alii R, *i.e. ut opinor*, exsalii *pro* exsilii (exilii
E, *Ps.-Cumm. II 26*)   sic *om.* E   15 annũ E. anno *Gildas c. 11*   17 suae *om.*
E   cum–perenni: peregrinationem E   19 mechatis labiis E   22 annis:
annos E   23 Qui: Si E   tantum *om.* E   24 in tres xlmas E   24 sq.
aspectũ coinquinatur E   26 peccantis: peccatis E; *lege* peccantie? peccati? ('of his
sin' *McNeill–Gamer*)   27 .vii.: .v. uel duo E   diu *om.* E   29 ⟨peniteat

his strength permits; he shall at all times deplore his guilt from his in-most heart, and above all things he shall adopt an attitude of the readiest obedience. After a year and a half he shall take the Eucharist and come for the kiss of peace and sing the psalms with his brethren, lest his soul perish utterly through lacking so long a time the celestial medicine.

3. If (the culprit) is a monk of inferior status, he shall do penance for three years, but his allowance of bread shall not be increased;[8] if he is a worker let him take a pint of Roman milk and another of whey and water as the intensity of his thirst requires.

4. If a presbyter or a deacon without monastic vow has sinned thus, he shall do the same penance as a monk not in holy orders. 5. But if after the offence he wants to become a monk he shall do penance in the strict form of exile[9] for a year and one-half; however, the abbot has authority to modify this, if his obedience is satisfactory to God and to his own abbot.

6. He who sins with a beast shall do penance for a year; if by him-self, for three forty-day periods, if he has (clerical) rank, a year; a boy of fifteen years, forty days.

7. He who defiles his mother shall do penance for three years, with perpetual exile.

8. Those who befoul their lips shall do penance for four years; if they are accustomed to the habit they shall do penance for seven years.

9. So shall those who commit sodomy do penance for seven years. 10. For femoral intercourse, two years.

11. He who merely desires in his mind to commit fornication, but is not able, shall do penance for one year, especially in the three forty-day periods. 12. He who is polluted by an evil word or glance, yet did not wish to commit bodily fornication, shall do penance for twenty or forty days according to the nature of his sin. 13. But if he is polluted by the violent assault of a thought he shall do penance for seven days. 14. He who for a long time is lured by a thought to commit fornication, and resists the thought too half-heartedly, shall do penance for one or two or more days, according to the duration of the thought.

15. He who is willingly polluted during sleep, shall arise and sing nine psalms in order, kneeling; on the following day he shall live on bread and water; or he shall sing thirty psalms, bending his knees at the end of each. 16. He who desires to sin during sleep, or is unintentionally polluted, fifteen[10] psalms; he who sins but is not polluted, twenty-four.

17. A cleric who commits fornication once shall do penance for one year on bread and water; if he begets a son he shall do penance for seven years as an exile; so also a virgin.

---

uel⟩ quantum exigerit E   peniteat *om.* E   30 cantet q̄ E   31 in ordine *om.* E
32 .xx. E   genua *om.* E   33 sine: siue RE   xii *del. McNeill–Gamer: om.* E;
cf. Lib. Dauidis, c. 9   34 sed *inserui ex Libro Dauidis*   35 genuerit E

18. Qui diligit aliquam feminam inscius alicuius mali praeter sermocinationes quasdam, .xl. diebus peniteat. 19. Osculatus autem et amplectans, annum .i., maxime in tribus xlmis. 20. Diligens mente tantum, .vii. diebus. 21. Si autem dixit sed non est susceptus ab ea, .xl.

22. Laicus fornicando et sanguinem effundendo conuersus tribus 5 annis peniteat; in primo et in tribus xlmis reliquorum cum pane et aqua et in totis sine uino, sine carne, sine armis, sine uxore.

23. Laicus maculans uxorem uel uirginem proximi sui, .i. anno cum pane et aqua sine uxore propria peniteat.

24. Si autem puellam Dei maculauerit et genuerit ex ea filium, tribus 10 annis inermis, in primo cum pane et aqua, in aliis uero sine uino carneque. 25. Si uero non genuit sed polluit, .i. annum et dimidio sine diliciis, sine uxore peniteat.

26. Qui autem ad suam intrat ancillam, uendat eam et .i. ann(o) peniteat. 27. Si genuerit ex ea filium, liberet eam. 15

28. Cuius uxor est sterilis, ambo, et ille et illa, in continentia sint.

29. Si ab aliquo sua discesserit uxor et iterum reuersa fuerit, suscipiat eam sine dote, et ipsa .i. annum cum pane et aqua peniteat, uel ipse, si aliam duxerit.

30. Qui in matrimonio, in tribus xlmis anni et sabbato et in dominico 20 nocte dieque et in duobus legitimis et concepto semine et in menstruo tempore continens fieri debet usque ad modum sanguinis consummandum.

31. Post partum abstineat, si filius, .xxxiii., si filia, .lxvi.

32. Cuius filius sine baptismo neglegentia mortuus fuerit, tribus annis, in primo cum pane et† uino, in aliis duobus sine diliciis coniugioque. 25

33. Si clericus de una plebe non eum susceperit, ann(um) .i. peniteat; si non de una plebe, semianno.

III. DE FILARGIRIA

1. Faciens furtuṁ semel, .i. ann(o) peniteat; si iterum, .ii. annis.
2. Si puer, .xl. uel .xxx. diebus, ut est aetas uel qualitas eruditionis. 30
3. Thesaurizans superflua in crastinum tempus per ignorantiam, tribuat illa pauperibus; si autem per contemptum arguentium, elymosina et ieiunio sanetur iudice sacerdote; permanens uero in auaritia alienetur.

---

23 *cf.* Leu. 12, 4–5   31 *cf.* Ex. 16, 20

3 in–xlmis: .iii. xlma E   5 sq. fundendo ⟨et postea⟩ conuersus ⟨fuerit ad penitentiam⟩ .iii. annos E   7 totis ⟨tribus⟩ E   uino ⟨et⟩ E   9 uxore sine E   11 sq. sine carne sine uino E   12 genuerit E   anno E   14 uenundet E   17 uxor: mulier E   18 dote sine E   anno E   20 matr. ⟨suo est⟩ E   tribus *om.* E   sabbatis E   21 *lege* duobus ⟨diebus⟩? (in diebus plurimis *Ps.-Cumm. III 18*)   22 usque–23 .lxvi. *om.* E   24 filius: paruulus E   neglegentiae R. neglegentiae ⟨causa⟩ *Zettinger* (in neglegentia *Ps.-Cumm. VI 19*)   25 uino: aqua E, *Ps.-Cumm. VI 19; fortasse lege* in primo cum pane et aqua, in aliis duobus sine uino diliciis coniugioque   aliis duobus: secundo anno E   26 susciperit (ci *s.s.*) E   27 de una plebe *om.* E   30 .xxx.: .xx. E   utista ętas E   31 superflua in: superfluam R   33 in: et R

18. He who loves any woman, (but is) unaware of any evil beyond a few conversations, shall do penance for forty days. 19. But if he kisses and embraces her, one year, especially in the three forty-day periods. 20. He who loves in mind only, seven days. 21. If, however, he has spoken but has not been accepted by her, forty (days).

22. A layman repenting of fornication and the shedding of blood shall do penance for three years; in the first, and in three forty-day periods of the others, with bread and water, and in all (three years) without wine, without meat, without arms, without his wife.

23. A layman who defiles his neighbour's wife or virgin (daughter) shall do penance for one year with bread and water, without his own wife.

24. But if he defiles a virgin of God and begets a son, (he shall do penance) for three years without arms; in the first, with bread and water, in the others without wine and meat. 25. If, however, he does not beget, but defiles, he shall do penance for one year and one-half without delicacies and without his wife.

26. But he who enters in unto his woman slave, shall sell her and shall do penance for one year. 27. If he begets a son by her, he shall set her free.

28. In the case of one whose wife is barren, both he and she shall live in continence.

29. If any man's wife deserts him and returns again, he shall receive her without payment,[11] and she shall do penance for one year with bread and water, or he shall do so if he has taken another wife.

30. He who is in (the state of) matrimony ought to be continent during the three forty-day periods of the year and on Saturday and on Sunday, night and day, and in the two appointed week days,[12] and after conception, and during the menstrual period to its very end.

31. After a birth he shall abstain, if it is a son, for thirty-three (days); if a daughter, for sixty-six (days).

32. A man whose child dies on account of neglect without baptism (shall do penance) for three years; in the first with bread and water,[13] in the other two without delicacies and without the married relationship.

33. If a cleric from the same parish does not accept him, he shall do penance for one year; if (he is) not of the same parish, for half a year.

III. OF AVARICE

1. He who commits theft once shall do penance for one year; if a second time, for two years. 2. If he is a boy, forty or thirty days, according to his age or state of knowledge.

3. He who hoards what is left over until the morrow through ignorance shall give these things to the poor; but if (he does this) through contempt of those who censure him, he shall be cured by alms and fasting according to the judgement of a priest; but if he persists in his avarice, he shall be sent away.

I

4. Qui repetit auferentem quae sua sunt contra interdictum Domini apostolique, tribuet ea egentibus quae repetit.

5. Qui aliena diripit quolibet modo, quadruplum reddat ei cui nocuit. 6. Si non habet unde reddat, peniteat ut supra diximus. 7. Furatus consecrata ut supra diximus peniteat, sed clausus.   5

8. Qui periurium iurat, .iiii. ann(os) peniteat. 9. Qui autem deducit alium in periurium ignorantem, .vii. ann(os) peniteat. 10. Qui deductus est ignorans et postea recognoscit, .i. ann(um). 11. Qui uero suspicatur quod in periurium deducetur et tamen iurat pro consensu, duos annos peniteat.   10

12. Falsum testimonium dicens primo placeat proximo suo qualeque fratri inposuit tali iudicio damnetur iudice sacerdote.

13. Qui non implet quodlibet eorum pro quibus Dominus dicit: *Uenite, benedicti Patris mei,* et cetera, quanto tempore sic mansit tanto peniteat largusque uiuat tenileto; sin autem, abscedatur.   15

14. Clericus habens superflua donet ea pauperibus; sin autem, excommunicetur. 15. Si postea penitet, quo tempore fuit in contradictione in poenitentia semotus uiuat.

16. Mendax pro cupiditate placeat largitate ei quem frustrauit. 17. Mendax uero per ignorantiam et non nouit, confitetur ei cui mentitus 20 est et sacerdoti et hora tacendi damnetur uel .xv. psalmis. 18. Si uero de industria, .iii. diebus tacendi peniteat uel .iii. psalmis, si praeest.

(IV.) V. DE IRA

1. Qui fratrem contristet iuste uel iniuste conceptum rancorem eius . satisfactione leneat et sic potest orare. 2. Si autem est inpossibile recipi 25 ab eo, sic tantum peniteat iudice sacerdoti. 3. Is uero qui non recipit eum quanto tempore inplacabilis fuit tanto cum pane et aqua uiuat.

4. *Homicida* ille *qui odit fratrem suum,* quamdiu non repellit odium in pane et aqua sit et ei quem oderat *caritate non ficta* copuletur. 5. Qui homicidium odii meditatione facit, relictis armis usque ad mortem 30 mortuus mundo uiuat Deo. 6. Si autem post uota perfectionis, cum

---

1 *cf.* Luc. 6, 30   14 Matth. 25, 34   28 1 Ioh. 3, 15   29 2 Cor. 6, 6

2 apostolique *om.* E; *sed fortasse ad* 1 *Cor. 13, 5 alluditur; cf. supra* I. 1   tribuat E
ea *om.* E   reppetiuit E   4 *et* 5 supra: sup̄ *bis* R, *sic saepius*   5 consacrata E
6 periurium iurat: periurat E   6. 7 annis, 8 anno *Syn. Luc. Uict. c. 5*
9 deducitur E   et *om.* E *cum Syn. Luc. Uict. c. 5*   11 ⟨qui⟩ falsum E
primo: ut E   15 ⟨et⟩ peniteat E   abscidatur E   17 quo: quantum E
18 ⟨tantum⟩ in p. E   19 cupiditate: cupidi R   ⟨ut⟩ placeat E   20 nocuit
E, *Bigot. III.* 5, *Ps.-Cumm.* V *12; cf. infra,* (IV) *11,* (XI) *13, et Pen. Hib. III. 17*
confiteatur E   21 .xv.: .xii. E *cum Big. et Pen. Hib.*   22 .iii. (2): xxx *Big.
III.* 5, 3; *Ps.-Cumm.* V *13;* '150' *Pen. Hib. l.c.* (*lege* .iiii. l, *i.e.* ter quinquaginta?)   potest R; *sed cf. Big. et Ps.-Cumm. l.c.*   23 *Numero* IV *praetermisso capita abhinc
perperam numerantur in* R   24 Qui *om.* E   fratrem: rem R   suum *add.* E   con-
tristat E, *Ps-Cumm.* IX *1*   25 leniat E   et–orare: *lege* si potest exorare?   est *om.* E
26 tantum: tamen E, *Ps-Cumm. l.c.*   sacerdote E   Is uero: ipsi (*i.e.* -e?) autem
E   27 fuit: sit E   tantum E   27 sq. uiuat homicida illa (*sic*). qui R
29 oderit E   30 relictis: reiectis E. *Cf.* (IX) *13 et Syn. Luc. Uict. c. 4*

4. He who recovers what is his own from one who is carrying it off, against the contrary command of the Lord and of the Apostle, shall give to the poor those things which he recovers.

5. He who plunders another's goods by any means, shall restore four-fold to him whom he has injured. 6. If he has not the means of making restitution, he shall do penance as we have stated above. 7. He who steals consecrated things shall do penance as we have said above, but in confinement.

8. He who swears a false oath shall do penance for four years. 9. But he who leads another into perjury unknowingly shall do penance for seven years. 10. He who is led into perjury unknowingly and afterwards finds it out, one year. 11. He who suspects that he is being led into perjury and nevertheless swears, on account of his consent, shall do penance for two years.

12. He who bears false witness shall first satisfy his neighbour, and with what he has wrongly charged his brother, with such judgement shall he be condemned, a priest being the judge.

13. He who fails to fulfil any of those things for which the Lord says:[14] *Come, ye blessed of my Father*, etc., for whatever time he has continued thus, for that time he shall do penance, and he shall live a liberal donor to the end of his life; but if he does otherwise, he shall be cut off.[15]

14. A cleric who has an excess of goods shall give these to the poor; but if he does not, he shall be excommunicated. 15. If he afterwards repents, he shall live secluded in penance for the same (length of) time as that in which he was recalcitrant.

16. One who lies because of greed shall make satisfaction in liberality to him whom he has cheated. 17. One who lies through ignorance, however, and does not know it, shall confess to him to whom he has lied and to a priest and shall be condemned to an hour of silence or fifteen psalms. 18. If, however, (he did it) by intention, he shall do penance by three days of silence, or three psalms if he is in authority.[16]

IV.[17] OF ANGER

1. He who makes his brother sad shall mollify by a satisfaction the rancour he has conceived, justly or unjustly, and so he shall be able to pray.[18] 2. But if it is impossible to be reconciled with him, then at least he shall do penance, a priest being judge. 3. He, however, who refuses to be reconciled shall live on bread and water for as long a time as he has been implacable.

4. That *murderer who hates his brother* shall go on bread and water as long as he has not overcome his hatred, and he shall be joined to him whom he hates in sincere charity. 5. He who commits murder through nursing hatred in his mind, shall give up his arms until his death, and dead unto the world, shall live unto God. 6. But if it is after vows of

peregrinatione perenni mundo moriatur. 7. Qui autem per furorem facit
et non ex meditatione, .iii. ann(os) cum pane et aqua, elimosinis oratio-
nibusque peniteat. 8. Si autem casu nolens occiderit proximum suum,
.i. ann(um) peniteat.

9. Qui per rixam ictu debilem uel deformem hominem reddit, 5
inpensa in medicos †curat et maculae pretium et opus eius donec sanetur
restituat et dimedium anni peniteat. 10. Si uero non habeat unde restituat haec, .i. annum peniteat. 11. Qui ictum proximo suo dederit et non
nocuit, .i. uel .ii. uel .iii. xlmis in pane et aqua peniteat.

12. Fratrem cum furore maledicens ei cui maledixerit placat et .vii. 10
diebus cum pane et aqua uiuat remotus. 13. Qui uerba aceruiora protulerit in furore, non tamen iniuriosa, satis faciens fratri superponat.
14. Si autem cum pallore uel rubore uel tremore tacuit tamen, .i. diem
cum pane et aqua sit. 15. Qui mente tantum sentit commotionem, satis
faciat ei qui illum commouit. 16. Qui uero non uult confitere ei qui se 15
commotauit, abscedatur pestifer ille a coetu sanctorum; si penitet,
quanto tempore contradicit tanto peniteat.

(V.) VI. DE TRISTITIA

1. Qui diu amaritudinem in corde retinet, hilari uultu et leto corde
sanetur. 2. Si autem non cito eam deponat, ieiunio iudice sacerdote 20
emendat. 3. Si autem iterat, abscedatur donec alacer laetusque in pane
et aqua agnoscat delictum suum.

(VI.) VII. DE ACCIDIA

1. Otiosus opere extraordinario oneretur et somnolentus uigilia
propensiori, id est, †tres uel† psalmis occupetur. 25

2. Uagus instabilisque quis sanetur unius loci mansione operisque
sedulitate.

(VII.) VIII. DE IACTANTIA

1. Contentiosus etiam alterius sententiae subdat se; sin autem, ana-
themazatur ut regno Dei est alienorum. 30

1 facit *om.* E   2 non *om.* E   ⟨et⟩ elemosinis ⟨et⟩ E   3 ⟨id est⟩ nolens E
5 reddit: fecerit reddat E, *Ps.-Cumm. VI 22, cf. Capit. Iudic. II. 2* (facit reddet
Big. IV. 3, 1)   6 inpensam E   curat *om.* E; *lege* ⟨pro⟩curat? (*i.e.* Qui . . .
reddit, inpensa . . . procurat R; Qui . . . fecerit, reddat inpensa E, *Ps.-Cumm. etc.*)
7 dimidio anno E   habet E   8 haec *om.* E   9 nouit R; *cf. Ps.-Cumm.
VI 24 et supra*, III. 17   *in fine* Si autem clericus est. anno .i. uel dimidio
peniteat *add.* E   10 ⟨est⟩ ei R   ei–placat: cui maledixit placeat (*sic etiam Ps.-
Cumm. IX 3; Big. IV. 5, 1*) ei E   11 remotus: semotus E *cum Big., sed* remotus
Ps.-Cumm.   12 fratri ⟨suo et⟩ E   13 uel (1) *om.* E   14 tantum: tam(en) R; *sed cf. Ps.-Cumm. IX 5; Capit. Iudic. XXIX. 2*
tacuit E   14 tantum: tam(en) R; *sed cf. Ps.-Cumm. IX 5; Capit. Iudic. XXIX. 2*
commotionem: commutatione E   15 faciet E   commouit: commutauit (*i.e.*
commot-) E   confiteri E   16 commutauit E (commouit *Ps.-Cumm.*)   abscidatur E   17 contradicat E   19 in *om.* E   20 ieiunium E   iudice sacerdotis R. sacerdote iudice E   21 abscidatur E   22 delicto suo E   24 et *om.* E
25 tres l- psalmis R. tres .l- expsalm' (*lege* sex psalmis?) E. tres uel .vii. psalmis

perfection, he shall die unto the world with perpetual exile. 7. But he who does this through anger, not from premeditation, shall do penance for three years with bread and water, with alms and prayers. 8. But if he kills his neighbour unintentionally, by accident, he shall do penance for one year.

9. He who by a blow in a quarrel renders a man incapacitated or maimed shall meet (the injured man's) medical expenses and shall make good the damages for the deformity and shall do his work until he is healed and do penance for half a year. 10. If he has not the wherewithal to make restitution for these things, he shall do penance for one year. 11. He who gives a blow to his neighbour without doing him harm, shall do penance on bread and water one or two or three forty-day periods.

12. One who curses his brother in anger shall make satisfaction to him whom he has cursed and live secluded for seven days on bread and water. 13. He who utters in anger harsh but not injurious words shall make satisfaction to his brother and keep a special fast. 14. But if (he expresses his anger) with pallor or flush or tremor, yet remains silent, he shall go for a day on bread and water. 15. He who merely feels incensed in his mind shall make satisfaction to him who has incensed him. 16. He, however, who will not confess to him who has incensed him, that pestilential person shall be cut off from the company of the saints; if he repents, he shall do penance for as long as he was recalcitrant.

V. OF DEJECTION

1. He who long harbours bitterness in his heart shall be healed by a joyful countenance and a glad heart. 2. But if he does not quickly lay this aside, he shall correct himself by fasting according to the decision of a priest. 3. But if he returns to it, he shall be cut off until, on bread and water, he willingly and gladly acknowledges his fault.

VI. OF LANGUOR

1. The idler shall be taxed with an extraordinary work, and the slothful with a lengthened (?) vigil; that is, he shall be occupied with three or ⟨seven?⟩ psalms.[19]

2. Any wandering and unstable man shall be healed by permanent residence in one place and by application to work.

VII. OF VAINGLORY

1. The contentious shall (not only mend his ways but) even subject himself to the decision of another; otherwise he shall be anathematized, since he is among the strangers to the Kingdom of God.

Ps.-Cumm. X 2; *fortasse* ter .l. psalmis   26 uagus: uagis R   29 anathematizatur E   30 alienus E

2. Iactans in suis benefactis humiliat se, alioquin quicquid boni fecerit humanae gloriae causa perdidit.

(VIII.) VIIII. DE SUPERBIA

1. Qui aliquam nouitatem extra scripturas, ut deuenerit in heresim, praesumit, alienetur. 2. Si autem penitet, suam publice sententiam 5 damnet et quos decipit ad fidem conuertat et ieiunet ad iudicium sacerdotis.

3. Qui †superbos ceteros qualibet dispectione arguit, primo satis faciat eis, deinde ieiunet iudicio sacerdotis.

4. Inoboediens maneat extra concilium sine cibo et pulset humiliter 10 donec recipiatur quantoque tempore inoboediens fuit tanto in pane et aqua sit.

5. Blasphemus etiam simili decreto sanetur.

6. Qui murmurat, separetur et opus eius abieciatur; cum semipane debe⟨t⟩o aquaque maneat.   15

7. Inuidus satis faciat ei cui inuidit; si autem nocuit, largitate placeat ei peniteatque. 8. Qui causa inuidie detrahit uel libenter audit detrahentem, iiiior diebus cum pane et aqua separatus ieiunet. 9. Si uero de eo qui praeest, .vii. diebus sic peniteat et seruiat ei libenter de reliquo. 10. Sed, ut quidam ait, non est detrahere uera dicere, sed secundum 20 euangelium *corripe eum inter te et ipsum solum* prius, et postea, *si te non audierit*, uoca alterum; si uos non audierit, *dic ecclesiae*.

11. Dilatus et dilator consimili persona. Si dilatus negauerit, ann(o) .i. simul peniteant, in una quaque ebdomada duobus diebus in pane et aqua, et biduo in fine unius cuiusque mensis, omnibus fratribus sub- 25 ponentibus et Deum eis iudicem fore contestantibus. 12. Permanentes autem in obstinatio⟨ne⟩ anno emenso altaris communioni sub iudice flamma sociantur et Dei iudicio relinquantur. 13. Si quando alter fuerit confessus, quantum alteri laboris intulerit tantum sibi multiplicetur.

14. Si quis autem uerbositate diligens fratrem deroget ei, ⟨.i.⟩ die uel 30 .ii. tacens peniteat. 15. Si autem confabulatione, .xii. psalmos canat.

16. Mala non recipientium sanitatem retractans, ne ceteri eis consentiant, uel uituperatione mali bonique confirmandi obtentu aut

21–22 *cf*. Matth. 18, 15–17 (te non R vg)

---

1 iectans E   2 perdet E   4–5 scripturas̀ cannonicas uel heresim p̄ (*eras.*) in ecclesia sumit E   5 sua R   6 damnat E   ⟨eos⟩ quos E   decepit Rᶜ 8 *i.e.* superbus? (superbę E. -e *Capit. Iudic. XXV*. superbia *Ps.-Cumm. XI 1*) quaslibet R   10 concilium *om.* E   12 sit ⟨in penitentiam⟩ E   13 decreto E *cum Ps.-Cumm. XI 8*: secreto R   14 separetur ⟨ad (*i.e.* a) mensa⟩ E   abiciatur E 15 debeo R: *correxi* (debito E. *Capit. Iudic. XXX*. 2)   aquaque maneat: et aqua maneat suspensus E   17 peniteatque: et peniteat iudice sacerdoti E   ⟨fratrem suum⟩ uel E   19 seruat R   21 prius: piis R   postea–22 ecclesiae: post dic ecclesiae si te non audeat (i *s.* e) et reliqua E   23 dilator: dilatur E* (de- Eᶜ) anno *Syn. Aquil. Brit. c. 5*   24 ebdomada: septimana E   25 biduo: biduana E   25 sq. subponentibus: supplicantibus E   27 obstinatio R. abstinatione E

2. One who boasts of his own good deeds shall humble himself; otherwise any good he has done he has lost on account of human glory.

VIII. OF PRIDE

1. He who allows himself any novelty outside the Scriptures, such as might lead him to heresy, shall be sent away. 2. But if he repents, he shall publicly condemn his own opinion and convert to the faith those whom he has deceived, and he shall fast at the decision of a priest.

3. He who proudly censures others for any kind of contempt shall first make satisfaction to them and then fast according to the judgement of a priest.

4. The disobedient shall remain outside the assembly, without food, and shall humbly knock until he is received; and for as long a time as he has been disobedient he shall go on bread and water.

5. The blasphemer, too, shall be healed by a similar decree.

6. He who murmurs shall be put apart and his work shall be rejected; he shall remain with the due half loaf of bread[19a] and water.

7. The envious shall make satisfaction to him whom he has envied; but if he has done him harm, he shall satisfy him with gifts and shall do penance. 8. He who for envy's sake defames (another) or willingly listens to a defamer shall be put apart and shall fast for four days on bread and water. 9. If the offence is against a superior, he shall do penance thus for seven days and shall serve him willingly thereafter. 10. But, as someone says, to speak true things is not to defame; but, according to the Gospel, first *rebuke him between thee and him alone*; afterwards, *if he will not hear thee,* call another; and if he will not hear you (both), *tell the Church.*

11. He who is informed on and he who lays the information are persons of the same status. If he who is informed on denies (his guilt) they shall do penance together for one year, two days in each week on bread and water, and two days at the end of each month, while all the brethren pledge them and call upon God as their judge. 12. But if they persist in obstinacy after the lapse of a year, they shall be joined to the communion of the altar, under the risk of (eternal) fire, and left to the judgement of God. 13. If at any time one of them confesses, to the extent to which he has inflicted hardship on the other his own (hardship) shall be increased.

14. If anyone, being garrulous, injures the good name of a brother whom he loves, he shall do penance in silence for one or two days. 15. But if he did it in conversation,[20] he shall sing twelve psalms.

16. One who recalls the evils of those who do not take to a sane life, lest others should consent to them, or for the sake of blaming the evil and confirming the good, or in sorrowful lamentation, is to be held

---

29 intulit E   30 .i. *addidi, cf. Ps.-Cumm. IX 9; Capit. Iud. XXX. 2*   30 sq. uno die uel duos E   31 fabulatione E   32 sanitate R

lugubri miseratione, medicus aestimandus est; si ista tria defuerint, detractor, et .xxx. in ordine canat psalmos.

17. Qui abbati excusationem praetendit uel yconimis, si ignarus regulae, .i. die peniteat; si uero gnarus, superponat.

18. Qui autem de industria cuicumque seniori flecti dedignatur, cena 5 careat.

19. Reticens peccatum fratris quod est ad mortem arguat eum cum fiducia et quanto tempore reticuit tanto in pane et aqua uiuat. 20. Si peccatum paruum reticuit, arguat quidem eum, sed psalmis siue ieiunio iudice sacerdote peniteat. 21. Qui alios proterue arguit, leniat primo 10 eos et .xxx. psalmos canat. 22. Qui peccatum pudendum fratri inputat priusquam seorsum arguat eum, satis faciens ei tres diebus (*sic*) peniteat.

23. Qui solus cum sola loquitur uel sub eodem tectu in nocte maneat, cena careat. 24. Si uero post interdictum, cum pane et aqua peniteat.

25. Alii statuunt .xii. triduana pro anno repensanda, quod ego nec 15 laudo nec uitupero. 26. Alii .c. dies cum semipane †mensurae et paxma-tiuo aquae† et sale, et .l. psalmos in una quaque nocte canet. 27. Alii quinquaginta superpositiones una interueniente nocte. 28. Alii paeni-tentiam aegris statuunt ut elemosinam dant, hoc est, praetium uiri uel ancillae; sed apt⟨i⟩us est si dimedium omnium que possidet unus quis- 20 que det, et si quem fraudauit, quadruplum reddat ei.

(IX.) X. DE MINUTIS CAUSIS

1. Si casu aliquo neglegens quis sacrificium perdat, relinquens illud feris et alitibus deuorandum, si excusabiliter, tres xlmis (*sic*), sin uero, ann(o) peniteat.　　　　　　　　　　　　　　　　　　　　　　　25

2. Qui communicauerit non ignorans ab ecclesia excommunicato, xl peniteat.

3. Sic qui manducauerit morticinam inscius; sin uero, ann(o) peniteat.

7–14 *cf.* Columbanus, Reg. coen. xv, p. 164, 1–11. 14 sq. Walker 13 sq., *cf.* *ibid.* c. xiii 15 *cf.* Can. Hib. II. 6 15. 18–21 *cf.* Theod. I. 7, 5 ('de libello Scottorum') 20 sq. *cf.* Luc. 19, 8 cc. 25–27 *sub titulo* De modis penetentiae *sic leguntur in Ps.-Cumm.* (*cf. pp. 462 sq. Wasserschl.*): alii statuunt .xii. triduanas pro uno anno quod in pane et aqua debet penetere, et hoc Theodorus conlaudauit. Alii .c. diebus cum simipane mensura paximacii cum sale et aqua et psal- .l. in una queque (*sic*) nocte. Alii .l. superpositiones una nocte interueniente. *In codice E, fol. 50ᵛ*, cc. 25–28 *iterum leguntur ad calcem textus Cummeani, sed his uerbis*: Item de modis penitentie. . . . Item alibi· alii statuunt .xii. triduanas pro anno repensando (*sic*). quod ego nec laudo nec uitupero. sed Theoderus (*sic*) laudauit. alii .c. dies cum semipani mensura paxˡmatio. aqua et sale et psalm(us) .xlta. in una quaque nocte alii .lta. super-positionis una nocte interueniente. alii penitentiam egens (*sic*). statuunt elemosinam praetium uiri uel ancille, sed posterior (*sic*) est. sed (*leg.* si) dimidium omnium quae possidet unus quisque det et siquidem aliquid fraudauit quadruplum reddat ei sicut Christus iudicauit. Theoderus quoque de egris praetium uiri uel ancille pro anno uel dimidium omnium que possidet dare et si quis alicuius aliquid fraudauerit reddere quadruplum ut Christus iudicauit

---

1 est estimandus E 　　　3 praecendit R 　　yconimis, si: equo animos E

a physician (of souls); if these three (motives) are lacking (he is considered) a detractor, and he shall sing thirty psalms in order.

17. He who offers an excuse to the abbot or the stewards, if he is ignorant of the rule, he shall do penance for one day; if he knows the rule, he shall keep a special fast.

18. He who intentionally disdains to bow to any senior shall go without supper.

19. He who is silent about a brother's sin which is unto death shall rebuke him with confidence, and for so long a time as he was silent he shall live on bread and water. 20. If it was a slight sin that he kept silent about, he shall indeed rebuke him, but he shall do penance with psalms or fasting according to the judgement of a priest. 21. He who rebukes others boldly shall first conciliate them and then sing thirty psalms. 22. He who imputes a shameful sin to his brother, before he rebukes him in private, shall make satisfaction to him and do penance for three days.

23. He who speaks with a woman alone, or remains under the same roof (with her) at night, shall go without supper. 24. If (he does this) after being forbidden, he shall do penance on bread and water.

25. Some (authorities) give the ruling that twelve three-day periods are the equivalent of a year,[21] which I neither praise nor blame. 26. Others, one hundred days with half a loaf of dry bread and an allowance of water,[22] and salt, and (the penitent) shall sing fifty psalms during each night. 27. Others, fifty special fasts, with one night intervening. 29. Others determine that the penance of the sick shall consist in the giving of alms, that is, the price of a man(servant) or a maidservant; but it is ⟨more⟩ fitting if anyone gives the half of all the things that he possesses, and if he have wronged anyone, that he restore him fourfold.

IX. OF PETTY CASES

1. If by some accident anyone negligently lose the host, leaving it for beasts and birds to devour, if it is excusable he shall do penance for three forty-day periods; if not, for a year.

2. He who not without knowing it holds communion with one who is excommunicate, shall do penance for forty (days).

3. So (shall) he (do penance) who eats of a dead thing unaware; but if not (unaware), he shall do penance for a year.

---

4 uno die E   gnarus *om.* E   8 tantum E   10 lineat E   12 tres: .iii. E
13 loquitur ⟨femina⟩ E   tecto E   14 cum–peniteat: .xl. diebus in pane et
aqua E   15 triduanas propter annum repensandas E   16 uituperato R
et *om.* E   paximatio E   16–17 *fortasse legendum* cum semipane paxmatiuo
et mensura aquae   19 ut *et* dant *om.* E   20 sed–21 ei *om.* E   aptius
ego: aptus R   24 tres: .iii. E   26 non: nec E   27 xlma E   28 inscius
om., xlta dies pen(itea)t *add.* E (*lege* qui . . . inscius, xlta dies, sin uero, anno peniteat*?*

4. Sciendum uero est quod quanto quis tempore moratur in peccatis tanto ei agenda paenitentia est.

5. Si cui iniungitur opus aliquod et contemptus gratia illud non fecerit, caena careat. 6. Qui non occurrit ad secundi psalmi consummationem, canat in ordine .viii. psalmos. 7. Si excitatus fuerit post 5 missam, quicquid cantauerint fratres replicet ex ordine et postulet ueniam. 8. Si uero secundo non ueniat, caena careat.

9. Si quis errans commutauerit aliquid de uerbis sacrorum ubi periculum adnotatur, tres superpositiones faciat.

10. Si sacrificium terratenus neglegendo ceciderit, superpositio sit. 10

11. Pro bonis regibus sacra debemus offerre, pro malis nequaquam.

12. Presbiteri uero pro suis episcopos (*sic*) non prohibentur offerre.

13. Qui praebent ducatum barbaris .xiiii. ann(os) peniteant, si tamen non accederit stragis Christianorum; sin uero, relictis armis usque ad mortem mundo mortui Deo uiuant.   15

14. Qui monasteria dispoliat se falso dicens captiuos redimere, .i. ann(o) cum pane et aqua, et omnia quaecumque traxerit pauperibus det et duobus annis sine uino carneque peniteat.

15. Qui creaturam perdiderit, .vii. diebus peniteat.

16. Animalis qui carnis morticinam manducauerit, cuius mortem 20 nescierit, tertia anni parte cum pane et aqua uiuat et reliqua sine uino carneque.

(X.) XI. PONAMUS NUNC DE LUDIS PUERILIBUS PRIORUM STATUTA PATRUM NOSTRORUM

1. Pueri soli sermocinantes et transgredientes statuta seniorum .iii. 25 superpositionibus emendantur. 2. Osculum simpliciter facientes, .vi. superpositionibus; inlecebrosum osculum sine coinquinamento, .viii.; si cum coinquinamento siue amplexu, .x. superpositionibus corrigantur. 3. Post autem annum .xx. [id est adulti] idem committentes .xl. diebus separati a mensa et extores ab ecclesia cum pane et aqua uiuant.   30

25–26 *Cf*. Columbanus, Reg. coen. c. viii, p.154, 5–7 W.

1–2 quantum quis tempore . . . tantum E   2 agenda: agenda in R. augenda E
(*sic Gildas c. 14*)   5 .viii. in ordine E *cum Gilda c. 19*   fuerit: ueniat E *cum Gilda*   6 replicet in ordine fratres E, *cf. Gildam* (*lege* replicet ex ordine fratres *cum Gilda?*)   6 et–7 ueniam *om.* E   7 secundo non ueniat: ad secundum uenerit E
10 sacrificium: sacrum E *cum Gilda c. 21*   superpositio sit E, *Ps.-Cumm. XIII 5*
(*cod. Vindob. 2233*): superpositi R (caena careat *Gildas c. 21*)   12 episcopis E   13 annis *Syn. Luc. Uict. c. 4*   14 strages E   reiectis E; *cf.* (IV) 5
15 mortuos (*i.e.* -us) Deo uiuat E   17 et–traxerit: omnia quae traxit E
19 peniteat–21 parte *sic corrupte in* E *leguntur*: tempore animalis iudicio sacerdotis damnetur. cv. Qui mortuum manducauerit cuius nesciuerit cannonem tertia parte anni, *etc.* (*Fortasse in exemplari tale aliquid legebatur quale est* (.vii. dierum) tempore iudicio sacerdotis damnetur. Animalis qui carnem manducauerit cuius nesciuerit mortem tertia parte anni, *etc.*)   20 carnis: *lege* carnem?   23 sq. nunc de ludis puerilibus priorum statuta ponam E   27 superexpositionibus R   .viii. ⟨superinpositiones peniteat⟩ E   28 si *om.* E   inquinamento E   siue: sine E   superex-

4. Now let it be understood that for whatever time anyone remains in his sins, for so long shall he do penance.

5. If any work is imposed on anyone and he does it not, on account of contempt, he shall go without supper. 6. He who does not arrive at the end of the second psalm shall sing eight psalms in order. 7. If he is aroused after the reading, he shall repeat in order whatever his brethren have sung and shall beg for pardon. 8. If, however, he does not come a second time, he shall go without supper.

9. If anyone in error has changed any of the words of the sacrifice, where (the word) 'danger'[23] is noted, he shall keep three special fasts.

10. If one by neglect lets fall the host to the ground, a special fast shall be assigned.

11. We ought to offer the sacrifice on behalf of good kings, never on behalf of evil kings.

12. Presbyters are not forbidden to offer on behalf of their bishops.

13. Those who furnish guidance to the barbarians shall do penance for fourteen years, provided there be no slaughter of Christians; but if (it turns out) otherwise they shall give up their arms and until death, being dead to the world, shall live unto God.

14. He who despoils monasteries, falsely saying that he is redeeming captives, (shall go) for one year on bread and water, and everything that he has taken he shall give to the poor, and he shall do penance for two years without wine and meat.

15. He who loses a consecrated object[24] shall do penance for seven days.

16. He who eats of the flesh of a dead animal, of whose (manner of) death he is unaware, shall live the third part of a year on bread and water and the rest (of it) without wine and meat.

X. LET US NOW SET FORTH THE DECREES OF OUR FATHERS BEFORE US ON THE (SINFUL) PLAYING OF BOYS

1. Boys talking alone and transgressing the regulations of the elders, shall be corrected by three special fasts. 2. Those who kiss simply shall be corrected with six special fasts; those who kiss licentiously without pollution, with eight (special fasts); if with pollution or embrace, with ten special fasts. 3. But if after the twentieth year [that is, as adults][25] they commit the same sin, they shall live, at a separate table and excluded from the church, on bread and water.

---

positionibus R. superpositionis E   29 annos E   id ÷ adultidē cōmedentes E *uerba* id est adulti *glossa uidentur esse* (*adsunt in Ps.-Cumm. II 14*)   idem committentes: id est continentes R; *correxi ex Ps.-Cumm. l.c., cf.* E   30 separata RE a *om.* E   (separati a mensa *Ps.-Cumm.*)   extores: et.ceterisque (*lege* exterresque) E

4. Minimi uero fornicationem imitantes et inritantes se inuicem, sed coinquinati non sunt propter inmaturitatem aetatis, .xx. diebus; si uero frequenter, .xl.

5. Puer qui sacrificio communicat peccans cum pecode, centum diebus.

6. Pueri autem .xx. annorum se inuicem manibus coinquinantes et confessi fuerint antequam communicant, .xx. uel .xl. diebus. 7. Si iterauerint post paenitentiam, .c. diebus; si uero frequentius, separantur et ann(o) peniteant.

8. Supra dicta aetas inter foemora fornicans, .c. diebus; id iterum faciens, annum.

9. Puer paruulus oppressus a maiore annum aetatis habens decimum, ebdomadam dierum ieiunet; si consentit, .xx. diebus.

10. Isdem aliquid furti comedens .vii. diebus peniteat. 11. Si post uicesimum annum aliquid modicum furti huic accederit, .xx. diebus peniteat. 12. Si uero in uirili aetate aliquid simile accederit, .xl. diebus; iteratum uero, .c. diebus; in consuetudinem uertunt, annum.

13. Uir semetipsum coinquinans, primo .c. diebus; iterans, annum. 14. Uiri inter femora fornicantes, primo ann(um), iterantes duobus annis. 15. In terga uero fornicantes, si pueri sunt, duobus annis; si uiri, tribus annis uel iiiior; si autem in consuetudinem uertunt, .vii. annis et modus penitentiae addatur iudice sacerdote. 16. Desideria labiis complentes, .iiii. ann(is); si in consuetudinem fuerant adsueti, .vii. ann(os).

17. Puer de saeculo ueniens nuper cum aliqua puella fornicari nitens nec coinquinatus, .xx. diebus; si autem coinquinatus est, .c. diebus; si uero, ut moris est, suam compleat uoluntatem, ann(o) peniteat.

18. Quidam commedens sui corporis cutem, id est scabiem, si⟨ue⟩ uermiculos qui pedecle nuncupantur suam nec non bibens urinam stercoraue comedens, cum inpositione manus episcopi anno integro cum pane et aqua peniteat.

19. Benedicens infantulum uice baptismi annum extra numerum peniteat siue cum pane et aqua expleat. 20. Si uero mortuus fuerit infans sub tali tantum benedictione, iudicio senatus peniteat homicida ille.

21. Paruuli se inuicem percutientes .vii. diebus peniteant; si autem maioris aetatis, .xx. diebus; si uero adoliscentes, .xl. diebus peniteant.

---

1 minimę R. minime E; *correxi e Ps.-Cumm. II 15*   imitantes *Zettinger*: mittantes R. emitantes E   (minimi . . . imitantes *Ps.-Cumm. II 15; Paen. Sangall. 15; Capit. Iudic. X. 1*)   2 non sunt: sunt non R; *cf. Ps.-Cumm. l.c.*   aetati R. aetatis inmaturitatem E *cum Ps.-Cumm.*   6 pueri ante annos. .xx. E   manibus *om.* E   7 uel .xl. *om.* E   10 super R   fornicantes E   13 ebdomata E   ieiunat E   si ⟨eum⟩ E   14 isdem: iste E   16 in uirili aetates R: in uirilitate E   .xl.: .xx. E   18 primum E   19 iterantes: iteratum uero E   21 tribus –iiiior: .iii. annos in penitentiam E   uertant E   .vii. annis *om.* E   22 ⟨suis⟩ labiis E   23 in consuetudine fuerint E *cum Vinniano (3)*   25 .xx.: .xl. E   27 siue *ego ex Ps.-Cumm. I 38*: si R. seu E   28 peducli E   non *om.* R   35 si–peniteant *om.* E

4. Children who imitate acts of fornication and stimulate one another, but are not defiled because of their immature age, twenty days; if frequently, forty.

5. A boy who takes communion in the sacrament although[25a] he has sinned with a beast, one hundred days.

6. But boys of twenty years who practice masturbation mutually and confess before they take communion (shall do penance) twenty or forty days. 7. If they repeat it after penance, one hundred days; if more frequently, they shall be separated and shall do penance for a year.

8. (One of) the above-mentioned age who practises femoral intercourse, one hundred days; if he does it again, a year.

9. A small boy misused by an older one, if he is ten years of age, shall fast for a week; if he consents, for twenty days.

10. A small boy, if he eats anything that he has stolen, shall do penance for seven days. 11. If after his twentieth year he happens to commit some small theft, he shall do penance for twenty days. 12. If, however, in the age of manhood he happens to do anything similar, forty days; if it is repeated, one hundred days; if it becomes a habit, a year.

13. A man who practises masturbation by himself, for the first offence, one hundred days; if he repeats it, a year. 14. Men guilty of femoral intercourse, for the first offence, a year; if they repeat it, two years. 15. Those practising homosexuality, if they are boys, two years; if men, three or four years; but if it has become a habit, seven years, and the manner of penance, moreover, shall be decided according to the judgement of a priest. 16. Those who satisfy their desires with their lips, four years. If it has become a habit, seven years.

17. A boy coming from the world recently who intends to commit fornication with some girl and has not been polluted, shall do penance for twenty days; but if he has been polluted, one hundred days; if, however, as it commonly happens, he fulfils his intention, for a year.

18. He who eats the skin of his own body, that is, a scab, or the vermin which are called lice, and also he who eats or drinks his own excreta—with imposition of hands of his bishop he shall do penance for an entire year on bread and water.

19. One who instead of baptism blesses a little infant shall do penance for a year apart from the number[26] or atone with bread and water. 20. If, however, the infant dies having had such blessing only, that homicide shall do penance according to the judgement of a council.

21. Small boys who strike one another shall do penance for seven days; but if (they are) older, for twenty days; if (they are) adolescents, they shall do penance for forty days.

(XI.) XII. DE QUESTIONIBUS SACRIFICII

1. Qui bene non custodierit sacrificium et mus comedit illud, .xl. diebus peniteat. 2. Qui autem perdiderit in ecclesia, id est, ut pars ceciderit et non inuenta fuerit, .xx. diebus. 3. Qui autem perdiderit suum crismal aut solum sacrificium in regione qualibet et non inuenia- 5 tur, tres xlmas uel annum. 4. Perfundens aliquid de calice super altare quando auferatur linteamen, .vii. diebus peniteat, aut si abundantius effuderit, superpositionibus .vii. diebus peniteat. 5. Si cadentis de manu sacrificium ceciderit in stramentum, .vii. diebus peniteat a quo ceciderit. 6. Qui effudit calicem in fine sollemnitatis misse, .xl. diebus peniteat. 10

7. Sacrificium euomens grauatus saturitate uentris, si in ignem proiecerit, .xx. diebus, sin autem, .xl. 8. Si uero canes comederint talem uomitum, .c. 9. Si autem dolore, et in ignem proiecerit, .c. psalmos canat.

10. Si uero neglexerit quis sacrificium accipere et non interrogat nec aliquid causae excusabilis exsteterit, superponat; et qui acciperit sacri- 15 ficium pollutus nocturno somno, sic peniteat.

11. Diaconus obliuiscens oblationem adferre donec auferatur lintea- men quando recitantur pausantium nomina similiter peniteat.

12. Qui dederit alicui liquorem in quo mus uel mustella mortua inuenitur, tribus superpositionibus peniteat. 13. Qui uero nouerit postea 20 quod tali abusus est potu, superponat. 14. Si autem in farina aut in aliquo siccato cibo aut in pultu uel in lacte coagolato istae inueniuntur bestiole, quod sit circa corpora illarum foras proieciatur, omne reliquum sana sumatur fide.

15. Qui non idonea manu tangit limphaticum alimentum, .c. emende- 25 tur animalibus plagis. 16. Si autem aliquid decoloratum fuerit liquoris, distributor .vii. emendatur ieiunio dierum. 17. Qui autem hoc sumpsit inscius et postea recognoscit, ter quinis diebus concauum cruciat in ieiunio stomachum.

18. Quicumque comederit uel biberit quod intinctum a familiari 30 bestia fuerit quae est muriceps, .iii. superpositionibus sanetur.

19. Qui neglegentiam erga sacrificium fecerit, ut siccans uermibusque consumptum ad nihilum deuenerit, tres xlm̄ (*sic*) cum pane et aqua peniteat. 20. Si autem integrum, sed inuentum fuerit in eo uermis,

---

3–4 *cf.* Columbanus, Reg. coen. c. xv, p. 162, 15 sq. Walker 32–p. 132, 6 *cf.* Colum- banus, Reg. coen. c. xv, p. 162, 17–25 Walker

---

2 non bene E   mus: *s.s.* surix E   8 effuderit *om.* E   diebus *om.* E   caden- tis: accedenti *Capit. Iud. XXXIV. 1.* accedentes E. accedentes, -ibus *codd. Ps.-Cumm. XIII 11* ('by accident' *McNeill–Gamer*)   9 ⟨et⟩ ceciderit R (et *om. Capit. Iud. l.c.; Ps.-Cumm. l.c.*); *sed fortasse legendum*: Si cadens de manu sacrificium, et ceciderit in stramentum . . .   stramen E   10 effudit: infundit E   .xl. diebus ⟨uel xl⟩ E 11 uentris–12 .xl.: uentris, .xx. diebus uel .xl. peniteat. Si quis sacrificium in ignem proiecerit .xx. diebus, sin autem, .xl. diebus peniteat E   12 Si uero–13 canat *om.* E   17 auferatur: afferatur E   19 mus uel *om.* E   20 .iii. superposi- tionis E   nouerit: nocuerit R, *cf.* III. 17, (IV) 11   21 aut: an R   22 pultū E.

XI. OF QUESTIONS CONCERNING THE HOST

1. He who fails to guard the host carefully, and a mouse eats it, shall do penance for forty days. 2. But he who loses it in the church, that is, so that a part falls and is not found, twenty days. 3. But he who loses his chrismal[27] or only the host in what place soever, and it cannot be found, three forty-day periods or a year. 4. One who pours anything from the chalice upon the altar when the linen is being removed shall do penance for seven days; or if he has spilled it rather freely, he shall do penance with special fasts for seven days. 5. If the host falls from one's hand on the straw,[28] he shall do penance for seven days from the time of the accident. 6. He who pours out the chalice at the end of the solemn Mass, shall do penance for forty days.

7. One who vomits the host because his stomach is overloaded with food, if he casts it into the fire, twenty days, but if not, forty. 8. If, however, dogs consume this vomit, one hundred. 9. But if it is with pain, and he casts it into the fire, he shall sing one hundred psalms.

10. If anyone neglects to receive the host and does not ask for it, and if no reason exists to excuse him, he shall keep a special fast; and he who, having been polluted in sleep during the night, accepts the host, shall do penance likewise.

11. A deacon who forgets to bring the oblation until the linen is removed when the names of the departed[29] are recited shall do penance likewise.

12. He who gives to anyone a liquor in which a mouse or a weasel is found dead shall do penance with three special fasts. 13. He who afterwards knows that he tasted such a drink shall keep a special fast. 14. But if those little beasts are found in the flour or in any dry food or in porridge or in curdled milk, whatever is around their bodies shall be cast out, and all the rest shall be taken in good faith.

15. He who with unfit hand touches liquid food shall be corrected with one hundred lively (?) blows. 16. But if any quantity of the liquor is discoloured, the distributor shall be corrected by a fast of seven days. 17. He who takes this unaware and afterwards recognizes it shall torture his empty stomach for fifteen days with fasting.[30]

18. Whoever eats or drinks what has been tainted by a household beast, namely, the cat,[31] shall be healed with three special fasts.

19. He who acts with negligence towards the host, so that it dries up and is consumed by worms until it comes to nothing, shall do penance for three forty-day periods on bread and water. 20. If it is entire but

---

pulto R^c coagulato uel lactę E 22 sq. inueniatur (*sic*) bestiolę E 23 corpora circa E 26 animalibus ('lively' *McNeill–Gamer*) *uix sanum*: manualibus E, *Capit. Iudic. XXIII. 3*; for a laim *Pen. Hib. I. 11* aliquod E 28 recognoscit: resciuit E 28 sq. in ieiunio: ieiunus E 33 .iii. quadragesima E 34 sed: sit et E

comburatur et cinis eius sub altari abscondatur, et qui neglexerit quater denis diebus suam neglegentiam saluat. 21. Si cum consummatione saporis decoloratur sacrificium, .xx. diebus expleatur ieiunium; conglutinatum uero, .vii. diebus.

22. Qui merserit sacrificium, continuo bibat aquam quae in crismali 5 fuerit sumatque sacrificium et per .x. soles emendat culpam. 23. Si sacrificium ceciderit de manibus offerantis terratenus et non inueniatur, omne quodcumque inuentum fuerit in loco in quo ceciderit comburetur et cinis eius ut supra abscondatur; sacerdos deinde demedio anno damnetur. 24. Si uero inuentum fuerit sacrificium, locus scopa mundetur 10 et stramen ut supra diximus igne comburetur et sacerdos .xx. diebus peniteat. 25. Si usque ad altare tantum fuerit lapsum, superponat. 26. Si uero de calice aliquid per neglegentiam stillauerit in terra, lingua lambetur, tabula radatur, igni sumatur, ut supra diximus celatur, .l. diebus peniteat. 27. Si super altare stillauerit calix, sorbeat minister stillam et 15 ternis peniteat diebus et linteamina quae tangerit stilla per tres abluat uices calice subter posito et aquam ablutionis sumat. 28. Si quando intra luitur calix stillauerit, prima uice .xii. a ministro canantur psalmi, si secunda uice, ⟨. . .⟩, si tertia, .iii.

29. Si titubauerit sacerdos super oratione dominica quae dicitur pericu- 20 losa, si una uice, .l. plagis emundatur, si secunda, .c., si tertia, superponat.

1. Sed hoc in omni paenitentia solerter intuendum est, quanto quis tempore in delictis remaneat, qua eruditione inbutus, qua inpugnatur passione, qualis existat fortitudine, qua uidetur adfligi lacrimabilitate, quali compulsus est grauatione peccare. 2. Omnipotens etenim Deus, 25 qui corda omnium nouit diuersasque naturas indidit, non aequali lance paenitudinis pondera peccatorum pensabit, ut est illud propheticum: *Non enim in serris triturabitur git neque rota plaustri super cimminum circuiet; sed in uirga excutitur git et chymminum in baculo, panis autem comminuetur;* ⟨uel⟩ ut est illud: *Potentes potenter tormenta patiuntur.* 30 3. Unde et quidam sapiens Domini ait: *Cui plus creditur, plus ab eo exigitur.* Discant igitur sacerdotes Domini qui in ecclesiis praesunt quia

---

28–30 Is. 28, 27. 28 (circuiet A. excutitur *cf.* LXX)   30 Sap. 6, 7 (patiuntur ASU *Lucifer*)   31 sq. *cf.* Luc. 12, 48

1 neglegit E   1 sq. quater denis: quaternis E   2 saluat: soluat E *cum. Ps.-Cumm.* *XIII 15; Capit. Iudic. XXXIV. 1 (b), p. 250, 10 Schmitz*   consummatione: amissione E   5 merserit: miserit E   6 soles–Si: dies culpas emendet. Soles (*sic*) si E   7 offerentis E   8 comburetur ⟨igne⟩ E   9 eius *om.* E super R   10 sacrificium: sacrum E, *cf.* (IX) 10   scupa mundatur E   11 igne comburetur: ignetur (*i.e.* -itur?) E   13 terram E   lambatur lingua E   14 igni: et hoc ipsum igne E   .l. *McNeill–Gamer cum Ps.-Cumm.* *XIII 18* : l- R. xl *Paen. Sangall. 32; Capit. Iudic. XXXIV. 1.* et minister qui neglexit xl E 16 tangerit: tetigerit E   18 inī RE (interluitur *Ps.-Cumm. XIII 20*)   psalmos R 19 si sec.–.iii. *om.* E; *fort. lege:* si secunda uice, ⟨bis⟩, si tertia, ter   22 intuendum est R, *Ps.-Cumm. pr.*: est intuendum E, *Big. pr. 2*   23 maneat E   inbutis R qua (2): quali E   24 qualis: quali E   26 lance *om.* R   28 ⟨tritura⟩ tritura-

if a worm is found in it, it shall be burned and the ashes shall be concealed beneath the altar, and he who neglected it shall make good his negligence with forty days (of penance). 21. If the host loses its taste and
is discoloured, he shall keep a fast for twenty days; if it is stuck together, for seven days.

22. He who wets the host shall forthwith drink the water that was
in the chrismal; and he shall take the host and shall amend his fault for
ten days. 23. If the host falls from the hands of the celebrant to the
ground and is not found, everything that is found in the place in which it
fell shall be burned and the ashes concealed as above; then the priest
shall be sentenced to half a year (of penance). 24. If the host is found,
the place shall be cleaned up with a broom, and the straw, as we have
said above, burned with fire, and the priest shall do penance for twenty
days. 25. If it only slipped to the altar, he shall keep a special fast.
26. If he spills anything from the chalice to the ground through negligence, it shall be licked up with the tongue; the board shall be scraped;
(what is scraped off) shall be consumed with fire (and the ashes) shall
be concealed as we have said above; he shall do penance for fifty days.
27. If the chalice drips upon the altar the minister shall suck up the
drop and do penance for three days,[32] and the linens which the drop has
touched he shall wash three times, the chalice being placed beneath, and
he shall drink the water used in washing. 28. If the chalice drips when it is
washed inside, the first time twelve psalms shall be sung by the minister;
if it happens a second time . . ., if a third time, three (?).[33]

29. If the priest stammers over the Sunday prayer which is called 'the
perilous,'[34] if once, he shall be cleansed with fifty strokes; if a second
time, with one hundred; if a third time, he shall keep a special fast.

1. But this is to be carefully observed in all penance: the length of time
anyone remains in his faults; what learning he has received; by what
passion he is assailed; how great is his strength; with what intensity of
weeping he is afflicted; and with what oppression he has been driven to
sin. 2. For Almighty God who knows the hearts of all and has bestowed
diverse natures will not weigh the weights of sins in an equal scale of
penance, as this prophecy saith: *For the gith*[35] *shall not be threshed with
saws, neither shall the cart wheel turn about upon the cummin; but the gith
shall be beaten with a rod and the cummin with a staff, but bread corn shall
be broken small,* ⟨or,⟩ as saith this passage: *The mighty shall be mightily
tormented.* 3. Whence a certain man, wise in the Lord,[36] said: 'To whom
more is intrusted, from him shall more be exacted.' Thus the priests of
the Lord, who preside over the churches, should learn that their share
is given to them together with those whose faults they have caused to be

---

bitur E   28 *et* 29 gith E   29 in (1) *om.* E *cum Ps.-Cumm.*   30 uel *addidi*
pacientur E, *cf. Ps.-Cumm.*   31 Domini *om.* E *cum. Ps.-Cumm.*

pars eis data est cum his quorum delicta repropitiauerunt. 4. Quid est autem repropitiare delictum, nisi, cum adsumpseris peccatorem [ad poenitentiam], admonendo, hortando, docendo, instruendo adduxeris eum ad poenitentiam, ab errore correxeris, a uitiis emendaueris et efficeris eum talem ut ei conuerso propitius fiat Deus, pro delicto repro- 5 pitiare diceris? 5. Cum ergo talis sacerdos sis et talis sit doctrina tua et sermo tuus, pars tibi datur eorum quos correxeris, ut illorum meritum sit tua mercis et illorum salus tua gloria.

FINITUS EST HIC LIBER SCRIPTUS A COMMINIANO

1 delicta–2 repropitiare: delectare propitiare *per homoeoteleuton* E   2–3 ad poenitentiam *om.* E; *haec uerba, quae desunt in praefationibus Bigotiana et Ps.-Cumm., e uersu sequenti hic irrepserunt in* R   3 admonendo: et monendo E *cum Ps.-Cumm. et Big.*   5 sq. repropitiasse E *cum. Ps.-Cumm.*   6 sis sacerdos E *cum Ps.-Cumm. et Big.*   8 tua ⟨sit⟩ gloria E *cum Ps.-Cumm. et Big.*   9 *om.* E

forgiven. 4. What is it, then, to cause a fault to be forgiven unless, when thou receivest the sinner, and by warning, exhortation, teaching, instruction, leadest him to penance, correctest him of his error, amendest him of his vices, and makest him such that God is rendered favourable to him after his conversion, thou art said to cause forgiveness for his fault? 5. When, therefore, thou art such a priest, and such is thy teaching and thy word, there is given to thee the share of those whom thou correctest, that their merit may be thy reward and their salvation thy glory.

HERE ENDS THIS BOOK WRITTEN BY COMMINIANUS

'CANONES WALLICI' [A]

INCIPIUNT EXCERPTA DE LIBRIS ROMANORUM ET
FRANCORUM

1 (P I) Si quis homicidium ex contentione commiserit, ancellas .iii. seruos .iii. reddat, securus fiat.

2. Si quis inuidia homicidium fecerit, ancellas .iiii. totidemque 5 seruos reddat et ipse securitatem habebit.

3. (P II) Si quis fuerit homicidi in iudicio conpulsus et praestandi ratione durus esse uoluerit, et †interfectus† fuerit, ancellas .v. seruos totidem reddi praecipimus.

Manum oculum et quodlibet membrum debilitatum faciet, accipiet 10 in iudicio.

4. (P 3) Si quis homicidi causa suspicatur et non est ei titulus conprobandi, .xlviii. homines nominatim congregabit, e quibus .xxiiii. in eclesia iurent eum esse ueracem, sic sine culpa excedat; si non iurauerint, ancellas .v. et .vii. seruos reddat, securus fiat.   15

5. (P 4) Si quis seruus ingenuum occiderit et plaga ingenuus aut de securi bidubio[q]ue aut cultello ⟨aut⟩ dexterali interfectus fuerit, homicida parentibus traditur et habent libertatem faciendi quod uoluerint.

6 (P 5) Si autem dominus seruo arma commiserit portare et in- 20 genuum hominem occiderit, ipsum et alium seruum se nouerit rediturum.

7 (P 6) Si quis ingenuus seruum alterius sine culpa occiderit, seruos duos domino restituat; quod si culpa serui fuerit, seruus pro seruo.

Leges Wallicae II. 49, 2–17 (A. Owen, Ancient Laws and Institutions of Wales, 1841, p. 843. Codicem Cottonianum Vespas. E. XI, saec. XIII med., ad usum nostrum denuo contulit uir clar. W. O'Sullivan)   2 Si quis inuidia hominem occiderit, ancellas quatuor totidemque seruos reddat et ipse securitatem habeat   3 Si quis fuerit in iudicio compulsus et dandi rationes durus esse uoluerit et inuitus fuerit, .v. ancillas totidemque seruos reddere precipimus   4 Manum oculum et quodcumque menbrum debilitatum fuerit, idem accipiet in iudicio, si non se redemerit   5 Si alicui homicidium imponitur et non est ei titulus comprobandi, .xlviii. hominum nominatorum iuramento se purgabit, ex quibus .xxiiii. in eclesia iurent eum esse ab homicidio immunem; quod si non iurauerint, ancellas .v. et tres seruos reddat et securus sit   6 Si quis seruus ingenuum occiderit, homicida parentibus tradatur et habeant potestatem faciendi de eo quod uoluerint   7 Si autem dominus seruo permiserit arma portare et ingenuum hominem occiderit, ipsum et alium seruum se nouerit redditurum   8 Si quis ingenuus seruum alterius sine causa occiderit, seruum pro seruo reddat

Codices: AB X HO   De glossis Britannicis codicis A cf. W. Stokes, The Breton glosses at Orléans, Calcutta 1880   Numeri in apparatu ad canones, non ad lineas, spectant
Titulus INCIPIUNT EXCERPTA DE LIBRIS (LIBRI X) ROMANORUM (ROMANIS A) ET FRANCORUM ABXH: SINOD̄ ROM̄(?) INCIPĪ PAUCA COLOMELLA O

1–4 om. X

'WELSH CANONS' [A][1]

HERE BEGIN EXCERPTS FROM THE BOOKS OF THE ROMANS AND
THE FRANKS

1. If anyone commits homicide as a result of strife, he shall pay three female slaves (and) three male slaves, (and) be safe.

2. If anyone commits homicide out of envy, he shall pay four female slaves, and he shall have immunity.

3. If anyone is brought before a homicide court and determines to be difficult about making statements and is slain,[2] we command that five female slaves (and) as many male slaves ought to be paid.

(If) his hand, eye, or any other member is maimed, he shall receive (due compensation) in judgement.[3]

4. If anyone has been suspected on account of murder and is not qualified to make proof,[4] he shall assemble forty-eight men chosen by name, twenty-four of whom shall swear in church that he is truthful, so he shall depart without blame; if they do not swear, he shall pay five female slaves and seven male slaves (and) be safe.[5]

5. If a slave kills a free man and the free man was killed by a blow, or with an axe or a bill-hook[6] or a knife, the murderer is given over to the (slain man's) parents and they have power to do (with him) what they will.

6. If, however, a master permits his slave to bear arms and he slays a free man, he shall be prepared to hand over that slave and another one.

7. If a free man kills another's slave without (the latter's) fault, he shall give two slaves to the owner in restitution; if it was the slave's fault, he shall give a slave for the slave.

ABHO   1 ex contentione commisserit (commiscerit H): committere uoluerit O
ancillas *etc. semper* B, *saepe* XO   seruosquet H   seruos .iii.: totidemque seruos O   ⟨et⟩
securus HO   2 .iiii.: .iii. AO   reddat *om.* HO   3 homicidi *scripsi, cf.* 4:
homicidia A. homicida BHO   ⟨et⟩ in O   rationes ABO   durus P, *Leg. Wall.*:
duras (i *s.* u H) HO. diras AB   esse *om.* B   noluerit B   interfectus A *cum* P:
inficiatus (infit- H) BHO   .v.: duas l- u. A (duas *fortasse ex uaria lectione* duras
ortum)   seruosque HO   praecepimus B*   Manuum oculorum et quamlibet
membrorum B (membrorum *etiam* A)   debilitatem AB   faciet: *lege* fiet?   accipiat
HO, *sed cf. Leg. Wall.*
   ABH   4 *om.* O   homicidii B. homicidia H   titulus ei AB, *sed cf.* P, *Leg. Wall.*
conprobandi: *s.s.* ⟨.i. B⟩ reuelandi BH   nominatim *ego*: nominati H. nominatos AB; *cf.*
31   excidat H   iurauerit BH   .vii.: .iii. H *cum Leg. Wall.*   reddat: reddet et AB
   ABXHO   5 *inc.* X   seruus *om.* A   et–fuerit *om.* X, *cf. Leg. Wall.*   ingenuus
aut: ingenui adēē A   de securi (-e O) *om.* A   c̄bidubioque (*s.s.* .i. guedom) A   -ue
pro -que *scripsi* (aut ⟨bi⟩dubio P)   aut cultello ⟨aut *addidi*⟩ dexterali: aut culter aut
cultello l- autello et O   dexterali *om.* BHO, *sed adest in* P   infectus HO   tradetur
HO   habebunt X
   6–14 *deest* O
   ABXH   6 autem *om.* A   commisserit: permisserit H, *cum* P *et Leg. Wall.*   redditurum BX. reddituram H   7 ingenuum A   restituet A   quod si *scripsi cum* P;
si quod AH. si pro qua BX   fuerit: fecerit BX

8 (P 7) Si quis in rixa manum uel oculum pedem[q]ue hominis maculauerit, ancellam siue seruum rediturum cognoscat.

9 (P 7) Si quis pollicem manus exciderit, medium dampni poni praecipimus.

10 (P 8) Si quis hominem lancea gladioue ferierit et interiora inspiciat, 5 argenti libras .iii. exsoluat.

11 (P 9) Si quis capud alterius percusserit usque ad cerebri pampas, libras argenti .iii. reddat.

12 (P 51) Si quis alapam alteri inpigerit nec sanguis nec libido appareat, .v. soltos argenti exsoluat.   10

13 (P 36) Si quis alterius in faciem alapam percusserit ut sanguis aut libido appareat, se ancellam nouerit rediturum.

14 (P 10) Si quis lancea aut in brachio aut in surra alterius foramen fecerit, tamen membro non noceat, argenti libras .ii. cognoscat reddere.   15

15 (P 12) Si quis homicidium fecerit et fugam petierit, parentes ipsius iura reddant intra dies paucos, postea parentes patriae restituuntur; aut ipsi de patria uadant; uel praetium demedium reddant et sic securi in sedibus sedeant.

Post haec si reus uenire uoluerit, reddat quod restat praetii, uiuat 20 securus.

Si interim occissus fuerit, mancipia quae acciperant debito restituantur.

16 (P 13) Si quis lanceam misserit et homo inlessus fuerit, argenti libram unam exsoluat; si plaga fuerit, legibus se nouerit rediturum.   25

17 (P XXVII) Si quis fornicatus fuerit cum alterius uxore aut sorore aut filia, morte moriatur; qui autem occiderit, nullam causam timeat habere.

Leg. Wall.   11 Si quis in rixa manum uel pedem aut oculum maculauerit, ancillam seruumque se redditurum nouerit   12 Si quis pollicem a manu exciderit, medium manus in precium reddere precipimus   13 Si quis hominem gladio aut lancea percusserit ita ut interiora appareant, duas libras persoluat   14 Si quis caput alicuius percusserit usque ad cerebrum, .iii. libras reddat   15 Si quis alicui dederit alapam nec sanguis nec liuor inde appareat, duos solidos inde persoluat   16 Si quis autem in facie alicui alapam dederit ita ut liuor aut sanguis inde manauerit uel appareat, ancillam reddat   17 Si quis in brachio uel sura lancea foramen fecerit, tamen menbrum non debilitauerit, .ii. libras reddat   9 Si quis homicidium fecerit et fugam petierit, parentes ipsius iura reddant aut patriam relinquant uel dimidium precii reddant. Post hoc si reus uenire uoluerit, dimidium quod restat de precio soluat. Qui si interim occisus fuerit causa eiusdem homicidii, totum galanas quod pro eo ante redditum fuerat retro reddatur   10 Si quis lanceam miserit et inde homo lesus fuerit (sic), argenti libram reddere debet

---

8 uel om. XH   -que om. AH. -ue pro -que scripsi, cf. P et Leg.Wall.   siue seruum: seruumque H, Leg. Wall.   redditurum BX   9 policem H   pollicem manus: manus l‾ pollicem A   damni BXH   percipimus XH   10 lancea uel gladio hominem A gladiouae H   11 caput BXH   pampas (s.s. i. cutem) A. pampas (s.s..i. scamas) B. papes (s.s. squamas) H. squamas X   argenti om. A   reddat om. X   12 alteri om. A

8. If anyone in a quarrel has injured a man's hand or eye or foot, he shall be prepared to pay a female slave or a male slave.[7]

9. If anyone cuts off the thumb of someone's hand, we command half that compensation to be paid.

10. If anyone strikes a man with a spear or sword and (one) can see the interior parts (of his body), he shall pay three silver pounds.[8]

11. If anyone strikes the head of another as deep as the scales[9] of his brain, he shall pay three silver pounds.

12. If anyone gives a slap to another so that neither blood nor bruise appears, he shall pay five silver solidi.

13. If anyone strikes another with a slap in the face so that blood or a bruise appears, he shall be prepared to pay a female slave.

14. If anyone with a lance pierces a hole in another's arm or into the calf of his leg, but does not disable the limb, he shall be prepared to pay two silver pounds.

15. If anyone commits murder and takes to flight, his relatives shall make satisfaction within a few days, then the relatives are reconciled to their country; or they shall leave the country; or they shall pay half the price and so stay secure in their places.

After this if the guilty man wishes to return, he shall pay the remainder of the price (and) live secure.

If meanwhile he has been killed, the slaves whom (his victim's kinsmen) have received shall duly be restored.

16. If anyone casts a spear (at somebody) and the man is not injured, he shall pay one silver pound; if there be a wound, he shall be prepared to make amends according to law.

17. If anyone commits fornication with another's wife or sister or daughter, he shall be put to death; and he who slays him, let him not fear that he will have any lawsuit.

---

inpigerit: s.s. deor A   nec (1) om. H   liuido B (sic et P). liuor X cum Leg. Wall. .v.: duos X cum Leg. Wall.   soltos A: saltos H*. solidos BXH^c   13 in faciem bis H percusserit om. H   liuido B cum P. liuor X cum Leg. Wall.   reditururum B 14 sura X

ABXHO   15 denuo inc. O   petierit: fecerit X   iura–ipsi om. X   iura: iure AHO, sed cf. Leg. Wall.   reddant AB: redeant H. reddeant O   patriae parentes (om. O) restituantur ⟨in statu priori O⟩ HO   dimedium B   et om. H   securi: securus A. scl-ari X   haec: hoc HO cum P, Leg. Wall.   uiuat securus: et securus in patria uiuat O Si ⟨quis⟩ HO ⟨a cognatis occisi (occisi X)⟩ occis(s)us BX, cf. HO inferius   occisus XHO   mancipia ⟨ancillae uel serui⟩ BX   acciperant: accipiant A*X. faciebant O   debitores BXHO   parentibus add. BX   restituantur: restaurantur (restaurent O) cognatis occisi HO

16–19 om. O ABH   16 om. X   miserit A   inlesus AB (inlesso P)   fuerit: erit AB, sed cf. Leg. Wall.   si: siue H   se om. H   redditurum BH

ABXH   17 fornicatus fuerit: fornicatur H   nullam–habere: nullam timeat occidere H

18 (P 11) Si quis capallum aut bouem aut quamlibet pecodem furti †quasi† ligatum uel quod occissum fuerit inuenerit in uillam, det is iuramento .iii. ideoneos, quod nihil habeat damni; si quis non iurauerit, soluat.

19 (P XXVIII) Si quis seruum seruam[q]ue uel quamlibet pecodem uel 5 rem aliquam conparauerit et cum ipso fuerit consignatum, si auctorem aut fideiusorem non habuerit, de furto se nouerit conponendum.

20 (P XXVIIII. 30) Si quis de †Calpeis uel de Saxonibus uel de qualibet gente capallum conparauerit in quamlibet speciem, testibus conprobet; si hoc consignatum fuerit et inuicem testes adequauerint, 10 sic ita aequale diuidant.

Si testes non habuerit et mendacium conatur inquirere, triplum se nouerit resti⟨tu⟩turum qui conatur.

21 (P 31. 14) Si quis animalia uicini sui in herba commisserit intacta et manserint in ea, pro animalia duo unum scriptulum reddat; si in 15 fastigium fuerint capta, pro animalia .iiii. scriptulum unum reddat; si in messe, quantum iurauerit dominus messis cum alio idoneo, quicquid dampni pertullerit sine dubio restauratur.

22 (P 15) Si porci per annonam noctuam manserint per maiorem noctis partem, quadrisextarium, si uero per minorem noctis partem, 20 sextarium reddat.

23 (P 16) Si quis causa fornicationis adprobatur, in .iii. prouincis iurat; si non iurauerit, ancellam reddat.

24 (P 17) Si quis sustullerit de homine aequum aut uacam uel quam-libet pecodem, quodcumque probatum fuerit recipiendum praecipimus, 25 et quodcumque eum repetierit, debitor reddat cum nutrimine suo.

25 (P 19) Si porci in glande ingressi, quotiens capti, porcastrum reddat; si ipse minauerit eos sponte, porcum maiorem reddat.

26 (P 18) Paruulus usque annum .xii. pro delicto nihil reddat nisi disciplinam accipiat; post hanc uero aetatem quicquid delinquat uel 30 furatur retribuat.

---

18 *Cf.* Leges Wall. II. 57, 1, p. 845 Owen: Si quis equum uel quodlibet furtum inuenerit, adducat illum cum quo inuenitur suum aduocatum, id est guarant

---

ABH   18 *om.* X   capallum B. capillum H*. caballum AH^c   boem B   furti quasi *om.* A. quasi *om.* B: furti causa *Binchy*   ligari H (*fort. lege* quod siue ligatum *etc.*) uillam AB: illa H   det is *ego*: detis BH. det A   habeant BH

ABXH   19 seruamue *ego*; *cf.* aut ancellam P   pecudem X   conparauerit: *s.s.* compri A   fuerit *om.* A   consignatum: *s.s.* cosoin A   fideiussorem ABX (fideiusores P) furtu X   conpuniendum H^c

ABXHO   20 *denuo inc.* O   Calpeis H. campis O; *cf.* calfaicum P: gallis ABXH^mg qualibet: quali H   caballum AXHO   hoc: autem ABX (hos P)   aequale: *s.s.* .i. adū (= aduerbium?) B; *cf. Gildam c. 1*   diuidant: diuida sit A   habuerint XH   resti-turum ABX: ⟨se O⟩ rediturum HO

21–25 *om.* X

ABHO   21 herba: erbam (h *s.l.*) H (*de* O *non constat.*)   commiserit O   intecta H   pro (1) *et* (2): propter BH   duo animalia O   scriptulum (t *priore loco eras.* in H): scripulum *bis* A   fastigium: *s.s.* i. guelto guat A, herbe H. fastigium herbae *in*

18. If anyone discovers on his farm a horse or an ox or any stolen animal[10] that has been either bound or slain, he shall provide three proper persons for swearing, so that he may have no damage (to pay); if anyone does not swear, he shall pay.

19. If anyone buys a male or female slave or any beast or anything, and he has no *auctor* (i.e. vendor) or guarantor, he shall be prepared to compound as for theft.[11]

·20. If anyone buys a horse of whatever breed from the †Calpei[12] or from the Saxons or from any tribe, let him establish this by witnesses; if conveyance thereof has been made to him and there is an equal number of witnesses for either party, let them then part on equal terms (?).[13]

If he has no witnesses and attempts to lie, let him who does so know that he is to make triple restitution.

21. If anyone lets his animals go into his neighbour's grass and they stay there unharmed, he shall pay one scripulus for every two animals; if they have been seized (and taken) under roof, he shall pay one scripulus for every four animals; if (they have been seized) on a crop, whatever quantity its owner with another fit person swears (to have been damaged), the amount of the damage he has suffered shall without question be restored.

22. If hogs stay in (another man's) grain field at night for the greater part of the night, (their owner) shall pay (for each hog) four pints; if for the lesser part of the night, one pint.[14]

23. If anyone is tried on account of fornication, he shall swear in three provinces;[15] if he does not swear, he shall pay one female slave.

24. If anyone has taken away from a man a horse or a cow or any beast, we command that (the owner) shall get back what has been proved (to have been taken), and whatever (the owner) demands of him the debtor shall pay without allowance for fodder.

25. If hogs trespass for acorns, whenever they are caught, (the owner) shall give a young pig;[16] if he of his own account drove them in, he shall give a full grown hog.

26. A boy up to the age of twelve years[17] shall give nothing for a fault, except that he shall receive discipline;[18] after that age, however, he shall make restitution for anything he defaults or steals.

textu B   fuerit AHO   .iii. (*sic*) animalia O   scrip(t)ulum unum AB   messis: de messe B   damni HO   pertulerit BO. protullerit (*s.s.* adi) A   restaurabitur O
22 Si ⟨quis⟩ H   porcus . . . manserit B   partem noctis HO   quadrisextariu A. quadrisextarii O. quadrisextim H* (quadrisextarium P): quatuor sextaria BH^c
23 in–iurat *om.* AB   prouinciis O   24 Si–pecodem *et* et–suo: *deest* O
sustullerit: *s.s.* doit A. sustulerit B   equum A   uaccam BH   pecc͗odem B   et–suo. quodcumque–praecipimus *codd.*: *transposui*   eum: etiam H   debitum H^c
cum nutrimine: cūru triminio H   sua B   25 grande (*s.s.* 1?) A   quoties O
porcastrum *scripsi cum* P: poractur (*s.s.* i. maciat) A. porcator BH^c. porceator H* (*deest* O)
redeat O   sponde H
ABXH   26 *denuo inc.* X, *om.* O   usque ⟨ad⟩ B   .xii.: *lege* xu? *cf.* P   nihil reddat nisi *scripsi, cf.* P: nihil reddat H. nihil nisi BX. nihil A   uero hanc B

27 (P 21. 22) Si quis ingenuus furtum fecerit et captus fuerit, ipse morietur; nullus ab eis accipiat questionem. Hoc usque ouem uel porcum; quod si minus, triplum restituet.

Fur per noctem occidi licet, per diem non licet; qui occiderit in nocte, nullam causam habet.   5

28 (P 23) Si quis causa furti suspicionem habuerit et non ei titulus, res ipsius in dies .xx. consignetur usque quo ueritas probetur.

29 (P 24) Si quis ad iudicium conpeditus uenire noluerit, hoc ⟨est⟩ ut in testibus probetur, argenti libram unam cogatur exsoluere et quicquid ad eum fuerit repetitum sine dilatione restituat.   10

30. Si quis tributum non oportune reddiderit ⟨et⟩ ad iudicem a tributario conpulsus fuerit, si mense ante praedicto neglexerit, pignus det, et si neglexerit mense secundo, duplum restituet.

31 (P 32) Si quis ancellam aut seruum perdiderit et suspicionem habuerit, .xxiiii. uiri nominatim congregentur, ex quibus .xii. iurent; 15 sic non reddat qui adprobatur.

32 (P 33) Si capallum, inuocandis uiris .vi. tres iurent et nihil sequitur.

33 (P 38) Si quis seruus seruum occiderit, uiuus commonis dominorum existat.   20

34 (P 39) Si bos uel uacca alium occiderit, uiuus ac mortuus in commune dominorum existant.

35 (P 39) Quod si taurus uel uaccam uel bouem occiderit, culpa prima non causam habeat; alteram causam conponat.

36. Si quis iurandi causa fuerit iudicio adductus a iudice uel maioribus 25 natu, †et nihil prodisse cognoscat se†, si uoluerit diuitare: hoc praecipimus iure permanere.

37 (P 46. 47) Si quis commisso delicto sponte et † ad confessionem uenerit sacerdoti, a nullo condempnari praecipimus, si quod abstullerit reddat; si ab alio fuerit conprobatus et repellis fuerit, praetium rei 30 abstractae reddat et triplum se nouerit conponendum.

(P 40. 41) Si clericus laicum conpetit, ad iudicis adstantiam debeant

---

27 *om.* O   captus: custus A   moritur A   accipiat *om.* A   ab eo X   questionem: *s.s.* emgruit A. questem H   restituat BH

ABXHO   28 *denuo inc.* O   eạ causa H   suspicionem H   et *om.* AH   res *scripsi cum* P: rei ABXHO   in: inter BX   consignetur: *s.s.* coso A   ⟨et⟩ usque X   29 conpetitus H, *cf.* P. inconpeditus X; O *incertus*   uoluerit H*   hoc ⟨est⟩ *ego.* ⟨et⟩ hoc X ut in testibus: per testes X   cognatur H   reppetitum H

ABXH   30 *om.* O   non oportune tributum H   rediderit B. redderit A   ⟨et⟩ ad BX a *scripsi cum* X: ā B. aut H. uel A   tributatorio (*s.s.* collot) A   menses .ii. X

ABXHO   31 *denuo inc.* O   perdiderit aut seruum HO   et *om.* A   suspicationem XHO   nominati XHO   sic: si ABX   32 Si ⟨quis⟩ BXH, *sed* quis *deest in* P; *cf.* 22 (*u.l.* H), 37 (*u.l.* H), 57 (*u.l.* HO), 62 (*u.l.* O).   capallum BO (caballum X): capallus H. capillus A .vi. tres: .vi. .iii. A. viiii B. .ix. X   .vi. tres iurent: .vi. (iii O) iurent (iuret O) .iii. HO   et *om.* ABX   33 seruus *om.* O   occiderit *om.* O   communis ABO   existant H   34 uaca B   uiuus *om.* O   comune B   existat X

35–36 *om.* X

27. If a freeborn man commits theft and is caught, he shall die; none of them (who have slain him) shall submit to an inquisition.[19] This (is valid) as far as a sheep or hog; if it is less, he shall restore it threefold.

A thief at night may be killed, (a thief) by day may not;[20] he who slays (one) at night does not have to stand trial.

28. If anyone is under suspicion on account of a theft and has no qualification (to make proof), his property shall be sealed[21] for twenty days until the truth is proved.

29. If anyone is sued at law and will not come (for trial), that is, in order that his case may be established by witnesses, he shall be compelled to pay one silver pound, and whatever is demanded of him he shall make good without delay.

30. If anyone does not deliver his tribute in time and is forcibly brought before a judge by the receiver, if he fails to deliver for one month after the tribute has been announced, he shall give surety; if he has failed to do so for two months, he shall pay double.

31. If anyone loses his female or male slave and has a suspicion, twenty-four men shall be assembled by name, of whom twelve shall swear; in that case he who is accused shall not pay.

32. If (he loses) a horse, of six men summoned three shall swear and there is no sequel.

33. If any slave kills a(nother) slave, the survivor shall be the joint property of the masters.

34. If an ox or a cow kills another (animal), the live and the dead one shall be the joint property of the owners.

35. But if a bull kills either a cow or an ox, the first offence shall incur no liability; on the second occasion (the owner) shall compound.

36. If anyone is brought to judgement by a judge or by his elders for the purpose of swearing an oath, let him know that it will be of no avail to him if he determines to avoid it: this we command to stay in force by law.

37. If anyone having committed a fault comes to a priest for confession of his own will, we command that he be not condemned by anybody, provided that he returns what he has taken; if he is proved by another (to be a felon) and is defiant, he shall pay the value of the object taken and be prepared to compound threefold.

If a cleric sues a layman they ought to come before the presence of

ABHO   35 quod *om.* AB, *sed ad. in* P   uel uaccam uel bouem: bouem uel uaccam HO, *sed cf.* P   altera BHO   36 fuerit *om.* A   maioribus: minoribus A   et: *lege* ei *et dele* se? *an lacuna ante* et *statuenda est?*   prodisse: prodesse B. *om.* A   se *s.l.* HO   deuitare B

ABXHO   37 denuo *inc.* X   sponde H   et *om.* BXO; *lege* et ⟨uoluntate⟩? *cf.* P 46   contem(p)nari AO   si quod ⟨aliis⟩ B. si quid ⟨ab aliis⟩ X   abstulerit BXO   si ab–rei *om.* O   rebellis X. pellis A   fuerit *om.* H   et triplum *om.* A   tripplum X   Quod–iudicium. Si–peruenire *codd.: transposui*   si ⟨quis⟩ H   conpetiit (*s.s.* ar) A. repetit XO   ad: a H. *om.* O   adstantiam (ast- B, asst- X): ad sententiam H. adsentiam (?) O

peruenire. Quod si laicus clericum causa repetierit, aepiscopi iudicant
inter illos in iudicium.

38 (P 42, cf. XXVI) Si quis in morte hereditatem dimisserit, quicquid
coram testibus commendauerit omnia permanere praecipimus nisi sint
iniqua.   5

39. Si quis seruum uel ancellam uel uernaculum sua uoluntate
libertate donauerit, nullus reppetere permittatur.

40. Si quis sponte sua quamlibet rem alteri donauerit, hoc priuate
praecipimus possidere.

41. Si qua causa ante iudicata, a nullo permittamus diiudicari.   10

42 (P 43) Si qua contentio circa finem territori fuerit exorta, ⟨a⟩
testibus requiratur et finis qui prius fuerat ipse permaneat.

43 (P 44. 45) Clericus uero si qua causa conpetitus fuerit et nullam
iam infamiam antea portauerat, in ipsius iuramento causa finiatur.
Quod si antea infamiam portauit, indictis iuratoribus secundum causam 15
laici ordine †libret.

44 (P 48) Si quis ⟨Deum⟩ fideiusorem inuocauerit et contempserit,
iudicii condictione damnetur.

45 (P 49. 50; cf. XXV) Si quis agrum aut uillam conparauerit et ipse
capitale furtum fecerit, morte morietur; terra quam emerat fisco 20
reuertatur.

Quod si filius aut frater †ex dono† furtum fecerit, pariter et fugam
fecerit, in⟨de⟩ ancellam et seruum fisco reddat et ex agro exul possideat.

Quod si innocens permanserit heres, hereditate relinquatur.

46 (P 52) Si quis ad aeclesiam arma portauerit et liti commisserit, 25
argenti libram unam aeclesiae cogatur exsoluere, et hoc aegentibus
aelimosina meretur uel sinatur.

47. Si quis filiam marito tradiderit, legitimam dotem accipiat. Quod
si cassus mortis illum demisserit et ipsa alteri uiro nubere uoluerit, filii
dotem accipiant. Quod si hos non habuerit, patri dari iubetur.   30

(ABXHO) quod *om.* O   clericum causa rep(p)etit HO: repetierit clericum causa
ABX (clericum qualibet causa conpetire P)   episcopi ABX   iudicent X   iudicio X

ABXH   38 *deest* O   dimiserit BX   praecipimus: precimus X   iniquos H
ABXHO   39 ancillam ABX   ⟨et⟩ libertate AB. libertate *om.* H; *de* O *non constat*
post nullus *add.* eam H, ea O   repetere BX   40 sponde H   41 causa ⟨est⟩ X
antea H   permitamus A   diiudicari: *s.s.* scarat A. deiudicari H   testatio *in*
fine canonis add. AHO   42 territori finem HO, *sed cf.* P   territori: *s.s.* terra A.
teritori B   quae HO   43 Clericus–fuerit: si uere causa clericus fuerit O
qua *om.* HO   causa *om.* A   infamiam: in familiam *bis* A   ⟨hac causa⟩ antea
habuerat O   portauerat antea A   portauerat: potuerat H   portauit: portauerat
O *cum* P   iurationibus HO   secundum: .ii. X. sed B   ordini H   liberet H*
44 Deum *suppleui ex* P   fideiussorem AXH (-iusorem P); *cf.* 19   condictione *scripsi*
cum P: condicione XHO. conditione B (ordine l- condicione O)   iudicii condictione:
in iudicio ne A   dampnetur X   45 aut: uel X   moriatur AO (morietur P)
⟨et⟩ terra O *cum* P   Quod si filius–relinquatur *om.* O   filios H   fructum
H*   pariter–fecerit *om.* A   fecerit (3): *lege* petierit *cum* P?   inde *ego*: in A, (*ex-*
punct.) H. *om.* BX   seruum: ferrum H   exul: nihil X   hereditati BXH^c; *lege*

a judge. But if a layman lodges a suit against a cleric, let bishops decide between them in judgement.[22]

38. If anyone disposes of an inheritance at his death, we command that whatever in the presence of witnesses he declares to be his will shall all remain unless it be illegal.

39. If anyone of his own will grants freedom to a male or female slave or to a slave born in the house, nobody shall be allowed to claim him back.

40. If anyone of his own will presents anything to another person, we command that (this person) shall own that object as private property.

41. If a case has already been decided, we would not permit it to be judged (again) by anybody.[23]

42. If any contention has arisen over the boundary of a piece of land, (information) shall be demanded from witnesses, and the boundary which existed before shall remain the same.

43. If a cleric has been sued in a case and he has had no bad reputation before, the case shall rest with his own oath. But if he previously bore an ill reputation, compurgators shall be summoned according to the case as if he were a layman.[24]

44. If anyone calls God to witness and despises Him, he shall be condemned by the solemn decision of the court.[25]

45. If anyone buys a field or farm[26] and if he commits a major theft,[27] he shall die; the land which he has bought shall be confiscated.
But if a son or brother commits the theft and he, at the same time, takes to flight, he shall, on the latter's behalf, give a female slave or a male slave to the fisc, and the person exiled from that piece of land shall own it (again).
But if the heir remains innocent, (the land) shall be bequeathed by inheritance.[28]

46. If anyone bears arms at church and makes strife, he shall be compelled to pay one silver pound to the church, and this shall be left[29] for the needy as alms.

47. If anyone gives his daughter to a husband, he shall receive the legal bride-price. But if (the husband) meets his death and she wants to marry another man, her sons shall receive the bride-price. If she does not have any sons, it is prescribed that (the bride-price) be given to her father.

---

hereditarie?   46 eclesiam A. aeclęsiam O   liti AH: litem BXO   commiserit X
eclesiae A   aegentibus B *cum* P: egentibus AX. a gentibus H. agentibus O   aelimosina HO *cum* P: ⟨in BX⟩ elemosi(-y- B)nam ABX   meretur uel sinatur *om.* X   signatur
O; *lege* feneratur? (feneretur P)   47 uiro l- marito O   legitimum AB   cassus:
casu BXO   emisserit AB. emiserit X. dimisserit H. dimiserit O   ipse X

48 (P 54. 55) Si quis ancellam aut seruum emerit et ante inpletum annum uitium in eo ⟨uel in ea⟩ apparuerit, proprio domino suo reddi iubemus. Quod si annus transierit, quidquid in mancipio uiti uidetur nullam habeat reieciendi causam.

49 (P 56) Si quis caballum conparauerit et usque ad mensem uitium 5 non habuerit, nullo modo non reiciatur.

50 (P 58) Si quis alterum fuste ferierit et sanguinem effunderit, uaccam reddat. Quod si maiorem plagam fecerit, secundum iudicium conponi praecipimus.

51 (cf. P 57) Si quis caballum a latrone abstullerit, si ualuerit 10 argenti libram, accipiat unchiam; sin autem minus, demedium unchiae accipiat.

52 (P 59) Si quis ancellam alterius adpraehenderit fugientem et a domino suo potuerit euadere, †stagnum ferrum† merito accipiat.

53 (P 60. 61. LXII) Si quis caballum alterius [non] indicauerit et ipse 15 potuerit capere, unciam dare debuit.

Nullus alterius siluam lessam et altam deuorat; quod si grauiter fecerit et ipse †effectionem reddere praecipimus.

54 (P LXIII) Si quis caballum alterius tullerit et in pedicam ruerit, suum proprium reddere praecipimus. 20

55 (P LXIIII) Si quis uillam uendere uicino capitali ei minante aut sponte uoluerit siue domum siue ortum, potestatem habeat praeter sepes quae †gignunt meses et herbam.

56 (P 66) Si quis clericus laicum ferierit, secundum plagam laici ordine sine dubio reddat. 25

57 (P LXV) Si laicus clericum percusserit, et dictis legibus manum suam redemat et penitentiam agat.

58 (P 67) Si quis intercidendo litem plagatus fuerit et mendax eum percuserit, secundum plagam se nouerit rediturum; quod si a ueraci, demedio uerax et demedio mendax iubemus mediate soluere. Simili 30 modo et de morte sic sancximus.

48 impletum BX   uitium–annus om. O   in eo uel in ea ego: in eo ABX. in ea HO; sed cf. in eum P   paruerit H   iubetur X   annum A   quicquid BXHO uitii ABXO, cf. homicidi 4, territori 42   habeat–51 latrone deest O   reieciendi (ex -am) H: reiciendi ABX; cf. 49
ABXH   49 deest O   comparauerit X   ullo H   non om. B   reiciatur A. reicitur H   50 deest O   fuste om. ABX, sed adest in P   effuderit ABX   redat B   quod: et ABX (quod P)
ABXHO   51 Si–latrone deest O   cabellum H   abstulerit BXO   libram ⟨unciam⟩ O   unciam BXH. deest O   sin: si A   unciae BXHO   52 suo om. HO   stagnum: s.s. mas A; lege stangnum ferri?   53 cabellum HO   non deleui, cf. P 60   potuerit: portauerit A   debet X. debebit O   lesam O. inlesam X   et: uel HO   altam A. alteram X: algam BHO cum P   deuoret XHO   (Nullus– deuorat fortasse sic accipiendum: Nullus alterius silua siue laesa siue integra ad sua animalia pascenda utatur)   si om. AB   post ipse (om. O) lacuna in exemplari uidetur fuisse   54 post 55 legitur in HO   cabellum H   tulerit BX   pedicam: s.s. arlup A   ruit X   ⟨ad⟩ suum B   55 bis extat in H: in textu ante 54, et in margine inferiore (H²)   capitali (s.s. er A) AHO: capitalem BXH²   uicino: in circo

48. If anyone buys a female slave or a male slave and a fault appears in him ⟨or in her⟩ before the completion of a year, we command that he be returned to his (former) master. But if a year has elapsed, whatever fault is seen in the slave, the buyer shall have no right to reject him.

49. If anyone buys a horse and it has no fault to the end of one month, it may on no account be rejected.

50. If anyone strikes another with a cudgel and sheds his blood, he shall pay a cow. If he strikes a heavier blow, we command that composition be made according to judgement.

51. If anyone recovers a horse from a robber, if its value is a silver pound, he shall receive one uncia; if, however, (it is worth) less, he shall receive half an uncia.

52. If anyone arrests another's female slave in flight and she had a chance of escaping from her master, he shall receive a reward . . . (?)[30]

53. If anyone spots another's horse and is able to catch it, (the owner) shall give him an uncia.

These two lines are corrupt beyond restoration; the provision must have been parallel to that of P 61.

54. If anyone takes away another's horse and fetters it, we command that he shall deliver up his own (?).[31]

55. If anyone decides to sell his farm to a neighbour either under a threat from the highman[32] or of his own will, or, (to sell) his house or his garden, he shall have power to do so, except the fences that surround the crops and the grass.[33]

56. If a cleric strikes a layman, he shall without question pay according to the blow as if he were a layman.

57. If a layman strikes a cleric, he shall do both: redeem his hand according to the stated laws and do penance.

58. If anyone interposing in a quarrel is struck and it is the lying one by whom he is struck, (the liar) shall be prepared to make restitution according to the blow; if the blow is struck by the one who is speaking the truth, we command that the truthful one and the liar pay one half each. In like manner we lay down the law in the case of (the peacemaker's) death.

(s.s. cir) A   capitali (-em) uicino (in circo) *codd.*: *transposui*   ei *ego*: et AXHO. *om.* BH²; *cf.* 36   minante aut sponte *om.* A   minante H: minantem O. minanti BXH² (*Uerba* Si–uoluerit *sic intellego*: si quis uicino uillam uendere uoluerit, quia capitalis ei minatur, aut sua sponte)   sponde H   hortum H   praeter: et BXH²   sepes: spes H quae: quem O. *om.* A   gignunt: unt O (circumit P; *lege* cingunt?)   meses A*H² (mesis P): messes AᶜBXHO   56 ferierit: . . ciderit O   secundum: sed AB   laici (-o *a.c.*) ordinē plagam O   57 si ⟨quis⟩ HO   clericus A   et: ex O   legibus *om.* X   redimat ABXO *cum* P

ABHO   58 *om.* X   intercedendo HO   lite H   plangatus A   percusserit BHO rediturus O. redditurum BH   a: aut AB   ueracio A   demedio (1): dimedio A. dimedium BO   demedio (2): dimedium ABO   mediate: mediatūe (-e *incerta*) H. mediatim O. medietatem AB   anximus H

59. Si quis legitimae legis uoluntate patrum nupto filiam iuncxerit et iuxta hoc concubinam ancellam sibi habere praesumserit, ipse ab aeclesia Dei et ab omni Christianorum mensa sit extraneus nisi ad penitentiam reuocetur.

60. Si quis ancellam suam in matrimonio sibi habere uoluerit et de 5 suis rebus habet potestatem, si noluerit postea habere eam, non conceditur; quod si eam uenundare uoluerit, eum uenundari iubemus et ancellam illam in sacerdotis ponimus potestatem.

61. Si quis catholicus capillos promisserit more barbarorum, ab aeclesia Dei alienus habeatur et ab omni Christianorum mensa donec 10 delictum emendat.

62. Si canis quidlibet manducet, prima culpa nihil reddatur pro illo nisi semet ipse; quod si iterum peccauerit, dominus canis quod commederit ille reddat.

Hic fortasse adicienda sunt ea quae leguntur post Canones Adamnani 1–7 15 *in codicibus AB:*

(63) Equus aut pecus si percuserit hominem in agro ciuitatis suae, demedium unciae reddet pro eo homini cuius sanguis effussus est. Si percuserit homo animal in agro suo, non reditur pro eo.

---

62 *cf.* Can. Hib. VI (V Wass.). 2

ABXHO   59 *denuo inc.* X   legitime A   nuto (*s.s.* aam) A   iuncxerit A: iunxerit HO, *ut uid.* X. iunc̨erit B   hoc: hanc O   concupinam B   habere–60 Si quis *deest* O   praesumpserit ABX   eclesia ABX   Dei *om.* A   ab *om.* H   60 sibi in matrimonio BX. sibi *om.* HO   et (1) *om.* X   et–uoluerit *om.* HO   noluerit *ego*: uoluerit ABX   habere: uenundare BX   concidetur A   uenundari: dam(p)nari BX ancillam ABXO   illam *om.* H   61 permisserit ABH. permiserit O. commiserit X: promiserit *Wasserschleben*   eclesia A   et–emendat *om.* O   omni: omnibus A BHO   62 *om.* AX   si ⟨quis⟩ O   canes H*   comederit H

AB   63 percusserit B^c demedium: se medium A. dimedium B   percuserit (2): percusserit B   homo: *lege* hominem?

59. If anyone in regular law has with the consent of the fathers joined his daughter to a bridegroom, and (the latter) takes the liberty of having in addition a slave woman as a concubine, he shall be excluded from the Church of God and from the table of every Christian[34] unless he is called back to penance.

60. If anyone who has power in his own affairs is resolved to have his slave woman in marriage, if he afterwards does not want to have her, it is not allowed; but if he is resolved to sell her, we command that he shall be sold, and we make that slave woman the ward of a priest.

61. If any Catholic lets his hair grow in the fashion of the barbarians, he shall be held an alien from the Church of God and from the table of every Christian until he mends his fault.

62. If a dog eats anything (belonging to one who is not his owner), this being his first offence, nothing is to be paid except himself;[35] but if he offends a second time, the master of the dog shall pay for what the dog ate.

63. If a horse or beast kicks a man in the territory of his own residence, (the owner) shall pay for it half an uncia to the man whose blood has been shed. If an animal kicks a man in its own territory, it is not to be paid for.

'CANONES WALLICI' [P]

INCIP(IT) IUDI(CIUM) CULPAR(UM)

I (A 1) Si quis homicidium ex intentione commisserit, ancellas .iii. et seruos .iii. reddat et securitatem accipiat.

II (A 3) Si quis iudicio fuerit conpetitus et praestando uerum durus esse uoluerit et ipsam intentionem fuerit †interfectus,† ancellas duas et 5 seruos .ii. reddi debere praecipimus.

Quod si manum aut pedem uel quodlibet membrum perdiderit similiter, duas partes praetii se nouerit accepturum.

3 (A 4) Si quis homicidii causa fuerit suspicatus et non ei titulus conprobandi, .xl. et .viii. uiris nominati⟨s⟩, ex quibus .xxiiii. in aeclesia 10 iurent eum esse ueracem, sic sine causa discedat.

Quod si non iuraueri⟨n⟩t, ancellas .iii. et seruos .iii. reddat et securitatem accipiat.

4 (A 5) Si seruus ingenuum occiderit et culpa ingenui fuerit, hoc ⟨est⟩ de fuste aut dexterali aut ⟨bi⟩dubio aut de cultello fuerit interemptus, 15 ipse homicida parentibus tradatur et quidquid faciendi uoluerint habeant potestatem.

5 (A 6) Si quis dominus seruum arma portare permisserit et ingenuum hominem occiderit, ipsum, et alium iuxta, se nouerit rediturum.

6 (A 7) Si quis ingenuus seruum alterius sine culpa occiderit, seruos 20 duos domino; quod si culpa fuerit serui, alius [alius] seruus domino reformetur.

7 (A 8. 9) Si quis rixa mactauerit hominem siue manum siue pedem siue oculum excusserit, ancellam siue seruum se rediturum cognoscat.

Quod si pullice manus excusserit, ancelle medium, id est demedium 25 praetii, siue serui medium reddat.

8 (A 10) Si quis hominem lancea aut gladio ferierit sic ut interiora inspiciat, argenti libras tres nouerit se rediturum.

9 (A 11) Si quis alterius caput percusserit sic ut cerebri cutem inspiciat, argenti libras sex cogatur exsoluere. 30

10 (A 14) Si quis alium lancea ferierit et brachium aut pedem forauerit sic ut membrum non noceat, argenti libras tres se daturum cognoscat.

Codex: P, foll. 135ʳ–138ʳ. *Numeri Romani in codice leguntur, ceteri sunt editorum. Numeri in apparatu ad canones spectant*

II *lege* ⟨in⟩ iudicio *cum* A? ipsam intentionem *fortasse pro ablatiuo scribitur, sed cf.* A 3 *uar. lect.* inficiatus*; lege* ipsam intentionem fuerit inficiatus et interfectus fuerit? ancellas *hic et saepius* Pᶜ 3 nominati, *sequente rasura*, P: *suppl. Wasserschleben, cf.* 32 iurauerint A, *Leg. Wall. II. 49, 5*: iurauerit P *cum* BH 4 et (1): *lege* nec? ⟨bi⟩dubio *suppletum ex* A: dubio P 7 redituram P: *corr. Wasserschleben* pollice Pᶜ. pollicem *Wasserschleben*

'WELSH CANONS' [P]*

1. If anyone commits homicide by intention, he shall pay three female slaves and three male slaves and shall receive immunity.

2. If anyone is sued at law and determines to be difficult about stating the truth and is slain for this intention, we command that two female slaves and two male slaves ought to be paid.

But if he has lost a hand or a foot or any other member in such circumstances, he shall be prepared to accept two-thirds of the price.

3. If anyone has been suspected on account of a murder, and is not qualified to make proof, forty-eight men shall be named, twenty-four of whom shall swear in church that he is truthful; so shall he depart without needing to stand suit.

If they do not swear, he shall pay three female slaves and three male slaves and shall receive immunity.

4. If a slave kills a freeman, and it was ⟨not⟩[1] the freeman's fault, and if he was slain with a cudgel or an axe or a bill-hook or with a knife, the murderer shall be given over to the (victim's) parents, and they shall have power to do (with him) what they will.

5. If any master permits his slave to bear arms and he slays a freeman, the master shall be prepared to hand over the slave and another with him.

6. If any freeman kills the slave of another without (the latter's) fault (he shall give) two male slaves to the master; but if the slave was to blame, another slave shall be restored to his master.

7. If anyone murders a man in a quarrel or cuts off his hand or his foot or (destroys) his eye, he shall be prepared to pay a female slave or a male slave.

But if he cuts off the thumb of his hand, the half of a female slave, that is, half the value, or the half of a male slave.

8. If anyone strikes a man with a spear or a sword so that (one) may see the interior parts, he shall be prepared to pay three silver pounds.

9. If anyone strikes the head of another so that (one) may see the membrane of his brain, he shall be compelled to pay six silver pounds.

10. If anyone strikes another with a lance and pierces his arm or his foot so that he does not disable the member, he shall be prepared to give three silver pounds.

11 (A 18) Si quis in uillam suam caballum aut bouem aut quod sibi libet furtum ligatum aut occissum inuenerit, dare idoneos iuratores praecipimus et nihil damni habeat; quod si non iurauerint, reddat.

12 (A 15) Si quis homicidium fecerit et fugam petierit, parentes ipsius habeant spacium intra dies .xv. ut aut partem restituant et securi 5 insedeant aut ipsi de patria uadant.

Post hoc si ipse interemptor uenire uoluerit, reddat medium quod restat et uiuat securus.

Quod si interim occisus fuerit, mancipium et quod acciperint faciant restaurari.   10

13 (A 16) Si quis ad alterum lanceam miserit inlesso homine, argenti libram cogatur exsoluere; ⟨si⟩ lesus, secundum plagam se nouerit rediturum.

14 (A 21) Si segitem alterius praesserit, quantum iurauerit dominus mesis cum alio idoneo, quidquid damni pertullerit sine dubio restauretur. 15

15 (A 22) Si porci alterius super annonam noctu manserint, per porcum maiorem quadrisextarium redat.

16 (A 23) Si quis causa fornicationis suspicionem habuerit et non est ei titulus adprobandi, in tribus bassilicis cum propinquis suis a minoribus usque ad maiorem omnibus iuret et nullam habeat causam; quod 20 ⟨si⟩ non iurauerint, ancellam reddat.

17 (A 24) Si quis aetiam aut uaccam aut quod sibi libet pecus perdiderit, cum quo eam inuenire potuerit et cum illo .iii. mensibus fuerit conprobatum, praecipimus triplum accipiendum.

18 (A 26) Si quis paruulus usque annos .xv. quodlibet dilectum 25 commisserit, nihil sub iudice reputatur nisi disciplinam accipiat; ⟨post⟩ hoc autem secundum aetatem et quod furabitur restituat.

19 (A 25) Si porci alterius glandes ingressi fuerint capti, porcastrum se daturum cognoscat.

Quod si spontaneus eos minauerit, porcum maiorem se daturum non 30 dubitet.

20 Si quis furtum seruus fecerit, secundum dilectum fragillis ca⟨e⟩datur et quae furabitur restituat.

21. 22 (A 27) Si quis ingenuus furtum fecerit et in ipso commisso morietur, nullus a suis habeat questionem.   35

(22) Si quis ingenuus aut seruus faciens furtum noctu et in ipso commisso lancea fuerit feritus et mortuus fuerit, qui eum occiderit nullam habeat causam reddendi.

---

16 *cf.* Heb. 8, 11 a minore usque ad maiorem

12 mancipium et quod: mancipia quae A; *lege* mancipium si quod?   13 si *addidi*; *uerba* lesus–rediturum *a can. XXVI transtuli, cf.* A   14 segetem P^c p̄s̄erit P messis P^c 16 si *suppl. Wasserschleben*   17 aetiam: *lege* aequam? (aequam A) *an* aetius *pro* ἔτεος *scribitur? cf. McNeill–Gamer ad loc.*   18 post *addidi, cf.* A
20 fragillis *i.e.* flagellis; *cf.* flagillo 53   22 feritos P

11. If anyone discovers on his farm a horse or an ox or any stolen animal that has been bound or slain, we command that he provide proper compurgators and then he shall have no damages (to pay); but if they do not swear, he shall pay.

12. If anyone commits murder and takes to flight, his relatives shall have a period of fifteen days in which they may make partial restitution and remain secure or themselves leave the country.

After this if the slayer himself wants to come, he shall pay the half that remains and live secure.

But if meanwhile he has been killed, (the victim's kinsmen) shall restore the slaves they have received.[2]

13. If anyone casts a spear at another and the man is uninjured, he shall be compelled to pay one silver pound; if the man was injured, he shall be prepared to make amends according to the blow.

14. If he tramples another's grain field, whatever quantity of the crop the owner with another fit person swears (to have been damaged), the amount of the damage that he suffered shall without question be restored.

15. If hogs stay on another man's grain field through the night, (their owner) shall pay four pints for each full-grown hog.

16. If anyone is under suspicion on account of (an act of) fornication and is not qualified to make proof, he shall swear in three churches with his kinsmen from the youngest to the oldest, and he shall have no trial; but if they do not swear, he shall pay a female slave.

17. If anyone loses a mare[3] or a cow or any beast, with whom he finds it, if it is proved to have been in the person's possession for three months, we command that he be paid by him threefold.

18. If any boy up to the age of fifteen years commits any offence, it is not held to be *sub iudice* except that he is to receive discipline; after this age, however, as befits his years, he shall also restore what he has stolen.

19. If a man's hogs have trespassed (for) acorns and are caught, let him be prepared to give a young pig. But if he on his own account drove them, he shall know for certain that he is to give a full-grown hog.

20. If any slave commits a theft, he shall be beaten with whips according to his fault and shall restore what he has stolen.

21. 22. If any freeborn man commits a theft and dies in the act of committing it, none of his relatives shall hold an inquisition.

(22) If any freeborn man or slave commits a theft by night and in the act of committing it is struck with a spear and killed, he who slays him shall have no need to make restitution.

23 (A 28) Si quis furti causa suspicione habuerit et non est ei titulus conprobandi, res ipsius intra dies aliquot signatur usque aut mendacium eius aut uerum peruenerit in lucem.

24 (A 29) Si quis iuditium conpetitus fuerit et uenire noluerit, hoc ⟨est ut⟩ testibus adprobatur, argenti libram unam cogatur exsoluere et 5 quicquid ad eum fuerit repetitum sine delatione restituat.

XXV (*cf.* A 45) Si quis agrum conparauerit, si culpam non fecerit, heres heredi hereditatem relinquat.

XXVI (*cf.* A 38) Si quis sponte relinquit, nullam habeat uim repetenti.

XXVII (A 17) Si quis causa fornicationis alterius uxorem infecerit, 10 capti morte moriantur et qui eos interfecerit nullam se timeat habere causam.

XXVIII (A 19) Si quis seruum aut ancellam aut quodlibet pecus aut aliquam rem conparauerit et cum ipso fuerit consignatum, nisi auctorem praesteterit aut fideiusores habuerit, furem se nouerit conponendum. 15

XXVIIII (A 20) Si quis †Calfaicum aut Saxonicum caballum conparauerit aut quamlibet speciem, hoc si in testibus conprobetur et cum ipso consignatum fuerit, inuicem sibi testes adequant; si⟨c⟩ ita equale[s] diuidant.

30 (A 20) Quod si quis repetit testes et non habuerit sed mendatium conatur inquirere, triplum se nouerit redditurum. 20

31 (A 21) Si cuius animalia in herba uicini sui intacta manserint, stagni libras .viii. reddat; quod si per istum fuerint capta, stagni libras .iiii. reddat.

32, *recte* XXXI? (A 31) Si quis ancellam aut seruum perdiderit et alium suspectum habuerit, .xxiiii. uiris nominatis et .xii. ex eis iurent 25 eum esse ueracem; quod [xxxi.] si non iurauerint, absque dubio reddat.

33 (A 32) Si caballum perdiderit, inuocatis uiris .vi., ex quibus .iii. iurent, et nihil damni consequetur.

34. Quod si uaccam aut bouem perdiderit, inuocatis ex omnibus .iiii., ex quibus duo iurent, et nihil damni conseque[n]tur. 30

35. Si quis percusserit alterum sic ut os suum superius fregerit, uaccas .iii. reddat.

36 (A 13) Si alterum in faciem alapa ferierit sic ut sanguis aut liuido appareat, argenti libram unam reddat.

37 (*cf.* A 58) Si quis intercedendo litem feritus fuerit, secundum 35 plagam mediam conpossitionem praecipimus accipere.

38 (A 33) Si quis seruus seruum alterius occiderit, uiuus commonis dominorum aexsistat.

---

24 *lege* ⟨*in uel* ad⟩ iuditium? (ad iudicium A)   conpetitur P*   est ut *addidi, cf.* A
XXVI repetenti *i.e.* repetendi. *Verba quae hic sequuntur ad 13 pertinent, ubi uide*
XXVIII aliquem P   XXVIIII hoc si in testibus *scripsi, cf.* A 20: hos ut tib; P
sic *scripsi cum* A   32 xxxi.: *numerus canonis in textum uidetur irrepsisse*   34 ex
omnibus: *lege* hominibus?   35 os suum *McNeill–Gamer*: ossuum P; *lege* ossum?
Cf. Legem Salicam XVII. 3: si quis alterum in caput plagauerit . . . et exinde tria ossa
quae super ipso cerebro iacent exierint   38 exsistat Pᶜ

23. If anyone is under suspicion on account of a theft, and is not qualified to make proof, his property shall be sealed for some days until either his falsehood or his truthfulness shall come to light.

24. If anyone is sued at law and will not come (to trial), that is, in order that his case may be established by witnesses (?), he shall be compelled to pay one silver pound, and whatever is demanded of him he shall make good without delay.

25. If anyone buys a field, if he does no wrong, the heir shall bequeath the inheritance to his heir.

26. If anyone voluntarily relinquishes (a property), he has no power to demand it back.

27. If anyone for the sake of fornication corrupts another's wife, when they are taken they shall be put to death; and he who kills them, let him not fear that he will have any lawsuit.

28. If anyone buys a male slave or a female slave or any beast or anything, and if conveyance has been made to him, unless he produces the *auctor* (i.e. the vendor) or has guarantors, he shall be prepared to compound as for theft.

29. If anyone buys a †4 or a Saxon horse or one of any (other) breed, this being established by witnesses and conveyance being made to him, let there be the same number of witnesses for either party; thus let them part on equal terms (?).

30. But if anyone demands witnesses and he has none, but is attempting to devise deception, he shall be prepared to restore threefold.

31. If anybody's animals stay on his neighbour's grass unharmed, he shall pay eight pounds of silver alloy;5 but if they have been seized by the other person, he shall pay four pounds of silver alloy.

32. If anyone loses his female or male slave, and if he suspects someone, twenty-four men shall be named and twelve of these shall swear that the latter is truthful; but if they do not swear, he shall pay without question.

33. If he loses a horse, six men shall be summoned of whom three shall swear, and no damages shall be awarded.

34. But if he loses a cow or an ox, four out of all shall be summoned of whom two shall swear, and no damages shall be awarded.

35. If anyone strikes another so that he fractures his forehead (?), he shall pay three cows.

36. If anyone strikes another with a slap in the face so that blood or a bruise appears, he shall pay one silver pound.

37. If anyone is struck when interposing in a conflict, we command that he receive half the (ordinary) compensation according to the blow.

38. If any slave kills another's slave, the survivor shall be the joint property of the masters.

39 (A 34. 35) Cuius animal siue bos siue uacca aliam ex cornu occiderit, uiuus et mortuus commones eius erunt.

Quod si taurus uacam aut bouem occiderit, dominus nullam habeat causam reddendi.

40 (A 37) Si laicus clericum qualibet causa conpetire uoluerit, aepi- 5 scopi ueniant arbitrio.

41 (A 37) Si clericus laicum conpetire uoluerit, ad iudicis †penitentiam debent uenire.

42 (A 38) Si quis in mortem hereditatem dimiserit, quicquid coram testibus demandauerit omnia manere praecipimus nec remoueri.   10

43 (A 42) Si qua contentio circa finem territori fuerit exorta, testes requirantur et finis qui prius fuerat ipse permaneat.

44 (A 43) Clericus uero si causa fuerit conpetitus et nulla in eum fama fuit cognita, ipsius iure causa difiniatur.

45 (A 43) Quod si antea famam portauerat, indictis iuratoribus laico 15 more causa difiniatur.

46 (A 37) Si quis commisso delecto ex spontanea uoluntate ⟨ad⟩ confessionem uenerit ad sacerdotem, a nullo eum damnari praecipimus.

47 (A 37) Quod si negare uoluerit et ab alio fuerit conprobatum et si in rebelli †tempore hoc fecesse cognoscetur, praetium suum in iuditio 20 reddat et triplum se daturum cognoscat.

48 (A 44) Si quis Deum inuocauerit in fideiusorem et contempserit eum, a iudici condictione dampnetur.

49 (A 45) Si quis agrum aut uillam conparauerit et ipse capitale furtum fecerit, morte morietur et terram quam emerat in fisco reuertetur. 25

50 (A 45) Quod si filius aut filia aut frater furtum fecerit et fugam petierit, ancellam aut seruum reddat et agrum possideat.

Quod si ⟨in⟩nocentes permanserint, heris heredibus derelinquat.

51 (A 12) Si quis alapa alium †occiderit sic ut nec sanguis nec liuido appareat, solidos .v. exsoluat.   30

52 (A 46) Si quis ante aeclesiam litem fecerit, argenti libram unam cogitur exsoluere et hoc aegentibus elimosina feneretur.

53 Si quis alterum flagillo percusserit, argenti libram exsoluat unam. Si ante aeclesiam, aeclesiae et elimosina deputetur.

54 (A 48) Si quis ancellam aut seruum emerit et ante impletum 35 annum uitium in eum apparuerit, priori domino reddi iubemus.

55 (A 48) Quod si annus transierit, quincquid (sic) in mancipium uitii fuerit, nullam uenditor habeat causam.

39 eius *i.e. domini uaccae mortuae; sed fort.* lege eorum, *cf.* A 34   40 conpetere P[c]
noluerit P   41 conpetere P[c]   penitentiam: *fort.* lege presentiam, *cf. lect. uar. ad.*
A 37   44 conpertitus P*   iure: iuramento A   45 famem P*   indicįtis P
46 ex spontanea *Wasserschleben*: exportare P (sponte A)   ad *suppleui cum McNeill–
Gamer, cf.* A   47 fecisse P[c]   49 capitale *scripsi cum* A: capitulas P   50 inno-
centes *ego, cf.* A: nocentes P (inocentes *sine adnotatione Wasserschleben*)   heres P[c]
51 occiderit: *lege* ceciderit?   52 elimonsina P*

39. If anybody's animal, whether ox or cow, kills another with its horn, the live one and the dead one shall be the joint property of the owners.[6]

But if a bull kills a cow or an ox, his owner shall have no need to make restitution.

40. If a layman wishes to sue a cleric in any cause, they shall seek the arbitration of a bishop.[7]

41. If a cleric wishes to sue a layman, they ought to come to a judge for decision.[8]

42. If anyone disposes of an inheritance at his death we command that whatever he has declared to be his will before witnesses shall all remain and not be rescinded.

43. If any contention has arisen over the boundary of a piece of land, witnesses shall be procured and the boundary which existed before shall remain the same.

44. If a cleric has been sued in a case and nothing is known against his reputation, the case shall be determined on his own oath.[9]

45. But if he previously bore an ill reputation, compurgators shall be summoned and the case shall be determined as if he were a layman.

46. If anyone having committed a fault comes to a priest for confession of his own will, we command that he be not condemned by anybody.

47. But if he is resolved to deny it and it is proved by another, even if he is known to have done this in time of rebellion,[10] he shall pay his own price in court and be prepared to give thrice (the ordinary compensation).

48. If anyone calls God to witness and despises Him, he shall be condemned by a solemn decision of the court.

49. If anyone buys a field or a farm, and if he commits a capital theft, he shall be put to death and the land which he has bought shall be confiscated.

50. But if his son or daughter or brother commits the theft and he takes to flight, he shall pay a female slave or a male slave and possess the field.

But if they remain innocent, the heir shall bequeath it to his heirs.

51. If anyone gives a slap to another so that neither blood nor bruise appears, he shall pay five solidi.

52. If anyone makes strife in front of a church, he is compelled to pay one silver pound, and this shall be given as alms to the needy.

53. If anyone strikes another with a whip, he shall pay one silver pound.

If in front of a church, alms shall also fall due to the church.

54. If anyone buys a female slave or a male slave, and if a fault appears in him before the completion of a year, we command that he be returned to his former master.

55. But if a year has elapsed, whatever fault there is in the slave, the vendor shall have no need (to make restitution).

56 (A 49) Si quis caballum conparauerit, in mense uno si uitium non apparuerit, nullo modo reuertetur.

57 (cf. A 51) Si quis caballum ante latronem excusserit, si in una patria, .ui. scripulos accipiat.

Si in alia, flumine transmisso, tertiam partem praetii eius accipiat.   5

58 (A 50) Si quis alterum fuste ferierit et sanguinem discurrerit, uaccam reddat. Quod si maiorem fecerit, secundum ⟨leges⟩ conponendum praecipimus aliam.

59 (A 52) Si ancellam aut seruum in fugam praeserit parte qua poterant euadere per dua milia siue .iii., tertiam partem praetii eorum 10 merito accipiat; aliter: si ancella fuit, libras argenti .ii. merito accipiat qui capit eam; si seruus, .iii. stagni libras accipiat.

60 (A 53) Si quis caballum indicauerit et eum capere potuerit, merito tertiam praetii eius accipiat siue unam unciam.

61 (A 53) Nullus uillae capitalis alterius siluam deteneat nec humidam 15 nec siccam nec algam maris nisi per boues per herba det.

LXII (A 53) Si quis fecerit aliud, reprobatur.

LXIII (A 54) Si quis caballum alterius †inpastoriauerit† et ⟨ut⟩ suum pastoriauerit, si pastoriam agnouerit sine dubio cum caballo, non dubitet inuadere et suum proprium eum esse praecipimus.   20

L⟨X⟩IIII (A 55) Si quis capitalis uicinum minauerit, etiam si uoluntarius ire uoluerit, siue domum siue hortum uendendi habet potestatem praeter sepis quae circumit mesis et herbas.

LXV (A 57) Si laicus clericum ferierit, et dictis ⟨legibus⟩ manum redimat et ad paenitentiam ueniat.   25

66 (A 56) Si quis autem clericus laicum ferierit, secundum plagam laico ordine sine dubio reddat.

67 (A 58) Si quis litem intercederit et a mendace feritus fuerit, secundum plagam legibus se nouerit conponendum.

Quod si ⟨a⟩ uerace fuerit feritus, mediam a uerace et mediam a 30 mendace conpossitionem iubemus accipere.

Hoc et de morte simili modo dicimus.

---

58 sanguinem discurrerit *mihi suspectum*   *lege* maiorem ⟨plagam⟩ *cum* A?   leges *addidi, cf.* 67   conponendum *ego, cf.* conponi A: conponendi P   59 .iii. (1) *McNeill–Gamer*: in P   libras (2) *McNeill–Gamer*: libẹra unam P; *fort. legendum* .iii. stagni ⟨libras et argenti⟩ libra⟨m⟩ unam   60 *lege* tertiam ⟨partem⟩? *cf.* 57. 59 61 alterius: altīī P, *cf.* A 53   LXIII: *quem canonem nemo iam probabiliter interpretatus est. Is qui legitur sub* A 54 *ex hoc uidetur fluxisse. Si Ducangius uocem* pastoriam *recte ut* pedicam *explanat (s.u.* Pastorium, *VI. 205* 'compedes quibus equi, ne aberrent in pascuis, impediuntur'), pastoriare *idem est atque in* pedicam *ruere* A 54. *Pro* inpastoriauerit *fortasse legendum est in* pastora (*i.e.* pasturam) minauerit. *Si quis equum alterius in suis pascuis alligauit, domino equum suum, si agnouit, sibi licet uindicare*   LXV legibus *add. McNeill–Gamer, cf.* A   67 ⟨a⟩ uerace *ego, cf.* A

56. If anyone buys a horse, if no fault appears in him during one month, he shall by no means be returned.

57. He who recovers a horse from a robber, if (it is) in the same country, he shall receive six scripuli.

If in another country, a river having been crossed, he shall receive the third part of its value.

58. If anyone strikes another with a cudgel and draws blood, he shall pay a cow. But if he inflicts a heavier (blow), we command that composition shall be made with a second cow according to the laws.

59. If (anyone) arrests a female slave or a male slave in flight in a place where they could escape for two miles or three, he shall receive in reward the third part of their value. Alternatively: if it was a female slave, he who captures her shall receive as a reward two silver pounds, if a male slave, three pounds of silver alloy.

60. If anyone spots a horse and is able to catch it, he shall receive as a reward the third part of its value, or one uncia.

61. No man shall hold the woodland of a farm of another high-man[11] whether (it is) wet or dry, nor his seaweed, unless he gives it for oxen as fodder.

62. If anyone does otherwise, he shall be censured.

63. If anyone has driven the horse of another to his (own) pasture and fettered it for grazing as if it were his own, if (the owner) recognizes beyond doubt his horse in fetters, he shall not hesitate to go into (the pasture) and we determine that the horse is his own.[12]

64. If any high-man threatens his neighbour, and also if he voluntarily decides to go away, he has power to sell either his house or his garden except the hedge that surrounds the crops and grass.

65. If a layman strikes a cleric, he shall both redeem his hand according to the stated ⟨laws⟩ and come to penance.

66. But if any cleric strikes a layman, he shall without question pay according to the blow as if he were a layman.

67. If anyone intercedes in a dispute and is struck by the one who is lying, he shall be prepared to make composition by the laws according to the blow.

But if he was struck by the one who is speaking the truth, we command that he receive composition half from the one who is speaking the truth and half from the liar.

In like manner also we say this (is to be done) in case of (his) death.

CANONES HIBERNENSES

I

DE DISPUTATIONE HIBERNENSIS SINODI ET GRIGORI NASASENI
SERMO DE INNUMERABILIBUS PECCATIS INCIPIT

1. Paenitentia parricidi .xiiii. anni, uel semis, si ignorantiae causa, in pane et aqua et satisfactione.

2. Haec est paenitentia homicidi, .vii. anni. In pane et aqua agitur. 5

3. Penitentia homicidi .vii. anni in pane et aqua, uel .x., ut dicit †monochoma.

4. Haec est poenitentia magi uel uotiui mali si⟨ue⟩ crudelis, †iddem ergach,† uel praeconis uel cohabitatoris uel heretici uel adulteri, id est .vii. anni in pane et aqua. 10

5. Poenitentia concoitus mulieri .vii. ⟨anni⟩ in pane et aqua. Poenitentia concoitus conuicinae .xiiii. anni uel .viiii.

6. Poenitentia perditionis liquoris matiriae filii in utero matris .iii. anni et semis.

7. Poenitentia perditionis carnis et animae .vii. et semis in pane et 15 aqua et castitate.

8. Praetium animae de perditione liquoris et mulieris .xii. ancillae.

9. xii. altilia uel .xiii. sicli praetium unius cuiusque ancillae.

10. Praetium animae de perditionem filii et mulieris .xii. ancellae.

11. Poenitentia de perditione mulieris de suo filio .xii. anni in pane et 20 aqua.

12. Poenitentia de bibitione sanguinis uel urinae .vii. anni et semis in pane et aqua et inpossitione manus aepiscopi postea.

13. Poenitentia essus carnis aequi .iiii. anni in pane et aqua.

14. Poenitentia essus carnis quam canes comederunt .xl. dies in pane 25 et aqua.

15. Poenitentia essus carnis morticini pecoris .xlii. in pane et aqua.

16. Poenitentia inlicite bibitionis canis annus unus.

Codex: P, fol. 138^{r-v}

---

1 Nasaseni, *i.e.* Nazianzeni *in exemplari uidetur fuisse, cf.* Nazasenus B, *p. 177*: hasasemi P   4 panis P   7 monochoma *uox incerta; de coniecturis u.* McNeill–Gamer, *pp. 118 sq.*   8 siue *ego*   crudelis Stokes *et dubitanter* O. Bergin, *cf.* McNeill–Gamer, *p. 119, adn. 14*: credulus P   8 sq. iddem ergach: id est díbergach Stokes, Thes. Palaeohib. *ii. 38*   9 praeconis: praedonis *K.* Meyer, Rev. celt. xv. *493*, adn. 2; sed cf. Coll. Hibern. XLIV. *8;* McNeill–Gamer, pp. *70; 119, adn. 15*   adulteri, id est *ego*: adulterii, *i.e.* adulteri .i., P   11 Poenitentia–aqua *in marg.* P anni *ins.* Wasserschleben   12 uel .viiii. *a scriba de exemplari dubitante additum esse suspicor*   18 can. *9 fortasse glossema erat canonis 8*   .xiii.: .xii. F. Seebohm, Anglo-Saxon Law, *p. 105*   19 ancillae P^c 22 urinae: urirę P

IRISH CANONS

I

OF THE DECISION OF AN IRISH SYNOD AND OF GREGORY NAZIANZEN. A DISCOURSE CONCERNING UNNUMBERED SINS[1]

1. The penance for parricide is fourteen years, or half as long if (it was committed) on account of ignorance, on bread and water and with satisfaction.[2]

2. This is the penance for homicide, seven years. It shall be performed on bread and water.

3. The penance for homicide (is) seven years on bread and water, or as Monochoma says, ten.[3]

4. This is the penance of a wizard, or of one who has vowed himself to evil, or a malefactor[4] or of a hawker, or of a cohabiter, or of a heretic, or of an adulterer: seven years on bread and water.

5. The penance for intercourse with a woman, seven years on bread and water. The penance for intercourse with a neighbour woman, fourteen years or nine.

6. The penance for the destruction of the embryo of a child in the mother's womb, three and a half years.

7. The penance for the destruction of flesh and spirit, seven and a half years on bread and water, in continence.

8. The life price for the destruction of the embryo and the mother, twelve female slaves.

9. Twelve fowls or thirteen[5] shekels[6] are the value of each female slave.

10. The life-price for the destruction of the child and the mother, twelve female slaves.

11. The penance for a mother's destruction of her own child, twelve years on bread and water.

12. The penance for drinking blood or urine, seven and a half years on bread and water, followed by the imposition of the hand of the bishop.

13. The penance for eating horseflesh, four years on bread and water.

14. The penance for eating flesh which dogs have been eating, forty days on bread and water.

15. The penance for eating the flesh of a dead beast, forty-two days[7] on bread and water.

16. The penance for the illicit drinking of (what has been contaminated by) a dog, one year.

---

25 carnis *bis* P*   27 morticinione (one *deletum*) P   .xlii.: .xl. dies *McNeill–*
Gamer, nescio an recte   28 inliciti P

17. Poenitentia bibitionis aquilae uel curbi uel graule uel galli uel gallinae .l. dies in pane et aqua.

18. Poenitentia bibitionis inlici⟨tae⟩ muricipis .v. dies in pane et aqua et superpossitio.

19. Poenitentia inlicitae bibitionis de morticina pecoris .xl. dies et 5 noctes in pane et aqua.

20. Poenitentia inlicitae bibitionis morticine muris .vii. dies in pane et aqua.

21. Poenitentia bibitionis inlicite laici uel laicae .l. dies in pane et aqua.

22. Poenitentia manducandi uel dormitandi in eadem domo uel in 10 uno lecto cum laico uel laica .xl. dies cum pane et aqua.

23. Poenitentia bibitionis inlicitae glantelle prignantis uel cohabitatoris sui .xl. diebus in pane et aqua.

24. Poenitentia manducationis in una domo uel in una singa cum eis .xl. diebus in pane et aqua. 15

25. Poenitentia dormiendi cum eis in una domo .xx. dies in pane et aqua.

26. Poenitentia bardigi †capalbiae post laicum uel laicam .l. dies in pane et aqua.

27. Si post glantellam in utero habentem uel post cohabitatorem suum, .xl. dies in pane et aqua. 20

28. Si post clericum plebis, .xx. dies in pane et aqua.

29. Si post hanchoritam uel episcopum uel scribam uel principem magnum uel post regem iustum, .xv. dies in pane et aqua.

II

P: B:

De arreis incipit.

1. Arreum superpossitionis .c. 25
ψalmi et .c. flectiones genuum uel
ter quinquageni et cantica .vii.

2. Arreum ⟨anni⟩ triduan⟨um⟩ i.   Arreum anni tridui dies et noctes
nox et dies in statione sine somno   sine sede et somno nisi paulisper

---

1 graule, *i.e.* gracule, *cf. Georges, Lexicon der lat. Wortformen, p. 305* (graculi *McNeill–Gamer; de formis* graulus, -a *cf. Thes. Ling. Lat. VI. 2133, 46;* W. Meyer-Lübke, *Roman. Etymol. Wörterbuch (1911), pp. 256 f.* 3 inlicī P 17 bardigi capalbiae: bardicationis glandellae *Poen. Bigot. IV. 6, 2* 2 diēm P 22 hanc horitam P

Codices: P, foll. 138ᵛ–139ʳ; B, p. 177
Titulus: De arreis incipit, *litteris minusculis sine intermissione,* P   CANONES
SENODI HIBERNIAE ET ḠḠ NAZASENUS B (*cf.* P, *fol. 138ʳ*)

P:

26 flecsiones Pᶜ   27 ter quinquageni
scripsi: .iii. quingenta P   28 anni *supplevi, cf.* B   triduanum i. *ego*; triduani P

17. The penance for the drinking of (what has been contaminated by) an eagle or a crow or a daw or a cock or a hen, fifty days on bread and water.

18. The penance for the illicit drinking of (what has been contaminated by) a cat, five days on bread and water and a special fast.

19. The penance for the illicit drinking of (what has been contaminated by) the carcass of a beast, forty days and nights on bread and water.

20. The penance for the illicit drinking of (what has been contaminated by) the dead body of a mouse, seven days on bread and water.

21. The penance for the illicit drinking of (what has been contaminated by) a layman or a laywoman, fifty days on bread and water.

22. The penance for eating or sleeping in the same house or in the same bed with a layman or a laywoman, forty days on bread and water.

23. The penance for the illicit drinking of (what has been contaminated by) a pregnant servant woman[8] or by him who cohabits with her, forty days on bread and water.

24. The penance for eating in the same house or in the same tent (?)[9] with them, forty days on bread and water.

25. The penance for sleeping in the same house with them, twenty days on bread and water.

26. The penance for the wailing . . . after (the death of) a layman or a laywoman, fifty days on bread and water.

27. If (the dirge is sung) after (the death of) a servant woman with child, or after (the death of) him who cohabits with her, forty days on bread and water.

28. If after (the death of) a cleric of the parish, twenty days on bread and water.

29. If after (the death of) an anchorite or a bishop or a scribe[10] or a great prince or a righteous king, fifteen days on bread and water.

II

OF COMMUTATIONS[1]

P:

1. The commutation of a special fast, one hundred psalms and one hundred genuflexions, or the three fifties and seven canticles.[2]

2. The commutation of a year, a three-day period (of penance), that is, a night and a day in a station[3] without sleep except

B:

2. The commutation of a year, days and nights of a three-day period without a seat or sleep except a little, and the one hundred

nisi paruum uel .iii.l. ψalmi cum canticis et cum missa horarum .xii. et .xii. flectiones in una quaque hora et manus sopinatae ad orationem.

3. Arreum anni triduanum cum mortuo sancto in sepulchro sine cibo et putu et sine somno sed cum uestimento circa se et cantatione ψalmorum et oratione horarum post confessionem et uotum sacerdoti.

4. Arreum anni triduanus in aeclesia sine cibo et potu et somno et ⟨cum⟩ uestitu sine sede et canticum ψalmorum cum canticis et oratione horarum et in eis .xii. genuculationes post confessionem peccatorum coram sacerdote et plebe post uotum.

5. Arreum anni .xii. dies et noctes super .xii. bucellos de tribus panibus, qui efficiuntur de tertia parte *coaid siir throscho*.

6. Arreum anni .xii. triduani.

7. Arreum anni mensis in dolore magno ut dubi[b]us sit de uita.

8. Arreum ⟨anni⟩ .xl. dies in pane et aqua, et superpossitio in singulis ebdomadibus et .xl. ψalmi et flectiones .xl. et horarumque oratio.

uel .cl. psalmi[s] cum .x. canticis stando et orando in omni hora, .xii. quoque flectiones genuum flectuntur in omni hora orandi, et palmae supernae ad orationem. 5

Arreum anni triduum cum mortuo sancto in uno sepulchro sine cibo potuque ac sine dormitatione, praecinctus uestimento suo, et cum cantico psalmorum et cum 10 [ad]oratione horarum post confessionem peccatorum sacerdoti et post uotum.

Arreum anni triduum in eclesia sine dormitatione cum uestimento 15 circa se sine sede, et canticum psalmorum cum canticis sine intermissione, et misa unius cuiusque horae et .xii. inflectiones unius cuiusque horae post confessionem 20 peccatorum coram sacerdote et plebe, et post uotum.

Arreum anni .xii. dies et noctes super .xii. bucellas mensurae de tribus panibus. 25

Arreum anni .xii. triduanas (*sic*).

Arreum anni mensis in dolore magno, sed de quo non moritur quis iterata postmodum uita ad 30 iudicium sacerdotis.

Arreum anni .xl. dies et noctes in pane et aqua et duae superpositiones uni cuique ebdomadae; .xl. psalmi et .xl. inflectiones in 35 una quaque hora horandi.

11 post *scripsi cum* B: per P   16 cum *addidi, cf.* B   26 *de uerbis Godelicis uide Thes. Palaeohib. ii. 38*   29 dubibus: *corr. McNeill–Gamer*   32 anni *suppleui, cf.* B   35 .xl. *scripsi cum* B: lx P, *cf. can. 9*

B:
    20 post *scripsi cum* P: per B   23–27: *can. 6 legitur ante 5 in* B

a little, or the three times fifty psalms with canticles, and the office[4] of the twelve hours, and twelve genuflexions in each hour, with the hands extended[5] for prayer.

3. The commutation of a year, three days with a dead saint in a tomb without food or drink and without sleep, but with a garment about him and with the chanting of the psalms and with the prayer of the hours, after confession of sins and after a vow (of amendment) made to a priest.

4. The commutation of a year, a three-day period in a church without food, drink, or sleep, ⟨with⟩ a garment, without a seat; and the chanting of the psalms with the canticles and the praying of the hours; and in these twelve genuflexions after confession of sins in the presence of priest and people, after a vow.

5. The commutation of a year, twelve days and nights on twelve biscuits[6] amounting to the size of three loaves, which are made of the third part of the food of long fasting.

6. The commutation of a year, twelve three-day periods.

7. The commutation of a year, a month in great pain, so that he is in doubt of his life.

8. The commutation ⟨of a year⟩, forty days on bread and water and a special fast in each week and forty psalms and forty[7] genuflexions and the praying of the hours.

and fifty psalms with ten canticles, standing and praying at every hour; also twelve genuflexions are made at every hour of praying, and the palms of the hands are turned upwards at prayer.

The commutation of a year, three days with a dead saint in one tomb without food and drink, without sleep, clad in one's garment, with the singing of the psalms and the praying of the hours after confession of sins to a priest and after a vow.

The commutation of a year, a three-day period in a church without sleep, with one's garment around one, without a seat; and the singing of the psalms with the canticles without a break, and the office of every single hour, and twelve genuflexions at every hour, after confession of sins in the presence of priest and people, and a vow.

The commutation of a year, twelve days and nights on twelve biscuits amounting to three loaves.

The commutation of a year, twelve three-day periods.

The commutation of a year, a month in great pain, but of which no one dies, (normal) life being afterwards resumed at the judgement of a priest.

The commutation of a year, forty days and nights on bread and water and two special fasts in each week; forty psalms and forty genuflexions at every hour of prayer.

M

9. Arreum anni .l. dies in longa superpossitione et .lx. ᵼalmi et flecti⟨ones et⟩ horarum oratio.

Arreum anni .l. dies et noctes in pane et aqua in mensura; .lx. psalmi et .lx. inflectiones in una quaque hora horandi.

10. Arreum anni .xl. dies *fordobor 7 ith* et superpossitiones due omnis ebdomadis; .xl. ᵼalmi et flecti(ones) et oratio omnis horae.

11. Arreum anni .c. dies in pane et aqua et oratio omnis horae.

Arreum anni dies .c. in pane et aqua; missa in omni hora horandi.

12. Haec omnia ieiunia sine carne et uino nisi paruum de herbisa in cella aliena per tempus.

Penitentia illorum annorum per lungum, quorum arreum in his praedictis emittitur, sine carne et uino et butyro et lacte dulci agatur.

III (Wasserschleben VI)

ITEM SYNODUS SAPIENTIUM: SIC DE DECIMIS DISPUTANT 15

1. Dicunt auctores decimas semel peccorum offerendas, et ob id *sanctum sanctorum erit*, id est, non debetur iterum offerri de illis decimam. Sed alii sana fide adfirmant ut omni anno decimas de uitalibus et mortalibus Deo demus, cum omni anno ipsius munera habemus.

2. Item: Omnia praeter fruges terrae ⟨de⟩ quibus decima semel 20 offeretur Domino ut dicitur *Quicquid consecratum fuerit semel* Deo *sanctum sanctorum erit Domino*, non iterum debet de illis offerri decimam, ut Colummanus doctor docuit. Fruguum uero terrae in uno quoque anno decima pars offerri debet quia in uno quoque anno nascuntur.

3. Item: Decimae non solum per animantia sed per mortalia fiunt. Ita et 25 primitiae, id est primus fructus omnis rei et animal quod primum nascitur in anno, similia quae sunt ut primitiua. Primogenita autem animalium tantum [non solum hominum sed animalium] quae licita sunt immolari.

17 Ex. 30, 10; Leu. 27, 28   21 sq. Leu. 27, 28 (XΩM)   27 sq. *cf.* Ex. 13, 2; 34, 19 sqq.

Codices: CB

5 dies *McNeill–Gamer*; añ. xl. añ P
5–6 fordobor 7 ith *Stokes, Thes. Palaeohib. ii. 38*; fordo bor fiit P

In B post 14 *adduntur haec*: Qui cum cane uel cum quo animali peccauerit .ii. anñ et dimedium. Qui facit scelus uirile ut sodomitae .iiii. anñ peniteat. Qui uero inferioribus (*lege* in femoribus) .iii. anñ peniteat in pane et aqua totum, si post uotum perfectionis. si autem ante, annus deminuitur de omnibus his tribus. *Cf. Syn. Luc. Uict. can. 7–9*

15 SAPIENTIUM *ego*: SAPIEÑ C. SAPIENTIA B   16 peͅcorum, -ibus *semper fere* B
18 sane C   20 de *inserui*   semel: simul C   22 domino. Non B
23 Columbanus (-banus *eras.*) manus C   frugum B   25 sed *scripsi, cf.* 28: sunt

9. The commutation of a year, fifty days in a long special fast and sixty psalms and genuflexions ⟨and⟩ the praying of the hours.

The commutation of a year, fifty days and nights on an allowance of bread and water; sixty psalms and sixty bows (?) at every hour of prayer.

10. The commutation of a year, forty days on a water diet[8] and two special fasts each week; (and) forty psalms and genuflexions and prayer every hour (*or*: the praying of every hour ?).

11. The commutation of a year, a hundred days on bread and water and prayer every hour (*or*: the praying of every hour ?).

The commutation of a year, a hundred days on bread and water; the office at every hour of prayer.

12. All these fasts (are) without flesh and wine, except a little beer in another's church on occasion.

The penance of those years, the equivalents of which are stated, (when performed) at length, is to be performed without meat, wine, butter, and sweet milk.

III

ALSO A SYNOD OF THE WISE: THUS THEY TEACH CONCERNING TITHES*

1. The authorities say that the tithes of the flock ought to be offered once, and therefore *it shall be most holy*, that is, a tithe ought not to be offered out of these a second time. But others in sound faith affirm that we are to give to God tithes, every year, of animals and human beings, since we have also His benefits every year.

2. Further: with respect to all (produce), except the fruits of the ground, of which a tithe is once offered to the Lord, (we should do) as it is said: *Whatever is once consecrated* to God *shall be holy of holies to the Lord*; for these the tithe ought not again to be offered, as saith Colman,[1] the teacher. Of the fruits of the ground, however, the tenth part ought to be offered each year, since they spring up each year.

3. Further: Tithes are not only for animal creatures, they apply to human beings (also). And so the 'first fruits', that is, the first fruits of everything, and the animal which is first born in the year, which is similar to the first fruits. The first-born, however, of those animals only which may be sacrificed.

CB (sunt C *fol. 62^r, b 2, ubi* sed *recte* B)   28 non–animalium *ut glossema*
(*ad l. 25 spectans?*) *deleui* inlicita C

4. Item: Decimae in peccoribus sunt et in fructibus terrae; uel: decimae in peccoribus, primitiae in fructibus. Primitiae sunt quicquid de peccoribus nascitur antequam nascentur alia hoc anno.

5. Sciendum quantum est pondus primitiarum, hoc est gomor; ut alii, .i. viiii. panes uel .xii. panes; deinde panes propossitionis materia .viiii. panium uel .xii. panium. De oleribus uero quantum pugnus capere potest. Hae res initio estatis reddi debent, et semel in anno ad sacerdotes Hierusalem offerebantur. In nouo autem unus quisque ad monasterium cui monachus fuerit. Et praeterea caritas habundat cum hisdem, et primogenita in masculis tantum, numquam in feminis fiunt.

6. Item ut alii: Si minus decimo substantiam habuerit, non reddet decimas.

7. Item ut alii: Quo modo conuenit offerre decimas aliquis Domino si non habuerit nisi unam uacam uel bouem? Diuidat praetium uacce in .x. et det decimam partem Domino; sic et reliqua.

8. Item: Uictimam uoluntariam Dominus praecipit. Ideo dicit: *Nemo tollat* animam *a me* et reliqua. De eo quod non uindicat Deus neque homines debent uindicari et in his qui cito conuertunt de culpa ad penitentiam in Exodo legitur †quod adoratione† uituli: Et stans Moyses in porta castrorum ait: *Si quis* †*deo iungatur mihi. Et congregati sunt ad eum omnes filii Leui, quibus ait: Haec dicit Dominus Deus Israel: Ponat uir gladium super femor suum* et reliqua usque dicit *Occidat unus quisque proximum et fratrem et amicum.* Et paulo post ait Moyses: *Consecrastis manus uestras hodie Domino unus quisque in filio et fratre suo ut detur uobis benedictio.* Finit amen.

Populus Israel debuerat constringui .x. mandatis legis dum causa ipsorum percusit Deus Egyptum .x. plagis; ideo decim mandata sunt. Ubi sunt in lege praecepta quae Deus non praecipit? Iethro socer Moysi elegere .lxx. principes qui iudicarent populum cum Moysi, et hoc iudicium est, quia si inuenerimus iudicia gentium bona, que natura bona illis docet et Deo non displicet, seruabimus.

---

4 gomor: *cf.* Ex. 16, 16. 36   5 panes propossitionis: *cf.* Ex. 25, 30
17 Ioh. 10, 18 (tollit VULG tollet D 1 δ)   20–25 Ex. 32, 26–29: *fere congruit cum*
VULG (*sed* 20 congregatique VULG, 23 fratrem et amicum et proximum suum
VULG)   28–29 *cf.* Ex. 18, 21–22

---

3 ⟨in⟩ hoc B   5 uel .xii. B: lxii C   p̄possitionis (-osi- B) CB
6 .xii. B: cxii C   7 ⟨in⟩ initio B, *cf.* 3   14 si *om.* C   uaccam B   uaccae B
18 *lege* conuert⟨er⟩unt?   19 quod (*per compendium scriptum*) adoratione C; pro
ad. B: *fort.* quod ⟨ad⟩ adoratione   20 deo CB; est Domini VULG *Ex. 32, 26*
23 moysen CB: *corr. Wasserschleben*   23 sq. consedastis C   24 ⟨in⟩ fratre B,
cf. Ex. 32, 29 Lugd. TEST VULG^pl *cum* LXX   27 ideo: deo C   28 Iethro
(inethro C)] *s.l. add.* .s. dixit CB

4. Further: Tithes are in the flocks and in the fruits of the ground; or, tithes are in the flocks, first fruits in the fruits (of the ground). First fruits are whatever is born of the flocks before others are born in that year.

5. To know what is the amount of the first fruits, that is, an omer;[2] as others (say), it is nine loaves or twelve loaves; then 'loaves of proposition', the material of nine loaves or of twelve loaves. Of vegetables, as much as the hand can hold. These things ought to be presented at the beginning of harvest, and they were offered once in the year to the priests at Jerusalem. In the new (dispensation), however, each person to the monastery of which he is a monk.[3] And besides charity abounds in these, and the first-born are in males only, never in females.

6. Further, as others say: if he has too little property for a tithe (*or*: less property than the amount of the tithe?) he shall not pay tithes.

7. Further, as others (say): How is it proper for anyone to offer tithes to the Lord if he has nought but one cow or ox? He shall divide the value of the cow in ten and give the tenth part to the Lord. So also in other cases.

8. Further: The Lord commands a willing victim. Therefore he saith: *No man may take* my life *away from me*, and so forth. Of the fact that God does not forcibly claim (anybody) and that men ought not to be so claimed it is read also in Exodus in the case of those who quickly turn⟨ed⟩ from guilt to penance, concerning the adoration of the calf:[4] 'And standing in the gate of the camp, Moses said: *If any man be for God, let him join with me; and all the sons of Levi gathered themselves together unto him, and he said unto them: Thus saith the Lord God of Israel: Put (every) man his sword upon his thigh*', and so forth, till he saith: *Let every man kill his neighbour and his brother and his friend.* And a little farther on Moses saith: *You have consecrated your hands this day to the Lord, every man in his son and in his brother, that a blessing may be given unto you.* Here endeth, Amen.[5]

The people of Israel had to be ruled by the Ten Commandments of the law, since for the sake of these God smote the Egyptians with the ten plagues; therefore are there ten commandments. Where are precepts in the law which God did not command? (For example) Jethro the kinsman of Moses told Moses to choose seventy leading men who would judge the people with Moses; and this is a judgement, (to the effect) that if we find judgements of the heathen good, which their good nature teaches them, and it is not displeasing to God, we shall keep them.

IV (Wasserschleben III)

1. Sanguis episcopi uel excelsi principis uel scribae qui ad terram effunditur, si colirio indiguerit, eum qui effuderit sapientes crucifigi iudicant uel .vii. ancellas reddat. 2. Si in specie, tertiam partem de argento et conparem uerticis de auro latitudinem nec non et similem 5 occuli de gemma praeciosa magnitudinem reddat; 3. et pro eius liuoris uel uulneris admiratione in conuentu uel in qualibet multitudine usque ad tertium annum aut eo amplius, si non indulgeat, praetium ancelle si qui comisit reddat.

4. Si uero sanguis episcopi ad terram non perueniat nec colirio indigeat, 10 manus percutientis abscidatur aut dimedium .vii. ancillarum reddat, si de industria; si autem non de industria, praetium ancille tribuat.

5. Qui uero episcopum sine effussione sanguinis peruserit uel eum motauerit, dimedium .vii. ancillarum praetium reddat.

6. Si autem aliquid de capillis eius carptum fuerit, sedatium unius 15 cuiusque capilli, id est duodecim scripuli, usque .xx. de utroque reddatur. Licet enim maius euulsum fuerit, quasi proprium reddi non dicitur.

7. Sanguis presbiteri qui ad terram effunditur donec colirium subfert, manus interfectoris abscidatur uel dimedium .vii. ancellarum reddat si de industria; si autem non de industria, ancellae pretio sanetur. 20

8. Si ad terram non perueniat, percusor ancellam reddat. Si in specie eius, tertiam partem de argento retribuat. Percusio eius ancelle praetio restituatur, motatio eius ut praediximus sanetur.

(9). PATRICIUS DICIT. Omnis qui ausus fuerit ea que sunt regis uel episcopi aut scribae furari aut rapere aut aliquod in eos committere 25 paruipendens dispicere, .vii. ancillarum praetium reddat aut .vii. annis peniteat cum episcopo uel scriba.

---

can. 6 *cf.* Ancient Laws of Ireland, iii. 353; iv. 363. 365　　　24–27 Coll. Hibern. XLVIII. 5 ('sinodus Hibernensis')

Codices: CB (C², fol. 70ᵛ; B², p. 305) W

2 sanguinem C²B²　　2–3 ad–effunditur *om.* W　　3 sic olirio B　indigerit W　　4 iudicant: dixerunt W　ancellas WC²: ancillas *cett.* redat W (*et saepius*) uel vii annis peñ *add.* W　　4 Si–reddat *om.* W　　in *bis* C　　6 occuli C: oculi *cett.*　　7 uel (1) *om.* C　usque: ut B²　　8 ancell- *hic et saepius* C² *solus*　　9 comisit C: com-(cum-)misit *cett.*　　10 peruenit C²B²W　indiget W　　11 abscidatur: interficiatur W demedium W　redat ⟨uel demedium .vii. añ. peñ.⟩ W　　11 sq. si de: sine C　　12 si-tribuat *om.* W　　non *om.* CB　　13 effusione B　percusserit BW　　13 sq. eum motauerit (mut- C²B²): comotauerit W　　14 demediam W　praetium: partem W re^ddat ⟨uel .iii. añ et dimedium peni-⟩ W　　*desinit* W　　16 cuiusque: quisque C id est *om.* C²B²　scripuli *ego*: discipuli *codd.* (de capillis *McNeill–Gamer*)　　17 non *om.* C　　18 subfert: suffret C. sufferth C². subferth B²　　20 de *om.* C² 21 percussor B　　22 retribuet B　percusio C: percussio *cett.*　　23 sane-tur *des.* C²B²　　24 PATRITIUS B　　25 aliquid B *cum Coll. Hib.*　　com-mittem C　　26 ⟨aut⟩ annis C

IV

DECREES OF AN IRISH SYNOD

1. The blood of a bishop, a superior prince, or a scribe which is poured out upon the ground, if he requires a dressing, wise men judge that he who shed the blood be crucified or pay seven female slaves.[1] 2. If (he pays) in specie, he shall pay the third part of silver and an amount of gold equal to the size of the crown, and also a like amount in a precious jewel the size of an eye; 3. for the embarrassment of his bruise or wound in a meeting or in any crowd to the third year or longer, if he does not waive his claim, he who has committed (the deed) shall pay the value of a female slave.

4. If, however, the blood of the bishop does not fall to the ground, and if he does not require a dressing, the hand of his assailant shall be cut off or he shall pay half (the value of) seven female slaves, if he did it on purpose; but if he did not do it on purpose, he shall pay the price of a female slave.

5. One who strikes or pushes a bishop without shedding blood shall pay half the price of seven female slaves.

6. But if any of his hairs are plucked out, satisfaction shall be made for every hair, that is, twelve screpalls for each, up to twenty. For even if more were plucked out, it is not stated that an approximate equivalent is due.

7. The blood of a presbyter which is poured out on the ground until the dressing checks it: the hand of the assailant[2] shall be cut off, or he shall pay half the value of seven female slaves, if he did it on purpose; but if not on purpose, he shall make amends with the value of a female slave.

8. If it does not go the ground, the striker shall pay a female slave. If, instead, (he pays) in specie, he shall pay the third part of it in silver. He shall make restitution for his blow with the value of a female slave; for pushing him he shall atone as we said above.

(9). PATRICK SAID: everyone who has dared to steal or seize those things that belong to a king, a bishop, or a scribe, or to commit any (other crime) against them, caring little about despising them, shall pay the value of seven female slaves or do penance for seven years with a bishop or a scribe.

V (Wasserschleben IV)

DE IECTIONE ECLESIE GRADUUM AB OSPITIO

1. Abraham et Loth de sua benignitate in acceptione hospitum sapiens
animaduertat quae bona acceperunt; Sodoma uero quam penam
meruerat de iectione eorum et opere nefando similiter sciat.

ITEM DE IECTIONE $\overline{AG}$ 5

2. Duo quoque episcopi in parte eremi erant, quorum nomina in
scriptura memorantur .i. Iustinus et Pauconius. Iustinus igitur Pau-
conium adit, sed eum non suscepit, non causa tamen inclementiae sed
consuetudine, quia hominem in ospicium non recipiat. Iectus autem
iectorem ad quendam senem accusauit dicens: Quam penitentiam hic 10
homo habet de opere prius memorato? Ipse uir Dei senex et sapiens
respondens ait: .vii. diebus debet penitere in pane et aqua, dum pro
consuetudine et imperitia illum non accipit; si pro inclementia hunc
iecisset, annus pro die hic acciperetur. Ita est sicut in simplici historia
ostenditur.   15

3. ITEM IN EUANGELIO APOSTOLI DIXERUNT: Mittamus ignem
super ciuitatem quae non nos suscipit; tamen exemplo indulgentiae
Christus eos ignem mittere prohibuit.

4. Est quidam uir in oriente, qui Christum accepit in hospitio cum
.xii. apostolis et ab illo tempore usque in hunc diem nec senior cum sua 20
muliere iuuencula non senescente, cui non deest aliquid boni et non
laborat, sed quomodo relinquit eum Christus sic est cum sua domu,
quem Gregorius testatur.

5. Et Christus dicit in euangelio: Si non uos recipiant, iecite puluerem
de pedibus uestris, .i. excommunicationis causa.   25

6 (Wass. 1). Item: qui iecit pauperem occidit eum, quia sexta aut
septima aut octaua aut nona pars occissionis eius iectio. Item qui soccurrere perituro ualet et non succurrerit, occidit eum †primum iugulum
hospitis esurientis quando enim cybus denegatur, quia non plus quam
octo dies esuriens sine cibo potuque uiuere non potest. Ideo autem 30
octaua pars occissionis eius de sua iectione exquiritur et aliquotiens pro
dignitate iecti quinta pars accipitur.

2–4 *cf.* Gen. cc. 18. 19   16–17 *cf.* Luc. 9, 54 sq.   24–25 *cf.* Matth. 10,
14; Marc. 6, 11; Luc. 9, 5

Codices: CBW (*can. 7 tantum*). Can. 1–5 *om. Wasserschleben*

---

1 OSPICIO B   2 hospitium C   3 animaduertat: enim aduertat B   quam:
quia CB; *correxi*   5 DE IECTIONE ITEM B   6 heremi B   9 hospicium B
10 senem *McNeill–Gamer*: semen C. sanem B   accusauit B   12 penitem C
12–14 si–acciperetur. dum–accipit CB: *ordinem restitui*   14 historia:
hostiaria C   17 nos *om.* C   18 mittem C   19 hospicio B   21 non
senescente: insenescente C   23 quem: *lege* quomodo? quem ⟨ad modum⟩?
24 iecite: *s.s.* l- i B   26 iecit: eicit B   27 occisionis C; *sic fere semper*

V

OF THE REFUSAL OF HOSPITALITY[1] TO PERSONS OF ECCLESIASTICAL RANK

1. Let the wise man observe what benefits Abraham and Lot received for their kindness in receiving strangers; but let him likewise be aware what punishment Sodom brought upon itself by rejecting them and for its wicked deed.

FURTHER, ON THE REFUSAL OF HOSPITALITY, AUGUSTINE[2] (SAYS):

2. Moreover there were two bishops in the desert whose names are recorded in a written work, namely, Justinus and Pauconius. Justinus, then, came to Pauconius, but he declined to receive him, not, however, by reason of unkindness, but from custom, since he would not receive a man to hospitality. He, however, that was cast out complained of him that cast him out to a certain old man, saying, 'What penance shall this man have for the deed just recited?' That aged and wise man of God answered and said: 'He ought to fast seven days on bread and water since he did not admit him because it was his custom and he lacked (human) experience; if he had cast him out because of unkindness, a year would then have been assigned for (each) day.' Thus it is as the simple story shows.

3. LIKEWISE THE APOSTLES SAID IN THE GOSPEL: 'Let us send fire upon the city which does not receive us', yet, as an example of forgiveness, Christ forbade them to send fire.

4. There is a certain man in the East who received into hospitality Christ with the Twelve Apostles, and from that time until this day he is no older, and his young wife does not age, and he lacks no good thing, and does not toil; but as Christ left him, so he is, with his house, as Gregory[3] attests.

5. And Christ says in the Gospel: 'If they will not receive you, shake off the dust from your feet,'—that is, in excommunication.

6 (Wass. 1). Further: One who casts out a poor man slays him, since the sixth or seventh or eighth or ninth part of his death is his rejection. Further, whoever is able to succour one who is about to perish and does not succour him, slays him; for[4] the throat of a hungry stranger perishes when food is denied him, as he cannot live more than eight days hungry, without food and drink. Therefore the eighth part of his death is required for his rejection, and sometimes the fifth part is received on account of the dignity of him who has been rejected.

27–28 quis occurrere CB: *distinx. McNeill–Gamer*   28 *ante* primum *lacunam suspicantur McNeill–Gamer; mihi uidetur ibi uerbum latere quale est* perit enim   29 enim: *lege* ei?   30 cybo B   31 eius *om.* B

7 (Wass. 2). Si quis occiderit episcopum et mortuus fuerit, si accipiatur ab eo praetium sanguinis eius, .l. ancellas reddat, id est .vii. ancellas
unius cuiusque gradus, uel .l. annis peniteat, et ex his accipiuntur .vii.
ancellae de iectione eius.

8 (Wass. 3). Ita et reliqua usque hostiarium. Quantum iudices 5
praetium sanguinis unius cuiusque gradus de his septem gradibus
iudicauerint, septima pars occissionis eius de sua iectione reddetur.

9 (Wass. 4). Si episcopus episcoporum iectus fuerit, quinta pars
occissionis eius iectio .i. est octo ancellae et due partes ancellae unius.

10 (Wass. 5). Si quis de minimis sine gradu de ecclesiastico ordine in 10
nomine Dei ambulantibus non susceptus fuerit in ospitio, nona pars
occissionis eius iectio, si fortis fuerit corpore; si autem infirmus fuerit,
octaua pars occissionis eius iectio.

11 (Wass. 6). Quicumque excelsum principem aut scribam aut
anchoritam aut iudicem non susciperit, quantum iudices iudicauerint 15
qui iudicabunt in illo tempore debitum occissionis eius, hoc est septima
pars in iectione eius accipietur.

VI (Wasserschleben V)

DE CANIBUS SINODUS SAPIENTIUM

1. Catenae autem canis quicquid in nocte mali fecerit non reddetur.
Canis peccorum quodcumque malum fecerit in bouello uel in pascuis 20
pecorum non reddetur. Si autem extra fines exierit, reddetur quod mali
fecerit.

2. Item: canis quodlibet manducet, prima culpa nihil reddatur nisi
ille solus. Si uero secundo uel tertio iterauerit, reddetur quod fecerit
uel commederit.   25

3. De his qui canem occident qui custodit peccora uel in domu manet
prudentes dicunt: Qui occidit canem qui custodit peccora, .v. uacas
reddat pro cane et canem de genere eius reddat, et quodcumque bestiae
commedent de peccoribus usque ad caput anni.

4. Item statuta prudentium: Qui canem .iiii. hostiorum, id est domus 30
ubi habitat dominus eius et caule ouium et uitulorum et bouum,
occidit, .x. uaccas reddat et canem de genere eius opera ipsius facientem
restituat.

10 de minimis: *cf*. Matth. 25, 40; (ex. min.) 10, 42   can. 1 *cf*. Coll. Hibern.
LIII. 5   can. 2 *cf*. ibid. LIII. 6

VI: *Codex*: B

1-4 *adest* W   1 occiderit: *s.s.* i. eiecerit CB   2 .l. ancillas reddet B.
reddet .l. ancillas W   id est: .i. C. id B   ancillas B   3 peniteat *des.*
W   4 ancillae B; *sic semper*   iectio C   5 hostiarum C   iudices ⟨iudi-
cant⟩ C   6 unius *om.* C   11 hospitio B   14 aut (1): aūt CB   15 quantum: qñdū B   20 bouello: *in marg.* buorch B

7 (Wass. 2). If anyone rejects[5] a bishop and if the latter has died, if the price of his blood is received from him, he shall pay (the value of) fifty female slaves, that is, seven female slaves for each rank, or he shall do penance for fifty years; and of these, seven female slaves are taken for his rejection.[6]

8 (Wass. 3). So also for the other (ranks), to (that of) sexton. Whatever the judges judge to be the blood price of each rank of those seven ranks, the seventh part of the death of each shall be paid for his rejection.

9 (Wass. 4). If a bishop of bishops has been rejected, the fifth part of his death is his rejection; that is, (the value of) eight female slaves and two-thirds of one female slave.

10 (Wass. 5). If one of the least ones who go about in the name of God without the rank of ecclesiastical orders is not received into hospitality, the ninth part of his death is his rejection, if he is bodily strong; if, however, he is weak, the eighth part of his death is his rejection.

11 (Wass. 6). Whoever does not receive a superior prince or a scribe or an anchorite or a judge, whatever the judges who shall judge at that time judge to be the due price of his death, that is, the seventh part, shall be taken for his rejection.

VI

A SYNOD OF WISE MEN: CONCERNING DOGS

1. Now a chained dog, whatever mischief he does in the night shall not be paid for. And whatever mischief a dog of the flocks does in the byre or in the pastures of the flocks shall not be paid for. But if he goes beyond bounds, what mischief he does shall be paid for.

2. Further: Whatever a dog eats, nothing is paid for his first offence except himself.[1] If he repeats the offence a second or a third time, what he does or eats shall be paid for.

3. Concerning those who kill a dog that guards the flocks or stays in the house wise men say: He who kills a dog that guards the flocks shall pay five cows for the dog and supply a dog of the same breed and restore whatever wild animals eat from the flock until the end of the year.[2]

4. Also, the constitutions of the wise: He who kills a dog of the four doors—namely, of the house where his master dwells, and of the fold of sheep, and of the byres of the calves and of the oxen—shall pay ten cows and substitute a dog of the same breed that will do the dead one's services.

INCIPIUNT CANONES ADOMNANI

1. Marina animalia ad litora delata quorum mortes nescimus summenda sunt sana fide nisi sint putrida.

2. Pecora de rupe cadentia, si sanguis eorum effussus sit, recipienda; sin uero, sed fracta sunt ossa eorum et sanguis foras non fluxerit, refutanda sunt ut morticina. 5

3. In aquis extincta morticina sunt quorum sanguis intrinsecus latet.

4. A bestis capta animalia et semiuiua bestialibus hominibus summenda sunt.

5. Animal semiuiuum subita morte praeraptum abscisa aure uel alia parte morticinum est. 10

6. Caro suellae morticinis crasa uel pinguis ut morticinum quo pinguescunt sues refutanda; cum uero decreuerit et ad pristinam maciem reuersa, summenda est. Si uero una uice uel .ii. uel .iii. morticinum manducauerit, post huius recessum de uentre earum sana fide summenda est. 15

7. Sues carnem uel sanguinem hominis gustantes inliciti sunt semper. In lege namque animal curnupetum si hominem occiderit inlicitum est; quanto magis quae comedunt hominem.

8. Gallinae carnem hominis uel sanguinem eius gustantes multum inmunde sunt et oua earum inmunda sunt; foetus tamen earum con- 20 seruandi licite, quos matrum inmunditia non polluit.

9. Puteus in quo inuenitur morticinum siue hominis siue canis siue animalis cuiuslibet primo euacuandus est et humus eius quam aqua madefecerat foras proicienda et mundus est.

17–18 *cf.* Ex. 21, 29. 36   22–24 *cf.* Leu. 11, 36

Codices: HO: AB²: PB¹: CB³

HO: AB²: *Titulum om.* B¹   ADOMANI H. Adamnani A. addamnari uel addomināri P
PB¹   1 maritima O   delata: cadentia P (*cf.* 3)   sumenda O.B¹.B²   2 sint
om. AB²   pudrida A   3 sanguines B¹   effussus sit H.AB²:
effus'sit P. effusus fuerit O. effusi sunt B¹   recipienda: sum(m)enda sunt PB¹
4 sed: siue O*   sanguinis O   non: si non P   fluxit AB². uenerit P   5 refutanda: refundanda H (restituenda *ut uid.* O). reputanta (*corr. in* -da) P; *cf.* 12
sunt *om.* PB¹   morticinum P   essent *add.* PB¹, sunt *add.* B²   6 morticina sunt
om. B²   7 bestis A: bestia H. bestiis *cett.*   animalia *om.* PB¹   sumenda
O.PᶜB¹   8 sunt *om.* B¹   9 animalia semiuiua P*   praeraptum P: p̄paratum B¹.
p̄reptum HO.A. p̄ceptum B²   abscissa OB²   11 caro suellae *ego*: carosuillę H.
carnesuille O. carnes suillae B². caro suella (suilla Pᶜ) PB¹. caro suilis A   morticinis: -us A. -ę O. si morticinum commedent B²   crassa H.B¹.B²   ut morticina O
quo: quod si O   12 pinguescit B¹   sues *om.* PB¹   refundanda P*. refundandae
B²; *add.* sunt P.B², est B¹   decreuerint O.AB²   ad: in PB¹   13 reuersae B².
reuersa sunt P   sumenda OB¹. *om.* B²   est: sunt HO.AB²   si–15 est *post* p. 180,
6 bestia *transp.* P   in una B¹   uel .ii. *om.* AB²   uel .iii. *om.* PB¹   morticina
O. -am B¹. -niam P   14 manducauerint O.AB².P   secessum PB¹. excessum AB²

HERE BEGIN THE CANONS OF ADAMNAN

1. Marine animals cast upon the shores, the nature of whose death we do not know, are to be taken for food in good faith, unless they are decomposed.

2. Cattle that fell from a rock, if their blood has been shed, are to be taken; if not, but if their bones are broken and their blood has not come out, they are to be rejected as if they were carrion.

3. (Animals) that have died in water are carrion, since their blood remains within them.

4. (Animals) seized by beasts and half alive are to be taken by bestial men.

5. A half alive animal seized by sudden death, an ear or other part being cut (or: torn?) off, is carrion.

6. Swine's flesh that has become thick or fat on carrion is to be rejected like the carrion by which the swine grow fat. When, however, it has been reduced and returned to its original thinness, it is to be taken. But if (a swine) has eaten carrion once or twice[1] or thrice, after this has been ejected from their intestines it is to be taken in good faith.

7. Swine that taste the flesh or blood of men are always forbidden. For in the Law an animal that pushes with the horn, if it kills a man, is forbidden; how much more those that eat a man.

8. Hens that taste the flesh of a man or his blood are in a high degree unclean, and their eggs are unclean; but their chicks may lawfully be preserved since the uncleanness of their mothers does not pollute them.

9. A cistern in which is found either the corpse of a man or (the carcass) of a dog or of any animal is first to be emptied, and the slime in it, which the water has moistened, is to be thrown out, and it is clean.

---

15 sumenda B¹. summendae B²   est B¹: sunt H.AB².P. *om.* O   16 canem H carnem homine̜m (-is B¹) uel sanguinem PB¹   homines A   gustantes *om.* O inlicita P   sunt reicende O   16 sq. semper in lege. Namque P   17 in lege–19 gustantes *deest* O   17 animal *om.* H   cornupetum *codd. pr.* H   inlicitum occiderit P   est *om.* PB¹   *post* est *des.* AB², *nisi quod addunt:* Equus aut pecus si percuserit (*altera* s *s.l.* B²) hominem in agro ciuitatis suae demedium (se medium A. dimedium B²) unciae reddet pro eo homini cuius sanguis effussus est. Si percuserit (-ss- B²) homo animal in agro suo non reditur pro eo   18 quando *codd. corr.* *Wasserschleben*   magis quae *Wasserschleben*: magisque P. magis qui B¹. magis sues q:- H   comedunt H: manducant P. -at B¹
: PB¹   19 hominem P*   uel sang. eius *om.* H   20 inmundae B¹   sunt *om.* H foetus–21 polluit *ante* 19 Gallinae *in* PB¹   tamen: quidem O   eorum B¹ 20 sq. obseruandi PB¹   21 sunt *ante* licite *add.* PB¹   licite B¹: licidae H. linquite P. *om.* O   matrum: mo̜gitum P   *post* polluit *add.* polli (pulli PᶜB¹) tamen con(ob- P) seruandi sunt PB¹   22 putheus H. puteos P*   homo H. homines P*   cane̜s H. canes P*   23 animales P*   cuiuslibet ⟨animalis⟩ P   euacuendus P   et–24 est *om.* O 23 eius quam aqua *ego*: eiusq H. eiusqᵘⁱ qua P. eius quia aqua B¹   putei *post* aqua *add.* PB¹

10. Intinctum a uaca sana conscientia summendum. Ut quid enim intinctionem uacce excommunicamus, cum a uitulo praemulgenti gustatum lac non refutemus? Sed tamen propter infirmas fratrum conscientias, non propter inmunditiam quoquendum est et tunc ab hominibus suscipiendum.   5

11. Intinctum uero suibus coquendum et inmundis hominibus summendum est. Sues namque munda comedunt et inmunda, uacae uero non nisi herbis et arborum fruntibus pascuntur.

12. Intinctum a coruo nulla coctione mundari potest propter nostram conscientiam. Quis enim nostrum scit quas inlicitas carnes prius come- 10 derat priusquam †nostrum inliquitum† intinxerit?

13. Intinctum †aduella nec sine coctione nec post coctionem suscipiendum est.

14. In aquis suffocta non manducanda sunt, unde Dominus carnem cum sanguine prohibuit manducari. In carne enim animalis suffucati in 15 aquis sanguis coagolatus perdurat. Hoc Dominus prohibet, non quod in illis temporibus homines crudam carnem comaederant quia non esset dulcior, sed quod carnem suffucatam et morticinam manducassent, et lex metrica scriptione scripta dicit: Carnem morticinam non manducetis.

15. Praedarum pecora a Christianis siue per commercia siue per 20 donationes non sunt summenda. Quod enim Christus reprobat, ut quid miles Christi suscipiet? Aelimosinam namque praedonis inuassi fletus extinguat.

16. De meretrice coiuge sic idem interpraetatus est, quod meretrix erit decusso proprii mariti iugo et secundi mariti iuncta uel tertii. Cuius 25 maritus illa uiuente alteram non suscipiet. Unde nescimus illam auctoritatem quam legimus in questionibus Romanorum utrum idoneis testibus an falsis ornatam fuisse.

15–16 *cf.* Gen. 9, 4; Leu. 17, 10–14; Deut. 12, 16. 23   19 *cf.* Gen. 9, 4; Leu. 5, 2; 17, 15; *al.*   21 *cf.* Eccli. 34, 23; *de uoce* reprobat *cf. adnotationem meam ad Patricii Epist. 8*

1 ⟨uero⟩ a H   ab OB¹   uaca: aqua O   summendum conscientia O   quid: si quis P   2 intinctione P. intentionem O   uache O. -ae B¹   excommunicemus PB¹   cum: et PB¹   a *om.* P   prᵉmulgenti B¹: p̄mulgendi H. promulgendi P. omulgendi O.   3 refutemus O: repuremus H. respuemus B¹. respuimus P; *cf. p.* 176, 5. 12   propter: pro H   4 inmunditias PB¹   coquendum B¹. coquentum P. consequendum O   5 hominibus: omnibus P   suscipiendum est PB¹   6 coquentum P   et: est et PB¹   6-7 summendum est uel tribuendum H. uel sumendum O. tribuendum est PB¹; *cf. p.* 176, 7 sq.   7 suis H   munda–inmunda: commedunt munda et inmunda commedunt P. munda et inmunda commedunt B¹   uache O. uacca P   8 fruntibus H: frontibus P*. frondibus *cett.*   frondibus arborum O   9 ⟨uero⟩ a P   cᵘruo P   coctione: contentione HO, *cf.* 2   mundare B¹. mondare P   10 *post* conscientiam *add.* dubiam PB¹   quas: qua P   inliquitas H   commederat *codd. pr.* H   11 priusquam: quam PB¹   nostrum inliquitum H. nostrum inlicitum O. nostrum lac B¹. *om.* P; *fortasse lege:* rostrum in liquidum   intincxerit PB¹   12 aduella HO. aduella uel aquila B¹ (*cf. Can. Hib. I. 17*). a mustella P. abdella ('*leech*') McNeill–Gamer   post coctione OP   nullo (ullo B¹) modo suscip. PB¹   14 In aquis–

10. That which is contaminated by a cow is to be taken with a clear conscience. For why should we exclude the contamination of a cow if we do not reject the milk tasted by a sucking calf? But nevertheless, on account of the weak conscience of the brethren, not on account of uncleanness, it is to be cooked, and then it is to be accepted by men.

11. That which is contaminated by swine is to be cooked, and distributed to unclean men. For swine eat things clean and unclean; but cows feed only on grass and the leaves of trees.

12. That which is contaminated by a crow can be cleansed by no cooking, on account of our ⟨doubtful *PB¹*⟩ conscience; for who of us knows what forbidden flesh he had eaten before he contaminated our liquid.¹

13. That which is contaminated by a leech is by no means to be taken, either without cooking or after cooking.

14. Things drowned in water are not to be eaten, since the Lord hath prohibited the eating of flesh that contains blood. For in the flesh of an animal drowned in water the blood remains coagulated. This the Lord prohibits, not because in those days men ate raw flesh, since it would be none too sweet, but because they had been eating drowned and carrion flesh. And the Law written in metrical form² says: 'Thou shalt not eat carrion flesh.'

15. Cattle seized in a raid³ are not to be taken by Christians whether in trade or as gifts: for what Christ rejects, how shall the soldier of Christ receive? For the weeping of the robber's victim would seem to make void his alms.

16. Of a wife who is a harlot, thus the same man⁴ explained, that she will be a harlot, who has cast off the yoke of her own husband, and is joined to a second husband or a third. Her husband shall not take another (wife) while she lives. For we do not know whether that verdict which we read in questions of the Romans⁵ was attested by acceptable or false witnesses.⁶

---

15 cum *om.* HO   soffocata B¹   15 sanguinem HO   manducari prohibuit B¹   suffocati *codd. pr.* H   16 sanguinis B¹   coagulatus (-ang- B¹ *a.c.*) O.PB¹ 17 comederant O. manducarent PB¹   18 quod: quia PB¹   suffocatam OP. soffocatam B¹   manducasent P   19 scriptione: scriptio H. ratione PB¹ scripta: scriptura OP   manducañ H   *post* manducetis *add.* O: De interdictione sanguinem manducandi   20 pecora: pecunia B¹   per *om.* HO   21 sunt: est B¹   Christus *om.* PB¹ (reprobat deus B¹)   ut quid ⟨enim⟩ HO   22 milis P*   elimosinam B¹. elimoisinam P   ꝑ̃ᵉ O   praedonis inuassi (in uasse O) fletus HO: praedonis fletus inuassi B¹. inuasit praedonis fletus P 23 extinguit PB¹   24 meretrica B¹   coniuge OB¹   quod: quia PB¹   meritrix P   25 de cusso P. de coitu O   iuncta H (*s.l.*). B¹: inito H*.P. *de* O *non constat*   26 unde: quia PB¹; *cf.* 14   27 autoritatem P   quessionibus O utrum idoneis: ut[ ]ūeris O   28 testibus an falsis: an testibus falsis H, an falsis testibus PB¹   ornatam: orta co. ēē O   fuise P

17. Carnem a bestiis commessam inmundam esse idem confirmat, non tamen morticinam, quia sanguis illius carnis, quamuis illicite, effussus est per bestias.

18. Laetali uero mursu tantum captum pecus nec in totum morti- ficatum peccoribus et bestialibus hominibus comedendum, abscisa 5 tamen aure uel qualibet parte et canibus data quam bestia dentibus intinxit. Aptum namque sibi uidetur ut carnem bestiis administratam humanae bestiae comederint.

19. Simili modo prohibet medullas ossuum ceruorum manducari quos lupi comederunt.   10

20. Similiter et ceruos quorum sanguinem quamuis paruum cernimus fluxisse per fracta in pedicis crura uetat manducari morticinam esse adfirmans, eo quod non fluxerat sanguis superior, qui custos et sedis animae erat, quia, licet extrimitas sanguinis per extrimum quodlibet membrum sit effussa, sanguis tamen crasior et solidior, in quo anima 15 sederat, intra carnem coagolatus manet. Itaque, quod si non causa uulneris inlissi sedem animae turbauerit, non est sanguinis effussio, sed tantum extrimae partis offensio; itaque et qui eam carnem comederit sciat carnem cum sanguine comedisse. Cum enim Dominus carnem prohibuit cum sanguine comedendam, non carnis coctio deerat, sed 20 sanguinis effussio, et praedictum intellegi debet et de peccoribus quae post abscisam uel tamen scisam aurem in extrima infirmitate mortua sunt. Adipem tamen et pelles in ussus uarios habebimus.

13–14 *cf.* Leu. 17, 14; Deut. 12, 16. 23   23 *cf.* Leu. 7, 24

1 commesam P   2 tamen: tantum *McNeill–Gamer*   quamuis: q P. *om.* B[1]
3 effussus O.PB[1]   per bestias: bestiis O   4 laetali: leto O   morsu O.B[1]
tantum H: tamen B[1]. tm̄ O.P.   nec H. *om.* O   nec B[1]. hec P: non H. *om.* O   5 peccoribus
ego, cf. 21: pecoribus H. peccatoribus *cett.*   et ⟨a⟩ B[1]   cumedendum H. comm-
PB[1]   abscissa P   6 tamen: tantum H   aure uel qualibet *om.* PB[1]; *cf. p.* 176, 9
carnibus P*   bestia: bestis (*ex* -ibus) P   7 intixit H. intincxerit B[1]   admini-
stratum H   8 c̄ederint H: commederint O.P. commedent B[1]

HO:PB[1]:   9 *inc.* CB[3]: ITEM ADOMPNANUS (ADUMNANUS: C). Medullas, *etc.*   ossuum P
CB[3]   seruorum P   non licet manducari CB[3]   10 commederunt (-ant P) *codd. pr.*
H.C   11 et *om.* PB[1]   paruum H. prauum O. paruulum CB[3]: peruenis P.
per uenas B[1]   11–12 fluxisse cernimus CB[3]   13 adfirmans: con(*s.s.* l-
ad C)firmans carnem CB[3]   eo quod: eoque P   fluxerit CB[3]   superor C   qui:
quia O   14 animae *om.* O   *post* erat *add.* B[1].CB[3]: Sed coagulatus (-ang- C) est
intra carnem (*cf.* 16)   quia licet PB[1]: quia libet HO. quamlibet B[3]. quam licet C
extremitas *codd. pr.* H; *sic semper* extrem- (extremittas C)   sanguis H   14–15 effusa
sit per . . . membrum (-orum C) CB[3]   15 sanguinis B[1]   crassior HO; *cf. p.* 176, 11
in *bis* C   16 coagulatus *codd. pr.* H   causa: crasa P   17 ulneris P   inlissi
P. inlessi B[1]: inlisi H.CB[3]. inlisise edem (*pro* inlissi sedem) O   animae turbauerit
(-int O) HO.B[3]: animetur lauerit P. animae lauerit B[1]   est *om.* HO   sanguis C
effussio sanguinis PB[1]   18 partis: portis P. partem O   offensio–19 comedisse
deest O   offensio H. offentio B[3]: effussio B[1]   itaque et B[3]: ita et H. ita ut PB[1]
eum H   commederit *codd. pr.* H.C   19 commedisse (cumm- P*) *codd. pr.* H.C
enim Dominus: dominus *om.* B[3]. dominus autem (h̄ *corr. in* hoc) P. autem dominus
B[1]   carnem *om.* PB[1].C   20 co sanguī H   commedendam O   cum sanguine
comedendam *om.* PB[1].B[3]   non carnis: nec B[1]   coctio HO.B[3]: equoctio P. et coctio
B[1]   deerat *om.* PB[1]   21 effussio ⟨dederat⟩ PB[1]   ⟨hoc⟩ praedictum PB[1].CB[3]

17. The same man firmly holds that flesh of which some has been eaten by beasts is unclean, though not carrion, since its blood, though illicitly, has been shed by beasts.

18. A beast that has only been seized with a deadly bite and not quite killed is to be eaten by beasts and by bestial men—the ear or any part which the beast contaminated with its teeth having been cut off and given to the dogs. For it seems to him[7] fitting that human beasts should eat the flesh that has been served to beasts.

19. In like manner he forbids the eating of the marrow of the bones of stags of which wolves have eaten.

20. Likewise he also forbids the eating of stags of whose blood we see a small quantity to have flowed out through their legs broken in a trap, affirming that they are carrion on the ground that the higher blood had not flowed, which is the guardian and seat of life; for, though the extremity of blood has flowed through whatever extreme member, yet the thicker and denser blood in which life had its seat remains clotted within the flesh. Thus, unless the infliction of a wound disturbs the seat of life, there is no shedding of blood but merely injury to an extreme part; and therefore he who eats such flesh shall know that he has eaten flesh with blood. For since the Lord has forbidden the eating of flesh with blood, what was lacking is not the cooking of the flesh but the draining of the blood; and what has been said above must be understood also of beasts that have died in extreme weakness after the cutting off or (simple) cutting of an ear. Their fat, however, and their hides we shall have for diverse uses.

---

intelligi B¹   debet *om.* PB¹   peccoribus O.B¹ *a.c.*: pecoribus *cett.*   22 abscisam (-ss-O.P)–aurem: abscisa (ul- tantum *s.l.m.* 2) aure H   uel–scisam *om.* O   scissam P. *om.* H   extrima P*.H: extrema *cett.*   23 ussūs H. usus O.P.CB³. usos B¹ habebimus ⟨manducetur. animalia coitu hominem⟩ C   Finiunt hec iudicia *ad calcem add.* PB¹·

TRES CANONES HIBERNICI

1. Si quis refugium crismalis alicuius sancti aut refugium baculis aut cimbalis fregerit aliquomodo uel per rapinam predam abstraxerit, uel homini aliqua ratione nocuerit, septempliciter restituet et in dura penitentia in peregrinatione extranea per .v. annos permaneat. Et si laudabilis penitentia eius fuerit, postea ad solum patrium perueniat. 5 Sin uero, in aexilio semper permaneat.

2. Si quis refugium euangelii fregerit uel per rapinam aliquid abstulerit, septempliciter restituet propter septiformem Christi gratiam et propter .vii. grados aecclesiasticos, sed et per .vii. annos in dura penitentia permaneat in peregrinatione. Si uero non egerit penitentiam, 10 excommunicandus est ab omni ecclesia catholica et a communione Christianorum omnium nec sepultura illi in loco sancto tribuenda est.

3. Si quis tirannus (s.s. rex) aliquem iuxta episcopum ligauerit, sanum soluat et restituat et .iii. alios uiros coaequales cum omni eorum substantia episcopo reddat et ipse solus usque ad .x. annos in durae pere- 15 grinationis penitentia permaneat, et si contigerit ut eum uulnerauerit, .vii. uiros cum omni substantia episcopo reddat et ipse solus per spatium .xx. annorum in peregrinatione permaneat. Si uero eum mortificauerit, omnem suam hereditatem et omnem substantiam cum hereditatibus et substantiis comitum Deo reddat et ipse in peregrinatione 20 perhenni uel humanius in .xxx. annorum peregrinatione absque carne et muliere et aequo in pane sicco uiuat et exiguo uestimento et per duas noctes in una mansione non maneat nisi tantum sollempnitatibus precipuis aut si infirmitas eum praeoccupauerit. Et si inuitos comites habuerit, omnem substantiam eorum inter Deum et hominem diuidant 25 et sic ipsi per spatium .vii. annorum in penitentia probabili permaneant.

Codex: X (Cambridge, C.C.C. 265, pp. 97 f.). Ed. M. Bateson, *E.H.R.* x. 721 sq.

5 solum patrium: solam patriam X

THREE IRISH CANONS

1. If anyone in any way breaks into the place of keeping of the chrismal of any saint, or a place of keeping for staves or cymbals, or takes away anything by robbery, or in any way injures a man, he shall make seven-fold restitution and remain through five years in hard penance in exile abroad. And if his penance is commendable, let him afterwards come to his own country; but if not, let him remain permanently in exile.

2. If anyone breaks into the place of keeping of a Gospel book or removes anything by robbery, he shall make sevenfold restitution, on account of the sevenfold grace of Christ and on account of the seven ecclesiastical ranks; but he shall also remain through seven years in hard penance in exile. But if he does not do penance he is to be excommunicated from the whole Catholic Church and from the communion of all Christians, and burial in holy ground is not to be accorded to him.

3. If any tyrant (i.e., king) binds anyone attached to a bishop, he shall release him safe and sound and make restitution, and he shall render to the bishop three other men of equal worth with all their substance, and he himself shall remain in the penance of hard exile alone for a period of ten years; and if he happens to wound him, he shall render to the bishop seven men with all their substance, and he himself shall remain alone in exile for the space of twenty years. But if he kills him, he shall render to God all his inheritance and all his substance with the inheritances and substance of his associates, and he himself shall go into perpetual exile, or, more mildly, into exile for thirty years, living without flesh and wife and horse, on dry bread, and with meagre clothing and not stay for two nights in one house save only in the principal festivals or if sickness lays hold of him. And if his associates have been unwilling, they shall divide all their substance between God and man, and so shall they themselves remain in commendable penance for the space of seven years.

CANONES SYNODI HIBERNENSIS S. PATRICIO PERPERAM ATTRIBUTI ('SYNODUS II S. PATRICII')

I. DE EO QUOD MANDASTIS DE QUOHABITATIONE CUM FRATRIBUS PECCATORIBUS

Audite apostulum dicentem: *Cum huiusmodi nec cybum quidem sumere.* Non eius esca, sed cum eo simul ad mensam. Ceterum, Si *bos* es et *trituras*, hoc est, si doctor es et doces, *non obduratur* tibi *os, et dignus es* 5 *mercedem tuam;* sed *olium peccatoris non inpinguat capud* tuum, sed *corripe* adhuc *et argue.*

II. DE OBLATIONIBUS EORUM.

Contentus tegmento et alimento tuo caetera *dona iniquorum reproba,* quia non sumit lucerna nisi quod alatur.   10

III. DE PENETENTIBUS POST RUINAS

Statuetur ut abbas uidet, cui a Domino tribuetur potestas alligandi et soluendi. Sed apcior est, iuxta scripture exempla, ⟨ad⟩ ueniam siuera cum fletu et lamentatione et lugubre ueste sub custodia paenitentia breuis quam longa et remissa cum teborem mentis.   15

IIII. DE EXCOMMUNICATIONEM

Audi Dominum dicentem: *Si* tibi *non audierit sit tibi uelut gentilis et*

---

3 1 Cor. 5, 11 cum eiusmodi (huiusmodi f g Iren. Ambrst. Aug. DFHΘ^cNORZ*) nec cibum ⟨quidem D *cum* Tert. Ambrst. Ambr. Hier. Aug.⟩ sumere   4–5 Deut. 25, 4 non ligabis os bouis terentis (triturantis A) in area fruges tuas (non infrenabis bouem triturantem Aug.); 1 Cor. 9, 9 non alligabis (obturabis Orig. Hil.) os boui trituranti; *cf.* 1 Tim. 5, 18   5–6 1 Tim. 5, 18 et dignus est operarius mercede sua (mercedem suam d r A*FHΘ*MN*T^c)   6–7 Ps. 140, 5 corripiet (-at Aug^{Spec}) me iustus . . . et increpabit (arguet R, arguat Aug^{Spec}) me; oleum autem peccatoris non im-pinguet caput meum   9 Eccli 34, 23; *cf.* Patric. Epist. 8, p. 94 Bieler   17 sq. Matth. 18, 17 si . . . non audierit sit tibi sicut ethicus (gentilis Q gat; gens e) et publicanus (publicanus et gentilis R).

II: Coll. Hib. II. 23 Wasserschleben: Sinodus Romana dixit de oblationibus eorum: Contentus tegmine tantum et alimento, caetera dona iniquorum reproba, quae reprobat altissimus, quoniam non sumit lucerna nisi quo alatur

III: Coll. Hib. XLVII. 8d Wass.: Romani de penitentia dicunt: Post ruinas statuitur ut abbas penitentiam prouideat, et si fiet cum fletu et lamentatione et lugubri ueste et sub custodia, melior est penitentia breuis reddenda quam longa et remissa cum tepore mentis.

IIII: *cf.* Coll. Hib. XL. 1 (1c: Sinodus Romana tribus modis excommunicari decreuit, hoc est, ex pace et mensa et missa; *cf.* I. 22a).

Codices: KQDJIY

CANONS OF THE ALLEGED SECOND SYNOD OF ST. PATRICK

I. CONCERNING WHAT YOU HAVE COMMANDED WITH RESPECT TO DWELLING AMONG SINFUL BRETHREN

Hearken unto the Apostle who says: *With such an one not so much as to eat.* (Not that one is) not to partake of his food, but that one may not share his table. Besides, if thou art an ox and treadest out the corn, that is, if thou art a teacher and teachest, *thy mouth shall not be muzzled and thou art worthy of thy reward,* but *let not the oil of the sinner fatten thy head, yet still rebuke and chastise.*

II. OF THEIR OFFERINGS

Be content with thy clothing and food, and *reject* all other *gifts of the wicked* since the lamp takes nothing but that by which it is fed.

III. OF PENITENTS AFTER FALL

It is determined that the abbot should take care, he to whom the Lord assigns the power of binding and loosing. But more fitting ⟨for⟩ pardon, according to the examples of the Scripture, is a short penance with weeping and lamentation and a garment of grief, under control, than a long and lax one with a lukewarm mind.

IV. ON EXCOMMUNICATION

Hearken unto the Lord when he saith: *If he will not hear* thee *let him*

Titulus deest in KQDJ   De synodo patricii tituli .xxxi. I. DE SYNODO PATRI-
CII CAPL- .XVII. DE DIUERSIS CAUSIS Y   *Tituli canonum litteris minusculis paullo largioribus scribuntur in* I, *litteris maiusculis in ceteris codicibus*   1 DE–MAN-
DASTIS *om.* I   MANDATIS QY   QUO HABITATIONE KJ. QUO HABI-
TATIONĒ Q. COHABITACIONE D. cohabitatione I   CUM: IN J   3 apostolum DJᶜI. (*per compendium* Y)   uiusmodi D   cibum DJIY   summere Q
4 escam Y   sed: sumis J   citterum Q. cęteris J   bos es: bos sis QY. bossis DJ.
possis I   5 nutrituras K   est *om.* K   obturatur DI. obturas J   tibi *om.* J
os: hos Q   et: &e Q   es (2): ēe I   6 mercede tua QDJI   oleum QDJIY   pec-
catores D   inpinguet I   caput DJIY   sed: se K. si J   7 corripes J   8 *titulus litteris minusculis scriptus in* J   OBLACIONIBUS J*   9 contentus:
contemptus Q. contenentur J   alimentuo J   cetera IY. cyttera Q   10 quia:
quae J   sumet QY   quod: quo *Spelman, cf. Coll. Hib.*   11–15 *om.* Y   11 *titulus cum textu coniungendus est, cf. can. i*   penitentibus I. POENITENTIBUS J
12 statuituʀ I   abba I   a Domino tribuetur: adtribuetur J   tribuitur I   aligandi
Q. allegandi J. ligandi I   13 sed: sit Q   apciorē K. abciorem Q. aptior est
DJI   scripturę I. scriptura Q   ad *suppleui*   14 confletu J   lucubre J. lucubri
uesti I   pęnitentiam K. penitentiae Q. paene(-i- J)tentiane DJ. paenitenti I: *corr.
Spelman*   15 cum teporem D. cum porem Q. contempore J. (cum–mentis: cum
temperamentis I)   16 *numerum om.* Y   EXCOMMUNICATIONE QDIY
17 si tibi: sit ibi Q   sit: sed D   tibi (2) *om.* J   uelud Y   gentiles Q. gentilibus J

publicanus. Non maledices; sed repellis excommunicatum a communione et mensa et missa et pace, et si *hereticus* est *post unam correptionem deuita.*

V. DE SUSPECTIS CAUSIS

Audi Dominum dicentem: *Sinite utraque crescere usque ad messem,* hoc est, *donec ueniat qui manifestauit consilia cordium,* ne iudicium ante 5 diem iudicii facias. Uidi Iudam ad mensam Domini et latronem in paradiso.

VI. DE UINDICTIS AECLESIAE

Audi item Dominum dicentem: *Qui effuderit sanguinem innocentem, sanguis ipsius effunditur.* †Sed ab eo qui portat gladio.† ⟨Uin⟩dicator 10 autem uindicte innocens habetur. De ceteris autem perlege euangelium ab eo loco in quo ait: et eum *qui auferit* aliquid a te *ne repetas.* Sed libenter si ipsi quae referat, humiliter recipias.

VII. DE BAPTISMATIS INCERTIS

Statuunt tenire: Baptizati, qui symbuli traditione a quocumque ac- 15 ciperunt, quia non infecit semen seminantis iniquitas; sin uero, non est rebaptizare sed baptizare.

VIII. NON ABSOLUENDUS AUTEM LAPSOS A FIDE CREDAMUS NISI PER INPOSITIONEM MANUS EPISCOPI.

VIIII. DE REIS AUTEM ABSTRACTIS AB AECLESIA.   20

Non ad reorum defensionem facta est aeclesia, sed iudicibus per-

---

1 *cf.* Rom. 12, 14   2 Tit. 3, 10 haereticum hominem post unam et secundam (et sec. *om.* m O Iren. Tert. Cypr. Lucif. Ambr. Hier. Aug.) correptionem deuita. 4 Matth. 13, 30.   5 1 Cor. 4, 5 quoad usque (donec f g D Ambrst. Ambr. Hier. Aug.) ueniat Dominus qui . . . manifestabit (-uit d AFHΘ*MNPRTZ*) consilia cordium 6–7 *cf.* Matth. 26, 21–25; Luc. 23, 43.   9–10 Gen. 9, 6 quicumque (qui m Hil.) effuderit humanum sanguinem, fundetur (effundetur CΠ. effunditur O) sanguis illius (ipsius CΦᴾ); *cf.* Ps. 105, 38 effuderunt sanguinem innocentem.   12 Luc. 6, 30 qui aufert (auferet b e f r aur AℲFFGJMZ) quae tua sunt ne repetas.
VIIII: Coll. Hib. XXVIII. 14d: Sinodus Romanorum: Non ad reorum defensionem facta est ecclesia, sed iudicibus persuadendum ut spiritali morte occidant eos qui ad sinum ecclesiae transfugerint.

---

1 maledicis DJY   sed: si J   2 *pro* et (1) *fort. legendum* id est (*pro .i. scriba archetypi legerat* 7)   et mensa *om.* QY *uerba* et missa *redundare suspicatur Harduinus*   3 *numerum om.* Y   4 sinete D. sine te I   utraque *om.* D 5 est *om.* K   manifestabit IY   consiliae J   6 facies QY   uide QDJIY   7 paradyso Q   8 ECCLESIE DQ. (-AE) IY   9 item: idem Y. iterum J. Dominum *bis in* I   sanguis: sanguinis KQ   10 effundetur QDJIY   Sed–gladio (-um JY) *corruptum; fortasse* Et ideo (*cf. can. xxx*): Qui portat ⟨gladium peribit⟩ gladio (*cf. Matth. 26, 52; Rom. 13, 4*)   Uindicator *ego, cf.* A. Souter, A Glossary of Later Latin, Oxoniae 1949 *s.u.*: dictatur KQDJ. dictator IY   11

be to thee as the heathen and the publican. Thou shalt not curse; but thou shalt reject an excommunicated person from communion and from the table and from the Mass and from the kiss of peace; and if he is *a heretic, after one admonition avoid him.*

V. OF SUSPECTED CASES

Hearken unto the Lord when he saith: *Suffer both to grow until the harvest,* that is, *until he cometh who will make manifest the counsels of the hearts,* that thou make not judgement before the Day of Judgement. Behold Judas at the table of the Lord, and the thief in paradise.

VI. OF THE PUNISHMENTS OF THE CHURCH

Hearken again unto the Lord when he saith, *Whosoever shall shed innocent blood, his blood shall be shed.* And therefore: *He who carries the sword shall perish by the sword.*[1] He, however, who punishes is held innocent in respect of the punishment. On other matters, however, read the Gospel from that place in which it says: And of him *that taketh away* any of thy goods, *ask them not again.* But, if he of his own restores anything, receive it in humility.

VII. CONCERNING DOUBTFUL BAPTISM[2]

They determine to hold: those who have received the tradition of the symbol are baptized, from whomsoever they have received it, since the seed is not defiled by the wickedness of the sower; but if they have not received it, it is not rebaptism, but baptism.

VIII. WE OUGHT TO BELIEVE THAT THOSE WHO HAVE LAPSED FROM THE FAITH ARE NOT TO BE ABSOLVED UNLESS THEY ARE RECEIVED WITH IMPOSITION OF HANDS BY A BISHOP.

IX. OF ACCUSED PERSONS TAKEN FROM A CHURCH.

A church is not made for the defence of accused persons; but judges

---

uindictę I. -ae Y   abetur Q habeatur Y   citteris Q   perlege euangelium *ego:* per legem euangelicam *codd.*   12 aufert I. auferet Y   sed: si J   13 si ipsi: seipsi D. si ipse Y. ipse I   quae: q; K. que Q. q̄ D. quem (m *in ras.*) J. quod I. qui Y. quid *Spelman*   recipis Y. suscipias I   14–17 *om.* Y   14 *titulus cum textu coniungendus, cf. i, iii, al.*   BAP(-B- J)TISMATIBUS DJI   15 tenere QDJI   babtizati J   simbuli Q. simboli DJ. symboli I   tradicione D   15–16 acceperunt DJI   16 quia: quae J   inficit DJI   semen *om.* I   simantes Q* (simenantes Qᶜ)   17 babtizare Q   18–19 *litteris minusculis scribunt codd. pr.* K 18 absoluendos IY   lapsus QDJI   19 PER: pro Q   inposit(-c- D)ione QDJ MANUS *om.* Y   20 *numeri abhinc desunt in* Y   REIS: RES Y. REBUS KQI AB ECLESIAE K. AB ECCLESIE Q. AB ECCLESIA DIY: ECLESIAE J 21 ad: a Q   defensione QDJ   *pro* ad – def. *habet* hebreorum difinitione J, hereorum defensione Y   aeclesia: ęc(ecc- Q)lesie KQ. ecclesia IY   sed iudicibus: sedicibus I iudicium J

suadendum est ut spiritali morte eos occiderint qui ad senum matris
aeclesie confugerunt.

X. DE LAPSIS POST GRADUM

Audi canonica statuta: Qui cum gradu cecidit, sine gradu surgat.
Contentus nomine tantum amittat ministerium, nisi qui [tantum] a 5
conspectu Domini peccans non recessit.

XI. DE SEPERATIONE SEXUUM POST LAPSUM.

Considerit unus quisque in conscientia sua si amor et desiderium
cessauit peccati, quia corpus mortuum non infecit corpus alterius
mortui; sin uero, separentur.   10

XII. DE OBLATIONE PRO DEFUNCTIS

Audi apostulum dicentem: *Est autem peccatum ad mortem: non pro
illo dico ut rogit quis.* Et Dominus: *Nolite dare sanctum canibus.* Qui
enim in uita sua sacrificium non meretur accipere, quomodo post
mortem illi poterit adiuuare?   15

XIII. DE SACRIFICIO

In nocte Paschae, si fas est ferre foras. *Non foras fertur*, sed fidelibus
deferatur. Quid aliud significat quod *in una domo* sumitur agnus quam:
sub uno fidei culmine creditur et communicatur Christus?

XIIII. DE ABSTINENTIA INSOLUBILE[QUE] A CIBIS   20

Statuunt ut Christi aduentus sponsi nullas nostras legis inueniat

12–13 1 Ioh. 5, 16 (*omissa uoce* autem; est enim q t)   13 Matth. 7, 6   17–18 Ex.
12, 46 in una domo comedetur nec efferetis de carnibus eius foras.
    X: *cf.* Coll. Hib. XI. 1b Patricius episcopus dicit: Qui sub gradu peccat, debet
excommunicari . . . ad priorem gradum uenire difficile. ⟨Item sinodus: Quicumque
sub gradu cecidit sine gradu consurget *Cod. Vallicell.*⟩
    XI: *cf.* Coll. Hib. XLVII. 20, adn. (g).
    XII: *cf.* Coll. Hib. XV. 8d et adn.(e).
    XIIII: Coll. Hib. XII. 15c De abstinentia insolubili a cibis statuunt Romani, ut
Christi aduentus sponsi nullas nostri ieiunii leges inueniat. Quid enim interest inter
Christianum et Nouatianum, nisi quod Nouatianus indesinenter abstinet, Christianus
uero per tempora ieiunat, ut locus et tempus et persona per omnia obseruetur.

    1 est ut *eras.* D   spiritale QDJ   occiderent QDJ. occidant Y   qui: q; Q   sinum
DJIY   2 aeclesiae J. ecclesie (-ae Y) QIY   confugiunt DJ. confugerint I. confugierunt Y (*sic fortasse archetypus*)   3 AUTEM *post* LAPSIS *add.* Y   4 kanonica Q
instituta QDJI (canonicam institutionem Y)   resurgat J   5 contus D
pro tantum *bis* tamen Y   amitat D. amitti J   mvsterium KY   qui *om.* J   tantum
(2) *deleui, cf. can. xxiii ex.*   7 DESPERATIONE K. DEPERATIONE D. DE

ought to be persuaded that they would slay with spiritual death those who have fled to the bosom of mother Church.[3]

X. OF THOSE WHO HAVE FALLEN AFTER ATTAINING TO CLERICAL RANK

Hearken to the canonical statutes: Whoever falls with rank shall arise without rank. Content with the name (of cleric) alone, he shall lose his ministry, except when by his sinning he has not withdrawn from the sight of God.

XI. OF THE SEPARATION OF THE SEXES AFTER FALL.

Each one shall consider in his conscience whether the love and desire of sin have ceased, since a dead body does not harm another's dead body; if this is not the case they shall be separated.

XII. ON OFFERING FOR THE DEAD

Hearken unto the Apostle when he saith: *There is a sin unto death: for that I say not that any man pray.* And the Lord (saith): *Give not that which is holy to dogs.* For he who did not in his life deserve to receive the sacrifice, how shall it be able to help him after death?

XIII. OF THE SACRIFICE

On the even of Easter, whether it is permissible to carry it outside. *It is not to be carried outside*, but to be brought down to the faithful. What else signifies it that the Lamb is taken *in one house*, but that Christ is believed and communicated under one roof of faith?

XIV. CONCERNING ABSTINENCE FROM FOOD WITHOUT BREAK

They decide that the coming of Christ the Bridegroom shall find none

SEPARATIONE IY   SEXU· Q. SEXUM DJ. sexus I   8 consideret DJY. considerat I   9 quia: q; J   inficit I. infigit Y   11 OBLATIONEM DJ   12 apostolum DI. (*per compendium* JY)   autem: aut D   ⟨et⟩ ad Y   13 roget QDJIY   sanctum dare DY   kanebus Q   14 merebitur QDJIY   accepere D 15 adiuuari I^c   16 *titulus cum textu coniungendus*   SACRIFICIUM QDJ 16-17 *uerba* De–foras (1) *ut titulus litteris largioribus scripta sunt in* I   17 IN NOCTE PASCHE *ut pars tituli* Q   pasce I*   ferre: referre J   foras (2): foris I sed: se K. si D; *cf. p.* 184, 6; 186, 1. 12; *al.*   18 defferatur D   aliut D   summitur Q   agnum QJ   19 Christus *om.* DJI, *nescio an recte*   20–*p.* 190, 3 *om.* Y   20 INSOLUBILE Q; A (QUIA: Q. Q̄ A: D. QUĀ: J) KQDJ. insolubili q: a I. (insolubili a *Coll. Hib.*); *leg.* De abstinentia insolubili quae est a cibis? CYBIS Q   21 statuit J   aduentum J   leges DJI   inueniant I ieiunii. Quid autem inter Nouatianum et Christianum interest nisi quod Nouatianus indesinenter, Christianus uero per tempus absteneat, ut locus et tempus et persona per omnia obseruitur?

XV. DE RELINQUENDA UEL DOCENDA PATRIA.

Docenda patria prius per exemplum Domini et derelinquenda postea, 5 si non proficiat, iuxta exemplum apostuli. Sed qui potest proficere, licet periclitatur, ubique doceat et se ostendat; qui uero non potest, taceat et abscondat. Alius quippe ab Iesu in domum suam mittitur, alius sequi iubetur.

XVI. DE FALSIS EPISCOPIS. 10

Qui non secundum apostulum electus est, ab altero episcopo est damnandus; deinde ad reliquam plebem declinandus, et degradandus.

XVII. DE PROPOSITO MONACHORUM.

Monachi sunt qui solitariae sine terrenis opibus habitant sub potestate episcopi uel abbatis. Non sunt autem monachi, ut aiunt, sed bactro- 15 periti, hoc est contemptoris sollicititŧ. Ad uitam perfectam in etate perfecta, hoc est xxx annorum, debit unus quisque constringere, non adtestando, sed uoto perficiendo, ut est illud: *Unus quisque sicut proposuit in corde* faciat, et ut: *Uota mea reddam in conspectu Domini*, et reliqua. Quae uero uita uiuitur? Situs locorum coartat, sed super- 20 habundantia in omnibus diuiditur in uita, quia *in frigore et nuditate* et *fame et siti, in uigiliis in ieiuniis* uocati sunt.

XVIII. DE TRIBUS SEMINIBUS EUANGELIORUM.

Centissime episcopi et doctores, quia omnibus omnia sunt; sexagissimum clerici et uiduae ⟨et⟩ qui contenentes sunt; xxxmi layci qui 25

5 *cf.* Matth. 15, 24   6 *cf.* Act. 16, 6 sqq.   8 sq. *cf.* Luc. 8, 39; Matth. 9, 9; *al.* 11 *cf.* 1 Tim. 3, 2 sqq.; Tit. 1, 7 sq.   18 sq. 2 Cor. 9, 7 unus quisque prout (sicut d e m Cypr. Hier.) destinauit (proposuit d e m Cypr. Aug.) ⟨in BPWZᶜ vg Hier. Pel.⟩ corde suo (*om.* d e m Cypr. Hier. Aug.)   19 Ps. 115, 18 uota mea Domino reddam in conspectu omnis populi eius   21 sq. *cf.* 2 Cor. 11, 27   24 sq. *cf.* Matth. 13, 8. 23 (LQR *al.*).

XVII: *cf.* Coll. Hib. XLVII. 20, adn.(g).   20 sq. *cf.* Ordo monasterii *ed.* de Bruyne, Rev. Bén. 1930, p. 319, 21 sq. (uita . . . uiuitur); Regula s. Benedicti c. 35 (positionem loci).

1 quid: quod Q   nouat(-c- D)ionum DJ   2 nouacianus D. nouationum J x̄pianum J   abstineat JI   3 obseruetur QDI. abstinetur J   4 DOCENDA: *litterae* nda *super rasuram, sequente rasura quattuor fere litterarum, in* I   5 delinquenda JI. relinquenda Y   6 apostoli QDI. apl-is J. ap-li Y   7 pereclitatur QDJ. periclitetur Y   docet (& *in ras.*) Q   qui–8 abscondat *om.* Y 8 abscendat Jᶜ; *lege* abscedat? aliis I   ab Iesu: abi** Y   mittetur DJY   11 apostolum DI. (*per compendium J*)   12 dampnatus K   ad: ab K   reliquem J 13–*p.* 192, 14 *om.* Y   13 *titulus litteris minusculis scribitur in* D   MANACHORUM Q*   14 solitariẹ K: -i QDJI   in *ante* terrenis K*   abitant Q   15 aitunt D 15–16 bactᵣo·periti Q. bactroperiti DJI. bactor periti K. bactro-peratae *coni. Haddan*–

of our laws of fasting. What else is the difference between a Novatian[4] and a Christian but that a Novatian abstains continually, a Christian does so for a time only, so that place, time, and person may in all things be observed.[5]

XV. OF LEAVING OR OF TEACHING ONE'S OWN COUNTRY.

One's country is first to be taught, after the example of Christ, and afterwards if it (*or*: one?) does not make progress, it is to be abandoned, according to the example of the Apostle. But he who is able to succeed, although he takes a risk, shall teach and show himself everywhere; but he who is not able, let him be silent and depart.[6] One, you recall, is sent by Jesus to his own house; another is commanded to follow Him.

XVI. OF FALSE BISHOPS.

He who is not chosen according to the Apostle, is to be condemned by another bishop; thereafter he is to be relegated to the rest of the people (*i.e.* the laity) and to be degraded.

XVII. OF THE WAY OF LIFE OF MONKS.

Monks are those who dwell in solitude without worldly resources, under the power of a bishop or an abbot. But they are not monks, as they say, only vagrant philosophers, that is, despisers of the world[7] . . .[8] Each one ought to be drawn to the perfect life at the perfect age, that is, of thirty years,[9] not in witnessing to, but in fulfilling, his vow: as saith this (passage): Let *each* do *as he hath purposed in his heart*, and: *I shall render my vows in the sight of the Lord*, and so forth. What sort of life do they live? the site of their place is narrow, but excess is to be avoided in all things in life,[10] for they are called *in cold and nakedness, in hunger and thirst, in vigils and fasts.*

XVIII. OF THE THREE SEEDS OF THE GOSPELS.

The hundredfold are the bishops and teachers, for they are all things to all men; the sixtyfold are the clergy and widows ⟨and⟩ those who are continent; the thirtyfold the lay folk who are faithful, who perfectly

---

Stubbs; lege bactroperitae   16 contemtoris D. contemptores QI. (bactroperitae . . . contemptores saeculi *Hier. in Matth. 10, 9–10, p. 58 Vallarsi, cf. Souter s.u.*)   solliciti: saeculi *cum Hier. scribunt, post lacunam indicant Haddan–Stubbs*   aetate Q. ẹtate I   17 perfectam QJ   hoc: ho D   xxx: a triginti J   debet DJI   18 sed: si DJ   illut D   18–19 proposui J   19 in (1) *om.* DJ   corde ⟨suo⟩ DJ   ⟨sic⟩ faciat I   20 quae: qui JI   uita uiuitur: uota uouunt J   cohartat J. h *s.s.* D   sed: si J. situs D   20–21 superabundantia QDI   21 diuiditur KQI (*cf. Acta 2, 45; 4, 35*). diuitetur (*i.e.* deuitetur) DJ   quia: q; J   22 in (2): et I   sunt: sumus DJI   24 centissimi J. centissim* D. centesimi I   doctoris D   quia: que Q. qui in (in *del.*) I   24–25 sexagisimum QD. sexagesimum JI; *lege* sexagissimi?   25 clereci D   uidue Q. -ẹ I.   et *suppleui; cf. Patric. Conf. 42*   continentes I   trigissime Q. tregissimi D. trigissimi J. trigesimi I.   laici QDJI   qui *om.* KJ

fidelis sunt, qui perfecte Trinitatem credunt. His amplius non est in messe Dei. Monachus uero et uirginis cum centissimis iungamus.

XVIIII. QUA ETATE BAPTIZANDI SUNT.

Octauo die caticumini sunt. Postea solempnitatibus Domini bapti- zantur, id est Pascha et Pentecosten et Aepiphania.   5

XX. DE PARROCHIAS

Cum monachis non est dicendum, quia malum est inauditum; qui unitatem uero plebis non incongrue suscipimus ⟨. . .⟩.

XXI. DE RETENENDIS UEL DIMITTENDIS MONACHIS.

Unus quisque fructum suum in aeclesia in qua inbutus est perfruat, 10 nisi causa maioris profectus ad alterius ferre permissu abbatis cogat. Si uero exigerit causa utilior, cum benedictione dicatur: *Ecce agnus Dei* —non *quae sua sunt* singuli *quaerentis sed quae Iesu Christi.* Uocationis autem causam non permittunt subditus discurrere.

XXII. DE SUMMENDA EUCHARISTIA POST LAPSUM.   15

Post examinationem carceris sumenda est, maxime autem in nocte Paschae, in qua qui non communicat fidelis non est. Ideo breuia sunt et stricta apud eos spatia, ne anima fidelis interiat tanto tempore ieiuna medicinae, Domino dicente: *Nisi manducaueritis carnem fili hominis non habebitis uitam in uobis.*   20

XXIII. DE IURAMENTO.

Non iurare omnino: de hoc consequens lectionis series docit non adiurandam esse creaturam aliam sed creatorem, ut prophetis mos est: *Uiuit Dominus et uiuet anima mea,* et: *Uiuit Dominus, cui adsisto hodie.*

12 Ioh. 1, 36.   13 Phil. 2, 21 omnes enim sua (quae sua sunt f g DFMOPSWZ* vg. Ambrst. Hier. Aug. Pel^B) quaerunt, non quae sunt (sunt *om.* d e f g LP Ambrst. Aug. Vigil.) Iesu Christi   19–20 Ioh. 6, 53   22 Matth. 5, 34   24 *inter alios locos cf.* 4 Reg. 2, 2. 4. 6 uiuit Dominus et uiuit anima tua (μου *pro* σου *u.l. in* GR). *cf.* 3 Reg. 17, 1 uiuit Dominus, cui adsisto ante conspectum (Lucif.); *cf.* cui assisto in conspectu eius Tert. (in cuius conspectu sto VULG).

2 *cf.* Hier. Epist. 123, 8   18 apud eos, *i.e.* apud Romanos? *cf.* Coll. Hib. XLVII. 8d   19 medicinae: *cf.* Cumm. II. 2

XXIII: Coll. Hib. XXXV. 3 Dominus in euangelio: Non iurabis omnino . . . Hieronimus: Haec consequentia lectionis docet nullam adiurandam esse creaturam sed creatorem, ut mos est prophetis dicere: uiuit Dominus, cui adsisto hodie, omne enim quod adiurabitur hoc et amatur (*cf.* Hier. in Matth. 5, 34 sqq., p. 30 Vallarsi, *ubi nulla prophetarum mentio fit, sed habes:* Qui iurat aut ueneratur aut diligit eum per quem iurat).

---

1 fideles I   perfecti K^cQ   his: is D   2 messe: mensi I   uirgines DJI   centesimis I   iungamur K. iungantur I. *om.* D   3 *Hic titulus post* De parrochias (6) *legitur in* I   QUE Q   AETATE Q. ętate I   BABTI- ZANDI J   4 octaua I   Octauo–sunt *litteris maiusculis scribit* D   solemnitati- bus Q. sollemnitatibus DJI   5 pasca I   et (1) *om.* D   pentecosten *codd.* (Pentecoste *Spelman.*) *De accusatiuo in enumerationibus cf.* B. Linderbauer, S. Benedicti

believe in the Trinity. Beyond these there is nought in the harvest of the Lord. Monks and virgins we may count with the hundredfold.

XIX. OF THE PROPER AGE FOR BAPTISM.

On the eighth day they are catechumens. Thereafter they are baptized on the solemn feast days of the Lord, that is at Easter, Pentecost, and Epiphany.

XX. OF PARISHES

With monks one must not even speak because it is an unheard-of evil; we who not improperly maintain the unity of the parish ⟨. . .⟩.[11]

XXI. OF MONKS TO BE RETAINED OR SENT OUT.

Let every one enjoy[12] his fruit in the church in which he has been instructed, unless the cause of greater success requires that he should bear (fruit) at another's (church) with the permission of his abbot.[13] If, indeed, the cause of greater (spiritual) profit demands this, it shall be said with blessing: *Behold the Lamb of God*, each one seeking not *the things that are his own but those which are Jesus Christ's*. But they do not permit their subjects to run about because of their vocation.

XXII. OF TAKING THE EUCHARIST AFTER A FALL.

After a proving of the flesh it is to be taken, but especially on the eve of Easter; for he who does not communicate at that time is not a believer. Therefore short and strict are the seasons (of penance) in their ranks,[14] lest the faithful soul perish, by abstaining from the medicine for so long a time, for the Lord saith: *Except you eat the flesh of the Son of Man, you shall not have life in you.*

XXIII. OF TAKING AN OATH.

Swear not at all: the lection beginning with these words teaches that no other creature is to be sworn by, but only the Creator, as is the custom of the prophets: *The Lord liveth, and my soul liveth*, and *The*

Regula, 1922, p. 232; P. B. Corbett, The Latin of the Regula Magistri, 1958, pp. 179, 194 sq. ephiphania Q. ephifania Dᶜ (epif- D*). epiphania JI 6–8 *distinxi lege* De parochianis (*uel* parochiarum) conmonachis? non est: nouē K 8 suscepimus DJ *lacunam indicaui* 9 RETENDIS K. retinendis I DEMITTENDIS QJ 10 ęclesie K. ecclesiis Q. ecclesia I inbutur J perfruat: *lege* proferat? 11 maiores Q profectus *om.* Q ad alterius *Wilkins*: ad altaris KQ. ad alteris DJI permisso DJI abatis Q 12 exegerit Q. exierit DJ benedictionem J 13 non: nam Jᶜ que *utroque loco* Q, *priore loco* I quae(-ę- I)rentes DJI. querentes Q sed: si DJ Iesum Q uocationes Q Uocationis–14 discurrere *om.* I 14 causam *recte pro ablatiuo sumunt McNeill–Gamer* 15 SUMENDA QDJIY 16 maximę I 17 pascha K. pasche Q qui: que Q* 18 spacia DIY intereat DJIY ieiunia QJI 19 medicine QY filii IY 20 abebitis Q 21–*p.* 194, 9 *om.* Y 22 consequens *ego*: consequente KQDJ. -ti I lectiones QJ serie I docet QDJI 23 adiuranda I sed: si J. *om.* D prophetę I 24 uiuet: uiuit QDJI hodiae Q

Finis autem *contradictionis adiuramentum est,* sed ⟨in⟩ Domino; omne enim quod amatur hoc [enim] et ⟨ad⟩iuratur.

XXIIII. DE CONTENTIONEM DUORUM ABSQUE TESTIBUS

Statuunt ut per sancta quattuor euangelia antequam communicet testetur qui ⟨a⟩dprobatur et deinde sub iudice[s] flamma relinquatur.   5

XXV. DE THORO FRATRIS DEFUNCTI

Audi decreta sinodi: Superstis frater thorum defuncti fratris non ascendat, Domino dicente: *Erunt duo in carne una*; ergo uxor fratris tui soror tua est.

XXVI. DE MERETRICE CONIUGE   10

Audi Dominum dicentem: *Qui adherit meretricem unum corpus efficitur.* Item: *Adultera lapidetur,* id est, huic uicio moriatur ut desinat crescere quae non desinebat mechari. Item: *Si adulterata fuerit mulier numquid reuertitur ad uirum suum priorem?* Item: *Non licet uiro dimittere uxorem suam nisi ob* quam *causam fornicationis,* hac si liciat ob 15 hanc causam. Unde, se ducat alteram, uelut post mortem prioris non uetant.

XXVII. DE UOLUNTATE UIRGINIS UEL PATRIS IN CONIUGIO.

Quid uult pater efficiat uirgo, *quia capud mulieris uir.* Sed quaerenda est a patre uoluntas uirginis, dum *Deus relinquid hominem in manibus* 20 *consilii sui.*

---

1 Heb. 6, 16 omnis controuersiae (contradictionis r) eorum finis . . . est iuramentum. 8 Gen. 2, 24; Matth. 19, 5; *al.*   11 1 Cor. 6, 16 qui adhaeret (adherit N*Z*) meretrici (-em Z*) unum corpus efficitur.   12 *cf.* Deut. 22, 21 (lapidabunt illam Mon., eam Aug.)   13 sq. *cf.* Ier. 3, 1 si contaminata fuerit mulier (*sic De promiss. c. 15*), numquid reuertetur ad eam (*uir eius*)? (*sic* VULG, *sed* GR: μὴ ἀνακάμπτουσα ἀνακάμψει πρὸς αὐτὸν ἔτι), *cf.* Oseas 2, 7 reuertar ad uirum meum priorem; Deut. 24, 4. 14 sq. Matth. 19, 3 si licet homini (ἀνδρί *u.l. in* GR, *cf.* Marc. 10, 2) dimittere uxorem suam quacumque ex causa (non dimittat illam 1 Cor. 7, 11). 9 nisi ob causam fornicationis a b ff₂ g₁ q r₁ aur Q (ob fornicationem VULGᵖˡ).   19 Eph. 5, 23 quoniam (quia d e Tert. Orig. quoniam uel quia g) uir caput est mulieris (caput mulieris uir Hier. *bis*; est *om.* Aug.).   20 sq. Eccli 15, 14 Deus . . . reliquit (relinquit *u.l.* m) illum (*i.e.* hominem) in manu consilii sui.

XXIIII: Coll. Hib. XVI. 14 Sinodus Romana: De contentione duorum sine testibus statuunt ut per quatuor sancta euangelia antequam commonicet testetur qui adprobatur, deinde sub iudice flamma relinquatur.

XXV: Coll. Hib. XLVI. 35b: Romani: Superstes frater thorum defuncti fratris non ascendat, dicente Domino: Erunt duo in carne una, ergo uxor fratris tui soror tua est.

---

1 contradictiones Q   sed: si J. *om.* I   in *addidi* (in *pro* sed *Wilkins*) 2 ⟨homo****⟩ hoc J   enim (2): est D; *deleui; cf. Coll. Hib. et supra p. 188, 5* adiuratur *ego:* iuratur *codd.; cf. Coll. Hib.*   3 *inde ab hoc titulo usque ad xxviiii numeros uno minores reddidit* Qᶜ   CONTENTIONE DJI   4 sancta *om.* I. *post* quattuor *ponunt* (*cum Coll. Hib.*) DJ   quottuor Q. quatuor D   euancielia (?) Q

Lord liveth in whose sight I stand to-day. Yet: *The end of controversy is the oath*, but ⟨in⟩ the Lord; for by all that a man loves, by this does he make oath.

XXIV. OF THE CONTENTION OF TWO WITHOUT WITNESSES

They determine that he who is to be proved (right) shall testify by the four holy gospels before he takes communion, and then he shall be left to the judgement of fire.

XXV. OF THE BED OF A DEAD BROTHER

Hear the decree of the synod: 'A surviving brother shall not enter the bed of a dead brother.' For the Lord saith: They shall be two in one flesh; therefore the wife of thy brother is thy sister.

XXVI. OF A PROSTITUTE WIFE

Hearken unto the Lord when he saith: *He who is joined to a harlot is made one body.* Also: *An adulteress shall be stoned*, that is, she shall die for this fault, that she may cease to increase who did not cease to commit adultery. Further: *If a woman has become corrupted, does she return to her former husband?* Further: *it is not permitted to a man to put away his wife, except because of fornication*—as if it were for that reason.[15] Hence, if he marries another, as if after death of the former, (authorities) do not forbid it.

XXVII. OF THE WILL OF THE MAIDEN AND OF THE FATHER IN MARRIAGE.

What the father wishes, the maiden shall do, *since the head of the woman is the man.* But the will of the maiden is to be inquired after by the father, since *God left man in the hand of his own counsel.*

5 ⟨et⟩ testetur Q*   testatur DJI   quid probatur *codd.: corr. McNeill–Gamer, cf. Coll. Hib.*   et *om.* I   iudicis DJI. (iudice *recte Coll. Hib., cf. Syn. Aqu. Brit. 6; Cumm. (VIII). 12*)   flammae J. fama I   6 TORO D*   FRATRES Q   7 synodi JI   superstis: super histis (istis I) QI   thorum *om.* I   8 ascedat J*   11 adheret D (h *s.s.*). IY   meretrice QDJ. meretrici IY   12 adaltera Q   lapidatur DJY   huic: hic Q*   uitio QIY   13 criscere Q   quae: qui DY   desinat DJ   me(-oe- JI)chare DJIY   adulteratam Q. adultera IY   14 reuertetur DJIY   demittere QDJ   15 suam *om.* DIY   quam *om.* QDJIY; *cf. Matth. 19, 9*   causa DJ   fornicationes Q. fornicacionis D   hac: ac IY   liceat DJIY   16 se ducat *ego:* seducat KQDJ. si ducat IY *Spelman*   uelud Y. uel I   18 UOLUNTATEM J   IN *om.* I   19 quod QDJIY   faciat QDIY. facit J   quia: quae J   caput DJIY   requerenda QD. requen/renda J. requirenda IY   20 relinquit DI. reliquit Y

XXVIII. DE PRIMIS UEL SECUNDIS UOTIS.

Eadem ratione obseruanda sunt prima uota et prima coniugia, ut
secundis prima non sunt inrita, nisi fuerint adulterata.

XXVIIII. DE CONSANGUINITATE IN CONIUGIO

Intellege quid lex loquitur, non minos nec plus; quod autem obserua- 5
tur apud nos, ut quattuor genera diuidantur, nec uidisse dicunt nec
legisse.

XXX. DE UINDICANDIS ADSUETIS

Numquam uetitur licet, uirum obseruande sunt legis iubelei, hoc
est quinquagissimi anni, ut non adfirmentur incerta ueterato tempore; 10
et ideo omnes neguti⟨ati⟩o subscriptione ⟨more⟩ Romanorum confir-
manda est.

XXXI. DE GENTILIBUS QUI ANTE BAPTISMUM CREDUNT QUAM PENETENTIAM HABENT.

Remittuntur quidem omnium peccata in baptismo; sed qui cum fideli 15
conscientia infidelem tempore uixit paene ut fidelis peccator iudicandus.

FINIT PATRICII SINODUS   DEO GRATIAS

XXX: Coll. Hib. XXXVI. 8: Sinodus ait de uenditis adsuetis: licet uerum numquam
ueteratur, obseruandae sunt tamen leges iubilei, id est anni quinquagesimi, ut non
affirmentur incerta tempore ueterato, et ideo omnis negotiatio subscriptione affirmanda
est.   11 more Romanorum: *cf.* Cod. Iustin. IIII. 21, 17 contractus uenditionum . . .
non aliter uires habere sancimus nisi instrumenta . . . subscriptionibus . . . partium
confirmata . . . sint.

2 ut: aut J   3 sunt K^cQDJI: sint Y *Spelman.* (*De* K* *non constat*)   irrita I. *om.* Y
fuerent J   adultera I   *Finit* Y   4 consanguinitat̄ I   5 intellegi J   quod Q   minus
QDJI   quod: quid J   6 quatuor D   diuidantur, *i.e.* deuitantur (*sic* Q); *cf. p. 190, 21*
8 *titulus, ut uidetur, cum textu coniungendus est; aliter Coll. Hib.*   *titulum om.* J
9 uetitus DJI. ueditus Q   uerum QDJI   obseruandẹ I   leges DI   iubelii Q   hoc:
id I   10 est *om.* K   quinquagesimi JI. quinquagesima Q   incerte K   11 omnis
Q. omni J. omñ D   negutio KQ. negotio DJI: negotiatio *Wilkins, cf. Coll. Hib.*
more *addidi*   13 BABTISMUM J   ⟨QUI ANTE⟩ CREDUNT D.   14
PENITENTIAM QI. PẸNITENTIAM J. POENITENTIAM D   ABENT Q
15 babtismum J   sed: si J   16 consciencia Q   temporem J. teporem DI;
fortasse legendum tepore (*cf. app. crit. ad p. 184, 15*) *uel* tempore ⟨uitae⟩   pene Q.
pẹne I   peccatore J   17 DEO GRATIAS *om.* DJI

XXVIII. OF FIRST AND SECOND VOWS.

First vows[16] and first marriages are to be observed in the same way, that is, the first are not made void for the second, unless they have been annulled by adultery.

XXIX. OF CONSANGUINITY IN MARRIAGE

Understand what the Law saith, neither less nor more: but what is observed among us, that they be separated by four degrees, they say they have never seen nor read.[17]

XXX. CONCERNING CLAIMS THAT HAVE BECOME OBSOLETE,

Although these are not forbidden at any time, yet the laws of the jubilee year, that is, of every fiftieth year, are to be observed, so that claims that have become uncertain through lapse of time may not be asserted; and therefore every business transaction should be confirmed by signature in the Roman manner.[18]

XXXI. OF PAGANS WHO BELIEVE BEFORE BAPTISM, WHAT OUGHT TO BE THEIR PENANCE.

The sins of all are indeed remitted in baptism; but he who with a believing conscience lives for some time as an unbeliever is to be judged almost as a believing sinner.

HERE ENDS THE SYNOD OF PATRICK
THANKS BE TO GOD

PAENITENTIALE QUOD DICITUR BIGOTIANUM

HIERONIMUS UIR BEATAE MEMORIAE ECLESIAE PASTORES ET
DOCTORES UT QUALITATES UITIORUM IN PECCANTIBUS ANIMAD-
UERTANT DILIGENTER AMONUIT DICENS:

1. Tanto maior potentia medici quanto magis creuit morbus egroti.
2. Hinc procurantibus aliorum sanare uulnera solerter intuendum est 5
cuius aetatis et sexus sit peccans, qua eruditione inbutus, qua fortitudine
exstat, quali grauatione conpulsus est peccare, quali pasione inpugnatur, quanto tempore in diliciis remansit, quali lacrimabilitate et labore
affligitur et qualiter a mundialibus separatur. *Cor* enim *contritum et*
humiliatum Deus non spernit. 3. Et hoc sapientibus in penitentia mode- 10
randa intuendum est, ne dignum scelus gladio ferula uindicent et
dignum peccatum ferula gladio percutiant; et secundum Gregorium
magnopere pastoribus procurandum, ne incauti alligauerint quod non
alligandum et non soluerint quod non soluendum.

4. His itaque de penitentia expraesis fateor quod, si in hoc paeni- 15
tentiae temperamento plus minusuae ante oculis creatoris uideatur,
non nostrae audaciae culpa est; maiorum enim decreta, non nostra
exposuimus.

5. Praetium anni .vii. diebus et noctibus ieiunare; ut alius dicit:
ieiuna .iii. ebdomadas continuas et saluus eris. 6. Item de remediis uaris 20
uulnerum, prout antiquorum auctorum approbatio tullit, conpendiosas
carptim caraxamus eglotas.

7. Omnis impius iniquus est et peccator; nec reciprocat, ut possimus
dicere: omnis peccator et iniquus etiam impius est. 8. Impietas enim
propriae ad eos pertinet qui Dei notitiam non habent uel cognitam 25
transgresione mutauerunt; peccatum autem et iniquitas pro qualitate
uitiorum post peccati et iniquitatis uulnera recipit sanitatem. 9. Unde
scriptum est: *Multa flagella peccatorum,* et non interitus sempiternus,
secundum illud Domini: *Quid enim prodest homini si uniuersum mundum*
lucretur, animam suam perdat aut detrimentum faciat? 10. Unde uidetur 30

---

4 sqq. *in s. Hieronymi scriptis non leguntur; de fonte cf. Wasserschleben, p. 441;*
McNeill–Gamer, p. 148. 9–10 Ps. 50, 19 (spernit PsV^{pl} Cypr. *semel*, Caes.
Arel. *bis.* spernet G: despiciet R. despicies VULG.) 12–14 *cf.* Greg. M. Hom.
in Euang. ii. 26, 5–6 (PL lxxvi. 1200 sq.) 28 Ps. 31, 10 (peccatorum Lugd.
G H Rom Moz Cassiod.) 29 sq. Matth. 16, 26; *cf.* Luc. 9, 25; 1 Cor. 3, 15;
u. etiam Patric. Epist. 8.

Codices: C, B

---

3 ammonuit B. 4 potentia: i. fiat *s.s.* CB. quando CB. 5 aliorum:
aborum C. 7 passione B. 8 quando CB. 10 non spernit: conspernit C.
12 percutient B. 13 incaute B. 16 oculos B. 17 audatiae B. 20 ieiunia

THE SO-CALLED BIGOTIAN PENITENTIAL

JEROME,[1] A MAN OF BLESSED MEMORY, CAREFULLY ADMONISHED THE PASTORS AND TEACHERS OF THE CHURCH THAT THEY SHOULD TAKE NOTE OF THE QUALITIES OF THE FAULTS OF SINNERS, SAYING:

1. Let the power of the physician become greater in the degree in which the fever of the sick man increases. 2. Hence those who take care to heal the wounds of others are to observe carefully what is the age and sex of the sinner, what instruction he has received, what is his strength, by what trouble he has been driven to sin, with what kind of passion he is assailed, how long he remained in sinful delight, with what sorrow and labour he is afflicted, and how much he is detached from worldly things. For *God despiseth not the contrite and humbled heart.* 3. Wise men, in regulating penance, are to look carefully also to this: not to punish with the rod a crime worthy of the sword and to smite with the sword a sin worthy of the rod; and according to Gregory, great care is to be taken by pastors lest they carelessly bind what ought not to be bound and loose what ought not to be loosed.

4. Now, having said this on penance, I confess that if in this apportionment of penance more or less should be approved before the eyes of the Creator, it is not our audacity that is responsible; for we have expounded the decrees of our elders, not our own.

5. The equivalent of a year: to fast seven days and nights; as another says: fast three continuous weeks and thou shalt be saved.[2] 6. We thus put down in writing, piece by piece, compendious selections on the various remedies of wounds, according to what has been approved by the ancient authors.

7. Every irreligious person is unrighteous and a sinner; but it does not follow conversely that we can say: every sinner and unrighteous person is also irreligious. 8. For irreligion properly appertains to those who have not the knowledge of God or have changed it by transgression; but sin and unrighteousness receive healing according to the nature of the (principal) vices after the wounds of sin and unrighteousness.[3] 9. Hence it is written: *Many are the scourges of sinners*, and not everlasting destruction, according to this (word) of the Lord: *For what doth it profit a man if he gain the whole world and lose or cast away his own soul?* 10. Whence it seems to be indicated that some sins involve loss, but not

---

CB.   uariis B.   21 conpediosas C.   22 eglotas, *i.e.* eclogas, *cf. Glossarium Amplonianum secundum (Corp. Gloss. Lat. V. 299, 47 sq.):* Haec egloge et exglotae cantiones in carminibus.   26 transgressione B.   27 sq. unde scriptum: ut descriptum C.

ostendi quod quedam peccata ad damnum quidem pertineant, nec
tamen ad interitum, quia qui damnum passus fuerit *ipse tamen saluari*
dicitur, licet *per ignem*. 11. Unde credo et Iohannis in epistola sua dicit
quaedam *esse peccata ad mortem*. 12. Quae uero *non ad mortem* sed ad
damnum, non puto facile a quoquam homine posse discerni; scriptum 5
namque est: *Delicta quis intellegit?* 13. Igitur qui *saluus erit, per ignem*
saluus erit, ut si quis aurum per ignem plumbis mixtum indignis
dequocat et resoluat, ut efficiantur omnes aurum bonum, quia *aurum*
terrae illius aurum *bonum esse* dicitur quam habitaturi sunt sancti, et
sicut *fornax probat* aurum ita *homines iustos temptatio*. 14. Ueniendum 10
est ergo omnibus ad ignem, ueniendum est ad conprobatorium; sed
etenim: *Et conflat et purgat filios Iuda*. 15. Sed illuc †cum uenitur†
sequi multa opera bona. Et si paruum aliquid iniquitatis adtullerit, illud
paruum tamquam plumbum igni resoluitur ac purgatur et totum
remanet aurum; et si quis plus illuc plumbi detulerit, plus exuritur, ut 15
amplius dequoquatur, ut et paruum aliquid auri purgati tamen resideat.
16. Quod si aliquis illuc totus plumbeus uenerit, fiet de illo hoc quod
scriptum est: *Demergitur in profundum tamquam plumbum in aqua*
ualidissima. 17. In cuius sacramento etiam in Leuitico inmunda fieri
mulier dicitur quae concepto semine peperit. 18. Non solum inmunda 20
erit, sed dupliciter inmunda; bis enim septenis diebus in inmunditia
scribitur permanere. 19. Sed interim: Quae peperit masculum, octaba
die et qui natus est circumciditur et illa sit munda. 20. Septima enim die
praesentis uitae tempus uideri potest. In septima enim die consummatus
est mundus. 21. In quo donec sumus in carne positi, ad liquidum puri 25
esse non possumus, nisi octaua uenerit dies, id est, nisi futuri saeculi
tempus aduenerit, in quo tamen die qui masculus est et uiriliter aget,
statim in ipso aduentu futuri saeculi purgatur. 22. Et statim munda
efficitur mater quae genuit eum; purgatam namque uitiis carnem ex
resurrectione suscipiet. 23. Si uero nihil in se habuit uirile aduersum 30
peccatum, si remissus et efeminatus fuerit in actibus suis, cuius peccatum
tale est quod non remittetur neque in praesenti saeculo neque in futuro,
iste transit et unam et alteram septimanam inmunditiae suae et tertia
demum incipiente aboriri septimana purgatur ab inmunditia quam
femina pariendo contraxit. 24. De quo fortassis et Esaias dicit: *Et erit,* 35
inquit, *in die ⟨illa⟩ uisitabit Dominus super militiam caeli in excelso et super*

2 sq. *cf.* 1 Cor. 3, 15　　　4 1 Ioh. 5, 16　　　6 Ps. 18, 13　　　6 1 Cor. 3, 15
8 sq. *cf.* Gen. 2, 12　　　10 *cf.* Eccli. 27, 6　　　12 *cf.* Mal. 3, 3 (conflat et purgat
VL[pi]); *cum nostro ad uerbum concordat* Rufinus, Orig. in Exod. hom. 6. 4 (p. 196,
8 Baehrens)　　　18 sq. Ex. 15, 10: de(di- *Breu. Moz.*)mersi sunt ⟨in profundum
Breu. Moz.⟩ tamquam (quasi *Hier.*) plumbum in aqua ualidissima *Breu. Moz.*, *Hier.*
in Ezech. 22.　　　19–23 *cf.* Leu. 12, 2–5　　　24 sq. *cf.* Gen. 2, 2–3　　　35 sqq. Is. 24,
21–22 (=VULG, *nisi quod illa habet:* in die ⟨illa⟩, *et* qui ⟨sunt⟩ super terram, *sed cf.*
τῶν ἐπὶ τῆς γῆς; congregatione *et* carcere *noster cum* vg. *contra* -em A)

1. 2. 5 dampnum B.　　　1 quidem: quid .ē. C.　　　pertinent B.　　　2 quia:

destruction; for he who has suffered loss *yet* is said *to be saved*, though (only) *by fire*. 11. Hence, I believe, it is that John in his Epistle also says that *there are* some *sins unto death*. 12. Which (sins), however, are *not unto death*, but unto loss, I do not think it easy for any man to be able to distinguish; for it is written: *Who can understand sins?* 13. Therefore he who *shall be saved* shall be saved *by fire*, as if one melts and dissolves by fire gold mixed with base lead, in order that all may be made good gold, since *the gold of that land* which the saints are to inhabit is said to be *good gold*; and as *a furnace tries* gold, so *temptation* tries *righteous men*. 14. Therefore all must come to the fire—must come to the proving; but truly: *It both melts and cleanses the sons of Juda*. 15. But if one comes thither, many good works should follow.[4] And if he brings but little unrighteousness, that little is dissolved and cleansed as is lead by fire, and what remains is all gold; and if anyone bears more of lead thither, he is burned more, so that he may be melted down more and yet that some little purified gold may remain. 16. But if anyone comes thither who is all lead, it happens to him as it is written: *He is plunged into the deep as lead in a mighty sea*. 17. It is in this mystical sense[5] that also in Leviticus a woman is said to become unclean who has conceived seed and borne a child. 18. Not only will she be unclean but doubly unclean; for it is written that she remains in uncleanness for twice seven days. 19. However: If she bears a male child, on the eighth day the child shall be circumcised and she shall be clean. 20. For the seventh day can be looked upon as the time of the present life.[6] For on the seventh day the world was completed. 21. While we are placed there in the flesh we cannot be to perfection, unless the eighth day come, that is, unless the time of the pure future world arrive; on which day, however, he who is a male and acts as a man is cleansed immediately on the coming of that future world. 22. And immediately the mother who bore him is made clean; for he shall receive in the Resurrection his flesh purified from its vices. 23. But if he had in him nothing manly with which to resist sin, if he was remiss and effeminate in his actions, whose sin is such that it is not forgiven either in the present world or in that which is to come, he passes through both the first and the second week of his uncleanness, and finally, with the beginning of the third week, he is cleansed from the uncleanness which the woman incurred by child-bearing. 24. Perhaps it is of this that Isaiah says: *And it shall come to pass*, saith he, *that in that day the Lord shall visit upon the host of heaven on high, and upon the*

---

quã B.   3 iohannes B.   ẹpistola B.   4 quaedam: quidam C.   10 sicut: sc̄i C.   12 cum (tum C) uenitur CB: *fort. lege* cum uenitur, ⟨conuenit⟩   13 sequi: sequantur *McNeill–Gamer*.   ad tullerit C. attulerit B.   14 resololuitur C.   22 interim: *lege* iterum?   octaua B.   23 *lege* die⟨s⟩?   25 aliquidum C.   28 munda: multa B.   30 aduersum *om*. C.   31 effeminatus B.   cuius *om*. B.   33 tertia *ego*: tertiam CB.   34 incipientem B.   aborriri B.   (tertiam demum incipientem adorsus septimanam *McNeill–Gamer*.)   36 uisitabit: instabit B.

reges terrae qui super terram, et congregabuntur in congregatione unius fascis in lacum et claudentur ibi in carcere et post multos dies uisitabuntur.
25. Itaque et diabolum ⟨dicit⟩ Dominus et satellites eius omnesque impios et praeuaricatores perire perpetuo; et Christianos, si in peccato praeuenti fuerint, saluandos esse post penas. 26. Quarum iterum quali- 5
tatem uel quantitatem poenarum non solum pro diuersitate, ut dixi, uitiorum sed pro unius cuiusque peccantium differentia uirium siue eruditione uel aetate iuste quidem, ut a Domino recto iudice, sed diuerse, ut a creatore conscio omnium, naturali non dubitamus libertate repensandam. 27. Etenim sicut sementibus †naturam certis legibus creator† ita 10
et hominibus secundum uirtutum seu qualitatum discrepantiam indulgebit, secundum illud prophetae: *Non enim in serris triturabitur geth neque rota plaustri super ciminum circumiet; sed uirga excutietur geth et ciminum in baculo, pannis autem comminuetur*; ⟨uel⟩ ut est illud: *Potentes potenter tormenta patientur; secundum mensuram peccati erit et plagarum modus.* 15
28. His igitur edoctus exemplis, dum et tibi cura in peccata ulciscendi, hoc est medendi animas, sane multiplex est et in eo quod diuersa sunt peccata et in discrepantia, ut dixi, uirtutum et qualitatum peccantium, sanctorum facta patrum ad Dominum reuertentium a suis medentium peccatis, simul omisa uerborum in breui circuitione merito 20
collegi uis, ut scilicet ferula dignum uitium gladio non uindices nec gladio dignum scelus ferula coerceas.
29. Ceterum quanti memento meriti tibi est *peccatorem ab errore conuertere uiae suae.* 30. Nam cum aliae peccatorum remissiones sint, quarum exemplis referta scriptura est, e quibus prima est qua baptiza- 25
mur in remissionem peccatorum, secunda in passione martyri, tertia quae per elemosinam datur, quarta per hoc quod et nos remittimus peccata fratribus nostris, quinta per abundantiam caritatis, sexta per penitentiam: 31. non est quoque harum extrema haec septima remissio, cum conuerterit quis peccatorem, ut dixi, ab errore uiae suae. 32. Ita 30
enim dicit scriptura diuina quia *qui conuertit peccatorem ab errore uiae suae saluabit animam suam a morte et cooperuit multitudinem peccatorum.*
Hoc est et in Leuitico scriptum: *Sacerdos qui offert illud et repropitiauit,*

---

3 sq. *cf.* Matth. 25, 41.   12–14 Is. 28, 27–28 (*fere* VULG); *de uariis lectionibus u. epilogum Cummeani, supra, p.* 132, 28–30   14 sq. Sap. 6, 7   15 Deut. 25, 2. (pro mensura VULG).   23–24 *cf.* Iac. 5, 20   24 sqq. *cf. Prologum Cummeani* 31–32 Iac. 5, 20; *de uariis lectionibus cf. praefationem Cummeani*   33 sq. *cf.* Leu. 7, 7–8; 19, 22

---

2 facis C.   claudentur: conlaudentur B.   ibi: ubi C.   3 dicit *addidi.* 4 perpetuo: ad(uerbium) *s.s.* C.   5 sq. qualitatem: quabilitate C.   8 ut a Domino: *s.s.* ⟨si C⟩ iudicetur CB.·   9 a creatore: accreatore C.   libertate B[c]: liberate C. liberrate B*, (liberalitate *McNeill–Gamer*); *fort. lege* ut a creatore conscio omnium naturali⟨um⟩, non dubitamus librate (*i.e. ad libram*) repensandam.   10 sq. *fort. lege*: Etenim sicut sementibus ⟨secundum⟩ naturam certis legibus creatam . . . 11 hominibus: omnibus B.   12. 13 gith B[c].   14 ⟨uel⟩ *suppleui, cf. epilogum*

kings of the earth who are on earth, and they shall be gathered together as in the gathering of one bundle into the pit, and they shall be shut up there in prison, and after many days they shall be visited. 25. Therefore also the Lord ⟨saith⟩ that both the devil and all his satellites and all wicked men and transgressors shall perish for ever; and the Christians, if they have been overtaken in sin, shall be saved after punishments. 26. The nature and extent of these punishments shall, we doubt not, be weighed, as I have said, not only according to the diversity of the faults but also according to the difference in strength of each of the sinners, or of training, or of age—justly, indeed, as by the Lord, the righteous judge, but diversely, as by the Creator who knoweth all in the freedom of his nature.[7] 27. For, indeed, as (He makes allowance) for the corn according to the laws of its created nature,[8] so also shall He make allowance to men according to their virtues or qualities, according to this word of the prophet: *For the gith shall not be threshed with saws, neither shall the cart wheel turn about upon cummin; but gith shall be beaten out with a rod and cummin with a staff; but bread corn shall be broken small*; ⟨or⟩ as this passage says: *The mighty shall be mightily tormented; according to the measure of the sin shall be the measure also of the stripes.*

28. Taught therefore by these examples, since for thee also the task of punishing sins, that is, of healing souls, is clearly manifold in view of both, the diversity of sins and the difference, as I have said, in the virtues and qualities of sinners, thou rightly wishest that the deeds of the holy fathers, the physicians of those who were returning to the Lord from their sins, together with their forgotten words, may be collected into brief space that thou, forsooth, punish not with the rod an offence worthy of the sword, nor with the sword one worthy of the rod.

29. Moreover, remember how great merit it is to thee to *convert a sinner from the error of his way.* 30. There are, of course, other remissions of sins of which the Scriptures are replete with examples. Of these the first is that in which we are baptized unto the remission of sins, the second consists in the passion of martyrdom, the third is that which is given through alms, the fourth lies in the fact that we forgive the sins of our brethren, the fifth in the abundance of charity, the sixth in penance. 31. Nevertheless, this seventh remission, (which occurs), as I said, when anyone converts a sinner from the error of his way, is not the least of these. 32. For thus saith the divine Scripture: *He that converteth a sinner from the error of his way shall save his soul from death and has covered a multitude of sins.* This also is written in Leviticus: *The priest who offers this and brings about reconciliation, it shall be for his own*

---

erit pro delicto ipsius. 33. Discant sacerdotes Domini qui eclesiis praesunt quia pars eis data est cum his quorum delicta repropitiauerint. 34. Quid autem repropitiare delictum? Si adsumseris peccatorem et monendo hortando docendo instruendo adduxeris eum ad penitentiam, ab errore coerc⟨u⟩eris, a uitiis emendaueris, et effeceris eum talem ut ei conuerso 5 propitius fiat Deus, pro delicto propitiare diceris. 35. Cum ergo talis sis sacerdos et talis sit doctrina tua et sermo tuus, pars tibi datur eorum quos correxeris, ut et illorum meritum tua merces sit et illorum salus tua sit gloria. 36. Ezechiel dicit: *Impietas impii super ipsum erit, et iustitia iusti super ipsum erit.* Et hoc iudicium est de eo quod non debent 10 iusti esse simul cum peccatoribus, et si habitauerint cum eis et occissi fuerint simul, non redetur ulli episcopo uel aecclesiae, dum dicitur: Tribus modis separantur iusti ab iniustis: misa mensa pace. Aliter in Ezechiele dicitur.

37. DE TURBA UITIORUM QUAE HUMANUM GENUS SEPARANT A REGNO 15 DEI APOSTOLUS AIT:

Manifesta sunt opera carnis, quae sunt

I	*ADULTERIA*	XI	*Heresses*	
II	*Fornicatio*	XII	*Animositas*	
III	*Inmunditia*	XIII	*Irae*	20
IIII	*Luxuria*	XIIII	*Rixae*	
V	*Idolatria*	XV	*Dissentiones*	
VI	*Homicidia*	XVI	*Sectae*	
VII	*Veneficia*	XVII	*Inuidiae*	
VIII	*Inimicitiae*	XVIII	*Odia*	25
VIIII	*Contentiones*	XVIIII	*Ebrietates*	
X	*Emulationes*	XX	*Commessationes*	

ET HIS SIMILIA.

Et: *Qui talia agunt regnum Dei non consequentur.*

38. ITEM APOSTOLUS AIT: 30

Nolite errare, quia neque fornicari neque idolis seruientes neque adulteri neque masculorum concubitores neque fures neque auari neque ebriosi regnum Dei possidebunt.

---

1 Discant–9 gloria = *epilogus Cummeani* 9 sq. Ezech. 18, 20 (*a* VULG *satis differt*; iustitia iusti super ipsum erit et iniquitas iniqui super ipsum erit *Iulianus apud Augustinum,* x. 1067e) 14 *cf.* Coll. Hib. XL. 1c 17–29 Gal. 5, 19–21 (adulteria *add* d e f g Iren TEST[pl]; ido(lo)latria e g Iren TEST[pl] D; ueneficia ⟨homicidia⟩ Cypr.) 31–33 1 Cor. 6, 9–10 (neque molles *om.* M; neque–rapaces *om.* m Hier.)

---

1 pro: quod C (*ex errore compendii*) 2 eis McNeill–Gamer, *cf.* Ps.-Cumm.: eius CB. 3 autem: aut C. adsumpseris C. 5 coercueris *ego*: coerceris C. coercens B. (correxeris *Cummeanus*.) 8 meritum–sit *ex Cummeano*:

sin. 33. The priests of the Lord, who preside over the churches, should learn that their share has been given to them together with those whose misdeeds they have caused to be forgiven. 34. But what is it to cause a misdeed to be forgiven? If thou take the sinner, and by warning, exhortation, teaching, instruction, lead him to penance, restrain him from his error, amend him of his vices, and render him such that God may be rendered favourable to him after his conversion, thou shalt be said to cause forgiveness for a misdeed. 35. When, therefore, thou art such a priest and such is thy teaching and thy word, there is given to thee the share of those whom thou hast corrected, that their merit may be thy reward and their salvation thy glory. 36. Ezekiel saith: *The wickedness of the wicked shall be upon him, and the justice of the just shall be upon him.* And this judgement means that the righteous ought not to be with sinners and that if they have dwelt with them and have been slain together with them no settlement with any bishop or church shall be made, as it is said: 'There are three ways in which the just are separated from the unjust—by the Mass, the table, and the kiss of peace.' It is differently stated in Ezekiel.

37. OF THE CROWD OF VICES WHICH SEVER THE HUMAN RACE FROM THE KINGDOM OF GOD THE APOSTLE SAYS:

The works of the flesh are manifest, which are

I	*ADULTERIES*	XI	*Heresies*
II	*Fornication*	XII	*Animosity*
III	*Uncleanness*	XIII	*Wraths*
IIII	*Luxury*	XIIII	*Quarrels*
V	*Idolatry*	XV	*Dissensions*
VI	*Murders*	XVI	*Sects*
VII	*Witchcrafts*	XVII	*Envies*
VIII	*Enmities*	XVIII	*Hatreds*
VIIII	*Contentions*	XVIIII	*Drunkenness*
X	*Emulations*	XX	*Revellings*

AND SUCH LIKE.

And: *They who do such things shall not obtain the Kingdom of God.*

38. LIKEWISE THE APOSTLE SAYS:

Do not err, for neither fornicators nor servants of idols nor adulterers nor liers with mankind nor thieves nor covetous nor drunkards shall possess the Kingdom of God.

---

interitus mer(mar- B)cescit CB.   11 habitauerit B.   occisi B.   12 reddetur B.
eclesiae B.   13 missa C.   18 Hereses B.   22 XV : X C.   30 AIT
om. B.   32 concupitores B.

HUCUSQUE APOSTOLUS. 39. ITEM ISSIODORUS:

Octo uitia sunt principalia, ex quibus uitiorum copiosa multitudo
exoritur:

I	Gula	VI	Tristitia	
II	Fornicatio	VII	Inanis gloria	5
III	Auaritia	VIII	Nouissima dux ipsa et	
IIII	Accedia		ipsorum regina super-	
V	Ira		bia.	

HUCUSQUE ISSIDORUS. 40. ITEM CASIANUS AIT:

De gastrimargia nascuntur   10

I	Commessationes	IIII	Multiloquium
II	Ebrietates	V	Hebitudo sensus
III	Inepta letitia	VI	Inmunditiae.

41. DE FORNICATIONE:

I	Turpiloquia	V	Inconstantia	15
II	Scurilitates	VI	Affectus praesentis	
III	Stultiloquia		saeculi	
IIII	Cecitas mentis	VII	Horror futuri.	

42. DE FILARGIRIA:

I	Mendacium	VI	Falsa testimonia	20
II	Fraudatio	VII	Violentiae	
III	Furta	VIII	Inhumanitas	
IIII	Periuria	VIIII	Rapacitas	
V	Turpis lucri appetitus	X	Inimicitiae.	

43 DE IRA: 25

I	Homicidia	V	Tumor mentis
II	Clamor	VI	Contumiliae
III	Indignatio	VII	Oppropria.
IIII	Rixae		

44. DE TRISTITIA: 30

I	Rancor	IIII	Disperatio
II	Pusillanimitas	V	Malitia
III	Amaritudo	VI	Torpor circa praecepta.

2–8 'Issiodorus': *recte* Cassianus, Conl. v. 2   10 sqq. *cf.* Cassianus, Conl.
v. 16, 5 sqq., *unde* Isid., Quaest. in Deuteron. c. 16 (PL lxxxiii. 366).   26 *cf.* Deut.
18, 22 tumor animi

I APOSTOLOS C.   4–8 *numeri desunt* in B.   7 Accidia B.   9 CASSIANUS B.
11–18 *numeri desunt in* B.   10–13 *sic distinguntur in* C: I De gastrimargia
nascuntur/ II Commessationes/ III Ebrietates/ IIII Inepta letitia/V Multiloquium/

SO FAR THE APOSTLE. 39. NOW ISIDORE:

There are eight chief vices, from which arises a copious multitude of vices:

I	Gluttony	VI	Dejection
II	Fornication	VII	Vainglory
III	Avarice	VIII	Lastly the very leader and
IIII	Languor		queen of these, Pride.
V	Wrath		

THUS FAR ISIDORE. 40. NOW CASSIAN SAYS:

Of gluttony are born

I	Revellings	IIII	Excessive talk
II	Drunkenness	V	Dullness of sense
III	Foolish gaiety	VI	Uncleanness.

41. OF FORNICATION:

I	Filthy speech	V	Inconstancy
II	Scurrility	VI	Love of the present world
III	Stupid talk	VII	Horror of the (world) to
IIII	Blindness of mind		come.

42. OF AVARICE:

I	Lying	VI	False testimonies
II	Fraud	VII	Acts of violence
III	Thefts	VIII	Inhumanity
IIII	Perjuries	VIIII	Rapacity
V	Greed of filthy gain	X	Enmities.

43. OF WRATH:

I	Murders	V	Pride of mind
II	Clamour	VI	Insults
III	Indignation	VII	Reproaches.
IIII	Quarrels		

44. OF DEJECTION:

I	Rancour	IIII	Despair
II	Smallness of mind	V	Malice
III	Bitterness	VI	Indifference about commands.

VI Hebitudo/ VII Sensus/Inmunditie   11 Multiloquiorum B.   12 Ebitudo B.   18 VII *om*. C.   27 Contumeliae B.   32 Pusillanimes (*s.s.* uel mitas) B.

45. DE ACCIDIA:

I	Otiositas	VI	Instabilitas mentis et
II	Somnolentia		corporis
III	Inportunitas	VII	Uerbositas
IIII	Inquietudo	VIII	Curiositas.
V	Peruagatio		

5

46. DE CENODOCTIA:

I	Contentiones	V	Hipocrissis
II	Heresses	VI	Pertinatia
III	Iactantia	VII	Discordiae
IIII	Presumptio nouitatum	VIII	Odium.

10

47. DE SUPERBIA:

I	Contemptus	V	Murmuratio
II	Inuidia	VI	Detractio
III	Inobedientia	VII	Ueneficia.
IIII	Blasfemia		

15

48. DE CONCORDIA UIRTUTUM QUE GENUS HUMANUM REPARANT AD REGNA CAELORUM APOSTOLUS:

FRUCTUS AUTEM SPIRITUS SANCTI

I	*Caritas*	VI	*Bonitas*
II	*Gaudium*	VII	*Mansuetudo*
III	*Pax*	VIII	*Fides*
IIII	*Patientia*	VIIII	*Modestia*
V	*Longanimitas*	X	*Continentia.*

20

Qui autem sunt Christi carnem suam cum uitiis et passionibus crucifixerunt. 25

HUCUSQUE PAULUS. 49. ITEM AMBROSIUS: UIAE AUTEM DOMINI ISTE SUNT

I	Fides	XIII	Longanimitas
II	Spes	XIIII	Sollicitudo
III	Caritas	XV	Contemptio uentris
IIII	Perseuerentia	XVI	Studium mentis
V	Bonitas	XVII	Castitas
VI	Timor Dei	XVIII	Benignitas
VII	Continentia	XVIIII	Misericordia
VIII	Patientia	XX	Libertas gloriae
VIIII	Lenitas	XXI	Studium scientiae legis
X	Quies		Dei
XI	Pax	XXII	Afectus aeternae.
XII	Oboedientia		

30

35

19–25 cf. Gal. 5, 22–24 cum apparatu Wordsworthiano.   26–39 *In Ambrosio non leguntur; ad pseudepigraphum Hiberni cuiusdam opus referri probabile est*

1 ACCEDIA B.   2 et om. C.   4 inoportunitas CB: *correxi ex Cassiano*

45. OF LANGUOR:

I	Idleness	VI	Instability of mind and
II	Drowsiness		body
III	Unseasonableness	VII	Verbosity
IIII	Restlessness	VIII	Curiosity.
V	Wandering about		

46. OF VAINGLORY:

I	Contentions	V	Hypocrisy
II	Heresies	VI	Obstinacy
III	Boasting	VII	Discords
IIII	Taking up with novelties	VIII	Hatred.

47. OF PRIDE:

I	Contempt	V	Murmuring
II	Envy	VI	Detraction
III	Disobedience	VII	Witchcrafts.
IIII	Blasphemy		

48. OF THE CONCORD OF VIRTUES WHICH RESTORE THE HUMAN RACE TO THE KINGDOM OF THE HEAVENS THE APOSTLE (SAYS): *BUT THE FRUIT OF THE HOLY SPIRIT IS*

I	*Charity*	VI	*Goodness*
II	*Joy*	VII	*Mildness*
III	*Peace*	VIII	*Faith*
IIII	*Patience*	VIIII	*Modesty*
V	*Longanimity*	X	*Continence.*

But they that are Christ's have crucified their flesh with its vices and passions.

THUS FAR PAUL. 49. NOW AMBROSE:[9] THE WAYS OF THE LORD, HOWEVER, ARE THESE:

I	Faith	XIII	Longanimity
II	Hope	XIIII	Solicitude
III	Charity	XV	Contempt of the belly
IIII	Perseverance	XVI	Zeal of mind
V	Goodness	XVII	Chastity
VI	Fear of God	XVIII	Kindness
VII	Continence	XVIIII	Mercy
VIII	Patience	XX	Freedom from ambition
VIIII	Mildness	XXI	Zeal for the knowledge of
X	Calmness		the law of God
XI	Peace	XXII	Love of the eternal (life?).
XII	Obedience		

7 *lege*: CENODOCXIA? *cf. c.* VII *tit.*   8 Hipocrisis B.   15 VII: VI B.
16 Blasphemia B.   17 CONCORDIA: CON *om.* C.   27 SUNT ⟨XXIIII⟩ C.
30 contempnatio C.   33 Benegnitas C*.   38 Affectus B. *lege*: ⟨uitae⟩ aeternae?

HUCUSQUE AMBROSIUS. 50. ITEM ESIODORUS

Ethica diuiditur in iiii. principales uirtutes: prudentiam, iustitiam, fortitudinem, temperantiam. Prudentia est agnitio uere scientiae scripturarum. 51. Iustitia Deum timere, relegionem uenerari, honorem deferre parentibus, patriam diligere, cunctis prodesse, nocere nulli, 5 fraternitatis uinculum amplecti, pericula aliena suscipere, opem ferre miserorum, boni accepti uicissitudinem rependere, aequitatem in iudiciis conseruare. 52. Fortitudo animi magnitudo, contemptus bonorum uel diuitiarum; haec aduersis aut patienter ⟨cedit⟩ aut resistit fortiter, nullius emolitur inlecebris, aduersis non frangitur, non eleuatur 10 secundis, inuicta ad laborem, fortis ad pericula, pecuniam neglegit, auaritiam fugit, nullis molestiis cedit, glorie cauet apetitus. 53. Temperantia est modus uitae in omni uerbo uel opere; haec uerecondie comes est, humilitatis regulam custodit, tranquillitatem animi seruat, continentiam et castitatem amplectitur, fouet decus et honestatem, restringit 15 ratione appetit⟨um⟩, iram comprimit nec rependit contumeliam.

54. ITEM ISSIDORUS:

Prudentia est in rebus qua mala discernuntur a bonis. Fortitudo est qua aduersa equanimiter tollerantur. Temperantia est qua libido concupiscentiaque rerum refrenatur. Iustitia est qua recte sua cuique distribuunt. 20

HUCUSQUE ISSIDORUS. 55. ITEM PAULUS:

Caritas patiens est, caritas non emulatur, non agit perperam, non inflatur, non est ambitiosa, non querit quae sua sunt, non irritatur, non cogitat malum, non gaudet super iniquitatem, congaudet autem ueritati. Omnia subfert, omnia credit, omnia sperat, omnia sustinet. Caritas 25 *numquam excidit.*

HUCUSQUE APOSTOLUS. 56. ITEM BENEDICTUS: QUE SUNT INSTRUMENTA BONORUM OPERUM.

In primis Deum dilige ex toto corde et ex tota mente et ex tota anima et ex tota uirtute. Deinde proximum tamquam te ipsum. 57. Deinde 30 non occidere; non adulterare; non furtum facere; non concupiscere; non falsum testimonium dicere; 58. honorare omnes homines et quod sibi fieri non uult ne alii faciat; 59. abnegare se ipsum sibi ut sequatur Christum; 60. corpus castigare, dilicias non amplecti, ieiunium amare,

2–16 Isidor. Diff. ii. 39   18–20 Isid. Etym. ii. 24, 6   22–26 1 Cor. 13, 4–8 (VULG, *sed desunt uerba* benigna est)   27 sqq. S. Benedicti Regula, c. 4.

1 ISSIODORUS B.   4 religionem B.   7 miseris *Isid.*   9 ⟨cedit⟩ *inserui ex Isidoro*   10 nullius C. nullus B: nullis *Isid.*   11 periculum B.   niglegit C. 12 cauet apetitus *scripsi cum Isidoro*: cauet apenitus C. cauta penitus B.   13 uerecundiae commes B.   16 rationem appetit CB. *correxi ex Isidoro*   cumprimit C. 17 ISSIODORUS B.   20 cuique *ego*: quique CB.   qua recte iudicando sua cuique distribuunt *Isid.*   23 flatur C.   est *om.* B.   24 gitat C.   autem *om.* C. 25 suffert B   34 dilitias B.   āmare B.

THUS FAR AMBROSE. 50. NOW ISIDORE

Ethics are divided into the four principal virtues: prudence, justice, fortitude, temperance. Prudence is the understanding of the true knowledge of the Scriptures. 51. Justice is this: to fear God, to respect religion, to show honour to one's parents, to love one's country, to be useful to all, to be harmful to none, to accept gladly the tie of brotherhood, to undergo dangers for others, to bring help to the distressed, to repay the good one has received, to retain equity in judgement. 52. Fortitude is greatness of mind, contempt of possessions and wealth; it either gives patiently way to adversity or resists it firmly, is not weakened by any lure, is not broken by bad luck, not elated by good luck, is invincible in the face of toil, strong in the face of dangers, does not care for money, flees from avarice, gives way to no hardships, bewares of the lust for fame. 53. Temperance is a life well measured in every word or deed; it is the companion of modesty, observes the humility of the rule, retains calmness of mind, embraces continence and chastity, fosters decency and honesty, restrains desire by reason, suppresses wrath and does not return insult for insult.

54. ALSO ISIDORE:

Prudence in things is (the quality) by which bad is distinguished from good. Fortitude is that by which adversity is endured with a steady mind. Temperance is that by which passion and the desire for things is bridled. Justice is that by which (men) give every one what is his according to right.[10]

THUS FAR ISIDORE. 55. NOW PAUL:

Charity is patient, charity envieth not, dealeth not perversely, is not puffed up, is not ambitious, seeketh not her own, is not provoked to anger, thinketh no evil, rejoiceth not in iniquity, but rejoiceth with the truth. It beareth all things, believeth all things, hopeth all things, endureth all things. Charity never falleth away.

THUS FAR THE APOSTLE. 56. NOW BENEDICT: WHAT ARE THE INSTRUMENTS OF GOOD WORKS.

First of all love God of thy whole heart and of thy whole mind and of thy whole soul and of thy whole strength. Then love thy neighbour as thyself. 57. Then: not to kill; not to commit adultery; not to commit theft; not to covet; not to bear false witness; 58. to honour all men and not to do to another what one does not want to be done unto oneself; 59. to renounce oneself that one may follow Christ; 60. to chastise one's body, not to give oneself to soft living, to love fasting, to sustain the

pauperes recreare, nudos uestire, infirmos uisitare, mortuos sepelire, in
tribulatione subuenire, dolentem consolari, seculi actibus se facere
alienum, nihil amori Christi praeponere, iram non perficere, dolum
corde non tenere, pacem falsam non dare, non relinquere caritatem,
(61) non iurare omnino, ueritatem ex corde et ore proferre, malum pro 5
malo non redere, iniuriam non facere sed et factam sufferre, inimicos
diligere, maledicentes non remaledicere sed magis benedicere, perse-
cutionem propter iustitiam sustinere; 62. non esse superbum, non
uinolentum, non multum edacem, non sumnolentum, non pigrum, non
murmurosum, non detractatorem; 63. spem suam ⟨Deo⟩ committere; 10
bonum aliquod cum uiderit in se, Deo adplicet non sibi, malum uero a
se factum sciat et sibi reputet; 64. diem iudicii timere, gehennam
expauescere, uitam aeternam omni concupiscentia spiritali desiderare,
mortem cotidiae ante oculos conspectam abere, actum uitae suae omni
hora custodire, in omni loco Deum ⟨se⟩ respicere pro certo scire; 65. 15
cogitationes malas cordi suo aduenientes mox ad Christum allidat et
seniori spiritali patefacere, uana uerba ac risui apta non loqui, risum
multum aut excusum non amare, os suum a prauo eloquio custodire,
multum loqui non amare, sanctas lectiones libenter audire, orationi
frequenter incu⟨m⟩bere, mala sua praeterita cum lacrimis uel gemitu 20
cotidie in oratione Deo confiteri, de ipsis malis de cetero emendare,
desideria carnis non perficere, uoluntatem propriam odire; 66. praeceptis
abatis in omnibus obedire, etiam si ipse aliter, quod absit, agat, memorantes illud praeceptum Dominicum: *Quae dicunt uobis facite, quae autem
faciunt nolite facere*; 67. non uelle dici sanctum antequam sit, sed prius 25
esse, quo uerius dicatur; praecepta Dei factis cotidie adimplere, castitatem amare, zelum et inuidiam non habere, contentionem non amare,
nullum odire, elationem fugere et seniores uenerare iuniores diligere in
Christi amore; 68. pro inimicis orare, cum discordante ante solis
occassum redire in pacem, et de Dei misericordia numquam disperare. 30

HUCUSQUE BENEDICTUS

69. De conpunctione cordis. iiii. cause sunt per quas omnes qui
praedicta a nobis uita currunt ad penitentiam confugiunt. 70.

GREGORIUS:

Quatuor quippe sunt qualitates quibus iusti uiri anima in con- 35
punctione uehementer accipitur: 71. cum malorum suorum reminiscitur,
considerans ubi fuit, ut Paulus ait: *non sum dignus uocari apostolus quia*

---

24 sq. *cf.* Matth. 23, 3   35 sqq. Greg. M., Moralia xxiii. 41   37 sq. 1 Cor.
15, 9 (quia TEST^pl).

---

6 reddere B.   9 uinolentum *Bened.*: uiolentum C. unolendum B.   10 detractorem *Bened.*   ⟨Deo⟩ *addidi e Benedicto*   11 aliquid C.   13 omni: ibi C.
considerare C.   14 habere B.   15 ⟨se⟩ *addidi e Benedicto*   19 multum
loqui *om.* C.   21 cetero: certo C.   26 quo *Bened.*; quod CB.   30 occasum
C.   33 confugunt B.   35 quattuor B.   36 accipitur: afficitur *Greg.*

poor, to clothe the naked, to visit the sick, to bury the dead, to assist in tribulation, to comfort a person in grief, to make oneself a stranger to deeds of the world, to put nothing before the love of Christ, not to do according to one's anger, to bear no falsehood in one's heart, not to give a false peace, not to abandon charity, (61) not to swear at all, to speak truth from one's heart and with one's mouth, not to return evil for evil, not to do wrong and to suffer the wrong incurred, to love one's enemies, not to curse those who curse us but rather to bless them, to endure persecution for the sake of justice; 62. not to be proud, not given to drinking, not greedy for food, not drowsy, not lazy, not murmuring, not a detractor; 63. to commit one's hope to God; if he sees any good in himself, let him attribute it to God, not to him, but let him know the evil to have been done by him and let him reckon it unto himself; 64. to fear the Day of Judgement, to be in horror of hell, to desire eternal life with all spiritual desire, to have death vividly before one's eye every day, to watch one's action every hour of one's life, to know for certain that God looks down on us in every place; 65. let him throw unto Christ bad thoughts that come to his heart and let him reveal them to a spiritual senior; not to utter idle words and such as are likely to arouse laughter, not to love much and loud laughter, to guard one's mouth against unprofitable talk, not to love much talking, to be fond of listening to holy readings, to pray often and diligently, to confess one's past sins to God in prayer daily with tears and sighing, to avoid those evils in future, not to fulfil the desires of the flesh, to hate one's own will; 66. to obey the abbot's commands in everything, even if he himself— God forbid—should act otherwise, thinking of that precept of the Lord: *Do what they say to you, but what they do do ye not*; 67. not to wish to be called holy before being so, but first to be so in order that it may be said all the more truthfully; to fulfil the commands of God daily by one's deeds, to love chastity, to have no jealousy or envy, not to love quarrel, not to hate anyone, to turn away from thinking oneself important, to show reverence to one's seniors, to love one's juniors with the love of Christ; 68. to pray for one's enemies, to restore peace after an argument before the sun sets, and never to despair of God's mercy.

THUS FAR BENEDICT.

69. On Compunction of the Heart. There are four causes why those who run the race of life as we have said before take refuge in penance. 70.

GREGORY:

There are four motives for which the soul of a just man feels vividly compunction:[11] 71. when he remembers his evils, considering where he was, as Paul says: *I am not worthy to be called an apostle because I*

persecutus sum eclesiam Dei; 72. aut iudiciorùm Dei sententiam metuens et secum querens cogitat ubi erit, ut illud Pauli: *Castigo corpus meum et seruituti subiecio, ne forte aliis praedicans ipse reprobus efficiar*; 73. aut mala uitae praesentis solerter adtendens merens considerat ubi est, ut illud supra dicti: *Dum sumus in hoc corpore peregrinamur a Domino*, et: 5 *Uideo aliam legem in membris meis repugnantem legi mentis mee*, et reliqua usque *quis me liberauit de corpore mortis huius peccati*; 74. aut cum bona superne patriae contemplatur, ⟨quae⟩ quia necdum adepiscitur languens conspicit ubi nullus non est, ut illud: *Uidemus nunc per speculum [et] in enigmate, tunc autem facie ad faciem.* 10

DE REMEDIIS UITIORUM CAPITULA OCTO

I. GULA. TEODORUS

1. Si quis episcopus aut aliquis ordinatus in consuetudine habuerit uitium ebrietatis aut desinat aut deponatur; et de penitentia ebrietatis satis supra diximus in questiuncula. 15

2. DE UOMENTIBUS TEODORUS:

1. Si monachus pro ebrietate uomitum facit, xxx dies peniteat; 2. si uero presbiter aut diaconus, .xl. peniteat; 3. si uero pro infirmitate uel quia longo tempore se abstinuerit aut pro gaudio in Natale Domini uel in Pascha uel pro alicuius sanctorum commemoratione faciat et tunc 20 plus non accipit quam decretum est a senioribus, nihil nocet. 4. Si laicus fidelis pro ebrietate uomitum fecerit, xv diebus peniteat.

3. DE UOMENTIBUS SACRIFICIUM.

1. Qui sacrificium euomit causa uoracitatis, .xl. diebus. Si uero obtentu insoliti cybi pinguioris et non uitio saturitatis sed stomachi, 25 .xxx. 2. Si infirmitatis gratia, xx peniteat. 3. Aliter alius dicit: Si infirmitatis causa, .vii. diebus; si in ignem proiecerit, .c. psalmos canet; si canis lambuerit talem uomitum, .c. diebus qui euomit poeniteat. 4. Qui accipit post cibum sacrificium, .vii. dies peniteat.

4. DE FURENTIBUS CIBUM 30

1. Furatus cibum .xl. diebus; si iterum, .iii. xl; si tertio, anno; si uero .iiii., iugi exilio sub alio abate peniteat. 2. Paruulus decim annorum

---

2–3 1 Cor. 9, 27 (seruituti subicio d e g m TEST^alq L; aliis praedicans g TEST^pl *cum* GR). 5 2 Cor. 5, 6 (in hoc corpore TEST^alq). 6 sq. Rom. 7, 23–24 (liberauit *ex betacismo* d Prisc ABF*G*HΘ*LNTZ^c; peccati *add.* L). 9 sq. 1 Cor. 13, 12. 13–22 Theodorus, Paenit. I. 1, 1–5. 15 questiuncula: *non uidetur exstare* 26 sqq. Cummean I. 9–11.

---

1 sententia C. 3 subiecio, ne *ego*: subietio ne C. subiectione B. 6 repugnatem C. 7 ⟨.iiii.⟩ aut C. *(in exemplari quattuor qualitates fortasse numeris distinctae erant.)* 8 quae *addidi e Gregorio* adepiscit C. adipiscitur B. languens: lugens *Greg.* 9 nullus C^cB. n,us C* *uix sanum, deest in Gregorio.* et *deleui.* 19 quia: qua C. 21 plus *om.* C. 23 SACRIFICII C. SACRIFICIIS B.

persecuted the church of God; 72. or, fearing the sentence of God's judgements and questioning himself, he asks where he will be, as is this (saying) of Paul: *I chastise my body and bring it into subjection lest perhaps when I have preached to others I myself should become a castaway*; 73. or, turning his mind's attention to the evils of the present life, considers with sorrow where he is, as is this word of the same: *While we are in this body we are absent from the Lord*, and: *I see another law in my members, fighting against the law of my mind*, and so forth unto *who shall deliver me from the body of this death of sin*? 74. or, when he contemplates the blessings of the fatherland on high, which, since he does not yet attain to them, he beholds with sorrowful longing for a place where he is not, as is this word: *We see now through a glass in a dark manner, but then face to face.*

EIGHT CHAPTERS ON THE REMEDIES OF VICES

I. GLUTTONY. THEODORE

1. If any bishop or anyone in (holy) orders has the vice of habitual drunkenness, he shall either break his habit or be deposed; on the penance of drunkenness we have said enough above in the short interrogation.[12]

2. CONCERNING THOSE WHO VOMIT. THEODORE:

1. If a monk vomits because of drunkenness, he shall do penance for thirty days; 2. if a priest or deacon, he shall do penance for forty days; 3. but if he does so because of sickness or because he abstained for a long time or after drinking the joy of Christmas or Easter or the commemoration of any of the saints[13] and on those occasions takes no more than what has been decreed by the seniors, it does not matter. 4. If a believing layman vomits because of drunkenness, he shall do penance for a fortnight.

3. OF THOSE WHO VOMIT THE HOST

1. He who vomits the host because of greediness, forty days. But if with the excuse of unusual and too rich food, and from the fault not of over-saturation but of the stomach, thirty (days). 2. If by reason of infirmity, he shall do penance for twenty (days). 3. Another (authority) says differently: If by reason of infirmity, seven days; if he ejects it into the fire, he shall sing one hundred psalms; if a dog laps up this vomit, he who has vomited shall do penance for one hundred days. 4. He who receives the host after (the taking of) food, shall do penance for seven days.

4. OF THOSE WHO STEAL FOOD

1. One who steals food, forty days; if again, three forty-day periods; if a third time, a year; if, indeed, a fourth time, he shall do penance in permanent exile under another abbot. 2. A boy of ten years who steals

---

25 cibi (*ex* -us) B.   29 Qui–peniteat *om*. B.   30 FURENTIBUS: *sic* CB.
30. 31 cybum B.   32 .iii. C.   decem B.

aliquid huius furti faciens vii diebus peniteat; si uero post .xx. annos aliquid furti huic acciderit, .xx. diebus. 3. Qui anticipat horam canonicam uel suauiora ceteris summat gulae tantum obtentu, cena careat uel duobus diebus in pane et aqua uiuat.

5. DE HIS QUI INLICITAS CARNES EDUNT ET BIBENTIBUS 5 INTINCTUM A BESTIIS ET AUIBUS CANONES SAPIENTIUM ET GREGORII:

1. Penitentia hominis bibentis urinam hominis seu et sanguinem, .vii. anni in pane et aqua et in consummatione ⟨ . . . ⟩.

2. Aliter Teodorus ait: Qui sanguinem uel semen biberit, .iii. 10 ann- peniteat.

3. Penitentia hominis uel urinam pecoris bibentis tres et semis anni in pane et aqua.

4. Penitentia hominis manducantis carnem inmundam uel morticinam uel delaceratam canibus uel bestiis .xl. dies in pane et aqua; si autem 15 necessitas cogit, nihil est.

5. Penitentia bibentis quod intincxit canis annus in pane et aqua.

6. Penitentia bibentis quod intincxerit aquila uel ingarrula uel gallus uel gallina .l. dies et noctes in pane et aqua.

7. Penitentia bibentis quod intinxit muriceps .v. dies et noctes in 20 pane et aqua.

8. Aliter Teodorus: Quod si cassu quis inmunda manu cibum tangit uel canis uel pilax uel mus uel inmundum animal quod sanguinem biberit, non nocet. 9. Sanguinem sorbere cum saliua non est peccatum.

10. Penitentia bibentis intinctum a mure unus dies in pane et aqua. 25

11. Penitentia bibentis liquorem in quo mus demersa obiit .vii. dies in pane et aqua.

12. Penitentia bibentis liquorem in quo fuit morticinum pecoris .xl. noctes et dies in pane et aqua.

6. DE CLERICIS BIBENTIBUS INTINCTUM LAICO UEL LAICA 30 CANONES PATRUM:

1. Penitentia bibentis quod laicus uel laica intinxerat .i. dies in pane et aqua.

2. Penitentia bibentis quod intinxerat glangella in utero habens filium uel cohabitationis cum ea .xl. cum pane et aqua. 35

---

10 sq. Theod. I. 7, 3.   14–16 Theod. I. 7, 6.   22–24 Theod. I. 7, 7. 11.

3 tantum *scripsi, cf. Ps.-Cumm. I. 10:* tamen CB.   caena B.   5 INLICITIS C. 8 hominis (1): homines C.   9 *in fine desideratur aliquid, uelut:* penitentiae inpositio manus episcopi, *cf. Can. Hib. I. 12.*   ann- *ambiguum*   12 penitentiam C.   *ante* uel *aliquid excidisse uidetur, cf. Pen. Hib. I. 2.*   urinam: utinam C.   anni *scripsi:* anñ B. añs C.   17 intinxit B.   18 intinxerit C. 19 .l. *ego*: l- C. uel B; *cf. Can. Hib. I. 17.*   22 casu B.   cybum B.   28 sq. *om.* C.   34 glancella B. *s.s.* ancilla CB.

any such thing shall do penance for seven days; if, indeed, after (the age of) twenty he happens to commit a theft, for twenty days. 3. He who anticipates the canonical hour or takes something more delicate than the others have, merely on account of appetite, shall go without supper or live for two days on bread and water.

5. OF THOSE WHO EAT FORBIDDEN MEATS AND DRINK WHAT HAS BEEN CONTAMINATED BY BEASTS OR BIRDS THE CANONS OF THE WISE AND OF GREGORY[14] (STATE):

1. The penance of a person drinking human urine or blood, seven years on bread and water, and after the performance (of this penance the imposition of the hand of the bishop).[15]

2. Differently Theodore says: He who drinks blood or sperm shall do penance for three years.

3. The penance of a person who even drinks the urine of an animal, three years and a half on bread and water.

4. The penance of a person who eats unclean flesh, or carrion, or flesh torn by dogs or beasts, forty days on bread and water; but if (he does so) under duress, it does not matter.

5. The penance of one who drinks what has been contaminated by a dog, a year on bread and water.

6. The penance of one who drinks what has been contaminated by an eagle or a magpie or a cock or a hen, fifty days and nights on bread and water.

7. The penance of one who drinks what has been contaminated by a cat, five days and nights on bread and water.

8. Differently Theodore: If anyone accidentally touches food with unclean hand, or (if) a dog (does so) or a watchdog or a mouse or an unclean animal that drinks blood, it does not matter. 9. To swallow blood with (one's) saliva is no sin.

10. The penance of one who drinks what has been contaminated by a mouse, one day on bread and water.

11. The penance of one who drinks liquor in which a mouse has been drowned, seven days on bread and water.

12. The penance of one who drinks liquor in which there has been the carcass of a beast, forty days and nights on bread and water.

6. OF CLERICS WHO DRINK WHAT HAS BEEN CONTAMINATED BY A LAYMAN OR LAYWOMAN THE CANONS OF THE FATHERS (STATE):

1. The penance of one who drinks what has been contaminated by a layman or a laywoman, one day[16] on bread and water.

2. The penance of one who drinks what has been contaminated by a pregnant servant woman, or for cohabitation[17] with her, forty days on bread and water.

7. DE COHABITANTIBUS CUM LAICIS

Penitentia manducandi et dormiendi in una domu uel spatula cum laico laicaue: xl dies in pane et aqua peniteat.

8. DE CONTEMPNANTIBUS IEIUNIA TEODORUS:

Qui contempserit indictum ieiunium in ecclesia, xl dies peniteat; si 5 in xl diebus, annum peniteat. Aliter in libro Regum Iohnathan ieiunium soluente reus fuit morti si non peteret populus uitam eius.

9. DE DIE DOMINICO

1. Si quis in die Dominico per neglegentiam ieiunauerit, ebdomadam totam debet ieiunare; si secundo, xl dies; si postea, lx. 2. Qui tribus 10 Dominicis non communicauerint, excommunicantur.

10. DE INFIRMIS

Infirmis licet omni hora cybum et potum summere.

⟨II.⟩ DE FORNICATIONE

1. Supra diximus in questiuncula de penitentia quo tempore et 15 labore adfligendi sunt clerici cadentes fornicatione; quedam tamen quae ibidem omisimus hic diligentius persequemur.

1. Item sacerdos si tangendo mulierem coinquinatus est, xl diebus peniteat; si osculatus est mulierem per desiderium, xx dies peniteat.

2. Si sacerdos per cogitationem semen effunderit, ebdomadam ieiunat; 20 si tangit manu, .iii. ebdomades peniteat; †à f̄ filios†, xl uel annum.

3. Qui sepe per uiolentiam cogitationis semen fudit, peniteat xx dies.

4. Qui in ecclesia dormiens semen fundit, .iii. dies peniteat. Si excitat ipse, primo xx dies, iterans xl.; si plus, addantur ieiunia.

5. Alius dicit: Qui concupiscit mente fornicari sed non potuit, anno 25 uno, maxime in tres xl peniteat. De tali enim Deus dicit: *Qui uidit mulierem ad concupiscendam eam* et reliqua.

6. Qui per turpiloquium uel aspectum coinquinatus non tamen uoluit fornicari corporaliter, .xx. uel .xl. diebus iuxta qualitatem peccantis peniteat.   30

7. Qui in somnis uoluntate pullutus est, surgat cantatque .viiii. psalmos et genua flectat et crastino cum pane et aqua uiuat uel xxx

---

5–7 Theod. I. 11, 4.   6 sq. *cf.* 1 Reg. 14, 43–45   9–11 Theod. I. 11, 2; 12, 1   13 Theod. II. 14, 14   15–24 Theod. I. 8, 1–3; 7–9   15 questiuncula: *u. supra*, I. 1   26 sq. Matth. 5, 28 (uiderit VL VULG; ad concupiscendam D Ep Q R *al.* uidirit . . . concupiscentum Pen. Hib. II. 15)

---

1 LACIS B.   5 eclesia B.   6 regnum C.   ionathan B.   7 p̄teret C. peteret B.   eius *om.* C.   16 adfligenti C. adflicti B.   18 tanguendo B. 20 ieiunet B.   21 ebdomadas B. ebdomes C.   23 eclesia B.   30 *leg.* peccati?   31 pollutus B.   viii. B.

7. OF THOSE WHO COHABIT WITH LAY PEOPLE

The penance for eating or sleeping in the same house or bed with a lay-man or a laywoman: he shall do penance for forty days on bread and water.

8. OF THOSE WHO DO NOT OBSERVE FASTS, THEODORE:

He who does not observe a fast announced in church, shall do penance for forty days; if it is in the forty days (of Lent), he shall do penance for a year. Differently in the Book of Kings, Jonathan by break-ing his fast became guilty of death had not the people begged for his life.

9. CONCERNING THE LORD'S DAY

1. If anyone by negligence fasts on the Lord's Day, he must fast for the entire week; if (he does so) a second time, forty days; if after that, sixty days. 2. Those who have not communicated for three Sun-days, are excommunicated.

10. CONCERNING SICK PEOPLE

Sick people are allowed to take food and drink at any hour.

⟨II.⟩ OF FORNICATION

1. We have said above in the short interrogation concerning penance for what time and with what hardship clerics are to be punished who have lapsed through fornication; some details, however, which we have left out there we shall set forth here more accurately.

1. If a priest has defiled himself by touching a woman, he shall do penance for forty days; if he has kissed a woman with desire, he shall do penance for twenty days.

2. If a priest, by (sinful) thoughts, has caused his sperm to flow, he shall fast for a week; if he touches (his member) with his hand, he shall do penance for three weeks; if . . .,[18] for forty days or a year.

3. He who often causes his sperm to flow by passionate thoughts, shall do penance for twenty days.

4. He whose sperm flows whilst he is sleeping in church, shall do penance for three days. If he stimulates himself, for the first offence twenty days, for the second one, forty; if more often, fasts shall be added.

5. Another (authority) says: He who wishes in his heart to commit fornication but cannot do so, shall do penance for one year, especially during the three forty-day periods. For it is of such a one that God says: *He who has looked at a woman to lust after her*, and so on.

6. He who has defiled himself by shameful words or by looking (at something shameful) yet did not intend to commit bodily fornication, shall do penance for twenty or forty days according to the nature of his sin.

7. He who is willingly polluted during sleep, shall arise and sing nine psalms in order, kneeling; and on the following day he shall live on bread and water, or he shall sing thirty psalms, bending his knee

psalmos flectando genua unius cuiusque in fine cantat. 8. Uolens in somnis peccare, si pollutus sine uoluntate, .xv. psalmos cantat.

9. Qui diligit aliquam feminam inscius alicuius mali praeter sermocinaciones quasdam, xl diebus peniteat. Osculatus autem et amplectans anno, maxime in .iii. xl.   5

2. DE FORNICATIONE NON NATURALI. I. TEODORUS:

Qui sepe cum masculo aut peccoribus coierit, .x. annis peniteat.

2. Uiri inter femora fornicantes .ii. ann- peniteant.

3. Manu uero semetipsos coinquinantes primo .c. diebus, iterantes anno peniteant.   10

4. Fornicantes labiis, quod dictu scelus, primo .iiii. annis, iterantes consuetudine .vii. annis peniteant.

5. Pueri autem xii ann- usque ad uigentisimum praefata scelera facientes dimedio penitentiae supradicte iuxta alios puniendi fiunt; iuniores uero leuius uindicandi.   15

3. DE FORNICANTIBUS CUM MATRE UEL SORORE.

1. Qui cum matre uel sorore fornicatus, vii uel xv ann- peniteat; sic et frater cum fratre naturali fornicans; aliter alius dicit.

2. Ducentem matrem aut sororem .iiii. ann- leuius solito poenitere iubet.   20

4. De laico fornicatore penitente in habitu laicali.

Laicus fornicans et sanguinem effundens si conuersus fuerit, .iii. ann- peniteat. In primo anno in pane et aqua, in totis .iii. sine uino carneque, sine armis, sine uxore propria sic uiuat.

5. DE UIOLENTE UXOREM UEL UIRGINEM ALTERIUS. 25 THEODORUS:

1. Qui maculat uxorem proximi sui, .iii. ann- ab uxore propria ieiunat; in ebdomada duos dies et in xl ieiunet.

2. Aliter quidam aiunt intollerabilius: paenitentia concoitus mulieris alicuius mariti uiui .vii. annis cum pane et aqua.   30

3. TEODORUS: Qui fornicatus fuerit cum uirgine, .iiii. annis peniteat.

---

7 Theod. I. 2, 2   17 sq. Theod. I. 2, 16. 17. 19   27 sq. Theod. I. 14, 9
31: *in Theodoro nihil simile legitur*

1 in fine *Wasserschleben, cf. Cummean. II. 15*: in hieme CB.   2 polutus C.
7 pecoribus B.   9 coinquinantes: qui inquinantes C.   13 autem: aut C.
xii: xv B.   uicessimum B.   15 iudicandi B.   16 FORNICANDIBUS B.   18 alius
om. C.   25 UIOLENTO C (*fort. lege* uiolendo); *cf. p.* 214, 30.   26 TEODORUS B.
28 ieiunet B. in ebdomada–ieiunet *om.* B.   29 quidam: qui C.   potentia C.   concuitus (*i.e.* concubitus?) C.

at the end of each. 8. He who desires to sin during sleep, if he is un-intentionally polluted, shall sing fifteen psalms.

9. He who loves a woman and is not conscious of any fault beyond some exchange of words, shall do penance for forty days. But if he has kissed and embraced her, for one year, especially during the three forty-day periods.

2. OF UNNATURAL FORNICATION. 1. THEODORE:

One who often has intercourse with a male or with beasts, shall do penance for ten years.

2. Men fornicating between their thighs shall do penance for two years.

3. Those who defile themselves with their hands shall, for the first time, do penance for one hundred days; if they repeat (their sin), for one year.

4. Those fornicating with their lips, which is a crime even to mention, shall at the first time do penance for four years, if they repeat it habitually, for seven years.

5. Boys, however, between the age of twelve and twenty who commit the same crimes are, according to others, to be punished by half the above mentioned penance; younger ones are to be punished (even) more lightly.

3. OF THOSE WHO COMMIT FORNICATION WITH THEIR MOTHER OR SISTER.

1. He who is guilty of fornication with his mother or sister shall do penance for seven or fifteen years; the same also a brother guilty of fornication with his natural[19] brother; another (authority) says differently.

2. He says that a man mating his mother or sister shall do penance for four years, and less strictly than is the rule.

4. OF A FORNICATING LAYMAN WHO DOES PENANCE IN LAY GARB.

If a layman committing fornication and shedding blood is converted, he shall do penance for three years. In the first year on bread and water, in all three without wine and meat, without arms and without his wife, so shall he live.

5. OF ONE WHO VIOLATES THE WIFE OR VIRGIN DAUGHTER OF ANOTHER. THEODORE:

1. He who defiles his neighbour's wife shall abstain from his own wife for three years; he shall fast for two days each week, and during the forty days (of Lent).[20]

2. Others say differently, and too severely: the penance for inter-course with a woman whose husband is still alive is seven years on bread and water.

3. THEODORE: He who has committed fornication with a virgin shall do penance for four years.

4. Alius alias temperauit: Laicus maculans uxorem uel uirginem proximi sui uno anno cum pane et aqua et sine uxore propria paeniteat.

5. Si autem puellam Dei maculauerit et genuerit filium ex ea, .iii. annis inermis, in primo cum pane et aqua et in aliis sine uino carneque peniteat.   5

6. Si autem non genuerit ex ea filium, sed pulluit eam, uno anno et dimedio sine diliciis sineque uxore peniteat.

6. DE DIMITTENTE UXOREM SUAM. TEODORUS:

1. Qui dimiserit uxorem suam alteri coniungens se, .vii. ann- peniteat cum tribulatione uel xii leuius. 2. Similiter mulier adultera vii annis 10 peniteat.

7. DE MULIERE DIMITTENTE UIRUM SUUM. TEODORUS:

Si ab aliquo sua discesserit uxor, uno anno paeniteat ipsa si inpolluta reuertitur, ceterum ipsa .iii.; ipse uero uno anno, si aliam duxerit, peniteat.   15

8. DE MULIERIBUS MENSTRUIS.
I. TEODORUS:

Mulieres menstruo tempore non intrent in ecclesiam nec communicent.

2. Qui menstruo tempore coierit, xx dies peniteat.

9. DE CONTINENTIA MATRIMONII   20

1. Qui ⟨in⟩ matrimonio sunt, .iii. noctes abstineant se a coniunctione antequam communicent.

2. Uir abstineat se ab uxore xl dies ante Pascha usque in octabas Pasce.

3. Mulier .iii. menses debet se abstinere a uiro quando concoepit ante 25 partum et post tempore purgationis, hoc est xl dies et noctes, seu masculum seu feminam genuerit. Aliter lex purgationis dicit.

10. DE NUBENDO IN DOMINICO

Qui nubit in Dominico, petat a Deo ueniam et uno uel duobus uel iii diebus peniteat aut amplius, si frequentat.   30

---

1 sq. *cf.* Vinnian c. 36.   9 sq. Theod. I. 14, 8   10 sq. Theod. I. 14, 14   13–15 Theod. I. 14, 13   17 sq. Theod. I. 14, 17   19 Theod. I. 14, 23   21–27 Theod. II. 12, 1–3   27 *cf.* Leu. 12, 2–5   29 sq. Theod. I. 14, 20

---

2 et sine *Wasserschleben*: et sic B. sic et C. *lege*: et sic sine? *cf. supra*, 4 *ex.* 6 non genuerit *Wasserschleben*: ingenuerit CB.   sed: sunt C.   pulluit eam *ego*: pullit C. pollutionem B.   7 deliciis B.   8 THEODORUS B.   14 uero *et* anno *om.* B.   17 eclesiam B.   20 MATRIMONIA C.   21 in *add. Wasserschleben.*   22 communicent: s.s. .i. sacr̄i B.   23 octauus C.   24 pasche B. 25 concepit B.   27 seu *om.* C.

4. Another (authority) has ruled differently: A layman who defiles his neighbour's wife or virgin daughter shall do penance for a year on bread and water and without his own wife.

5. But if he has defiled a virgin of God and has begotten a child by her, he shall do penance for three years without arms, in the first year on bread and water, and in the others without wine and meat.

6. If, however, he does not beget a child of her, but has defiled her, he shall do penance for one year and a half without delicacies and without his wife.

6. OF HIM WHO DIVORCES HIS WIFE. THEODORE:

1. He who divorces his wife and marries another shall do penance for seven years in hardship or for twelve years less strictly. 2. Similarly an adulterous wife shall do penance for seven years.

7. OF A WIFE DIVORCING HER HUSBAND. THEODORE:

If anyone's wife deserts her husband, she shall do penance for one year if she returns undefiled; otherwise, she (shall do penance) for three (years); he, however, shall do penance for one year if he has taken another wife.

8. CONCERNING THE MONTHLY PERIOD OF WOMEN.
1. THEODORE:

During their monthly period women should not enter a church nor receive holy communion.

2. He who has intercourse with his wife during her monthly period shall do penance for twenty days.

9. OF CONTINENCE IN MARRIAGE

1. Those living in wedlock should abstain from intercourse three nights before receiving holy communion.

2. A man should abstain from his wife during the forty days before Easter and until the octave of Easter.

3. A woman who has conceived must abstain from her husband for three months before childbirth and during the period of purgation afterwards, that is, forty days and nights, whether she has given birth to a male or female child. The law of purgation says differently.

10. OF MARRYING[21] ON SUNDAY

He who marries on Sunday shall ask God's forgiveness and do penance for one or two or three days or for more, if he does so repeatedly.

11. DE MORTUIS INFANTIBUS. I. THEODORUS:

Si moritur infans trium annorum sine baptismo, .iii. annos peniteant pater et mater eius. In primo cum pane et aqua et in duobus sine diliciis coniugioque, sine carne uinoque.

2. Si clericus de una plebe eum non suscipit, uno anno; si non de 5 una plebe, semianno peniteat.

HUCUSQUE DE FORNICATIONE. NUNC DE FILARGIRIA.

III

Filargiria iuxta Cassianum decim subdiuissionibus†, ut praediximus, e quibus sunt furta, periuria, mendacia, falsa testimonia, rapacitas, inhumanitas. 10

DE HOC UITIO PAULUS AIT:

Radix omnium malorum cupiditas.

1. DE FURTO. I. TEODORUS:

Qui sepe furtum fecerit, .vii. annis peniteat uel quomodo sacerdos iudicauerit peniteat. 15

2. Aliter alius sapiens iudicat dicens: Furtum semel uno anno, iterum faciens .ii.

3. Si puer, xl uel xx diebus poeniteat, ac ut est aetas et qualitas facientis iudicandum est.

2. DE RAPACITATE: 20

1. Qui diripit aliena quolibet modo, reddat quadruplum ei cui nocuit; si non habet unde reddat, peniteat ut supra diximus.

2. Qui repetit auferentem quae sua sunt Domini contra interdictum, tribuat egentibus quae repetiuit.

3. DE PERIURIO. I. THEODORUS: 25

Qui periurium fecit in ecclesia xi ann- peniteat.

2. Qui uero necessitate coactus sit, iii annis peniteat.

3. Qui in manu hominis periurat, apud Grecos nihil est; si uero in manu episcopi uel presbiteri uel diaconi seu in altari uel in cruce non consecrata, uno anno. 30

2–4 *cf.* Theod. I. 14, 29   8 *cf. supra, p.* 206, 20 sqq.   12 1 Tim. 6, 10; *cf.* Vinnianus c. 29   14 sq. Theod. I. 3, 3   16 sq. Cummean III. 1.   23 *cf.* Luc. 6, 30 (*u. etiam* 'Syn. II. S. Patr.' *c. 6*).   26–30 Theod. I. 6, 1–4.

---

1 IMFANTIBUS B.   TEODORUS C*B.   5 una: uno C.   8 casianum B. *post* subdiussionibus *desideratur uerbum, e.g.* diuiditur.   11 sq. *om.* C.   18 aetas: eas C.   26 ann- *om.* C.   27 coactus *Wasserschleben*; conatus CB.

11. OF DEAD CHILDREN. I. THEODORE:

If a child of three years dies without baptism, the child's father and mother shall do penance for three years. In the first year on bread and water, in the other two without delicacies and the marital union, without meat and wine.

2. If a cleric of the same parish does not accept him he shall do penance for one year; if (he is) not of the same parish, for half a year.

THUS FAR OF FORNICATION. NOW OF AVARICE.

III

According to Cassian, avarice has ten subdivisions, among which are thefts, perjuries, lies, false testimonies, rapacity, inhumanity.

OF THIS VICE PAUL SAYS:

The desire of money is the root of all evils.

1. OF THEFT. I. THEODORE:

He who commits theft often, shall do penance for seven years or as the priest shall judge.

2. Another wise man judges differently, saying: Committing theft once, one year, doing it again, two years.

3. If (it is) a boy, he shall do penance for forty or twenty days, and his penance is to be decided according to his age and quality.

2. OF RAPACITY

1. He who plunders another's goods in whatever way shall render it fourfold to him whom he has damaged; if he has not the means for paying, he shall do penance as we have said above.

2. He who recovers from one who is carrying it off what is his own against the contrary command of the Lord shall give to the poor those things which he has recovered.

3. OF PERJURY. I. THEODORE:

He who swears a false oath in a church shall do penance for eleven years.

2. He who does so under duress shall do penance for three years.

3. Swearing a false oath into the hand of an (ordinary) man does not matter according to the Greeks; if, however, (this is done) in the hand of a bishop or priest or deacon or at the altar or before an unblessed cross, one year.

4. Aliter alius dicit: Qui periurat, .vii. ann- peniteat. Qui deducit alium in periurium ignorantem, .vii. ann- peniteat similiter. Qui autem ductus est ignorans et postea recognoscit, anno .i. Qui uero suspicatur quod in periurium ducitur, tamen pro consensu iurat, .ii. annis.

4. DE FALSO TESTE. 5

Falsum testimonium dicens placeat proximo suo primo et quale fratri inposuit tali iudicio dampnetur iudice sacerdote.

5. DE MENDACIO. 1. SOLOMON AIT:

Os quod mentitur occidit animam.
2. Qui mentitur pro cupiditate, placeat largitate quem frustrauit. 10
3. Mendax uero per ignorantiam et non nocuit, confiteatur ei· cui mentitus est et sacerdoti, et hora tacendi damnetur uel xii salmos cantet. Si uero non per ignorantiam, .iii. diebus taceat, uel xxx salmos si·praeest cantet; praesules enim tacere non possunt.

6. DE INHUMANITATE 15

1. Qui non implet quodlibet eorum pro quibus Dominus dicet: *Uenite benedicti patris mei*, et reliqua, quanto tempore sic mansit tanto peniteat largusque uiuat de cetero; sin autem, abscidatur.
2. Clericus habens superflua donet ea pauperibus; sin autem, excommunicetur. Si uero post peniteat, tempore quo in contradictione 20 fuit in penitentia semotus uiuat.

⟨IV. DE IRA⟩

Ira, ut praediximus, gignit homicidia, clamorem, indignationem, rixam, tumorem mentis, contumelias, obprobria.

1. DE UARIIS HOMICIDIIS. 25

1. Parricidium faciens .xiiii. ann- cum pane et aqua peniteat.

2. THEODORUS DE GREGIS DICIT:

Si pro ultione amici occiderit hominem, .vii. annis uel .x. peniteat. Si reddere uult propinquis peccuniam, demedio spatio peniteat. Qui uero pro uindicta fratris occiderit hominem, .iii. annis peniteat. Qui 30

1–4 Cummean III. 8–11.   9 Sap. 1, 11   17 Matth. 25, 34
23: *u. supra*, Praef. *c.* 43   27–p. 228, 5 Theod. I. 4, 1. 2. 5. 6.

---

5 TESTE: TESTIMONIO B.   8 SOLAMON C*.   9 quo C.   11 nocui C.
12 xi C.   12. 13 psalmos B.   13 Si–taceat *om.* B.   praeest: p̄.ē. CB;
cf. ⟨VIII⟩. 2, 2 *et app. crit. ad p.* 118, 22.   15 HUMANITATE C.   22 DE IRA
add. Wasserschleben.   23 ut: aut B.   clamorem: da mortem C.   24 rixa CB:
corr. Wasserschleben.   29 pecuniam B.   spatio *bis* B.

4. Differently another (authority) says: He who swears a false oath shall do penance for seven[22] years. He who leads another into perjury unknowingly shall do penance similarly for seven years. But he who is led into perjury unknowingly and afterwards finds it out, one year. He, however, who suspects that he is led into perjury and nevertheless swears on account of his consent, two years.

4. OF A FALSE WITNESS

He who bears false witness shall first satisfy his neighbour, and with what he has wrongly charged his brother with such judgement shall he be condemned, a priest being the judge.

5. OF LYING. I. SOLOMON SAYS:

The mouth that lieth killeth the soul.

2. One who lies because of greed shall make satisfaction in liberality to him whom he has cheated.

3. If one lies through ignorance, however, and does no harm, he shall confess to him to whom he has lied and to a priest, and shall be condemned to an hour of silence or twelve[23] psalms. If, however, (he did it) not through ignorance, he shall be silent for three days or, if he is in authority, he shall chant thirty psalms; for those in authority cannot keep silence.

6. OF INHUMANITY

1. He who fails to fulfil any of those things for which the Lord will say: *Come, ye blessed of my Father*, etc., for whatever time he has continued thus he shall do penance, and he shall live a liberal donor henceforward; but if he does otherwise, he shall be cut off.

2. A cleric who has an excess of goods shall give these to the poor; if he does not he shall be excommunicated. If, however, he afterwards does penance, he shall live secluded in penance for the same (length of) time as that in which he was recalcitrant.

⟨IV. OF ANGER⟩

Anger, as we have said before, begets murders, clamour, indignation, strife, pride of mind, insults, and reproaches.

1. OF VARIOUS MURDERS

1. He who commits parricide shall do penance for fourteen years on bread and water.

2. THEODORE, REFERRING TO THE GREEKS, SAYS:

If anyone has killed a man in revenge for a friend, he shall do penance for seven years or ten. If he is willing to pay a fine in money to the relatives (of his victim), he shall do penance for half that time. If, however, he has killed a man in revenge for a brother, he shall do

monachum uel clericum occiderit, iuxta indulgentiam Noui Testamenti arma relinquat et Deo seruiat uel .vii. annis peniteat.

3. DE OCCISSIONE EPISCOPI

Qui episcopum uel presbiterum occiderit, regis iudicium de eo est.

4. Qui in puplico bello hominem occiderit, xl dies peniteat.   5

2. DE OCCIDENTIBUS SEMET IPSIS. I. THEODORUS:

Si homo uexatus a diabolo ⟨et⟩ nescit aliquid nisi discurrere semet ipsum occidit quacumque causa, potest ut oretur pro eo, si ante relegiosus erat. Si autem pro disperatione uel pro timore aliquo uel pro causis ignotis, Deo relinquendum est hoc iudicium et non ausi sumus orare 10 pro eo. Qui uoluntariae semet ipsum occiderit, misam pro eo facere non licet, sed tamen orare et elymosinas largiri pro eo.

2. Penitentia perditionis liquoris materiae infantis in utero mulieris .iii. anni in pane et aqua.

3. Penitentia perditionis carnis et animae in utero: .xiiii. peniteat in 15 pane et aqua.

4. Praetium animae mulieris morientis de perditione carnis cum anima: xiiii. ancelle.

3. DE RIXANTIBUS

1. Qui per rixam iectu debilem uel deformem hominem facit reddet 20 inpensa in medicos, et macule praetium et opus donec sanetur restituat, et demedio anni peniteat. Si uero non habuerit unde restituat hoc, uno anno peniteat; in quadragessimis in pane et aqua peniteat. Si autem clericus, uno anno uel demedio anni.

2. Et non praetereundum quod si quis per furorem et rixas et non ex 25 meditatione odii alium occiderit, iii annis debeat penitere.

3. Si autem casu nolens occiderit proximum suum, anno uno peniteat.

4. Si quis autem ex meditatione odii et post uota perfectionis alium occiderit, cum peregrinatione perenni mundo moriatur.   30

4. DE INDIGNATIONE

Qui fratrem contristet iuste uel iniustae conceptum rancorem eius satisfactione leniat, et sic potest orare; sin autem inposibile recipi ab eo, sic tamen peniteat iudice sacerdote. Is autem qui non recipit eum quanto

---

7–12 Theod. II. 10, 1–3   27 *cf.* Theod. I. 4, 7

6 HOCCIDENTIBUS B.   TEODORUS B.   7 ⟨et⟩ *suppleui ex Theodoro.*   8 religiosus B.   10 ausi: causis C.   sumus: *lege* simus?   18 ancillae B.   22 unde *Wasserschleben*: de C. inde B.   23 quadragesimis C.   in quadr.–peniteat *fortasse mancum; cf. Cumm. (IV) V. 11.*   24 dimedio B.   26 alienum C.   27 nolens *ego*: uolens CB.   31 DI INDIGNATIONE C. DE INDULGENTIA B.   34 quando B.

penance for three years. He who has killed a monk or a cleric shall, according to the spirit of forgiveness of the New Testament, lay down his arms and serve God, or do penance for seven years.

3. OF SLAYING A BISHOP

He who has slain a bishop or priest comes under the judgement of the king.

4. He who has killed a man in open war shall do penance for forty days.

2. OF THOSE WHO KILL THEMSELVES. I. THEODORE:

If a man is vexed by the devil and can do nothing but run about, and kills himself for whatever reason, one may pray for him if before he was religious. If, however, (he kills himself) because of despair or of some fear or for some unknown reason, judgement in this matter must be left to God and we should not dare to pray for him.[24] One who has killed himself of his own will, for him Mass must not be said, yet it is permitted to pray for him and give alms.[25]

2. The penance for the destruction of the embryo of a child in the mother's womb, three years on bread and water.

3. The penance for the destruction of flesh and spirit in the womb: to do penance for fourteen years on bread and water.

4. The life price for a woman who dies of the destruction of flesh and spirit: fourteen female slaves.

3. OF PERSONS ENGAGED IN STRIFE

1. He who by a blow in a quarrel renders a man incapacitated or maimed shall meet (the injured man's) medical expenses and shall make good the price of his deformity and shall do his work until he is healed, and do penance for half a year. If he has not the wherewithal to make restitution for these things, he shall do penance for one year; during the forty-day periods he shall do penance on bread and water. If, however, he is a cleric, he shall do penance for a year and a half.[26]

2. It must not be left unmentioned that if anyone has killed another through anger and quarrels and not from premeditation out of hatred, he must do penance for three years.

3. But if he kills his neighbour unintentionally by accident, he shall do penance for one year.

4. But if anyone kills another from premeditation out of hatred, and after vows of perfection, he shall die unto the world with perpetual exile.

4. OF INDIGNATION

He who makes his brother sad shall mollify by a satisfaction the rancour he has conceived, justly or unjustly, and so he shall be able to pray; if, however, it is impossible to be reconciled to him, then at least he shall do penance, a priest being judge. He, however, who refuses to

Q

tempore inplacabilis sit tanto tempore cum pane et aqua uiuat. Ac *homicida* ille *qui odit fratrem suum* quandiu non repellit odium in pane et aqua sit et ei quem odierit *caritate non ficta* copuletur.

5. DE OBPROBRIIS

1. Fratrem cum furore maledicens cui maledixerit placeat illi et .vii. 5 diebus semotus pane et aqua peniteat.

2. Qui uerba aceruiora in furore, non tamen iniuriosa, protulerit, ⟨post⟩ satisfactionem fratri superponat. Si cum pallore rubore uel tremore, tamen tacuit, una die in pane et aqua uiuat.

6. DE CLAMORE CANONES PATRUM: 10

1. Clamor excitatus cum tanto terrarum spatio a loquente, si cui dicitur separatus aut cum surdus sit salutatus, nullius inpedimenti est. Clamor uero iracundia commotus silentio et ieiunio quantum sacerdos iudicauerit sanetur. Et clamor dolore excitatus non praetermittendus, de quo pauca dicimus.   15

2. Penitentia bardicationis glandellae post obitum laici uel laicae .l. dies et noctes in pane et aqua;

3. si post glandellam morientem in partu uel cohabitatorem uel cohabitatricem fidem habentem, xl dies in pane et aqua;

4. si post clerici plebilis obitum, xx dies in pane et aqua;   20

5. si post anchoritae uel scribae uel episcopi uel principis magni uel regis magni obitum, .xv. dies in pane et aqua;

6. si sanctimonialis quedam huiusmodi uocibus turbata clamauerit, duplici penitentia emendetur predicta.

7. DE LUCTO FACIENDO ET PRO BONO MERITO REPUTANDO 25 IN LEGE DICITUR:

Iacob filius Isaac xl diebus in Egypto luctatus est et tota ebdomada in terra Canaan; et Christus in Nouo, plorauerunt eum feminae; et pene innumerabilibus scripturarum exemplis inuenitur scriptum in canone, et pro malo merito inputatur illi pro quo non ploratur.   30

7. DE EO QUOD NEMO DEBET ACCIPERE SACRIFICIUM NISI SIT MUNDUM ET PERFECTUM ET NIHIL MORTALE IN EO INUENTUM

Christus autem cum surrexit puellam, sibi iusit dari manducare .i. postquam perfecta sana esset et non infirma .i. sana a Christo praesente

---

2 1 Ioh. 3, 15   3 2 Cor. 6, 6   26 *cf.* Gen. 50, 3–10   27 Luc. 23, 27
33–*p.* 232, 1 *cf.* Marc. 5, 43. 37. 40

---

2 hodit B.   repellat B*.   4 OPROBRIIS B.   7 protulerit *Wasserschleben*,
cf. Cumm. (IV) V. 13; Ps.-Cumm. IX. 4: pertulerit CB.   8 post . . . superponat
ego, cf. satis faciens . . . superponat *Cumm., Ps.-Cumm. ibid.*; s.f. suo p̄ponat CB.
11 cum ⟨ea⟩ C.   14 praetermitendus C.   18 quohabitatorem B.   19 coabitatricem B.   20 obitum *post* dies CB.   23 huismodi B.   25 LUTO C.
PRO BONO: PRONO C.   28 canan B.   32 mundus et perfectus *McNeill–Gamer*
probabiliter   33 com C.   iussit B.   34 *lege* perfecte?

be reconciled to him shall live on bread and water for as long a time as he has been implacable. And that *murderer who hates his brother* shall go on bread and water as long as he does not overcome his hatred, and he shall be joined to him whom he hates in sincere charity.

5. OF REPROACHES

1. One who curses his brother in anger shall placate him whom he has cursed and shall do penance for seven days secluded, on bread and water.

2. He who utters in anger harsh but not injurious words shall make satisfaction to his brother and then keep a special fast. If (he expresses his anger) with pallor or flush or tremor, yet remains silent, he shall live for a day on bread and water.

6. OF CLAMOUR, THE CANONS OF THE FATHERS:

1. To raise one's voice in shouting, if the person addressed is far away from the speaker, or if one greets a deaf person, is not at all forbidden. Shouting, however, that is prompted by quick temper shall be healed by silence and fasting for such a period as the priest may decide; also, we must not pass over clamour aroused by grief, of which we shall say a few things.

2. The penance for the wailing of a female dependant after the death of a layman or laywoman, fifty days on bread and water;

3. if (the dirge is sung) after (the death of) a servant woman who died in childbirth, or of him who cohabits with her,[27] they being believers, forty days on bread and water;

4. if after (the death of) a cleric of the parish, twenty days on bread and water;

5. if after (the death of) an anchorite or a scribe or a bishop or a great prince or a great king, fifteen days on bread and water;

6. if any nun becomes excited and shouts with sounds of this sort, she shall be corrected with double the penance prescribed above.

7. CONCERNING THE MAKING OF LAMENTATION AND ITS BEING RECKONED AS GOOD MERIT, IT IS SAID IN THE LAW:

Jacob the son of Isaac was lamented for forty days in Egypt and for a whole week in the land of Canaan; and so was Christ in the New (Testament), the women wept for Him; and it is found written in the Canon with almost innumerable examples of the Scriptures, and for whom no lament is made to him it is reckoned as bad merit.

7. OF THE FACT THAT NO ONE OUGHT TO RECEIVE THE SACRIFICE UNLESS HE IS CLEAN AND PERFECT[28] AND NOTHING MORTAL IS FOUND IN HIM

When Christ had raised up the young girl He commanded to give her to eat, that is, after she had been perfect, whole, and not infirm, that is, made whole by Christ in the presence of Peter and James and

Petro et Iacobo et Iohanne et patre et matre, id ⟨est⟩ unus quisque postquam confessus fuerit uitia et postquam ea subplantauerit et postquam gratia Dei uenerit et pater celestis et aecclesia fuerint praesentes ei, tunc sanus in bono opere accipiat sacrificium.

V. DE TRISTITIA

1. 1. Tristitiae genera duo sunt: unum salutiferum, alterum mortiferum. 2. Salutiferum, cum nos nostra peccata uel aliorum contristant et nobis lacrimarum habundantiam digna penitentia inducant. De hoc genere tristitiae Saluator dicit: *Beati qui lugent nunc quoniam ipsi consolabuntur.* 3. Mortiferum, cum orbitate amicorum aut demptione rerum corporalium aut dampno, si demptae sunt, contristamur. 4. †Sanctae Sinclitae non dissimilia his in exemplis sanctorum loquor dicens†: Est tristitia utilis et est tristitia quae corrumpit. 5. Tristitia uero utilis est, ut pro peccatis gemescamus et pro ignorantia proximorum et ut non cadamus a proposito et ut perfectionem bonitatis adtingamus. 6. Hae sunt species uere tristitiae. Est enim aduersari nostri ad has quedam coniunctio; inmittit enim tristitiam sine aliqua ratione, quam tedium quidam appellauerunt. Oportet ergo talem spiritum sepius orando et sallendo depellere.

2. DE MALEDICTIONE QUAE INFERT UITAM ETERNAM IN EUANGELIO

Beati estis cum maledixerint uos homines et persecuti uos et reliqua usque *merces uestra copiosa est in caelis.*
3. De tristitia uero mortifera rancor, pussillanimitas, amaritudo, disperatio, malitia, torpor circa praecepta, ut praediximus, nascuntur.

1. Cum enim amaritudinem in corde retinet, hilari uultu et leto corde sanetur; si autem non cito eam deponat, ieiunio sacerdote iudicante se emendat; si autem iterauerit, abscidatur donec alacer letusque in pane agnoscat delictum suum.

2. Et hoc uitium, ut quidam sapiens ait, emendatur sono psalmorum frequenter et praeceptis canonicis ex labiis iusti, sicut apostolus dicit: *Et te ipsum saluum facies et eos qui te audiunt.* Tristitia enim quae mortem operatur, †id est,† circa uoluntatem suam: si diminuetur in hoc, tristis

---

9 sq. Matth. 5, 5 (nunc *add.* DE Ep LRY^gl; *sic etiam* Pen. Hib. VI. 1b)   12–19 Vitae Patrum V. 10, 71 (Syncletica)   22 sq. Matth. 5, 11 sq. (uos ER. homines *add.* DLR *al.*)   25 *cf.* Praef. 44   31 *cf.* Prou. 10, 21. 32.   32 1 Tim. 4, 16

1 est *addidi.*   2 postquam (1) *om.* C.   confessus: *s.s.* i. petrus CB. subplantauerit: *s.s.* i. iacob(um) CB.   3 gratia: *s.s.* i. iohs̄ B.   eclesia B. 7 nos *om.* C.   aliorum: amborum C.   ⟨et nobis lacrimarum penitentiam⟩ et nobis CB.   10 dempnatione C.   11 sq. *fortasse lege*: Sancta Sinclit⟨ic⟩a ... loquitur dicens.   12 disimilia C.   16 aduersarii B.   18 appellauerunt *Vitae Patrum*: appellati (-ant B) uerum CB.   19 psallendo B.   24 ranchor B. pusillanimitas B.   25 tupor C.   28 alacerat CB: *correxi, cf.* Cumm. (V). 3

John and her father and mother; that is to say, every one, after confessing his faults and destroying them, and after the grace of God has come and the heavenly Father and the Church are present with him, shall then, being whole in good works, receive the sacrifice.

V. OF DEJECTION

1. 1. There are two kinds of dejection: one that brings salvation, the other that brings death. 2. The one that brings salvation (is found in us) when we are sorry for our sins and for the sins of others and (these sins) move us to an abundance of tears with due penance.[29] Of this kind of dejection the Saviour says: *Blessed are they that mourn now: for they shall be comforted.* 3. It brings death when we grieve because we are deprived of friends or have suffered damage or loss of bodily goods. 4. In the examples of the saints, Saint Syncletica[30] says much the same, putting it thus: 'There is a dejection that is for our good and a dejection that corrupts. 5. Dejection for our good (means) that we should sigh for our sins and for our neighbours' ignorance, and that we should not fall short of our vocation, and that we should attain to the goal of perfect goodness. 6. These are forms of true dejection. For our enemy also has something to do with these things; he brings over us dejection without reason, which some have called disgust. One must therefore frequently drive away such a spirit by prayer and the chanting of psalms.'

2. OF THE MALEDICTION WHICH, ACCORDING TO THE GOSPEL, BRINGS ETERNAL LIFE.

Blessed are ye when men shall revile you, and persecute you, and so on unto *your reward is very great in heaven.*

3. Of dejection that brings death are born rancour, smallness of mind, bitterness, despair, malice, indifference about commands, as we have said above.

1. For when (someone) harbours bitterness in his heart he shall be healed by a joyful countenance and a glad heart; but if he does not quickly lay it aside he shall correct himself by fasting according to the judgement of a priest; if he returns to it he shall be cut off until, on bread, he willingly and gladly acknowledges his fault.

2. This vice, then, as a certain wise man says, is healed by the sound of psalms often recited and the precepts of the Canon, coming from the lips of the just, as the apostle says: *Thou shalt both save thyself and them that hear thee.* Dejection that works death concerns one's will: if a person is thwarted in this, he is dejected; but he ought to rejoice daily in

---

33 id est: .i. ē CB. *fortasse lege* tristitia enim quae mortem operatur est circa uoluntatem suam.

est; sed oportet eum gaudere cotidie in mandatis Dei, sicut dicit Dauid: *Gaudete iusti et iterum gaudete.*

⟨VI.⟩ DE ACCEDIA

Accedia otiositatem, sumnolentiam, inoportunitatem, inquietudinem, peruagationem et reliqua gignit. 5

1. De otiositate

1. Otiosus opere plus omnibus honeretur et secundum apostolum *laborat manibus suis, ut habeat unde communicet indigentibus.* Nam otiositas omne opus bonum disipat,

2. sicut in exemplis sanctorum abbas Pastor loquitur dicens: Quia 10 sicut fumo expelluntur apes, ut tollatur dulcitudo earum operis, ita et corporalis quies timorem Domini expellit ab anima et auferet ab ea omne opus bonum.

2. DE SOMNOLENTIA. I. SAPIENS AIT:

Si mortem odis, cur somnum dilegis? Nam somnus assiduus emitatio 15 mortis.

2. Sumnolentus cum uigiliis et orationibus sanetur .i. iii uel vi. psalmis occupetur.

3. In exemplis sanctorum frater quidam dicit: Si contigerit grauari me somno et transierit hora ministeri mei, anima mea pro uerecondia 20 iam non uult implere opus suum, et dixit senex: Si contigerit usque mane dormire, quando euigilas surge, claude hostium et fenestras tuas et fac opus tuum; scriptum est enim: *Tuus est dies et tua est nox.* In omni tempore glorificatur Deus.

3. De uagatione 25

1. Uagus instabilisque mantione unius loci operisque sedulitate sanetur.

2. Item alius: Accedia per stabilitatem corporis et cordis et cogitationis adiuuare potest.

3. In exemplis sanctorum frater quidam applicuit in Sciti ad abatem 30 Moysen petens ab eo sermonem, et dixit senex ei: Uadens sede in cella tua et cella tua docebit te uniuersa.

4. In eodem libro dixit abbas Antonius: Sicut pisces, si tardauerint in sicco, moriuntur, ita et monachi tardentes extra cellam aut cum uiris saecularibus inmorantes a quietis proposito resoluuntur. 35

2 *in Psalmis non legitur, cf.* Phil. 4, 4.   8 *cf.* Eph. 4, 28 (suis *add.* c d f g t TEST^{alq} VULG^{pl}.   communicet: *cf.* communicare Victor. Hier. Pel^B)   10–13 Vitae Patrum V. 4, 32   19–24 Vitae Patrum V. 10, 98   23 Ps. 73, 16   30–32 Vitae Patr. V. 2, 9   33–35 Vitae Patr. V. 2, 1

2 gaudete (2): gaude C.   4 somnolentiam B.   *lege* inportunitatem. 10. 11 sic C.   10 albas CB.   11 et: ut C.   12 aufert *Vitae Patr.* 15 diligis B.   sompnus B.   asiduus C.   17 cum sumnolentus (somnolentes B*) CB: *transposuit Wasserschleben.*   20 ministri CB. (ministerii *Vitae Patr.*)

the commandments of God, as David says: *Rejoice, ye just, and again rejoice.*

⟨VI.⟩ OF LANGUOR

Languor brings forth idleness, drowsiness, unseasonableness, restlessness, wandering about, and the rest.

1. OF IDLENESS

1. The idler shall be taxed with more work than all the others, and shall, according to the apostle, *labour, working with his hands, that he may have someting to give to them that suffer need.* For idleness wastes every good work,

2. as in the examples of the Fathers abbot Pastor says: 'As bees are expelled by smoke so that their sweet labour might be taken from them, so rest of the body expels from the soul the fear of God and will take away from it every good work.'

2. OF SLOTH. I. A WISE MAN SAYS:

1. 'If thou loathest death why dost thou love sleep? For continuous sleep is the image of death.'

2. The slothful is to be healed by vigils and prayers, that is, he shall be occupied with three or six psalms.

3. In the examples of the saints a certain brother says: 'If it so happens that sleep has befallen me and the hour of my ministry has gone by, my soul, in shame, no longer wants to carry out its work', and an elder said: 'If it happens that thou hast slept until morning, rise as soon as thou awakest, shut thy door and windows, and do thy work; for it is written: *Thine is the day and thine is the night.* God is glorified at any time.'

3. OF WANDERING ABOUT

1. A wandering and unstable man shall be healed by permanent residence in one place and by application to work.

2. Also another (authority says): Languor can be overcome by steadiness of body, heart, and thought.

3. In the examples of the saints a certain brother approached abbot Moyses in Scythe, asking of him a sermon, and the old man said: 'Go and sit down in thy cell, and thy cell will teach thee all things.'

4. In the same book abbot Anthony has said: 'As fish die if they tarry on dry land, so also monks staying for long away from their cells or conversing with men of the world lapse from their vocation for a retired life.'

---

uerecundia B.   21 ⟨te⟩ contigerit *Vitae Patr.*   22 euigilias CB: *corr. Wasserschleben.*   30 emplis C.   insciti C. inscitia B, *sed s.s.* i. nomen patriȩ CB.   33 abas B.   35 reuoluuntur *Vitae Patr.*

5. In eodem libro dixit sancta †ecclesia†: Si in monasterio cum aliis conuersaris non motes locum; lederis enim omnino si facias hoc. Etenim sicut gallina quae dereliquerit oua foeta [et] sine pullis ea exire faciet, ita monachus uel uirgo frigescit et mortificatur in fine de loco ad locum transeundo.   5

6. ITEM IN EODEM LIBRO:

Frater interrogauit senem dicens: Nutant cogitationes meae et tribulor; et ille dicit: Tu sede in cella tua et cogitationes iterum ueniunt. Si⟨cut⟩ enim si assina ligata sit et stringatur, pullus eius currit huc atque illuc, semper autem ad matrem suam reuertitur ubicumque illa erit, ita et erunt et cogitationes eius qui propter Deum tollerabiliter in cella sua residerit, quia etsi ad modicum nutant sed iterum reuertuntur ad eum.   10

7. Etiam si quis cogitationes uarias habuerit quando orat et quando cantat psalmos, sibi proficit oratio, quia †omnes ruminatio quae ruminat homo eam gustat† corporaliter; ita et hoc spiritaliter intellegimus in psalmis canendis. Haec sufficiunt de admonitione ut nullus uagus sit.   15

⟨VII.⟩ DE CENODOCXIA

Caenodoxia, id est uana gloria, contentiones, heresses, iactantiam et reliqua gignit.

1. DE CONTENTIONE.   20

Contentiosus alterius scientiae etiam se subdeat; sin autem, anathemazetur, ut regno Dei sit alienus.

2. DE HERESI.

Qui aliam doctrinam extra scripturas uel heressim praesummit, alienatur ab ecclesia; si peniteat, suam puplice sententiam damnet et quos decipit ad fidem conuertat et ieiuniat ad iudicium sacerdotis.   25

3. DE IACTANTIA.

Iactans in sua beneficia se humiliat; alioquin quicquid bonum fecerit causa humanae gloriae perdidit.

4. DE REMEDIO HUIUS UITII QUIDAM SAPIENS AIT: 30

Cenodoxiae uitium ita curatur, id ⟨est⟩ ut non quis contentiosus siue inueritate siue inquietate fiat, ut heressis temptatio distruatur; quia quis

---

1–5 Vitae Patr. V. 7, 15   7–12 Vitae Patr. V. 7, 30

1 eclesia B. *lege:* Syncletica.   3 foeta: *lege* fota *cum Vitis Patr.?*   et *deleui cum Vitis Patr.; sed fortasse post* ita *transponenda est, cf. p. 234, 34; 236, 10 sq.*   4 in fine: in fide *Vitae Patr.*   7 meae: me C.   9 sicut *Vitae Patr.*: si CB.   si *om.* B.   10 illa erit: ierit *Vitae Patr.*   11 intollerabiliter CB: *correxi ex Vitis Patr.*   13 sq. quando orat et quando cantat: quando cantat (*in marg.*: . . . ndo orat) B.   14 sq. omnes (-is B)–gustat *corruptum; nescio an in Leu. 11, 3 sqq. tale quid apud Hibernos lectum sit quale est*: omnis (bestia) ruminationem quae ruminat,

5. In the same book Saint Syncletica says: 'If thou livest with others in a monastery do not change thy place; thou wilt surely be harmed if thou dost this. For as the hen that deserts her (half-)hatched eggs will cause them to be without chickens, so a monk or virgin turns lukewarm and in the end dies (spiritually) by wandering from one place to another.'

6. ALSO IN THE SAME BOOK:

A brother asked an elder, saying: 'My thoughts stray and I am worried'; and he says: 'Thou sit down in thy cell and thy thoughts will come again. For as it is with the mother ass: if she is tied to the plug, her foal runs hither and thither, but wherever it is it always returns to its mother, so it will be with the thoughts of him who for the sake of God sits patiently in his cell: even though they stray a little they return again to him.'

7. Even if someone has all sorts of thoughts when praying or chanting psalms, the prayer has its value; for, †as what is ruminated is tasted bodily† so we understand this also of the chanting of psalms.[31] These things are sufficient admonition that nobody must wander about.

⟨VII.⟩ OF VAINGLORY

Vainglory brings forth contentions, heresies, boasting, and the rest.

1. OF CONTENTION

The contentious shall subject himself even to the knowledge[32] of another; otherwise he shall be anathematized as a stranger to the kingdom of God.

2. OF HERESY

He who dares to follow another doctrine beside the Scriptures, or a heresy, is a stranger from the Church; if he repents he shall publicly condemn his opinion and shall convert to the faith those whom he has deceived and shall fast according to the judgement of a priest.

3. OF BOASTING

One who boasts of his good deeds shall humble himself; otherwise any good he has done he has lost on account of human glory.

4. CONCERNING A REMEDY OF THIS VICE, A CERTAIN WISE MAN SAYS:

The vice of vainglory is healed in this way, namely, that no one is contentious by either untruthfulness or quarrelsomeness, so that all

---

homo eam gustet; *hic tamen exspectatur*: omnis ruminatio quam ruminat †homo†, eam gustat.   15 intelligimus B.   17 CENODOXIA C.   18 hereses B.   21 sq. anatemazetur B.   22 sit *fortasse delendum*.   24 scriptura C.   heresim p̄sumit B.   25 eclesia B.   dampnet B.   26 ieiunat B.   31 est *suppleui*. 32 inquietate: iniquitate B.   heresis B.

non nisi ex contentione hereticus fiat ut nemo sit cupidus nisi facultate
saeculi. Deinde cenodoxia non crescit in nobis, quae in sacerdotibus et
regibus et in his qui in sublimitate constituti sunt uegit, et de modico
uerborum et ciborum et de nuditate saeculi et humilitate saluatur hoc
uitium cenodoxiae.   5

⟨VIII. DE SUPERBIA⟩

Superbie progenies haec est: contemptus, inuidia, inobedientia,
blasfemia, mormor aut detractationes, ueneficia.

1. Quidam sapiens ait: Qui superb[i]ae ceteros qualibet dispectione
arguit, primo satisfaciat eis, deinde ieiunat iudice sacerdote.   10

2. **1.** Inuidus satisfaciat ei cui inuidit; si autem nocuit, largitate placeat
ei et peniteat iudice sacerdote.

2. Qui causa inuidiae detrachit uel libenter detrahentem audit, .iiii.
diebus cum pane et aqua separatus uiuat; si uero qui praeest, vii. diebus
peniteat et seruiat ei libenter de cetero. Sed ut ait quidam, non est   15
detrahere uera dicere, secundum euangelium: *Corripe eum inter te et
ipsum solum primus, et postea si te non audiat dic ecclesiae.*

3. Ut blasfemiam detractationis diuitemus, audiemus quid in exemplis
sanctorum abas peritus dixit; ait enim: Bonum est monacho manducare
carnem et bibere uinum quam manducare in obtractatione carnes   20
fratrum; et iterum dicit: Susurrans serpens ad Euam de paradisso eam
eiecit; huic ergo similis qui proximo suo obloquitur quando et audientis
se animam perdit et suam non saluat.

4. Inobediens maneat extra concilium sine cibo et pulsat humiliter
donec recipiatur; quanto tempore inobediens fuit tanto uiuat donec   25
sanetur in pane et aqua.

5. Qui mormorat separetur et opus eius abiciatur; in pane et aqua uiuat
donec sanetur.

6. Cauendum est nobis hoc uitium, quod numquam uirtutibus crescit,
hoc est ieiunio et uigiliis et abstinentia, ministratione uero indigna et   30
seruili et maxime humilitate euanescit et oratione pura, ut intimo corde
quomodo psalmista ait dicamus: *Ab ocultis meis munda me, Domine.*
FINIT DE UITIIS.

---

9 sq. Cummean (VIII). 3   16–17 *cf.* Matth. 18, 15–17   19–23 Vitae Patr.
V. 4, 50. 52 (Hyperichius)   32 Ps. 18. 13 (Domine *add* , *cum* COPT, GR
2035, PsV Rom. Moz. Cypr. Aug.)

---

1 sit: *lege* fit?   3 uegit, *i.e. uiget* C.B.   4 saluator C.   hoc *om.* C.
6 *titulum suppl. Was serschleben.* (.vii. *textui adscribunt* CB.)   8 blasfēā C. blas-
phemĩa B.   9 superbae, *i.e.* superbe; *cf. adn. ad Cumm.* (*VIII*) .3.   11 cui:
cum C.   16 corripere C.   17 eclesiae B.   20 quam *Vitae Patr.*; quia
CB.   21 de: da C.   paradiso B.   22 eicit C.   quando: quoniam *Vitae Patr.*
25 quando B.   27 murmurat B.   29 *lege* ⟨non⟩ numquam?   32 occultis B.

temptation of heresy be destroyed; for nobody is likely to become a heretic except through contention, just as nobody is likely to be greedy except because of a worldly disposition (?). Further, vainglory does not grow in us, whereas it is strong in priests and kings and in those who are in high places, and it is by restraint in talk and food and by stripping ourselves of the things of the world and by humility that this vice of vainglory is healed.

⟨VIII. OF PRIDE⟩

The offspring of pride is this: contempt, envy, disobedience, blasphemy, murmuring or detraction, witchcrafts.

1. A certain wise man says: He who proudly censures others by any kind of contempt shall first make satisfaction to them and then fast according to the judgement ot a priest.

2. 1. The envious shall make satisfaction to him whom he has envied; but if he has done harm, he shall satisfy him with gifts and do penance according to the judgement of a priest.

2. He who for envy's sake defames (another) or willingly listens to a defamer shall be put apart and shall fast for four days on bread and water; but if the offence is against a superior, he shall do penance for seven days and shall serve him willingly thereafter. But, as someone says, to speak true things is not to defame, according to the Gospel: *Rebuke him between thee and him alone first, and afterwards if he will not hear thee tell the Church.*

3. In order that we may avoid the blasphemy of detraction, let us hear what an experienced abbot has said in the examples of the saints; for he says: 'It is better for a monk to eat meat and to drink wine than to eat the flesh of his brethren by defamation'; and again he says: 'The serpent, whispering to Eve, caused her to be ejected from Paradise; similar to it is he who speaks against his neighbour because he destroys the soul of him who listens and does not save his own.'

4. A disobedient person shall stay outside the assembly, without food, and shall humbly knock until he is received; and for as long a time as he has been disobedient he shall go on bread and water until he is healed.

5. He who murmurs shall be put apart and his work shall be rejected; he shall live on bread and water until he is healed.

6. We should beware of this vice, which sometimes[33] thrives on virtuous exercises, that is, on fasting, vigils, and abstinence; which, however, by lowly and ignoble service and above all by humility and pure prayer, fades away, so that we may say from the inmost heart, with the Psalmist: *From my secret sins cleanse me, O Lord!*   OF VICES, THE END.

NOTES ON TRANSLATION

'FIRST SYNOD OF ST. PATRICK'

1. The present translation is reproduced, in a slightly revised form, from my *Works of St. Patrick* (Ancient Christian Writers, vol. 17, 1953), pp. 50–54. It is here included by kind permission of the editor of the series, Rev. Prof. Dr. J. Quasten, and the publishers (Newman Press, Westminster, Md., and Messrs. Longmans, Green & Co., London).

2. *Denique*, which follows here in the Latin, is probably a mere particle of transition. On the assumption that it has a more specific meaning, it might be translated either 'at long last' (implying previous admonitions to the same effect) or 'finally' (suggesting that this canon was quoted mechanically from another set where it occurred at the very end—so McNeill–Gamer, p. 77, n. 1).

3. In ancient Ireland, as in all primitive communities, suretyship was an important institution which involved those who undertook it in far-reaching obligations. For the various types of surety, see R. Thurneysen, *Die Bürgschaft im irischen Recht* (Abh. d. Preuss. Akad., 1928, phil.-hist. kl. Nr. 2), pp. 35 ff.; D. A. Binchy in *Early Irish Society* (Dublin, 1954), pp. 63 f.

4. The *Collectio Hibernensis* quotes this canon with the variant 'cleric' for 'Christian'. However, St. Patrick, Epist. 7, refers to the same prohibition as binding also on lay people.

5. On *lamia* 'vampire' see my 'Works of St. Patrick', p. 98, n. 11. Cf. also the Edictum Rotharii, *c.* 376: 'nullus presumat haldiam . . . quasi strigam, quam dicunt mascam, occidere; quod Christianis mentibus nullatenus credendum est nec possibilem (*sic*) ut mulier hominem uiuum intrinsecus possit comedere.'

6. The practice of paying a bride-price (Ir. *tinnscra, tochra, coibche*) was common in early Indo-European society. For references, see Thurneysen in 'Studies in Early Irish Law' (1936), pp. 112–23, and my 'Works of St. Patrick', p. 98, n. 14.

7. *Parruchia*, i.e. diocese.

8. The words *offerat tantum susceptione* evidently mean 'he shall offer the holy sacrifice only on the grounds, or under the title, of a *susceptio*'. J. Hardouin, *Conciliorum Collectio Regia* I (1715), col. 1793, compares c. 33 of the Fourth Council of Carthage, A.D. 398 (Mansi III. 954): 'episcopi uel presbyteri si causa uisitandae ecclesiae ad alterius ecclesiam uenerint, in gradu suo suscipientur et . . . ad oblationem consecrandam inuitentur.'

9. Or: 'is not allowed to be served'? Cf. c. 34. This provision was possibly a safeguard against the infiltration of semi-Pelagianism. On this assumption the canon might well be genuine. On certificates for travelling clergy see McNeill–Gamer, p. 80, n. 35.

10. I suspect the words *inconsultu suo abbate* of having intruded here from the final clause. The words *Diaconus . . . uindicetur* would then refer to the secular clergy.

THE PREFACE OF GILDAS ON PENANCE

1. *Superpos(s)itio, superponere* denote a special fast which seems to have consisted in forgoing the principal meal of the day; this is suggested by the fact that of the two otherwise identical canons Gildas 10 and Cummean I. 4 the latter has *superponat* where the former has *caena priuatur*. For a discussion of this term see McNeill–Gamer, p. 31, with references; P. B. Corbett, 'The Latin of the Regula Magistri' (Louvain 1958), pp. 275 f. Metaphorically, St.

Columbanus in his *Regula coenobialis* (cc. 4. 5. 6. 15) and in his *Penitential* (A 9) enjoins a *superpositio silentii*.

2. The fifty days are the time between Easter and Pentecost, during which the severe discipline of the Irish monasteries was slightly relaxed (see J. Ryan, *Irish Monasticism*, pp. 346, 387). The expression *post passionem* is not quite accurate; perhaps we should read *post Pascha*. Cummean, who reproduces the entire paragraph verbatim (II. 2), has: *exceptis quinquagesime diebus; post superpositionem pane sine mensura utatur*, etc. I am inclined to believe that this is what Gildas originally wrote.

3. McNeill–Gamer translate 'dish' (David 7 'repast'). However, *ferculo* in both places (and in Cummean II. 2) is almost certainly a continental misreading of *serculo*, the latinized form of Ir. *sercol* (see RIA Contributions, S, col. 190) 'titbit', 'delicacy'. In an old law-tract (Críth Gablach 149) this word is used of extra rations to be supplied on Sunday; the plural *sercla tírmai* 'dry relishes' occurs in the *OI Penitential* II. 3, which corresponds roughly to the present paragraph. If *serculo* was the original reading, then the two documents ascribed to Gildas and David must, at least in their present form, be of Irish provenance.

4. That is, monks employed in manual work, the *operarii fratres* of Adamnán, *Vita S. Columbae*, iii. 23 (24) in.; cf. Reeves, *Life of St. Columba* (1857), p. 342.

5. That is, the forty days before Christmas, before Easter, and after Pentecost: *Paenitentiale Theodori*, II. 14, 1 'Three periods of fast during the year are prescribed for the people at large: the forty days before Easter, when we pay our tithes, the forty days before the Nativity of the Lord, and the forty days and nights after Pentecost.'

6. I have inserted here the word *ieiuna* on the strength of the parallel passages Cummean II. 2 ex., Ps.-Cummean II. 23, and '*Synodus II S. Patricii*', c. 22. As the text stands it would read a little strained. Cf. McNeill–Gamer, p. 175, n. 16.

7. Cummean, it would seem again, had before him a better text: 'if, however, after his sin he wants to become a monk . . . .' (II. 5). The earnestness of the sinner's conversion as proved by this resolution justifies a shortening of his formal penance. Cummean's reading is recommended also by the context: c. 3 refers to an actual sin committed by a cleric who is not a monk; c. 4, as it stands, would refer to a monk intending to commit a sin which he actually does not commit. A change of two particulars in one provision would be strange in this type of text.

8. *Misa*, i.e. *missa*. In the language of early monasticism, this term is commonly applied to parts of the sacred office: *missa psalmorum, missa de cantico, missa scripturae*, but in particular to the lessons and concluding prayers at Matins; cf. Caesarius of Arles, *Regula ad monachos*, c. 20 (*PL* lxvii. 1102A) *duos nocturnos faciant et tres missas. Ab una missa legat frater folia tria et orate; legat alia tria et leuet se*; Aurelian of Arles (d. 551), *Regula* (Holstenius, *Codex Regularum*, I, p. 153, col. 1) *Post dictos (nocturnos) . . . quotidie ad librum facite missas tres. Unus frater legat paginas tres aut quatuor . . . et fiat oratio: iterum legat tantum, fiat alia oratio: tertio legat idem tantum, et surgite. . . . Iterum legat alius frater: et sic impletis tribus missis dicite matutinarios canonicos.* On the subject see Dom C. Gindele, *Revue Bénédictine*, 1954, p. 17; *Studia Anselmiana*, xlii (1957), pp. 178, 186, 191, 195 f., 214. On the term *missa* see Chr. Mohrmann, *Vigiliae Christianae*, xii (1958), pp. 67–92, esp. pp. 81 ff.

9. Perhaps we should read, with Cummean (IX) 8, *si uero secundo non uenerit* 'if he does not come a second time'.

10. On the *periculosa oratio*, i.e. the prayer of consecration, see *The Stowe Missal*, 65ᵛ 24–66ʳ 3, vol. ii (*HBS*, vol. xxxii), p. 40; W. Stokes, *Thesaurus*

Palaeohibernicus, ii. 252. Cf. also Welsh *periglawr* 'mass-priest' (Lewis, *Glossary of Welsh Medieval Law*, p. 246); 'the priest who reads the *oratio periculosa* at Mass' (Stokes, *Bezz. Beitr.* ix. 91).

11. Here the text seems to be corrupt. My tentative emendation (see the critical apparatus) would read: 'and in contempt, as it were, retorts.'

THE SYNOD OF NORTH BRITAIN

1. We have probably to understand North Wales, see A. W. Wade-Evans, *Life of St. David* (1923), p. 112.

2. MS. B has 'four years'—probably a misreading of the Roman numeral *uii* as *iiii*.

3. In the *OI Penitential* this phrase (= Cumm. I. 12) has apparently been misunderstood; it is rendered there (I. 9) 'under the yoke of a strange abbot'.

4. Canons 5 and 6 must, I think, be understood in the light of canon 7, viz. as a means of bringing moral pressure to bear on both the informer and the person informed on if the latter denies the charge. First they are made to fast for a year, then to receive the Eucharist at the risk of sacrilege. On this assumption the speculations of McNeill–Gamer, p. 171, nn. 14 and 15 seem unnecessary. *Paenitentiale Vallicellanum*, I. 74, which they quote as a parallel, throws no light on the present passage. It reads: *Si quis delatus et delator negauerit, unum annum peniteat et in ebdomada ii dies in pane et aqua; biduana in fine unius cuiusque mensis faciat.* McNeill–Gamer, who translate 'if the informer denies that he has laid the information', envisage a rather improbable situation. In my opinion, the canon of the *Vallicellanum* is merely an unintelligent abridgement of Cummean VIII. 11.

THE SYNOD OF THE GROVE OF VICTORY

1. Perhaps we should read *sed* 'but'.

2. Apparently a reference to Anglo-Saxon invaders.

3. MS. B: 'fourteen.'

4. The second half of this canon seems to be textually corrupt. The crimes are apparently listed in order of gravity, and the penances increase in proportion. The words 'for the rest of life' are thus an intruder on their first occurrence, and *non ad uota sibi* should read *hoc ad uota sibi* ('if this was according to his wishes'). If a person acts as guide to the invaders, and his action does not result in the slaughter or captivity of Christians, his penance is thirteen years; if such things happen, the guide is to go without arms for the duration of his penance (cf. Vinnian c. 35, Cummean II. 22, *al.*); if he voluntarily offers his services, he is to do penance for the remainder of his life.

EXCERPTS FROM THE BOOK OF DAVID

1. The text seems corrupt; read: *si non satis fecerit* 'unless he apologizes'?

2. Cf. '*Synodus I S. Patricii*', c. 22; Vinnian, c. 44; Columbanus, B 16.

3. MS. B: 'fifteen.'

4. I translate the text as tentatively reconstructed in my apparatus. A fast from nones to nones would allow the penitent only one meal a day.

PENITENTIAL OF VINNIAN

1. The four paragraphs which are printed here in small type are prefixed to the *Penitential of Vinnian* in the Vienna MS. only. They correspond almost verbatim to Cummean (X) 5. 15–17. It is doubtful whether they formed part of the original compilation of Vinnian.

2. MS. S reads 'pardon'.

3. *Aut illi aut illę*: so MSS. V and S; cf. Cummean II. 28 *et ille et illa*. It is more probable, however, that this is a gloss on the first few words of the continuation, preserved only in MSS. P and B, as (tentatively) emended in the app. criticus. The canon would then read as follows: 'A cleric, however, must not give money. His penance shall therefore be a necessary supplication. If, then, he becomes a novice (*conuersus*) with sighs and enters into a covenant with the eternal God, from that day onwards the faults which he has committed in the world shall not be remembered.'

4. The 'crown' is a cleric's virginity; see below, cc. 21, 37.

5. *Homonum*: an early Latin form. The accusative *homonem* is quoted from Ennius, *Annales*, 141, by Priscian, VI. 15; cf. *homonis* in Probus, *Catholica*, p. 10, 28 f. Keil. Such rare forms, which are found occasionally in the Latin writings of Irish authors, derive from their study of the Latin grammarians.

6. See the critical apparatus. Here and elsewhere *quadragesimae* denote the three forty-day periods of fast during the ecclesiastical year; cf. note 5 on Gildas.

6a. The phrase *iungere altario*, which is peculiar to Vinnian and Columbanus (but is found only twice in parallel passages: Vi 12–Co B. 2; Vi 35–Co B. 13), means neither restoration to ecclesiastical office (see Vi 15) nor readmission to sacramental communion (see Vi 35); it seems to designate the act of rejoining the congregation as an equal member.

7. This interpretation of the words *partum alicuius* seems to be required in view of the opening of c. 21. Otherwise, the words might be understood as meaning 'some (other) woman's child'.

8. The words within brackets here and in c. 22 are found in MS. S only.

9. 'City': *urbe* V. The variant *orbe* S would seem to be merely a vulgar Latin spelling. *Urbs* here probably is an equivalent of the commoner *ciuitas*, meaning an ecclesiastical, in particular a monastic, establishment. As an alternative, Prof. Binchy would consider some influence of OI *orb(a)e* (neutr.), lit. 'patrimony, hereditary estate', but often = 'territory, region'.

10. The slayer must take upon himself the obligations which the slain person would have had regarding his parents, above all their maintenance or support in old age. On this obligation (Ir. *goire*), cf. *Ancient Laws of Ireland*, i. 124, 10; RIA, *Contributions towards a Dictionary of the Irish Language, G*, col. 130 f., s.v. *goire* (b); D. A. Binchy, *Celtica*, iii (1956), pp. 228 f. In Adamnan, *Vita S. Columbae*, ii. 39, a certain Libranus, having done seven years' penance, and wishing to become a monk, must first fulfil the *pietatis obsequia* to his father and mother. Nowhere, however, except in the present passage and in Columbanus (B 1), who depends on Vinnian, is there a reference to the vicarious *goire* of the slayer for his victim.

11. Here MS. P adds: 'But if he has killed a man out of envy or for pay, he shall set free seven handmaids and four (read 'seven': *uii* for *iiii*?) servants.'

12. *Clentella* (*cleuentella* S; *cleantilla* Columbanus, *Epist.* i. 6; *clientel(l)a* Columbanus, *Paenit.* B 8): Linguistically, *clentella* and similar forms might be vulgar Latin spellings of *clientela* (cf. *clientella* Terence, *Eun.* 1039, cod. A; *clientilla* Corpus Gloss. IV. 216, 43; 495, 17; V. 179, 44); there is, however, no evidence to show that this abstract noun ever had the meaning 'dependant'. I therefore regard *cl(i)entella*, etc., as a diminutive of *clienta* (found in Plautus, Fronto, the Latin grammarians; cf. *clientula* Ps.-Asconius on Cicero, *in Verrem*, p. 193; Apollinaris Sidonius, *Epist.* ii. 2, 10), and regard *clientela* in the *Penitential of St. Columbanus* as a scribal 'correction'. Cf. also the obviously identical word *glantella, glandella, glangella* of Can. Hib. I. 23. 27 = Paenit. Bigot. I. 6, 2; IV. 6, 2. 3. In the present context, however, as in the *Penitential of St.*

Columbanus (which is based on Vinnian's) *clentella* does not denote a female dependant in general; it clearly means 'his (former) wife'. It is easy to see why the author wished to avoid the word *uxor* or *coniux*; but why did he choose *clentella*? Professor Binchy suggests the following explanation: 'The Irish word *cé(i)le*, originally "fellow, companion, *socius*", has developed several specialized meanings. One is "vassal" or "client" (MacNeill, *Early Irish Laws and Institutions*, pp. 118 ff., argues that the Irish *céile* and the Roman *cliens* occupied more or less the same position). The second meaning is "spouse", "partner"; nowadays it is used of either husband or wife indifferently, but in the oldest Irish *céle* is used of the male, and *sétig* of the female partner. Yet quite early (already in the Old Irish period) we find *céle* applied to the female partner by prefixing *ban-*, the normal feminine prefix; hence *ba(i)n-ché(i)le*. Could *clentella*, *cleantilla* be an attempt to Latinize this, the translator being confused between the two meanings? I should add that *céle* and *banchéle* are informal expressions, used about any kind of sexual union, whether legitimate or not.—As far as Irish Law is concerned, an ordained husband has no duties to his wife or even to the child he begets after taking orders.'

13. 'After their vow': *post uotum suum*. My translation of *suus* throughout this passage has been prompted by the plural forms of the verb. It is, then, implied that both husband and wife had to take vows of virginity on the former's ordination.

14. The idea that a vice is best cured by the practice of the 'opposite' or 'contrary' virtue is probably derived from Cassian, who develops it at some length in his *Conlationes*, xviiii. 14 (CSEL, vol. xiii, pp. 547 ff.). See also c. 29.

15. The expressions *si* and *si non conuersus fuerit* here and c. 31 respectively doubtless refer to a repentant and an unrepenting sinner. McNeill–Gamer understand *conuersus* as meaning a new-comer to the monastic life (on *conuersus* in that sense, see J. Ryan, *Ir. Monasticism*, p. 216). This strange misunderstanding can be explained at least partly by the fact that Wasserschleben and Schmitz, against the manuscript evidence, place c. 31 after c. 32, and that the translators, also without manuscript authority, omit *non* in c. 31. There can be little doubt that cc. 30 and 31 belong together.

16. I assume that *fenerari* here and in c. 32 derives its meaning from the Gospel parables of the unjust steward and of the talents (Luke xvi. 1–9; Matth. xxv. 14–30, cf. esp. 27 *recepissem utique quod meum est cum usura*). According to McNeill–Gamer's translation, money should be *lent* to the poor; but *fenerari* does not mean lending without interest, and money-lending to the poor at a rate of interest would be entirely contrary to the Church's teaching.

17. On compunction, see Cassian, *Conlationes*, viiii. 26 ff. (CSEL, vol. xiii, pp. 273 ff.).

18. 'Fruit of his penance': the savings made by fasting (cf. c. 36).

19. The words within brackets are found in MS. S only.

20. The text seems to be defective; in the critical apparatus I have suggested a supplementation which makes this canon refer to intercourse without issue; cf. c. 40.

21. According to the emendation proposed in my apparatus, the text would say: 'it will turn out well for them on the last day.'

22. *Dos* here apparently denotes a gift from the bridegroom to the bride (Ir. *coibche*).

23. *Creaturam*: cf. Cummean (IX) 15. The term is explained in a penitential ascribed to the Venerable Bede by Dom B. Albers (*Archiv für katholisches Kirchenrecht*, lxxxi. 399–418), XV. 1: 'He who loses a consecrated object (*creaturam*), that is, incense, thuribles, tablets, or a sheet for writing, or salt

that has been blessed, bread newly consecrated, or anything of this sort, shall do penance for seven days' (translation by McNeill–Gamer, p. 230). With this meaning, *creatura* would seem to be the Latin equivalent of OI *cretair* (Middle Welsh *creir*), which originally meant 'halidom, talisman', and later 'relic, sacred object', occasionally 'holy water': see Vendryes, *RC* xliv. 90–96. In *Bethu Phátraic* 2743 *cretra* (plural) corresponds to *aqua benedicta* of the Vita IV, c. 87 (cf. E. Hogan, *Todd Lectures Series*, v, 1894, pp. 58, 121). Ir. *cretair* is not derived from Lat. *creatura*; the use of the latter as an equivalent of the Irish word might have been suggested by such expressions as *creatura aquae, creatura salis* in liturgical formulae of benediction and exorcism.

24. The concluding words would appear to be an echo of some hymn:

> ut ab omnibus omnia
> deleantur facinora.

Cf. the hymn *In memoriam abbatum Benchorensium* (Antiphonary of Bangor, fol. 36ᵛ), stanza vi. 5–6:

> uti possimus omnia
> nostra delere cremina.

PENITENTIAL OF ST. COLUMBANUS

* This translation is substantially that of Dr. Walker (SLH, vol. ii, pp. 169 ff.), with such minor changes as were suggested by details of my textual restoration, or seemed desirable in the interest of conformity throughout this volume.

1. The real penance is the perfect Christian life; but since this perfection is rarely, if ever, achieved, special penances are necessary.

2. I translate the text as emended in my critical apparatus.

3. Canons 9–12 are closely parallel to some sections in St. Columbanus's *Regula coenobialis*; see the references under the Latin text.

4. Cf. Vinnian, cc. 28, 29, with footnote.

5. For the *sicail* (from Lat. *sicli*) as the price of virginity, see Thurneysen, *Studies in Early Irish Law*, p. 124, who suggests that the idea was borrowed from Deut. xxii. 28–29.

6. *Oppraesserit*: cf. Cummean (X) 9.

7. *Bonosiaci* (with the characteristic Celtic suffix, for *Bonosiani*, cf. Eoin MacNeill, *Phases of Irish History*, 1920, p. 152) are the followers of Bonosus, bishop of Naïssus. On their doctrines see the references given by Dr. Walker, p. 179, n. 1; J. Laporte, *Le Pénitentiel de saint Colomban* (Tournai, 1958), pp. 62 f.

8. *Absolute*, i.e. the entire body.

9. *Tonitruum euangelii*. The translation is Dr. Walker's. A different translation is perhaps suggested by Petrus Chrysologus, serm. 79 (P. L. lii. 422 B): 'modo qui⟨d⟩ hinc (= super dominicam resurrectionem) intonuerit Lucas exquiramus.' The 'thunder of the Gospel' is the mighty word of God. Cf. also Propertius ii. i, 39 f., and the standard commentaries *ad loc*.

PENITENTIAL OF CUMMEAN

1. On this Prologue, see Introduction, pp. 6, 18 f.

2. *Vitae*, as in our text, is the reading also of *Codex Amiatinus* and of the Book of Armagh (Vulgate: *uiae*).

3. *Canon* here denotes the (canonical books of the) Bible, both the Old and the New Testament; cf. Columbanus, *Epist.* v. 3 *discipulorum diuinum canonem spiritu sancto scribentium*; *Instruct.* x. 1 *diuini canonis testimonia*. The same meaning might be presumed for *Bethu Phátraic* (K), p. 16 Mulchrone: *coro legh in*

R

canoin n-eclasdacdae laiss (with Germanus); *Genair Pátraic 12 legais canoin la German.* (Dr. J. Gwynn understands *canon* of the New Testament only, *Liber Ardmachanus*, p. xxxi.)

4. This Penitential and some others (e.g. Ps.-Cummean and the so-called *Paenitentiale Bigotianum*) arrange their material according to Cassian's *ogdoas* of capital sins (*Inst.* v. 1; *Coll.* v. 18; see also Paenit. Bigot. pr. 40–47). The same scheme underlies the short treatise *De octo uitiis* (*S. Columbani opera*, ed. G. S. M. Walker, pp. 210 ff.); cf. Dom J. Laporte, *Revue Mabillon*, 1955, p. 5.

5. That is, the mealtime laid down by the Rule.

6. The bracketed passages in this canon are probably glosses, cf. Zettinger, *Archiv für katholisches Kirchenrecht*, lxxxii. 508. The exact meaning of *quadrans* is open to conjecture. According to Roman usage, it would be a quarter-pound or 3 ounces. This interpretation is supported by the references in the following glosses to the Roman pint (*sextarius*) and half-pint (*hemina*), and by the duo-decimal system underlying the subdivision of measures, which seems to reflect the division into 12 ounces of the Roman *as*. On the equation of the liquid ounce with the capacity of an eggshell see K. Meyer, *Contributions to Irish Lexicography*, s.v. *bochtan*.

7. For *polenta* as a measure see Du Cange, *Glossarium*, v. 331.

8. Gildas c. 2 has 'shall be increased'; Gildas c. 1, however, imposes on the fornicating priest or deacon the same penance (three years) as on the monk of lower rank, contrary to Cummean, who assigns to the former a penance of seven years.

9. In Christian Latin *propositum* is often used of a chosen, or willingly accepted, way of life, especially of the monastic life. The sinner who wants to become a monk is to spend part of his penance in the 'strict life' of exile.

10. The manuscript reads *xii. xv.* One figure is obviously a correction of the other. Following McNeill–Gamer, I have accepted the number *xv*, in accord-ance with the *Excerpts from the Book of David*, c. 9.

11. That is, a bride-price, see above, pp. 240, n. 6; 244, n. 22.

12. That is, Wednesday and Friday.

13. The manuscript has: 'in the first with bread and wine', which is contrary to all penitential practice. My restoration would make the text to say: 'in the first with bread and water, in the other two without wine, delicacies, etc.'

14. *Dicit* might stand here for *dicet* (so Paenit. Bigot. III. 6, 1) 'he will say'— at the Last Judgement.

15. Here and below (IV. 16; V. 3) *abscedatur* represents either *abscaedatur* or, more probably, *abscidatur*, which is the corresponding variant in the Paenit. Bigot., III. 6, 1; V. 3, 1. The expression echoes Gal. v. 12.

16. For *potest* we should probably read *praeest*, see the parallels quoted in the apparatus. A superior cannot keep silence for days, so his penance must be com-muted. In this case the singing of thirty psalms is a more likely penance than the singing of merely three. Cf. the *Paenitentiale Bigotianum* and Ps.-Cummean.

17. In MS. R this chapter is numbered V, the following VI, etc. The *OI Penitential*, which is closely related to Cummean's, inserts before *De ira* a chapter *De inuidia*, the matter of which is partly incorporated in Cummean (VIII) IX. Is there a connexion between the jump in the numbering of R and the additional chapter, at this point, in the *OI Penitential*?

18. For *et sic potest orare* I suggest reading *si potest exorare* 'if he can prevail on him'.

19. The singing of three or seven psalms would seem little for an extended vigil. Perhaps we should read *tres l-* as *ter .l.* 'thrice fifty', i.e. the whole Psalter; cf. Can. Hib. II. 1. 2.

19*a*. Or: 'with half his ration of bread'? Cf. the *OI Penitential*, IV. 7.

20. The difference between *confabulatio* here and *uerbositas* in § 14 is not quite clear. Perhaps the one person is merely garrulous and is easily made to talk; the other, though not malicious, is a gossip-monger.

21. This is a reference to the practice stated in Can. Hib. II. 6; the following two 'commutations' seem to have no independent parallel. The provision of c. 25 is quoted also in the *Penitential of 'Theodore'*, I. 7, 5, and is followed there by the remark: *Theodorus laudauit.*

22. The translation follows my tentative reconstruction of the text.

23. See note 10 on Gildas.

24. See note 23 on Vinnian.

25. McNeill–Gamer regard the words *id est adulti, id est continentes* as two glosses not originally connected. They are certainly right with regard to the former. The words *id est continentes*, however, are a corruption of *idem committentes*, the reading of the parallel canon in Ps.-Cummean II. 14.

25*a*. For *puer qui sacrificio communicat* the *OI Penitential* has 'an acolyte'.

26. That is, in separation from his community; cf. *Synodus I S. Patricii*, c. 28.

27. The *crismal* ('pyx') is referred to also in the Rule of St. Columbanus (see Dr. Walker's note, p. 149, 5) and in other penitential texts, cf. McNeill–Gamer, p. 114, n. 83.

28. My very tentative emendation of the corrupt text (see the apparatus) assumes a tautology of some sort, and a common vulgar Latin construction (see my *Libri S. Patricii*, ii. 143 f.) which would inevitably invite scribal tampering.

29. This is a reference to the reading of the diptychs after the offertory; see F. E. Warren, *Liturgy and Ritual of the Celtic Church* (1881), pp. 105, 262; L. Duchesne, *Origines du culte chrétien* (1898), pp. 199 ff.; *The Stowe Missal*, ed. G. F. Warner, ii. 14 f.; Lawlor-Best, 'The Ancient List of Coarbs of Patrick', *Proc. RIA* xxxv C 9, p. 333.

30. The words *ter quinis diebus concauum cruciat in ieiunio stomachum* have an 'Hisperic' ring; cf. *Hisperica Famina*, A 170 *concauos sennosis motibus replent toraces.*

31. *Muriceps* 'mouse-catcher' is found also in Can. Hib. I. 18 = Bigot. I, 5, 7. Cf. *Corpus Glossariorum*, V. 422, 39 *cattus muriceps* and the references in Du Cange s.v. The word is neither classical, nor patristic, nor 'Hisperic'.

32. In the *Capitula Iudiciorum*, XXXIV. 1, this provision is specified as follows: If only the uppermost linen is wetted the penance of the priest is three days; if also the second linen, the penance is seven days; if the third, nine days; if the fourth, fifteen days.

33. The text is defective. According to my restoration it would say: 'the first time twelve psalms shall be sung by the minister; if it happens a second time, twice that number; if a third time, thrice.'

34. See above, (IX) 9, and note 10 on Gildas.

35. That is, vetches.

36. *Quidam sapiens Domini.* Such expressions as *Deum sapere, diuina sapere*, etc., are common in Christian Latin. In the present passage, however, *Domini* might have intruded from the following line. McNeill–Gamer, without commenting on the text, translate: 'a certain wise man saith.'

'*WELSH CANONS*' [A]

1. In the notes on this text no attempt has been made to go into details of Early Welsh Law; I intend to do no more than interpret the Latin text and illustrate, as far as possible, its Latin background.

2. In the place of the words 'and is slain', MSS. BHO read 'and denies the charge' (Welsh Laws: 'and is unwilling'). Perhaps the two readings should be combined: '. . . and denies the charge, and is slain.'

3. Welsh Laws: '(the guilty person) shall suffer the same unless he buys himself free.'

4. *Et non est ei titulus conprobandi*, i.e. if he is not of such rank that his assertion overrules the counter-assertion. Cf. A 43.

5. On the custom of compurgation by the oath of kinsmen see T. P. Ellis, *Welsh Tribal Law and Custom in the Middle Ages*, ii (1926), 303 ff.; T. A. Levi, *The Laws of Hywel Dda in the Light of Roman and Early English Law* (Aberystwith Studies, x, 1928), p. 54.

6. Cf. *Corpus Glossariorum*, III. 368, 64 *uidobium* δίκελ⟨λ⟩α, and the note ibid. VI. 140. This Gallo-Latin word (Ir. *fidb(a)e*, Mid. Welsh *gudif*, etc., its first element being Celt. *widu* 'wood') means 'bill-hook'. It is also glossed *falcastrum*; cf. H. Pedersen, *Vergl. Gramm. d. kelt. Sprachen*, I. 165, 389.

7. On the grounds of comparative law studies one would expect: 'If anyone . . . has maimed a man or deprived him of his hand', etc.

8. The Roman pound, *libra (pondo)*, was divided into 12 *unciae* at 24 *scripula* each; cf. below, A 21. 22. 51, P 15. 51. 52. 57. 59. 60. The persistence in some form of the Roman metronomic and monetary system is characteristic of this and other 'sub-Roman' civilizations. See also Gildas c. 2, and below, A 12.

9. *Pampa scala* Du Cange VI. 124 (quoting the present passage); cf. the gloss *.i. scamas* in B, and *squamas* as a gloss in H and in the text of X. P 9 reads *cerebri cutem*.

10. *Quamlibet pecodem furti* = P 11 *quod sibi libet furtum*. Both expressions are unusual. Perhaps we should read, with Prof. Binchy, *bouem aut quamlibet pecodem furti causa ligatum* 'an ox or any animal bound because of theft'.

11. The interpretation of this paragraph is problematical. I understand *consignare* as denoting the act of conveying property from the vendor to the purchaser in the presence of witnesses, i.e. of actually handing over the property in question; cf. *Leges Visigothorum*, V. 2, 6, p. 215, 17 ff. Zeumer, *Certe si quisquis ille rem donatam siue per traditionem conditae scripturae siue per consignationem uel traditionem rerum in iure suo perceperit*, where the *consignatio* is clearly distinguished from the *traditio scripturae*, or grant by deed. If anyone has acquired property by sale without a written contract he must, when his title to ownership (*auctoritas*) is challenged, be prepared to point out the person who has sold him the property (*auctor*) and the witness (*fideiusorem*) of the transaction. The P-text (28) is more explicit: *nisi auctorem praesteterit aut fideiusores habuerit*. *Auctor* is used regularly of the issuer of a deed (in contradistinction to the *testes* who sign with him) in *Leges Visigothorum* (pp. 112 b 16–18. 23; 115, 15; 116, 18; *al.*); here the term seems to be applied to the vendor (Welsh *arddelwr*) irrespective of the existence or otherwise of a deed of sale.—Cf. note 21.

12. *De Calpeis*, cf. P 29 *Calfaicum*; MSS. ABXH^mg read *de Gallis*, but how could a plain reading have become so strangely corrupted? The reference here would be to a tribe with whom the Welsh had regular commercial relations. Nearer the original, it seems to me, is the P-version, which reads: *Calfaicum aut Saxonicum caballum aut quamlibet speciem*. The reference would then be to different breeds of horses, which can no longer be identified. (I wonder can *Calpeis, Calfaicum* be related to Greek κάλπη 'trot of a horse'?)

13. The meaning of the words *sic ita aequale diuidant* is not quite clear. The word *aequale* is glossed *.i.adū* in B. If, as is likely (cf. the gloss on Gildas c. 1), this abbreviation stands for *aduerbium*, the phrase *aequale diuidant* would have a parallel in *Leges Visigothorum*, IV. 2, 8 (*heredes*) *equali per capita diuidant*

portionem; Lex Alamannorum, p. 24, 8; 149 b 5 Lehmann *aequale (-i) partiant*. In the paragraph under discussion, however, there can be no question of either sharing or dividing property. The Latin phrase might be intended to mean: 'the witnesses (equal in number for either party) shall see to it that a fair price is paid for the horse'; but if this is meant, the Latin is awkwardly vague—much vaguer, in fact, than is my translation.

14. This provision and the parallel one, P 15, seem to be both incomplete. As has been pointed out by McNeill–Gamer, the amount of four pints or one pint respectively has probably to be paid in respect of each hog (*per porcum maiorem*). A phrase to this effect might have been omitted here through *homoiotes*.

15. For *prouincis*, P has *bassilicis*; *prouincia* must then mean the same as the Hibernian *paruchia*. The suspected person must swear by three different saints.

16. *Porcaster* 'young pig' is found in Aldhelm, *De uirginitate carmen* 2779: *porcaster obesus*; the phrase was borrowed from Aldhelm by Albarus, *De Leobegildi bibliotheca* 125 (*Poetae Latini Aeui Carolini*, iii, p. 135); the feminine *porcastra*, with the same meaning, is quoted from Oribasius, *Synopsis*, 9, p. 400, by Souter, *Glossary of Later Latin*, s.v. However, *porcastrum* is read only in the parallel version, P 19; the A-text reads *porcator* (*porceator, poractur*), which is glossed in A as *maciat* 'swineherd' (cf. W. Stokes, *Breton Glosses*, p. 74). In the original behind the two recensions the text probably ran like this: *quotiens capti, porcator porcastrum reddat* 'as often as they are caught the swineherd shall pay a young pig'. A subject actually expressed is demanded by the following *si ipse minauerit eos*.

17. For *.xii.* we should perhaps read *.xu.* (*.xv.* P 18). In early Welsh society a son became *sui iuris* on reaching the age of fourteen (T. P. Ellis, *Welsh Tribal Law*, i (1926), p. 382 ff.). We might therefore translate: 'A boy before entering his fifteenth year . . . .'

18. Obviously a beating. The principle of different scales of punishment for minors and adults was established in Roman Law from the earliest times, cf. *Twelve Tables*, VIII. 9. 14.

19. The phrases *nullus ab eis accipiat questionem* and (P 21) *nullus a suis habeat questionem* obviously mean the same thing: the slayers of a thief do not have to stand trial. The literal meaning of either phrase is not quite easy to determine. According to classical usage (which, to be sure, need not be presumed here), *quaestionem habere* means 'to hold an inquisition'; *quaestionem accipere*, after the analogy of classical *iudicium accipere* 'to submit to trial', would mean 'to submit to an inquisition'. *Ab eis* (A 27) would then refer to the slayers, *a suis* (P 21) to the kinsmen of the slain thief.

20. Cf. *Twelve Tables*, VIII. 12 *Si nox furtum factum sit, si im occisit, iure caesus esto*. 13 *Furem luci* (by day) *occidi uetant XII Tabulae . . . nisi se telo defendit*; cf. ibid. 14.

21. *Consignetur*. The suspect person shall be on bail.

22. Or: 'let judges decide between them in a bishop's court'? Cf. P 40.

23. This is a well-known principle of Roman Law.

24. The text seems corrupt but the meaning is beyond doubt.

25. *Iudicii condictione damnetur*: so both A 44 and P 48. My translation is merely tentative. It seems to me that perjury, being considered an extraordinarily grave offence, as is evident from the very terms in which it is here referred to, would call for a special act of condemnation on the part of the court where it was committed. It is difficult to see, however, what exactly *condictio*, a technical term of Roman Law, could mean in this context. Possibly the person who drafted '*Canones Wallici*' had in mind some such gloss as *Corpus Glossariorum*, II. 394, 15 ff., where *condictio* is said to mean any *actio in*

personam. This gloss (an inaccurate and misleading extract from Gaius IV. 18) or a similar one might have suggested a far wider meaning of *condictio* than this term ever had.

26. I interpret *uilla* here and elsewhere in these texts as denoting the individual farm or homestead, not the *tref* or rural community (*uillata*).

27. *Capitale furtum*, i.e. theft that carries the death penalty. See A 27.

28. The text should probably be emended in accordance with P 50.

29. *Meretur uel sinatur* 'is due and shall be left'? P 52 has *feneretur* 'shall be given' (see note 16 on Vinnian). The A-recension is probably corrupt; perhaps we should read *meretur uel feneretur*.

30. The text is corrupt; P 59 does not quite correspond.

31. Or: 'return (to the owner) his property'? Cf. P 63.

32. *Capitalis*; probably the landowner (*uchelwyr*) of the *tref*, or possibly the *penngur*.

33. The fences protecting the fields and pastures are common property of the neighbours.

34. Cf. below, '*Synodus II S. Patricii*', c. 1.

35. The idea here and in the corresponding provision, *Can. Hib.* VI. 2, seems to be that the offending animal is forfeited (and may be killed).

'WELSH CANONS' [P]

* Notes on corresponding sections of the A-text are not repeated here. See ref. in text.

1. I translate: *nec culpa ingenui fuerit.*

2. I translate: *mancipium si quod acciperint.*

3. *Aetiam* is probably a scribal blunder for *aequam* (*aequum* A 24). McNeill–Gamer suggest that *aetia* might stand for Greek ἔτειος 'yearling', but there is no other trace of this supposed loan-word.

4. The manuscript reads Calfaicum. See note on A 20.

5. *Stagnum*, i.e. *stannum*. On the meaning, see McNeill–Gamer, p. 378, n. 58.

6. McNeill–Gamer point out that this provision is a parallel to A 34. This is suggested also by the strange phrase *commones eius erunt*. I translate *commones eorum erunt*—the reading suggested in my apparatus.

7. Or: 'bishops shall come for arbitration'? Cf. A 37.

8. The text is corrupt. See also the variants under the A-text.

9. *Iure* is probably to be understood as *iure iurando*. The A-text (A 43) has *iuramento*.

10. I suspect the reading *in rebelli tempore*. The A-text (A 37) reads *et repellis fuerit*.

11. The interpretation of the words *uillae capitalis alterius* is uncertain. McNeill–Gamer translate: 'of another's capital villa'.

12. To the emendation suggested in the apparatus, and to my translation on this basis (see also *Medieval Studies presented to A. Gwynn, S.J.*, Dublin, 1961, pp. 390 f.), Père Grosjean (letter, dated 30–XI–1961) objects that the confusion of two words, one being the ancestor of French *pâture*, the other the ancestor of *empêtrer*, seems unlikely. I am inclined to agree. An alternative solution might be found on the assumption that *pastoriauerit* was glossed by the more usual *impastoriauerit* ('empêtrer'). The original would then have read: *Si quis caballum alterius ut suum pastoriauerit* 'If anyone has fettered the horse of another for grazing as if it were his own . . . .'

IRISH CANONS

I

1. My punctuation of the title follows the manuscript. The literal meaning of the words is anything but clear. The term *disputatio* might refer to a discussion of certain topics by the members of a synod which resulted in the decrees that follow here below; cf. *sic de decimis disputant* in the title of *Can. Hib.* III. St. Gregory of Nazianzus has probably as little to do with these canons as has St. Basil with the *Penitential of Cummean* (see the *Incipits* of Cummean's prologue, and Introduction, p. 6).

2. That is, the compensation due to the relatives of the victim, consisting of (1) the fixed wergild (*éraic*), and (2) a series of payments (*dîre*), based on their 'honour-price', due to certain close relatives; cf. Thurneysen, *Irisches Recht*, p. 14 f.

3. *Monochoma* is almost certainly a corruption of the name of some Irish saint or ecclesiastic. No convincing identification has been suggested so far; cf. McNeill–Gamer, pp. 118 f., n. 11.

4. Latin: *crudelis* (for *credulus* P), glossed *iddem ergach*, for which Stokes suggests 'id est *dîbergach*'. (Cf. Muirchú, *Life of St. Patrick*, A i. 23, where Macuil maccu Greccae is described as *mente crudelis*, who, as head of a band of robbers, assumes *signa* (s.l. *diberca*) *nequissima crudelitatis*.) However, a scribal misreading such as assumed by Stokes is very difficult to explain. *Credulus* for *crudelis* would be a very common blunder of the *uox ecclesiastica* type.

5. For 'thirteen' we should probably read 'twelve'; see the apparatus.

6. The Anglo-Saxon *siclus* was equal to two silver *denarii*: Du Cange, s.v.

7. McNeill–Gamer plausibly suggest to read 'forty' instead of 'forty-two'.

8. On *glantella* see note 12 on Vinnian.

9. McNeill–Gamer tentatively equate *singa* with Ir. *scing* (from Old Norse *skinn*) 'hide', and translate it, hesitatingly, 'table-rug'. The context, however, rather suggests the meaning 'bed-spread', 'couch', as in Cormac's *Glossary* (ed. Meyer), no. 28. See RIA Contributions, S, col. 94. If the equation is correct, this canon cannot be older than the middle of the ninth century. Binchy plausibly suggests that it might be a doublet of c. 22.

10. The *scriba* (OI *fer légind*) is the director of studies in a monastic school; see the references in McNeill–Gamer, p. 122, n. 33.

II

1. On *arreum*, Ir. *arra*, see Binchy, *supra*, p. 50 f.

2. On the 'canticles', see McNeill–Gamer, p. 122, n. 37.

3. The term *statio* was inherited from the ascetic and penitential vocabulary of the early Church. See especially Chr. Mohrmann, 'Statio', in *Vigiliae Christianae*, vii (1953), pp. 221–45.

4. On *missa* 'office' see note 8 on Gildas.

5. Probably a cross-vigil; the penitent would have to say prayers with hands stretched out, the palms of the hands being turned upwards.

6. *Bucellos* (*-as* B), literally 'mouthfuls', 'morsels': bread of small size, three pieces equalling one normal loaf. Cf. McNeill–Gamer, p. 123, n. 45.

7. MS. P reads 'sixty', but B has 'forty', which corresponds to the number of psalms.

8. Cf. the *OI Penitential*, II. 2: *for dobrit* 'on water diet'.

III

* Dr. R. Kottje draws my attention to the fact that cc. 1, 2, and 5 have close parallels in the last two paragraphs of a tract *De decimis in lege* (MSS. Cologne 210, fol. 47ᵛ, and Vallicellanus XVIII, fol. 75ᵛ).

1. It seems impossible to identify the Colman here mentioned because the name was very common. See McNeill–Gamer, p. 129, n. 93.

2. One tenth of an *ephah*—the daily provision of manna which the Israelites in the desert were allowed to collect.

3. McNeill–Gamer plausibly interpret this detail as a reference to the custom of presenting a male child to the monastery with which his family was traditionally connected.

4. The idea of this sentence, which is not quite clear, seems to be that a man (in particular, one would be inclined to think, those human 'first-fruits' referred to in canons 3 and 5) ought to offer himself to God of his own free will as did the tribe of Levi in the Book of Exodus.

5. With *Finit amen* the decrees of the synod come to an end. There follows a learned postscript—a specimen of Irish biblical exegesis. The idea that the Ten Commandments correspond to the ten plagues of Egypt is further developed in a Bible commentary of Irish origin (see B. Bischoff, in *Sacris Erudiri*, vi. 223 ff.), which for the greater part is still unpublished. At my request Professor Bischoff has kindly copied the relevant section from MS. Munich, Clm 14276 (saec. IX in., from Ratisbon). It reads: (fol. 55ʳ) INCIP(IUNT) PAUCA. DE EXODO.i.A̅G̅ DIC(IT) . . . (fol. 55ᵛ) .iii. Cur .x. praecepta dixit et non plus. Ideo propter x plagas aegyptiorum. que (*s.s.* as) fecit propter illos. inposuit illis .x. praecepta legis. INDE A̅G̅S̅ DIC(IT). Non est sine causa quod praeceptorum legis dei numerus .x. Cum numero .x. plagarum quibus aegyptus percutitur exequari uidetur. Consideremus ergo. cur ibi .x. precepta et hic .x. plage memorentur ideo quia in illis erant uulnera in istis medicamenta. et opus erat ut tam periculosis plagarum .x. uulneribus .x. preceptorum medicamina subuenerint (*last e corrected to* i). ITE(M) A̅G̅. Ita uos cognoscitis .x. ista precepta illis .x. plagis per ordinem se. esse contraria. Nam de primo precepto prima plaga percutitur sic usque .x. (There follows a long paragraph, fol. 55ᵛ–57ʳ, in which each of the ten plagues is represented as a punishment for the transgression of one of the Ten Commandments.) Similarly, the ten plagues are given as the reason for the Jewish law of tithes in the tract *De decimis in lege* (see above, note *). Reasoning and formulation have a parallel in a tract, preserved in MSS. BC, *De decimis et primogenitis et primitiuis* (B, p. 274): primogenita dantur deo de hominibus et iumentis quia percussit primogenita hominum et iumentorum in egypto. omne masculum datur quia femine non occisse sunt in egypto. ideo non dantur femine.

IV

1. The payment of seven female slaves or of their equivalent in money would appear to have been the normal alternative of the death penalty. In the *Tripartite Life of Patrick*, l. 2494 Mulchr., St. Patrick prophesies to Cellachán: *numquam tu et gens tua euadet aut reum morti aut .uii. ancellas redere.*

2. Literally 'murderer' (*interfectoris*).

V

1. *Iectio* would seem to be a latinization of OI *esáin* 'driving out, expulsion', which is used in the law tracts to denote the offence of refusing hospitality to strangers; see Binchy, *Críth Gablach*, pp. 76, 88 f. The cautionary examples drawn from biblical and hagiographic sources which have been prefixed to this section are doubtless an attempt to invest this indigenous rule with a religious background. On the other hand, the penalties for *iectio* do not tally with those prescribed for *esáin* in the native tracts.

2. A̅G̅ in Irish manuscripts is the normal abbreviation of *Augustinus*. I have

not succeeded in tracing this story either in the works of St. Augustine or elsewhere. *Pauconius* is possibly a misspelling of *Pachomius*.

3. This story is very similar to that in the *Tripartite Life of Patrick*, ll. 263 ff. Mulchr. St. Gregory the Great does not tell the story as it is told here; he has a similar though less extravagant one in his *Homiliae in Evangelium*, XXIV. 2 (*PL* lxxvi. 1183 B): A pious man who often receives pilgrims in his house is once visited by Christ in a pilgrim's guise. While the stranger is waited on he suddenly disappears. At night Christ appears to the man in a vision (cf. the similar story about St. Martin) and says to him: 'So far thou hast received me in my members; this day thou has received me in person.' Did the more developed story as told in *Bethu Phátraic* travel in Ireland under the name of St. Gregory?

4. 'For . . . perishes . . . him': I translate the emendations which I have suggested in the apparatus.

5. The manuscripts read *occiderit*, glossed *.i.eiecerit*. The 'gloss' might originally have been a correction.

6. With this canon compare the penalty for refusing hospitality to the bishop of Armagh as stated in the *Book of the Angel* (LA, fol. 21ᵛ, a 22–26): *Item qui non reciperit praedictum praesulem in hospitium eundem* (sic) *et reclusserit habitationem contra illum .uii. ancellas siue .uii. annos poenitentiae similiter reddere cogatur.*

VI

1. Cf. the corresponding phrases *nisi semet ipse*, 'Welsh Canons', A 62, and *nisi forte semet*, Coll. Hib. LIII. 6. On the first occasion the marauding dog, if caught, may be killed, but there is no obligation on his owner to replace his depredations. On the other hand, if he gets away and returns to the same property again for fresh thieving, then his owner must pay the value of what he has eaten.

2. *Caput anni*, literally 'the beginning of the (new) year'.

THE CANONS OF ADAMNÁN

1. The Latin text is uncertain, and probably corrupt. Assuming that *nostrum* has intruded from the line above, we might translate 'has contaminated the liquid'; or else, taking *nostrum* for a misreading of *rostrum*, we might understand: 'has dipped its beak into the liquid.'

2. The words *lex metrica scriptione scripta* can mean only one thing: that the passage referred to was written in verse in the Hebrew Old Testament. The fact that certain portions of the Old Testament were versified was known from St. Jerome, cf. *Chronicon*, Praef. p. 3 b 14–4 a 11 Helm; *Praefatio in Iob, Biblia Sacra* (the new Vatican Vulgate), vol. ix, p. 71, 8–72, 6. However, as the Rev. Professor Dermot Ryan kindly informs me, none of the biblical passages in which this law is laid down is written in verse. The first reference to it, Gen. ix. 4, does stand in close vicinity to a versified passage (Gen. ix. 6); confusion of the two verses might thus account for the slightly inaccurate statement of our canon. On what authority an Irish writer of the period could have stated that a particular verse of the Old Testament was metrical we do not know. The knowledge of Hebrew in the Irish schools appears to have been slight; it was derived mainly from such secondary sources as the *Interpretationes* and *Commentarii* of St. Jerome; and a Latin, or even a Greek, text of Genesis distinguishing between verse and prose sections of the original would, to my knowledge, be unparalleled.

3. That is, cattle taken from their owners in the course of a *crech*.

4. From this phrase and the similar ones at the beginning of canons 17, 19,

20 as well as from the expression *aptum sibi uidetur* (c. 18) one might conclude
that these canons were not actually drawn up by Adamnán but merely rest on
his (real or supposed) authority.

5. The *Romani* here referred to are probably supporters of the 'Roman' party
among the Irish clergy.

6. I have translated, to the best of my ability, the Latin text as printed, but
I gravely doubt whether the latter is correct. Should we perhaps read: *Unde
noscimus* (for *nescimus*) *illam auctoritatem quam legimus in questionibus Romanorum
'Utrum idoneis testibus an falsis' ortam* (*orta co.* O) *fuisse?* A husband deserted
by his wife, who wishes to marry again, must establish the death of his former
wife by reliable witnesses. The question arises out of the principle stated above
by 'Adamnán'. In his later years, Adamnán was a supporter of the 'Roman' party.

7. McNeill–Gamer, whom I follow in my translation, seem to take *sibi* as an
equivalent of *ei*, and thus to interpret this passage as another reference to the
authority behind these canons. The phrase *aptum sibi uidetur* need not, however, mean more than 'it seems consistent'; cf. *sibi absurdum* 'inconsistent' in
Rufinus, *Apologia contra Hieronymum* II. 34.

'SECOND SYNOD OF ST. PATRICK'

1. I translate my tentative restoration of the text; see the apparatus.

2. *Baptismatis* (KQ) is the ablative plural, for *baptismatibus* (DJI).

3. The meaning of this canon is obscure. There can be no question of
renouncing the Church's right of asylum, which was recognized in principle
in Ireland as it was elsewhere. The canonist contemplates an attempt to remove
by force a criminal who has sought asylum in a church. By granting asylum, the
Church does not defend or excuse his guilt, but would substitute a spiritual
penalty for the physical penalty that awaits the culprit in a secular court. The
judges, instead of trying to get hold of that person by the use of force, are urged
to 'slay him with spiritual death', that is, to give him an opportunity of sub-
mitting to ecclesiastical penance rather than to secular punishment. The words
spiritali morte are probably a reference to the principle of *spiritu facta carnis
mortificare* (Rom. viii. 13), of 'dying to the world and to sin'.

4. On Novatian, an early schismatic (*c.* 250 A.D.), see Pauly–Wissowa–Kroll,
Realencyclopädie der classischen Altertumswissenschaft, vol. xvii, part i (1936),
coll. 1138–56 (with bibliographical references). He was known as a rigorist, but
there is no evidence to show that he either practised or advocated perpetual
fasting.

5. On the pattern *locus tempus persona* in Irish learning see B. Bischoff in
Sacris Erudiri, vi (1954), pp. 205 f.

6. *Abscondat* (*abscedat* J^c) must be a scribal blunder for *abscedat*. This is
implied in McNeill–Gamer's translation, which I follow.

7. The term *bactroperiti* (probably corrupted from *bactroperitae* 'staff-and-
wallet-men') is used by St. Jerome of those itinerant philosophers of Hellenistic
and later times who popularized philosophy, especially that of the Cynic and
Stoic brand, by preaching it in the market-place; it is applied here to unworthy
monks (one thinks of the *gyrouagi* of the rules of the Master and of St. Benedict,
c. 1). McNeill–Gamer follow Jerome in substituting *saeculi* for *solliciti*, but the
latter might be part of the original text: *contemptores saeculi solliciti* 'despisers
of the world, yet worldly' (for *solliciti* see Matth. vi. 25, sim.)—a condensation
of Jerome's *quod contemptores saeculi . . . cellarium secum ferebant*.

8. Some words describing 'those who are not monks' seem to have been
omitted here in our source. See previous note.

9. The age of thirty is the perfect age because at this age Christ began His public teaching (Luke iii. 23). In the same sense the Pauline phrase (Eph. iv. 13) *in uirum perfectum, in mensuram aetatis plenitudinis Christi* is applied to St. Patrick by Muirchú (I. 4).

10. My translation (which is that of McNeill–Gamer), corresponds to the reading *diuitetur* (= *deuitetur*) of MSS. DJ. The reading of KQ, *diuiditur*, is possibly a mere spelling variant of the same word. In the opinion of the Rev. Prof. Cyrille Vogel (Strasbourg), however, *diuiditur* could be accepted as meaning 'is distributed', that is, anything in excess of the barest necessities should be shared by all. The interpretation which I have adopted seems preferable on account of the words *in uita*, which are explained in terms of 2 Cor. xi. 27 as the strict observance of a life of poverty.

11. This canon, it seems to me, objects to monks living outside the monastery as members of a parish community. The objection is made in the interest of the unity of the parish. Cf. Vinnian, c. 50, who forbids monks to baptize and to accept alms. Are these the 'false monks', *bactroperiti*, of c. 17? *Parrochia* in the title of this canon would seem to mean 'parish' rather than 'diocese' and to be synonymous with *plebs* in the text.

12. *Perfruat.* This might be a reminiscence of Rom. xv. 24; cf. St. Patrick, *Confessio*, 53. A plainer meaning would be obtained, however, by reading *proferat* 'let him bring forth his fruit'.

13. I understand *ad alterius ferre* = *ad alterius aeclesiam fructum suum ferre*; see previous note.

14. The group here referred to is probably the 'Roman party' in seventh-century Ireland; cf. Coll. Hib. XLVII. 8d (quoted in the apparatus under c. 3).

15. The text as I understand and punctuate it says that a husband may divorce his adulterous wife and then marry again. With this view the words *hac* (= *ac*) *si liciat ob hanc causam* do not agree. They are probably the criticism of a reader, who, like Vinnian (c. 43 f.) advocated the stricter observance, and have crept into the text in the course of its transmission.

16. The vows here referred to are probably vows of betrothal (so McNeill–Gamer).

17. This canon is probably another instance of criticism levelled by the 'Roman party' against its opponents. Marriage within the forbidden degrees was customary in ancient Ireland; the enforcement of Canon Law in this matter was opposed by the Irish throughout the Middle Ages.

18. I understand this canon as an attempt to compromise between the strict demand to return all property to its former owner during the jubilee year of the Old Testament (Lev. xxv. 8 ff.) and the generally accepted legal principle that a valid sale creates a title of permanent ownership on the part of the purchaser. This canon, however, concerns not so much the purchaser's right to ownership as the claim of either party that a contract should be honoured by the other party. Legally, our canon says, the claim never expires by superannuation, but after fifty years a claim that can no longer be clearly established ought not to be pressed. As a precaution against this danger it is suggested to transact all business in writing and to have deeds of sale signed by the several parties in the Roman manner.

THE 'BIGOTIAN' PENITENTIAL

1. The passage here attributed to St. Jerome is not found in the genuine works of this writer. It has parallels in other penitential texts of Irish origin or affiliation (see the references under the Latin text). Ps.-Patristica of Irish origin are numerous, cf. note 9 below.

2. This paragraph is clearly an interpolation; it might have been prompted by the phrase 'more or less' in par. 4. Pars. 4 and 6 form one whole.

3. This paragraph, if not corrupt, is badly styled as a result of over-condensation. The argument might be expected to run as follows: 'Irreligion properly appertains to those who have no knowledge of God; sin and iniquity even to those who, having this knowledge, change (i.e. pervert) it by transgression, The irreligious (who persist in that state) are doomed; the sinners and the unrighteous may be healed after the wounds of sin and iniquity, (by penance) according to the nature of the several *uitia* (i.e. the eight principal vices which serve for the classification of sins in this and other Penitentials)'. Emendation along these lines would be easy but could claim no authority.

4. I translate my tentative emendation of the text, see the apparatus.

5. For *sacramentum* 'mystical meaning' cf. Souter, *A Glossary of Later Latin*, s.v.; *cuius* refers loosely to the idea of cleansing by fire.

6. As suggested in my apparatus, I read *dies.*—§§ 20–21 have a parallel in John Scottus, *Periphyseon* V. 39 ex. The idea, found already in St. Augustine (*Ciu. Dei*, xxii. 30 ex.), was probably current in Ireland. Cf. also Sedulius Scottus, *Collectaneum in Apostolum, prologus*, p. 110, 79–82 Frede.

7. The emendation suggested in my apparatus might be translated as follows: 'shall, we doubt not, be weighed in scales . . . as by a Creator who knoweth all nature.'

8. My translation follows the emendation suggested in the apparatus.

9. In actual fact the reference is to another pseudepigraphum, most probably of Irish origin.

10. The text of Isidore reads: 'by which men, judging rightly, give everyone what is his.'

11. I translate St. Gregory's *afficitur*; see apparatus.

12. *Questiuncula*. The text here referred to has not come down to us. McNeill–Gamer think of a document similar in form to Ps.-Bede or to the *Corrector* of Burchard—a set of questions addressed to the penitent by his confessor, each, when answered in the affirmative, to be followed by the pronouncement of the appropriate penance.

13. Drinking the 'joy' of one of the great mysteries of the faith on a special feastday, or the memory of a great saint, was apparently a monastic custom of semi-liturgical character, from which nobody was to hold himself excused. This custom is known from continental sources since the Carolingian period, and referred to as *caritas* in monastic *Consuetudines* from the tenth century onwards (see B. Bischoff, *Caritas-Lieder*, in *Liber Floridus*, 1950, pp. 165 ff.). There is no unambiguous reference to this custom in genuine Irish sources. Wine was allowed in the Irish monasteries on the principal feast days of the ecclesiastical year (J. Ryan, *Irish Monasticism*, p. 389). A passage in the *OI Penitential* (III. 15) 'after rejoicing on the eight (chief) festivals of the year' possibly refers to a special allowance of beer. The present passage is taken from the *Penitential of 'Theodore'*.

14. Cf. note 1 on Can. Hib. I.

15. The text is incomplete, but can be supplemented from the parallel canon, Can. Hib. I. 12.

16. The numeral seems wrong; Can. Hib. I. 21 has 'fifty'. The scribe of the exemplar of CB apparently misread *.l.* as *.i.* The mistake might, of course, be in Can. Hib. I, which has survived in a single, and rather inaccurate, copy (P).

17. It is strange to find a sexual sin mentioned in this context. We should probably read, with Can. Hib. I. 23, *et cohabitatoris cum ea* 'and (or) by him who cohabits with her'.

18. The reading of the manuscripts is defective and obscure.

19. Since most of these penances were intended for monks this specification was desirable in order to avoid ambiguity.

20. Or: 'during the forty day-periods' (*in quadragesimis*)?

21. The word 'marrying' (*nubere*) here denotes the exercise of marital rights.

22. In Cummean, who is probably referred to here, the duration of the penance is four years. The Roman numeral *.iiii.* could easily be misread as *.uii.* However, *.uii.* must have been found in the parent of our manuscripts as is evident from the word 'similarly' (not in Cummean) in the following clause.

23. According to Cummean III. 17, fifteen psalms.

24. I translate *non ausi simus* as suggested in my apparatus.

25. It seems strange that one may pray for one who has killed himself in cold blood but not for one who has done so with a mind disturbed by fear or despair. Should we not read in the second instance, here as well as in Theodore, *inuoluntarie* 'unintentionally'?

26. *Uel demedio anni*: The penance of the cleric must be greater than that of the layman; hence *uel* is either a scribal blunder for *et*, or has the force of *et*.

27. In my translation I have left out the words *uel cohabitatricem*, which are not in the parallel, Can. Hib. I. 27, and would appear to be a gloss on *glandellam*.

28. I translate *mundus et perfectus*, the reading suggested by McNeill–Gamer.

29. The meaning of the text is clear but I doubt its verbal correctness. Read either *cum digna penitentia*, or *digna⟨m⟩ penitentia* ('a flood of tears appropriate to penance').

30. My translation follows the text as emended in the apparatus; I have, however, adopted the correct spelling of the name of Syncletica. On St. Syncletica, foundress of a community of nuns in the Egyptian desert, see F. G. Holweck, *A Biographical Dictionary of the Saints* (1924), p. 942; her Vita is found in *Acta Sanctorum*, Ian. vol. i, pp. 242–57 (3rd ed.).

31. The Latin text is corrupt beyond restoration. The author apparently wants to compare praying (or chanting) with a distracted mind to rumination. Rumination, he means to say, does not bring new food to an animal's body and yet helps to feed it; so (if I understand correctly) distracted prayer does not 'feed' the soul but is, as it were, a rumination of previous attentive prayer. For the wording of this idea some biblical passage seems to have been adapted *tant bien que mal* but the required model is not provided by either Vulgate or Old Latin. The closest parallel is Novatian, *De cibis Iudaicis* 2 (*Archiv für Lateinische Lexicographie*, xi. 229, 2): *et mundorum quidem hanc formam dedit, ut ruminatione ruminent et ungulas findant.* The paronomasy *ruminatione(m) ruminare* is not attested in the Latin Bible; it is found, however, in the Septuagint at Deut. xiv. 8, in the Hebrew also at Lev. xi. 3. 7; Deut. xiv. 6. (This information has been kindly supplied by Dom B. Fischer, O.S.B., Beuron). Perhaps one of these verses was known in Ireland in a Latin translation that resembled more closely the Greek or Hebrew text.

32. For 'knowledge' (*scientiae*) Cummean has 'decision' (*sententiae*) which makes better sense. *Scientiae* is possibly a scribal blunder in the exemplar of CB.

33. Reading ⟨non⟩*numquam* as suggested in the apparatus.

APPENDIX

By D. A. Binchy

THE OLD-IRISH PENITENTIAL

FOR the bulk of this text we are dependent on a single manuscript: P = RIA 3 B 23 (now no. 1227, see Catalogue, pp. 3360 f.), saec. xv, scribe Tadcc ua Rigbardáin, pp. 16ᵃ25–28ᵃ26. Edited with translation, notes, and a brief glossary by E. J. Gwynn in *Ériu* vii (1914), pp. 121–95; most of Gwynn's translation has been reprinted in McNeill–Gamer, pp. 157–68. Corrigenda by Gwynn himself in *Ériu* xii (1938), pp. 245–9; cf. also Meyer, *Miscellanea Hibernica* (Illinois, 1916), p. 39. Apart from obvious scribal neologisms, the language is Old Irish throughout, certainly not later than the end of the eighth century.

The text in P is acephalous, lacking the general introduction to the Penitential and the homiletic preface to cap. I; accordingly the first folio of the exemplar, which contained these, had been lost before P was written. The missing material can be supplied, however, from R (see *infra*). The original second folio of the exemplar was obviously misplaced, for the scribe of P has copied it after the third. The seventh chapter, dealing with *vana gloria*, is incomplete, breaking off in the middle of the homiletic preface, and a final chapter on *superbia*, which almost certainly concluded the original Penitential, is altogether lacking. From this Gwynn infers (doubtless rightly) that the final folio of the exemplar had also been lost.

A homily on the deadly sins based on this Penitential survives in three further manuscripts:

(1) R = Rawlinson B 512, saec. xiv–xv (in which there is also a copy of the *Table of Commutations*, ff. 39ᵃ2–40ᵇ2, printed by Meyer in *ZCP* iii (1901), pp. 24–28; the general introduction and the homiletic preface to cap. I reprinted and translated by Gwynn in *Ériu* vii. 135–7).

(2) Q = RIA 23 P 3 (now no. 1242, see Catalogue, pp. 3433 f.), saec. xv, scribe Uilliam mac an Lega (who wrote this section of the manuscript in 1467), ff. 15ᵃ1–15ᶜz; the more important variants are cited by Gwynn in his edition of the relevant passages of P.

(3) C = NLI Phillipps MS. 1026, saec. xv (see Stokes, *Martyrology of Oengus*, p. ix); subsequently collated with his edition of P by Gwynn in *Ériu* xii. 245–6.

In all three manuscripts the homiletic material which begins each chapter of P has been abstracted to make a separate text. But Gwynn has pointed out an important difference between them. Since R alone has the general introduction and the homiletic preface to cap. I, it must have been transcribed either from the original Penitential (which Gwynn calls *X*) or from an early copy which still contained the opening folio, whereas Q and C both derive, not indeed from P, but from its immediate exemplar (Gwynn's *x*). For details see *Ériu* vii. 123 f., xii. 247 f. On the other hand, the original final folio must have been lacking in R's exemplar, for it breaks off at the same word as PQC.

The present translation is a revised version of Gwynn's; it incorporates, in addition to the corrigenda already published by him, a number of other corrections, not all of which, however, are certain. Any detailed justification of these would obviously be out of place here; accordingly I have confined my notes on linguistic problems to a minimum. I have omitted the citations from Latin penitentials appended by Gwynn to each section, for these, though affording at the time of their publication most valuable aid in establishing the sources of our Penitential, have now been rendered superfluous by the concordance provided in the present volume. The initial lacuna in P has been supplied from R, and the original order of the exemplar has been restored on the lines established by Gwynn himself. I have also retained (with some minor modifications) his Latin translation of certain sections of cap. II. Latin citations incorporated in the Irish text are given in the manuscript orthography.

The venerable of Ireland have drawn up from the rules of the Scriptures a penitential for the annulling and remedying of every sin, both small and great. For the eight chief virtues, with their subdivisions, have been appointed to cure and heal the eight chief vices, with whatsoever springs therefrom.

Moderation, with abstinence, against gluttony and drunkenness. Continence, with chastity, against lust and adultery. Generosity, with charity, against avarice, and benevolence of heart against envy and hatred. Meekness, with gentleness, against anger and strife. Spiritual joy against worldly sorrow. Fear of death and perishing against vain glory. True humility, with the fear of the Lord, against haughtiness and pride.

Now these are the names of the chief vices whereof comes for every man the death of body and soul: Gluttony, Lust, etc.

CAP. I § 1a. These are the names of the subdivisions that spring from Gluttony: immoderate joy, excess of talking, wanton folly, lewdness of thought, impurity of mind, despair, drinking without stint, unbridled drunkenness.

b. But these are the subdivisions that spring from abstinence: spiritual joy, decency of body, purity of soul, silence till need (of speech), comprehension of wisdom, abundance of intelligence, application to the mysteries of God.

c. These following are the remedies of Gluttony: moderate fasting, remorse of heart, rare meals, frequent self-questioning, watching, feasting the poor, solacing all the hungry, confinement at certain hours with a specified allowance, patience in regard to everything until it be considered.

§ 2 Anyone who eats the flesh of a horse, or drinks the blood or urine of an animal, does penance for three years and a half.

§ 3 Anyone who eats flesh which dogs or beasts have been eating, or who eats carrion, or who drinks the liquid in which the carrion is, or who drinks the leavings of hawk[1] or raven or scaldcrow or domestic cock, or who drinks the leavings of a layman or laywoman or of a pregnant woman, or who eats a meal in the same house with them, without separation of seat or couch, does penance for forty nights on bread and water.

§ 4 Anyone who drinks liquid in which there is a dead mouse does seven days' penance therefor.

Anyone who drinks the leavings of a cat does five days' penance.

Anyone who drinks or eats the leavings of a mouse does penance for a day and a night. Theodore says that although food be touched by the hand of one polluted or by dog, cat, mouse, or unclean animal that drinks blood, this does the food no harm.

§ 5 Anyone who breaks a fast that is proclaimed in church keeps a double fast as penance for it.

§ 6 Anyone who is sick is allowed to eat meals at any hour of the day or night.

§ 7 Anyone who drinks beer till he is tipsy in spite of the prohibition of Christ and the Apostles, if he be in orders, does forty days' penance. If he be in lawful wedlock, seven days. If anyone out of good fellowship constrains another to get tipsy, he who provokes his tipsiness does penance along with him. If it is through enmity that he does it, he who provokes the tipsiness does penance as if he were a homicide. If his tipsiness does not hinder him (from his duties) except that he is unable to chant the Psalms, or say Mass, or such-like, he keeps a fast therefor.

§ 8 Anyone who takes without permission meat or drink from his brother while tipsy keeps a fast therefor, as well as the punishment for his tipsiness. If it be the brethren's evening meal (?)[2] that he takes, it is three fasts or a fortnight's strict penance.

§ 9 Anyone who steals food gets forty days the first time, and forty more the second time, a year the third time, and exile under the yoke of a strange abbot the fourth time. If it be boys of ten years old, they get seven days: if over twenty years, twenty days' penance.

§ 10 Anyone who eats till he makes himself ill, or till his skin gets tight, keeps a fast or two days on bread and water. If he vomits, it is seven days.

§ 11 Anyone who ⟨touches⟩ food with unclean hands, a hundred lashes are laid on his hand. If the colour of the liquor be at all troubled with some unclean thing, the cook does forty days' penance. The man who drinks it unwittingly, and afterwards learns what he has done, does five days' penance.

§ 12 Anyone who gives another anything in which there has been a dead mouse or dead weasel, three fasts are laid on him who gives it,

[1] See pp. 275–7 for notes.

and he who thereafter learns what has been done, a fast on him. If it is in any other dry food, in porridge or in thickened milk, the part round it is thrown away, the rest is consumed.

§ 13 Anyone who resolves to keep a fast ⟨for one day⟩ or three days or forty nights or a year, and breaks it of himself without being compelled by anyone else, does double penance.

§ 14 Anyone who takes a vow that he will not eat flesh or bacon or butter, or will not drink beer or milk, is bound to take three morsels or three sips of each of them at Easter and Christmas against the occurrence of disease and suffering; or against excess of famine or scarcity falling upon the people,[3] so that all the victuals they have perish, except the particular thing which he has vowed ⟨not⟩ to partake of; or in case of a repast provided by a confessor, who has no other sort of victuals which the man may eat who has taken that vow of abstinence for God's sake: in such cases it is for God's sake that the relaxation is practised, so that it is a reward that he has for it.

§ 15 Anyone who eats food and drinks beer until he vomits, if he be a regular monk, does thirty days' penance. If this is caused by disease, or if it happens after a long fast, or after rejoicings at the eight festivals of the year, or if it be a confessor's repast, or if it be on saints' days, if they do not drink beyond the measure which their confessor prescribes—in all such cases there is no harm.

§ 16 Anyone who fasts on a Sunday through carelessness or austerity does a week's penance on bread and water.

§ 17 Anyone who drinks the leavings of a dog, or of one red with (the blood of) men, or of a robber, or of one that slays his mother or father or brother, or lies with his mother or sister or daughter, or of a contumacious (?) bishop or priest after he has violated his orders without repenting, does a year's penance on bread and water.

§ 18 Anyone that is sickly is allowed a meal at any hour of day or night.

§ 19 Anyone who eats before the rest, or eats food that is daintier than the brethren's food, unless it be disease or natural infirmity that causes him to do so, or unless he is unable to eat anything else habitually, must keep a fast therefor or (do penance for) two days on bread and water.

§ 20 Anyone who is suddenly seized by an attack of disease, a fast for him the first night: if it comes of a demon, he is the lighter thereby; if of God, let the cause of it be seen.

§ 21 Anyone who drinks the blood of a cat, three fasts therefor. Anyone who eats his vermin or the scurf[4] of his body, a hundred nights on bread and water.

CAP. II § 1*a*. *Luxuria*, that is the name of the second vice that kills the soul of man; either because it does violence to every will, both the will of God and the will of man, except that which is accordant with itself,

s

or because it does violence to the man himself, and leaves no ⟨will⟩ in any one, whether man of learning or bishop or sage, because the man who is constantly under its power and dominion has no thought of learning or piety or wisdom.

b. Also, he takes no thought of honour nor of his soul nor of heaven nor earth nor penalties nor rewards: for the nature of this vice is likened to fire, because it burns up every virtue that is in man, like fire, so that men perceive no trace thereof in him.

c. Now this is the offspring that is born of this vice, to wit, filthiness of words, shameless scurrility, blindness of mind, fickleness of nature, rude discourse, relapse into ruin, multiplicity of counsels, promising without performance, promiscuous concupiscence, care for man, neglect of God.

d. This again is the virtue that has been appointed to quench this vice, to wit, perseverance in chastity, with what springs therefrom, namely, steadfastness of counsel, quiet discourse, steadfastness as opposed to fickleness (?),[5] faithful promises, keeping of troth, meditation on God, modesty of nature, confirming of faith, hatred of this world, love of the world to come.

e. These are the remedies against fleshly lust, namely, subduing of gluttony, moderate meals, moderation in drink, avoidance of drunkenness, hatred of conviviality, mastering of nature, heedfulness in solitude, cheerfulness in company, attendance on elders, avoidance of young folk, a fixed measure of labour or reading or prayer, hatred of the rabble with unclean words, a stable mind with purity of conversation, desire of rewards so as to win them, contemplation of penalties so as to avoid them.

§ 2 Anyone holding the rank of a bishop who transgresses in respect of a woman is degraded and does penance twelve years on water diet, or seven years on bread and water.

§ 3 If he be a priest or a deacon who has taken a vow of perpetual monkhood, he spends three and a half years on bread and water, with a fast in every week of the time except between the two Christmases and between the two Easters and at Pentecost; and such persons have relaxation on the high festivals of the year, and on Sundays and on the fifty nights between Easter and Pentecost: that is to say, a *bochtán*-measure[6] of fresh milk, or a fair quarter of a *selann*[7] if there be no milk, and they are allowed dry relishes of all sorts of fruit at all seasons, and they are also allowed an extra portion of bread in the Saturday night's fast, and a quarter ration of gruel and whey-water on which there is no cream of curds or buttermilk every day; a goblet of fresh milk, if the nature of a man's constitution be sickly, and a scrape of gruel on bread. If, however, he be not sickly, the allowance is bread and water or thin beer or the whey water we have mentioned if it be within reach. He may not lie on feathers nor on a cushion nor on a good bed. He may not take off his shirt except it be to stitch or wash or cleanse it of vermin.

§ 4 Additional labour is laid on penitents in the three Lents of the year, as their strength can bear it. Obedience and humility are required of them, besides going to Communion at the end of three and a half years for the higher orders, at the end of a year and a half for the lower orders generally, so that their souls may not perish for want of Christ's body by reason of the long period of penitence; and thereafter they receive the kiss of peace from the brethren, and they sing the Psalms in their place among the rest of the brethren.

§ 5 There is required of them also remorse and lamentation for their sins, and that they should desire their brethren to pray God for them that their sins may be forgiven through penance and penitence.

§ 6 If it be a man of a lower rank than a priest or deacon who transgresses in this point through lust, he does penance three years, but the measure of his bread and whey-water is increased that it may suffice him for vigils and labour: that is, he gets a prime *bochtán* of fresh milk, besides whey-water, as much as he needs.

§ 7 For the rations of those in orders who are doing penance have been appointed, if they do not do labour, as follows: they are to get six ounces' weight of bread, with a little gruel spread on it, and kitchen herbs, and a few hard-boiled (lit. 'dry') eggs, a jug of fresh milk, if a man is sickly, and a *bochtán* of buttermilk or curds.

§ 8 If it be a priest or deacon not having taken monastic vows, the penance of a monk not in orders is what he performs. If they take such a vow after committing the transgression, they do penance for a year and a half living on bread and water in penitence.

§ 9 If it be a pious abbot (who is over them), he is empowered to curtail these penances, according to the strength and self-abnegation and obedience of him who has committed the sin.

§ 10 One of the wise said, on account of the fewness of persons in orders: All these orders are reconsecrated after doing penance, with the same functions; and they go under the hand of a bishop, i.e. a bishop of the tribe, and they vow perpetual monkhood under the yoke of a pious abbot.

§ 11 Clericus qui feminam semel adit, annum poeniteat in pane et aqua: si genuerit prolem, quattuor annos. Similis est poenitentia sanctimonialis quae virginitatem suam polluit.

§ 12 Sacerdos qui feminam osculatur et eam tangendo coinquinatur, quadraginta noctes durae poenitentiae solvat.

Si per cogitationem coinquinatur, septem dies durae poenitentiae. Si manu excitat, viginti noctes.

§ 13 Qui per violentiam (?)[8] cogitationum incessanter coinquinatur, decem dies poeniteat in pane et aqua.

§ 14 Qui in ecclesia dormiens coinquinatur, tres dies poeniteat: si excitat ipse, viginti noctes.

§ 15 Qui cordis ac mentis affectu fornicari concupiscit, et non potest, annum poeniteat. De illo dicit Cristus: *qui vidirit mulierem ad concupiscentum eam ⟨jam moechatus est eam⟩ in corde suo* (Matt. v. 28).

§ 16 Qui per turpiloquium vel mulieris partes aspiciendo vel corpus ejus tangendo coinquinatur, sine proposito peccandi, jejunium agat.

§ 17 Qui somnium carnale videt cum expletione voluntatis ac libidinis, si ante somnum talia cogitabat, jejunium agat. Si non cogitabat, duodecim *Pater* canat in cruce, et duodecim genuflectiones faciat.

§ 18 Qui sine advertentia (?)[9] coinquinatur genuflectionem faciat et *Pater* ter canat in cruce.

§ 19 Qui mulierem sollicitat, et non impetrat, quinquaginta noctes vel annum poeniteat.

§ 20 Qui colloquium frequens cum mulieribus amat duodecim dies poeniteat.

§ 21 Qui cum matre aut filia aut sorore fornicatur quattuor decem annos poeniteat, dicit Theodorus; similiter si frater cum fratre. Secundum Cumineum Longum autem, quattuor annos poenitentiae cum peregrinatione perenni. Tres annos et dimidium propter ceteros consanguineos.

§ 22 Fornicans labiis quattuor annos primo poeniteat: si fit consuetudo et usus, septem annos.

§ 23 Qui in os feminae semen suum effundit, ambo quinque annos poeniteant: si fit consuetudo, septem annos.

§ 24 Qui cum pecoribus fornicatur duo annos poeniteat.

§ 25 Viri qui inter femora aut in terga inter se fornicantur duo annos poeniteant. Similiter etiam si mulieres aut puellae eadem faciunt inter se.[10]

§ 26 Qui manibus aut femoribus actum libidinis ipse secum committit, imprimis septem dies durae poenitentiae agat, atque insuper ter quadraginta noctes sequentes poeniteat.

§ 27 Si quis impugnatione cogitationis pollutus fuerit invitus membra sua manu aut femore tangendo, idque sine proposito peccandi acciderit, septem dies tantum poeniteat et ieiunium atrum vel arreum ieiunii in medio observet. Si autem cum proposito libidinoso, annum poeniteat vel arreum solvat.

§ 28 De lascivia parvorum puerorum inter se. Acolyti qui osculantur mulieres aut puellas propter suam simplicitatem ieiunium agant: si autem cum affectu libidinoso, quattuor ieiunia.

Si osculum illecebrosum dederint cum plena membrorum connexione sine coitione, septem ieiunia.

§ 29 Si post vicesimum annum ea facinora committunt, quadraginta noctes cum pane et aqua poeniteant, vel ab illo loco quo ea committunt separentur dum poenituerint.

§ 30 Parvi pueri fornicationem inter se imitantes, priusquam natura impellit, viginti ⟨dies⟩ poeniteant.

§ 31 Acolytus qui cum pecoribus fornicatur centum noctes poeniteat.

§ 32 Puer semet ipsum manibus coinquinans et confessus antequam communicet, viginti dies poeniteat. Si iteraverit, centum noctes poeniteat. Si fit consuetudo, separentur ab illa ecclesia in qua peccaverunt et annum cum pane et aqua poeniteant.

§ 33 Pueri qui supradictam aetatem attigerint, si inter femora fornicati sint, primo centum noctes poeniteant, altera vice dimidium annum, tertia vice annum integrum.

§ 34 Puer decem annorum validioris oppressione (?)[11] violatus septem dies poeniteat. Si consentit, viginti noctes poeniteat.

§ 35 . . .[12] si pollutus fuerit, centum noctes. Si libidinem expleverit ut moris est, annum integrum.

§ 36 Anyone that lives in lawful wedlock, these are his rules of conduct: continence during the three Lents of the year, and on Fridays, Wednesdays and Sundays, and between the two Christmases and between the two Easters, if he goes[13] to the Sacrament on Christmas Day and Easter Day and Whitsun Day. Also they are bound to observe continence at the time of their wives' monthly sickness, and at the time of pregnancy, and for thirty nights after the birth of a daughter, twenty nights after the birth of a son. They are also bound to go without bacon or fresh meat during the three Lents of the year.

Women do not go to the Sacrament when their monthly sickness is upon them. Anyone who has intercourse with them at such times does penance for twenty nights.

Persons living in lawful wedlock spend forty nights continuously in continence, without eating bacon or fresh meat, before going to the Sacrament, except at Pentecost: then it is only ten days. They live in continence also between the two Christmases and between the two Easters, as well as the Monday after the lesser Easter.

CAP. III § 1a. *Auaritia* is the name of the third vice that kills the soul of man, that is, avarice: for it may be compared to Hell as to its extent and capacity, and because it gives up nothing that is cast into it: so likewise the maw of avarice, though the world's whole wealth were poured into it, could not be filled, and would give nothing back again. For it is a fire to burn and a sea to drown, an earth to swallow up, a lion to ravish, a beast to devour, a sword to spoil, a serpent to spring, a dungeon to keep, a chain to fetter, a pitfall to compass (?) the destruction of body and soul.

b. For from this root of avarice grow all the vices, and on its account are most souls of the human race brought to Hell. For its sake the son kills his father and mother: for its sake men suffer red martyrdom and white martyrdom and green martyrdom, even slaying and burning and drowning. For its sake men go to Hell with its pains, and desert the kingdom of Heaven with its rewards.

c. ⟨This is the offspring and issue that is born of this vice,⟩* even desire without measure, corruption with despair, raidings without ceasing, robbing without mercy, falsehood without control, perjury without restraint, derision of every good thing, pleasure in every evil thing, blindness of mind, denying of nature, oppression of the wretched, incitement of the strong, covetousness of earthly things, deceit concerning the soul.

d. Now this is the virtue that has been appointed to combat this vice, namely liberality with charity, and what springs therefrom, that is to say, mercy with forgiveness, rectitude with truthfulness, bounty with gentleness, without pride, without hatred, without malice; compassion with eagerness, without treachery, without deceit, without cunning (?); benevolence without loquacity, without falsehood, without perjury, without insolence.

e. These again are the remedies against avarice, to wit, service of Christ's strangers,[14] feasts for the poor, labouring for one's food, a mind set on poverty, trust in a blessing, prevision of punishment, hope of reward, expectation of judgement in presence of the Creator on the Day of Judgement.

§ 2 Anyone who makes a habit of thieving and stealing through covetousness and graspingness, Theodore says, seven years' penance therefor. According to Cummine Fota it is a year the first time, two the second time. If boys do such things, it is forty nights of penance, or twenty nights, or else their penance is according to their age. If the culprit can pay the mulcts which God has appointed in law and rule,[15] his penance is correspondingly less.

§ 3 If anyone steals a sheep, he must restore four sheep in its place; if an ox, five oxen; if a horse, two horses in its place; if a pig, two pigs in its place. If each of these animals be kept in the thief's possession alive, he pays double, that is, a beast in addition to the other. He pays double also for inanimate chattels, that is, a (second) chattel together with the original chattel.

§ 4 If he has nothing that he can pay for it, he gives service in place of it. If he offers it to God and does penance as his confessor prescribes, and does not possess anything that he can pay (as fine), he pays nothing to man, save only penance with a token of reconciliation.

§ 5 The apostle Paul says: Let him who has lived by robbery and theft cease therefrom, and let him labour with his hands, so that he may have what he can give...[16] in alms to the poor and needy. For as water quenches fire, so almsgiving quenches sins. Christ says: Anyone who has much wealth or substance should distribute half of it to the poor and needy.

* *Supplied from R.*

§ 6 As for him who desires to reach the pitch of perfectness, he distributes all he has to the poor and needy and goes on a pilgrimage or lives in destitution in a communal church till he goes to Heaven.

§ 7 Anyone who plunders an altar or shrine, or steals a Gospel-book, seven years' penance. If it be a bell, or crozier or service-set, it is forty years on bread and water.

§ 8 Anyone who breaks into an oratory, four years' penance therefor. If it be into a refectory, four years on bread and water.

§ 9 Anyone who takes a reward to kill a man or to bear false witness or to bring a false suit or to give false judgement, does three and a half years' penance.

§ 10 Anyone who persists in avarice to the end of his life [17]must go on a pilgrimage or must distribute the value of seven cumals to the poor and needy for his soul's sake.[17]

A cleric or nun who lives in a communal church and has somewhat more than suffices him, whatever it be, let him give it to the poor and needy of the church where he lives. If he does not, let him be excommunicated from the church where he lives. If he repents, he is to do penance apart for as long as the sin has been on his conscience without express command of the superior: for it is worse for a communal church in which there is the worth of a *dirna* of private property or stolen goods than if a fire were burning it, by reason of the amount it causes of murmuring and envy and ill-feeling towards the man that owns it, as John Cassian stated.[18]

§ 11 Anyone who does not pay what he owes does penance therefor as for theft, as if what he owes were a theft he had committed.

§ 12 Anyone who takes a false oath in church on a book of the four Gospels does ten years' penance: fourteen years according to Colum Cille, seven—or four—according to Cummine.

§ 13 Anyone who leads his fellow into perjury does seven years' penance. He who commits perjury in ignorance, a year's penance.

§ 14 If he knows that it is perjury, but commits it through friendship or connivance, a year's penance. If for a bribe, seven year's penance. If under compulsion laid upon him, a year's penance. If under the hand of a bishop or priest or deacon, or at an altar or consecrated (cross), three years' penance.

§ 15 Cummine Fota says: Whatever be the emblem on which a downright perjury is sworn, the man who swears it is bound to seven years' penance, unless it be through his folly or dotage.

If little boys (commit perjury) through fear or connivance, a year of strict penance on bread and water, or the commutation for it, is laid upon him who takes the oath. If it be light women or girls, three years or the commutation.

§ 16 Anyone who gives false testimony or false witness or false judgement against his neighbour, must ask his pardon in his presence, and pay the value of anything he may testify against him, or else do penance according to the liability he swears to against his fellow.

§ 17 If the falsehood is uttered in ignorance, and does no harm to the person about whom it is uttered, full penitence is required thereupon, and a silent fast is kept as well, or twelve psalms, or a hundred blows with a lash on the hand of him who utters the falsehood in ignorance.

If anyone utters such a falsehood deliberately, without doing harm, he spends three days in silence except for the appointed prayers or readings; or else he receives seven hundred blows of a lash on his hands and keeps a half-fast or recites the hundred and fifty psalms.

§ 18 Anyone who utters a falsehood in words whereof good results, by giving a false description to a man's enemies, or by negotiating peace between disputants, or by anything that rescues a man from death,[19] there is no heavy penance (?) provided it is done for God's sake.[19]

§ 19 Anyone who is himself conscious of any falsehood or unlawful gains let him confess privately to a confessor or to an elder who may be set over him. If there be none such, let him make his own confession to God, in whose presence the evil was done, so that He shall be his confessor; and let him perform a vigil and a fast and pray to God diligently.

§ 20 Anyone who hides from his confessor the sins he should confess and someone else discovers them, double penance upon him. If no one does so (?),[20] he is to be expelled from the community of the brethren.

§ 21 Anyone who conceals a capital sin committed by his fellow, let him do penance on bread and water for as long a time as he hid it; for the guilt is the same in God's eyes, whether a man does the evil or conceals it when done by another, if he do not publish and correct it. If the sin that is concealed be trivial, both do penance for that sin according to the penance assigned to it.

§ 22 When two persons of equal rank and equal standing have a dispute without witnesses, and one of them asserts something false, both do penance for the space of a year, or until one of them admits the lie, and they are put on bread and water for two days in every week, and keep a two days' fast every month, and they pray to God diligently that He may pass just judgements upon them, and they fast a whole year for their dispute; they (then) receive the body of Christ, who shall be their judge at the Doom, and the matter is left to God's judgement. If it comes to pass that one of them makes full confession, his penance is increased according to the amount of labour he has brought upon his neighbour, and he earnestly begs forgiveness of him and of the brethren generally.

§ 23 Anyone who disputes violently about anything, and says 'I did not do this or that'—or anyone who imagines something which he does not see or know, but rather for purposes of contention, and does not say 'unless perchance' or 'under correction'—does penance therefor with three fasts.

CAP. IV § 1*a*. *Inuidia*, envy: this is the name of the fourth vice that kills the soul of man, for this is the vice which caused Cain to kill Abel son of Adam, and the Jews to kill Christ. By it chiefly is each man led to kill his fellow in this world. Now the nature of envy, with malice, is likened to the nature of fire. For it is the way of fire that it burns indifferently what is below and above and about it; so also envy assails indifferently him that is lower and him that is higher and him that is equal, so that it is an enemy to every man whether good or bad, near or far.

b. Anyone in whom is the nature of envy and malice, there is no dwelling for God in his heart, and so there will be no dwelling for him with God in Heaven.

c. This is the offspring and issue that is born of this vice, namely, hate of one's neighbour, murmuring at every good thing, thanksgiving for every evil thing, backbiting of friends, chagrin at their winning honour, joy over their loss of esteem.

d. This is the virtue that has been appointed to combat this vice, namely kindliness of heart without malice, with all kinds of virtue that spring therefrom, such as brotherly love, helpfulness to our neighbour, speaking well of everyone, hatred of reviling, rejection of murmuring, magnifying of everything good, rebuking of everything evil, kindly words, a mind compassionate to all men, save for aught that involves sin.

§ 2 Anyone who is envious, or malicious, or offensive to his brethren, let him ask pardon penitently and earnestly of him whom he has offended in envy and malice, and let him do penance on bread and water for as long a time as there had been hatred in his heart. If evil has resulted from his envy, let him replace as much as was lost by his fault, if he have the wherewithal: if not, let him ask pardon tearfully and penitently.

§ 3 Anyone who reviles his mother or father or sister or brother or his prince or superior or an elder who is above him in age or instruction, let him make confession and do penance seven days on bread and water, or perform the commutation which wipes it out. If he reviles anyone else, three days and a half. If it becomes a fixed habit with him, so that he does not remember to restrain himself, he is to be expelled from the church to a place of penance until he shall have given up that vice.

If the words are spoken not in carping nor in envy, but out of compassion for the body and soul of him about whom they are said, no penance is imposed in respect of any man, but it is reckoned as meritorious,[21] if no other profit results . . . in labour and prayer.[21]

§ 4 Anyone who is guilty of envious fault-finding, or anyone who loves to hear it, let him do penance for four days on bread and water, and let him make amends to him against whom he makes mischief. If it is against one who is set over him that the mischief-making is directed, seven days' penance is imposed therefor. But some say that telling the truth is not mischief-making, if it be done according to the Gospel rule, that is: Speak your mind first between you twain: if he does not amend, then call in someone else to support thee; if this does not mend matters, let the thing be spoken before all the people.

§ 5 Anyone who makes mischief against his brother through (love of) talk or drunkenness, let him spend a day in a silent fast. If it be through gossiping that he finds fault, he recites twelve psalms, or receives a hundred blows on his hands.

There are, however, four cases in which it is right to find fault with the evil that is in a man who will not accept his cure by means of entreaty and kindness: either to prevent someone else from abetting him in this evil; or to correct the evil itself; or to confirm the good; or out of compassion for him who does the evil. But anyone who does not do it for one of these four reasons is a fault-finder, and does penance four days, or recites the hundred and fifty psalms for it (?).[22]

§ 6 Anyone who rails at his fellow through envy and malice, let him ask pardon with gentleness and recite thirty psalms or do penance for a day and a night on bread and water.

§ 7 Anyone who murmurs without just cause, and one who prompts another to do so, and one who likes to listen to murmuring and does not examine into it—all such persons do three days' penance on bread and water, and he who actually commits the offence is separated, and his work ⟨is rejected⟩, and he is put on a half-ration of bread, or half the brethren's allowance of bread only, and a little water therewith, until he be cured of murmuring; since everyone is allowed (?)[23] to make a request to his senior in regard to anything he may need, whether clothing or food.

§ 8 Care must be taken to check murmuring about food for this reason, because it was this sin that the Devil first prompted in Adam and Eve in the beginning of the world, whereby they ate the forbidden apple, and on this account they were driven out of Paradise to hunger and poverty and thirst and death and Hell thenceforth.

§ 9 It was this moreover that he prompted in the Lord's people in the desert so that only two of them reached the land of promise, Joshua and Caleb, out of 700,000 armed men besides women and children, so that it was their grandchildren and great-grandchildren who reached it afterwards.

§ 10 It was this moreover that he first prompted in Judas Iscariot, whereby Christ was afterwards crucified: for in whatever place there has been murmuring and envy and reviling and hate of one's neighbour and mischief-making and exultation in everything evil and chagrin at everything good, that place has never been left without vengeance[24] from Heaven and earth.

§ 11 Therefore is envy to be shunned beyond everything, because it creates enmity between son and father, and between daughter and mother, and between king and queen, and between two kinsmen so that each of them slays the other. It causes enmity also between monk and abbot, between disciple and master. It makes an enemy also of everyone a man sees and does not see, out of envy for the good that is in him, so that it incites strife (even) among anchorites one with another.

CAP. V § 1*a*. *Ira*, anger, this is the name of the fifth vice that kills the soul of man. As the edge of a weapon pierces a man's body, so the sharp point of anger pierces the soul and causes its death.

b. This is the offspring and issue that is born of this vice of anger, to wit, man-slaying without humanity, persecution of one's neighbours without mercy, conceit of mind without abasement, haughty speech without subordination, contentiousness without end, accusations without compassion, reproaches without reflection, contumely without restraint.

c. Now the virtue that has been appointed to combat this vice is meekness with gentleness and all that springs therefrom, to wit, soundness of heart, shunning of contention, gentle speech, repression of conceit, docility of nature, silence amid talkativeness, patience amid sufferings, hatred of reviling, zeal without chiding, benevolence without guile, munificence (?) without malice.

d. This is the remedy against anger,[25] with all that springs from it.

§ 2 Anyone who kills his son or daughter does penance twenty-one years. Anyone who kills his mother or father does penance fourteen years. Anyone who kills his brother or sister or the sister of his mother or father, or the brother of his father or mother, does penance ten years: and this rule is followed to the seventh man both of the mother's and father's kin—to the grandson and great-grandson and great-great-grandson, and the sons of the great-great-grandson, as far as the finger-nail.[26] The foregoing applies to cases of kin-slaying. Seven years of penance are assigned for all other homicides; excepting persons in orders such as a bishop or a priest, for the power to fix their penance rests with the king who is over the laity, and with the bishop, whether it be exile for life, or penance for life. If the offender can pay fines, his penance is less in proportion.

§ 3 Anyone who kills a man in revenge for his father or mother or brother or sister does four years' or forty nights' penance therefor.

§ 4 Anyone who kills a man in battle or in a brawl or by lying in wait for him, a year and a half or forty nights, provided he does not pursue the slaughter after the fight is won.

§ 5 Anyone who kills himself while insane, prayers are said for him, and alms are given for his soul, if he was previously pious. If anyone has killed himself[27] in despair or for any other cause, he must be left to the judgement of God, for men dare not offer prayers for him—that is a Mass—unless it be some other prayer, and almsgiving to the poor and miserable.

§ 6 A woman who causes miscarriage of that which she has conceived after it has become established in the womb, three years and a half of penance. If the flesh has formed, it is seven years. If the soul has entered it, fourteen years' penance. If the woman dies of the miscarriage, that is, the death of body and soul, fourteen cumals (are offered) to God as the price of her soul, or fourteen years' penance.

§ 7 Anyone who gives drugs or makes a bogey or gives a poisonous drink so that someone dies of it, seven years' penance, as for a homicide. If no one dies of it, three years' penance.

§ 8 Anyone who hurts his fellow in a quarrel so as to leave a blemish on him, has to pay the leech's fee, and to do his work until he is well, and does half a year's penance and pays a price for the blemish according to what a righteous leech judges. If he has not the price to pay, he does a year's penance instead.

§ 9 Anyone who strikes his fellow, but not deliberately, forty or sixty [days'] penance. If it be a cleric who thus strikes another, it is thrice forty nights or a year of penance.

§ 10 Anyone who kills his kinsman without premeditation, without quarrel, without wrath, yet it happens by his deed, that is a year of penance. If he does it in anger, without premeditation, three years' penance.

§ 11 Anyone who, after taking a vow of renunciation, kills his fellow in anger and with premeditation and intent, the penance for him is a life of exile in destitution, unless pious confessors grant him remission.

§ 12 Anyone who vexes his fellow about any matter, reasonable or unreasonable, let him beg his pardon[28] that he may be healed in spirit: for God hearkens to prayer on this condition, that our neighbour's spirit be healed. If he will not accept his excuses, let (the offender) himself do penance in proportion to the vexation he causes to his fellow, or according as an elder adjudges: and let him who will not accept his excuses do penance on bread and water until he shall have accepted them, and as long as there be hatred in his heart.

§ 13 Anyone who curses his neighbour, let him beg his pardon, and let him undergo a week's strict penance.

Anyone who speaks bitter words to his fellow, though not from his heart, let him ask his pardon and keep a fast. If his brother turns red or pale before him, or if he is taken with a trembling, yet keeps silence and does not contradict him, his penance is a day on bread and water.

§ 14 Anyone who feels a stirring (of anger) in his mind only, let his mind make peace with (his brother).

Anyone who does not make confession to him who has stirred his anger cannot remain in the community of the brethren of the church, lest a plague come thereof. The nature of concealed anger is likened to fire in wood.

§ 15 Anyone who cannot reach him with whom he is angry (to ask his pardon), let him forgive him in his heart ⟨and⟩ repent earnestly before God.

§ 16 If anyone raises his voice in speaking to someone at a distance or to a deaf man, there is ⟨no⟩ penance. If the raising of his voice is attended with anger, whether at a distance or near by, penance is done according to the sin and the transgression. If it be illness that provokes any outcry, it is not to be passed over for the moment.[29]

§ 17 A married woman or a concubine (?)[30] who makes lamentation over a layman or laywoman, fifty nights' penance. If it be over a married woman or a concubine (?) who dies in childbed, or a member of the household, forty nights' penance. If over a secular cleric, twenty nights' penance. If over a bishop or king or anchorite or head of a great monastery, fifteen nights' penance.

§ 18 If it be a cleric who happens to commit one of the offences here mentioned, he has double penance, compared with a married woman.

CAP. VI § 1*a*. *Tristitia*, that is the name of the sixth vice that kills the soul of man. Now there are two forms of this vice, namely, worldly sadness with despair and lack of faith; godly sadness with love of God and serene faith. One of them causes eternal joy in eternal life in Heaven: the other causes eternal grief in the eternal pains of Hell.

b. The sadness which causes the soul's joy in Heaven is that which comes of lamenting over sins, with faith in forgiveness, and that which comes of pitying every strong man and every miserable man and every neighbour of ours who is in the power of sin and vice so that he falls into vileness and misery, without faith, without penitence. For he who deplores his own sins and his neighbour's sins shall be joyful with God in Heaven. It is of him that Christ says: *beati qui lugent* n*unc* q*uoniam ipsi consulabunt*ur.

c. But of worldly sadness there are three forms. The first is sadness and grief at parting with carnal friends for loss of their human affection, and for love and attachment to them; or because of parting with one's guilt and sins and fleshly lusts. Again, the second form of worldly sadness is the grief and despair that arise from every desire that a man desires, because he cannot satisfy it, save only the will of God. The third form of worldly sadness again is the grief and despair which arise from every good thing a man gets, through fear of its being taken away from him, and of its perishing, and through fear of parting with it, even later on,[31] so that he is never free from grief and sadness while he lives, and he goes thereafter to find eternal grief, to everlasting torment without end.

d. Now this is the offspring and issue that is born of worldly sadness—bitterness with malice, lovelessness with insolence, miserliness with gaingetting, much talking after silence, idle volatility without thrift (?), unsteadiness of nature, restlessness of body, wandering of mind towards everything base, readiness to engage in everything evil, sluggishness and slackness towards everything good, despair along with inattention to the commands of God, joy and vigour in doing the works of the Devil.

e. These now are the remedies of this vice: spiritual joy, with serenity of heart and mind, against worldly sadness; fervency of prayer, with fasting and watching, against sluggishness and torpor; liberality with openness of mind toward God against inattention; a fixed measure of labour and prayer against idle volatility; faith with works, joy with gentleness, against despair and malice of mind.

§ 2 Anyone therefore whom the Devil has mocked by means of grief and sorrows, such as the loss of friends or relatives or of anything else, so that he allows him to do nothing good, but (only) to despair, let him first keep a three days' fast without food or drink; if he relapses into the same state afterwards, it is forty nights on bread and water.

§ 3 If he should be in grief and sadness so that he cannot be roused, the monk does penance in another place on bread and water, and returns no more into the community of the brethren, until he be joyful in body and soul.

CAP. VII § 1*a.* *Uana Gloria,* that is, vain glory, is the name of the seventh vice that kills the soul of man ...[32] but any good thing that a man does with his body in the world is lost through vain glory, unless men are on their guard against it. For whatever we do for the sake of pomp or praise from men is called vain glory, and the only reward we gain from it is the praise we have from men, as Christ himself says: *Am*en *dico uobis percipierunt mercedem suaam.*

b. This is the offspring and issue that is born of this vice: disobedience with contumacy, pride with arrogance, readiness for strife, a guise of simulation, upholding of heresy unlawfully, boasting of one's good deeds, pompousness of speech, disguising of appearance, exaltation of the body, debasing of the soul.

c. These again are the remedies that have been appointed to cure it: obedience without contumacy, humility with quietness, shunning of strife, smoothness without simulation, learning from the venerable, steadfastness of nature, a lowly mind, respect for God . . . .

NOTES

1. Reading *sinéoin* for MS. *sinain* (it corresponds to *aquila* in Bigot. I. 5, 6, p. 216 *supra*, but the Irish word for eagle is *ilar*, older *irar*).

2. For MS. *cen* read *cena* (Lat.) = 'the evening meal on weekdays', *Mon. Tall.*, p. 166? Or was this word borrowed into Irish, like Welsh *cwyn*? If so, its earliest form would have been **cēn*.

3. Under the rigorous Culdee discipline a monk who had taken a perpetual vow of abstinence from flesh-meat was advised to keep it even if 'famine or heathen' had left the monastery without a sufficiency of other foods; he was given the comforting assurance that death by starvation in such circumstances was equivalent to martyrdom (*Mon. Tall.*, § 51). To guard against this extreme contingency, however, it was recommended that all such persons should consume a token morsel of meat on Easter Day in order to be able to claim a dispensation from their vow in the event of war or famine during the following year (*Mon. Tall.*, § 12, *RCD*, § 25). In our text the practice is extended to other kinds of food and drink also.

4. MS. *gauin* is doubtless a mistranscription of *gainn* in the exemplar. This renders unnecessary Gwynn's successive emendations to *gur* ('scab') and *gamin* ('skin').

5. Reading *anfostai* (cf. *anfostaigh* Q). But PRC all have *anfontai*, which is obscure to me.

6. Reading *bochtán* for MS. *brothchan* (which would mean 'porridge', as Gwynn translates); cf. § 6 *infra*, *Mon. Tall.*, § 68, &c. The *bochtán* was one of the smaller liquid measures; the word occurs *Laws*, I. 106, 2, where it is glossed (106, 24) 'a small vessel which contains twelve times the full of a hen-egg'. The *b.* corresponds to *sextarius de lacte Romanus* and the *cingit* ('goblet') to *hemina* in the Latin Penitentials.

7. For *selann* see RIA Contrr. S s.v., Gwynn, *Rule of Tallaght*, p. 89. The Irish glossators (e.g. Cormac 1051, 1053, O'Davoren 1484, &c.) take it to be the name of a measure. But here and in *Mon. Tall.* (§§ 22, 49, 52, &c.) it seems to mean an extra allowance of food, more particularly of butter or honey.

8. Here *tri oirndecht* MS. = *tri foirndecht*; cf. RIA Dict. F s.v. *forndecht*.

9. I take *cen orchlisin* MS. as = *cen forcloisin*, lit. 'without overhearing', hence 'unawares, inadvertently'. But this meaning, though it seems to be supported both by the context and by a few of the exx. cited in RIA Dict. F s.v. *forcloisin*, is by no means certain. Cf. Cummean II. 16 (p. 114 *supra*), which has *sine uoluntate*.

10. After this the MS. has the words *daingin sin a pennadoir* 'this is severe, O Penitentiary!', obviously a marginal comment in the scribe's exemplar which he has incorporated in the text.

11. Gwynn's emendation of *faindecht* MS. to *an-écht* 'facinus' is unconvincing. The word is possibly an abstract noun formed from *faenaid* 'prostrates, throws down', which would suit the context here.

12. As Gwynn points out (*Ériu* vii. 180), this and the previous section correspond to Cap. Jud. x. 1 (=Cumm. (X). 17, p. 128 *supra*), but the scribe has inadvertently omitted an entire sentence. For *ainnas* (Gwynn) the MS. reads *amnas*, apparently a mistranscription of *am̃ as* (= *amail as*) in the exemplar.

13. For *mani teis* MS. we must read either *ma téis* or *mani téi*. Gwynn translates the latter, but the former seems more probable to me.

14. For *nuigen* P I read *n-uigedh* (= *n-oiged*) with C. Cf. *fuirired n-aíged Dé* 'feeding God's strangers' (or 'guests') *Laws*, III. 18, 18. Cf. further 'Christus in eis (sc. hospitibus) adoretur qui et suscipitur' *Reg. S. Ben.*, cap. 53. But R has

nuiden (= *noíden*) 'infants', so Gwynn's translation 'Christ's babes' may be right.

15. This is not a reference to the penalties for theft laid down in native Irish law but rather to the rules given in Exod. xxii. 1, 4, which are summarized in § 3.

16. I do not understand *chomraicc* in the present context. Since the sense is complete without it, it may be mere dittography of the last word in § 4.

17–17. I have left Gwynn's translation unchanged since I cannot mend the text. Both verbs are perfect indic. with an infixed neuter pronoun, but so far as I know, Gwynn's proposal to take these forms as = 'must' is not admissible. Besides, if the man has remained a miser 'to the end of his life', how can he then go on a pilgrimage? One would expect rather that the almsgiving and other good works 'for his soul's sake' would be performed by his next of kin after his death; but if so, the text is extremely corrupt. For *fothrodail set* read *fo-rodailset* (pl.)?

18. This dictum does not occur in the extant works of Cassian; see Gwynn's note, loc. cit., p. 185.

19–19. Translation uncertain. Assuming that the modern idiom *ní mór* goes back to the Old-Irish period, the meaning may be rather 'penance is ⟨still⟩ necessary except it (the action) has been done for God's sake'. But normally *acht rop* means 'provided it be'.

20. The force of *manip é-side* (read *mani bé-side?*) in the present context is obscure to me. As Gwynn remarks, 'If the sinner does not confess, and if nobody else detects his sins, how are they to become known?' It is doubtful whether the protasis could mean 'if this be of no avail', i.e. if he is again convicted of a similar offence.

21–21. The Irish clause is obscure, and I can make no sense of *fou* in the context. Perhaps something has fallen out, as Gwynn suggests.

22. In the right-hand margin the scribe has added at the end of this paragraph *īd* and immediately above it *n̄t*. Gwynn's expansion as *ind nocht* is doubtful, and his translation 'naked' is quite impossible. Perhaps one should take *ind* as the conjugated preposition (acc. neut.) 'for it', and *nt* as = *nota*, a frequent marginal sign in legal and other MSS. Or *ind nocht* 'that night'?

23. I cannot improve on Gwynn's emendation of MS. *conarectar* to *con-airleicther*, but this is far from certain; indeed the whole clause appears to be out of context.

24. MS. *digu | uil* stands for *díguil* (= *dígail*). The emendation to *digu uilc* 'the utmost evils' (Gwynn) is unnecessary.

25. In the other chapters we find a number of 'remedies' against the relevant vice listed in a separate paragraph. As *in so* (P) normally means 'this (or these) following', one might be tempted to conclude, with Gwynn, that (*d*) is incomplete here. But C reads *annsin* (= *in sin*) 'the foregoing', obviously identifying the 'virtue' described in (*c*) with the 'remedy' (note that this word is sg. here, whereas elsewhere it is always pl.). The fact that R omits (*d*) altogether suggests that there was no such sub-section in the original (X) and that this attempt to supply one is due to *x*, the immediate exemplar of P and C.

26. For the *ingen ar méraib*, lit. 'nail in front of [the] fingers', the final degree of kinship recognized in Irish law, see RIA Contrr. I s.v. *ingen*. After this degree the homicide ceases to be 'kin-slaying' (*fingal*) and thus entails a shorter period of penance. I take *hissin fingail sin* as a separate sentence (lit. 'This is for kin-slaying').

27. Reading *ra-n-orr nech* for MS. *ronoirnecht*.

28. Reading *da-nguideth* for MS. *ica guideth*.

29. As Gwynn points out, this is a misunderstanding of a Latin sentence corresponding to Bigot. IV. 6, 1 (p. 230 *supra*): 'Et clamor dolore excitatus non praetermittendus, de quo pauca dicimus.' The Irish adapter has taken *dolor* to mean 'pain' instead of 'sorrow' for the dead, with which the next two sections are concerned.

30. Gwynn's translation of *caillech aithirgi* (rectius *aithrige*) as 'a penitent nun' is justified by the MS. reading. But, as he himself points out, one would expect a word meaning 'concubine' as opposed to *cétmuinter* 'lawful spouse'. Since *caillech* is used elsewhere of a woman living with a man (e.g. *ZCP* xiii. 20, 22, Anecdota from Ir. MSS. I. 7, 25, &c.), I suggest reading *caillech airige*, the second word being gen. (of apposition) of *airech*, the old native word for 'concubine' (see *Studies in E. Ir. Law*, p. 64); but this is, of course, quite uncertain.

31. Reading *íar mbaull* for MS. *iarma | ul*.

32. Here some words seem to be omitted, but if so, the lacuna is common to all the MSS., including R.

THE OLD-IRISH TABLE OF COMMUTATIONS

THIS work is preserved in two manuscripts: (1) R = Rawlinson B 512, saec. XIV–XV (cf. Stokes *VT* I. xiv–xlv), ff. 42ᶜ12–44ᵃ2. Edited with translation by Kuno Meyer in RC xv. 485–98; corrigenda, ibid. xvii. 320. Meyer is responsible for the title *De arreis* (taken from the Latin text in MS. Par. 12021), for the division of the material into thirty-two sections (followed in the present translation), and for the insertion of occasional cross-headings in Latin and English (omitted here). His translation, which has been reprinted in McNeill–Gamer, pp. 142–7, needs correction on several points. (2) B = Royal Ir. Ac. 3 B 23, now 1227 (see Catalogue, pp. 3360 f.), saec. xv, scribe Tadcc ua Rigbardáin, pp. 13ᵃ1–16ᵃ21. In general this provides a better text than R, the older linguistic forms being normally preserved. It is also fuller, containing five additional sections, three of which are found in *De arreis* (15 A = DA 5, 16 A = DA 7, 32 A = DA 3). This additional material has been printed by E. J. Gwynn in *Ériu* v. 45–48, where there is also a collation of the remainder of the text with Meyer's edition of R. The order of the sections differs somewhat from that of R: 1–13, 21–31, 33, 32, 32 A, 15–19 A, 14, 20.

B would seem to be closer to the original than R, which represents a somewhat shortened recension. But since the full text of B is not yet available in print,[1] I have thought it better to give a fresh translation of R, keeping Meyer's order and division of sections and intercalating the additional matter in B as 15 A, &c. This new material is printed in italics, as are also words and phrases found only in B in the sections common to both manuscripts. Discrepancies between the readings of R and B are given in the footnotes.

The language of the treatise, allowing for scribal modernizations (particularly in R), is Old-Irish throughout and closely resembles that of the Penitential (p. 258 ff. *supra*), which follows it in B. None of the verbal forms is later than the eighth century. It seems almost certain that both works were

---

[1] An edition and translation have since appeared in *Ériu* xix (1962), pp. 47–72.

compiled in the monastery of Tallaght (or perhaps in one of the older foundations which had accepted the 'Culdee' reform movement, such as Terryglass) in the second half of the century before the death of Mael Ruain (792). For the meanings of OI *arre*, see pp. 50 f. *supra*.

Here follow the commutations:

1. A commutation for rescuing a soul out of hell: three hundred and sixty-five Paters and three hundred and sixty-five genuflexions and three hundred and sixty-five blows of the scourge every day for a year, and a fast every month—this rescues a soul out of hell. For it is in proportion to the number of joints and sinews in the human body[1] that this commutation to save a soul which has merited torments (while) in the body has been devised.

2. Another commutation: (reciting the) Three Fifties daily, ending with the *Beati*, for seven years rescues a soul out of hell.

3. Another commutation which is shorter:[2] (to recite the Psalter with) *Lauda* and the *Beati* and a Pater at the end of each psalm for three years.

4. Each of the foregoing commutations rescues a soul out of hell if intercession for it be permissible at all.

5. Every penance is determined, both as to its severity and the length of time one is engaged in it, by the magnitude of the sin, the length of time it is persevered in, the motive for which it is committed, and the fervour with which it is eventually abandoned. For there are certain sins which are not entitled to any remission of the penitence due for them, however long be the period prescribed[3] for them, unless God Himself shorten it by means of death or a message (?)[4] of sickness or the amount of (extra?) mortification a person takes on himself. Such are, for example, kin-slayings, homicides, and secret murders; also brigandage, druidism, and satirizing; further, adultery, incest, perjury, heresy, and violation of (the duties of one's ecclesiastical) grade. There are other sins which are atoned for by (performing) half the (prescribed) penance together with half the commutation, others by the (full?) commutation together with one-third of the penance, still others by the commutation alone.

6. The sages enumerate four reasons why the commutations are practised: (1) for a speedy separation from the sin with which one has been united;[5] (2) for fear of adding to the sin[6] in the future; (3) for fear that one's life be cut short before the end of the penance decided by a soul-friend; (4) in order to (be free to) approach[7] the Body and Blood of Christ by restricting (?)[8] (the period of) penance. *As the body (which is left) for long periods of time without food and drink perishes, so does the soul (which is left) throughout the whole of its present life[9] without the Body and Blood of Christ, without the food of the soul.*[10]

7. As there is a difference between laymen and clerics and between

nuns[11] and laywomen, so too there is a difference between the (kind of) mortification and penance due from them, as well as between the commutations which may properly be performed by them.

8. First, commutations proper for former lay men and women: spending the night in water or on nettles or on nutshells, or with a dead body—for there is hardly a single layman or laywoman who has not[12] some part in manslaughter. On the other hand these are the commutations proper for clerics and nuns except such of them as have slain a man (who are required to perform the first kind)—unless, indeed (a commutation of the first kind) be performed for the purpose of increasing one's reward:[13] spending the night in cold churches or remote[14] cells while keeping vigils and praying without respite, *i.e.* (without) leave to sit or lie down or sleep—as though one were at the very gates of hell—unless a little weariness chance to occur between two cycles of prayer, when one may sit.[15]

9. These, now, are the commutations of a black fast (due) after grievous sin, as the saints have prescribed:[16] a hundred blows with the scourge or (recitation of) the Three Fifties together with their hymns and canticles.[16]

10. Another commutation (of the same): a hundred Paters (said while) in cross-vigil,[17] and *Deus in adiutorium* as far as *festina* thrice at the conclusion of each Pater, and a genuflexion after each *Deus*, and diligent meditation on God. For him who does this thrice it is a commutation of a three days' black fast.

11. Commutation of a three-day fast[18] for one who can read:[19] (reciting) the Three Fifties standing and celebrating each canonical hour, twelve genuflexions with arms outstretched towards God at each canonical hour, and diligent meditation upon heaven.

12. Commutation of a black fast (due) for grievous sin for one who cannot read: three hundred genuflexions and three hundred properly administered blows with a scourge, at the end of each hundred a cross-vigil until the arms are weary. 'I beseech pardon of God', 'May I receive mercy', 'I believe in the Trinity'—that is what one sings without ceasing until the commutation is completed; further, frequent striking of the breast and perfect contrition to God. To do this thrice is a commutation of a three-day fast.

13. Commutation of a fast for ordinary minor sins: *Alleluia, Alleluia, in manus* [20]*tuas Domine*[20] as far as *veritatis* and a complete Pater Noster. This is sung thirty times in cross-vigil, and thirty genuflexions and thirty blows with a scourge afterwards.

14. A commutation of seven years' strict penance consisting of expiatory prayers in order to rescue a soul from the pain of hell: a hundred Masses, a hundred and fifty psalms, a hundred *Beati*, a hundred genuflexions with each *Beati*, a hundred Credos, a hundred Paters, a hundred soul-hymns.[21]

15. Another commutation of a year (of penance):[22] a black fast for three days without eating, drinking, or sleeping: one night (spent) in water, another naked on nettles, the third on nutshells.

15A. *Commutation of a year of strict penance: twelve days on twelve morsels[23] of a standard loaf along with their condiment of skim-milk, while performing the labour (mortifications?) which have been established in the book[24] or praying and celebrating each canonical law.*

16. Another commutation (of the same): twelve fasts of three days, one after the other; a full meal between every two fasts.

16A. *Another commutation (of the same): A month (passed) in grievous illness after a vow of perpetual amendment (made) under the hand of a person in orders.*

17. Another commutation (of the same): to chant twelve *Beati* in cross-vigil without lowering the arms while doing so.

18. Yet another commutation (of the same): to chant *Miserere mei Deus* forty times in cross-vigil or (simply) standing, and a Pater after every psalm and *Deus in adiutorium* as far as *festina* thrice at the conclusion of each psalm.

18A. *A commutation of seven years' strict penance: seven months (passed) in grievous illness after a vow of perpetual amendment (made) under the hand of a person in orders.*

19. Another commutation (of the same): seven months (passed) in confinement on bread[26] and water (prostrate?) on the soil or on the floor from one period of nones to another, together with fervent prayer and celebration of each canonical and a vow of perpetual amendment.

19A. *Another commutation (of the same): to spend seven months on bread and water in gyves or fetters without being loosed day or night.*

20. The following is a commutation of (chanting the) hundred and fifty psalms: (to say) a Pater twelve times and *Deus in adiutorium* as far as *festina* after each Pater; (then) a Pater fifteen times and the whole of *Deus in adiutorium* after each Pater. This atones for every (kind of) sin (if) accompanied by keen and heartfelt repentance. *It is a commutation of (chanting the) Three Fifties, and heals him who transgresses against his clerical orders provided there be keen repentance.*

21. A commutation of a three-day fast for one who cannot read: a day and night without sleep, without sitting down save only when he lowers himself to genuflect. 'I beseech pardon of God', 'May I receive mercy', 'I believe in the Trinity'—that is what he sings without ceasing. A Pater Noster and Credo twelve times in cross-vigil and three genuflexions at the end of each, and *Deus in adiutorium* as far as *festina* three times after each prayer. Such is the commutation of a three-day fast. Thirty three-day fasts (compounded for?) in this manner are a commutation of a year's penance for young clerics, as Gregory has laid down.

22. Commutation of a fast[28] by means of scourging: seven hundred properly administered lashes seven times.

23. Another commutation (of the same) by means of genuflexions: two hundred genuflexions properly made, bending the body *to the ground* scrupulously.[29]

24. Another commutation (of the same): to remain standing without a staff in one's hand or (other) support until the Three Fifties and their canticles have been chanted.

25. Another commutation (of the same): (to remain in) a cross-vigil until the chanting of fifty psalms or of the *Beati* four times has been finished, and the arms are not to touch the sides until the chanting is over, even though there be nothing else to support him (?).[30]

26. A commutation of a week's strict penance on bread and water: seven *Beati* (recited) in a properly performed cross-vigil, with a Credo, a Pater, and *Hymnum dicat* after each *Beati*.

27. A commutation of a week (of strict penance) for one who cannot read: seven hundred properly made genuflexions and seven *hundred*[31] properly administered lashes, and a cross-vigil after each hundred until the arms are weary.

28. A commutation of a fortnight (of the same): to do this twice.

29. A commutation of three weeks (of the same): to do it three times.

30. A commutation of forty days on bread and water: to do it (all) in one day (?).[32]

31. If there be danger of death, the following is a commutation of a year (of penance) when accompanied by intense contrition: to chant 365 Paters standing with both arms extended (?) towards heaven and without the elbows ever touching the sides, together with fervent concentration on God. And the words are not spoken aloud.[33] And to recite the *Beati* in a stooping position with thy two arms laid flat by thy sides. Or the *whole* body is stretched out along the ground face downwards and both arms laid flat by the sides. Patrick has recommended this (type of) vigil and Colum Chille and Maedóc of Ferns and Molacca Menn and Brénainn moccu Altae and Colum mac Crimthain and Mocholmóc of Inis Celtra. And this tradition was deposited with Enda in Aran. The four chief sages of Ireland, viz. Ua Minadan and Cumaine Fota and Murdebur and Mocholmóc mac Cumain[34] from Arran, have recommended its continual practice to every son of life[35] who desires to obtain heaven.

32. A commutation of a year's strict penance which Ciarán son of the wright prescribed for Ennu moccu Laigsi . . . :[36] for three days and three nights one is engaged in it in an unlighted house or in any other place where no distraction can penetrate, and the normal allowance for a three-day fast is not (consumed) but only three sips of water each day. And this is the (actual) commutation: to chant each day the hundred

and fifty psalms standing without a staff *in the hand*, and a genuflexion at the end of each psalm and a *Beati* after each fifty, a genuflexion after every two chapters, and (reciting) *Hymnum dicat* after every *Beati* in cross-vigil (?):[37] and there is no lying down . . .[38] but only sitting; and in addition to this, keeping each canonical hour, and diligent concentration on the sufferings of Christ with anguish of heart and perfect contrition to God and calling to mind all the sins he can remember.

32A. *A commutation of a year's strict penance: (to spend) three days and three nights in a grave with a dead body without drinking, eating, or sleeping; to make earnest confession to God and man at every hour of the day and night, together with a vow to abandon all sin under the direction of a pious soul-friend; to chant the Three Fifties each day and keep each canonical hour. If he cannot read, he prays in his heart with mental ardour, with tears and repentance.*

33. A commutation of fifty nights of strict penance capable of being performed in a single day which Colum Chille and Mobí Clárenech have laid down with the counsel of the Archangel Michael: (to recite) *Dominus regnauit, Exaudi Domine iustitiam meam,* [39]*Dominus regit me,*[39] *Domini est terra, Beatus qui intellegit, Deus noster refugium, Exaudi Deus deprecationem, Nonne Deo, Exaudi Deus orationem meam cum* [40]*deprecor,*[40] *Te decet, Domine refugium, Domine exaudi, Domine probasti, Eripe me* [41]*Domine*[41]*, Domine clamavi, Uoce mea* [40]*ad Dominum*[40]*, Domine exaudi* [40]*orationem meam auribus*[40]*. Gloria* [41]*et honor*[41] *Patri et Filio et* [41]*Spiritui Sancto*[41] at the conclusion of each psalm, and seven genuflexions, and *Deus in adiutorium* [41]*as far as festina*[41] three times, and one Pater (to be said) between every second psalm until the whole commutation is completed.

NOTES

1. For the notion that the body contained this number of 'joints and sinews' see *Revue Celtique* xii. 68 § 35, and Joyce, *A Social History of Ancient Ireland* I. 598.

2. lit. 'not longer'.

3. Reading *con-mestar* with B.

4. Ir. *eipistil* < *epistola*. See now *Ériu* xix. 68.

5. Lit. 'after cohabitation with it'.

6. Perhaps rather 'of committing further sins' during the period of penance which would entail further penances?

7. Reading *ascnam* with B.

8. *cuinnriuch* R means 'checking, constraining, correcting'; *comeicniugad* B means 'forcing, constraining'.

9. Lit. 'life today'.

10. Cf. Cummean II 2 and parallels.

11. Lit. 'young nuns' (*mac-caillecha*).

12. Reading *dunā bē* with B.

13. i.e. clerics are free to perform the 'commutations' proper to *conversi* in order to acquire additional merit.

14. Lit. 'hidden'.

15. Lit. 'save that a little oppression may occur seated between two prayers'; the sense seems to be as I have translated.

16–16. 'a hundred psalms and a hundred genuflexions and a hundred blows' B (cf. *De arreis*, c. 1).

17–17. Om. B.

18. *sic* B, 'of a fast' R.

19. Reading *legas* with B.

20–20. Om. R.

21. I do not know which hymn is referred to here. But see *Ériu* xix. 72.

22. Meyer has wrongly expanded *blīā* as *bliadan* and translated 'a year of three days' black fasts'; bliad*na* B.

23. Reading *déc* for MS. *du*; cf. *De arreis*, c. 5 (*supra*, p. 164).

24. Reading *la mmoth dorónad i lebur* (lammoth duro nadilebuir MS.).

25. *sic* B, 'two' R.

26. 'cress' B.

27. 'ten' B (*recte*?).

28. = a three-day fast?

29. Lit. 'without neglect'.

30. Translation uncertain.

31. Om. R. in error.

32. 'to do it in one day, if at the need of death' Meyer, who takes *mad ri ēcin mbáis* as part of the sentence. But see now *Ériu* xix. 62, 70.

33. Lit. 'voice does not come into sound'; cf. Thes. II. 253. 7 (mistranslated).

34. = Colmán s. of Comman, † 751 (AI); cf. Fél. Oeng. 21 Nov.

35. i.e. every Culdee, cf. *Mon. Tall.*, § 1, &c.

36. *ó chomsola o dibrig* R, *do chomsola huadib ire* B, both unintelligible to me. Meyer takes the reading of R as a proper name.

37. Lit. 'cross'.

38. *commain* R, *comoin* B, obscure to me in this context.

39–39. Om. R.

40–40. Om. R.

41–41. Om. B.

SIGLA

Ad	Canones Adamnani
Aq	Synodus Aquilonaris Britaniae
Bi	Paenitentiale Bigotianum
Ca	Tres Canones Hibernici
Co A, B	Paenitentiale S. Columbani A, B
Cu	Paenitentiale Cummeani
Da	Excerpta de libro Dauidis
Gi	Praefatio Gildae
Hi I–VI	Canones Hibernenses I–VI
Lu	Synodus Luci Victoriae
Pa I	'Synodus I S. Patricii' (i.e. Patricii, Auxilii, Isernini)
Pa II	'Synodus II S. Patricii'
Vi	Paenitentiale Vinniani
Wa A, P	Canones Wallici, Textus A, Textus P

tit.	titulus
pr.	praeambula, prologus
ps.	postscriptum
ssc.	subscriptio

INDICES

I. CONCORDANTIAE CANONUM

Cu III. (cont.)

5–6	Bi III. 2, 1
8–11	Lu 5. Bi III. 3, 4
12	Bi III. 4
13–15	Bi III. 6, 1–2
16–18	Bi III. 5, 2–3
(IV). 1–4	Bi IV. 4
5–6	Bi IV. 3, 4
7–8	Bi IV. 3, 2–3
9–10	Bi IV. 3, 1
12–14	Bi IV. 5, 1–2
(V). 1–3	Bi V. 3, 1
(VI). 1	cf. Bi VI. 1, 1; 2, 2
2	Bi VI. 3, 1
(VII). 1	Bi VII. 1
2	Bi VII. 3
(VIII). 2	Bi VII. 2
3	Bi VIII. 1
4	Bi VIII. 4
6	Bi VIII. 5
7–10	Bi VIII. 2, 1–2
11–13	Aq 5–7
25	Hi II. 6
(IX). 1	Gi 9
2–5	cf. Gi 12–15
6–10	Gi 19–21
11–12	Gi 23–24
13	cf. Lu 4
14	Vi 30 (V)
15	cf. Vi 52
(X). 5; 15–17	Vi (1)–(4)
(XI). 29	cf. Gi 20
ps. 1	Bi pr. 2
3–5	Bi pr. 33–35
Da 3–4	Cu I. 2–3
6	cf. Co B 16
7	cf. Co B 4
8–9	Cu II. 15–16. Bi II. 1, 7–8
10	cf. Gi 5
Gi 1–4	Cu II. 2–5
5	cf. Da 10
7	cf. Co A 6
9	Cu (IX). 1
10	Cu I. 4
11	cf. Cu II. 6
12–15	cf. Cu (IX). 2–5

19–21	Cu (IX). 6–10
20	cf. Cu (XI). 29
23–24	Cu (IX). 11–12
Hi I. 1	Bi IV. 1, 1
5	Bi II. 5, 2
6–8	Bi IV. 2, 2–4
12	Bi I. 5, 1
16–18	Bi I. 5, 5–7
19	Bi I. 5, 12
20	Bi I. 5, 11
21	Bi I. 6, 1
22	Bi I. 7
23	Bi I. 6, 2
26–29	Bi IV. 6, 2–5
II. 6	Cu (VIII). 25
Lu 1	Cu III. 1. Bi III. 1, 2
4	cf. Cu (IX). 13
5	Cu III. 8–11. Bi III. 3, 4
6	Cu II. 7
7–9	cf. Hi II ex. (B)
Vi (1)–(4)	Cu (X). 5; 15–17
(3)	Cu II. 8
1–3	cf. Co A 2
8–9	cf. Co B 9; 21
10–11	cf. Co B 4
12	cf. Co B 2
17	cf. Co B 11; 23
18–20	cf. Co B 6
22	cf. Co A 4a; B. 5; 21
23	cf. Co A 3; B 1
25	cf. Co A 4
25–26	cf. Co B 7; 19
27	cf. Co B 8
30 (V)	Cu (IX). 14
35	cf. Co B 13. Bi II. 4
36	cf. Co B 14; 16. Bi II. 5, 4
37–38	Bi II. 5, 5–6
39–40 (V)	Cu II. 26–27
41	cf. Cu II. 28
42–45 (V)	Cu II. 29
48	Bi II. 11, 2
52	cf. Cu (IX). 15

Paenitentiale Hibernicum	Cummeanus	Paenitentiale Bigotianum
I. 2–3		I. 5, 3–6; 6, 1–2; 7
4		5, 7. 8. 10. 11
5		8
6		10
7	I. 1–4 (E)	
9	12–14	
10	6–7	
11	(XI). 15–17	

Paenitentiale Hibernicum	Cummeanus	Paenitentiale Bigotianum
I. 12	(XI). 12–14	
15		I. 2, I. 3
16		9, 1
18		10
19	I. 5	
21	(X). 18	
II. 1 c		pr. 41
2–6	II. 1–3	
8–9	4–5	
11	17	
12–13	13–14	II. 1, 1–3
14		4
15–16	11–12	5–6
17–18	15–16	7–8
19–20		9
21		3, 1
22	8	2, 4
24	6	1
25	(X). 14–15	
28–34	2–9	
35	17	
36		8, 1–2; 9, 1–3
III. 2	III. 1	III. 1, 1–3
10	3	
13–14	9–11	3, 4
16	12	4
17	17–18	5, 3
21	(VIII). 19–20	
22	11–13	
IV. 2	7	
4	8–10	
5	14–16	
7	6	
V. 2–3		IV. 1, 1–3
4		4
5		2, 1
6		2–4
8	(IV). 9–10	3, 1
9–11	5–8	2–4
12	1–3 (4)	4
13–14	12–16	5, 1–2
16–18		6, 1–6
VI. 1		V. 1
3	(V). 3	3, 1
VII. 1a, b	(VII). 2	VII. pr.+3

II. INDEX BIBLICUS

Asterisco (*) indicatur textus a Vulgata diuersus

III. INDEX NOMINUM PROPRIORUM

IV. INDEX RERUM UERBORUM LOCUTIONUM

apparet sanguis, libido (i.e. liuido) Wa A 12 (P 51). A 13 (P 36). uitium Wa A 48 (P 54), P 56.
applicuit frater ad abatem Moysen Bi VI. 3, 3.
adpraehendere ancellam fugientem Wa A 52.
adprobari causa fornicationis Wa A 23. *absolute* Wa A 31. Pa II. 24. — testibus adprobatur Wa P 24 (in . . . probetur A 29). — titulus adprobandi Wa P 16 (conprobandi A 4, P 3, *al.*).
approbatio antiquorum auctorum Bi pr. 6.
aptum . . . sibi uidetur Ad 18.
aqua: humus quam a. madefecerat Ad 9. in -is extincta Ad 3. animal, -ia in -is suffocata Ad 14 (*bis*). pane et -a, pane aquaque, cum (in) pane et -a *paenitere passim.* mensura -ae Cu (VIII). 26. -am (-a Cu) quantum sufficit Gi 2 = Cu II. 3. talimpulum -ae Gi I = Cu II. 2. — bibat -am quae in crismali fuerit Cu (XI). 22. -am ablutionis sumat Cu (XI). 27. — baptizamur in -a Cu pr. 2.
aquila: bibitio -ae Hi I. 17. *cf.* Bi I. 5, 6.
aquilonalis Britania Aq tit.
arbitrari: quantum -tus fuerit sacerdos Vi 9.
arbitrium: aepiscopi ueniant -o Wa P 40.
arborum fruntibus (*i.e.* frondibus) pascuntur *uaccae* Ad 11.
argentum reddere *sim.* Hi IV. 2. 8. -ti libram (-as) reddere, *sim.* Wa *passim.* ualere -ti libram Wa A 51. .v. soltos -ti exsoluat Wa A 12.
arguere *peccatorem* Vi 30 (S). Cu (VIII). 19. 20. 22. per contemptum -ntium Da 1. Cu III. 3. dispectione Cu (VIII). 3 = Bi VIII. 1. alios proterue Cu (VIII). 21.
arma portare Wa A 6 (P 5). ad aeclesiam Wa A 46. -is conpugnare Pa I. 8. -is reiectis, relictis *paenitere* Lu 4. Cu (IV). 5. (IX). 13. *cf.* Bi IV. 1, 2. sine -is *paenitere* Cu II. 22.
arreum Hi II *passim.*
ascendere thorum defuncti fratris Pa II. 25.
assina ligata Bi VI. 3, 6.
aspectu coinquinari Cu II. 12. Bi II. 1, 6.
assiduus somnus emitatio mortis Bi VI. 2, 1.
adstantia: ad iudicis -am Wa A 37.
assuesco: in consuetudine adsueti Vi (3) = Cu II. 8. de uindicandis -tis Pa II. 30.
adsumere peccatorem Cu ps. 4 = Bi pr. 34.

attestari: non adtestando ad uitam perfectam constringere Pa II. 17.
adtingere perfectionem Bi V. 1, 5.
auaritia Vi 27. Cu III. 3.
auarus clericus Vi 28.
auctor *uenditionis* Wa A 19 (P 28). auctores *canonum* Hi III. 1. antiqui Bi pr. 6.
auctoritas canonis Cu pr. 14. in questionibus Romanorum Ad 16.
audacia: nostrae -ae culpa Bi pr. 4.
audacter accedere ad iudicium tribunalis Co B 30.
audire libenter detrahentem Cu (VIII). 8 = Bi VIII. 2, 2. *obloquentem* Bi VIII. 3. *admonentes* Cu (VIII). 10. -emus quid abas peritus dixit Bi VIII. 3. *u. Ind. Gramm. sub* **formulae.**
auferre linteamen *altaris* Cu (XI). 4. 11. aliquid per rapinam Ca 2. si quod abstullerit reddat Wa A 37. qui repetit -entem quae sua sunt Cu III. 4 = Bi III. 2, 2. caballum a latrone Wa A 51 (excusserit P 57). quies -et omne opus bonum ab anima Bi VI. 1, 2.
augere *pro* agere, *ut uid.,* Gi 14. Co B 6. 25.
auis: intinctum a bestiiis et -bus Bi I. 5 tit.
auris abscis(s)a Ad 5. 18. 20.
aurum: de -o latitudo Hi IV. 2. *in comparatione* Bi pr. 13. 15.
auxilium Dei Vi 29.
axis: super -em iacere Da 11.

bactroperiti (*u. app. crit.*), hoc est contemptores solliciti Pa II. 17.
baculum: refugium -is . . . frangere Ca 1.
baptisma (bab- J): de -tis (-ibus DJI) incertis Pa II. 7.
baptismus (babt-): de gentilibus qui ante -um credunt Pa II. 31. remittuntur . . . peccata in -o Pa II. 31. *infans moriens* absque -um Vi 47. sine -o Cu II. 32. Bi II. 11, 1. benedicens infantulum uice -i Cu (X). 19.
baptizare (babt-): baptizamur in aqua Cu pr. 2. in remissionem peccatorum Bi pr. 30. non rebaptizare sed b. Pa II. 7. -ti, qui symbuli traditione . . . acciperunt Pa II. 7. qua etate -ndi Pa II. 19. solempnitatibus Domini -ntur Pa II. 19. non debet uocari clericus qui non potest b. Vi 49 (V). monachi non debent b. Vi 50 (V). *praeterea* Pa I. 24. 27. 29.
barbaros ad Christianos educere, ducatum praebere -is Lu 4. Cu (IX). 13.

barbaros (*cont.*)
   capillos promittere more -orum Wa A
   61.
bardicatio glandellae Bi IV. 6, 2.
bardigium (?): poenitentia bardigi
   †capalbiae Hi I. 26.
bas(s)ilicis sanctorum ministrandum est
   Vi 33. in tribus -is . . . iuret Wa P 16.
bat(t)uti lactis sextarius Gi 1 = Cu II. 2.
beati sunt . . . casti corpore Vi 41.
   Hieronimus uir -ae memoriae Bi pr. tit.
bellum: qui in puplico -o hominem
   occiderit Bi IV. 1, 4.
bene agere Vi 23. 34. si b. egerit paenitentiam Co B 1. qui b. non custodierit
   sacrificium Cu (XI). 1. se b. humiliare
   Co A 11. b. illis in nouissimo †direge-
   tur Vi 41.
benedicens infantulum uice baptismi Cu
   (X). 19.
benedictio infantis Cu (X). 20. cum -ne
   dicatur Pa II. 21. creaturam uel -nem
   Dei perdere Vi 52.
benefactum: iactans in suis -is Cu (VII).
   2.
beneficium: iactans in sua -a Bi VII. 3.
benignitas Bi pr. 49. Abraham et Loth
   Hi V. 1.
bestia: a -is capta animalia Ad 4. caro a
   -is commessa Ad 17. *cf.* Ad 18. intinctum a -is, *sim.* Ad 18. Bi I. 5 tit. caro
   delacerata canibus uel -is Bi I. 5, 4.
   sanguis effussus per -as Ad 17. quodcumque -ae commedent de peccoribus
   Hi VI. 3. humanae -ae Ad 18. familiaris
   b. quae est muriceps Cu (XI). 18.
bestiales homines Ad 4. 18.
bestiole, *i.e. mus uel mustella* Cu (XI). 14.
bibat aquam quae in crismali fuerit Cu
   (XI). 22. bibere sanguinem uel semen
   Bi I. 5, 2. urinam Cu (X). 18. urinam
   hominis seu et sanguinem Bi I. 5, 1.
   urinam pecoris Bi I. 5, 3. animal quod
   sanguinem -erit Bi I. 5, 8. bibere uinum
   Bi VIII. 3. intinctum a bestiis Cu
   (XI). 18. Bi I. 5 tit. I. 5, 5. 6. 7. 10. 11.
   12. a glangella Bi I. 6, 2. a laico uel
   laica Bi I. 6 tit. I. 6, 1. — iuxta fana Co
   B 24. usque ad uomitum Co B 22.
bibitio inlicita Hi I. 16. 18. 19. 20. 21. 23.
   sanguinis uel urinae Hi I. 12. aquilae
   uel curbi *al.* Hi I. 17.
biduano paenitere Aq 5 (biduo Cu
   (VIII). 11 (R: biduana E)).
bidubium 'axe' Wa A 5 (P 4).
blasph(-f-)emare clericos Pa I. 32.
   regulam Co A 11.
blasfemia Bi VIII. pr. VIII. 3.
blasphemus Cu (VIII). 5.

bonitas Bi pr. 49. perfectio -tis Bi V. 1, 5.
bonus: iudicia gentium -a quae natura -a
   illis docet Hi III ps. -um meritum Bi
   IV. 6, 7 tit. -um opus Pa I. 10. Bi IV. 7.
   VI. 1, 1. 2. -a opera Vi 46. Bi pr. 15.
   quicquid -i (-um Bi) fecerit Cu (VII).
   2 = Bi VII. 3. ut efficiantur omnes
   aurum -um Bi pr. 13. reges -i Gi 23 =
   Cu (IX). 11. — bonum confirmare Cu
   (VIII). 16. -a accipere Hi V. 1. —
   bonum est . . . quam Bi VIII. 3.
bos: caule bouum Hi VI. 4. algam per
   -ues per herba dare Wa P 61. decimae
   de una uaca uel -ue Hi III. 7. -uem
   furare Co B 7. 19. -uem ligatum
   inuenire Wa A 18 (P 11). -uem perdere Wa P 34. si bos alium occiderit
   Wa A 34 (*cf.* P 39). si taurus -uem
   occiderit Wa A 35 (P 39). si bos es Pa
   II. 1.
bouellum 'byre' Hi VI. 1.
brachium forare Wa P 10. in -o foramen
   facere Wa A 14. in lumento -a discooperire Co B 28.
breuis paenitentia Pa II. 3. -ia *paenitentiae*
   spatia Pa II. 22. omissa uerborum in -i
   circuitione . . . collegi uis Bi pr. 28.
breuitatis causa Vi ps.
bucellus, -a 'morsel, biscuit': super .xii.
   -os (-as B) de tribus panibus Hi II. 5.
butyrum (-erum) *paenitentibus conceditur*
   Gi 1 = Cu II. 2. Hi II. 12 (B).

cab(-p-)allum conparare Wa A 20 (P 29).
   A 49 (P 56). perdere Wa A 32 (P 33).
   -um ligatum . . . inuenire Wa A 18
   (P 11). *auferre* Wa A 54. impastoriare
   Wa P 63. -um *raptum* indicare, capere
   Wa A 53 (P 60). a latrone auferre,
   excutere Wa A 51 (P 57). *alibi semper*
   equus *legitur.*
cadere: pecora de rupe -ntia Ad 2. -ns
   sacerdos Cu (XI). 5. si sacrificium
   ciderit de manu (-ibus) offerentis,
   sim. Cu (XI). 2. 5. 23. — *translate*: ruina
   maxima c. Vi 12. 27. Co B 2. ruina
   fornicationis c. Vi 10. clerici -ntes
   fornicatione Bi II. 1 pr. cadere
   absolute = peccare Vi 21 (*ter*). Pa II.
   10. non -amus a proposito Bi V. 1, 5.
caedere: seruus *qui* furtum fecerit fragilis
   -atur Wa P 20.
caelestis medicina Gi 1 = Cu II. 2. pater
   celestis Bi IV. 7. uirtutes -es Vi 29.
caelum: regna -orum Bi pr. 48.
caligines 'eye sicknesses' Co B pr.
calix *sacrificii*: -cem tenere Da 12. perfundere aliquid de -ce, stillat aliquid
   de -ce, *sim.* Cu (XI). 4. 6. 26. 27. 28.

causa (*cont.*).
　utilior Pa II. 21. aliquid -ae excusabilis
　Cu (XI). 10. — c. ante iudicata Wa A
　41. finiatur, difiniatur Wa A 43 (P 44,
　45). sine -a discedat Wa P 3. -am con-
　ponat Wa A 35. -a *aliquem* con-,
　repetere Wa A 37, 43 (P 40, 44). nullam
　habeat -am, *sim.* Wa A 17. 27. 35. 48.
　P 16. 22. 27. 39. 55. — *redundat*: c.
　breuitatis Vi ps. profectus Pa II. 21.
　uulneris Ad 20. *u. Ind. Gramm.*
　(**praepositiones**).
celari hominibus Vi 10. celare (=
　abscondere) *cinerem* Cu (XI). 26.
caeleri medicina penitentiae preuenire
　perpetuas poenas Vi 22.
celeritate penitentiae adiuuari Vi 13.
cella *monachi* Bi VI. 3, 3. 4. 6. in -a aliena
　ieiunare Hi II. 12 (P).
c(a)ena: -am faciat seruis Dei Vi 35. -am
　suam non praesummat Gi 7. -a priua-
　tur Gi 10. -a careat *u.* carere *et Ind.
　Gramm.* (**formulae**).
c(a)enodoxia Bi VII. tit. pr. VII. 4 (*ter*).
centissimi *in ecclesia fructus* Pa II. 18.
cerebri cutis, pampae Wa A 11 (P 9).
certe: uel c. Co A 2.
ceruis(s)a: Gi 22. Da 11. Cu I. 1. paruum
　de herbisa Hi II. 12 (P).
cerui, -orum medullae *non manducandae*
　Ad 19. 20.
cessauit desiderium peccati Pa II. 11. non
　-ndum est eripere predam *diabolo* Vi
　34.
ceteri: ne c. *malis* consentiant Cu (VIII).
　16. suauiora -is sumere Cu I. 5 = Bi
　I. 4, 3. ceterum 'otherwise' Bi II. 7.
　de -o Vi 21. Bi VIII. 2, 2.
chrismal: aqua quae in crismali fuerit Cu
　(XI). 22. cr. alicuius sancti Ca 1. per-
　dere suum crismal Cu (XI). 3.
cibus (cy-): Da 11. pinguior Bi I. 3, 1.
　siccatus Cu (XI). 14. infirmis licet
　omni hora -um summere Bi I. 10.
　inmunda manu -um tangere Bi I. 5, 8.
　uti -is Co B. 20. qui accipit post -um
　sacrificium Bi I. 3, 4. c. denegatur
　hospiti Hi V. 6. -um furari Aq 4 = Cu
　I. 12 = Bi I. 4, 1. *cf.* de furentibus -um
　Bi I 4 tit. — de modico -orum saluatur
　cenodoxia Bi VII. 4. abstinens se a -is
　suculentioribus Co B 14. abstinentia
　insolubilis a -is Pa II. 14. sine -o Cu
　(VIII). 4 = Bi VIII. 4. sine -o potu-
　que, *sim.* Hi II. 3. 4. V. 6. *u.* **formulae**
　in Ind. Gramm.
cinis *sacrificii* Cu (XI). 20. 23.
circuitio: omissa uerborum in breui -ne
　collegere Bi pr. 28.

circumciditur qui natus est *mystice inter-*
　pretatur Bi pr. 19.
cito conuertere Hi III. 8.
ciuitas quae non suscipit *apostolos* Hi V.
　3. in agro -tis Wa (AB) 63.
clam commedere Co A 2.
clamare: si sanctimonialis turbata -uerit
　Bi IV. 6, 6.
clamor Bi IV. pr. IV. 6 tit. 6, 1 (*bis*).
claude hostium et fenestras tuas Bi VI. 2,
　3. clausus peniteat Aq 1. 2. Cu III. 7.
　u. carcer.
clericatus: accipere, amittere -us officium
　Vi 10. 11. 15. 21. sine ministerio,
　officio -us Vi 8. 12.
clericus *passim in* Pa I. Vi. Co B. *praeterea*
　Cu II. 17. III. 14 (= Bi III. 6, 2). Pa
　II. 18. Bi II. 1 pr. IV. 3, 1. c. de una
　plebe, non de una plebe Cu II. 33 =
　Bi II. 11, 2. c. plebis Hi I. 28. plebilis
　Bi II. 6, 4. -i bibentes intinctum a laico
　Bi I. 6 tit. clericus (*cum laico*) *litigans*
　Wa A 37. 43. 56. 57. P 40. 41. 44. 65.
　66. -um occidere Bi IV. 1, 2.
clerus Pa I pr.
cl(i)entel(l)a: Vi 27 *bis.* Co B 8. *u.*
　glantella.
coaequales uiros reddere Ca 3. -i peni-
　tentia utatur Pa I. 11. iuxta quod
　meretur quoaequalia sentiat Co A 12.
coagulatum lac Cu (XI). 14. sanguis -us
　Ad 14. 20.
coaptare: opusculum quod -uit Uinniaus
　'suis . . . filiis Vi ps.
coartare: situs locorum -at Pa II. 17.
coctio carnis Ad 12. 13. 20.
cocus *monasterii* Co B 29.
cenubium (*i.e.* coenobium): si carne
　habundat c. Gi 22. alterius patriae -o
　uiuat Aq 1.
co(h)ercere se a licitis Cu pr. 15. *pecca-*
　torem ab errore Bi pr. 34. scelus ferula
　Bi pr. 28.
coetus sanctorum, *i.e. ecclesia* Cu (IV). 16.
cogere: qui -it aliquem ut inebrietur Da 3
　= Cu I. 2. *cf.* Da 4. si sacrificium
　uomere -atur Co A 6. nisi causa maioris
　profectus . . . -at Pa II. 21. necessitas
　-it Bi I. 5, 4. necessitate coactus Bi III.
　3, 2. — reddere, exsoluere cogatur,
　sim. Co B 21. Wa A 29. 46. P 9. 13. 24.
　52.
cogitare *mala, peccatum* Vi 2. 3.
cogitatio: stabilitas -nis Bi VI. 3, 2.
　nutant -nes Bi VI. 3, 6 (*bis*). iterum
　ueniunt *ibid.* -nes uarias habere Bi VI.
　3, 7. — c. maligna Vi 2. *cf.* Cu II. 14.
　per -nem peccare Vi 1. Co A 2. in-
　pugnatione -nis coinquinari Cu II. 13.

com(-n-)pellere: uestro amore conpulsus Vi ps. quali -pulsus est grauatione peccare Cu ps. I = Bi pr. 2. — si quis fuerit homicidi in iudicio -pulsus Wa A 3. *cf.* 30.

conpendiosas caraxamus eglotas Bi pr. 6.

conpendi ratione intimare Cu pr. 1.

conpeti iudicio, ad iudicium Wa P 2. A 29 (P 24). (causa) *aliquem* conpetere Wa A 37 (P 40. 41). A 43 (P 44).

complere desideria labiis Vi (3) = Cu (X). 16. uoluntatem Vi (4) = Cu (X). 17. paratus ad -nda *peccata* Co A 2.

conponere medicamenta Co B pr. — ('to compound'): causam Wa A 35. de furto (furem P) se nouerit -endum Wa A 19 (P 28). secundum iudicium (leges P) -i (-endum P) Wa A 50 (P 58). legibus Wa P 67. triplum Wa A 37.

conpossitionem accipere Wa P 67.

com(-n-)probari *de paenitentibus* Vi 23. Co B 1. *emptionem* testibus -et Wa A 20. *cf.* P 29. si -tum fuerit *delictum* Wa P 17. 47. (-tus A 37). titulus -ndi Wa A 4. P 3. 23.

conprobatorium Bi pr. 14.

conpugnare armis Pa I. 8.

conpunctio cordis Bi pr. 69.

conpungi Vi 31 (S).

concedere: non -itur *ancillam coniugem dimittere* Wa A 60. matrimonium non ad libidinem -ssum est Vi 46.

concilium 'assembly, community' Cu (VIII). 4 = Bi VIII. 4.

concipere filium Vi 46. *absolute* Bi II. 9, 3. concepto semine Cu II. 30. Bi pr. 17. c. rancorem Cu (IV). 1 = Bi IV. 4.

concoitus mulieri Hi I. 5. mulieris Bi II. 5, 2.

concordia uirtutum Bi pr. 48.

concubina Vi 40 (S). -am ancellam habere Wa A 59.

concupiscentia carnalis Vi 46.

concupiscere feminam, *sim.* Vi 16. 17 (perseueranter). Co B 11. uxorem proximi Co B 23. qui -it mente tantum fornicari Cu II. 11. Bi II. 1, 5. si quis concupierit hominem occidere Co A 2.

condemnare: *confitentem delictum* a nullo condempnari (damnari P) praecipimus Wa A 37 (P 46).

condictione damnetur Wa A 44 (P 48).

confabulatio *monachi et uirginis* Pa I. 9. -ne fratrem derogare Cu (VIII). 15.

confessio criminum, peccatorum, *sim.* Cu pr. 6. Hi II. 3. 4. Wa 37 (P 46). plena -ne ueniam petere Vi 5. -nes de commotionibus animi Co B 30. dari diligentius Co B 30.

confestim penitere Vi 1. *cf.* Co A 11.

confirmare: omnes negutiatio subscriptione -nda est Pa II. 30. boni -ndi obtentu Cu (VIII). 16. confirmat *auctor canonis* Ad 17. Iacobo -nte Cu pr. 11.

confiteri culpam Co B 23. peccatum Gi 17. uitia Bi IV. 7. *absolute* Aq 7 = Cu (VIII). 13. Cu (X). 6. qui non uult c. ei qui se commotauit Cu (IV). 16. -atur ei cui mentitus est et sacerdoti Cu III. 17 = Bi III. 5, 3.

confractiones Co B pr.

confugere ad senum aeclesiae Pa II. 9. ad penitentiam Bi pr. 69.

confundere *proximum* Da 4. *peccatorem* Vi 30 (S).

conglobare: toti *monachi* simul sint -ti Co B 29.

conglutinatum *sacrificium* Cu (XI). 21.

congregare homines nominatim Wa A 4. *cf.* 31. *spolia ecclesiarum* Vi 30 (S).

congruum est Pa I. 31.

coniugales = mariti Co B 16.

coniugium: uoluntas uirginis uel patris in -o Pa II. 27. consanguinitas in -o Pa II. 29. prima -a Pa II. 28. mulieres a -o liberae Co B 16. xxx^m fructum Saluator -is deputauit Vi 46. sine diliciis -oque Cu II. 32 = Bi II. 11, 1.

coniunctio *coniugum*: abstineant se a -ne antequam communicent Bi II. 9, 1. — pacis c. Co B 30. — est aduersari nostri ad has *species tristitiae* quedam c. Bi V. 1, 6.

coniungere se, coniungi = coire Co B 16. Bi II. 6, 1.

co(n)iux: de meretrice -ge Ad 16. Pa II. 26.

consanguinitas: de -itate in coniugio Pa II. 29.

conscientia: considerit in -a sua Pa II. 11. sana -a (*abl.*) Ad 10. fidelis Pa II. 31. propter infirmas -as Ad 10. *cf.* 12.

conscius creator omnium naturali⟨um⟩ Bi pr. 26.

conscripta = scripta Pa I. pr.

consecrare: postquam -ti sunt a (*om.* ?) Deo Vi 27. se Domino c. Co B 8. periurare in cruce non -ta Bi III. 3, 3. c. aecclesiam Pa I. 23. *absolute* Pa I. 24. 28. -ta furatus Aq 3. Cu III. 7.

consensus: ex -u abstinere se Vi 46. iurare pro -u Lu 5 = Cu III. 11 = Bi III. 3, 4.

consentimus et sequemur Vi ps. ne *malis* -ant Cu (VIII). 16. -it *peccato* Cu (X). 9.

consequens lectionis series Pa II. 23.

misericordiam -atur a Deo Vi 8. nihil damni -etur Wa P 33. 34.

conseruandi foetus *gallinarum inmundarum* Ad 8.

consignare *aliquid* cum aliquo Wa A 19. 20 (P 28. 29). res ipsius -etur Wa A 28.

considerit (-et DJY. -at I) in conscientia sua Pa II. 11.

consimili persona iudicentur Aq 5. *cf.* Cu (VIII). 11.

consortium femine Vi 14.

conspectus: a -u Domini non recedere Pa II. 10.

constringere ad uitam perfectam Pa II. 17. -gui .x. mandatis legis Hi III ps.

consuesci Co B 7. 19.

consuetudine, pro consuetudine hospites non recipere Hi V. 2. malae -inis culpa Co B 19. in -ine peccati esse Vi 11. *cf.* 26. Cu (X). 12. Cu (X). 15 = Vi (2). Cu (XI). 16. si in -ine fuerint adsueti Vi (3) = Cu II. 8. in -ine habere uitium Bi I. 1. iterantes -ine Bi II. 2, 4.

consumere: sacrificium uermibus -ptum Cu (XI). 19. tristitia -it animam Vi 29.

consummare: in cena -bitur *paenitens siue paenitentia* Vi 35. usque ad modum sanguinis consummandum *maritus* continens fieri debet Cu II. 30. in septima die -tus est mundus Bi pr. 20.

consummatio saporis Cu (XI). 21. secundi psalmi c. Gi 19 = Cu (IX). 6. *paenitentiae* Bi I. 5, 1.

contemnere Deum fideiusorem Wa A 44 (P 48). ieiunium Bi I. 8 tit. I. 8.

contemptio uentris Bi pr. 49.

contemptor: bactroperiti hoc est -es solliciti Pa II. 17.

contemptus *inter superbiae progeniem nominatur* Bi VIII. pr. -us gratia Gi 15. Cu (IX). 5. per -um Co B 24. 25. Da 2. per -um arguentium Da 1. Cu III. 3.

contentio circa finem territorii Wa A 42 (P 43). caenodoxia -nes gignit Bi VII. pr. de -ne(m) Pa II. 24. Bi VII. 1 tit. homicidium ex -ne committere Wa A 1. ex -ne hereticus fiat Bi VII. 4. ex -ne (*u. app. crit.*) *contradicere* Co A 9.

contentiosus Cu (VII). 1 = Bi VII. 1. Bi VII. 4.

contentus tegmento et alimento Pa II. 2. nomine tantum amittat ministerium Pa II. 10.

contestari: Deum eis iudicem -ntibus Aq 5 = Cu (VIII). 11. euangelio -nte Cu pr. 1.

conti(-e-)nens fieri debet Cu II. 30. -tes Pa II. 18.

continentia Bi pr. 49. cordis et lingue Vi

29. in matrimonio Vi 46 (*bis*). matrimonii Bi II. 9 tit. *coniuges steriles* ambo manere in -am suam Vi 41. *cf.* Cu II. 28.

contingit *absolute* 'it happens' Vi 10. c. grauari me somno, dormire Bi VI. 2, 3.

continuus: ieiuna .iii. ebdomadas -as Bi pr. 5. continuo 'at once' Cu (XI). 22.

contradicere Co A 9. Cu (IV). 16.

contradictio Cu III. 15 = Bi III. 6, 2. finis -nis adiuramentum est Pa II. 23.

contrahere inmunditiam Bi pr. 23.

contraria humanae saluti uitia Cu pr. 15. (e) -is -a curare Vi 28. 29. sanare Cu pr. 15. quecumque dederit Deus siue prosperum siue -um Vi 41.

contrauenire *absolute* Pa I. 26.

contristare fratrem Cu (IV). 1 = Bi IV. 4. peccata -nt Bi V. 1, 2. -ri *miseriis temporalibus* Bi V. 1, 3.

contumeliae Bi IV. pr.

conuenire: iterum *coniuges* -ent Vi 46. discordare -it (= contingit) Pa I. 31. -it (= debet) offerre decimas aliquis Hi III. 7.

conuentus 'assembly' Hi IV. 3.

conuersari in monasterio Bi VI. 3, 5.

conuersio et salus aliorum Cu pr. 11. post -nem suam (*i.e. postquam clericus factus est*) Co B 8.

conuertere ad fidem Cu (VIII). 2. Bi VII. 2. peccatorem Bi pr. 31. si -sus fuerit *moribundus* in hunc mundum Vi 34. si -sus fuerit ('changes his mind') Vi 30 (S). *cf.* 31 (S). -ti ad Deum Vi 35. Co B 20. ad penitentiam Vi 44 (S). Hi III. 8. -sus *peccator* Vi 9 ex. (PB). Cu ps. 4 = Bi pr. 34. -ti *ad propositum castitatis* Pa I. 17 (*bis*). — laicus -sus Cu II. 22.

conuicina Hi I. 5.

copu(-o-)lari alio uiro Vi 45 (S). ei quem oderat caritate -etur Cu (IV). 4 = Bi IV. 4.

coquendum est intinctum a uacca, a suibus Ad 10. 11.

cor mundum non habere Co B 30. disposuit in -de suo Vi 6. paratus ad haec -de conplenda Co A 2. in -de peccare Vi 1. 3. mechatus est eam in -de suo Vi 17. amaritudinem in -de retinere Cu (V). 1 = Bi V. 3, 1. diuuersantur *peccata* in -dibus nostris Vi 29. det Deus penitentiam in -de uiri eius Vi 45 (S). intimo c. dicamus Bi VIII. 6. donec c. sanum fuerit Co B 30. leto -de sanetur *tristis* Cu (V). 1 = Bi V. 3, 1. euellantur peccata de -dibus Vi 29.

cor (*cont.*)
    consortium femine de -de suo absciderit
    Vi 14. mundemus *uitia* de -dibus nostris
    Vi 29. conpunctio -dis Bi pr. 69. con-
    tinentia -dis Vi 29. *Deus* -da omnium
    nouit Cu ps. 2. — in -de non in cor-
    pore Vi 17. studium -dis et corporis Vi
    10. adflictio -dis et corporis Cu pr. 7.
    stabilitas corporis et -dis Bi VI. 3, 2.
cornu *bouis* Wa P 39.
cornupetum (cu- H) animal Ad 7.
coronam suam perdere Vi 10. 37. renouare
    -am Vi 21.
corporalis quies Bi VI. 1, 2. demptio
    rerum -ium Bi V. 1, 3. -iter fornicari Cu
    II. 12. Bi II. 1, 6. gustare -iter Bi VI.
    3, 7.
corporum medici Co B pr. si adhuc in -re
    sunt Vi 23. pro fragilitate -ris istius
    eui Gi 1 = Cu II. 2. casti -re Vi 41. si
    fortis fuerit -re Hi V. 10. -ris cutem
    comedere Cu (X). 18. c. mortuum non
    infecit c. alterius mortui Pa II. 11. -ra
    bestiolarum Cu (XI). 14. — c. Christi
    Co B 30. Domini Vi 46. — *u.* cor *ad
    calcem.*
correptio: hereticum post unam -nem
    deuita Pa II. 4.
corrigere *peccatorem* Cu ps. 4. 5 = Bi pr.
    35. -gi superpositionibus Cu (X). 2.
corrumpere: tristitia quae -it Bi V. 1, 4.
coruus: bibitio curbi Hi I. 17. intinctum
    a -uo Ad 12.
cotidianus uictus *monachi* Gi 15.
cotidie gaudere in mandatis Dei Bi V. 3, 2.
crassus: caro suellae morticinis crasa Ad 6.
    sanguis -ior Ad 20.
crastinus: thesaurizans superflua in -um
    tempus Cu III. 3. in -o Cu II. 15.
creator Bi pr. 26. ante oculis -is Bi pr. 4.
    non iurandam esse creaturam sed -em
    Pa II. 23.
creaturam non iurandam esse Pa II. 23.
    -am uel benedictionem Dei perdere
    Vi 52. *cf.* Cu (IX). 15.
credere: cui plus -plus ab eo exigitur
    Cu ps. 3. sub uno fidei culmine -itur
    Christus Pa II. 13. fideles qui Trini-
    tatem -unt Pa II. 18. gentiles qui ante
    baptismum -unt Pa II. 31. non
    absoluendus lapsos a fide -amus nisi . . .
    Pa II. 8. credo . . . diregetur Vi 41.
crescere desinat quae non desinebat
    michari Pa II. 26. quanto magis -uit
    morbus egroti Bi pr. 1. *superbiae* uitium
    uirtutibus -it Bi VIII. 6. cenodoxia non
    -it in *monachis* Bi VII. 4.
cri(-e-)men (magnum), *i.e. peccatum graue,*
    Vi 12. 22. 28. 47 (*bis*). reuocare Pa I. 16.

plur. Pa I. 14. Co B pr. (capitalia).
    criminum confessio Cu pr. 6.
crucifigi iudicant sapientes eum qui
    sanguinem episcopi . . . effuderit Hi
    IV. 1.
crudelis id est díbergach Hi I. 4.
crudus: -am carnem comedere Ad 14.
cruentus latro *in cruce* Cu pr. 13.
crura ceruorum in pedicis fracta Ad 20.
crux: periurare in -ce non consecrata Bi
    III. 3, 3.
culmen: sub uno fidei -ine Pa II. 13.
culpa ingenui Wa P 4, serui Wa A 7 (P 6).
    sine -a occidere Wa A 7 (P 6). sine -a
    excedat Wa A 4. culpa prima *animalis*
    non causam habeat Wa A 35. prima -a
    nihil reddatur *pro cane* Wa A 62. Hi
    VI. 2. iudicium -arum Wa P tit. — c.
    laici leuior Vi 7. nostrae audaciae c. Bi
    pr. 4. malae consuetudinis c. Co B 19.
    deflere -am Gi 1 = Cu II. 2. delere
    Gi 7. diluere Gi 11. Co B 25. Cu I. 1.
    emendare Cu (XI). 22. conuertere de
    -a ad penitentiam Hi III. 8. confiteri
    -am sacerdoti Co B 23. c. per sacer-
    dotem abstergatur Co B 14. dimittatur
    c. Co B 15. diuersitas -rum Co B pr.
    magnitudo -rum Co A 1.
cultello interfici, interimi Wa A5 (P4).
cultus daemonum Co B 24.
cuncta cognoscere, curare Co B pr.
    uti . . . cibis . . . -is Co B 20.
cupiditas Vi 29. Cu III. 16. Bi III. 5, 2.
cupidus *clericus* Vi 29. facultate saeculi
    Bi VII. 4.
cura in peccata ulciscendi Bi pr. 28.
curare e contrariis contraria Vi 28. 29.
    uarietas curandorum Vi ps. cuncta c.
    debet confessor Co B pr. uitium Bi VII.
    4.
curationum genera Co B pr.
currere: qui praedicta a nobis uia -unt
    Bi pr. 69.
currus: in uno -u monachus et uirgo *ne*
    discurreant Pa I. 9.
custos animae *sanguis superior* Ad 20.
custodia: sub -a *paenitere* Pa II. 3.
custodire sacrificium Cu (XI). 1. canis
    qui -it peccora Hi VI. 3.
cutis cerebri Wa P 9 (*cf. glossam* A 11).
    commedens sui corporis -em Cu (X).
    18.
cymbalum: refugium cimbalis frangere
    Ca 1.

daemonum cultus Co B 24.
daemoniorum mensa Co B 24.
dam(p)nare: *confessum sacerdoti* a nullo -ri
    praecipimus Wa P 46. falsus episcopus

est -ndus Pa II. 16. condictione -etur
periurus Wa A 44 (P 48). *haereticus
conuersus* suam publice sententiam -et
Cu (VIII). 2 = Bi VII. 2. — damnari *paenitentia* Co A 12. Cu III. 12
= Bi III. 4. Cu III. 17 = Bi III. 5,
3. Cu (XI). 23.

dam(p)num rerum corporalium Bi V. 1, 3.
d. reddere Co B 19. medium -i poni
Wa A 9. nihil habeat -i Wa A 18 (P 11).
nihil -i consequetur Wa P 33. 34. quicquid -i pertullerit Wa A 21 (P 14).
quedam peccata ad d. quidem pertinent nec tamen ad interitum Bi pr.
10.

dare iuramento (iuratores) idoneos Wa A
18 (P 11). nisi algam per boues per
herba det Wa P 61. confessiones dari
praecipitur Co B 30.

debere *absolute*: quod -mus non negabimus Vi 34. — debito *adu.* Wa A 15. —
debitum (*subst.*) soluere Pa I. 8. 20.
fraudare 20. d. occissionis eius . . .
accipiatur Hi V. 11.

debilis: qui -em hominem reddit Cu
(IV). 9. (facit) Bi IV. 3, 1. ad integrum
salutis statum -a reuocare Co B pr.

debilitare proximum Co B 21. -tum
membrum Wa A 3.

debitor Wa A 24.

decernat abas *de offensione* Gi 18. antiqui
-creuere sancti Da 10. sinodus Hibernensis -creuit Hi IV tit. decreta
maiorum Bi pr. 4. *cf.* -um a senioribus
Bi I. 2, 3. -a sinodi Pa II. 25. simili -o
sanetur Cu (VIII). 5 (*u. app. crit.*).

decimae 'tithes' Hi III *passim.*

decimum: si minus -o substantiam
habuerit non reddet decimas Hi III. 6.

decipere: *haereticus conuersus* quos -it ad
fidem conuertat Cu (VIII). 2 = Bi
VII. 2. maleficio *aliquem* d. Vi 18. *cf.*
19. mulieris partum Co B 6.

declinandus ad plebem falsus episcopus
Pa II. 16.

decolorare: si -tur sacrificium Cu (XI).
21. *cf.* 16.

decoquere aurum Bi pr. 13. 15.

decresco: cum -uerit *sus morticinis crassa*
Ad 6.

decutere: meretrix -sso proprii mariti
iugo Ad 16.

dedignari seniori flecti Cu (VIII). 18.

deducere in periurium Lu 5 = Cu III.
9–11 = Bi III. 3, 4.

deesse: ut nullus desit numero praeceptum audientium Co B 29.

defendere: si aetas non defendit *peccantem*
Co B 10.

defensio: non ad reorum -nem facta est
aeclesia Pa II. 9.

deferatur fidelibus sacrificium Pa II. 13.
marina animalia ad litora delata Ad 1.
si quis plus illuc plumbi detulerit Bi
pr. 15. dilatus, *i.e.* delatus Aq 5 = Cu
(VIII). 11.

difiniatur (*i.e.* definiatur) causa Wa P 45.

deflere culpam Gi 1 = Cu II. 2. admissa
Co A 1.

de(di-, dif-)finitio 'ruling' Pa I pr. Cu pr.
1. per -nem (= intentionem) Vi 4.

deformem hominem reddere (facere) Cu
(IV). 9 = Bi IV. 3, 1.

defuncti fratris thorus Pa II. 25. oblatio
pro -is Pa II. 12.

degradandus *falsus episcopus* Pa II. 16.

dilator (*i.e.* delator) Gi 27. Aq 5 = Cu
(VIII). 11.

delere culpam Gi 7. facinora Vi ps.

diliciae (*i.e.* deliciae): in -is (delictis Cu
ps. 1) remanere Bi pr. 2. sine -is
paenitere Cu II. 25. 32. Bi II. 11, 1.

delictum committere Wa P 18. A 37
(P 46). gerere Vi 9 ex. (PB). commemorare -a Vi 9 ex. remanere in -is
Cu ps. 1. agnoscat -um suum Cu (V).
3 = Bi V. 3, 1. -um emendat Wa A 61.
-um, -a, pro -o repropitiare Cu ps.
3. 4 = Bi pr. 33. argui pro -o Gi 25.
secundum -um caedi Wa P 20. pro -o
disciplinam accipiat Wa A 26.

delinquere Wa A 26.

de(di-)luere culpam Gi 11. Co B 25.
Cu I. 1.

demandare *aliquid testamento* Wa P 42.

demere: res corporales si -ptae sunt Bi
V. 1, 3.

demergere *animam* in profundum inferni
Vi 29. liquor in quo mus -sa obiit Bi I,
5, 11.

demittere: si cassus mortis illum demis
(s)erit (di- HO) Wa A 47.

demptio rerum corporalium Bi V. 1, 3.

denegare cybum Hi V. 6.

dens: pars *animalis* quam bestia -tibus
intinxit Ad 18.

denuntiare 'to give warning' Co B 25.

depellere spiritum *tristitiae* Bi V. 1, 6.

deponatur *episcopus ebrius* Bi I. 1. -ere
amaritudinem Cu (V). 2 = Bi V. 3, 1.

deputare xxx^m fructum Saluator coniugiis -uit Vi 46. aeclesiae elimosina
-etur Wa P 53.

derelinquat heris heredibus Wa P 50.
-enda *patria* Pa II. 15. gallina quae
-iquerit oua Bi VI. 3, 5.

derogare fratri Cu (VIII). 14.

desiderium: redire ad carnis d. Vi 27.

desiderium (*cont.*).
osculari mulierem per d. Bi II. 1, 1. -a
labiis complere Vi (3) = Cu (X). 16.
d. peccati Pa II. 11.
desinat crescere quae non -ebat michari
Pa II. 26. *episcopus ebrius* aut -at aut
deponatur Bi I. 1. diabulus *animam
praedari* non -it Vi 34.
dispectione (*i.e.* despectione) ceteros
arguere Cu (VIII). 3 = Bi VIII. 1.
disperare (*i.e.* desperare): penitere et non
d. Vi 22.
disperatio (*i.e.* desperatio) Bi IV. 2, 1. V.
3 pr.
dispicere (*i.e.* despicere) praepositum Co
A 11. regis uel episcopi aut scribae
priuilegia Hi IV. 9.
disponsare (*i.e.* desponsare) mulierem
Christo maritoue Da 5. uirgo necdum
-ta Da 6.
destitutor Co A 12.
dispoliare (*i.e.* despoliare) monasteria Vi
30 = Cu (IX). 14.
distruatur (*i.e.* destruatur) heressis
temptatio Bi VII. 4.
detinere: nullus uillae capitalis alterius
siluam deteneat Wa P 61. superbiae
morbo detenetur Co A 11.
detractatio, -nes Bi VIII. pr. VIII. 3.
detractator Bi pr. 62 (detractorem *Bened.*).
detractio Vi 29.
detractor *clericus* Vi 29. d. *definitur* Cu
(VIII). 16.
detrahere proximo Vi 29. Co A 10. Cu
(VIII). 8 = Bi VIII. 2, 2. non est d.
uera dicere Cu (VIII). 10 = Bi VIII.
2, 2.
deuenire in heresim Cu (VIII). 1. ad
interitum Cu (XI). 19.
diuuersantur (*i.e.* deuersantur) *peccata* in
cordibus nostris Vi 29.
de(di-)uitare hereticum post unam correptionem Pa II. 4. quattuor genera
consanguinitatis Pa II. 29. blasfemiam
detractationis Bi VIII. 3. super-
habundantiam Pa II. 17 (DJ). *iuramentum* Wa A 36.
deuorare: relinquens *sacrificium* feris et
alitibus -ndum Gi 9 = Cu (IX). 1.
nullus alterius siluam -at Wa A 53.
dexterale 'axe' Wa A 5 (P 4).
diabo(-u-)lus: instincto -i Vi 24. uexari
a -o Bi IV. 2, 1. eripere predam de ore
-i Vi 34. -um perire perpetuo Bi pr. 25.
diaconus Pa I. pr. Pa I. 34. Gi I. 3. 5. Aq
1. 2. Da 7. 10. 11. 12. Vi 27. 49 (*bis*).
Co B 4. 6. 8. Cu II. 2. 4. (XI). 11. Bi
I. 2, 2. III. 3, 3.
dicere *idem fere ac* loqui: per labia Vi 16.

cf. 17. si cui dicitur separatus est Bi
IV. 6, 1. — falsum testimonium -ns
Cu III. 12 = Bi III. 4. dictis (*i.e.*
latis) legibus Wa A 57 (P 65). *u. Ind.
Gramm. sub* **formulae.**
dies: .xii. horis noctium -rumque Deum
suplicare Da 11. dies dominicus, -a Pa
I. 30. Gi 1. Da 7. Co B 28. 29. Cu II. 2.
Bi I. 9 tit. 9, 1. sabati Da 7. annus pro
die *iectoris paenitentia* Hi V. 2. diei
superpossitio Gi 8. ebdomadam -rum
peniteat Vi 5. 7. bis septenis -bus
inmunda *est mulier* Bi pr. 18. septima,
octaua dies *mystice accipitur* Bi pr. 20.
21. d. iudicii Pa II. 5. *cf.* Bi pr. 21. *u
Gramm. sub* **formulae.**
differentia uirium Bi pr. 26.
dignitas clerici Vi 49.
dignus: -a penitentia Bi V. 1, 2. -i sunt
Domini corpore Vi 46. d. es mercedem
tuam Pa II. 1. -um scelus gladio, d.
peccatum ferula Bi pr. 3. 28.
diiudicari causa ante iudicata *non debet*
Wa A 41.
dilacerare: caro delacerata canibus Bi I.
5, 4.
di(-e-)latio: sine -ne Wa A 29 (P 24).
dilectio Dei Vi 29. -nis gratia Vi ps.
diligens: studium -tius cordis et corporis
Vi 10. -ter amonuit Hieronimus Bi tit.
quae omisimus -tius persequemur Bi II.
1 pr. confessiones dari -tius praecipitur
Co B 30.
diligentia: cum omni -a Pa I. 16.
diligere fratrem Cu (VIII). 14. feminam
Cu II. 18 = Bi II. 1, 9. -ns mente
tantum Cu II. 20. somnum Bi VI. 2,
1.
dimidius: demedia paenitentia Co B 18.
u. Ind. Orthogr.
diminuitur annus de *paenitentia* Lu 9. si
-etur *circa uoluntatem*, tristis est Bi V.
3, 2.
dimittere uallum apertum in nocte Co B
26. monachos Pa II. 21. uxorem Vi 41.
45 (S). Bi II. 6 tit. 6, 1. de muliere
uirum suum Bi II. 7 tit. — in morte(m)
hereditatem Wa A 38 (P 42). neglegenter d. *sacrificium* Co B 12. saeculum
Co B 20. — culpam Co B 15.
diripere aliena Cu III. 5. Bi III. 2, 1.
diabulus predam nostre anime d. non
desinit Vi 34.
dirus: -a captiuitas Lu 4.
discedere *a monasterio* Co A 2. 3. si ab
aliquo -sserit sua uxor Vi 42–45 (V) =
Cu II. 29 = Bi II. 7. sine causa -at *qui
compurgatur* Wa P 3.
disciplina 'punishment' Wa A 26 (P 18).

discooperire genua aut brachia in lumento Co B 28.

discordare per discordiam Pa I. 31.

discrepantia qualitatum Bi pr. 27. uirtutum Bi pr. 27. 28.

discurrere non permittunt subditus (*i.e.* -os) Pa II. 21. homo uexatus a diabolo nescit aliquid nisi d. Bi IV. 2, 1. in uno curru Pa I. 9. — sanguinem d. (effundere A) Wa P 58.

displicere: bona natura Deo non -et Hi III ps.

disponere in corde Vi 6.

disputant de decimis Hi III tit.

disputatio Hibernensis sinodi Hi I tit.

dissipare: otiositas omne opus bonum disipat Bi VI. 1, 1.

distentio uentris Cu I. 6.

distributor *liquoris* Cu (XI). 16.

districtus: in -o proposito exalii Cu II. 5 (*u. app. crit.*).

diuersitas culparum, paenitentiarum Co B pr. uitiorum Bi pr. 26.

diuersis medicamenta generibus conponunt Co B pr. -a curationum genera *ibid.* -a peccata Bi pr. 28. -as naturas *Deus hominibus* indidit Cu ps. 2. *paenitentiam* -e repensandam Bi pr. 26.

diuidat praetium uacce in .x. Hi III. 7. substantiam inter Deum et hominem -ant Ca 3. sic ita aequale (equales P) -ant Wa A 20 (P 29). superhabundantia -itur Pa II. 17 (KQI).

diuina lectio Vi ps. scriptura Bi pr. 32.

diuturnitas cogitationis Cu II. 14.

docere patriam Pa II. 15. *peccatorem* Cu ps. 4 = Bi pr. 34. cella tua -bit te uniuersa Bi VI. 3, 3. iudicia quae natura bona -et Hi III. ps. lectionis series -it (-et QDJI) Pa II. 23. *u.* doctor.

doctor Columannus docuit Hi III. 2. si d. es et doces Pa II. 1. -is iudicio Aq 1. -es eclesiae Bi tit. *cf.* Pa II. 18.

doctissimorum quorundam opinio Vi ps.

doctrina *sacerdotis* Cu ps. 5 = Bi pr. 35. extra scripturas Bi VII. 2.

dogma ecclesiasticum Vi 32.

dolorem saturitatis sentire Cu I. 6. -e *euomere sacrificium* Cu (XI). 9. mensis in -e magno Hi II. 7. clamor -e ('mourning') excitatus Bi IV. 6, 1. -es animarum Co B pr.

dolum facere Da 7.

dominicus: oratio -a quae dicitur periculosa Cu (XI). 29. in nocte -a Vi 46. in -o Cu II. 30. Bi II. 10 (*bis*). qui tribus -is non communicauerint excommunicantur Bi I. 9, 2. *u.* dies.

dominus ancillae, serui Wa A 6. 7. 33. 48. 52. P 5. 6. 38. 54. canis Wa A 62. Hi VI. 4. *gregis* Wa A 34. P 39. messis Wa A 21 (P 14).

domus ubi habitat dominus Hi VI. 4. -um uendere Wa A 55 (P 64). canis qui in -u manet Hi VI. 3. in -bus suscipiendi sunt peregrini Vi 33. dormire, manducare in una -o cum laicis Hi I. 22. 24. 25. *cf.* Bi I. 7. in una -o sumitur agnus Pa II. 13. — domus = familia: sic est cum sua -u Hi V. 4.

donare rem alteri Wa A 40. res suas uendat et -et pauperibus Co B 20. *cf.* Cu III. 14 = Bi III. 6, 2. seruum ... libertate d. Wa A 39.

donationes Ad 15.

donum: pontificalia -a Pa I. 25. inuadere -a I. 26.

dormire in una -o cum laicis Hi I. 22. 25. *cf.* Bi I. 7. qui -ens semen fudit Bi II. 1, 4. si contigerit *monachum* usque mane d. Bi VI. 2, 3.

dormitatio: sine -ne *paenitere* Hi II. 3. 4 (B).

dos 'bride-price' Pa I. 22. Da 6. Wa A 47 (*bis*). — 'dowry' Vi 44 (S). Cu II. 29.

draco, *i.e.* diabolus Vi 34.

dubitat facere Vi 2. non -et inuadere Wa P 63.

dubius de uita Hi II. 7. absque -o Wa P 32. sine -o Wa A 21. 56. P 14. 63. 66.

ducatum praebere barbaris Lu 4 = Cu (IX). 13.

ducere alteram uxorem Pa II. 26. Bi II. 7. matrem aut sororem Bi II. 3, 2. — uitam solitariam Cu pr. 11.

dulce lac Hi II. 12 (B).

dulcitudo operis *apium* Bi VI. 1, 2.

duplex penitentia Bi IV. 6, 6. -iciter inmunda Bi pr. 18. -iter uindicetur Pa I. 28.

duplum restituet Wa A 30.

dura penitentia in peregrinatione Ca 1. 2. *cf.* 3. praestandi ratione (praestando uerum) durus Wa A 3 (P 2).

ebibatus (*i.e.* epibata) 'layman' Da 10.

ebriari Da 3 (inebr. Cu I. 2).

ebrietas Gi 10. Da 4. Bi I. 1 (*bis*). per (a)ebrietatem sacrificium uomere Co B 12. uomitum facere Bi I. 2, 1. 4.

ebrius Da 3 = Cu I. 2.

(a)ec(c)lesia: -am aedificare Pa I. 24. consecrare Pa I. 23. suam cognoscere Pa I. 2. indicere ieiunium in -a Bi I. 8. perdere *sacrificium* in -a Cu (XI). 2. *cum* pontifex in singulis habitauerit -is Pa I. 25. mulieres menstruo tempore

exul paeniteat Co B 1. 13. 20. Cu II. 17.
ex agro e. Wa A 45.
exterminari de patria Vi 31 (S).
exterris Vi 23 (V), *cf.* Cu (X). 3 *app. crit.*,
pro extorris.
extor(r)is de patria sua Vi 12. 23 (extorem
S). -es ab ecclesia Cu (X). 3.
extraneus ab omni Christianorum mensa
Wa A 59. -a femina Vi 36. peregrinatio
Ca 1.
extraordinarium opus Gi 22. 26. Cu
(VI). 1, 1.
extrimitas sanguinis Ad 20.
extre(-i-)mus: per -um quodlibet membrum Ad 20. -ae partis offensio *ibid.* in
-o fine uite Vi 34. in -a infirmitate Ad
20. in -o Christianorum ordine Co B
25. -a haec septima remissio Bi pr. 31.
exundante uentre Gi 7.
exurere *aurum e plumbo* (*in comparatione*)
Bi pr. 15.

facere cenam seruis Dei Vi 35. foramen
in brachio Wa A 14. plagam Wa A 50
(P 58). osculum Cu (X). 2. luctum Bi
IV. 6, 7 tit. misam Bi IV. 2, 1. orationem
Pa I. 28. homicidium, fornicationem,
furtum, *sim. passim; u. Ind. Gramm.*
bonum Bi VII. 3. — quod si grauiter
fecerit Wa A 53, si cogitat et dubitat f.
Vi 2. donec se -iat emendatum Pa I. 28.
diuersitas culparum diuersitatem -it
paenitentiarum Co B pr.
facies: alterius in -em alapam percutere
Wa A 13.
facile: non puto f. a quoquam homine
posse discerni Bi pr. 12.
facinus: ut deleantur -ora Vi ps.
facto peccare Co A 3. sanctorum -a
patrum Bi pr. 28.
facultas prohibuit *cogitantem peccare* Vi 3.
nemo *est* cupidus nisi -te saeculi Bi
VII. 4. ex -tibus nostris conpatiendum
est nobis *miseris* Vi 33.
falsi episcopi Pa II. 16. testes Ad 16. Bi
III. 4. -um iuramentum Vi 22. testimonium Co A 8. Cu III. 12 = Bi III.
4. -a testimonia Bi III pr. se -o dicens
captiuos redimere Vi 30 (V) = Cu
(IX). 14. sub -o nomine redemptionis
captiuorum Vi 30 (S).
fama 'bad reputation' Pa I. 16. Wa P 44.
45 (infamia A 43).
familiaris bestia quae est muriceps Cu
(XI). 18.
familiaritas femine, -arum Vi 14. 15.
fanum: manducare aut bibere iuxta -a
Co B 24.
farina Cu II. 2. (XI). 14.

fas: si f. est ferre foras *sacrificium* Pa II.
13.
fastigium: si in -um fuerint capta animalia
Wa A 21.
femina: primogenita numquam in -is
fiunt Hi III. 5. seu masculum seu -am
genuerit Bi II. 9, 3. inmunditia quam
f. pariendo contraxit Bi pr. 23. *Christum*
plorauerunt -ae Bi IV. 6, 7. — concupiscere -am Vi 16. diligere -am Cu II.
18 = Bi II. 1, 9. consortium -e Vi 14.
familiaritas -e, -arum Vi 14. 15.
fornicari cum extranea -a Vi 36.
femineus: cum masculo coitu femineo
peccare Co B 15.
femur: in -oribus, inter -a *fornicari* Lu 8.
Cu II. 10. (X). 8. 14. Bi II. 2, 2.
fenerare pauperibus Vi 30 (S). egenis Vi
32. aegentibus Wa P 52.
fenestras *cellae* claudere Bi VI. 2, 3.
fenum: lectum non multo -o instructum
habeat Gi 1 = Cu II. 2.
feris et alitibus deuorandum relinquens
sacrificium Gi 9 = Cu (IX). 1.
ferculum Gi 1 (*u. app. crit.*) = Cu II. 2.
Da 7.
ferire *aliquem* fuste Wa A 50 (P 58). lancea
gladioue Wa A 10 (P 8). lancea P 10. 22.
alapa alterum in faciem Wa P 36.
praeterea Wa A 56. P 65. 66. 67.
ferre foras sacrificium Pa II. 13. *fructum*
Pa II. 21. antiquorum auctorum approbatio tullit Bi pr. 6.
ferula dignum peccatum Bi pr. 3. uitium
Bi pr. 28.
festinemus curare contraria e contrariis
Vi 29.
foetus (*i.e.* fetus) *gallinarum* Ad 8.
adiect.: gallina quae dereliquerit oua
-a (*lege* fota?) Bi VI. 3, 5.
fideiusor Pa I. 8. Wa A 19 (P 28). Deum
(in) -em inuocare Wa A 44 (P 48).
fidelis anima Pa II. 22. cum -i conscientia
infidelem uiuere Pa II. 31. laicus f.
Bi I. 2, 4. layci -es Pa II. 18. f. peccator
Pa II. 31. si manseremus -es Vi 41. qui
non communicat in nocte Paschae f.
non est Pa II. 22. fideles *subst.* Pa II.
13. -issime frater Cu pr.
fides Bi pr. 49. -em habere Bi IV. 6, 3.
ad -em conuertere Cu (VIII). 2 = Bi
VII. 2. sub uno -ei culmine creditur
Christus Pa II. 13. -ei meritum Cu pr.
10. lapsi a -e Pa II. 8. sana -e adfirmant
Hi III. 1. sana -e sumatur *cibus* Cu
(XI). 14. *cf.* Ad 1. 6.
fiducia: cum -a arguere Cu (VIII). 19.
fiet de illo hoc quod scriptum est Bi pr.
16.

X

fraudare *aliquem* Cu (VIII). 28. debitum Pa I. 20.

fraude uesci Da 14.

frequentare *peccatum* Bi II. 10.

frequenter cogitare *mala* Vi 2. *peccare* Cu (X). 4. -tius Cu (X). 7. emendatur sono psalmorum -ter Bi V. 3, 2.

frigescit monachus uel uirgo de loco ad locum transeundo Bi VI. 3, 5.

frons: uacae arborum fruntibus pascuntur Ad 11.

fructus horti sicci Co B 15. terrae Hi III. 4 (*bis*). primitiae, id est primus f. omnis rei Hi III. 3. elymosinarum Cu pr. 4. penitentie Vi 35. 36. accipiant xxx^m -um Vi 46. -um perfrui (*u. app. crit.*) Pa II. 21.

fruges terrae Hi III. 2 (*bis*).

frustrare *aliquem* Cu III. 16 = Bi III. 5, 2.

fugam facere Wa A 45. petere Wa A 15. P 12. 50. ancellam aut seruum in -a praendere Wa P 59.

fugientem ancellam adpraehendere Wa A 52.

fumo expelluntur apes Bi VI. 1, 2.

fundere sanguinem Co A 5. B 9. 21. semen Bi II. 1, 3. 4.

fur per noctem occidi licet Wa A 27. -em se nouerit conponendum Wa P 28.

furare, -i Vi 24. Co A 2. 4. B 7. 19. Wa A 26 (P 18). P 20. Hi IV. 9. cibum Aq 4 = Cu I. 12 = Bi I. 4, 1. consecrata Aq 3. Cu III. 7.

furor Gi 17. Cu (IV). 7 = Bi IV. 3, 2. Cu (IV). 12 = Bi IV. 5, 1. Cu (IV). 13 = Bi IV. 5, 2.

furtum Pa I. 15. 32. Lu 1 = Cu III. 1 = Bi III. 1, 2. Vi 25. Co B 7. 19. Wa A 18. 19. 27. 28. 45. P 11. 20. 21. 22. 23. 50. Bi III tit. 1, 1. 2. capitale Wa A 45 (P 49). aliquid -i Cu I. 13 = Bi I. 4, 2. modici -i Cu I. 14. *cf.* Bi I. 4, 2. Cu (X). 10. 11. furta Bi III pr.

fuste ferire *aliquem* Wa A 50 (P 58). de -e interemptus Wa P 4.

futurum saeculum Bi pr. 21 (*bis*). 23. in -o Vi 22 (*bis*). 46.

gallina quae dereliquerit oua Bi VI. 3, 5. -ae carnem hominis gustantes Ad 8. quod intincxerit gallus uel g. Bi I. 5, 6. bibitio galli uel -ae Hi I. 17.

gallinaceus: plenitudo . . . ouorum -orum Cu II. 2 *bis* (*glossa?*)

gallus: quod intincxerit g. Bi I. 5, 6. bibitio -i Hi I. 17.

gaudere in mandatis Dei Bi V. 3, 2.

gaudium spiritale Vi 29. suscipiemus gloriam Dei in -o Vi 41. — 'drink of joy' Bi I. 2, 3.

gemescere pro peccatis Bi V. 1, 5.

gemma: de -a praeciosa magnitudo Hi IV. 2.

generare filium Co B 4.

generatio filiorum Vi 46.

genuculationes (*i.e.* geniculationes) Hi II. 4 (P).

gens: de Saxonibus uel de qualibet -te Wa A 20. gentes 'pagans' Pa I. 13. Hi III. ps. 'lay people' Pa I. 24.

gentilis homo Pa I. 8. — *subst.*: Pa I. 8. 14. 20. Pa II. 31.

genua in lumento discooperire Co B 28. flectere Cu II. 15 (*bis*). flectiones -um Hi II. 1 (P). 2 (B).

genus humanum Bi pr. 37. 48. — canem de -ere eius reddat Hi VI. 3. (restituat) 4. — quattuor -era *consanguinitatis* Pa II. 29. — diuersis medicamenta -eribus Co B pr. curationum -era *ibid.* tristitiae Bi V. 1, 1. *cf.* 2.

gerere dilecta (*i.e.* delicta) Vi 9 ex. (PB).

gignere *de uiro* Vi 12. 27. 37. 38. 40. Co B 2. 8. 14. Cu II. 17. 24. 25. 27. — *de femina* Vi 21. 46. Bi pr. 22. II. 9, 3. — ira -it homicidia &c. Bi IV. pr. *cf.* VI. pr. VII. pr.

gladium portare Pa II. 6. hominem -o ferire Wa A 10 (P 8). scelus -o dignum Bi pr. 3. 28.

glandella, glangella *u.* glantella.

glans: porci in -de (-des) ingressi Wa A 25 (P 19).

glantela (gland-, glang-): bibitio -e Hi I. 23. bardigium (?) post -am Hi I. 27. *cf.* Bi I. 6, 2 (*s.s.* ancilla). IV. 6, 2. 3.

gloria: suscipiemus -am Dei Vi 41. humana -a Cu (VII). 2 = Bi VII. 3. uana -a Bi VII. pr. libertas -ae Bi pr. 49. — illorum salus tua *sit* g. Cu ps. 5 = Bi pr. 35.

glorificare Deum Bi VI. 2, 3.

gnarus regulae Cu (VIII). 17.

gomor: pondus primitiarum, hoc est g. Hi III. 5.

gradus ecclesiasticus: Vi 27. Co B 8. Hi V tit. V. 7. 8. Ca 2. inferior Gi 2 = Cu II. 3. sublimior Da 12. lapsi post -um Pa II. 10. cum -u *peccare* Cu II. 6. sine -u Da 7. Cu II. 4. Hi V. 10. *cf.* si -um non habet Co B 10. qui cum -u cecidit sine -u surgat Pa II. 10.

grandis: si -e sit (*i.e. peccatum*) Co A 9.

gratia Christi septiformis Ca 2. g. Dei Bi IV. 7.

grauari saturitate uentris Cu (XI). 7.

lectus (*cont.*)
cf. 47. *monachus* cum laico uel laica Hi
I. 22.
legitimus: in duobus -is (diebus?)
abstineant coniuges Cu II. 30. -a dos
Wa A 47. *persona* -ae legis Wa A 59.
matrimonium sine continentia non
ligitimum est Vi 46.
leguminis talimpulo uesci Da 11.
lenire rancorem *fratris* Cu (IV). 1 = Bi
IV. 4. *cf.* Cu (VIII). 21.
lenitas *uirtus* Bi pr. 49.
leo: eripere predam ex ore -nis (*i.e.*
diaboli) Vi 34.
lepra esse inuidia iudicatur Vi 29.
laetali (*i.e.* letali) mursu captum pecus
Ad 18.
leuior culpa *laici* Vi 7. -ius paenitere Bi II.
3, 2. 6, 1. iuniores -ius uindicandi Bi
II. 2, 5.
lex: legis animaduersio Co B pr. legitimae
-gis *persona* Wa A 59. -gibus, secundum -ges conponere, reddere, *sim.*
Wa A 16. 57. P 58. 65. 67. — leges
ieiunii Pa II. 14. iubelei Pa II. 30. —
scientia -gis Dei Bi pr. 49. lex = sacra
scriptura Vi 29. Hi III ps. Ad 7. Pa II.
29. Bi IV. 6, 7 tit. lex metrica scriptione scripta dicit Ad 14. purgationis Bi
II. 9, 3.
libenter audire detrahentem Cu (VIII).
8 = Bi VIII. 2, 2. expetere Vi 44 (S).
referre *ablata* (= sponte) Pa II. 6.
seruiat ei l. Cu (VIII). 9 = Bi VIII.
2, 2.
liber Regum Bi I. 8. in eodem -ro (*i.e. in
Vitis Patrum*) Bi VI. 3, 4. 5. 6 tit.
excerpta de libro Dauidis Da tit. de -is
Romanorum et Francorum Wa A tit.
libera fieri oportet ancilla Vi 40 (S).
mulieres a coniugio -ae Co B 16.
liberare ancillam(-as), seruum(-os) Vi 22.
24. 40 = Cu II. 27.
libertas faciendi quod uoluerint Wa A 5.
gloriae Bi pr. 49. seruum uel ancellam
uel uernaculum -te donare Wa A 39.
libido: non ad -inem concessum est
matrimonium Vi 46. concupiscentiae
carnalis *ibid.* — *u.* liuido.
libram, -as argenti reddere Wa *passim.*
stagni Wa P 31 (*bis*). argenti -am ualere
Wa A 51.
licenter inlicita committere Cu pr. 15.
licere: a licitis licet ('even') cohercere se
debuit Cu pr. 15.
licita Cu pr. 15. Hi III. 3. -te Ad 8. -to
Co B 18. 27.
ligare aliquem iuxta episcopum Ca 3.
assina -ta Bi VI. 3, 6.

lingua lambetur *stilla sacrificii* Cu (XI).
26. continentia cordis et -e Vi 29.
linteamen, -ina *altaris* Cu (XI). 4. 11. 27.
liquidus: ad -um puri Bi pr. 21.
liquor *contaminatus* Cu (XI). 12. Bi I. 5,
11. 12. aliquid decoloratum -is Cu
(XI). 16. obsceno -e maculatus Gi 22.
perditio -is matiriae filii Hi I. 6, *cf.*
Bi IV. 2, 2. -is et mulieris Hi I. 8.
litem (-i AH) committere Wa A 46. facere
P 52. interci(-e-)dere Wa A 58 (P 67).
litus: ad -ora delata animalia Ad 1.
libido (*i.e.* liuido) Wa A 12 (P 51). 13
(P 36).
liuor Hi IV. 3. -es Co B pr.
locus in quo cecidit *sacrificium* Cu (XI).
23. 24. de -o ad -um transire. Bi VI. 3,
5. non motes -um *ibid.* unius -i mansio
Cu (VI). 2 = Bi VI. 3, 1. situs -i,
-orum *monasterii* Vi ps. Pa II. 17.
sepultura in -o sancto Ca 2. locus et
tempus et persona Pa II. 14. ab eo -o
euangelii Pa II. 6.
longanimitas Bi pr. 49.
longitudo paenitentiarum Co A 1.
longa consuetudo Vi 26. *paenitentia* Pa II.
3. *cf.* Hi II. 12 (B). superpossitio Hi II.
9 (P). -o tempore se abstinere Bi I. 2, 3.
loqui: qui solus cum sola -itur Cu (VIII).
23. tantum terrarum spatium a -ente
Bi IV. 6, 1. lex -itur Pa II. 29.
lucerna Pa II. 2.
luctare 'mourn' Bi IV. 6, 7.
luctum facere Bi IV. 6, 7 tit.
ludi pueriles *amatorii* Cu (X). tit.
luere: quando intra -itur calix Cu (XI).
28.
lugubris miseratio Cu (VIII). 16. uestis
paenitentis Pa II. 3.
lumentum Co B 27. 28.
lupi comederunt ceruos Ad 19.
lutum Co B 27. 28.
lux: usque uerum peruenerit in -cem
Wa P 23.
luxuria Da 4.
limphaticum (*i.e.* lym-) alimentum Cu
(XI). 15.

macies *suis* Ad 6.
mactare rixa hominem Wa P 7.
maculae pretium Cu (IV). 9 = Bi IV. 3, 1.
maculare uxorem proximi sui aut uirginem
Vi 36. Cu II. 23. *cf.* Bi II. 5, 1. puellam
Dei Vi 38. Cu II. 24. -i obsceno liquore
Gi 22. in rixa manum . . . hominis m.
Wa A 8. se communione sinistrae partis
Co B 25.
madefacere: humus quam aqua -fecerat
Ad 9.

magis = plus: si magis inueniat Vi ps.

magnitudo: similem occuli de gemma -inem reddere Hi IV. 2. m. culparum Co A 1.

magnopere pastoribus procurandum Bi pr. 3.

magus Hi I. 4.

maior plaga Wa A 50. *cf.* P 58. porcus Wa A 25 (P 19). profectus Pa II. 21. aetas Cu (X). 21. puer paruulus oppressus a -e Cu (X) 9. cum propinquis suis a minoribus usque ad -em Wa P 16, -es natu Wa A 36. -um decreta Bi pr. 4.

maledicere Cu (IV). 12 = Bi IV. 5, 1. Pa II. 4.

maledictio quae infert uitam eternam Bi V. 2.

maleficium Vi 18. 20. Co B 6.

maleficus Vi 18. Co B 6. -a Vi 18.

maligna cogitatio Vi 2.

malitia Bi V. 3 pr.

malus: poenitentia uotiui -i Hi I. 4. reges -i Gi 23 = Cu (IX). 11. -i actus Vi 35. pro -o merito inputatur Bi IV. 6, 7. — malum *subst.*: non obtinebit eum m. Vi 21. si omne m. egerit Vi 35. m. inauditum Pa II. 20. -a non recipientium sanitatem Cu (VIII). 16. -i uituperatio *ibid.* inscius alicuius -i Cu II. 18 = Bi II. 1, 9. canis quicquid, quod(cumque) -i, -um fec(er)it Hi VI. 1 (*ter*).

mancipium, -a Wa A 15 (P 12). 48 (P 55).

mandare: de eo quod -stis Pa II. 1.

mandata Christi, Dei Vi 33. 46. Bi V. 3, 2. .x. -a legis Hi III ps.

manducare: Christus *filiae Iairi* iusit dari m. Bi IV. 7. carnem Bi VIII. 3. usque ad uomitum Co B 22. cum laico uel laica Hi I. 22. *cf.* Bi I. 7. iuxta fana Co B 24. morticinam Gi 13 = Cu (IX). 3. 16. Ad 14 (*bis*). *cf.* 20. Bi I. 5, 4. morticinum Ad 6. in aquis suffocata non -nda sunt Ad 14. carnem cum sanguine prohibuit -i Ad 14. medullas ossuum ceruorum Ad 19. — canis quodlibet -et Wa A 62. Hi VI. 2. — *translate*: m. in obtractatione carnes fraᴛrum Bi VIII. 3.

manducatio Hi I. 24.

mane: usque m. dormire Bi VI. 2, 3.

manere: per duas noctes in una mansione non -eat Ca 3. extra concilium Cu (VIII). 4 = Bi VIII. 4. *ne* sub eodem tectu in nocte *cum femina* Cu (VIII). 23. *ne* in uno lecto -eant *coniuges paenitentes* Vi 45 (S). *cf.* 47. non -eat cum uxore sua *paenitens* Vi 35 (*bis*). non -eat cum alio in aeternum Co B 3. *coniuges steriles* manere in continentia(m) Vi 41. cum semipane . . . aquaque -eat Cu (VIII). 6. — m. fideles Vi 41. *in peccato* Cu III. 13 = Bi III. 6, 1. — animalia si intacta -serint Wa A 21 (P 31). si porci super (per A) annonam -serint Wa A 22 (P 15). — sanguis intra carnem coagulatus -et Ad 20. — omnia coram testibus *commendata* m. (perm. A) praecipimus Wa A 38 (P 42).

manifestum peccatum Vi 21.

mansio unius loci Cu (VI). 2 = Bi VI. 3, 1. per duas noctes in una -ne non maneat Ca 3.

mansuetudo Vi 29. Co A 12.

manus percutientis, interfectoris abscidatur Hi IV. 4. 7. -um suum redimere Wa A 57 (P 65). -um debilitatum facere Wa A 3. excutere P 7. maculare A 8. perdere P 2. pollicem -us excidere A 9. excutere P 7. uirga in -u *paenitentis* Vi 35. non idonea, inmunda -u tangere alimentum, cibum Cu (XI). 15. Bi I. 5, 8. -us sopinatae ad orationem Hi II. 2 (P). si sacrificium de -u (-ibus) *sacerdotis* ceciderit Cu (XI). 5. 23. tangere -u mulierem Bi II. 1, 2. -u, -ibus coinquinari Lu 8. Cu (X). 6. Bi II. 2, 3. in -u hominis, episcopi, presbiteri periurare Bi III. 3, 3. det fructum penitentie in -u sacerdotis Vi 35. 36. -us inpositio Co B 25. Cu (X). 18. Hi I. 12. Pa II. 8.

mare: alga -is Wa P 61.

marina animalia Ad 1.

marito tradere filiam Wa A 47. mulier disponsata -o Da 5. suum torum *post paenitentiam* maritus cognoscat Co B 18. m. *adulterae* Da 11. Bi II. 5, 2. Ad 16 (*bis*). dans praetium pudicitiae -o uxoris uiolatae Co B 14.

martyrii passio Cu pr. 13. Bi pr. 30.

masculum parere, gignere Bi pr. 19. II. 9, 3. primogenita in -is tantum fiunt Hi III. 5. *translate*: qui m. est et uiriliter aget Bi pr. 21. — fornicari cum -o Da 5. *cf.* Co B 15. Bi II. 2, 1.

mater: patri et -ri *occisi homicida* uicem pietatis reddat Vi 23. pater et m. *infantis sine baptismo mortui* Bi II. 11, 1. materia filii in utero -ris Hi I. 6 = Bi IV. 2, 2. m. *post partum* munda efficitur Bi pr. 22. fornicari cum -re Bi II. 3 tit. 3, 1. *cf.* 2. — mater aeclesia Pa II. 9. — pullus asinae ad -rem reuertitur Bi VI. 3, 6. foetus -rum inmunditia non polluit Ad 8.

materia panium Hi III. 5. m. filii in utero matris Hi I. 6 = Bi IV. 2, 2.

matrimonium: ancellam suam in -o sibi habere Wa A 60. continentiam esse in -o Vi 46. *cf.* Cu II. 30. Bi II. 9 tit. 9, 1. cum bonis operibus expleant -um Vi 46.

mederi animas Bi pr. 28. *cf.* Gi 18.

mediate (-im O) *pretium* soluere Wa A 58.

medicamina sacri eloqui Cu pr. 1.

medicamenta conponunt medici Co B pr.

medicina salutaris animarum Cu pr. tit. penitentiae Vi 22. caelestis Gi 1 = Cu II. 2. *cf.* Pa II. 22.

medici corporum Co B pr. potentia -i Bi pr. 1. -um quaerat *qui proximum uulnerauit* Co B 21. inpensa in -os Cu (IV). 9 = Bi IV. 3, 1. — spiritales -i Co B pr. *cf.* Cu (VIII). 16.

meditatio: (ex) -ne odii Lu 2. Cu (IV). 5. 7 = Bi IV. 3, 2. Bi IV. 3, 4.

medium (*i.e.* dimidium) ancelle siue serui Wa P 7. dampni A 9. *pretii* P 12. -a conpossitio P 67.

medulla ossuum ceruorum Ad 19.

meliora proferre Vi ps.

membrum 'limb' Wa A 3. 14. P 2. 10. Ad 20. propriis -is se ipsum uiolare Co B 17.

memorantur nomina *duorum episcoporum in eremo* Hi V. 2.

memoria: Hieronimus uir beatae -ae Bi pr. tit.

mendacium Wa P 23. Bi III. 5 tit. -a Bi III pr. -um inquirere Wa A 20 (P 30). iurare Da 16.

mendax Cu III. 16. 17 = Bi III. 5, 3. Wa A 58 (P 67).

mens: studium -tis Bi pr. 49. tepor Pa II. 3. tumor Bi IV pr. diligens -te tantum Cu II. 20. concupiscere -te tantum Cu II. 11. *cf.* Bi II. 1, 5. -te tantum sentire commotionem Cu (IV). 15.

mensa: separari a -a Cu (X). 3. *cf.* Pa II. 4. Bi pr. 36. Wa A 59. 61. ad -am *peccatoris sedere* Pa II. 1. Iudas ad -am Domini Pa II. 5. -ae daemoniorum communicare Co B 24.

mense ante praedict*um* tributum neglegere Wa A 30. si usque ad -em uitium non habuerit caballus Wa A 49. *cf.* P 56. — mulier. iii. -es debet se abstinere a uiro ante partum Bi II. 9, 3. — m. in dolore magno Hi II. 7.

menstruae mulieres Bi II. 8 tit. (in) -o tempore Cu II. 30. Bi II. 8, 1. 2.

mensura: per -a(m) *panis et aquae paenitere* Vi *passim. cf.* Co B 6. Hi II. 9 (B). — m. aquae Cu (VIII). 26. panis

Gi 1. 2 = Cu II. 2. 3. pane sine -a Gi 1 = Cu II. 2. bucelli -ae de tribus panibus Hi II. 5 (B). — -ae paenitentiae Co A 1.

mentiri Cu III. 17. Bi III. 5, 2. 3.

merces *confessoris* Cu ps. 5 = Bi pr. 35. dignus es -em tuam Pa II. 1.

merere: Sodoma penam -uerat Hi V. 1. aelimosina aegentibus -tur Wa A 46 (*cf.* P 52). — mereri Co A 12. Pa II. 12.

meretrix coniunx Ad 16. Pa II. 26.

mergere sacrificium Cu (XI). 22.

merito Wa A 52. P 59 (*bis*). 60. Bi pr. 28.

meritum fidei Cu pr. 10. *paenitentium* Cu ps. 5 = Bi pr. 35. luctus pro bono -o reputandus Bi IV. 6, 7 tit. pro malo -o inputatur illi pro quo non ploratur Bi IV. 6, 7. quanti memento -i tibi est Bi pr. 29.

mes(s)is: dominus -is Wa A 21 (P 14). sepes quae circumit -es Wa P 64. *cf.* A 55. — m. Dei Pa II. 18.

metricus: lex -a scriptione scriptus Ad 14.

miles Christi Ad 15.

minare, -i: capitali ei minante Wa A 55 (*si recte interpretatus sum*). si quis capitalis uicinum -uerit P 64. — minare porcos in glande Wa A 25 (P 19).

minor, minimus: a minoribus usque ad maiorem Wa P 16. minimi fornicationem imitantes Cu (X). 4. si quis de -is sine gradu . . . non susceptus fuerit Hi V. 10.

minister, *i.e. sacerdos*: Cu (XI). 27. 28.

ministerium clericatus Vi 8. *cf.* Pa II. 10. hora -i *monastici* Bi VI. 2, 3.

ministrare in uinculis constitutis Vi 33. *clerico* Pa I. 33. cibum Pa I. 34. basicilis sanctorum Vi 33. — *absolute de sacerdotibus* Da 1.

ministratio indigna Bi VIII. 6.

minuitur (*i.e. subtrahitur*) de reliquis *paenitentiis* dum non nouit Lu 9. — de -tis morum inconditorum Co A 8. de -tis causis Cu (IX). tit. de -tis sanctionibus Co B 25.

miscere: aurum plumbis mixtum Bi pr. 13.

miseratio lugubris Cu (VIII). 16.

misericordia Dei, Domini Vi 8. 12. 22. 29. — m. *uirtus* Cu pr. 10. Bi pr. 49.

missa 'mass' Co B 30. Bi IV. 2, 1. sollemnitas -e Cu (XI). 6. tribus modis separantur iusti ab iniustis: missa mensa pace Bi pr. 36. *cf.* Pa II. 4. — mis(s)a = lectio: Gi 19 = Cu (IX). 7. missa horarum, *sim.* Hi II. 2 (P). 4 (B). 11 (B).

mundare (*cont.*)
  coruo nulla coctione -ri potest Ad 12.—
  -emus *uitia* de cordibus nostris Vi 29.
mundialis: qualiter a -bus separatur Bi
  pr. 2.
mundus in septima die consummatus est
  Bi pr. 20. in hoc -o Vi 7. in hunc -um
  Vi 34. mori, mortuus -o Da 5. Cu (IV).
  5. 6. 13. Bi IV. 3, 4.
munda *est* mulier *post partum masculi* Bi
  pr. 19. 22. -us est puteus *humo proiecta*
  Ad 9. sues -a comedunt et inmunda Ad
  11. sacrificium sit -um Bi IV. 7 tit. —
  cor -um Co B 30.
munus: empti causa -eris Vi 24 (P). *Dei*
  -era Hi III. 1.
muriceps 'cat' Cu (XI). 18. Hi I. 18 =
  Bi I. 5, 7.
mormor (*i.e.* murmur) Bi VIII pr.
murmu(-o-)rare Co A 9. Cu (VIII). 6 =
  Bi VIII. 5.
mus Cu (XI). 1. 12. Hi I. 20. Bi I. 5, 8.
  10. 11.
mustella 'weasel' Cu (XI). 12.
mutare: notitiam Dei cognitam transgresione m. Bi pr. 8. si in monasterio
  conuersaris non motes locum Bi VI. 3, 5.

nasci: primitiae, id est . . . omnis animal
  quod primum -tur Hi III. 3. *cf.* 4.
  fruges terrae in uno quoque anno -untur
  Hi III. 2. maiores natu Wa A 36. —
  patientia pro ira . . . n. debet Vi 29. de
  tristitia rancor . . . -untur Bi V. 3 pr.
natura bona gentium Hi III ps. diuersae
  -ae Cu ps. 2.
naturalis frater Bi II. 3, 1. fornicatio Gi
  1 = Cu II. 2. non n. fornicatio Bi II.
  2 tit. creator conscius omnium -ium
  Bi pr. 26 (*u. app. crit.*).
necessaria suplicatio Vi 9 ex. (PB).
necessitas: si n. cogit Bi I. 5, 4. -te coactus
  Bi III. 3, 2. n. luti abstergendi Co B 27.
  cf. 28. certis -tibus conglobati Co B
  29. — in -tibus constituti Vi 33.
nefandum opus *Sodomitarum* Hi V. 1.
negare: non n. *communionem* Vi 34. quod
  debemus *ibid.*
neglegentia erga sacrificium Cu (XI). 19.
  cf. 20. ussus Pa I. 7. per -am, -a *peccare*
  Da 1. 2. Vi 21. Cu II. 32. (XI). 26.
  ieiunare Bi I. 9, 1. perire. Vi 47.
neglegere tributum Wa A 30 (*bis*). sacrificium accipere Cu (XI). 10. *bene custo-*
  dire Cu (XI). 20. -ns sacrificium perdere
  Gi 9 = Cu (IX). 1. *cf.* Gi 21 = Cu
  (IX). 10. -nter dimittere *sacrificium* Co
  B 12.

negu(-o- DJI)tiatio Pa II. 30.
nequaquam facere promittat Co B 19.
nescire mortem *animalis* Cu (IX). 16. *cf.*
  Ad 1. homo uexatus a diabolo -it aliquid
  nisi discurrere Bi IV. 2, 1.
nihil est Bi I. 5, 4. III. 3, 3. n. nocet Bi
  I. 2, 3.
nimis: saturatus nimis Co A 6.
nitens fornicari Vi (4) = Cu (X). 17.
  nitendum eripere predam *diabolo* Vi 34.
nocere homini Ca 1. Bi III. 2, 1. *cf.* Cu
  (VIII). 7 = Bi VIII. 2, 1. ictus . . .
  non -uit Cu (IV). 11. si quis . . .
  membro non -eat Wa A 14 (*cf.* P 10).
  nihil, non -et Bi I. 2, 3. 5, 8.
noctu *u.* nox.
nocturno somno pollutus Cu (XI). 10.
noctuus: si porci per annonam -am
  manserint Wa A 22.
nolens occidere proximum Cu (IV). 8 =
  Bi IV. 3, 3.
nomina episcoporum in parte eremi Hi
  V. 2. quando recitantur pausantium -a
  Cu (XI). 11. contentus -ine amittat
  ministerium Pa II. 10. sub falso -ine
  redemptionis captiuorum Vi 30 (S).
nominatim homines, uiros congregare
  Wa A 4. 31 (*u. app. crit.*); *sed* uiris
  nominatis Wa P 3. 32.
nona Da 11 (*u. app. crit.*).
noscere: qui nouerit postea quod tali
  abusus est potu Cu (XI). 13. *Deus*
  corda omnium nouit Cu ps. 2. se
  nouerit redditurum, *sim.* Wa *passim;*
  u. Ind. Gramm. sub **formulae.**
notescere: notuit coram Deo Vi 10.
notitiam Dei non habere Bi pr. 8. in -am
  homonum, hominum non uenerit Vi
  11. Co B 4.
nouitatem extra scripturas praesumere
  Cu (VIII). 1.
nouus: in tribus annis nouissimis *paeni-*
  tentiae Vi 12. in -issimo die Vi 41 (*u.*
  app. crit.).
nox: fur per -tem occidi licet, per diem
  non licet Wa A 27. per maiorem,
  minorem -tis partem Wa A 22. canis
  quicquid in -te mali fecerit Hi VI. 1.
  solus cum sola . . . in -te *ne* maneat Cu
  (VIII). 23. *abstineant coniuges* in -te
  dominica uel sabbati Vi 46. .iii. noctes
  antequam communicent Bi II. 9, 1. per
  duas -tes in una mansione non maneat
  paenitens Ca 3. in -te Paschae Pa II. 13.
  22. .l. psalmos in una quaque -te canere
  Cu (VIII). 26. .l. superpositiones una
  interueniente -te Cu (VIII). 27. —
  ingenuus faciens furtum -tu Wa P 22.
  si porci alterius super annonam -tu

manserint Wa P 15. — nox et dies, *sim.*
u. Ind. Gramm. sub **formulae.**
nubere carnalem sponsum Pa I. 17. alteri
uiro Wa A 47. nupto filiam iungere
Wa A 59. — nubere (*i.e.* coire) in
dominico Bi II. 10.
nuditas saeculi Bi VII. 4.
numerus: nullus desit -o praeceptum
audientium Co B 29. annum extra -um
peniteat Cu (X). 19.
nuncupare uirginem *puellam lapsam post
paenitentiam* Vi 21.
nutant cogitationes Bi VI. 3, 6 (*bis*).
nutrimen: debitor reddat *pecudem* cum
-ine suo Wa A 24.
nutrit furor homicidium Gi 17.

obire: liquor in quo mus -iit Bi I. 5, 11.
obitus: bardicatio post -um *certarum
personarum* Bi IV. 6, 2. 4. 5.
ob(o)edientia Gi 1. 4 = Cu II. 2. 5. Vi
23. Bi pr. 49.
oblatio pro defunctis Pa II. 12. diaconus
obliuiscens -nem adferre Cu (XI). 11.
de -nibus *peccatorum* Pa II. 2.
obliuiscens diaconus oblationem adferre
Cu (XI). 11.
obliuio Gi 15.
obloqui proximo suo Bi VIII. 3.
obreptio *diabuli* Vi 24 (V).
obsceno liquore maculari Gi 22.
obseruande sunt leges iubelei Pa II. 30.
locus et tempus et persona -itur Pa II.
14. -nda sunt prima uota et prima
coniugia Pa II. 28. quattuor genera
consanguinitatis Pa II. 29.
obstinatio Aq 6 = Cu (VIII). 12.
obtentu insoliti cybi Bi I 3, 1. boni confirmandi Cu (VIII). 16. gulae Cu I.
5 = Bi I. 4, 3. religionis Vi ps.
obtinere: non -bit eum malum Vi 21.
obtractatio Bi VIII. 3.
occidere *absolute* Pa I. 14. fratrem,
hominem, proximum, *sim.* Lu 2. Vi 8.
23. Co B 1. Bi IV. 3, 2. (parentes occisi
Co B 13.) *fornicatorem* Wa A 17. furem
Wa A 27 (P 22). *homicidam* Wa A 15
(P 12). episcopum uel presbiterum Bi
IV. 1, 3. monachum uel clericum Bi
IV. 1, 2. filium Vi 12. 13. si seruus
ingenuum -erit Wa A 5 (P 4). 6 (P 5).
si ingenuus seruum Wa A 7 (P 6). si
seruus seruum Wa A 33 (P 38). — si
quis -erit i. eiecerit episcopum Hi V.
7. — o. canem Hi VI. 3. 4. capallum
...-ssum inuenire Wa A 18 (P 11).
animal si hominem *uel aliud animal*
-iderit Ad 7. Wa A 34. 35 (P 39). —

uenenis hominem o. Da 11. in puplico
bello Bi IV. 1, 4. pro uindicta fratris,
pro ultione amici Bi IV. 1, 2. subito Vi
24. casu nolens Cu (IV). 8 = Bi IV. 3,
3. ex meditatione odii Bi IV. 3, 4. ex
odio Vi 24. concupiscere hominem o.
Co A 2. disponere in corde proximum
o. Vi 6. si iusti *cum peccatoribus* -ssi
fuerint Bi pr. 36. — de occidentibus
semet ipsis Bi IV. 2 (*ter*). — qui eicit
pauperem -it eum Hi V. 6. qui perituro
non succurrerit -it eum *ibid.* — spiritali
morte o. Pa II. 9. peccata capitalia -unt
animam Vi 29. tristitia -it animam Vi 29.
occissio Hi V. 6 (*bis*). 8. 9. 10. 11. Bi IV.
1, 3 tit.
occupare: somnolentus uigilia -etur Cu
(VI). 1. *cf.* Bi VI. 2, 2.
occurrere ad collectas Pa I. 7. ad secundi
psalmi consummationem Gi 19 = Cu
(IX). 6.
octaua dies, id est futuri saeculi tempus
Bi pr. 21. *cf.* 19. usque in octabas Pasce
Bi II. 9, 2.
octo principalia uitia Cu pr. 15. Bi pr. 39.
non plus quam o. dies esuriens sine
cibo potuque uiuere non potest Hi V. 6.
oc(c)ulum debilitatum facere, excutere,
maculare Wa A 3. 8. P 7. similem -i de
gemma magnitudinem reddat Hi IV.
2. — ante -is creatoris Bi pr. 4.
hodibilis Vi 21.
odisse: ei quem -ierat caritate copuletur
Cu (IV). 4. *cf.* Bi IV. 4.
(h)odium repellere Cu (IV). 4 = Bi IV.
4. (ex) odii meditatione Lu 2. Cu (IV).
5. Bi IV. 3, 2. 4. ex -o Vi 24. effectu
hodii Da 4. odii causa Cu I. 3.
oeconomus: excusationem praetendere
yconimis Cu (VIII). 17.
offensus quis ab aliquo Gi 18.
offensio extrimae partis (*i.e. laesio*) Ad 20.
offerre *absolute* Pa I. 23. 24. 27. 28. 30.
Gi 24 = Cu (IX). 12. (sacra o. *passim.*)
sacrificium o. Cu (XI). 23. decimas Hi
III. 1. 5. 7.
officium *filii* Co B 13. — clericatus Vi 10.
11. 12 (*bis*). 15. 21.
(h)olera Gi 1 = Cu II. 2. Hi III. 5.
omisa uerborum collegi uis Bi pr. 28.
quae ibidem -simus hic persequemur
Bi II. 1 pr.
omne malum agere Vi 35. episcopi et
doctores, qui -ibus -ia sunt Pa II. 18.
(h)onerare: otiosus opere extraordinario
-etur Cu (VI). 1. *cf.* Bi VI. 1, 1.
operari: tristitia quae mortem -tur Bi V.
3, 2.
operarius Gi 1. 2 = Cu II. 2. 3.

opes: monachi sine terrenis -ibus habitant Pa II. 17.

opinio quorundam doctissimorum Vi ps.

oportere: non -et = non licet Vi 43 (S). 45 (S).

opportunus: tributum non oportune reddere Wa A 30.

opprimere infantem Co B 18. puer paruulus oppressus a maiore Cu (X). 9.

obprobrium Bi IV pr. 5 tit.

opus bonum Pa I. 10. Bi IV. 7. VI. 1, 1. 2. bona -era Vi 46. Bi pr. 15. *malum* Hi V. 2. nefandum *Sodomitarum* Hi V. 1. — o. *monachorum* Gi 15. 16. Cu (IX). 5. Bi VI. 2, 3 (*bis*). extraordinarium Gi 22. 26. Cu (VI). 1. o. *murmurantis* abiciatur Cu (VIII). 6 = Bi VIII. 5. uagus sanetur -eris sedulitate Cu (VI). 2 = Bi VI. 3, 1. — -era proximi *uulnerati* agat Co B 21. *cf.* Cu (IV). 9 = Bi IV. 3, 1. canem -era ipsius facientem restituat Hi VI. 4. opus *apium* Bi VI. 1, 2.

opusculum quod coaptauit Uinniaus Vi ps.

orare Vi 8. Co B 15. Cu (IV). 1 = Bi IV. 4. V. 1, 6. VI. 3, 7. *utrum* o. *liceat pro suicida* Bi IV. 2, 1 (*ter*). — orare in omni hora Hi II. 2 (B). hora (h)orandi Hi II. 2 (B). 8 (B). 9 (B). 11 (B).

oratio, -nes Vi 2. 12. 46. Cu (IV). 7. Bi VI. 2, 2. si quis cogitationes uarias habuerit quando orat, *tamen* sibi proficit o. Bi VI. 3, 7. o. pura Bi VIII. 6. o. dominica quae dicitur periculosa Cu (XI). 29. manus sopinatae ad -nem Hi II. 2. — o. omnis horae Hi II. 10. 11 (P). horarum Hi II. 3. 4 (P). 8 (P). 9 (P).

orbitas amicorum Bi V. 1, 3.

ordinare 'ordain' Pa I. 30. Bi I. 1.

ordo: ex, in -ine canere psalmos, *sim.* Gi 19 = Cu (IX). 6. 7. Cu II. 15. (VIII). 16. -ine .xii. horis . . . Deum suplicare Da 11. o. *paenitentiarum* Co A 1. — ordo ecclesiasticus Hi V. 10. *cf.* Aq 1. in extremo Christianorum -ine Co B 25. — laici(-o) -ine Wa A 43. 56 (P 66).

oriens: uir in -te Christum accepit in hospitio Hi V. 4.

ornare: utrum idoneis an falsis testibus †ornatam† fuisse Ad 16.

os: patres Domini ore subrogati Cu pr. 14. eripere predam ex ore leonis uel draconis Vi 34. de ore diabuli *ibid.*

os superius frangere Wa P 35. fracta ossa Ad 2. medullae ossuum Ad 19.

oscu(-o-)lari Vi 14. Cu II. 19 = Bi II. 1, 9. per desiderium Bi II. 1, 1.

oscu(-o-)lum simpliciter facientes Cu (X). 2. cum amplexu Cu (X). 2. in secreto praebere Da 15. inlecebrosum, -a inlecebrosa Vi 15. Cu (X). 2.

ostendere se Pa II. 15. incoeptum boni operis Pa I. 10. in simplici historia -itur Hi V. 2.

hostiarius Pa I. 6. Hi V. 8.

hostium *cellae monachi* Bi VI. 2, 3. canis .iiii. -orum Hi VI. 4.

otiositas Bi VI pr. 1 tit. 1, 1.

otiosus Cu (VI). 1 = Bi VI. 1, 1.

ouem furare (-i) Vi 24. Co B 7. 19. usque ouem uel porcum *fur moriatur* Wa A 27. caule ouium Hi VI. 4.

oua gallinacea Cu II. 2 (*bis in glossis*). Ad 8.

pactum cum Deo aeterno iniuit *conuersus* Vi 9 ex. (PB).

paene ut fidelis peccator iudicandus Pa II. 31.

p(a)enitentia *passim; haec tantum notamus:* laudabilis p. Ca 1. dura Ca 1. 2. *cf.* 3. integra et perfecta Vi 35. probabilis Ca 3. sincera Pa II. 3. demedia p. non debet esse Co B 18. p. per lungum Hi II. 12 (B). — -am iudicare Co B 19. tradere *alicui* Co B 18. in -a moderanda Bi pr. 3. — -am habere Hi V. 2. Pa II. 31. implere Vi 38. 53. submittere se ad -am Vi 4. -a uti Pa I. 11. — medicina -ae Vi 22. remedia Vi ps. modus Vi (2) = Cu (X). 15. temperamentum Bi pr. 4. tempus Co B 18. labor Vi 21. *cf.* Aq 7 = Cu (VIII). 13. fructus Vi 35. 36. — diuersitas -arum Co B pr. longitudo Co A 1.

p(a)enitere *passim; haec tantum notamus:* clausus -eat Aq 1. 2. cum fratribus Aq 2. 3. 4. exul Co B 1. Cu II. 17. inermis exul Co B 13. 20. peregrinus Co B 2. non -eant simul *clericus et clentella* Vi 27. — p. cum episcopo uel sacerdote Co B 1. cum episcopo uel scriba Hi IV. 9. — cum, in pane et aqua (per mensuram), *sim. u. Ind. Gramm. sub* **formulae.** cum tribulatione Bi II. 6, 1. in habitu laicali Bi II. 4 tit. — paenitentes *ordo Christianorum* Co B 25.

paenitudo Cu ps. 2.

pallor: cum -e *irasci* Cu (IV). 4 = Bi IV. 5, 2.

palmae supernae ad orationem Hi II. 2 (B).

pampa: capud percutere usque ad cerebri -as (.i. cutem, scamas) Wa A 11.

panes qui efficiuntur de tertia parte coaid siir throscho Hi II. 5 (P). bucellos mensurae de tribus -ibus Hi II. 5 (B). *u. Ind. Gramm. sub* **formulae.** — panes propossitionis Hi III. 5.

paradis(s)us: latro in -o Pa II. 5. serpens Euam de -o eiecit Bi VIII. 3.

parentes: homicida -ibus *occisi* traditur Wa A 5 (*cf.* P 4). satis faciat -ibus *occisi* Co B 1. reddens uicem -ibus occisi pietatis et officii Co B 13. parentes *homicidae* iura reddant Wa A 15 (*cf.* P 12). — *fornicator uirginis* dotem det -ibus Da 6. reddito humiliationis eius praetio -ibus Co B 16.

parere: inmunda fit mulier quae . . . peperit Bi pr. 17. *cf.* 19. 23.

(parochia): parruchia Pa I. 30. 34. de parrochias cum monachis Pa II. 20.

parricidium Hi I. 1. Bi IV. 1, 1.

pars *corporis animalis* Ad 5. 20. *sacrificii* Cu (XI). 2. — duae -tes ancellae unius Hi V. 9. -tem *compositionis* restituant Wa P 12. — pars eis data est cum his quorum delicta repropitiauerunt Cu ps. 3 = Bi pr. 33. *cf.* Cu ps. 5 = Bi pr. 35. — parte (*i.e.* regione) qua poterant euadere Wa P 59. in -te eremi Hi V. 2. — communio sinistrae -tis Co B 25.

partum perdere Vi 20. mulieris -um decipere Co B 6. mulier .iii. menses abstin*eat* a uiro ante -um Bi II. 9, 3. *uir a coniuge* post -um Cu II. 31. glandella moriens in -u Bi IV. 6, 3.

paruipendens dispicere Hi IV. 9.

parumper Cu II. 2 (parum Gi 1).

paruulus puer oppressus a maiore Cu (X). 9. — si p. absque babtismum abscesserit Vi 47. si clericus non susciperit -um Vi 48 (V). p. decem annorum aliquid furti faciens Cu I. 13 = Bi I. 4, 2. p. usque annum .xu. pro delicto nihil reddat Wa A 26 (*cf.* P 18). -i se inuicem percutientes Cu (X). 21.

paruum sanguinem cernimus fluxisse Ad 20. sine somno nisi -um Hi II. 2. -um aliquid iniquitatis Bi pr. 15. p. peccatum Cu (VIII). 20.

pasci: uacae herbis -untur Ad 11.

pascua pecorum Hi VI. 1.

pas(s)io: qua inpugnatur -ne Cu ps. 1 = Bi pr. 2. — p. martyrii Cu pr. 13. Bi pr. 30. — .l. diebus post -nem Gi 1.

pastores eclesiae Bi tit. pr. 3.

pastoria 'fetter' Wa P 63 (pedica A 54).

pastoriare caballum Wa P 63.

pater: de uoluntate uirginis et -ris in coniugio Pa II. 27 (*ter*). dos -ri dari iubetur Wa A 47. p. et mater hominis *occisi* Vi 23. *infantis sine baptismo mortui* Bi II. 11, 1. — p. celestis Bi IV. 7. —

antiqui -res Gi 5. sanctorum facta -rum Bi pr. 28. canones -rum Bi IV. 6 tit. priorum -rum diffinitiones Cu pr. 1. -rum statuta Cu pr. 14. (X). tit. uoluntate -rum Wa A 59. ordo *paenitentiarum* a sanctis traditur -ribus Co A 1.

patientia Vi 29. 45 (S). Bi pr. 49.

patria: extorris de -a Vi 12. *cf.* 23. exterminari de -a Vi 31 (S). non in sua -a Vi 24. *parentes homicidae* de -a uadant Wa A 15 (P 12). recipiatur in -a(m) Vi 23. Co B 1. -ae restituuntur Wa A 15. relinquenda uel docenda p. Pa II. 15. — ('country', *Gall.* 'pays':) alterius -ae cenubio uiuat Aq 1. si in una -a . . ., si in alia Wa P 57.

patrius: ad solum -um peruemiat Ca 1.

paulisper: sine somno nisi p. Hi II. 2 (B).

pauper uictus Gi 22. qui iecit -em occidit eum Hi V. 6. dare (donare, erogare, *sim.*) -ibus Vi 22. 30 (S). 32. 36 (V). Co B 19. 20. Cu III. 3. 14 = Bi III. 6, 2. Cu (IX). 14. *cf.* Vi 30 (V).

pausantium nomina recitantur Cu (XI). 11.

pax Bi pr. 49. — 'kiss of peace' (*Hib.* póg) Gi 1 = Cu II. 2. Co B 30. Pa II. 4. Bi pr. 36.

paxmati(ui) panis mensura Gi 1 = Cu II. 2. cum semipane -iuo Cu (VIII). 26. (paximatiui, -tio Cu (E) II. 2. (VIII). 26.)

peccare *passim; haec tantum notamus*: per cogitationem p. Co A 2. uoluntate iam -uit in corde suo Vi 3. uerbo p. per inreptionem Vi 4. peccatis praeualentibus facto p. Co A 3. — peccare *i.e. fornicari*: Gi 3 = Cu II. 4. Vi 27. Co B 8. cum puella aliena Vi 27. Co B 8. cum uirgine uel uidua Da 6. cum muliere uel cum uiro Aq 1. cum masculo coitu femineo Co B 15. cum pecode Gi 11. Co II. 6. Vi (1) = Cu (X). 5. cum cane uel animali Lu 7. in sompnis Da 9 = Cu II. 16. — si *canis* iterum -uerit Wa A 62. — peccans = peccator: Cu II. 12 = Bi II. 1, 6 (*u. app. crit.*). Bi tit. pr. 2. 26. 28.

peccator Vi 34. Cu ps. 4 = Bi pr. 34. Pa II. 1. 31. Bi pr. 7. 31. 36.

peccatrix Vi 34.

peccatum *passim; haec tantum notamus*: capitalia a Da 10. magna et capitalia Vi 29. capitalia et carnalia Co B 30. p. paruum Cu (VIII). 20. pudendum Cu (VIII). 22. sodomiticum Co A 3. — matrimonium sine continentia est p. Vi 46. p. *et* scelus *distinguuntur* Bi pr.

peccatum (*cont.*).
3. quedam -a ad damnum pertinent nec tamen ad interitum Bi pr. 10. in -o praeueniri Bi pr. 25. pro -is gemescere Bi V. 1, 5. pondera -orum pensare Cu ps. 2.

pectus percutere Vi 1.

pec(c)unia Vi 9. 35. Bi IV. 1, 2.

pecus (*in casibus obliquis et in plurali saepe* pecc- *scribitur*): p. perdere Wa P 17. praedarum -ora Ad 15. canis -orum Hi VI. 1. qui custodit -ora Hi VI. 3. pascua -orum Hi VI. 1. quodcumque bestiae commedent de -oribus Hi VI. 3. decimae -orum Hi III. 1. *cf.* 4. morticina (-um) -oris Hi I. 19. Bi I. 5, 12. -ora de rupe cadentia Ad 2. in extrima infirmitate mortua Ad 20. laetali mursu captum p. -oribus comedendum Ad 18. urinam -oris bibere Bi I. 5, 3. cum -oribus coire Bi II. 2, 1. p. si percuserit hominem Wa (AB) 63.

pecus (*gen.* -udis): pecodem conparare Wa A 19. tollere Wa A 24. pecodem furti (*uid. app. crit.*) inuenire Wa A 18. cum -odibus fornicari Da 11. peccare cum -ode Gi 11. Vi (1) = Cu (X). 5. Cu II. 6.

pedica: caballum in -am ruere Wa A 54. fracta in -is crura *ceruorum* Ad 20.

pedecle (*i.e.* pediculae) Cu (X). 18 (peducli E).

pelles in ussus uarios habebimus Ad 20.

pendat ('let him atone') extraordinario opere Gi 22.

penitus: ne p. anima intereat Gi 1 = Cu II. 2.

pensare pondera peccatorum Cu ps. 2.

penuria ingenii Vi ps.

percus(s)io Co B 26. Hi IV. 8.

percusor Hi IV. 8.

percutere *aliquem* Vi 6. 8. Co A 2. Wa A 57. P 35. Hi IV. 4. 5. per rixam Co A 5. B 9. flagillo Wa P 53. se inuicem Cu (X). 21. alterius in faciem alapam Wa A 13. capud alterius Wa A 11 (P 9). animal Wa (AB) 63. equus aut pecus si -serit hominem Wa (AB) 63. -sit Deus Egyptum .x. plagis Hi III ps. *translate*: peccatum gladio Bi pr. 3. — -iat pectus suum Vi 1.

perdere aliquem maleficio Co B 6. animam Vi 47. Bi VIII. 3. partum alicuius Vi 20. — ancellam aut seruum Wa A 31 (P 32). capallum Wa P 33. pecus Wa P 17. *cf.* 34. manum &c. Wa P 2. creaturam uel benedictionem Dei Vi 52. *cf.* Cu (IX). 15. crismal Cu (XI) 3. sacrificium Gi 9. Co A 6.

B 12. Cu (IX). 1. *cf.* 2. usuram accipiens -at ea quae accipit Da 13. quicquid boni (bonum) fecerit *iactans* -idit Cu (VII). 2 = Bi VII. 3. coronam suam p. Vi 10. 37.

perditio illius rei Co A 8. — carnis et animae Hi I. 7 = Bi IV. 2, 3. carnis cum anima Bi IV. 2, 4. filii et mulieris Hi I. 10. liquoris et mulieris Hi I. 8. liquoris matiriae filii Hi I. 6 = Bi IV. 2, 2. mulieris de suo filio Hi I. 11.

perdurat sanguis coagolatus in carne animalis suffucati Ad 14.

peregrinatio Ca 1. 2. 3 (*bis*). perennis Lu 6 = Cu II. 7. Cu (IV). 6 = Bi IV. 3, 4. Ca 3.

peregrinus Vi 33. Co B 2.

perennis peregrinatio Lu 6 = Cu II. 7. Cu (IV). 6 = Bi IV. 3, 4. Ca 3.

perfectionis uotum, u. Lu 9. Cu (IV). 6 = Bi IV. 3, 4. -nem bonitatis adtingere Bi V. 1, 5.

perfectus: -a (*leg.* -e?) sana *facta est* puella Bi IV. 7. uita -a in etate -a Pa II. 17. penitentia Vi 35. -um sacrificium Bi IV. 7 tit. — -e Trinitatem credere Pa II. 18.

perferre: quicquid dampni pertullerit Wa A 21 (P 14).

perficere uotum Pa II. 17. *absolute* Vi 46 (V).

perfrangere sarculum Gi 26.

perfruat fructum in *sua* aeclesia Pa II. 21 (*u. app. crit.*).

perfundere aliquid de calice super altare Cu (XI). 4.

perfusio (*lege* profusio) lacrimarum Cu pr. 5 (*codices praeter* E).

periclitari Pa II. 15.

periculosa oratio Cu (XI). 29.

periculum: ubi p. adnotatur Gi 20 = Cu (IX). 9.

perire: soccurrere -turo Hi V. 6. si paruulus absque babtismum -erat Vi 47. p. perpetuo Bi pr. 25. cum plurimis Cu pr. 11.

peritus abbas Bi VIII. 3.

periurare Co A 4a. B. 5. 20. Bi III. 3, 3. 4.

periurium Lu 5 = Cu III. 8. 9–11 = Bi III. 3, 4. Bi III pr. 3 tit. 3, 1.

perlege euangelium Pa II. 6 (*u. app. crit.*).

permanere in exilio Ca 1. in peregrinatione Ca 1. 2. 3. in peregrinationis penitentia Ca 3. — in auaritia Cu III. 3. in inmunditia Bi pr. 18. in obstinatione Aq 6 = Cu (VIII). 12. in penitentia probabili Ca 3. — si -nserint casti Vi

Y

refugium crismalis, euangelii Ca 1. 2. baculis aut cimbalis Ca 1.

refutare morticina Ad 2. 6. *cf.* 10.

regio 'place' Cu (XI). 3.

regnare cum Christo Vi 46.

regnum Dei Cu (VII). 1 = Bi VII. 1. Bi pr. 37. caelorum Bi pr. 48.

regulae ueritatis exsecutor Gi 27. ignarus, gnarus -ae Cu (VIII). 17. -am blasphemare Co A 11.

reicere *rem emptam* Wa A 48. 49. reiectis armis *paenitere* Lu 4. Cu (E) (IV). 5. (IX). 13.

reiterare = iterare ('to do again') Co B 24.

reli(-e-)gio Bi pr. 51. -nis obtentu Vi ps.

reli(-e-)giosus Pa I. 25. Bi IV. 2, 1. ('in religious orders') Da 11.

relinquere hereditatem Wa A 45. *cf.* P 50. sacrificium feris et alitibus deuorandum Gi 9 = Cu (IX). 1. patriam Pa II. 15. *agrum* Wa P 26. *hominem* sub iudice flamma Pa II. 24. Dei iudicio Aq 6 = Cu (VIII). 12. Deo iudicium Bi IV. 2, 1. arma -at Bi IV. 1, 2. relictis armis Lu 4 (B). Cu (IV). 5. (IX). 13.

reliquus: ad (ab K) -am plebem declinandus *falsus episcopus* Pa II. 16. de -o Vi 4. Cu (VIII). 9. de -o uitae suae Vi 22. et -a (usque) *u. Ind. Gramm. sub* **formulae.**

remanere in delictis Cu ps. 1. in diliciis Bi pr. 2. totum -et aurum Bi pr. 15.

remedia penitentiae Vi ps. curandorum *ibid.* uitiorum Bi tit. *cf.* VII. 4 tit. uulnerum *animae* Cu pr. 1. Bi pr. 6.

remis(s)io peccatorum Vi 12. Bi pr. 30. *cf.* Cu pr. 2. Bi pr. 31. indulgentia et r. nostra Cu pr. 12.

remissus et efeminatus Bi pr. 23. -a *paenitentia* Pa II. 3.

remittere peccatum, -a Pa II. 31. Bi pr. 23. 30.

remouere: coram testibus *commendata* manere praecipimus nec -i Wa P 42. -tus uiuat Cu (IV). 12 (semotus E. Bi).

renouare coronam Vi 21. in ecclesiam renuetur Pa I. 15.

reparare genus humanum ad regna caelorum Bi pr. 48.

repellendus foras *superbus* Co A 11. -is excommunicatum a communione Pa II. 4. -re odium Cu (IV). 4 = Bi IV. 4.

repensare .xii. triduana pro anno Cu (VIII). 25. qualitatem uel quantitatem poenarum Bi pr. 26.

repetere auferentem quae sua sunt Cu III. 4 = Bi III. 2, 2. quodcumque eum

-ierit debitor reddat Wa A 24. r. *seruum libertate donatum* Wa A 39. *agrum* Wa P 26. quicquid ad eum fuerit -itum restituat Wa A 29 (P 24).— si laicus clericum causa -ierit Wa A 37. testes r. Wa P 30. — ('repeat') Co B 24.

replicet quicquid cantauerunt Gi 19 = Cu (IX). 7.

repraesentare ('restore') rapta Pa I. 15.

reprobat Christus *oblata spolia* Ad 15.

repropitiare delictum, -a, pro delicto Cu ps. 3. 4 = Bi pr. 33. 34.

repugnans tepidius *cogitationi malae* Cu II. 4.

repulsio 'expulsion' Co A 12.

reputare: nihil *quod puer deliquit* sub iudice -atur Wa P 18. de luctu pro bono merito -ando Bi IV. 6, 7 tit.

requiratur *finis* a testibus Wa A 42. *cf.* P 43.

rem alteri donare Wa A 40. de suis -bus habere potestatem Wa A 60. praetium rei abstractae Wa A 37.

residere in cella Bi VI. 3, 6. ut aliquid auri purgati -eat Bi pr. 15.

residuus: in -is tribus annis Vi 18. -o uitae *paenitere* Lu 4 (*bis*).

resoluetur *paenitens* a sacerdote Pa I. 14. a quietis proposito -untur Bi VI. 3, 4. aurum plumbis mixtum -re Bi pr. 13. *cf.* 15.

restare: reddat quod -at praetii Wa A 15. *cf.* P 12.

restaurare mancipium Wa P 12. dampnum Wa A 21. P 14.

restituere sanum *aliquem* Ca 3. seruos domino Wa A 7. mancipia Wa A 15. canem Hi VI. 4. *furtum* Wa P 18. 20. quicquid fuerit repetitum Wa A 29 (P 24). — maculae pretium Cu (IV). 9 = Bi IV. 3, 1. partem *pretii homicidii* Wa P 12. duplum Wa A 30. triplum Wa A 20. 27. septempliciter Ca 1. 2. — percusio eius ancelle praetio -atur Hi IV. 8. illud extraordinario opere -at Gi 26. si non habeat unde -at Cu (IV). 10 = Bi IV. 3, 1. — restitui altario Vi 14. patriae Wa A 15. officio Vi 12. statui priori se r. Pa I. 10.

resurgere a ruina Vi 27.

resurrectio Bi pr. 22.

reticere peccatum fratris Cu (VIII). 19. 20.

retinere monachos Pa II. 21. amaritudinem in corde Cu (V). 1 = Bi V. 3, 1.

retractare mala Cu (VIII). 16.

retribuere: quicquid delinquat uel furatur

retribuere (*cont.*).
-at Wa A 26. tertiam partem de argento Hi IV. 8.

reuerentia Gi 16.

reuertere *caballum* Wa P 56. — reuertitur, -untur: assinae pullus ad matrem Bi VI. 3, 6. cogitationes ad orantem *ibid.* uxor *adultera* ad uirum Vi 42–45 (V) = Cu II. 29. Bi II. 7. -atur in sua *paenitens* Co B 13. patres ad Dominum -ntes Bi pr. 28. *caro suilla* ad pristinam maciem reuersa Ad 6. terra ⟨in P⟩ fisco -atur (-etur P) Wa A 45 (P 49).

reuocare *crimen* Pa I. 16. -ri ad penitentiam Wa A 59. ad integrum salutis statum debilia r. Co B pr.

reus homicidii Co B 6. morti Bi I. 8. si r. uenire uoluerit Wa A 15. rei abstracti ab aeclesia Pa II. 9. non ad reorum defensionem facta est aeclesia Pa II. 9.

rex: quae sunt -gis furari Hi IV. 9. post -gem iustum bardigium Hi I. 29. cf. Bi IV. 6, 5. -gis iudicium Bi IV. 1, 3. -ges boni, mali Gi 23 = Cu (IX). 11. cenodoxia in -gibus uegit Bi VII. 4.

ritu gentilium Pa I. 20.

rixa Vi 5. Co A 5. 9. B 9. Cu (IV). 9. Wa A 8 (P 7). Bi IV pr. 3, 1. 2.

rixari Bi IV. 3 tit.

rubor: cum -re tacere Cu (IV). 14 = Bi IV. 5, 2.

ruere caballum in pedicam Wa A 54. presbiteri -ntis poenitentia Da 11.

ruina maxima cadere Vi 12. 27. Co B 2. cf. Vi 10. se seruare a -a Vi 15. penetentes post -as Pa II. 3.

†ruminatio quae ruminat† Bi VI. 3, 7.

rumpit fragilitas *paenitentiam ueram* Co A 1.

rupes: pecora de -e cadentia Ad 2.

sab(b)ato Cu II. 30. in die -i Da 7. in nocte -i Vi 46.

sacri eloqui medicamina Cu pr. 1. sacrum 'host' Gi 21 (sacrificium Cu (IX). 10.) -a offerre *passim*, uerba -orum Cu (IX). 9.

sacerdos Pa I. 6. Aq 2. Da 1. Co B 4. 6. 18. Cu (XI). 23. 24. Bi II. 1, 2. 2. -tes *Iudaeorum* Hi III. 5. s. praedicat Co B 24. denuntiat et prohibet Co B 25. si titubauerit s. super oratione periculosa Cu (XI). 29. ancellam illam in -tis ponimus potestatem Wa A 60. confiteri -ti, *sim.* Co B 23. Cu III. 17 = Bi III. 5, 3. Hi II. 3. 4. ad confessionem uenire -ti, ad -tem Wa A 37 (P 46). s. paenitentiam iudicans Co B 17. cf. Vi 9. Bi III. 1, 1. IV. 6, 1. iudice -te,

iudicio, ad iudicium -tis *u. sub* iudex, iudicium. -ti committitur *paenitens* Vi 23. Co B 1. cf. -tis cum quo paenituit *ibid.* det fructum penitentie in manu -tis Vi 35. 36. resolui a -te Pa I. 14. culpa per -tem abstergatur Co B 14. s. oret pro *paenitente* Co B 15. s. *confessor admonetur* Cu ps. 3. 5. = Bi pr. 33. 35.

sacramentum 'mystical meaning' Bi pr. 17.

sacrificium 'host': si s. ceciderit in stramentum Cu (XI). 5. terratenus Cu (XI). 23. si decoloratur Cu (XI). 21. questiones -i Cu (XI). tit. -um accipere Cu (XI). 10 (*bis*). Pa II. 12. Bi I. 3, 4. IV. 7 tit. 7. communicare Vi (1) = Cu (X). 5 (-o). sumere Cu (XI). 22. bene non custodire Cu (XI). 1. (e)uomere Gi 7. cf. 8. Co A 6. B 12 (*bis*). Cu I. 8 = Bi I. 3, 1. Cu (XI). 7. Bi I. 3 tit. perdere Gi 9. Co A 6. B 12. Cu (IX). 1 (XI). 3. mergere Cu (XI). 22. inuenire Cu (XI). 24. neglegentia erga -um Cu (XI). 19. de -o in nocte Paschae Pa II. 13.

sacrilegium Co B 24.

saeculares uiri Bi VI. 3, 4.

saeculum 'world' Pa I. 16. Co B 8. Vi (4) = Cu (X). 17. Vi 7. 9 ex. (PB). cupidus facultate -i Bi VII. 4. nuditate -i Bi VII. 4. omni dimisso -o Co B 20. neque in praesenti -o neque in futuro Bi pr. 23. aduentus, tempus futuri -i Bi pr. 21.

sepes (*i.e.* saepes) quae gignunt (*lege* cingunt?) meses et herbam Wa A 55. *cf.* P 64.

sal: cum pane et aqua et -e Da 11. Vi (V) 5. 8. 23. 26. 35. Co B 15. cf. Cu (VIII). 26.

saliua: sanguinem sorbere cum -a Bi I. 5, 9.

saluari post penas Bi pr. 25. -e animam Bi VIII. 3. neglegentiam Cu (XI). 20. uitium Bi VII. 4.

Saluator, *i.e.* Christus Vi 46. Cu I. 1. Bi V. 1, 2.

salus animarum Vi 46. aliorum Cu pr. 11. *peccatorum* Cu ps. 5 = Bi pr. 35. ad integrum -tis statum debilia reuocare Co B pr. aeternae -tis compago Co B 30. spes unica -tis *Christus* Cu pr. 13. octo uitia humanae -ti contraria Cu pr. 15.

salutare: clamor *licitus* cum surdus sit -tus Bi IV. 6, 1.

salutaris animarum medicina Cu pr. tit.

salutiferum genus tristitiae Bi V. 1, 1. 2.

saluus Bi pr. 5. 13.

sanare animarum uulnera Co B pr. *cf.* Bi
pr. 2. uitia Cu pr. 15. *cf.* Bi IV. 6, 1.
contraria contrariis Cu pr. 15. —
peccator -etur elymosina, *sim.* Cu III. 3.
(V). 1 = Bi V. 3, 1. Cu (VI). 2 = Bi
VI. 3, 1. Cu (VIII). 5. (XI). 18. Bi
VI. 2, 2. donec sanetur Cu (IV). 9
= Bi IV. 3, 1. Bi VIII. 4. 5. ancell(a)e
pr(a)etio -etur Hi IV. 7. 8.
sancire de criminibus Co B pr. de morte
Wa A 58.
sanctimonialis Bi IV. 6, 6.
sanctiones monachorum Co B 25.
sanctitatis uotum Cu I. 1.
sanctus Abraham Vi 46. -a Syncletica Bi
VI. 3, 5. cum mortuo -o in sepulchro
Hi II. 3. alicuius -orum commemoratio
Bi I. 2, 3. -orum facta patrum Bi pr. 28.
terra quam habitaturi sunt -i Bi pr.13 .
antiqui decreuere -i Da 10. basilicae
-orum Vi 33. intercessio -orum Cu pr.
9. exempla -orum (*i.e. Vitae Patrum*)
Bi V. 1, 4. VI. 1, 2. 2, 3. 3, 3. VIII. 3.—
coetus -orum, *i.e. monachorum* Cu
(IV). 16. — sepultura in loco -o Ca 2.
per -a quattuor euangelia testari Pa II.
24.
sane: cura in peccata ulciscendi s. multiplex Bi pr. 28.
sanguis *Christi* Co B 30. — s. *uxoris
menstruae* Cu II. 30. — -nis *humani
effusio* Lu 4. Vi 8. 35. Co A 5. B 9. 21.
Cu II. 22. Wa A 12 (P 51). 13 (P 36).
50 (P 58). (AB) 63. Hi IV. 1. 4. 5. 7.
praetium -nis Hi V. 7. 8. bibitio -nis
humani Hi I. 12. cf. Bi I. 5, 1. 2. -nem
sorbere cum saliua non est peccatum
Bi I. 5, 9. sues, gallinae -nem hominis
gustantes Ad 7. 8. — sanguis *animalium*
Ad 2 (*bis*). 3. 14. 17. 20 *passim.*
sanitatem recipere Cu (VIII). 16. Bi pr.
8. post -tem Co B 21.
sanus: in bono opere Bi IV. 7. -um
aliquem soluere Ca 3. -a puella *Iairi*
Bi IV. 7. s. *a peccato* Vi 1. 2. cor -um
Co B 30. -e uirtutis Gi 22. -a conscientia Ad 10, fide *cibum* sumere Cu
(XI). 14. Ad 1. 6. -a fide adfirmant Hi
III. 1.
sapiens Domini Cu ps. 3. *cf.* Hi V. 2. Bi
pr. 3. s. ait Bi V. 3, 2. VI. 2, 1. VII. 4
tit. VIII. 1. iudicat dicens Bi III. 1, 2.
-tes iudicant Hi IV. 1. canones -tium
Bi I. 5 tit. sinodus -tium Hi III tit.
VI tit.
sapor: si cum consummatione -is decoloratur sacrificium Cu (XI). 21.
sarculum perfrangere Gi 26.
satellites *diaboli* Bi pr. 25.

satis ac libenter expetere Vi 44 (S). satius
est nobis Pa I pr. s. agere = s. facere
Vi 23. s. agant ut adsint Co B 29. s.
facere Vi 1. *alicui* Vi 23. Co B 1. Cu
(IV). 13. 15. (VIII). 3 = Bi VIII. 1.
Cu (VIII). 7 = Bi VIII. 2, 1. Cu
(VIII). 22.
satisfactio Co B 13. Cu (IV). 1 = Bi IV
4. Bi IV. 5, 2. — (= *éric*) Hi I. 1.
saturatus nimis Co A 6.
saturitas Cu I. 6. (XI). 7. Bi I. 3, 1.
scabiem *cutis* commedere Cu (X). 18.
scandalum Vi 6. Co B 21. 30.
scelus dignum gladio Bi pr. 3. 28. pueri
praefata -era facientes Bi II. 2, 5.
fornicantes labiis, quod dictu s. Bi II.
2, 4. s. uirile Lu 8. Cu II. 9.
scientia legis Bi pr. 49.
scindere aurem Ad 20.
scopa mundetur locus *ubi sacrificium
cecidit* Cu (XI). 24.
scriba (*Hib.* fer légind) Hi I. 29. IV. 1.
9 (*bis*). V. 11. Bi IV. 6, 5.
scribere meliora Vi ps. liber -ptus a
Comminiano Cu ssc. lex metrica
scriptione -pta Ad 14. -ptum est Bi pr.
16. VI. 2, 3. inuenitur -ptum in canone
Bi IV. 6, 7.
scriptio: lex metrica -ne (ratione PB¹)
scripta Ad 14.
scriptura ait, dicit Vi 8. 21. 29. Bi pr.
32. — exemplis referta s. est Bi pr. 30.
-ae exempla Pa II. 3. -arum exempla
Bi IV. 6, 7. — nouitas extra -as Cu
(VIII). 1. doctrina extra -as Bi VII. 2.
opusculum de -arum uenis redundans
Vi ps. sententia -arum Vi ps. — *de
libro non sacro:* episcopi quorum
nomina in -a memorantur Hi V. 2.
scrip(t)ulum, -os accipere, reddere Wa 21
(*bis*). P 57. Hi IV. 6.
scrutator diuine lectionis Vi ps.
secretus: osculum -o praebere Da 15
-e lauare Co B 28.
securis: de -i interfici Wa A 5.
securitatem accipere Wa P 1. 3. habere A 2.
securus fiat Wa A 1. 4. uiuat A 15 (P 12).
-i in sedibus sedeant A 15. *cf.* P 12.
sedatium 'satisfaction' Hi IV. 6.
sedere in lumento Co B 28. in sedibus
Wa A 15. in cella Bi VI. 3, 3. sanguis
crasior in quo anima -erat Ad 20.
sedes: sine -e *paenitere* Hi II. 2 (B). 4.
sedis, -em animae Ad 20. securi in
-ibus sedeant Wa A 15.
sedulitas operis Cu (VI). 2 = Bi VI. 3, 1.
semen fundere Bi II. 1, 3. 4. concepto
-ine Cu II. 30. Bi pr. 17. s. bibere Bi
I. 5, 2. non infecit s. seminantis

semen (*cont.*).
  iniquitas Pa II. 7. — de tribus -inibus euangeliorum Pa II. 18.
sementum Bi pr. 27.
semiannus *paeniteat* Da 14. -o Cu II. 33 = Bi II. 11, 2.
seminare: -ntis iniquitas Pa II. 7.
semipanis Cu (VIII). 6. 26.
semis: .iii. (.vii., .xiiii.) anni et s. Hi I. 1 6. 7. 12. Bi I. 5, 3.
semiuiuum animal Ad 5. *cf.* 4.
semotus peniteat Bi IV. 5, 1. (remotus Cu (R)) uiuat Cu III. 15 = Bi III. 6, 2.
sempiternus interitus Bi pr. 9.
senatus: iudicio -us peniteat Cu (X). 20.
senescere: cum muliere iuuencula non -nte Hi V. 4.
senex Hi V. 2 (*bis*). Bi VI. 2, 3. 3, 3. 6.
senior: nec s. cum sua muliere non senescente Hi V. 4. s. *monachus* Gi 6. Cu (VIII). 18. statuta -um Cu (X). 1. -um traditiones Co B pr. decretum est a -ibus Bi I. 2, 3.
sententiae alterius subdere se Cu (VII). 1 = Bi VII. 1. suam publice -am damnet Cu (VIII). 2 = Bi VII. 2. secundum istam -am Vi 46. secundum -am scripturarum Vi ps.
sentire dolorem saturitatis Cu I. 6. commotionem Cu (IV). 15. iuxta quod meretur quoaequalia -iat Co A 12.
seorsum *fratrem* arguat Cu (VIII). 22.
separatus a loquente *clamare permittitur* Bi IV. 6, 1. -ri a mensa Cu (X). 3. *cf.* Bi pr. 36. ab aliis -tus Christianis Co B 25. a mundialibus Bi pr. 2. uitia humanum genus -ant a regno Dei Bi pr. 37. -re *paenitentes* Vi 27 (V). 40 (S). Cu (X). 7. Pa II. 11. qui murmurat -etur Cu (VIII). 6 = Bi VIII. 5. -tus ieiunet, uiuat Cu (VIII). 8 = Bi VIII. 22.
separatim peniteant Vi (S) 27. 45.
separatio sexuum post lapsum Pa II. 11.
septempliciter restituere Ca 1. 2.
septiformis Christi gratia Ca 2.
septimana Aq 5. Cu (VIII). 11 (E). Bi pr. 23. -a p(a)eniteat(ur) Co A 9. 10. B 22.
septima dies *mystice accipitur* Bi pr. 20.
sepulchrum: cum mortuo sancto in -o Hi II. 3.
sepultura in loco sancto Ca 2.
sequestrari ab ecclesia Pa I. 26.
sequi: nihil -tur Wa A 32. consentimus et -emur (-eremur *cod.*) Vi ps.
series lectionis Pa II. 23.
sermo *boni confessoris* Cu ps. 5 = Bi pr. 35. s. de innumerabilibus peccatis Hi I. tit. frater petens -nem Bi VI. 3, 3.

sermocinantes pueri soli Cu (X). 1.
sermocinationes *cum femina* Cu II. 18 = Bi II. 1, 9.
serpens susurrans ad Euam Bi VIII. 3.
serua: seruum -amue conparare Wa A 19.
seruare iudicia gentium bona Hi III ps. se -uit a ruina Vi 15. -et se fortiter, ne . . . Vi 21.
seruilis ministratio Bi VIII. 6.
seruire Deo in monasterio Co B 20. arma relinquat et Deo -iat Bi IV. 1, 2. uiro suo *uxor adultera paenitens* Vi 44 (S). -iat *detractor uictimae* Cu (VIII). 9 = Bi VIII. 2, 2.
seruitutis iugum Pa I. 7. Co B 20.
seruus furtum *faciens* Wa P 20. si ingenuum occiderit Wa A 5 (P 4). si dominus -o arma commisserit portare . . . A 6. *cf.* P 5. si ingenuus -um occiderit A 7 (P 6). si s. -um occiderit A 33 (P 38). -um aut ancellam (seruam) conparare A 19. P 28. emere A 48 (P 54). liberare Vi 22. *cf.* 24. libertate donare Wa A 39. seruitutis iugo absoluere Co B 20. perdere Wa A 31 (P 32). in fugam praemere P 59. ancellas, -os reddere A 1. *cf.* 6 (P 5). 45 (P 50). P 7. alius s. domino reformetur P 6. -os duos domino restituat (-et A) A 7. uicem -i (*lege* -e?) uel ancille expleat *adultera paenitens* Vi 44 (S). — -i Dei, *i.e. sacerdotes* Vi 35.
sextarius Romanus Gi 1. 2 = Cu II. 2. 3. -um reddat Wa A 22.
sexagissimum (*u. Ind. orth.*) clerici sunt Pa II. 18.
sexus peccantis Bi pr. 2. -um separatio post lapsum Pa II. 11.
siccans sacrificium Cu (XI). 19.
siccus: silua -a Wa P 61. in pane -o uiuere Ca 3. cum fructibus horti -is *paenitere* Co B 15. pisces in -o moriuntur Bi VI. 3, 4.
sicera Da 1.
sicli .xiii. praetium ancillae Hi I. 9.
signatur res intra dies aliquot Wa P 23 (consignetur A 28).
silentii superpositio Co A 9. clamor -o sanetur Bi IV. 6, 1.
silua Wa A 53. P 61.
simplex: in -ici historia Hi V. 2. osculum -iciter facientes Cu (X). 2.
simul non peniteant Vi 27. si *iusti cum peccatoribus* occissi fuerint s. Bi pr. 36.
simulacrum: pro honore -orum Co B 24.
sincera paenitentia Pa II. 3.
sinatur hoc aegentibus aelimosina Wa A 46.
singa 'tent'(?) Hi I. 24.

singulus: in anno -o Vi 46.
sinistrae partis communio Co B 25.
senus (*i.e.* sinus): ad -um matris aeclesiae
    confugere Pa II. 9.
situs loci Vi ps. locorum Pa II. 17.
socer Moysi Iethro Hi III. ps.
sociari altaris communioni Aq 6 = Cu
    (VIII). 12.
sodomitam fornicationem faciens Gi 1.
sol: per .x. -es emendat culpam Cu (XI).
    22.
solidus: .v. soltos (-idos) argenti exsoluat
    Wa A 12. *cf.* P 51.
solidus *adi.*: sanguis -ior Ad 20.
solitaria uita Cu pr. 11. monachi -ae (-i
    QDJI) habitant Pa II. 17.
sol(l)em(p)nitates Domini Pa II. 19.
    precipu*ae* Ca 3. -tas misse Cu (XI). 6.
solerter intuendum est Cu ps. 1 = Bi pr.
    2.
sollicitudo Bi pr. 49.
sollicitus: contemptores -i Pa II. 17.
soluere *aliquem* sanum Ca 3. potestas
    alligandi et -ndi Pa II. 3. *cf.* Bi pr. 3. —
    s. debitum Pa I. 8. 20. *pretium* Wa A
    58. si quis non iurauerit, -at Wa A 18.
    si non habet unde -at Co B 21.
solum patrium Ca 1.
solus cum -a loquitur Cu (VIII). 23. s. in
    peregrinatione permaneat Ca 3. pueri
    -i sermocinantes Cu (X). 1.
so(-u-)mnolentia Bi VI pr. 2 tit.
so(-u-)mnolentus Co A 12. Cu (VI). 1 =
    Bi VI. 2, 2.
som(p)nus: in -is cum uoluntate pollutus
    Da 8 = Cu II. 15. in -is peccare Da
    9 = Cu II. 16. pollutus nocturno -o
    Cu (XI). 10. sine -o *paenitere* Hi II. 2.
    3 (P). 4. s. assiduus emitatio mortis Bi
    VI. 2, 1. grauari -o Bi VI. 2, 3.
sonus psalmorum Bi V. 3, 2.
sorbeat minister stillam *quae* super altare
    cecidit Cu (XI). 27. sanguinem -re cum
    saliua Bi I. 5, 9.
soror: uxor fratris tui s. tua est Pa II. 25.
    cum -e fornicari Da 11. Bi II. 3 tit. 3,
    1. *cf.* ducentem -em Bi II. 3, 2. cum
    alterius -e Wa A 17.
spatium terrarum Bi IV. 6, 1. — habeant
    -um intra dies .xv. Wa P 12. per -um
    .vii., .xx. annorum Ca 3. *paenitentiae* -a
    Pa II. 22. demedio -o peniteat Bi IV.
    1, 2.
spatula 'bed' Bi I. 7.
species *caballi* ('breed') Wa A 20 (P 29).
    uere tristitiae Bi V. 1, 6. in -e *reddere*
    Hi IV. 2. 8.
spes Bi pr. 49. unica salutis *Christus* Cu
    pr. 13.

spiritus: in ultimo -u constitutus Vi 34.
    sp. *tristitiae* Bi V. 1, 6.
spiritalis mors Pa II. 9. gaudium -e Vi
    29. -es medici Co B pr. -iter intellegere
    Bi VI. 3, 7.
sponsa ('married woman'): fornicare cum
    -a Co B 23.
sponsus carnalis Pa I. 17. Christi aduentus
    -i Pa II. 14.
spontaneus: si sp. *porcos* minauerit Wa
    P 19. ex -a uoluntate Wa P 46.
sponte Wa A 25. 37. 55. P 26.
stabilitas corporis et cordis et cogitationis
    Bi VI. 3, 2.
stagni (*i.e.* stanni) libras reddere Wa P 31
    (*bis*). accipere P 59. †stagnum ferrum†
    A 52.
stare: secrete -ndo pedes lauare Co B 28.
    stet inter catecuminos Co B 25. -ndo
    uigilare, orare, *sim.* Gi 22 (*bis*). Hi II.
    2 (B).
statim penitere Vi 4.
statio: in -ne *paenitere* Hi II. 2 (P).
statuere paenitentiam, *sim.* Co A 1. Cu
    (VIII). 28. *cf.* Pa II. 3.
statui priori se restituere Pa I. 10. integer
    salutis status Co B pr.
statuta canonica Pa II. 10 (K). patrum
    Cu pr. 14. (X). tit. prudentium Hi VI.
    4. seniorum Cu (X). 1. sinodi Pa I ssc.
stercora comedens Cu (X). 18.
sterilem uxorem *uir* non debet demittere
    Vi 41. *cf.* Cu II. 28.
sterilitas Vi 41.
stilla *sacrificii* Cu (XI). 27 (*bis*).
stillare: si de calice aliquid -uerit Cu (XI).
    26. *cf.* 27. 28.
stomachi uitio *sacrificium euomere* Bi I.
    3, 1.
stragis Christianorum Lu 4 = Cu (IX).
    13.
stramen Cu (XI). 24.
stramentum Cu (XI). 5.
stricta *paenitentiae* spatia Pa II. 22.
striga 'witch' Pa I. 16.
stringere asinam Bi VI. 3, 6.
studium diligentius cordis et corporis Vi
    10. *euellere peccata* per -um nostrum
    Vi 29. st. mentis, scientiae legis Bi pr.
    49.
stupens elinguis Gi 10 = Cu I. 4.
suauiora ceteris sumere Cu I. 5 = Bi I.
    4, 3.
subdere se alterius sententiae Cu (VII).
    1 = Bi VII. 1. subditi *monachi* Pa II.
    21.
subdiaconus Da 11.
subdiuissiones filargiriae Bi III pr.
subfert colirium *sanguinem* Hi IV. 7.

uitium (*cont.*).
purgatam -is carnem suscipiet Bi pr. 22.
Finit de -is Bi ssc. — ferula dignum u.
gladio non uindices Bi pr. 28. -o
moriatur Pa II. 26. — *ad* uitium
singulare (*ebrietatem, gulam, superbiam,
sim.*) *refertur* Co B 24. Bi I. 1. 3, 1.
III pr. V. 3, 2. VII. 4 tit. 4 (*bis*).
VIII. 6.
uitulus: a -o praemulgenti gustatum lac
Ad 10. caule -orum Hi VI. 4. —
adoratio uituli *in deserto* Hi III. 8.
uituperare: nec laudo nec -o *com-
mutationes paenitentiarum* Cu (VIII).
25.
uituperatio mali Cu (VIII). 16.
uiuere: non plus quam octo dies esuriens
. . . u. non potest Hi V. 6. maritus illa
-nte alteram non suscipiet Ad 16. uita
-itur Pa II. 17. ut iustus iuste -at Co A
12. qui infidelem tempore -xit Pa II.
31. largus -at Cu III. 13 = Bi III. 6, 1.
semotus Cu III. 15 = Bi III. 6, 2.
separatus Bi VIII. 2, 2. -a(n)t Deo Cu
(IV). 5. (IX). 13. -at donec sanetur in
pane et aqua Bi VIII. 4. *sim. u. sub*
formulae *in Ind. Gramm.* in peregrinatione -at Ca 3. -at securus Wa A
15. (P 12.) — eradicabitur de terra
-ntium Vi 29.
uiuus: mulier alicuius mariti -i Bi II. 5, 2.
uxor *mariti* -a prima Vi 43 (S). si seruus
seruum occiderit, u. commonis dominorum existat Wa A 33 (P 38). si bos
alium occiderit u. et mortuus in
commune dominorum existant Wa A 34
(commones eius erunt P 39).
ultio: pro -ne amici occidere hominem
Bi IV. 1, 2.
unc(h)ia Wa A 51. 53. demedium -ae Wa
51. (AB) 63.
unde: si non habet unde reddat, restituat,
soluat Co B 21. Cu III. 6 = Bi III.
2, 1. Cu (IV). 10 = Bi IV. 3, 1.
unitas carnis *in matrimonio* Vi 46. plebis
Pa II. 20.
uoca alterum *ad corripiendum fratrem* Cu
(VIII). 10. -ti sunt *monachi* in frigore
et nuditate . . . Pa II. 17.
uocatio *monachorum* Pa II. 21.
uoluntarius: si u. ire uoluerit Wa P 64.
uictimam -am Dominus praecipit Hi
III. 8. — qui -ae (*aduerb.*) semet
ipsum occiderit Bi IV. 2, 1.
uoluntas patris et uirginis in coniugio Pa
II. 27 (*bis*). tristitia operatur circa -tem
Bi V. 3, 2. si compleat suam -tem Vi
(4) = Cu (X). 17. uoluntate = sponte
Gi 22. Da 7. 8 = Cu II. 15. sua -te

Wa A 39. ex spontanea -te Pa 46. —
-te iam peccauit in corde suo Vi 3. sine
-te pollutus Da 9 = Cu II. 16. — -te
patrum Wa A 59.
uomere Co A 6. Bi I. 2 tit. sacrificium Co
B 12 (*bis*). Bi I. 3 tit. *u.* euomere.
uomitus: usque ad -um manducare aut
bibere Co B 22. distendi Cu I. 7. si
canes lambuerint talem -um Cu I. 11 =
Bi I. 3, 2. Cu (XI). 8. pro ebrietate -um
facere Bi I. 2, 1. 4.
uoracitas Gi 7. Co B 12. Bi I. 3, 1.
uotiuus malus Hi I. 4.
uotum: si ad -a sibi Lu 4. — de primis uel
secundis -is Pa II. 28. obseruanda sunt
prima -a Pa II. 28. — *de uoto religionis*:
si promiserit -um suum Deo Vi 34. -o
perficiendo Pa II. 17. -um habere Co
B 10. -um sanctitatis habere Cu I. 1.
-um irritum facere Vi 27. Co B 8. -a
frangere Co A 3. praelato ante monachi
-o Gi 1 = Cu II. 2. sine monachi -u
(-o) Gi 3 = Cu II. 4. post, ante -um
perfectionis Lu 9. post -a perfectionis
Cu (IV). 6 = Bi IV. 3, 4. post -um
peccare Vi 27. Co B 8. post confessionem et -um sacerdoti Hi II. 3. *cf.* 4.
uouere: impleat quod -erit Vi 34 (*bis*).
absolute de uoto monachi Lu 9.
uox: sanctimonialis huiusmodi -cibus
turbata Bi IV. 6, 6.
urbs: in alia urbe (in alio orbe S) *paenitere*
Vi 23.
urinam bibere Cu (X). 18. Bi I. 5, 1. 3.
bibitio -ae Hi I. 12.
usuram accipere Da 13.
ussus neglegentia Pa I. 7. ad -um necessarium Pa I. 25. adipem et pelles in -us
uarios habebimus Ad 20.
uterus: perditio liquoris in -o matris Hi
I. 6 = Bi IV. 2, 2. *cf.* 3. in -o habere
Hi I. 27. Bi I. 6, 2.
uti: coaequali penitentia -antur Pa I. 11.
utilis tristitia Bi V. 1, 4. 5.
uulnerare Co B 21. Ca 3.
uulnus Hi IV. 3. Ad 20. — animarum -era
Co B pr. peccati et iniquitatis Bi pr. 8.
remedia -erum Cu pr. 1. Bi pr. 6.
aliorum sanare -era Bi pr. 2.
uultus: hilari -u sanetur *tristis* Cu (V).
1 = Bi V. 3, 1.
uxor clerici Pa I. 6. u. fratris tui soror tua
est Pa II. 25. non oportet adducere -em
aliam quandiu fuerit u. uiua prima Vi
43 (S). -rem sterilem non debet demittere Vi 41. u. sterilis *caste cum marito
uiuat* Cu II. 28. -rem (non) habere Co
B 16. 17. laicus cum -re Vi 39 (S). si ab
aliquo discesserit sua u. Vi 42–45 (V) =

Cu II. 29 = Bi II. 7. u. fornicata cum alio Vi 51. dimittere -rem Bi II. 6 tit. 6, 1. concupiscere -rem proximi Co B 23. cum mariti -re fornicari, *sim.* Da 11. Vi 36. Co B 14. Cu II. 23. Wa A 17. *cf.* P 27. Bi II. 5 tit. 5, 1. de alterius -re filium gignere Co B 14. non intret amplius ad concubinam sed iungatur propriae -ri Vi 40 (S). — non maneat cum -re(m) *paenitens, sim.* Vi 35 (*bis*). 36. 37. 38. 39 (S). Co B 14. 18. sine -re Cu II. 22. 23. 25. Bi II. 5, 1. *facta paenitentia* intret ad -rem suam Vi 35. uir non intrabit *ad uxorem praegnantem* Vi 46. abstineat se ab -re *in quadragesima* Bi II. 9, 2.

V. INDEX GRAMMATICUS

Graeca, Hebraica, Celto-Latina, Hibernica: *V. Ind. uerborum s.u.* abbas, ac(c)edia (accidia), amen, anathema, anathemazare, (h)anchorita, apostolus, bactroperiti, baptisma, baptismus, (re-) baptizare, basilica, blasphemare, blasphemia, blasphemus, butyrum, canon, canonicus, caraxare, catecuminus, catholicus, c(a)enodoxia, chrismal, clericatus, clericus, clerus, cenobium, colirium, cymbalum, daemo, daemonium, diabolus, diaconus (subdiaconus), dogma, ebibatus, ecclesia, ecclesiasticus, eglota, elemosina, episcopus, epistola, eremus, aetia ('yearling'?), euangelium, eucharistia, gomor, heres(s)is, hereticus, (h)ebdomada, historia, idolatria, laicus, lamia, lepra, limphaticus, martyrium, monachus, monasterium, yconomus, paradis(s)us, parruchia, pausare, pax(i)mati(u)um, filargiria, pilax, pr(a)esbiter, propheta, propheticus, psallere, psalmista, psalmus, sab(b)atum, symbulum, synodus, thesaurizare, tirannus; *Ind. nominum s.u.* Aepiphania, Pascha, Pentecoste. — (?) abdella 'leech' Ad 13. arreum Hi II *passim.* bardicatio Bi IV. 6, 2. bardigium (?) Hi I. 26. caballus, capallus Wa 14^ies. †capalbia Hi I. 26. ceruis(s)a Gi 22. Da 11. Cu I. 1. Hi II. 12 (P). clentella, glantella, *sim. u. Ind. uerb.* singa 'tent' (?) Hi I. 24. — buorch (*in marg.* B) Hi VI. 1. díbergach Hi I. 4 (P). coaid siir throscho Hi II. 5 (P). fordobor 7 ith Hi II. 10 (P).

Formatio substantiuorum: portarius Co B 29. tributarius Wa A 30. — porcaster Wa A 25 (P 19). — cohabitator Hi I (*ter*). Bi IV. 6, 3. contemptor Pa II. 17. dilator Gi 27. Aq 5 = Cu (VIII). 11. destitutor Co A 12. detractator Bi pr. 62. detractor Vi 29. Cu (VIII). 16. distributor Cu (XI). 16. exsecutor Gi 27. fideiusor Pa I. 8. Wa (*quater*). fornicator Bi II. 4. iector Hi V. 2. ingresor Pa I. 27. interemptor Wa P 12. interfector Hi IV. 7. iuratores Wa A 43. P 11. 45. lauator Co B 28. m(o)echator Lu 6 = Cu II. 7. percusor Hi IV. 8. porcator Wa A 25 (*app.*). praeuaricator Bi pr. 25. scrutator Vi ps. uindicator Pa II. 6. — clericatus Vi (*sexies*). ducatus Lu 4 = Cu (IX). 13. incoeptus Pa I. 10. — abrenuntatio Cu pr. 8. acceptio Hi V. 1. admonitio Bi VI. 3, 7. animaduersio Co B pr. approbatio Bi pr. 6. bibitio Hi I (*octies*). cantatio Hi II. 3 (B). circuitio Bi pr. 28. combustio

Co B pr. commansio Vi 15. confabulatio Pa I. 9. Cu (VIII). 15 (fabulatio E). confractio Co B pr. coniunctio Co B 30. Bi II. 9, 1. V. 1, 6. conpossitio Wa P 67. consummatio Gi 19 = Cu (IX). 6. Cu (XI). 21. Bi I. 5, 1. contemptio Bi pr. 49. contradictio Cu III. 15 = Bi III. 6, 2. Pa II. 23. curatio Co B pr. dispectio Cu (VIII). 3 = Bi VIII. 1. detractatio Bi VIII. pr. 3. distentio Cu I. 6. donatio Ad 15. dormitatio Hi II. 3. 4 (B). †effectio Wa A 53. effussio Lu 4. Hi IV. 5. Ad 20 (*bis*). examinatio Pa II. 22. excommunicatio Hi V. 5. Pa II. 4. excusatio Cu (VIII). 17. flectio Hi II *passim.* fornicatio *passim.* genuculatio Hi II. 4 (P). grauatio Cu ps. 1 = Bi pr. 2. humiliatio Co B 16. iectio Hi V (*nouies*). inpositio Co B 25. Cu (X). 18. Hi I. 12. Pa II. 8. inpugnatio Cu II. 13. increpatio Gi 8. inflectio Hi II (B). 4. 8. 9. intermissio Hi II. 4 (B). intinctio Ad 10. irreptio Vi 4. *cf.* 24 (SP). lamentatio Hi I. 24. maledictio Bi V. 2. manducatio Hi I. 24. mansio Cu (VI). 2 = Bi VI. 3, 1. meditatio Lu 2. Cu (IV). 5. 7. Bi IV. 3, 2. 4. ministratio Bi VIII. 6. miseratio Cu (VIII). 16. motatio Hi IV. 8. negutiatio Pa II. 30. obreptio Vi 24 (V). obstinatio Aq 6 = Cu (VIII). 12. obtractatio Bi VIII. 3. occissio Hi V (*sexies*). Bi IV. 1, 3 tit. percus(s)io Co B 26. Hi IV. 8. perditio *nouies.* perfusio (?) Cu pr. 5. peruagatio Bi VI. pr. praedicatio Co B 29. redintegratio Co A 8. repulsio Co A 12. sanctio Co B 25. satisfactio Co B 13. Cu (IV). 1. Hi I. 1. Bi IV. 4 ; 5, 2. scriptio Ad 14. sermocinatio Cu II. 18 = Bi II. 1, 9. subdiuissio Bi III. pr. subiectio Vi 44 (S). subscriptio Pa II. 30. superpos(s)itio *passim.* traditio Co B pr. Pa II. 7. transgresio Bi pr. 8. tribulatio Bi II. 6, 1. uagatio Bi VI. 3 tit. uituperatio Cu (VIII). 16. uocatio Pa II. 21. — adstantia Wa A 37. iactantia Cu (VII). tit. Bi VII. 3 tit. pr. inobedientia Bi VIII. pr. ob(o)edientia Gi 1. 4. Vi 23. Cu II. 2. 5. Bi pr. 49. perseuerantia Bi pr. 49. — consanguinitas Pa II. 29. diuersitas Co B pr. 26. diuturnitas Cu II. 14. extrimitas Ad 20. familiaritas Vi 14. 15. fragilitas Gi 1 = Cu II. 2. Co A 1. inmaturitas Cu (X). 4. inportunitas Bi VI. pr. (*ex Cassiano*). inquietas Bi VII. 4. inueritas Bi VII. 4. lacrimabilitas Cu ps. 1 = Bi pr. 2. longanimitas Bi pr. 49. otiositas Bi

VI (*bis*). possibilitas Vi ps. pussillanimitas Bi V. 3 pr. sedulitas Cu (VI). 2 = Bi VI. 3, 1. sterilitas Vi 41. sublimitas Bi VII. 4. taciturnitas Co A 12. uarietas Vi ps. uerbositas Cu (VIII). 14. uoracitas Gi 7. Co B 12. Bi I. 3, 1. — cohabitatrix Bi IV. 6, 3. — amaritudo Cu (V). 1. Bi V. 3 pr. 3, 1. dulcitudo Bi VI. 1, 2. inquietudo Bi VI. pr. paenitudo Cu ps. 2 (*alias semper* p(a)enitentia). turpitudo Pa I. 6. — adiuramentum Pa II. 23. coinquinamentum Cu (X). 2. linteamen Cu (XI). 4. 11. 27. lumentum Co B 27. 28. nutrimen Wa A 24. sementum Bi pr. 27. stramen Cu (XI). 24. stramentum Cu (XI). 5. — conprobatorium Bi pr. 14.

Substantiua composita : cohabitator Hi I. 4. 23. 27. Bi IV. 6, 3. cohabitatrix Bi IV. 6, 3. commansio Vi 15. concoitus Hi I. 5. Bi II. 5, 2. confabulatio Pa I. 9. Cu (VIII). 15. confractio Co B pr. conuicina Hi I. 5. inueritas Bi VII. 4. superhabundantia Pa II. 17.

Deminutiua : bestiole Cu (XI). 14. bucellus, -a Hi III. 5. columellum Wa A tit. (O). cultellus Wa A 5 (P 4). formellus Gi 1 = Cu II. 2. infantulus Cu (X). 19. iuuencula Hi V. 4. opusculum Vi ps. paruulus *passim.* pedecle Cu (X). 18. questiuncula Bi I. 1. II. 1 pr. uermiculus Cu (X). 18. uernaculus Wa A 39. — uagulus Pa I. 34. — talimpulum Gi 1 = Cu II. 2. Da 11.

Abstracta pro concretis : supradicta aetas . . . fornicans Cu (X). 8. clerus = clerici Pa I. pr. euum = generatio : pro fragilitate corporis istius -i Gi 1 = Cu II. 2. concilium 'assembly' Cu (VIII). 4 = Bi VIII. 4. nouitas = noua doctrina Cu (VIII). 1. — abundantia caritatis = abundans caritas Bi pr. 30. *similiter :* abundantia lacrimarum Bi V. 1, 2. celeritas penitentie Vi 13. commansiones feminarum Vi 15. diuersitas culparum, paenitentiarum Co B pr. uitiorum Bi pr. 26. dulcitudo operis *apium* Bi VI. 1, 2. extrimitas sanguinis Ad 20. inmaturitas aetatis Cu (X). 4. odii meditatione Cu (IV). 5. perfectio bonitatis Bi V. 1, 5. operis sedulitas Cu (VI). 2 = Bi VI. 3, 1. turpitudo uentris Pa I. 6. ueritas regulae Gi 27. uiolentia cogitationis Bi II. 1, 3.

Formae nominum, declinatio : ebibatus Da 10. — *nom. sg.* mercis Cu ps. 5 (-es Bi pr. 35). sedis Ad 20. stragis Lu 4 = Cu (IX). 13. superstis Pa II. 25. — *acc. sg.* heres(s)im Bi VII. 2. — *abl. sg.* insolubile (-i I) Pa II. 14. lugubre (-i Q) Pa II. 3. Natale Bi I. 2, 3. spiritale

(QDJ) Pa II. 9. tale Cu III. 12 (E : -i R). — igni Bi pr. 15. sacerdoti Cu (VIII). 7 (E). — consequenti (I) Pa II. 23. inferiori (-e E. Gi 2) gradu Cu II. 3. uigilia propensiori Cu (VI). 1. a ueraci Wa A 58. uesti (I) Pa II. 3. — *gen. pl.* homonum (-inum S) Vi 11. ossuum (-ium P^c) Ad 19. — *acc. pl.* diffini⟨ti⟩onis Cu pr. 1 (E). sermocinationis Cu II. 18 (E). superpositionis Cu (VIII). 27 *et saepius* (E). — *abl. pl.* cum filiis et filiabus Vi 27. Co B 8. — *Heteroclita, metaplasmus :* (h)ebdomas, -da *u. Ind. uerb.* inpensam Cu (IV). 9 (E). Pascha *semper fem. nisi* ante Pascha Bi II. 9, 2. tria xlma Cu II. 2 (E). (XI). 19 (E). *al.* triduani, -as *u. Ind. uerb.* — de baptismatis (-ibus DJI) Pa II. 7. diaconus *semper nisi* diaconibus Pa I. pr. (*gen. sg.* -nis Vi 27 (V).) — *abl. sg.* domo Hi I. 22. 24. 25. domu Hi V. 4. VI 3. Bi I. 7. *cf.* grados Ca 2. inconsultu Pa I. 34. instincto (-u SP) Vi 24. lucto Bi IV. 6, 7 tit. permissu(-o DJI) Pa II. 21. tectu Cu (VIII). 23 (-o E). uotu Gi 3. Cu II. 2. (uoto Gi 1. Cu II. 4.) usos Ad 20 (B^1 : us(s)us *cett.*). — pultu Cu (XI). 14. fruguum Hi III. 2 (C). — *Contaminatio declinationum :* sementibus (*dat. pl.*) Bi pr. 27. — *Nomina Hebraica :* socer Moysi . . . cum Moysi Hi III. ps. Io(h)nathan ieiunium soluente Bi I. 8. — *V. Ind. orthogr.* (e–i, o–u).

Genus substantiuorum : dies *u. Praefationem p.* 31 sq. sues . . . inliciti Ad 7 ; *sed cf.* de uentre earum Ad 6.

Numerus : epula Co B 19.

Appositio : sub iudice flamma Aq 6 = Cu (VIII). 12. Pa II. 24. cum fratribus peccatoribus Pa II. 1. meretrix coniunx Ad 16. Pa II. 26.

Casus : Genitiuus : *g. criminis :* homicidii reus Co B 6. homicidi conpulsus Wa A 3 (*u. app. crit.*). uindicte innocens Pa II. 6. — *g. partitiuus legitur plus uicies ; notamus* regno Dei est alienorum Cu (VII). 1 ; *cf.* **Nominis cum pronomine structura.** — *g. qualitatis :* puer decem annorum Cu I. 13 = Bi I. 4, 2. si postea .xx. annorum . . . huic accederit Cu I. 14 (post .xx. annos Bi I. 4, 2). maioris aetatis *pueri* Cu (X). 21. si sane uirtutis est Gi 22. si quis legitimae legis Wa A 59. hae paucorum sunt Co B pr. bucellae mensurae de tribus panibus Hi II. 5¹ (B). — .iii. diebus tacendi Cu III. 18. pecodem furti Wa A 18. praedarum pecora Ad 15. catenae canis Hi VI. 1. septimana inmunditiae Bi pr. 23. — *g. relationis :* sapiens Domini Cu ps. 3. opem ferre miserorum Bi pr. 51. anima

z

Casus (*cont.*).

. . . ieiuna medicinae Pa II. 22. libertas gloriae Bi pr. 49. de nuditate saeculi Bi VII. 4. — *Hic adiungendum uidetur*: superpositiones due omnis ebdomadis Hi II. 10 (P). cum missa horarum .xii. Hi II. 2 (P); *cf.* Hi II. 3. 4. 8 (P). 9 (P). 10 (P). 11 (P). (*dubium:*) xl (= quadraginta? quadragesimam?) dierum (*sic* S: dies VPB) peniteat Vi 8. — *g. inhaerentiae*: libido concupiscentiae carnalis Vi 46. passio martyrii Cu pr. 13. — episcopus episcoporum Hi V. 9. — *Datiuus*: clerico fallat Pa I. 8. celatum est hominibus Vi 1c. iuuare captiuo Pa I. 32. quae natura bona illis docuit Hi III. ps. quomodo . . . illi poterit adiuuare? Pa II. 12. — (*pro* ad *cum acc.*) iudicio adduci Wa A 36. ad confessionem uenerit sacerdoti Wa A 37 (ad sacerdotem P 46). — *Datiuus e substantiuo pendet*: concoitus mulieri, c. conuicinae Hi I. 5. refugium crismalis . . . aut refugium baculis aut cimbalis Ca 1. duae superpositiones uni cuique ebdomadae Hi II. 8 (B). — *Accusatiuus*: *loco nominatiui*: Pentecosten Pa II. 19. adherit (-et DIY) meretricem Pa II. 26 (K: -e QDJ. -i IY). sacrificium communicare Vi (1), *cf.* sacrificio communicare Cu (X). 5. si hoc consueuit Co B 7. ut membrum non noceat Wa P 10. nubserit carnalem sponsum Pa I. 17. fructum . . . perfruat (*leg.* proferat?*) Pa II. 21. satisfactionem fratri superponat Bi IV. 5, 2 (*lege* in satisfactionem? *cf.* satis faciens fratri superponat Cu (IV). 13). — *Dubium*: se (= sibi? a se?) nouerit conponendum Wa A 19. 37. P 28. 67. — *Accusatiuus et ablatiuus confunduntur*: si pullice manus excusserit Wa P 7. iteratum *pro* -ò Cu (X). 12. absque babtismum Vi 47. cum sanctum Abraham Vi 46. de perditionem Hi I. 10. de par(r)oc(h)ias Pa II. 20 (-is I). iactans in sua beneficia Bi VII. 3 (in suis benefactis Cu (VII). 2). si in fastigium fuerint capta Wa A 21. si ancellam . . . in fugam praeserit Wa P 59. ancellam illam in sacerdotis ponimus potestatem Wa A 60. maxime in tres xl peniteat Bi II. 1, 5. non maneant in unum tectum Vi 47. si quis capallum . . . inuenerit in uillam Wa A 18 (*cf.* P 11). det Deus penitentiam in corde uiri Vi 45 (S). porci in glande ingressi Wa A 25. si quis animalia uicini sui in herba commiserit Wa A 21. in manu hominis periurat Bi III. 3, 3. det . . . fructum penitentie in manu sacerdotis Vi 35. 36. recipiatur in patria

sua Vi 23. si . . . aliquid . . . stillauerit in terra Cu (XI). 26. nisi . . . per herba det Wa P 61. pro animalia duo Wa A 21. titubare super oratione Cu (XI). 29. (*dubium:*) ipsam intentionem fuerit interfectus Wa P 2. — *Dissentiunt codices*: demedio, -um Wa A 58 (*bis*). ieiunio (-um E) . . . emendat Cu (V). 2. delictum (-o E) suum (-o E) Cu (V). 3. dignus es mercedem tuam (-a S) Pa II. 1. det pecunia (-am S) Vi 35. comprobatus fuerit testimonium (-o S) Vi 23. ab (K: ad *cett.*) reliquam plebem degradandus Pa II. 16. ad reorum defensionem (-e DJ) Pa II. 9 (a -e Q; *u. app. crit.*). ante oculis (-os B) creatoris Bi pr. 4. cum benedictione (-em J) Pa II. 21. cum teborem (contempore J) mentis Pa II. 3. cum uxorem (-e S) Vi 35. de quohabitationem Pa II. 1 (Q: -e *cett.*). de contentionem (-e DJI) Pa II. 24. de excommunicationem (-e QDIY) Pa II. 4 de oblatione (-em DJ) Pa II. 12. de uoluntate (-em J) Pa II. 27. remittuntur . . . omnium peccata in baptismo (-um J) Pa II. 31. in consuetudine uertunt Vi (2); in -em Cu (X). 15. si in consuetudine fuerint adsueti Vi (3) = Cu II. 8; *sed* in -em Cu (X). 16. manere in continentiam (-a S) Vi 41. in mancipio uidetur Wa A 48; in -um fuerit Wa P 55. in morte (-em P) hereditatem dimisserit Wa A 38 (P 42). per inpositionem (-e DJ) Pa II. 8 (pro -e Q). per mensura V, per -am SPB *semper in* Vi. per obreptione (inreptionem SP) Vi 24. pro redemptionem (-e S) Vi 35. super terra (-am C) iacere Da 11. *Cf.* foris Pa II. 13 (I: foras *cett.*). — *Accusatiuus et ablatiuus iunguntur*: dispoliare ecclesias et monasteriis Vi 30 (S). sextario Romano et alium Cu II. 3 (E). tres uel vii psalmis occupetur Cu (VI). 1. tres diebus peniteat Cu (VIII). 22. cum pane et aqua et sal Vi 23. pro suis episcopos Cu (IX). 12 (episcopis Gi 24). — *De accusatiuo et ablatiuo temporis u. Praefationem, p.* 32. — *Ablatiuus*: *abl. nudus pro* in *cum abl.*: alterior patriae cenubio uiuat Aq 1. inferiore gradu possitus Gi 2 = Cu II. 3. intimo corde dicamus Bi VIII. 6. *cf.* Cu (V). 1 (E). si quis iudicio fuerit conpetitus Wa P 2. *cf. Praepositiones* (in). — *abl. comparationis*: suauiora ceteris sumat Cu I. 5 = Bi I. 4, 3. si minus decimo substantiam habuerit Hi III. 6. his amplius Pa II. 18. leuius solito poenitere Bi II. 3, 2. duplici penitentia emendetur predicta Bi IV. 6, 6. plus omnibus honeretur Bi VI. 1, 1. — *abl. causae*: peccatis praeualentibus facto peccare Co A 3. si gulae uitio hoc fecerit Co B 24; *cf.* Bi I. 3, 1. qui homicidium odii meditatione facit Cu (IV). 5. uituperatione mali *mala retractans* Cu (VIII). 16. inuidia homicidium facere Wa A 2. si . . . semet ipsum occidit quacumque causa Bi IV. 2, 1. secundis prima *uota* non sunt irrita Pa II. 28. causa, gratia *c. gen. pro abl. causae: u.* **Praepositiones.** — *abl. instrumenti:* remisio . . . qua baptizamur Cu pr. 2. incerta ueterato tempore Pa II. 30. — *abl. modi:* petat ueniam plena confessione et humilitate Vi 5. coitu fęmineo peccare Co B 15. caritate . . . copuletur Cu (IV). 4 = Bi IV. 4. facto peccare Co A 3. rixa mactare hominem ('in the course of') Wa P 7. homicidium uoluntate facere Da 7. uoluntate patrum nupto filiam *iungere* Wa A 59. multa increpatione plectatur Gi 8. — *abl.* = secundum *cum acc.:* ecclesiastico dogmate egenis . . . fenerandum est Vi 32. iudicio doctoris Aq 1. episcopi uel sacerdotis Vi 12. sacerdotis Vi (2). Co B 2. 13. 18. Cu (VIII). 3. (ad iudicium sacerdotis Cu (VIII). 2. Hi II. 7 (B). Bi VII. 2.) senatus Cu (X). 20. legibus se nouerit rediturum Wa A 16. dictis legibus manum suam redemat Wa A 57 (P 65). — *abl. qualitatis:* diuersis medicamenta generibus conponunt Co B pr. — *abl. limitationis:* maiores natu Wa A 36. casti corpore Vi 41. si fortis fuerit corpore Hi V. 10. qualis existat fortitudine Cu ps. 1. praestando uerum durus Wa P 2. — paratus corde Co A 2. — *abl. absolutus: u.* **Praefationem,** *p.* 32 *sq.* — **Attractio inuersa casus:** non sumit lucerna nisi quod (quo *Coll.Hib.*) alatur Pa II. 2. — *Cf.* **Praepositiones** (ad, cum, de, in, per, pro, sub).

Formatio adiectiuorum: animalis Cu (XI). 15. aquilonalis Aq tit. bestialis Ad 4. 18. carnalis Co A 8. coniugales Co B 16. laicalis Bi II. 4. laetalis Ad 18. mundialis Bi pr. 2. principalis Cu pr. 15. Bi pr. 39–47. uisceralis Vi ps. uitalis Hi III. 1. — triduanus *septies.* — fornicarius Vi 45 (S); *u.* **Formatio substantiuorum.** — femineus Co B 15. gallinaceus Cu II. 2. — mortiferum Bi V (*ter*). pestifer Cu (IV). 16. salutiferum Bi V. 1, 1. 2. — excusabilis Cu (XI). 10. hodibilis Vi 21. plebilis Bi IV. 6, 4. — elinguis Gi 10 = Cu I. 4. excommonis Pa I (*septies*). septiformis Ca 2. — contentiosus Cu (VII). 1 = Bi VII. 4. inlecebrosus Vi 14. 15. 19. Cu (X). 2. iniuriosus Cu (IV). 13 = Bi IV. 5, 2. — curnupetus Ad 7. — noctuus Wa A 22.

Adiectiua et aduerbia composita: coaequalis Pa I. 11. Co A 12. Ca 3. compar Hi IV. 2. conscripta = scripta Pa I. pr. consimilis = similis Aq 5 = Cu (VIII). 11. inconditus Co A 8. inconsultans Gi 25. inconsultu abbate Pa I. 34 (*bis*). inpollutus Bi II. 7. insolubilis Pa II. 14. — inibi = ibi Co B 30. incongrue Pa II. 20. indesinenter Pa II. 14.

Formatio aduerbiorum: corporaliter Cu II. 12. Bi II. 1, 6. Bi VI. 3, 7. excusabiliter Cu (IX). 1. indesinenter Pa II. 14. licenter Cu pr. 15. perseueranter Vi 17. septempliciter Ca 1. 2. tollerabiliter Bi VI. 3, 6. mixtim Co B 12. nominatim Wa A 4. 31. — fortassis Bi pr. 24. — parumper Cu II. 2. — postmodum = postea Pa I. 19. Hi II. 7 (B). — tenileto Cu III. 13.

Aduerbiorum usus: casu = forte Cu (IV). 8 = Bi IV. 3, 3. hinc 'therefore' Bi pr. 2. unde = ea causa quod Ad 14. *cf.* 16 (quia PB[1]). ita = ea condicione Vi 12. 14. 15. sic = ea condicione Pa I. 15. 16. Vi 5. 6. 23. Cu (IV). 1 (*sed u. app. crit.*) = Bi IV. 4. Wa A 4, sic ut = ita ut Wa P 8. 9. *De uoce* sic *proleptice usurpata u.* **Pleonasmus.** — *Cf.* **Praepositiones** (ante, post).

Adiectiua pro substantiuis usurpata: coniugales = mariti Co B 16. nupto filiam iuncxerit Wa A 59. communicare ab ecclesia excommunicato Cu (IX). 2. peccans = peccator Bi pr. 2. recti 'the righteous' Pa I. 31. — *neutra:* biduanum Aq 5. dimedium annum . . . dimedium aliud Vi 15. medium ancelle Wa P 7. dampni Wa A 9. debendo (= -um) *pretii* Wa A 58. missum 'dish' (?) Gi 1 = Cu II. 2. modicum furti Cu (X). 11. uerborum Bi VII. 4. morticinum pecoris Bi I. 5, 12. in profundum inferni Vi 29. siue prosperum siue contrarium Vi 41. de reliquo uitae Vi 22. residuo uitae Lu 4 (*bis*). triduanum, -a Gi 20. Da 15. Cu (VIII). 25. Hi II (P). 2. 3. triduum Hi II (B). 2. 3. 4. — aliena diripere Cu III. 5. contraria Vi 28. 29. Cu pr. 15. excerpta Da tit. extincta Ad 3. inlicita Cu pr. 15 (*opp.* licita). inpensa Cu (IV). 9. interiora Wa A 10 (P 8). meliora proferre Vi ps. de minutis morum inconditorum Co A 8. mortalia Hi III. 3 (*opp.* animantia). *cf.* 1. munda . . . inmunda Ad 11. omisa uerborum Bi pr. 28. primitiua = primitiae Hi III. 3. primogenita Hi III. 5. de uerbis sacrorum Cu (IX). 9. superflua Cu III. 3. 14. Bi III. 6, 2. decimas de uitalibus et mortalibus . . . demus Hi III. 1.

Adiectiua pro aduerbiis usurpata:
largus uiuat Cu III. 13 = Bi III. 6, 1.
semiannus paeniteat Da 14. si spontaneus
minauerit Wa P 19. triduanus in aecclesia
Hi II. 4 (P). uoluntarius ire Wa P 64. —
*Neutrum adiectiui cum praepositione pro
aduerbio positum:* ad liquidum Bi pr. 21.
ad modicum Bi VI. 3, 6. ad purum Co B
pr. (*cf.* 3 Reg. 14, 10). de cetero Vi 21.
Bi VIII. 2, 2. de reliquo Da 5. Vi 4. *cf.*
22. Cu (VIII). 9. ex integro Co B 20. in
aeternum Co B 3. in totum Ad 18.
in absconso Vi 10, *cf.* in secreto Da 15. in
crastino Cu II. 15. in futuro Vi 22 (*bis*).
46. in nouissimo Vi 41 (*u. app. crit.*). in
primo Vi 22.

Aduerbium e nomine pendet: sono
psalmorum frequenter Bi V. 3, 2.

Comparatio: multum inmunde Ad 8.
— bonum est monacho manducare carnem
. . . quam manducare in obtractatione
carnes fratrum Bi VIII. 3. — uerba
aceruiora proferre Cu (IV). 13 = Bi IV.
5, 2. studium diligentius cordis et corporis Vi 10. obtentu insoliti cybi pinguioris
Bi I. 3, 1. si abundantius *aliquid* effuderit
Cu (XI). 4. confessiones dari diligentius
Co B 30. inferius = infra Pa I. pr.
saepius Co A 3. Bi V. 1, 6. satius Pa I. pr.
tepidius repugnans Cu II. 14. *Hic fortasse
adiungendum:* quidam aiunt intollerabilius Bi II. 5, 2. — his amplius non est
in messe Dei Pa II. 18. si . . . magis
(= plus) inueniat Vi ps.

Numeralia: dua milia Wa P 59.
uigentisimus Bi II. 2, 5 (C). quater denis
diebus Cu (XI). 20. bis septenis diebus
Bi pr. 18. ter quinquageni (*i.e.* psalmi)
Hi II (P). 1. *cf.* 2. — ternis (= tribus)
peniteat diebus Cu (XI). 27.

Pronomina: *Pron. reflexiuum
generaliter usurpatum:* triduanum . . .
cum uestimento circa se Hi II. 3 (P). —
sibi, se = ei, eum: Aq 7 = Cu (VIII). 13.
Cu (IV). 16. Ad 18. Bi IV. 7. — se *pro
datiuo:* de furto se nouerit conponendum
Wa A 19. *cf.* 37. P 28. 67. — **Pron. reci-
procum:** inuicem *pro* inter se: Pa I. 9.
Wa A 20, *cf.* P 29. separari ab inuicem Vi
40 (S). — abstinere se (ab) inuicem Vi
46 (*bis*). inritantes, coinquinantes, percutientes se inuicem Cu (X). 4. 6. 21. —
Pron. possessiuum: suus sine ui reflexiua
usurpatur: in caput suum erit Vi 34. non
debet demittere uxorem *sterilem* propter
sterilitatem suam Vi 41. si ab aliquo discesserit sua uxor Vi 42–45 (V) = Cu II.
29 = Bi II. 7. dimittatur illi sua culpa
Co B 15. altero pedes suos (*i.e.* senioris)

lauante Co B 28. bibitio glantelle uel
cohabitatoris sui Hi I. 23. *cf.* 27. *uice
uersa:* omnem substantiam eorum
(= suam) . . . diuidant Ca 3. — proprius
= suus Vi 39 (S). 40 (S). Co B 14. 17.
Cu II. 23. Ad 16. Bi II. 5, 1. — ex
clentella propria sua Vi 27. non intret
ad uxorem suam propriam, *sim.* Vi 36. 37.
39 (S). proprio domino suo Wa A 48. —
Pron. demonstratiuum: filii dotem
accipiant. Quod si hos non habuerit . . .
Wa A 47. ex his quae Vi 30 (S); *cf.* 41.
cum his quorum Cu ps. 3. si . . . hunc
iecisset Hi V. 2. hoc = id: Gi 18. Lu 9.
Cu (X). 11. Pa II. 23. Bi I. 4, 2. hoc est
Cu pr. 8. (VIII). 28. Hi V. 11. Pa II. 5.
17 (*bis*). Bi II. 8, 3; *sed* id est Vi 34. Co
B 15. Cu (X). 18. Hi I. 4. III. 1. IV. 6.
Bi IV. 7. V. 3, 2 (?). VII. 4. (i. *uel* .i.
Hi II. 2 (P). III. 5. V. 2. 5. 9. Bi IV. 7.) —
iste (*locos selectos damus*): quicumque
super animam famam istam inposuerit
Pa I. 16. si . . . istae inueniuntur bestiole
Cu (XI). 14. — *idem fere quod* is:
secundum istam sententiam Vi 46. finit
istud opusculum Vi ps. si per istum
fuerint capta Wa P 31. si uero nihil in se
habuerit uirile . . ., iste transit Bi pr. 23.
uiae Domini iste (= hae) sunt Bi pr. 49. —
ille = is Co B 15. Cu III. 3. Wa A 47. 62.
Hi III. 1. ps. Ca 2. — ipse = idem: finis
qui prius fuerat ipse permaneat Wa A 42
(P 43). — in ipsius iuramento ('in his
oath alone') causa finiatur Wa A 43, *cf.*
P 44. adulter quoque et ipse ('he, too')
triannio Lu 3. diuine lectionis scrutator
ipse ('he, on his part') Vi ps. — ipsius
(= Dei) munera Hi III. 1. si ipse (=
dominus) minauerit eos Wa A 25. —
*Distinctionis personarum causa ipse pro is
aut ille ponitur* Wa A 2. 6 (P 5). 15 (P 12).
47. 53 (*bis*). 59. *cf.* Hi V. 2 ipse uir Dei.
— ipse = is: Vi 12. Wa A 15 (P 12).
19 (P 28). 28 (P 23). P 29. Hi VI. 4
(*uariatio*). — semet ipse: nihil reddatur
pro *cane* nisi semet ipse Wa A 62. de
occidentibus semet ipsis Bi IV. 2 tit. —
isdem = idem Cu (X). 10. — talis = is:
si . . . canes lambuerint talem uomitum
Cu I. 11, *cf.* Bi I. 3, 3. — **Pron. interro-
gatiuum:** qualis = quae Cu ps. 1 =
Bi pr. 2. ut quid (ἵνα τί) Ad 10. 15. —
Pron. relatiuum: omittitur antecedens:
quadruplum pro quo iurauerat Da 16.
det pecuniam quem percutit Vi 9. placeat
largitate quem frustrauit Bi III. 5, 2. si
cui dicitur separatus (*i.e.* si ab eo cui
dicitur separatus est) Bi IV. 6, 1. si uero
qui praeest (de eo qui Cu (VIII). 9) Bi

VIII. 2, 2. — omnis qui *pro* quicumque Vi 30 (V). Hi IV. 9. omnia quaecumque Vi 30 (S). — quidam commedens = quicumque comedit Cu (X). 18. — quilibet = quicumque Wa *passim*. Bi III. 2, 1. Cu (VIII). 1 = Bi VIII. 1. — qui . . . cuicumque seniori flecti dedignatur Cu (VIII). 18. — **Pron.** *indefinitum:* aliquis, aliquid, aliqui *in enuntiatis negatiuis et condicionalibus passim*. aliquod = aliquid (*sic* B) Hi IV. 9 si quis episcopus aut aliquis ordinatus Bi I. 1. — offensus quis (= si quis offensus est) ab aliquo debet hoc indicare abati Gi 18. *similiter*: uagus instabilisque quis Cu (VI). 2. — quia quis non nisi ex contentione hereticus fiat Bi VII. 4. — in fine cuiusque mensis Aq 5 (unius cuiusque Cu (VIII). 11). — in una quaque hebdomada Gi 1 = Cu II. 2. uni cuique ebdomadae II. 8 (B: in singulis ebdomadibus P). in una quaque hora Hi II. 2 (P: omni B). 9 (B). *cf.* 4 (B *bis*). in uno quoque anno Hi III. 2 (*bis*; omni anno 1 *bis*). unius cuiusque capilli *pretium* Hi IV. 6. unius cuiusque gradus Hi V. 7. 8. unius cuiusque *psalmi* in fine Bi II. 1, 7. — iustus quisque Vi 9. — unus . . . alia Pa I. 9. non . . . creaturam aliam sed creatorem Pa II. 23. alius = aliquis (*Hib.* alaile) Pa I. 5 (?). 11 (?). Wa P 32. Bi IV. 3, 2. 4. — alter = alius *u. Praefationem, p.* 37 *sq.* — homo *pronominis indefiniti instar*: *u. Ind. uerborum*. — nullus = nemo Wa A 27 (P 21). A 39. P 61.

Nominis cum pronomine structura: aliquid causae Cu (XI). 10. liquoris Cu (XI). 16. idem creminis Pa I. 16. quidquid uiti Wa A 48 (P 55). mali Hi VI. 1. quod mali fecerit Hi VI. 1. — aliquid furti Cu I. 13 = Bi I. 4, 2. aliquid modici furti Cu I. 14. aliquid modicum furti Cu (X). 11. paruum aliquid iniquitatis Bi pr. 15. — alicuius sancti Ca 1. alicuius sanctorum Bi I. 2, 3.

Esse, fieri, uerba auxiliaria: absolui esse peccata Vi 10. *De copula omissa u. Praefationem p.* 43 *sq.* — existere *pro* esse: *u. Ind. uerborum, p.* 307. — *Pro participio uerbi q.e.* esse *ponitur* constitutus Vi 29. 33 (*bis*). 34 (*ter*). Bi VII. 4. pos(s)itus Gi 2 = Cu II. 3. Bi pr. 21. — fieri *pro uerbo contingentiae usurpari uidetur*: continens fieri debet Cu II. 30. pueri . . . praefata scelera facientes . . . puniendi fiunt Bi II. 2, 5. conuerso propitius fiat Deus Cu ps. 4 = Bi pr. 34. *cf.* securus fiat Wa A 1. 4. posse *abundat*: cum quo eam inuenire potuerit Wa P 17. — posse *absolute*

ponitur: si concupiuit et non potuit Vi 17, *cf.* Cu II. 11 = Bi II. 1, 5. dicimus posse renouare coronam Vi 21. potest, ut oretur pro eo Bi IV. 2, 1. — **debere**: *abundat*: reddi debere (*om.* Wa A) praecipimus Wa P 2 (A 3). — non debetur . . . offerri decimam Hi III. 1 (non debet III. 2). — conuenit (= debet) offerre decimas aliquis Hi III. 7. oportet (= debet) . . . libera fieri ancilla Vi 40 (S). — *De uerbo q.e.* facere *u. Praefationem, p.* 31.

Verborum formatio: anathemazare Pa I. 16. debilitare Co B 21. Wa A 3. notescere Vi 10. pastoriare Wa P 63. plagare Wa A 58. — iustificare Vi 22. mortificare Ad 18. Ca 3. Bi VI. 3, 5. testificari Co A 8.

Verba composita: cohabitare Bi I. 7 tit. consignare Wa (*quinquies*). contestari Aq 5 = Cu (VIII). 11. discooperire Co B 28. paruipendere Bi IV. 9. rebaptizare Pa II. 7. repropitiare Cu ps. 3. 4 = Bi pr. 33. 34. — *Pro simplicibus fere usurpantur*: aboriri Bi pr. 23. abrenuntiare Co B 19. ad(at-)testari Cu pr. 6 (LFM). conscripta Pa I pr. denegare Hi V. 6. derelinquere Pa II. 15 (relinquenda Y, tit.) dispoliare Vi 30 ≐ Cu (IX). 14. diuitare Wa A 36. Pa II. 4. 17 (DJ). 29. Bi VIII. 3. educere Lu 4. efficere Pa II. 27. emundare Cu (XI). 29. euomere Cu I. 8, *cf.* Bi I. 3, 1. Cu I. 11 = Bi I. 3, 3. exoriri Wa A 42 (P 43). exposcere Vi 34. exsoluere Wa (*undecies*). inpastoriare Wa P 63. perdurare Ad 14. perfrangere Gi 26. permanere Wa A 38 (manere P 42). praemulgere Ad 10. recognoscere Cu (XI). 17. referre Pa II. 13 (J). reiterare Co B 24. resurgere Pa II. 10 (J). superaddere Gi 1 = Cu II. 2. — *Simplex uerbum pro composito ponitur*: ebrietur Da 3 (inebriatur Cu I. 2). fundendo Cu II. 22 (E: effundendo R).

Coniugatio: odis Bi VI. 2, 1. tundatur Co B 20. uegit Bi VII. 4. — (conuertat et) ieiuniat (ieiunat B) Bi VII. 2. subdeat Bi VII. 1 (-dat Cu (VII). 1). diripet *forma incerta* Bi III. 2, 1. — effunderit Vi 8 (S). Wa A 50 (-fud- ABX). Bi II. 1, 2. expeterit Vi 44. euomerit Cu I. 8. uomerit Co A 6 (Tii*). lambuerint Cu I. 11 (-berint E), *cf.* Bi I. 3, 3. odierit Bi IV. 4. relinquit (*perf.*) Hi V. 4. tangerit Cu (XI). 27 (tetigerit E). statuere Gi 5. — furentibus = furantibus Bi I. 4 tit. *Sim.* tardentes Bi VI. 3, 4. uiolente Bi II. 5 tit. contempnantibus Bi I. 8 tit. offerantis Cu (XI). 23.

Verbum intransitiuum uel absolutum: abscondat Pa II. 15 (*u. app. crit.*).

Verbum intransitiuum (*cont.*).
abstineat Cu II. 31; *sed* abstineat se Vi
14. 46. Co B 14. si . . . testes adequauerint
Wa A 20 (sibi testes adequant P 29). ad
uitam perfectam . . . debit unusquisque
constringere Pa II. 17. ieiunio . . .
emendat Cu (V). 2 (se emendat Bi V. 3, 1).
iactans in sua beneficia Bi VII. 3. (surgere
transitiue usurpatur Bi IV. 7.) — si aetas
non defendit Co B 10. spe unica salutis
indulgente Cu pr. 13. occidere *absolute*
Pa I. 14. — *uerb. reflexiuum*: caueat se
Vi 4 (V). — *Tertia persona absolute usurpari uidetur*: si . . . interiora inspiciat
Wa A 10 (P 8). ut cerebri cutem inspiciat
Wa P 9, *cf*. A 11 ('if, that one sees').

Genera uerbi : amantissimi fratres Vi
ps. anno emenso Aq 6 = Cu (VIII). 12.
confitere (-i E) Cu (IV). 16. fornicauerit
Co A 3. B 3. 4. 10. 15. 16. 17. fornicare
Co B 23. *alias* fornicari. furauerit Co A 4.
B 7. 19 (furatus fuerit *ubique* Ti). furat
Cu I. 12. (furatus Aq 4 = Bi I. 4, 1.) *alias*
furari. moechare Pa II. 26 (mechari K).
testificauerit (?) Co A 8 (Tii*). uescit Da
14. — perpetratus fuerit Cu I. 12 (E).

Tempora uerbi : *Praesens pro futuro*:
non facio Co A 9. tu sede in cella tua et
cogitationes iterum ueniunt Bi VI. 3, 6.
uouerit permanere kasta Pa I. 17. se falso
dicens captiuos redimere Vi 30 (V) = Cu
(IX). 14. non maledicis (-es KQI) Pa II.
4. — *praesens absolutum*: eum non suscepit . . . quia hominem non recipiat Hi V.
2. — *Futurum pro coniunctiuo praesentis*:
resoluetur Pa I. 14. roget . . . faciet Gi 1 =
Cu II. 2. ut . . . fiet Cu pr. 7 (E). exilium
patietur Aq 3. percutiet Vi 1 (S : -at V). —
uice uersa: accipiant . . . fructum Vi 46.
Cf. si . . . capitale furtum fecerit morte
morietur (-atur AO), terra quam emerat
fisco reuertatur (-etur P) Wa A 45 (P 49).
ne . . . uindicent et . . . percutiant (-ent B)
Bi pr. 3. — *Perfectum: coniunctiuus perfecti
coniunctiui aoristi instar est*: consortium
femine de corde suo absciderit Vi 14.
si . . . sacrificium euomerit Cu I. 8
(euomit Bi. I. 3, 1). si quis foramen
fecerit, tamen membro non noceat Wa A
14. iudicibus persuadendum est ut . . .
occiderint (-ent QDJ) Pa II. 9. ne incauti
alligauerint . . . et non soluerint Bi pr. 3.
— *perfectum pro praesenti*: in eodem libro
dixit Bi VI. 3, 4. 5. *Cf*. qui concupiscit . . .
fornicari sed non potuit Cu II. 11. — *Plus-
quamperfectum*: si . . . conpetitus fuerit
et nullam iam infamiam antea portauerat
(P *differt*) . . . si antea famam portauit
(-erat O.P 45) . . . Wa A 43 (P 44. 45). finis

qui prius fuerat permaneat Wa A 42
(P 43). quis . . . scit quas . . . carnes . . .
comederat Ad 12. Sodoma quam pe-
nam meruerat . . . sciat Hi V. 1. — *ppf.
pro imperfecto*: populus Israel debuerat
constringi Hi III ps. in illis temporibus
homines crudam carnem comaederant
Ad 14. — *V.* etiam **Enuntiata secundaria** (postquam).

Modi : *V.* Praefationem, *pp*. 34 *sqq*.,
38 *sqq. infra*, **Enuntiata secundaria**.
*Praeterea haec pauca notamus: Coniuncti-
uus*: *c. potentialis*: ceterique malint Da
11. aelimosinam praedonis inuassi fletus
extinguat (-it PB[1]) Ad 15. quia quis non
nisi ex contentione hereticus fiat Bi VII.
4. — *c. subiectiuus*: quia hominem . . . non
recipiat Hi V. 2. non quia . . . crudam
carnem comaederant quia non esset
dulcior Ad 14. — *c. concessiuus*: aut uictor
aut uictus fuerit Vi 2. — *coniunctiuus
uerbi q.e.* debere: debeant (per)uenire
Wa A 37 (debent P 41). debeat peniterc
Bi IV. 3, 2.

Verbum infinitum: 1. *Infinitiuus
sine accusatiuo subiecti usurpatur*: uouerit
permanere kasta Pa I. 17. nequaquam
facere promittat Co B 19. nullam causam
timeat habere Wa A 17 (se habere P 27).—
inf. finalis: festinemus curare Vi 29. non
intret amplius fornicari Vi 36. qui diu
inluditur fornicari Cu II. 14. quali compulsus est grauatione peccare Cu ps. 1,
cf. Bi pr. 2. iusit dari manducare Bi IV.
7. — *inf. e uerbo uolendi pendet*: disposuit . . . proximum percutere aut occidere Vi 6. concupierit hominem occidere
Co A 2. — *inf. post uerbum cum signi-
ficatione negatiua*: non cessandum est
eripere Vi 34. si . . . neglexerit quis sacrificium accipere Cu (XI). 10. non prohibentur offerre Gi 24 = Cu (IX). 12.
Christus eos ignem mittere prohibuit Hi
V. 3. prohibet, prohibuit . . . | manducari
Ad 14. 19. — *notamus praeterea*: meruit
excommunicare Pa I. 1. si . . . dona
inuadere fuerit depraehensus Pa I. 26. —
Infinitiuus passiuus: si uoluerit uenundari
eam Vi 40 (S). elemosinam . . . recipi non
licet Pa I. 13. fur . . . occidi (non) licet
Wa A 27. monachus . . . decet uindicari
Pa I. 34. decet suscipi eam Vi 44 (S).
V. etiam *supra, p*. 345 (debere). *Similis
structura inuenitur post uerba iubendi*: quasi proprium reddi non dicitur Hi IV. 6.
(*similiter*: eum . . . crucifigi iudicant IV.
1.) confessiones dari . . . praecipitur Co B
30. medium dampni poni praecipimus
Wa A 9. conponi praecipimus Wa A 50

(conponendum P 58). — *Duae structurae contaminantur*: homicida congruum est nominari Pa I. 31. — 2. **Gerundium, Gerundiuum:** siue ad ussum necessarium siue aegentibus distribuendum Pa I. 25. neglegendo = neglegentia Gi 21 = Cu (IX). 10. oscolando illecebroso Vi 14. .iii. diebus tacendi (= silentii) Cu III. 18. — *Gerundium pro participio praesenti usurpatur*: qui . . . maculatus fuerit dormiendo (= dormiens) Gi 22. stando uigilet, canet *ibid.; similia*: Vi 14. 35. Co B 27. 28 (*bis*). Cu II. 15 (*bis*). 22. Bi VI. 3, 5. *Hic fortasse adiungendum*: praestando uerum durus Wa P 2. stando et orando in omni hora Hi II. 2 (B). — *Gerundiuum pro participio praes. pass.*: elemosinam a gentibus offerendam . . . recipi Pa I. 13. cum mandatis Dei implendis et uitiis expellendis Vi 46. usque ad modum sanguinis consummandum Cu II. 30. inuocandis (-atis P 33) uiris Wa A 32. — saluandos esse = saluari posse Bi pr. 25. — 3. **Supinum:** maiores natu Wa A 36. quod dictu scelus Bi II. 2, 4.

Praepositiones: *a, ab:* ab iuuentute Co B 8. ab Iesu Pa II. 15. — extores ab ecclesia Cu (X). 3. ab uxore . . . ieiunat Bi II. 5, 1. cum . . . peccatorem ab errore correxeris, a uitiis emendaueris Cu ps. 4 = Bi pr. 34. purgatur ab inmunditia Bi pr. 23. — inluditur fornicari a cogitatione Cu II. 14. a iudici condictione dampnetur Wa P 48. — ab hinc, ab aliunde Pa I. 9. ab inuicem Vi 46. — *absque* babtismum Vi 47. absque necessitate Co B 28. absque carne . . . uiuat Ca 3. absque dubio Wa P 32. — *ad* uomitum distendi Cu I. 7. ad aruspicem iurare Pa I. 14. submittere se ad penitentiam Vi 4. si quis ad alterum lanceam miserit Wa P 13. frater applicuit ad abatem Bi VI. 3, 3. — *aduersum* peccatum Bi pr. 23. — *ante* inpletum annum = anno non iam inpleto Wa A 48 (P 54). si quis caballum ante latronem excusserit Wa P 57. — *ui aduerbiali*: praelato ante monachi uoto Gi 1 = Cu II. 2. *sim.* Gi 26. 27. Vi 24. 27. Co B 18. Bi IV. 2, 1. mense ante praedicto *tributo* Wa A 30. — *apud*: omnia quaecumque inuenta fuerint apud eum Vi 30 (S). — *causa c. gen.*: anteponitur decies, postponitur nouies, interponitur semel (empti c. muneris Vi 24 P). *pro ablatiuo causae*: ussus neglegentiae c. Pa I. 7. infirmitatis c. Gi 7. Cu I. 9. Bi I. 3, 3. ebrietatis c. Gi 10. odii c. Cu I. 3. c. inuidie Cu (VIII). 8 = Bi VIII. 2, 2. ignorantiae c. Hi I. 1. non c. . . . .

inclementiae sed consuetudine Hi V. 2. uocationis causam (*sic*) non permittunt sub ditus discurrere Pa II. 21. c. uoracitatis Bi I. 3, 1; *cf.* Gi 7. — c. ipsorum percusit Deus Egyptum Hi III. ps. *matrimonium* c. filiorum . . . concessum est Vi 46. si quis c. fornicationis alterius uxorem infecerit Wa P 27. iecite puluerem de pedibus uestris, .i. excommunicationis c. Hi V. 5. — c. furti (furti c. P) suspicionem habere Wa A 28 (P 23). c. fornicationis Wa P 16. quicquid bonum fecerit c. humanae gloriae perdidit Bi VII. 3. *Cf.* effectu, gratia, obtentu. — *circa:* contentio c. finem territori Wa A 42 (P 43). cum uestimento c. se Hi II. 3 (P: praecinctus uestimento suo B). Hi II. 4 (B: cum uestitu, *om.* circa se, P). *postponitur* Cu (XI). 14 (E). — *cum:* testimonio . . . episcopi uel sacerdotis cum quo paenituit Co B 1. laicus cum uxore propria 'a married layman' Vi 39 (S). si . . . cum ipso fuerit consignatum Wa A 19 (P 28). P 29. — peniteat cum tribulatione Bi II. 6, 1. clamor excitatus cum tanto terrarum spatio a loquente Bi IV. 6, 1. peniteat . . . cum pane Pa I. 29. paenitere cum pane et aqua Vi *passim; u.* **Formulae.** — cum *c. abl. pro abl. causae aut instrumenti*: cum suo praetio illi subueniat Pa I. 32. si cum bonis operibus expleant matrimonium Vi 46. fratrem cum furore maledicens Cu (IV). 12 = Bi IV. 5, 1. sumnolentus cum uigiliis et orationibus sanetur Bi VI. 2, 2. — anathema sit cum (*Hib.* le) omnibus Christianis Vi 31 (S). — *de* furto se nouerit conponendum Wa A 19. dubius de uita Hi II. 7. de †Calpeis uel de Saxonibus uel de qualibet gente capallum conparare Wa A 20. si quis sustullerit de homine aequum aut uacam Wa A 24. de hoc consequens lectionis series Pa II. 23. — de c. abl. pro instru*mentali*: de fuste . . . interfectus Wa P 4; *sed cf.* A 5. de modico uerborum et ciborum et de nuditate saeculi et humilitate saluatur hoc uitium Bi VII. 4. — de *partitiuum*: si quis . . . de clericis aut de ministris Dei Vi 5. *sim.* Vi 27 (S). Co B 16. Hi V. 10. sextarius de lacte . . . de tenucla Gi 2 = Cu II. 3. himina de ceruissa Da 11. paruum de herbisa Hi II. 12 (P). plenum uas de farina Cu II. 2 (*glossa?*). de oleribus quantum pugnus capere potest Hi III. 5. bibitio de morticina pecoris Hi I. 19. quicquid de peccoribus nascitur Hi III. 4. quodcumque bestiae commedent de peccoribus Hi VI. 3. canem de genere eius reddat Hi VI. 3. si aliquid de capillis

Praepositiones (*cont.*).

eius carptum fuerit Hi IV. 6. conparem uerticis de auro latitudinem reddat Hi IV. 2, *sim. ibid. bis.* 8. si . . . commotauerit aliquid de uerbis Gi 20 = Cu (IX). 9. pauca de penitentiae remediis, alia . . . de remediis aut de uarietate curandorum testimonia Vi ps. haec sufficiant de admonitione Bi VI. 3, 7. — de *c. abl. pro genitiuo praeter partitiuum*: bucellos (-as B) mensurae (*om.* P) de tribus panibus Hi II. 5. paenitentia de perditione mulieris de suo filio Hi I. 11. *sim.* Hi I. 12. V. 2. praetium animae de perditionem filii Hi I. 10. *cf.* Bi IV. 2, 4. confessiones . . . de commotionibus animi Co B 30. quantum iurauerit dominus de messe Wa A 21 (B: messis *cett.*). *Ex contaminatione fortasse explicatur*: prologus de medicinae salutaris Cu tit. (R). — *effectu*: hodii seu luxuriae Da 4 (odii causa Cu I. 3). — *erga*: neglegentia e. sacrificium Cu (XI). 19. — *ex* (e *perraro legitur*: e duobus Pa I. 31. e contrariis Vi 28. 29. e quibus Wa A 4. Bi pr. 30; *sed* ex quibus Wa A 31. P 3. 33. 34. Bi pr. 39): mulier . . . dimissa . . . ex uiro suo Vi 45 (S). ex ore leonis . . . id est de ore diabuli Vi 34. ex facultatibus nostris conpatiendum est nobis Vi 33. — *cum notione partitiua*: si quis . . . ex clericis Vi 14. — *cum notione causali*: ex odio, ex meditatione odii *aliquem* occidere Vi 24. Bi IV. 3, 4. ex contentione Co A 9 (*u. app. crit.*). — *extra*: alia doctrina extra scripturas Bi VII. 2. — *gratia semper postponitur*: humanitatis g. Da 3 = Cu I. 2. — (= causa, *pro abl. causae*) sitis g. Gi. 1 = Cu II. 2. *sim.* Gi 7. 10. 15 (= Cu (IX). 5). Da 1. Bi I. 3, 2. — *in*: terra . . . in (*om.* A) fisco reuertatur Wa A 45 (P 49). Deum in (*om.* A) fideiusorem inuocare Wa A 44 (P 48). in caput suum erit Vi 34. — in pane et aqua paenitere, *sim. u.* **Formulae.** in fletu et lacrimis Vi 29. *cf.* 12. in omni pietate atque subiectione Vi 44 (S). in omni patientia et castitate Vi 45 (S). — in femoribus scelus uirile facere Lu 8. *cf.* Cu II. 10. — fideiusor in quacumque quantitate Pa I. 8. — concupiscere in anima sua Vi 16. in corde, in corpore peccare Vi 1. 17 (*bis*). *sim.* Cu (V). 1 = Bi V. 3, 1. baptizamur in aqua Cu pr. 2. ut in testibus probetur Wa A 29 (ut t. adprobatur P 24). in testibus conprobetur Wa P 29 (*u. app. crit.* testibus conprobet Wa A 20). gaudere in mandatis Dei Bi V. 3, 2. sanus in bono opere Bi IV. 7. — *c. abl. loci*: in loco in quo ceciderit Cu (XI). 23. — *c. abl.*

temporis: in presenti tempore Vi 22. in omni tempore Bi VI. 2, 3. in illo tempore Hi V. 11. in illis temporibus Ad 14. — in *aut ponitur aut omittitur*: nocte Pascharum Pa I. 18. in nocte Paschae Pa II. 22. in nocte dominica Vi 46. uallum apertum in nocte dimittere Co B 26. *cf.* Cu (VIII). 23. — diebus ac (et) noctibus, die ac nocte Vi 2. 12. 14. 29. nocte dieque Cu II. 30. *sed*: in die Co B 26. in septima die Bi pr. 20. — in omni hora Hi II. 2 (B) — in primo anno Vi 35. primo (anno) . . . in alio Vi 36 (V). in vii anno Vi 27. Co B 6. in duobus annis Vi 37. in residuis tribus annis Vi 18. per duos annos in quibus . . . Co B 20. — in (B: *om.* C) initio estatis Hi III. 5. in tribus xlmis anni et sabbato et in dominico . . . et in duobus legitimis et concepto semine et in menstruo tempore Cu II. 30. — *iuxta*: aliquem i. episcopum ligare Ca 3. — (= secundum:) i. qualitatem peccati Cu II. 12 = Bi II. 1, 6. i. indulgentiam Noui Testamenti Bi IV. 1, 2. — *obtentu* = causa *pro abl. causae*: gulae o. Cu I. 5 = Bi I. 4, 3. boni confirmandi o. Cu (VIII). 16. o. insoliti cybi Bi I. 3, 1. — *per*: culpa illius per sacerdotem abstergatur Co B 14. si *animalia* per istum fuerint capta Wa P 31. sanguis . . . effussus . . . per bestias Ad 17. qui facit per se aliquid Cu A 9. per se ipsum fornicare Co B 10. — per sancta . . . euangelia . . . testetur Pa II. 24. — si porci per annonem manserint Wa A 22. euadere per dua milia Wa P 59. — per duas noctes Ca 3. per maiorem, minorem noctis partem Wa A 22. fur per noctem occidi licet, per diem non licet Wa A 27. per duos annos Co B 20. per spatium .vii. annorum Ca 3. linteamina . . . per tres abluat uices Cu (XI). 27. — per *c. acc.* *pro abl. modi aut causae*: per astutiam fallere Pa I. 8. discordare per discordiam Pa I. 31. per furtum captiuum inuolare Pa I. 32. per cogitationem peccare Vi 1. Co A 2. *cf.* Bi II. 1, 2. 3. per contemptum Da 1. 2. Cu III. 3. per infirmitatem Co A 6. B 12. per ignorantiam Da 1. 2. Co B 24. 25. Cu III. 3. 17 (= Bi III. 5, 3). per neglegentiam Da 1. 2. Vi 21. 47. Cu (XI). 26. Bi I. 9, 1. per penitentiam uindicetur Pa I. 34. *cf.* Vi 10. 12. 18. 47 (V). per rapinem predam abstrahere Ca 1. aliquid auferre Ca 2. percutere per rixam fratrem, proximum Co A 5. B 9. per furorem et non ex meditatione Cu (IV). 7 = Bi IV. 3, 2. per turpiloquium uel aspectu coinquinatus Cu II. 12 = Bi II. 1, 6. *sim.* Vi 2. 4. 24 (*bis*). 29. Co A 11. B 12. 20.

Pa II. 15. Bi pr. 69. II. 1, 1. — dicere per labia Vi 16. unum est peccatum per corpus et animam Vi 17. per difinitionem aliquid loqui Vi 4. praedarum pecora . . . siue per commercia siue per donationes non sunt summenda Ad 15. — per scandalum sanguinem fundere Co B 21. — remissio peccatorum per elemosinam datur Bi pr. 30. — blasfemantur multi clerici per unum latronem Pa I. 32. — *ad notionem praepositionis* pro *accedit*: per singula cremina annum penitentiae agat Pa I. 14. matrimonium . . . concessum est . . . per generationem filiorum et non libidine Vi 46. decimae . . . per animantia, per mortalia fiunt Hi III. 3. per porcum maiorem quadrisextarium redat Wa P 15. algam . . . per boues per herba det Wa P 61. — penitentia per lungum (= longa) Hi II. 12 (B). locus et tempus et persona per omnia obseruitur Pa II. 14 — *post* sanitatem eius . . . peniteat Co B 21. post manus inpositionem . . . altario iungatur Co B 25. post uota perfectionis Cu (IV). 6 = Bi IV. 3, 4. lapsi post gradum Pa II. 10. saluari post penas Bi pr. 25. — post *c. acc. pro abl. absoluto*: post paenitentiam transactam Co B 18. post abscisam uel tamen scisam aurem Ad 20. — (*ui aduerbiali?*) ante partum et post tempore purgationis Bi II. 9, 3. — *pro c. abl. causae*: pro consuetudine et imperitia illum non accipit Hi V. 2. pro inlecebroso amore *maleficus* Vi 19. *cf.* Co B 6. mendax pro cupiditate Cu III. 16. *cf.* Bi III. 5, 2. — pro honore (= in honorem) simulacrorum Co B 24. pro cultu daemonum *ibid.* — *sine postponitur* Cu I. 7. II. 23 (E). 29 (E). — *sub* falso nomine redemptionis Vi 30 (S). si mortuus fuerit infans sub tali tantum benedictione Cu (X). 20. — *super idem fere quod in* (*Gall.* sur): uagus et profugus sit super terram Co B 1 (*cf. Gen.* **4, 12**). super altare effundere, stillare Cu (XI). 4. 27. si porci alterius super annonam . . . manserint Wa P 15. — si titubauerit sacerdos super oratione dominica Cu (XI). 29. — .xii. dies et noctes super .xii. bucellos Hi II. 5. — *supra* possibilitatem meam . . . temptaui scribere Vi ps. — *usque* (*ad:*) si . . . usque ad mensem uitium non habuerit Wa A 49 (in mense uno P 56). usque mane dormire Bi VI. 2, 3.

Coniunctiones: 1. *Coni. copulatiuae*: et *in enumeratione ultimo loco ponitur*: Wa A 3. Bi pr. 2. et reliqua Bi VI. pr. VII. pr. — pane aquaque Aq 5. sine uino carneque Cu II. 24. (IX). 16. sine cibo potuque Hi II. 3 (B). sine carne uinoque Bi II. 11, 1. -que *passim in* Cu. -que = etiam: sunt praeterea aliaque Vi ps. et . . . -que: .xl. ψalmi et flectiones. xl. et horarumque oratio Hi II. 8 (P). — ac, atque: satis ac libenter Vi 44 (S). uiuus ac (et P) mortuus Wa A 34 (P 39). a scandalo ac inuidia Co B 30. sine cibo potuque ac (et P) sine dormitatione Hi II. 3. (B). resoluitur ac purgatur Bi pr. 15. *praeterea* Bi III. 1, 3. IV. 4. — hac (= ac) si Pa II. 26. — in fletu et lacrimis atque orationibus Vi 12 12 (S). in omni patientia atque subiectione Vi 44 (S). huc atque illuc Bi VI. 3, 6. *praeterea* Pa I. 6. — *uel idem fere quod et*: dilectionis gratia uel religionis obtentu Vi ps. de primis uel secundis uotis Pa II. 28. — *uel pauca* Co B pr. — 2. *Coni. causales*: itaque *secundo loco* Cu pr. 2. 15. — scilicet = nam Vi 29. — 3. *Coni. aduersatiuae et concessiuae*: nisi 'except', 'but': inermis existat nisi uirga tantum in manu eius Vi 35. ieiunia sine carne et uino nisi paruum de herbis a Hi II. 12 (P). tempore paenitentiae non illis liceat suas cognoscere uxores nisi post paenitentiam transactam ('but only . . .') Co B 18. pro delicto nihil reddat nisi disciplinam accipiat Wa A 26. *cf.* P 18. — tamen: reddito tamen . . . praetio Co B 16. data tamen ante . . . helemosina Co B 19. abscisa tamen aure Ad 18. post abscisam uel tamen scisam aurem Ad 20. — tamen si Lu 4. — licet: a licitis licet ('even') cohercere se Cu pr. 15. *cf.* **Enuntiata secundaria.** — *Plura u. sub lemm.* **Polysyndeton, Variatio.**

Negatio: nec *semper et ante consonantes et ante uocales legitur nisi* neque offerat Pa I. 24. neque homines Hi III. 8. — nec = non: nec ordinare praesumat Pa I. 30. nec (non R) ignorans Cu (IX). 2 (E). nec senior Hi V. 4. nec tamen = non tamen Bi pr. 10. necdum = nondum Da 6. — nec = ne . . . quidem Pa I. 12. 18. — *iunguntur* non . . . nec . . . nec Pa I. 9. non . . . nec Pa I. 17. non . . . neque . . . nec . . . nec . . . †nec Pa I. 24. non . . . nec . . . nec Pa I. 28. nec . . . nec Wa A 12 (P 51). non . . . nec Pa II. 29. (nullus . . . nec . . . nec . . . nec Wa P 61.) — non, nullus, *sim. cum coni. hortatiuo aut iussiuo*: carnem morticinam non manducetis Ad 14. (*sed* non maledices Pa II. 4 (KQI).) officium . . . non amittat Vi 10. *cf.* 15. non intret ad uxorem Vi 36. 37 (*bis*). 38. ad concubinam Vi 40 (S). *cf.* 36. *sim.* Bi II. 8, 1. non maneat cum uxore sua Vi 35. nec in uno lecto maneant Vi 45 (S). *cf.*

Negatio (*cont.*).

47. non maneat cum alio Co B 3. *praeterea*
Pa I. 3. 4. 9. 17. 24. 27. 28. 29. 30. Gi 27.
Vi 23. 27. Pa II. 25. (nullus:) Wa A 17
(P 27). A 27 (P 21. 22). A 39. P 61. (num-
quam) Co B 5. nullo modo non reiciatur
Wa A 49, *cf.* P 56. ne . . . alligauerint . . .
et non soluerint Bi pr. 3. — ut non *pro* ne:
Pa II. 30. Bi pr. 28. VII. 4. ut nullus =
ne quis Co B 29. Bi VI. 3, 7. — si . . .
neminem perdiderit Co B 6.

Enuntiata secundaria : 1. *Enuntiata
declaratiua:* discant . . . sacerdotes . . .
quia Cu ps. 3 = Bi pr. 33. (*aliter accipiendum*: dicit scriptura diuina quia Bi pr.
32, *cf.* Gr. ὅτι.) — sciendum quod Gi
14 = Cu (IX). 4. suspicatur quod . . .
deducitur Lu 5 = Cu III. 11 = Bi III.
3, 4. fateor quod . . . est Bi pr. 4. praedicauit quod sacrilegium hoc erat Co B
24. promittat . . . quod numquam reiteret
ibid. uidetur ostendi quod . . . pertineant
Bi pr. 10. sciendum est . . . quod . . .
non . . . liceat Co B 18. non praetereundum quod . . . debeat Bi IV. 3, 2. —
adfirmant ut . . . demus (= dandas esse)
Hi III. 1. — 2. *In enuntiatis interro-
gatiuis indicatiuus uerbi legitur*: quali
compulsus est grauatione peccare Cu ps.
1, *cf.* Bi pr. 2. sapiens aduertat quae bona
Abraham et Loth acceperunt Hi V. 1.
Sodoma . . . quam penam meruerat . . .
sciat *ibid.* quis . . . nostrum scit quas
inlicitas carnes *coruus* prius comederat
Ad 12. *sim.* Pa II. 19. 29. 31. Bi pr. 2
(*ter*). 29. 56. II. 1 pr. VIII. 3. *cf.* quid (K:
quod *cett.*) uult pater efficiat uirgo Pa II.
27. — considerit . . . si amor et desiderium
cessauit peccati Pa II. 11. de sacrificio . . .,
si fas est ferre foras Pa II. 13. — 3.
Enuntiata relatiua: nullum crimen
quod non potest ridimi Vi 47 (V).
peccatum tale est quod non remittetur Bi
pr. 23. *sed*: capitalia crimina, quae etiam
legis animaduersione plectantur (-untur
Fleming) Co B pr. quod sit circa corpora
illarum foras proiiciatur Cu (XI). 14. —
Coniunctiuus usurpatur post quisquis, quicquid, quicumque, &c.: Pa I. 6. 7. 11. 14.
15. 16. 17. 21. Vi 30 (V). 41. Cu (VII).
2 = Bi VII. 3. Cu (IX). 7 (cantauerint:
-unt Gi 19). 14. Wa P 4. A 38 (P 42).
Hi VI. 2. *post* prout Gi 1 = Cu II. 2.
*Sed ubique exceptis locis Pa I. 6 et Hi
VI. 2 aut coni. perfecti aut ind. futuri ex-
acti intelligi potest.* — 4. *Post* **uerbum
timendi** *legitur infinitiuus*: nullam causam
timeat habere Wa A 17 (nullam se timeat
habere causam P 27). — *Pro* ut *finali*

ponitur quod: det iuramento .iii. idoneos
quod (et P 11) nihil habeat damni Wa A
18. — *Post* ut *legitur indicatiuus*: anathe-
mazatur ut regno Dei est alienorum Cu
(VII). 1 (sit alienus Bi VII. 1). ut secundis
prima uota non sunt inrita Pa II. 28. —
ut *c. coni.* = 'as if': unum est ut occiderit
eum Vi 8. non minus peccatum eius est
ut esset clericus Vi 27. — 5. *Enuntiata
temporalia:* postquam *c. ind. plus-
quamperfecti:* Co B 25. *c. fut. exacto:* Vi
46. Bi IV. 7 (*quater*). — postquam perfecta sana esset Bi IV. 7. — antequam,
priusquam *c. coni.*: Pa I. 23. Co B 30
(*bis*). Cu (VIII). 22. Hi III. 4. Pa II. 24.
Bi II. 9, 1. nec (non) ante . . . quam ut
Pa I. 16. 29. *sed*: antequam communicant
Cu (X). 6. — *Coniunctiuus legitur post*
quamdiu Vi 14 (V). 43 (S). Bi IV. 4. *cf.*
quanto tempore inplacabilis sit Bi IV. 4
(fuit Cu (IV). 3). *post* donec = quamdiu
Bi pr. 21. *post* donec 'until': Pa I. 17. 18.
20. 28. Vi 2. 29. 38. 51. 53. Co B 30. Cu
(IV). 9 = Bi IV. 3, 1. Cu (XI). 11. Cu
(VIII). 4 = Bi VIII. 4. Bi VIII. 5. *post*
usque quam Vi 30 (S). *post* usquequo Vi
31 (S). 41. 46. *post* quando Cu (XI). 4. —
dum 'since' *cum notione fere causali:* Hi
V. 2. Bi pr. 28. 36. *similiter usurpatur*
quando Bi VIII. 3. — 6. *Enuntiata
concessiua:* etsi *c. coni.*: Pa I. 33. licet *c.
coni.* Vi 34. (*sed* licet periclitatur Pa II.
15.) *cf.* licet per ignem Bi pr. 10. a licitis
licet coercere se debuit Cu pr. 15. — 7.
Enuntiata condicionalia: si, nisi (forte)
c. coni. Pa I. 7. 27. Gi 9 = Cu (IX). 1.
Gi 16. Vi (4) = Cu (X). 17. Vi 12. 27.
44 (S). 45 (S). Co A 6. 7. 9. B 6. 29. Cu
(V). 2 = Bi V. 3, 1. Cu (VIII). 28. *cf.*
(XI). 3. Wa P 61. hac si liciat (-at DJIY)
Pa II. 26. *dissentiunt codices*: sint Vi (2),
sunt Cu (X). 15. facit Vi 5 (V: faciat
SPB). sunt Vi 23 (V: sint P). si bos es Pa
II. 1 (K: bos sis QY; *cf.* DJI). *De modo
dubitari potest*: si quis quesierit Pa I. 1.
sim. Pa I. 5. 8. 17. 18. 22. 23. 24. 25. 26.
28. 29. 30. 31. 32. Vi 2 (S). Cu pr. 11. I. 1.
sed cf. si quis . . . acciperit et collectum sit
Pa I. 4. si . . . uisus fuerit . . . et . . . non
tegat Pa I. 6. si . . . ostenderit . . . et . . .
habeat Pa I. 10. *similiter* cum (si Bi)
adsumpseris peccatorem Cu ps. 4 = Bi pr.
34. cum talis sacerdos sis et talis sit
doctrina tua Cu ps. 5 = Bi pr. 35. *sed*:
cum . . . retinet . . . sanetur Bi V. 3, 1
(qui Cu (V). 1). qui (= si quis) fratrem
contristet Cu (IV). 1 = Bi IV. 4. qui . . .
necessitate coactus sit Bi III. 3, 2. *Cf.
Praefationem, p.* 34 *sqq.*

Constructio ἀπὸ κοινοῦ, **zeugma** : qui repetit auferentem quae sua sunt Cu III. 4 = Bi III. 2, 2. — ab interioribus uitiis . . . abstinendum est et abstergendum Co B 30. qui corda omnium nouit diuersasque naturas indidit Cu ps. 2.

Constructio ad sensum : lectores cognoscant unus quisque aecclesiam in qua psallat Pa I. 2. dicatur : Ecce agnus Dei — non quae sua sunt singuli quaerentis (-es QDJI) Pa II. 21. quicquid . . . omnia Wa A 38 (P 42). si . . . manducauerit (*uar. lect.* -int), . . . de uentre earum Ad 6. supra dicta aetas . . . fornicantes Cu (X). 8 (E). offensus quis ab aliquo debet hoc (*i.e.* offensionem) indicare abati Gi 18.

Contaminatio syntactica : Christianus cui dereliquerit aliquis et prouocat eum . . . qui sic fecerit alienus sit Pa I. 21. clericus habens superflua donet ea pauperibus Cu III. 14 = Bi III. 6, 2. si quis uerbositate diligens fratrem deroget ei Cu (VIII). 14. cui maledixerit placeat illi Bi IV. 5, 1 (cui maledixerit placat, *omisso pronomine demonstratiuo,* Cu (IV). 12). susurrans serpens ad Euam de paradisso eam eiecit Bi VIII. 3. — qui bene non custodierit sacrificium et mus comedit illud Cu (XI). 1. cum quo eam inuenire potuerit et cum illo fuerit conprobatum Wa P 17. si quis ancellam alterius adpraehenderit et a domino suo potuerit euadere Wa A 52. cum puella fornicari nitens nec coinquinatus est Vi (4) = Cu (X). 17 (*om.* est). mendax . . . per ignorantiam et non nocuit, confiteatur Cu III. 17 = Bi III. 5, 3. pueri . . . se inuicem . . . coinquinantes et confessi fuerint . . ., .xx. uel .xl. diebus Cu (X). 6. *similiter in protasi* : si quis homicidi causa suspicatus et non est ei titulus conprobandi Wa A 4 (fuerit suspicatus P 3; *fortasse copula subaudiri debet*). si quis ingenuus faciens furtum noctu uel in ipso commisso lancea fuerit feritus Wa P 22. *cf.* .xxiiii. uiris nominatis et .xii. ex eis iurent Wa P 32. *sim.* 33. 34. si homo uexatus a diabolo (⟨et⟩ *Theod.*) nescit aliquid nisi discurrere Bi IV. 2, 1 (*copula omissa?*). — uolens peccare, sed non potuit, .xv. psalmos Da 9. irritantes se inuicem, sed coinquinati non sunt Cu (X). 4. — cogitationes . . . etsi ad modicum nutant sed iterum reuertuntur ad eum Bi VI. 3, 6 (sed *idem fere est quod* tamen). — qui per turpiloquium . . . coinquinatus non tamen uoluit fornicari corporaliter Bi II. 1, 6 (est *add.* Cu II. 12). *cf.* qui (*om.* R) falsum testimonium dicens Cu III. 12 (E).

Inconcinnitas, anacoluthon : mulier quae . . . iunxerit se adultero, quae haec facit excommonis sit Pa I. 19. *sim.* Christianus qui . . . quicumque Pa I. 16. si quis clericus uel si qua mulier . . . si aliquem . . . deciperat Vi 18. qui conuersus ingemuit . . . non commemorabuntur (eius *add.* B) dilecta quae gessit Vi 9 ex. (PB). — quantum iudices praetium sanguinis . . . iudicauerint, septima pars occissionis eius de sua iectione reddatur Hi V. 8. *cf.* 11. — clericus . . . nouus, baptizare . . . illum non licet Pa I. 27. clericus . . ., etsi habitet in plebe, non licitum ministrare Pa I. 33. *cf.* 34. sanguis presbiteri qui ad terram effunditur . . ., manus interfectoris abscidatur Hi IV. 7. — primo anno super terra, secundo lapidi capud inponendum, tertio super axem iaceat Da 11, quod si a ueraci, demedio uerax et demedio mendax iubemus mediate soluere Wa A 58 (*sed cf.* P 67). arreum anni triduum . . . praecinctus uestimento suo Hi II. 3 (B). eum qui effuderit sapientes crucifigi iudicant uel .vii. ancellas reddat Hi IV. 1. de gentilibus . . . quam penetentiam habent Pa II. 31. quae peperit masculum, octaba die et qui natus est circumciditur et illa sit munda Bi pr. 19.

Variatio : refugium crismalis . . . aut refugium baculis aut cimbalis Ca 1. — in nocte dominica uel sabbati Vi 46. matrimonium sine continentia non ligitimum sed peccatum est Vi 46. — non ad libidinem sed causa filiorum concessum est *ibid.* non causa . . . inclementiae sed consuetudine Hi V. 2. contemptus gratia . . . obliuione Gi 15 = Cu (IX). 5. uituperatione mali bonique conformandi obtentu Cu (VIII). 16. per generationem filiorum et non libidine Vi 46. per turpiloquium uel aspectu Cu II. 12 = Bi II. 1, 6. primo *anno* . . . in alio Vi 36 (V). in tribus xlmis anni et sabbato et in dominico . . . et in duobus legitimis et concepto semine et in menstruo tempore Cu II. 30. cura . . . et in eo quod diuersa sunt peccata et in discrepantia . . . uirtutum Bi pr. 28. pro infirmitate uel quia longo tempore se abstinuerit aut pro gaudio Bi I. 2, 3. — prius . . . postea Pa II. 15. — canem de genere eius opera ipsius facientem Hi VI. 4. — uenerit . . . aduenerit Bi pr. 21. — si . . . non interrogat nec aliquid causae . . . exsteterit Cu (XI). 10. si confitetur . . . et si . . . persistat Gi 17. si . . . sint, si . . . uertunt Vi (2). si quis surrexerit et disposuit Vi 6. qui . . . loquitur uel . . .

Variatio (*cont.*).

maneat Cu (VIII). 23. — osculatus et amplectans Cu II. 19 = Bi II. 1, 9. de his qui . . . edunt et bibentibus Bi I. 5 tit. — ex ore leonis . . . de ore diabuli Vi 34. per furorem et non ex meditatione Cu (IV). 7 = Bi IV. 3, 2. — et . . . -que Bi pr. 25. et . . . atque Vi 12 (S). uel . . . aut Vi ps. aut . . . aut . . . aut . . . uel certe . . . siue . . . uel Co A 2. aut . . . uel Co B 8. aut . . . aut (an R) . . . uel Cu (XI). 14. uel . . . -ue Wa A 8 (*u. app. crit.*). aut . . . uel Wa P 2. uel . . . aut Hi IV. 9. Bi I. 2, 3. uel . . . uel . . . seu . . . uel Bi III. 3, 3.

Ellipsis: *u. Praefationem, p.* 41 *sqq.*

Ordo uerborum: si quis animalia uicini sui in herba commisserit intacta et manserint in ea Wa A 21 (= et intacta manserint, *cf.* P 31). — iuxta nostram ex parte intellegentiam Co B pr. — *Chiasmus:* si quis clericus uel si qua mulier malefica uel maleficus Vi 18. si quis in ultimo spiritu constitutus fuerit uel si qua constituta sit licet peccatrix uel peccator fuerit Vi 34. — *Hyperbaton:* impleto cum testibus ueniat anno penitentiae Pa I. 14. quicquid cantauerunt replicet ex ordine fratres Gi 19. antiqui decreuere sancti Da 10. ebdomadam peniteat dierum Vi 5. paratus ad haec corde conplenda Co A 2. diuersis medicamenta generibus conponunt Co B pr. priorum statuta patrum nostrorum Cu (X). tit. sana sumatur fide Cu (XI). 14. ancellam illam in sacerdotis ponimus potestatem Wa A 60. Abraham et Loth . . . sapiens animaduertat quae bona acceperunt Hi V. 1. Christi aduentus sponsi nullas nostras legis (-es DJI) inueniat ieiunii Pa II. 14. aurum per ignem plumbis mixtum indignis decoquere Bi pr. 13. quanti memento meriti tibi est Bi pr. 29. Domini contra interdictum Bi III. 2, 2 (c. interd. Domini Cu III. 4). quidquid faciendi uoluerint habeant potestatem Wa P 4 (*mihi dubium*).

Asyndeton: stupens elinguis Gi 10 = Cu I. 4. inermis exsul Co B 13. 20. sine diliciis, sine uxore Cu II. 25. — animarum uulnera morbos dolores aegritudines infirmitates sanare Co B pr. sine uino, sine carne, sine armis, sine uxore Cu II. 22. (*polysyndeton per asyndeton continuatur:*) cum . . . Abraham et Isaac et Iacob Iob Noe omnibus sanctis Vi 46. — eucharistiam summat, ad pacem ueniat, psalmos cum fratribus canat Gi 1 ex. cuncta cognoscere, curare, ad integrum salutis statum debila reuocare Co B pr. stet . . . inter paenitentes, insanae

communionis culpam diluat Co B 25. — qui . . . suspicatur quod . . . deducitur, tamen iurat Lu 5 = Cu III. 11 = Bi III. 3, 4. morte morietur; terra . . . fisco reuertatur Wa A 45 (et O. P 49). magnum est crimen; aut uix aut non potest redimi Vi 22. homines congregabit *qui* iurent eum esse ueracem, sic sine culpa excedat Wa A 4. ancellas .iii. seruos .iii. reddat (et *add.* HO) securus fiat Wa A 1. *cf.* 4. 15. — *pro periodo condicionali:* praeda uel fraude uescit, semiannus Da 14. furat cibum, .xl. diebus Cu I. 12 in consue-. tudinem uertunt, annum Cu (X). 12. manum oculum et quodlibet membrum debilitatum faciet, accipiet in iudicio Wa A 3; *cf.* Cu (X). 2 (E). — credo . . . dirigetur Vi 41. ita oportet fieri: quod uult faciat Vi 39. *cf.* 41.

Iuncturae bimembres: in fletu et orationibus Vi 12 (V). in omni pietate atque subiectione Vi 44 (S). — post integram et perfectam penitentiam Vi 35. iudicium uerum et iustum Vi 41. pauperibus et egenis Vi 22. *cf.* 32. — satis ac libenter Vi 44 (S). — euellantur et eradicentur Vi 29. erogentur et fenerentur Vi 30 (S). consentimus et seque[re]mur Vi ps. — adfectandum et nitendum Vi 34.

Polysyndeton: locus et tempus et persona Pa II. 14. per furorem et rixas et non ex meditatione odii Bi IV. 3, 2. sine cibo et putu (potuque B) et (ac B) sine somno Hi II. 3. — aut de securi bidubioue aut cultello aut dexterali Wa A 5, *cf.* P 4. cum alterius uxore aut sorore aut filia Wa A 17. *sim.* Wa P 28. 29. 50. Hi IV. 9. V. 11. siue . . . siue . . . siue Wa P 7. cum pallore uel (*om.* Bi) rubore uel tremore Cu (IV). 14 = Bi IV. 5, 2. *sim.* Wa A 19. 20. 39. (uel . . . uel . . . uel . . . uel) Hi I. 17. 29. (uel *ter*) Bi I. 5, 6. (*quater*) Bi IV. 6, 5. Cf. *lemmata* **Coniunctiones, Variatio.**

Anaphora: aliter *octies* Co B pr. sine *bis* Cu II. 24 (E). 25. *quater: ibid.* 22. ueniendum est . . ., ueniendum est Bi pr. 14. — *repetitio, sed non anaphora:* iterum suam cognouerit clientelam et filium iterum de ea genuerit Cu B 8. inmunda . . . dupliciter inmunda Bi pr. 18.

Allitteratio, assonantia: cordis et corporis Vi 10. corporis et cordis Bi VI. 3, 2. medicina penitentiae preuenire perpetuas poenas Vi 22. praeuaricatores perire perpetuo Bi pr. 25. — cuncta cognoscere, curare, ad integrum salutis statum debila reuocare Co B pr. contemptio uentris, studium mentis Bi pr. 49.

Pleonasmus: in consuetudine(m) adsueti Vi (3) = Cu II. 8. Cu (X). 16. iterantes consuetudine Bi II. 2, 4. tertia *septimana* incipiente aboriri Bi pr. 23. — inuicem confabulationem exerceant Pa I. 9. iterum . . . reuocat Pa I. 16. praelato ante monachi uoto Gi 1 = Cu II. 2. insuper augeat Co B 6 (*u. app. crit.*). saepe . . . consueuit Co B 19. simul sint conglobati Co B 29. — *Verbum* posse *abundat*: inuenire potuerit Wa P 17. — in his quaecumque dederit Deus Vi 41. penitentia eorum hec est, id est . . . Vi 45 (S). saturatus nimis sacrificium per hoc euomuerit Co A 6. haec septima remissio, cum . . . Bi pr. 31. omne . . . quod amatur hoc et adiuratur Pa II. 23. si pro inclementia hunc iecisset, annus pro die hic ('in that case') acciperetur Hi V. 2. si ipse minauerit eos sponte Wa A 25. omnia quaecumque Vi 30 (S). Cu (IX). 14. omne quodcumque Cu (XI). 23. quicquid . . . omnia Wa A 38 (P 42). — *Abundat aduerbium* sic: et sic peragat, si iubetur Gi 16. sicut monachus . . . sic peniteat Gi 3. *sim.* Da 4. Vi 41. Co B 13. Cu II. 5. Cu (IV). 2 = Bi IV. 4. Wa A 15. 58. P 3. Ad 16. Bi II. 4. sic ut = ut Wa P 9. 10. 36 (ut A 13). — *Abundat* ita: ita debet fieri, ambo manere in continentiam suam Vi 41. *sim.* Vi 39 (S). Co B 20. 25. Bi VII. 4. sic ita aequale diuidant Wa A 20, *cf.* P 29. — *Abundat negatio*: nec nocte pascharum non introeat Pa I. 18. nullo modo non (*om.* B) reiciatur Wa A 49, *sed cf.* P 56. non plus quam octo dies . . . uiuere non potest Hi V. 6. — *Abundantia coniunctionum*: et horarumque oratio Hi II. 8 (P). — pariter et Wa A 45. et praeterea Hi III. 5. — blasphemus etiam simili decreto sanetur Cu (VIII). 5. (contentiosus etiam alterius sententiae subdat se Cu (VII). 1 = Bi VII. 1 *sententia nimis concisa est*: contentiosus non solum ad pacem reuocetur sed etiam . . .). — adulter quoque et ipse Lu 3. urinam hominis seu et sanguinem Bi I. 5, 1. — prius . . . priusquam Ad 12. — *Abundat uerbum dicendi*: accusauit dicens Hi V. 2. *sim.* Bi tit. III. 1, 2. V. 1, 4. VI. 1, 2; 3, 6. — *Abundat uerbum eundi*: uadens sede in cella tua Bi VI. 3, 3 (*ex usu biblico*). — eius dilecta quae gessit Vi 9 ex. (P). — tunc, ita primum Co B 2. 18. — contentus nomine tantum Pa II. 10. — tunc in uii anno Vi 27. *cf.* Co B 6. *sim.* Vi 36. 46. — solus non in eadem domo Pa I. 28. separatim nec in uno lecto Vi 45 (S). qui facit per se aliquid sine interrogatione

Co A 9. ambo, et ille et illa Cu II. 28. *hic fortasse ponendum*: aliam doctrinam extra scripturas Bi VII. 2.

Litotes: non tamen iniuriosa *uerba* Cu (IV). 13 = Bi IV. 5, 2. non (nec E) ignorans Cu (IX). 2. non incongrue Pa II. 20. non dissimilia his Bi V. 1, 4. — nec non Cu (X). 18.

Figura etymologica et synonymica: iurare iuramentum falsum Vi 22. falsum testimonium testificatus Co A 8. praecepta quae Deus non praecipit Hi III ps. flectiones genuum flectuntur Hi II. 2 (B). uita uiuitur Pa II. 17. — uirgis uirgeatur Vi 31 (S). peniteat equali penitentia Vi 51 (V). morte moriatur, -etur Wa A 17 (*cf.* P 27). A 45 (P 49). ruina fornicationis, ruina maxima cadere Vi 10. 12. 27. Co B 2.

Paronomasia: discordare . . . per discordiam Pa I. 31. iustus iuste uiuat Co A 12. in sedibus sedeant Wa A 15. iurandi causa iudicio adductus a iudice Wa A 36. iudicant . . . in iudicium Wa A 37. heres hereditate relinquatur Wa A 45, *cf.* P 50. legitimae legis Wa A 59. doctor docuit Hi III. 2. iectus iectorem . . . accusauit Hi V. 2. quantum iudices . . . iudicauerint Hi V. 8. 11. in una mansione non maneat Ca 3. uindicator . . . uindicte innocens habetur Pa II. 6. non infecit semen seminantis iniquitas Pa II. 7. aliter alius dicit Bi I. 3, 3. III. 3, 4. aliter alius sapiens iudicat dicens Bi III. 1, 2. alius alias temperauit Bi II. 5, 4.

Polyptoton: diuersitas culparum diuersitatem facit paenitentiarum Co B. pr. uirgo uirgini coniunctus est Co B 16. si quis seruus seruum occiderit Wa A 33 (P 38). — qui omnibus omnia sunt Pa II. 18. — contraria contrariis sanantur Cu pr. 15 (*bis*). *sim.* Vi 28. 29. — uerbum contra uerbum simpliciter prumptum Co A 9. solus cum sola loquitur Cu (VIII). 23. seruus pro seruo Wa A 7. frater cum fratre naturali fornicans Bi II. 3, 1. a uilla in uillam Pa I. 9. de loco ad locum transeundo Bi VI. 3, 5.

Lusus uerborum: qui inlicita licenter commisit a licitis licet cohercere se debet Cu pr. 15. in acceptione hospitum . . . quae bona acceperunt Hi V. 1.

Formulae: 1. *Formulae quibus ad locos biblicos refertur:* ait Moyses Hi III. 8. quomodo psalmista ait Bi VIII. 6. Solomon ait Bi III. 5, 1. ut Paulus ait Bi pr. 71. (*e Greg. Magno*). Paulus ait Bi III. pr. apostolus ait Bi pr. 37. *cf.* Bi pr. 38. sicut ait scriptura Vi 21. euangelium . . .

Formulae (*cont.*).
ait Pa II. 6. — Deus dicit Bi II. 1, 5.
Dominus dicit Cu III. 13. pro quibus
Dominus dicet Bi III. 6, 1. Christus dicit
in euangelio Hi V. 5. Saluator dicit Bi V.
1, 2. Esaias dicit Bi pr. 24. Ezechiel dicit
Bi pr. 36. in euangelio apostoli dixerunt
Hi V. 3. dicit enim apostolus Vi 41.
Iohannis in epistola sua dicit Bi pr. 11.
quia dicit scriptura Vi 8. dicit enim
scriptura Vi 29. lex metrica scriptione
scripta dicit Ad 14. *cf.* Bi II. 9, 3. — sicut
dicit Dauid Bi V. 3, 2 (*u. app. bibl.*). sicut
Solamon dicit Vi 21. sicut apostolus
dicit Vi 29. 46. Bi V. 3, 2. ita enim dicit
scriptura diuina quia Bi pr. 32. —
fructum quem Saluator in euangelio
enumerans . . . deputauit Vi 46 (*allusio*).
Dominus prohibuit Ad 14. 20. — audite
apostulum dicentem Pa II. 1. 12. audi
Dominum dicentem Pa II. 4. 5. (audi
item . . .) 6. 26. perlege euangelium ab eo
loco in quo ait Pa II. 6. — Solamone
dicente Pa I. pr. Domino dicente Cu pr.
5. Pa II. 22. 25. *cf.* apostolo consolante
Cu pr. 7, *et* Cu pr. 6. 8. 11. 12. 13.
matrimonium Deo auctore concessum est
Vi 46. — dicitur Bi pr. 10. ut dicitur Cu
I. 1. Hi III. 2. sicut in scripturis dicitur
Vi 29. in lege dicitur Bi IV. 6, 7. in
Leuitico . . . dicitur Bi pr. 17. in Exodo
legitur Hi III. 8. — sicut praeceptum est
a Deo Vi 33 (*allusio*). — sicut scriptum
est Vi 46. unde scriptum est Bi pr. 9.
scriptum namque est Bi pr. 12. quod
scriptum est Bi pr. 16. est in Leuitico
scriptum Bi pr. 32. scriptum est enim Bi
VI. 2, 3 (*ex Vitis Patrum*). — ut illud Bi
pr. 74 (*e Gregorio*). ut illud supra dicti
(*i.e.* Pauli: *ibid.*) Bi pr. 73. ut illud Pauli
Bi pr. 72 (*ibid.*). ut est illud Cu ps. 2 =
Bi pr. 27. Cu pr. 3. 9. Pa II. 17. ut est hoc
Cu pr. 10. ut est illud propheticum Cu
ps. 2. *cf.* homicida ille qui odit fratrem
suum Cu (IV). 4 = Bi IV. 4. secundum
hoc Cu pr. 4. secundum illud Cu pr. 2.
14. secundum illud prophetae Bi pr. 27.
secundum illud Dei Bi pr. 9. secundum
euangelium Cu (VIII). 10 = Bi VIII. 2,
2. secundum apostolum Vi 42 (S). Bi VI.
1, 1. — memorantes illud praeceptum
Domini Bi pr. 66 (*ex regula s. Benedicti*).
— contra interdictum Saluatoris, ut
dicitur Cu I. 1. contra Domini interdictum Bi II. 2, 2. contra interdictum
Domini apostolique Cu III. 4 (*u. app.
crit.*). per exemplum Domini . . . iuxta
exemplum apostuli Pa II. 15 (*allusiones*).
more Cain (*cf.* Gen. 4, 12) Co B 1. ut

prophetis· mos est Pa II. 23. — (*ellipsis
uerbi:*) de concordia uirtutum . . .
apostolus Bi pr. 48. — (*coniunctio tantum
legitur:*) enim Bi pr. 2. igitur Bi pr. 13.
itaque Bi pr. 25. namque Co B pr. *cf.* in
lege namque Ad 7. quia Vi 28. quoniam
V. 22. — *Locus loco iungitur:* et Dominus
Pa II. 12. et paulo post ait Moyses Hi
III. 8. contra interdictum Saluatoris (*u.
supra*) . . . apostolique Cu I. 1. — *uox et
nuda habetur* Pa II. 23. Bi pr. 73 (*e Greg.
Magno*). et postea Cu (VIII). 10. et ut
Pa II. 17. *similiter:* ceterum Pa II. 1.
item Cu pr. 14. Pa II. 26 (*ter*). item
apostolus ait Bi pr. 38. item Paulus Bi
pr. 55. audi item Pa II. 6. ⟨uel⟩ ut est
illud Cu ps. 2 = Bi pr. 27. — *Alius locus
ex alio explanatur:* hoc est Pa II. 5. —
Locus loco opponitur: aliter in libro
Regum Bi I. 8. aliter lex purgationis dicit
Bi II. 9, 3. aliter in Ezechiele dicitur Bi
pr. 36. sed . . . sed . . . Pa II. 1. — 2.
Formulae paenitentiales: (*a*) *de
peccatoribus et peccatis:* praelato ante
monachi uoto Gi 1 = Cu II. 2. sine
monachi uotu (-o) Gi 3 = Cu II. 4. post,
ante uotum(-a) perfectionis Lu 9. Cu
(IV). 6 = Bi IV. 3, 4. post uotum peccare
Vi 27. Co B 8. *u. etiam* uotum *in Indice
uerborum.* — ruina maxima cadere Vi 12.
27. Co B 2. *cf.* ruina fornicationis cadere
Vi 10. — si in consuetudine fuerint
adsueti Vi (3) = Cu II. 8. *cf.* Cu (X). 16.
Vi 11. — in notitiam homonum (-inum)
non uenerit Vi 11. Co B 4. — magnum
crimen est sed redimi potest per penitentiam Vi 12. *cf.* 28. 29. 47. magnum est
crimen; aut uix aut non potest redimi Vi
22. — qui si sic non faciat (fecerit) Pa I.
27. 28. *cf.* 19. 21. — (*b*) *de paenitentia:*
penitentia eius ipsa est Vi 3. p. (eius) haec
est Vi 14. 17. 22. *cf.* 28. 29. 45 (S). —
unum est peccatum sed non eadem
penitentia Vi 3. 17. *cf.* 8. minus peccatum
sed eadem penitentia Vi 13. — petat a
Deo ueniam Vi 1. 2 (S: adiutorium V).
Bi II. 10. *cf.* Vi. 5. 29. ueniam . . . roget
Gi 1 = Cu II. 2. postulet ueniam Cu
(IX). 7. — cum fletu et lacrimis Vi 8. in
fletu et (lacrimis atque *add.* S) orationibus
Vi 12. in fletu et lacrimis Vi 29. —
coronam suam perdere Vi 10. *cf.* 37.
renouare coronam Vi 21. — officium
clericatus (non) amittat Vi 10. 11. 15. sine
officio (ministerio) clericatus Vi 8. 12. —
de forma et tempore paenitentiae: ebdo-
madaı peniteat dierum Vi 5. 7. — abstineat (se) a uino et (a) carnibus (-e) Vi
16ies. Co *septies.* sine carne et uino Hi

II. 12. sine uino carneque Cu II. 24. (IX). 16. cf. Bi II. 11, 1. sine uino et carnibus Vi 30 (V). — sine diliciis, sine uxore Cu II. 25. sine diliciis coniugioque Cu II. 32 = Bi II. 11, 1. cf. absque carne et muliere et aequo Ca 3. — relictis (reiectis E) armis usque ad mortem mortuus mundo uiuat Deo Cu (IV). 5. cf. (IX). 13. cum peregrinatione perenni mundo moriatur Cu (IV). 6 = Bi IV. 3, 4. — pane aquaque Aq 5. pane et aqua et sale Da 11. cum pane et aqua (⟨et sale⟩) Vi passim. Co B 3. 6 (bis). 7. 15. Cu (X). 19. in pane et aqua Co passim. Cu I. 5 = Bi I. 4, 3. Cu (IV). 4 = Bi IV. 4. — per mensura(m) Vi passim. Co B 6. in mensura Hi II. 9 (B). cf. paxmati panis mensura Gi 1 = Cu II. 2. mensura grauetur panis Gi 2 (Cu II. 3). sine mensura Gi 1 = Cu II. 2. — si operarius (est) Gi 1. 2 = Cu II. 2. 3. — sine cibo et putu (potuque B) et (ac B) sine somno Hi II. 3. cf. 4. (sine cibo potuque uiuere non potest Hi V. 6. cybum et potum summere Bi I. 10.) — cena careat Gi 15. 19. 21. 25. Cu I. 5 = Bi I. 4, 3. Cu (VIII). 18. 23. (IX). 5. 8. caena priuatur Gi 10. — canat ... in ordine psalmos Cu II. 15. cf. (VIII). 16. psalmos in ordine canere Gi 19 = Cu (IX). 6. (replicet ex ordine Gi 19 = Cu (IX). 7.) — similiter peniteat Cu (XI). 11. cf. simili decreto sanetur Cu (VIII). 5. — quadragesimas ieiunet, sim. Vi 12. 20. 23. 36 (V). maxime in tribus xlmis Cu II. 11. 19. — annum (-o) integrum (-o), totum (-o) Vi, Co passim. — (principium talionis:) quantum ... tantum, quanto (tempore) ... tanto (tempore) Gi 14 = Cu (IX). 4. Aq 7 = Cu (VIII). 13. Co B 21. Cu III. 13 = Bi III. 6, 1 (cf. 2). Cu (IV). 3 (cf. Bi IV. 4). 16. (VIII). 4 (= Bi VIII. 4). 7 (E). 19. cf. Cu III. 15. (IV). 4. ps. 1. quale ... tali Cu III. 12 = Bi III. 4. tamdiu ... quam Vi 29. (quantum ... quidquid Wa A 21, P 14). Cf. Praefationem, p. 45 sq. — (c) de reconciliatione: si ... bene egerit Vi 23. (agat) 34. — iudicio sacerdotis Vi (2). 12. Co B 2. 13. 18. Cu (VIII). 3. (doctoris iudicio Aq 1. iudicio senatus Cu (X). 20.) ad iudicium sacerdotis Cu (VIII). 2. Hi II. 7. Bi VII. 2. iudice sacerdote Cu III. 3. 12 (= Bi III. 4). (IV). 2 (= Bi IV. 4). (V). 2. (VIII). 20. (X). 15. Bi VIII. 1. 2, 1. — det . . . fructum penitentie in manu sacerdotis Vi 35. 36. — sanus sit Vi 1. 2. — recipiatur ad communionem Vi 35. 36. Co B 6. (non recipietur in aeternum Vi 23.) — iungat se altario Vi 15. iungatur

altario Vi 21. 27. 35. Co B 2. 13. 15. 18. 25. — altario reconciliabitur Vi 6. restituatur altario Vi 14. Deo reconciliari et proximo Vi 5. — 3. **Formulae excommunicationis:** ab ecclesia separentur Pa I 6. excludendus, -antur Pa I. 10. 22. sequestretur 26. extores ab -a Cu (X). 3. extraneus Wa A 59. alienus Wa A 61. alienatur ab -a Bi VII. 2. extra -am conputetur Pa I. 8. alienus habe(a)tur, sit, est Pa I. 7. 21. 24. 31. excommonis sit, fuerit Pa I. 17. 18. 19. 20. 27. 32. Vide Indicem uerborum sub abscidere, anathemazare, excommunicare. — in ecclesiam renuetur Pa I. 15. recipiendus Pa I. 16. — 4. **Formulae iudiciales:** non est ei titulus conprobandi Wa A 4 (P 3). (A 28) P 23. (adprobandi) P 16. — homines nominatim congregabit Wa A 4. uiri nominatim congregentur Wa A 31. uiris nominatis P 3. 32. — nullam causam habe(a)t Wa A 27. P 16. 22. 55. (se) timeat habere Wa A 17 (P 27). — cogatur exsoluere Wa P 13. se nouerit conponendum Wa A 19. 37. P 28. 67. se daturum cognoscat Wa P 10. 19. 47. (se P) rediturum cognoscat Wa A 8 (P 7). se daturum non dubitet Wa P 19. se nouerit rediturum Wa A 6 (P 5). A 16 (P 13). A 13. 58. P 8. 30. restituturum Wa A 20. se nouerit accepturum Wa P 2. (merito accipiat Wa A 52. P 59 bis. 60.) — sine dubio Wa A 21. 56 (P 66). absque dubio Wa P 32. — securus fiat Wa A 1. 4. (uiuat) A 15 (P 12). cf. securitatem accipiat P 1. 3. habebit A 2. — si non habet unde reddat, sim. Co B 21. Cu III. 6 = Bi III. 2, 1. Cu (IV). 10 = Bi IV. 3, 1. — 5. **Formulae ad matrimonium aut adulterium spectantes:** non suscipit eum mulier Co B 11. 23. non est susceptus Cu 11. 21. — non intret ad uxorem suam (propriam) Vi 36. 37 (bis). 38. 39 (S). cf. 51. non intret amplius ad concubinam suam Vi 40 (S). — nec in uno lecto maneant Vi 45 (S). cf. 47. — 6. **Formulae iniungendi:** dicimus Vi 10. 21. 34. 42 (S). Wa P 67. non dicitur Hi IV. 6. dum dicitur Bi pr. 36. — iubemus Wa A 48 (P 54). A 58. 60. P 67. dos dari iubetur Wa A 47. — permittamus Wa A 41. -atur ibid. 39. — penitentiam quam supra posuimus Vi 51. cf. ps. ponamus nunc . . . priorum statuta patrum Cu (X). tit. cf. ancellam . . . in sacerdotis ponimus potestatem Wa A 60. — praecipimus Wa A 3. 9. 24. 36. 37. 38. 40. 50. 53. 54. P 2. 11. 17. 42. 46. 58. 63. precipimus et exortamur Vi 32. 46. — sancximus Wa

VI. INDEX ORTHOGRAPHICUS

Recompositio : adaltera Pᵇ II. 26 (Q). consacrata Cu III. 7 (E). exalii (= exilii) Cu II. 5. obtractatione Bi VIII. 3. praeraptum Ad 5. triannio Lu 2. 3. — exsteterit Cu (XI). 10 (R). praesteterit Wa P 28. — *Sic fortasse accipienda*: redemi Vi 22 (S: redimi V). redemat Wa A 57 (redimat *codd*. ABXO. P 65). collegi Bi pr. 28. dilegis (diligis B) Bi VI. 2, 1. elegere Hi III ps. intellegi (-ligi Bᴵ) Ad 20. *cf*. Bi VI. 3, 7. insedeant Wa P 12. absteneant (-tin- JI) Pa II. 14. contenentes (-i- I) Pa II. 18. detenetur Co A 11 (-tin- Ti. Tiiᶜ). deteneat Wa P 61. retenendis (-ti- I) Pa II. 21. *Dubito de* requerenda Pa II. 27 (-qui- IY. quaerenda K). *V. etiam* **Voces** (di-, demedium).

Assimilatio, dissimilatio : 1. *Praefixa:* adfectandum Vi 34. affectus Bi pr. 41. — affirmante (*pro* conf.) Cu pr. 11 (F). adfirmant Hi III. 1. -ans Ad 20. -entur Pa II. 30. — adflictio (affl- EFN) Cu pr. 7. adfligi Cu ps. 1. *cf*. Bi pr. 2. -endi Bi II. 1 pr. (*u. app. crit*.). — administratam Ad 18. — admiratione Hi IV. 3. — amiserit *pro* admiserit Cu II. 2 R (m *pro* mm?). — admonendo Cu ps. 4 = Bi pr. 34. admonitione Bi VI. 3, 7. — adnuntiabit, -uit Cu pr. 4 (RSL: ann- N). — adprobatur Wa A 23. Pa II. 24 (*u. app. crit*.). approbatio Bi pr. 6. — adsidue Pa I. 9. adsidua Cu pr. 9 (E). assiduus Bi VI. 2, 1. — adstantiam Wa A 37 (ast- B. asst- X). — adtendite Cu I. 1. adtendens Bi pr. 73. — adtestante Cu pr. 6 (L: att- FM. testante *cett*.). adtestando Pa II. 17. — adtingamus Bi V. 1, 5. — adtullerit Bi pr. 15. — conburatur Cu (XI). 20 (E). combustiones Co B pr. — commanendo Vi 12. cūmmansionibus (cum m. V) Vi 15. — commissus (P: cumm-, cūm- VS) Vi 23. commisso Wa P 22. conmissus Co B 1. — commouit, -tauit, -tio Cu (IV). 15–16. — communio *semper*. — conpago Co B 30. — conparem Hi IV. 2. — conparauerit Wa A 19 (P 28). 20. (P 29) A 45 (P 49). A 49 (comp- X), P 56. — conpatiendum Vi 33. — conpendii Cu pr. 1 (SL). conpendiosas Bi pr. 6. — conpetitus Wa A 29 (-ped-), P 24. A 43 (P 44). P 2. conpetit Wa A 37, *cf*. P 41. — conplentes Vi (3). conplenda Co A 2. compleat Vi (4) = Cu (X). 17. — conponunt Co B pr. -at Wa A 35. -nendum Wa A 19. 37. P 28. 58. 67. -ni A 50. conpossitionem P 67. — comprimit (cum- C)

Bi pr. 53. — comprobatus (P: cum pr. VS) Vi 23. conprobatus Co B 1. conprobandi Wa A 4 (P 3). *sim*. A 20 (P 29). A 37 (P 47). P 17. conprobatorium Bi pr. 14. — conpugnauerit Pa I. 8. — conpulsus Vi ps. Wa A 3. compulsus Cu ps. 1 (*sed* conpulsus Bi pr. 2). — conpunctus Vi 31. conpunctione Bi pr. 69. — conputetur Pa I. 8. — exsecutor Gi 27. — exalii Cu II. 5. exilium Aq 3. aexilio Ca 1. — existat Vi 12. 35. 37. Cu ps. 1. Wa A 33. (-nt) 34. aexsistat Wa P 38. — exsoluat Wa A 10. A 12 (P 51). A 16, *cf*. P 13. -ere Wa A 29 (P 24). A 46 (P 52). P 9. — expectabit Vi 45 (S). -are Co B 30. — exstat Bi pr. 2. exsteterit Cu (XI). 10 (R). — exul Co B 1. 20. Cu II. 17. Wa A 45. exsul (*sed* exul Ti) Co B 13. — exsurgere Vi 27 (V *solus* exstat). — extinguat Ad 15. — inbutus Cu ps. 1 = Bi pr 2. Pa II. 21. — imfantibus B (inf- C) Bi II. 11 tit. — inlecebris Bi pr. 52. inlecebrosa Vi 15. illecebroso Vi 14. inlecebroso (ill- P) Vi 19. -um Cu (X). 2. — inlicita, -(a)e, -i, *sim*. Hi I. 16. 18. 21. 23. Ad 7 (*bis*). 12. Bi I. 5 tit. illicite Ad 17. — inluditur Cu II. 14. — inmane Vi 18. — inmaturitatem Cu (X). 4. — immolare Hi III. 3. — inmorantes Bi VI. 3, 4. — inmunditia Ad 8. (-am) 10. Bi pr. 18. 23 (*bis*). (-ae) 40. inmundus, -e Ad 8. 11 (*bis*). 17. Bi pr. 17. 18. I. 5, 8. — inpastoriauerit Wa P 63. — inpediat Da 7. inpedimenti Bi IV. 6, 1. — imperitia Hi V. 2. — impietas Bi pr. 8. impius Bi pr. 7. 25. — inpigerit Wa A 12. — inpinguato Gi 1 = Cu II. 2. — inplacabilis Cu (IV). 3 = Bi IV. 4. — impleatur, *sim*. Vi 12. 23. 33 (*sed* inpl- S). 34 (*bis*) 38. 46. 53. Cu III. 13 = Bi III. 6, 1. Bi VI. 2, 3. inpletum Wa 48 (*sed* impl- P 54). inpolluta Bi II. 7. — inponendum Da 11. -ent Cu pr. 9 (*loc. bibl.*, *in* R *solo*). inposuerit Pa I. 16. -uit Cu III. 12 = Bi III. 4. — inportunitas Bi pr. 45. VI. pr. — inpos(s)ibile Cu (IV). 2 = Bi IV. 4. — inpos(s)itione(m) Co B 25. Cu (X). 18. Hi I. 12. Pa II. 8. — inpugnatur Cu ps. 1 = Bi pr. 2. -tione Cu II. 13. — inputat Cu (VIII). 22. -tur Bi IV. 6, 7. — inreptionem Vi 4 (*u. app. crit*.). 24 (*u. app. crit*.). — irridere Da 4. — inritantes Cu (X). 4. — inritum Vi 27. -ta Pa II. 28 (irr- I). irritum Co B 8. *Non assimilatur* in *priuatiuum praeter exempla quae dedimus*. — obmissa Bi pr. 28 (B). — oppropria Bi pr. 43.

A a

Assimilatio (*cont.*).
obprobria Bi IV. pr. obprobriis (oppr- B)
Bi IV. 5 tit. — subfert Hi IV. 7. Bi pr. 55
(suff- B). — submittere Vi 4. — subplantauerit Bi IV. 7. — 2. *Alia composita:*
quicquid Wa A 21. 26. A 29 (P 24). A 38
(P 42). quidquid (quicquid BXHO.
quincquid P 55) A 48. — namque Co B
18. — nunquam Co B 1 (Tii); *sed* numquam *ib.* 5 (Ti, Tii). — quaecunque Co
B 1 (Tii). quicunque *ib.* 13 (Tii). —
quamdiu Vi 14. 36 (quandodiu S). 47.
quandiu Vi (S) 44. 45. quamdiu Cu (IV).
4, *sed* quandiu Bi IV. 4. — uenundet Vi
39 (V). Cu II. 26 (E: uendat R). -dari Vi
39 (S). 40 (S). -dare Wa A 60. — 3. *Varia:*
babtismus, -zare, *sim.* Vi 47. 49 (V). 50
(V) *bis.* Pa II. 7 (J; Q). 19 (J). 31 (J) *bis.* —
nubserit Pa I. 17. — stagni (*i.e.* stanni)
Wa P 31 (*bis*). 59. *cf.* A 52. — menbris
Co B 17 (Tii).
 Syncope: (h)anchoritae, -am Hi I. 29.
V. 11. Bi IV. 6, 5. pedecle Cu (X). 18.
soltos (saltos H*. solidos BXHᶜ. P 51)
Wa A 12. tegmento Pa II. 2. tenucla Gi
1. 2 = Cu II. 2. 3.
**Haplographia et dittographia con-
sonantium**: abas, &c. Gi 4. 12. 16. 18
(*bis*). 27 (*ter*). Aq 4. Pa II 21 (Q). Bi pr. 66.
I. 4, 1. VI. 3, 3. VIII. 3; *alibi* abbas. sabati
(-bb- B) Da 7. — acce(-i-)dia *semper, u.
Ind. uerborum.* brachia Co B 28. -o Wa A
14. -um Wa P 10. occuli Hi IV. 2 (C).
peccuniam Bi IV. 1, 2 (C). peccŏdem Wa
A 24 (B). peccora, -um, &c. Hi III. 1 *et
passim fere cod.* C (pęcora *semper fere* B).
Hi VI. 1. 3 (*bis*). Ad 18. 20 (OB¹). Bi II.
2, 1 (C). *sed* pecoris Hi I. 19. uaca, &c.
Wa A 24. P 39 (*sed* uacca *ibid.*). Hi III. 7
(C). VI. 3. Ad 11 (*u. app. crit.*); *alibi* uacca.
V. etiam **Voces** (ecclesia). — redat Wa A
50 (B). P 15. Hi IV. 4 (W). rediderit Wa A
30 (B). reditur Wa (AB) 63. redetur Bi pr.
36 (C). *cf.* Bi 61 (C). rediturum *codd. aut
omnes aut praestantiores* Wa A 6 (P 5).
A 8 (P 7). A 16 (P 13). A 58. P 8. (*sed*
redditurum P 30.) — afectu Gi 18 (C).
Bi pr. 49 (C). efeminatus Bi pr. 23 (C).
diffinicionem Vi 4 (S: difinitionem V).
diffinitionem Cu pr. 1 (S, *cf.* E). -es *ibid.*
R (defin- LN). *cf.* defferatur Pa II. 13
(D: deferatur *cett.*). — aligandi Pa II.
3 (Q). colirio, -um Hi IV. 1. 4. 7. polutus
Bi II. 1, 8 (C). solem(p)nitatibus Pa II. 19
(KQ: sollemn- DJI). solerter Cu ps. 1 =
Bi pr. 2. Bi IV. 3. tollerantur Bi pr. 54.
tollerabiliter Bi VI. 3, 6. intollerabilius
Bi II. 5, 2. tullerit Wa A 54 (-l- BX). tullit
Bi pr. 6. (abstullerit Wa A 37 *praeter codd.*

BXO. A 51. adtullerit Bi pr. 15. pertullerit
Wa A 21 *praeter* BO. P 14. sustullerit
Wa A 24 *praeter cod.* B.) *V. etiam* **Voces**
(clentella). — āmare Bi pr. 60 (B).
ammittat (= amittat) Vi 11 (S). amiserit
(= admiserit) Cu II. 2. amonuit Bi
tit. (C). ciminum, -o Cu ps. 2 (E). commedere, &c. Co A 2. Wa A 62. Hi VI. 2.
3. Ad 11 (PB¹). 17. 18 (OP, *cf.* B¹). 20 (*u.
app. crit. ad p.* 180, 18–20). commedens
Cu (X). 18 (R). -unt Ad 7. -erit Cu (XI).
18 (E). commes Bi pr. 53 (B). commessationes Bi pr. 40. comisit Hi IV. 3 (C).
excominicatus Pa I. 12. cimmina (=
hemina) Cu II. 2 (himina Gi 1). comune
Wa A 34 (B). summere, &c. Gi 1 (C).
2 (C). (praesummat) 7. 16. Ad 1 (-m- OB).
4 (*u. app. crit.*). 6 (-m- B¹). *ib.* (-m- OB¹).
10. 11 (-m- O). 15. Pa II. 1 (Q). 13 (Q). 22
(K). Bi I. 4, 3. 10. (praesummit) VII. 2
(-m- B). sumat Cu I. 5. — cannonicas Cu
(VIII). 1 (E). pannis (= panis) Bi pr. 27.
V. etiam **Voces** (Britannia, -i, -icus). —
apetitus Bi pr. 52 (*u. app. crit.*). oportune
Wa A 30. reppetere Wa A 39 (*praeter* BX).
suplicare Da 11. suplex Gi 22. suplicatione Vi 9 ex. (P). — extorem Bi 23 (S).
-es Cu (X). 3. offere Bi I. 28 (offerre 27).
parruchia Pa I. 30. 34. parrochias (-is I)
Pa II. 20 (parocias D). scurilitates Bi
pr. 41. surra (sura X) Wa A 14. — abscisa
(-ssa OB²) Ad 5. 18. *cf.* 20. accussantis
Gi 18 (B). asidue Cu pr. 9 (S*), asiduus
Bi VI. 2, 1 (C). assina Bi VI. 3, 6. bassilicis Wa P 16. cassus (casu BXO) Wa A 47.
cassu Bi I. 5, 8 (C). Casianus Bi pr 40 (C).
III pr. (B). centissi(-esi- I)me (-i) Pa II.
18. -is *ibid.* (*similiter* quadragressimas Vi
20 (S). -is Bi IV. 3, 1 (B). quinquagissimi.
(-esimi QJI) Pa II 30. sexagissimum (-isi-
QD, -esi- JI) Pa II. 18. tre(tri-)gissimi
(-e) *ibid.* (-esi- I). uigentisimum (uicessimum B) Bi II. 2, 5.) ceruissa Da
11. confesus Aq 7 (B). crasa (-ss- HB)
Ad 6. -ior (*praeter* HB) Ad 20. disipat
Bi VI. 1, 1. effussio Lu 4. Hi IV. 5. Ad
20 (*bis*). effussus Wa (AB) 63. Ad 2 (*u.
app. crit.*). 17 (-s- OPB¹). -a (-s-CB³) 20.
essus Hi I. 13. 14. 15. (commessam,
praeter P, Ad 17.) excusum Bi pr. 65.
(excusserit Wa P 57.) fideiusor Pa I. 8.
cf. Wa A 19 (P 28). Wa A 44 (P 48). fuise
Ad 16 (P). heresses, -is, -im Bi pr. 37. 46.
VII. pr. 2. 4. hipocrissis Bi pr. 46 (C).
ingresor Pa I. 27 (*sed* ingressus 24).
(transgresione Bi pr. 8 (C).) inlissi Ad 20
(*u. app. crit.*). inposibile Bi IV. 4. inuassi
Ad 15 (*u. app. crit.*). Isserninus Pa I. tit.
pr. Issiodorus Bi pr. 39. 50 (B: Esiodorus

C). 54. lessam (-s- O) Wa A 53. inlessus, -o Wa A 16 (-s- AB), P 13. manducaset Ad 14 (P). meses, -is Wa A 55 (P 64). P 14. (messis, -e A 21.) misa, &c. Gi 19. Hi II. 4 (B). Bi pr. 36 (B). IV. 2, 1. (sed missam Cu (IX). 7.) miso Gi 1 = Cu II. 2 (u. app. crit.). misserit Wa A 16 (-s- A, P 13). commisserit Wa A 1 (AB), P 1. A 6 (u. app. crit.). 21. 46 (u. app. crit.). P 18. conmissus Co B 1. demisserit Wa A 47 (u. app. crit.). dimisserit (-s- BX) Wa A 38 (P 42). omisa Bi pr. 28 (C: obmissa B). permisserit Wa A 6 (H), P 5. permisione Pa I. 1 (alibi permiss-). promisserit Wa A 61 (u. app. crit.). remisisti Cu pr. 6 (FN). remisio (-ss- LM. om. N) Cu pr. 2. (remissio ib. 12.) occassum Bi pr. 68 (B). occissio, &c. Hi V. 6 (bis). 8. 9. 10. occissus, -um Wa A 15 (-s- P 12). A 18 (P 11). Bi pr. 36 (C). paradisso Bi VIII. 3 (C). pasione Bi pr. 2 (C). percusio Hi IV. 8 (C). percusor ib. (C). percuserit Vi 8 (B). 9 (B, cf. P*). Wa (AB) 63 (-ss- Bᶜ). Hi IV. 5 (-ss- BW). possitus Gi 2 (B). conpossitionem Wa P 67. inpossitione Hi I. 12 (alibi inpos-). propossitionis Hi III. 5 (C). superpossitio Gi 1 (u. app. crit.). 7 bis (u. app. crit.). 8 (u. app. crit.). Hi I. 18. II. 1 (P). 8. 9 (P). 10 (P). superpositio, &c. Gi 20. Cu II. 2. (IX). 9. praesserit Wa P 14. praeserit Wa P 59. (expraesis Bi pr. 4). pussillanimitas Bi V. 3 pr. subdiuissionibus Bi III. pr. ussus, -um Pa I. 7. 25. Ad 20 (u. app. crit.). sed usuram Da 13. — abremitatur Co B 19. batuti Cu II. 2 (-tt- Gi 1). dimitatur (Tii*) Co B 15. quatuor Pa II. 24 (D). 29 (D). sodomittam Gi 1 (C). V. etiam Voces (Britannia, &c.) — diuuersantur Vi 29 (u. app. crit.).

Vocales:

a–o: quottuor Pa II. 24 (Q). Solamone Pa I. pr. Solamon (Sa- S) Vi 21. Bi III. 5, 1 (C*: Solomon CᶜB). abstinatione Cu (VIII). 12 (E). manachus Gi 2 (B*). manachorum Pa II. 17 (Q*). ofamiliari pro a fam. Cu (XI). 18 (E).

a–e: contempnantibus Bi I. 8 tit. offerantis Cu (XI). 23 (R). — cabellum Wa A (H) 51. (HO) 53. (H) 54. iecite Hi V. 5. iecit Hi V. 6. iectio, &c. 1, Hi V tit. 6 (bis). 7. 8. 9. 10. 11. iectus, -i Hi V. 6. 9. iectu Bi IV. 3, 1. iectans Cu (VII). 2 (E). perseuerentia Bi pr. 49. similiter: furentibus (= furantibus) Bi I. 4 tit. tardentes Bi VI. 3, 4. uiolente (= uiolante) Bi II. 5 tit. (u. app. crit.). seperatione Pa II. 11 (u. app. crit.).

ae (ę)–e–oe (y): cęnubium Gi 22 (B: ce- C). cenubio Aq 1. concoepit Bi II. 9, 3 (C: -cep- B). incoeptum Pa I. 10. foemora Cu (X). 8. feno Gi 1. Cu II. 2 (E). foeno Cu II. 2. foeta Bi VI. 3, 5. mechator Lu 6 (u. app. crit.). moechator Cu II. 7 (mechatur E). moechantes Cu II. 8 (mechatis E). moechare Pa II. 26 (JI: mechari, -e cett.). obedire Bi pr. 66 (C: -oe- B). inobedientia Bi pr. 47. inobediens Bi VIII. 4 (-oe- Cu (VIII). 4). poenitentia, -am, &c. Pa I. 16. Gi tit. Cu ps. 1 (E), Pa II. 1 (I). 31 (D). pae-, pę-, penitentia, &c., passim. yconimi Cu (VIII). 17.

ae (ę)–e: aebrietatem Co B 12 (Tii). aec(c)lesia u. Voces. aegentibus Pa I. 25. Wa A 46 (u. app. crit.), P 52. ae(ę-)limosinam, sim. u. Voces. Aepiphania Pa II. 19 (K: u. app. crit.). ae(ę-)piscopus, &c. Pa I. 27. 30 (ep- 24. 25). Wa A 37 (e-ABX), P 40. Hi I. 12. ępistola Bi pr. 11 (B). aequus (= equus), &c. Co B 7. 19. Wa A 24. Hi I. 13. Ca 3. aetiam Wa P 17. aexilio Ca I. aexsistat Wa P 38. — adpraehenderit Wa A 52.¹ depraehensus Pa I. 26. cęlare Gi 27 (C). caeleri Vi 22 (V). caena(cę-) Gi 10. 19. 21. Cu (VIII). 18 (E). 23 (E). (IX). 5 (R). 8. Bi I. 4, 3 (B). caenodoxia Bi VII pr. (alibi ce-). cęteris Gi 1 (C). caeterum Co A 8. 12. (alibi cet-). comaederant Ad 14 (u. app. crit.). depraecatio Cu pr. 9 (R). fęmineo Co B 15 (Tii). interpraetatur Pa I. 16. -us Ad 16. laetali Ad 18. pęcodibus Da 11 (B). pęcora, &c., semper fere cod. B in Hi III. praesserit Wa P 14. praeserit P 59. (expraesis Bi pr. 4. oppraesserit Co B 18.) pr(a)esbiter u. Voces. praeciosa Hi IV. 2. praetium (prę-, p̄-), &c., Pa I. 4. 32. Co B 14. Cu (VIII). 28. Wa A 15. A 37 (P 47). P 7. 57. 59. 60. Hi I. 8. 9. 10. III. 7. IV. 3. 4. 5. 7. 8. 9. V. 7. 8. Bi pr. 5. IV. 2, 4. 3, 1. pretium Cu (IV). 9. — errorę Cu pr. 11 (S). — cotidiae Bi pr. 64 (C). hodiae Pa II. 23 (Q). iniustae (adu.) Bi IV. 4. libentissimę Cu II. 2. maximę Pa II. 22 (I). propriae Bi pr. 8. solitarię (K: -i cett.) Pa II. 17. superbae Cu (VIII). 3 (E). Bi VIII. 1 (u. app. crit.). uoluntariae Bi IV. 2, 1. — itaquę Cu pr. 15 (S). gladiouae Wa A 10 (H). minusuae Bi pr. 4.

egris Cu (VIII). 28 (E). egroti Bi pr. 1. Egypto, -um Hi III ps. Bi IV. 6, 7. emulationes Bi pr. 37. emulatur Bi pr. 55. enigmate Bi pr. 74. equali Vi 51 (V solus). equanimiter Bi pr. 54. eque Gi 6. estatis

---

¹ Siglum q.e. p̄ semper resolui *prae*; u. Praefationem, p. 26.

ae (ę)–e (*cont.*).

Hi III. 5. estimandus Cu (VIII). 16 (E).
etate (ae- Q, ę- I) Pa II. 17. 19. eternam
Bi V. 2. eui Gi 1 = Cu II. 2. — adherit
(-et DIY) Pa II. 26. cecitas Bi pr. 41.
celestis Bi IV. 7. Grecos Bi III. 3, 3.
Gregis Bi IV. 1, 2. heres(s)es, *&c.*, Bi pr.
37. 46. VII. pr. 2 tit. 2. 4. hereticus
Hi I. 4. Pa II. 4. Bi VII. 4. *sed* haereticis
Co B 25. iubelei Pa II. 30. lederis Bi VI.
3, 5. Iesus Wa P 13. Iessam Wa A 53 (-s-
O). inlessus, -o Wa A 16 (P 13). Ietus, *&c.*,
Cu (V). 1. 3 (E) = Bi V. 3, 1. merens
Bi pr. 73. pene Pa II. 31 (Q). Bi IV. 6,
7. precipuis Ca 3. predicta Bi IV. 6, 6.
querentes Pa II. 21 (Q). quesierit Pa I. 1.
querit Bi pr. 55. questionem Pa I. 1. Wa A
27 (P 21). -es Cu (XI). tit. questiuncula Bi
I. 1. II. 1 pr. seculi Bi pr. 60. sepe Bi II. 1,
3. 2, 1. sepius Bi V. 1, 6. sepes Wa A 55
(-is P 64). *dubium*: requerenda Pa II. 27
(QDJ). — ance(-i-)lle Hi IV. 3. 4. 8. Bi
IV. 2, 4 (C). bestiole Cu (XI). 14 (R: -ę E).
caule Hi VI. 4. cause Bi pr. 69. due Hi II.
10 (P). eclesie Hi V tit. Pa II. 6 (QD). glantelle Hi I. 23. inlicite Hi I. 16. 21. inmunde
Ad 8. iste Bi pr. 49. macule Bi IV. 3, 1.
medicine Pa II. 22 (QY). mee Bi pr. 73
(C). morticine Hi I. 20. Pasc(h)e Pa II.13
(QI*). 22 (Q). Bi II. 9, 2. que Pa I. 25. Hi
IV. 9. Bi pr. 48. 56. quedam Bi pr. 10. II.
1 pr. IV. 6, 6. sane (*gen.*) Gi 22. scripture
Pa II. 3 (*u. app. crit.*). superbie Bi VIII pr.
superne Bi pr. 74 (C). uacce (-ae B) Hi
III. 7. Ad 10. uere (*gen.*) Bi V. 1, 6. uidue
Pa II. 18 (Q). uindicte Pa II. 6 (*praeter*
IY).

au–a: augenda = agenda Gi 14.
augendum = agendum Co B 25. *dubium*
Co B 6. Pauconius = Pachomius (?) Hi
V. 2.

e–i: accederit Cu (IX). 13 (acciderit
Lu 4). (X). 11. 12. accedat (RE, *Sang.* 550)
Cu pr. 8 (-i- SFM). ancella, *&c.*, Vi 24
(-i- Pᶜ). 39 (V) = Cu II. 26. Wa *passim*
(*sed* -i- semper *cod.* B, *multis locis* XO,
hic illic Pᶜ). Hi I. 10 (P*). IV. 1. 3 (C²
solus). 7 (*bis*). 8 (*bis*). V. 7 (*bis*). 9 (*bis*).
ancillae Cu (VIII). 28. Hi I. 8. 9. acce-
pere (*inf.*) Pa II. 12 (D). benegnitas Bi pr.
49 (C*). cremina, -is Pa I. 14. 16.
dilectum (= delictum) Wa P 20. dilecta
Vi 9 ex. (P). fecesse Wa P 47 (fecisse Pᶜ).
elari (= hilari) Cu (V). 1 (E). inlessi Ad
20 (Bᴵ *solus*). peneteant Cu (VIII). 11
(E*). se = si Pa II. 6 *et* 26 (*u. app. crit.*).
sed = sit Pa II. 4 (D). sit = sed Pa II.
3 (Q). senum Pa II. 9 (KQ). suella Ad 6
(*u. app. crit.*). *u. etiam* **Voces** (di-,

demedium). — abscedatur (= abscidatur)
Cu III. 13. (IV). 16. (V). 3. (-i- *semper*
E. Bi). adepiscitur Bi pr. 74 (*u. app.
crit.*). allegandi Pa II. 3 (J: -lig- *cett.*).
commessationes Bi pr 40. delaceratam
Bi I. 5, 4. delatione Wa P 24 (di- A 29).
demittere Vi 41 (V). Pa II. 21 (QJ). 26
(QDJ). denumera(n)s Cu I. 11 (E).
emitantes Cu (X). 4 (E). emitatio Bi VI.
2, 1. iubelei (-ii Q) Pa II. 30. penetentibus
Pa II. 3 (KQD). -tiam Pa II. 31 (K).
paenetentiane Pa II. 3 (D). pereclitatur
Pa II. 15 (QDJ). relegionem Bi pr. 51 (C).
relegiosus Da 10 (B). Bi IV. 2, 1 (C).
simenantes = seminantis Pa II. 7 (Qᶜ).
sterelitatem, sterelem Vi 41 (S). tregissimi
Pa II. 18 (D). audeat (-i- Eᶜ) Cu (VIII).
10 (E: audierit R). — butero Gi 1 (C) =
Cu II. 2. clereci Pa II. 18 (D). infecit (*pr.*)
Pa II. 7 (KQ: -fic- DJI). 11 (-fic- I. -fig-
Y). kanebus Pa II. 12 (Q). leneat Cu
(IV). 1 (-i- E. Bi IV. 4; *cf.* Cu (VIII).
21 E). pedecle Cu (X). 18. putredum Gi
17. *Cf.* **Recompositionem.** *Dubium*:
requerenda Pa II. 27 (*u. app. crit.*).
— canes (*nom. sg.*) Vi 21 (S). gentiles Pa
II. 4 (Q). *gen. sg.*: contradictiones (Q: -is
cett.) Pa II. 23. fornicationes Pa II. 26
(Q). fratres Pa II. 25 (Q). homines Bi I.
5, 1 (C: -is B). lectiones Pa II. 23 (QJ).
maiores, uocationes Pa II. 21 (Q). sacerdotes Co B 1 (Tii). hereditate (*dat.?* -i
BXHᶜ) Wa A 45. libidine (*dat.?*) Vi 46.
sacerdote (*dat.?* Cu (IV). 2 (E). meretricem K, -e QDJ (-i IY) Pa II. 26; *u.
Ind. gramm. Ablatiui* insolubile (-i I),
lugubre (-i Q), spiritale, tale, Natale
(Pa II. 14. 3. 9 DJ. Cu III. 12 E. Bi I.
2, 3), consequente (-i I) Pa II. 23 *ad
declinationem fortasse spectant; cf. Ind.
gramm.* centissime (KQ: -i JI), trigissime
(Q: -i *cett.*) Pa II. 18. horte Cu II. 2 (E).
minime (E), -ę (R) Cu (X). 4. debeto *ex
coniectura* Cu (VIII). 6 (*cf.* R: debito E).
licete Cu pr. 15 (S*). diripet (*praes.*)
Bi III. 2, 1. sumet (-it KDJI) Pa II. 1.
uiuet (K: -it QDJI) Pa II. 23. abscideret
(*pro* -it) Vi 14 (S). scripseret Vi ps.
manseremus (*pro* -imus) Vi 41 (V).
fuerent (*i.e.* -int) Pa II. 28 (J). sinete
Pa II. 5 (D, *cf.* I). mittetur (*praes.* -itur
KQI) Pa II. 15. *sic* statuetur Pa II. 3
(-i- I). tribuetur (-i- I) *ibid.; cf.* deducetur
Cu III. 11 (R: -i- E). *Dubia*: illi poterit
adiuuare Pa II. 12. (accedia . . . adiuuare
potest Bi VI. 3, 2.) prodisse (-esse B)
Wa A 36. intercidendo litem Wa A 58
(-ced- HO. intercederit P 67).

accidia Cu (VI) tit. Bi pr. 39 (B). 45

i–y (*cont.*).
IV tit. VI tit. Pa II. 25 (-y- JI). ssc.
(synodus Hi III tit.) tirannus Ca 3.
cybus, &c. Aq 4. Da 11. Co B 14 (Tii).
Cu (E) *semper*. Hi V. 6. Pa II. 1 (KQ). Bi
I. 3, 1 (C). 4, 1 (B). 5, 8 (C). 10. Elysabet
Vi 41 (S). layci Pa II. 18 (K). paradyso
Cu pr. 13 (SFN). Pa II. 5 (Q). *V. etiam*
Voces (elymosina, *sim.*).
   i–o : yconimis Cu (VIII). 17.
   i–u : genuculationes Hi II. 4 (P). —
excominicatus Pa I. 12.
   o–u : adoliscentes Cu (X). 21. coagolato
Cu (XI). 14 (R : -u- E). coagolatus Ad 20
(H). colomella Wa A tit. (O). commonis
(-munis ABO) Wa A 33 (P 38). commones
P 39. excommonis, -icari, &c., Pa I. 1. 11.
17. 18. 19. 20. 27. 28. 32. copolari Vi 45
(S). commotauerit Gi 20 (-mut- Cu (IX).
9). iracondia Lu 2. *sim.* uerecondia, -ae
Bi pr. 53 (C). VI. 2, 3 (C). luxoria (R) Cu
I. 1. mormor Bi VIII pr. murmorat Co
A 9 (Tii). mormorat Bi VIII. 5 (C:
murmurat B. Cu (VIII). 6). motes Bi VI.
3, 5. orbe (= urbe) Vi 23 (S). oscola, -is
Vi 15 (osculis S). oscolando Vi 14 (V).
pecodem, &c. Gi 11. Da 11. Vi (1) = Cu
(X). 5 (R). Cu II. 6 (R). Wa A 18. 24.
pecŏniam Vi 9 (P) *bis*. soccurrere Hi V. 6
(*sed* succurrerit *ibid.*). soffocata, -am Ad
14 (B¹). sopinatae Hi II. 2 (P). talimpolo
Da 11 (B*). — *nom. sg.* diaconos Co B 4
(Ti*). mortuos Cu (E) (IX). 13 (-i R).
(X). 20. saluos Cu pr. 7 (E). *sic fortasse*
superbos Cu (VIII). 3. — minos Pa II.
29 (K: -us *cett.*). — (*heteroclisis?*) usos Ad
20 (B¹).
   apostulum Pa II. 1 (KQJ*). 12 (KQ). 16
(KQ). -i 15 (KQ). ce(cę-)nubium Gi 22. -o
Aq 1. commutauit Cu (IV). 15 (E: commouit R). 16 (E: -mot- R). commutatione
Cu (IV). 15 (E: -mot- R). concuitus Bi
II. 5, 2 (-co- B). curbi (= corui) Hi I. 17.
curnupetum Ad 7 (H). diabuli Vi 24 (V).
34. di–, delatur Cu (VIII). 11 (E: -or R).
fruntibus Ad 11. lungum Hi II. 12 (B).
mechatur Cu II. 7 (E: moechator R).
mursu Ad 18 (mo- OB¹). negutio Pa II.
30 (KQ). parruchiam Pa I. 30. 34. *sed*
par(r)oc(h)ias Pa II. 20. prumptum Co
A 9 (Tii*). pullice Wa P 7 (po- Pᶜ).
pullutus Cu (R) II. 15. 16 (*bis*). Bi II. 17
(C). pulluit Bi II. 5, 6 (*u. app. crit.*;
polluit Cu II. 25). putu Hi II. 3 (P).
renuetur (= renouetur) Pa I. 15. scupa
Cu (XI). 24 (E): *cf. Hib.* scúap. suffucatam Ad 14 (-foc- OP). -i *ibid.* (H).;
sed ibid. suffocata. sumnolentiam Bi VI
pr. (C). -tus Bi VI. 2, 2 (*u. app. crit.*); *sed*

somnolentus Cu (VI). 1. sy(-i-)mbuli Pa
II. 7 (KQ). — *acc. pl.* absoluendus (-os
IY) . . . lapsus (-os KY) Pa II. 8. medicus
Cu (IV). 9 (E). monachus Pa II. 18.
psalmus Cu (E) *passim*. subditus Pa II. 21.
— (*heteroclisis?*) inconsultu Pa I. 34 (*bis*).
tectu Cu (VIII). 23 (R). uotu Cu II. 2
(R). — cum- *pro* com-, con- *u.* **Assimila-**
tionem. *Quae scripturae partim ex usu*
compendiorum explicantur.
   u–uu : sexum Pa II. 11 (DJ). *cf.*
renuetur (= renouetur) Pa I. 15.
   y–u : chymminum Cu ps. 2 (*loc. bibl.*).
   Aspiratio : abetur Pa II. 6 (Q). -bitis
Pa II. 22 (Q). abere Bi pr. 64 (C). abitant
Pa II. 17 (Q). aruspicem Pa I. 14. coabitatricem Bi IV. 6, 3 (B). ebdomas, -ada, &c.,
Vi 5. 7. Cu II. 2. (VIII). 11. (X). 9. Hi II.
8. 10 (P). Bi pr. 5. I. 9, II. 1, 2 (*bis*). 5, 1.
IV. 6, 7. *sed* hebdomada Gi 1. ebitudo Bi
pr. 40. is (= his) Pa II. 18 (D). exortamur
Vi 32. 46. elari (= hilari) Cu (V). 1 (E).
ortando Cu ps. 4 (E). ortum Wa A 55
(hortum H. P 64). ospitio (-cio), -um Hi V
tit. 2 (ho- B). 10 (ho- B). uiusmodi Pa II.
1 (D). — habundat Gi 22. Hi III. 5.
habundantiam Bi pr. 30 (B). superhabundantia Pa II. 17 (KJ). hac (ac IY)
Pa II. 26. hanchoritam Hi I. 29. cohartat
Pa II. 17 (J. h *s.s.* D). helemosina *u.*
Voces. perhenni Ca 3. cohercere Cu pr.
15. heremi Hi V. 2 (B). inhermis Vi 35
(S; *sed* inermis Co B 20). Cu II. 24 (E).
cf. app. crit. ad Pa II. 25 superstis. *huc*
fortasse spectat hisdem (*pro* isdem) Hi III.
5. hoccidentibus Bi IV. 2 tit. hodibilis
Vi 21 (V), hodit Bi IV. 4 (B). hodii Da 4.
Cu (IV). 5 (E). holeribus Gi 1 (oleribus
Cu II. 2). honeretur Bi VI. 1, 1 (on- Cu
(VI). 1). hora horandi Hi II (B). 8. 9. 11.
hostiarium, -o Pa I. 6. Hi V. 8. hostium,
-orum Hi VI. 4. Bi VI. 2, 3. humidam
Wa P 61. *Nomina Hebraica*: Elishabet Vi
41 (S). Iohnathan Bi I. 8. Samuhel Vi 41.
Sathane Cu pr. 7 (F: satan- *cett.*)
   catecumini, -os Co B 25. Pa II. 19.
crismal, &c., Cu (XI). 3 (R). 22. Ca 1.
Pasca, &c., Pa II. 13 (I*). Bi II. 9, 2
(C). *alibi* Pascha, &c. parocias Pa II. 20
(D). — chymminum Cu ps. 2. detrachit Bi
VIII. 2, 2. inchoat Pa I pr. unchiae, -am
Wa A 51 (unc- BXHO). — herbisa *pro*
ceruisa Hi II. 12 (P). cimmina (= he-,
himina) Cu II. 2 (R). chrastino Cu II.
15 (E).
   pilax Bi I. 5, 8. — epʰifania Pa II. 19
(D).
   anatemazetur Bi VII. 1 (B). toro Pa II.
25 (D*). T(h)eodorus: *u. Ind. nominum.*

Consonantes :

Media *eliditur* : exierit Cu II. 14 (R: -igerit E). Pa II. 21 (DJ: -igerit KI: -egerit Q).

Nasalis *non exprimitur* : ascedat Pa II. 25 (J*). circuiet Cu ps. 2 (R). coiuge Ad 16 (con- OB¹). fudit (*pr.?*) Bi II. 1, 3. iugamus Pa II. 18 (Q). Nasaseni Hi I tit. quatoque Cu (VIII). 4 (E). trasactam Co B 18 (Tii). adiuranda (= -am) Pa II. 23 (I). — *inseritur* : coniungio Co B 16 (Tii). effunderit Wa A 50 (-fud- ABX). Bi II. 1, 2. mensi *pro* messe Pa II. 18 (I). adulteratam Pa II. 26 (Q). causam Pa II. 21. perfectam Pa II. 17 (QJ). — *Incertum* : tempore KQ, temporem J: teporem DI Pa II. 31.

b–p : ebibatus Da 10. teborem Pa II. 3 (K). —babtizo, *&c.* : *u.* **Assimilatio, dissimilatio.**

b–u : curbi Hi I. 17. herbisa Hi II. 12 (P). libido Wa A 12 (-u- B. P 51). 13 (-u- B. P 36). octaba, -as Cu pr. 9 (R). Bi pr. 19 (C). II. 9, 2 (B). — aceruiora Cu (IV). 13 = Bi IV. 5, 2. — (-bit *et* -uit:) saluabit (*pf.*) Bi pr. 32. *cf.* emendaberis Cu ps. 4 (E). adnuntiauit (*fut.*) Cu pr. 14 (RL); *u. app. bibl.* liberauit (*fut.*) Bi pr. 73. *sic* manifestauit (-bit IY) Pa II. 5. pensauit Cu ps. 2 (E). saluauit ... alleuauit Cu pr. 9 (R.) saluauit *ibid.* 11 (-bit FS).

c–ǵ : docmate Vi 32 (S). lucubre (-i) Pa II. 3 (QJ). — eglotas Bi pr. 6. Gregis Bi IV. 1, 2. infigit Pa II. 11 (Y). tre-, trigissimi (-e) Pa II. 18 (*u. app. crit.*)

c–k : kanonica Pa II. 10 (Q). kanebus Pa II. 12 (Q). kasta Pa I. 17.

c–qu : consecuntur Cu pr. 10 (N). licorem, -is Cu (E) (XI). 12. 16. relicorum Cu II. 22 (E). — quoaequalia Co A 12. quohabitatione (co- DI) Pa II. 1. quohabitatorem (*sed* coabitatricem) Bi IV. 6, 3 (B). quoinquinauerit Aq 2. Co A 7 (Tii). -tus, -ti Cu (E) (X). 4. 17. dequoquatur Bi pr. 15. *cf.* equo animos *pro* economis Cu (VIII). 17 (E).

cx–x : cenodocxia Bi VII tit. (B). intincx(er)it Bi I. 5, 5 (C). 5, 6 (B); *sed* intinxit 5, 7. iuncxerit Wa A 59 (*praeter codd.* HOB). sancximus Wa A 58 (sanximus H).

d–t : capud Wa A 11 (A). Pa II. 1 (KQ). 27 (KQ). conpeditus Wa A 29 (-t- H. P 24). fornicandibus Bi II. 3 tit. (B). glandellam *u.* **Voces.** idem = item Pa II. 6 (Y). obduratur Pa II. 1 (obt- DJI). relinquid Pa II. 27 (KQJ: -it *cett.*). uelud Pa II. 4 (Y). 26 (Y). ueditus (Q: uet- DJI, cf. K) Pa II. 30. — ebdomata Cu

(E) II. 2. (X). 9. fruntibus (H), frontibus (P*) *pro* frondibus Ad 11. illut Cu pr. 2 (S). 3 (S). 14 (N). Pa II. 17 (D). motus *pro* modus Cu (X). 15 (E). quanto *pro* quando Cu (VIII). 13 (E). repetenti (*pro* -di) Wa P 26. soltos *pro* solidos Wa A 12 (A. saltos H*).

f–ph : blasfemantur Pa I. 32. blasfemia Bi pr. 47 (C). VIII pr. (C). (-am) VIII. 3. ephifania Pa II. 19 (D). filargiria Cu III tit. Bi pr. 42. III tit. pr.

p–b : capallum Wa A 18 (-b- AHᶜ. P 11). A 20 (-b- AXHO. P 29). A 32 (-b- X. P 33). *alibi semper* caballus, *&c.* concupinam Wa A 59 (B). erupuit Vi 17 (V). oppropria Bi pr. 43. puplico, -e Bi IV. 1, 4. VII. 2. repellis Wa A 37 (-b- X. rebelli P 47).

s–z : Nasaseni Hi I tit.

ci–ti : apcior Pa II. 3 (K, abcior Q). consciencia Pa II. 31 (Q). diffinicionem Vi 4 (S). exercicium Vi 29 (S *solus*). fornicacionis Pa II. 26 (D). (h)ospicio Hi V tit. (B). 4 (B); *sed* -tio 10. in iusticium Cu pr. 6 (F). pacientur Cu ps. 2 (E). percucientes Cu (X). 21 (E). praeciosa Hi IV. 2. sermocinaciones Bi II. 1, 9. spacium Wa P 12. -a Pa II. 22 (DIY). uiciorum Cu pr. 8 (F). uicio Pa II. 26 (-t- QIY). — audatiae Bi pr. 4 (B). dilitias Bi pr. 60 (B) iuditium, -o Wa P 24. 47. mendatium Da 16 (C*). pertinatia Bi pr. 46. printipalia Cu pr. 15 (S). santiendum Co B pr. (Tii).

si–ci : reconsiliari, -bitur Vi 5 (B). 6 (B). — cicera *pro* sicera Da 1 (B).

ti–si : mantione Bi VI. 3, 1 (mans- Cu (VI). 1 (E). propentiori Cu (VI). 1 (E). *cf.* cenodoctia Bi pr. 46.

pt–p : scriptulum Wa A 21 (*bis*); *sed* scripulos Wa P 57.

s–ps : sallendo Bi V. 1, 6 (C). salmos Bi III. 5, 3 (C).

t–ct : luto Bi IV. 6, 7 tit. (C: lucto B).

mpn–mn : condempnari Wa A 37 (*u. app. crit.*). contempnentur Pa I. 6. contempnantibus Bi I. 8 tit. (contemptus = contentus Pa II. 2 (Q).) dampnare, *&c.*, Wa A 60 (*u. app. crit.*). P 48 (A 44 *cod.* X). Pa II. 16 (K). Bi III. 4. VII. 2 (B). dampnum, *&c.*, Co B 19 (Tii). Wa A 9 (-mn- BXH). Bi pr. 10 (B). V. 1, 3. sol(l)empnitatibus Ca 3. Pa II. 19 (K). sompnus, -is Da 8 (B). Bi VI. 2, 1 (B). —

ms–mps : adsumseris Bi pr. 34 (B). praesumserit Wa A 59 (-mps- ABX).

ǵu–g : constringui Hi III ps. tanguendo Bi II. 1, 1 (B).

Varia : ψalmi, *&c.*, Hi II (P). 1. 2. 3. 4. 8. 9. 10.

Voces *frequentiores uarie scribuntur:*
Britanis Pa I. 33. Britaniae Aq tit. (C).
Britanniae *ibid.* (B). Britannico Gi 1.
Brittannico Cu II. ?.

   ceterum *etc.*: citterum Pa II. 1 (Q).
cyttera *ibid.* 2 (Q). citteris *ibid.* 6 (Q).

   clientela Co B 8 (-ll- Tii*?*). clentella
Vi 27 *bis* (V: cleuentella S). glantelle,
-am Hi I. 23. 27. glandellae, -am Bi IV.
6, 2. 3. glangella (C), -cella (B) Bi I. 6, 2
(*s.s.* ancilla).

   demedium, *&c.,* Pa I. 15. Gi 15. Co
B 18 (Ti). Cu (XI). 23. Wa A 51. P 7.
Bi IV. 1, 2. 3, 1. dimedium, *&c.,* Gi 1. 4.
Lu 7. Vi (V) 3. 6. 15 (*bis*). (V *solus*) 38.
Cu (IV). 9. Hi IV. 7. Bi II. 2, 5. 5, 6.
Dissentiunt codices: di- (V), de- (S) Vi 20.
demed- (Tii*), demid- (Tiiᶜ), dimid-
(Ti) Co A 2. Wa A 15 (di- B). 58 (di-
ABO). 63 (se- A, di- B). Hi IV. 4 *et* 5 (de-
W). Bi IV. 3, 1 *secundo loco* (di- B).
dimidium, *&c.,* Vi 3 (S). 6 (SP). 15 *bis*
(S). Co A 2 (Ti). B 6. 11. 17. 18 (Tii).
Cu II. 2. Cu (E) *semper.*

   aecclesia, *&c.* Pa I. 2. 22. 23. 24. 25.
(*sed* eccl- 26.) Da 16 (C). Cu pr. 9 (F).
Hi II. 4 (P). Bi pr. 36 (C). IV. 7 (C).

aecclesíasticos Ca 2. aeclesia, *&c.* Wa A
46 (ecl- A), P 52. A 59 (ecl- ABX). P 3. 53
(*bis*). Pa II. 6 (eccl- QDIY). 9 *ter* (*u. app.
crit.*). 21 (KDJ). eclesia, *&c.* Wa A 46 (A).
59 (ABX). Hi II. 4 (B). V tit. Bi tit. 33. 36
(B). I. 8 (B: eccl- C). II. 1, 4 (B: eccl- C).
IV. 7 (B). VI. 3. 5 (B: eccl- C). VIII. 2,
2 (B). *alibi* ecclesia.

   elemosina Cu (VIII). 28. Bi pr. 30
(eli- Cᶜ). helemosina Co B 19. -as 20.
elimosina, *&c.* Pa I. 12. 13. Vi (V *solus*)
36. 46. 50. Cu (IV). 7. Wa P 53. Bi pr.
30 (Cᶜ). *sic semper fere* Cu (E). elymosina, *&c.,* Vi 28 (V). 36 (V). Cu III. 3.
Bi IV. 2, 1. (helym- *cod.* S: Vi 28. 36.)
Dissentiunt codices: elymosinarum Cu pr.
4 (R: ẹlemosyn- S. elemosin- ELFG.
helemosin- M. elemosyn- N). elymosina
ibid. (R: elẹmosyna S. elemosina ELF.
helemosina M. elemosyna N). aelimosina
Wa A 46 (HO: elemosinam AX. elemo-
synam B. elimosina P 52). aelimosinam
Ad 15(*praeter* elimosinam Bʳ. elẹmosinam
P).

   presbiter, *&c., semper, exceptis* praesbit-
Pa I. 23. 34. Gi 1 (B). presbyter Gi 1 (C).

VII. GENERAL INDEX TO THE OLD-IRISH TEXTS

elder adjudging penance P V. 12. reviling of an e. P IV. 3.

Enda in Aran A 31.

Enna moccu Laigsi A 32.

envy: its nature, effects, remedies P IV. 1a–d. its various forms P IV *passim*.

Eucharist: see 'communion'.

Eve P IV. 8.

exile for life P V. 2. 11. under the yoke of a strange abbot P I. 9.

false assertions P III. 22. f. witness, suit, judgement P III. 9. 16 ff. f. oath P III. 12 ff.

falsehood to a good purpose P III. 18.

fast as penance *passim*. on Sunday P I. 16. long f. P I. 15. silent f. P III. 17. in confinement A 19. in darkness A 32. black f. A 15. commutations of same A 9 f. 12. of ordinary f. A 13. of three days' f. A 11. 21. breaking of f. P I. 5. 13.

fault-finding P IV. 4 f.

festivals, eight, of the year P I. 15. high f. P II. 3.

fetters, wearing of (commutation) A 19A.

fifty nights between Easter and Pentecost (relaxation of penance) P II. 3.

fine: payment of f. lessens penance P V. 2. See also 'mulcts'.

flesh, forbidden: of horse P I. 2. touched by dogs or beasts P I. 3. abstinence from f. P I. 14. II. 36.

food: dry f. P I. 12. daintier f. than have others P I. 19, excessive f. P I. 15. f. touched by polluted hand P I. 4. stealing of f. P I. 9.

fornication P II. *passim*. penances of f. according to status P II. 11 f.

Friday, continence on P II. 36.

genuflexions A 10–14. 21. 23. 27. 32 f.

gluttony P I. *passim*.

Gospel-book, stealing of P III. 7.

hawk, leavings of P I. 3.

Hell: rescuing a soul out of H. A 1 ff.

heresy A 5.

homicide P V. 2. A 5.

horse-flesh P I. 2.

hurting one's fellow P V. 8.

illness, a (partial) commutation A 16A.

impurity in thought or word P II. 12 f. 15–17. in dream P II. 17. See also 'fornication'.

incest A 5. with mother, sister, or daughter P I. 17. II. 21. of brother with brother P II. 21.

Joshua P IV. 9.

Judas Iscariot P IV. 10.

keening: see 'lamentation'.

killing P V. 2–4. 7. 10 f.

kin-slaying P V. 2. A 5.

king and bishop fix penance for persons in orders P V. 2 keening over k. P V. 17.

kiss of peace P II. 4.

lamentation, woman's, over dead P V. 17.

lashes P I. 11. III. 17. A 27. See also 'blows'.

lay people: leavings of l. p. P I. 3. meals with them *ibid*. different penances for l. p. and religious A 7. commutations for l. p. A 8.

leavings of birds P I. 3. of cat P I. 4. of dog P I. 17. of lay people P I. 3. of pregnant women *ibid*. of murderer or robber P I. 17. of incestuous men *ibid*. of bishop or priest violating his order *ibid*.

leech P V. 8.

Lents, the three of the year P II. 4. 36.

liquid contaminated by carrion P I. 3. by dead mouse P I. 4.

luxuria: its effects and remedies P II. 1a–e.

Maedóc of Ferns A 31.

manslaughter P V. 10. A 8.

marriage, continence in P II. 36.

martyrdom, kinds of P III. 1b.

Mass: tipsiness prevents priest from saying M. P I. 7. offering M. for one who has killed himself P V. 5.

meals with lay people P I. 3. allowed to the sick at any time P I. 6. having a meal before the rest P I. 19.

meat: see 'flesh'.

Michael, archangel A 33.

milk allowed to penitents P II. 3. 7. A 15A. abstinence from P I. 14. thickened m. P I. 12.

mischief-making P IV. 4 f. 10.

Mobí Clárenech A 33.

Mocholmóc of Inis Celtra A 31.

Mocholmóc mac Cumain from Aran A 31.

Molacca Menn A 31.

monastery, head of, keening over P V. 17.

monastic vows P II. 8.

Monday after the lesser Easter P II. 36.

monk P I. 15. performing the penance of a m. P II. 8. m. given to sadness P VI. 3

monkhood, perpetual P II. 10.

mouse, dead P I. 12. in liquid P I. 4. leavings of a m. *ibid*. pollution by a m. *ibid*.

mulcts compensate in part for penance P III. 2.

Murdebur A 31.

murder, secret A 5.

murmuring P IV. 7 ff.